The
Effortless
Economy
of
Science?

SCIENCE AND CULTURAL THEORY

A Series Edited by Barbara Herrnstein Smith

and E. Roy Weintraub

The Effortless Economy of Science?

Philip Mirowski

Duke University Press

Durham & London

2004

We would like to thank the following for permission to use material previously published in different form:

"On Playing the Economics Trump Card in the Philosophy of Science: Why It Didn't Work for Michael Polanyi" is reprinted with permission of the Philosophy of Science Association through the University of Chicago Press.

"Economics, Science, and Knowledge: Polanyi versus Hayek" is reprinted with permission of *Tradition & Discovery: The Polanyi Society Periodical*.

"What's Kuhn Got to Do with It?" is reprinted by permission of Sage Publications Ltd from *History of the Human Sciences* 14 (May 2001).

"The Economic Consequences of Philip Kitcher" is reprinted with permission of the editors of *Social Epistemology*.

"Re-Engineering Scientific Credit in an Era of the Globalized Information Economy" is reprinted with kind permission of *First Monday* and originally appeared in *First Monday*, vol. 6, no. 12 (December 2001); http://firstmonday.org/issues6_12/mirowski/index.html.

"Looking for Those Natural Numbers: Dimensionless Constants and the Idea of Natural Measurement" is reprinted courtesy of *Science in Context*, Cambridge University Press.

"A Visible Hand in the Marketplace of Ideas: Precision Measurement as Arbitrage" is reprinted courtesy of *Science in Context*, Cambridge University Press.

"What Econometrics Can and Can't Tell Us about the Historical Actors," in *Economics Broadly Considered: Essays in honor of Warren Samuels*, is reprinted with permission of Routledge and Jeff Biddle, John Davis, and Steve Medema, editors.

"Why Econometricians Don't Replicate (Although They Do Reproduce)" is reprinted with permission of *Review of Political Economy*.

"From Mandelbrot to Chaos in Economic Theory" appears with permission of the *Southern Economic Journal*.

"Smooth Operator: How Marshall's Demand and Supply Curves Made Neoclassicism Safe for Public Consumption But Unfit for Science," in *Alfred Marshall in Retrospect*, is reprinted with the permission of Edward Elgar Publishing Ltd. and Rita McWilliams Tullberg, editor.

"Problems in the Paternity of Econometrics: Henry Ludwell Moore" is reprinted with permission of *History of Political Economy*.

"Refusing the Gift," in *Postmodernism, Economics and Knowledge*, appears with permission of Routledge and Steven Cullenberg, Jack Amariglio, and David Ruccio, editors.

Other portions of this book have previously appeared in different form in *Review of Political Economy* 7 (1995): 227–41; Michael Szenberg, ed., *Passion and Craft: Economists at Work* (Ann Arbor: University of Michigan Press, 1998); and Philip Mirowski, ed., *The Economic Writings of William Thornton*, vol. 1 (London: Pickering & Chatto, 1999).

Contents

The
Effortless
Economy
of
Science?

Part One
From
Economics
to Science
Studies

Introduction:
Cracks, Hidden
Passageways, and
False Bottoms:
The Economics of
Science and Social
Studies of Economics

He once remarked that mistaking science for technology deprived the nonscientist of one of the greatest sources of awe, replacing it with a diet as filling as Tantalus's fruit. I had only to hear the man talk for fifteen minutes to realize that he believed science had no purpose. The purpose of science, if one must, was the purpose of being alive: not efficiency or mastery, but of the revival of appropriate surprise . . . [If he] lamented the commercialization of science, he despaired even more over the science of commerce.—Richard Powers, *The Gold Bug Variations*

The revival of appropriate surprise

Living in the Cracks

This is a collection of essays, all of which in one way or another have fallen into those in-between spaces where prudent academics dare not tread. The reader is undoubtedly aware that there exist established disciplinary academic formations of hallowed lineage, such as the fields called "economics" and "philosophy," not to mention "physics" and "statistics"; and then, there are also the disciplinary groupings of rather more recent and tenuous purchase, such as the "social studies of science," the "history and philosophy of science," "science policy," "metrology," and the "history of economic thought"; but protracted experience has now convinced me that almost none of my contemporaries' mental maps has commodious space set aside for the social study of the history of economics, the economics of the philosophy of science, the history of the economics of science, the political history of the analytical philosophy of science, or the comparative philosophy of quantification in physics and economics. I have encountered people in the course of my travels who apparently felt that conducting a critical and historical inquiry into the political and economic underpinnings of science would be tantamount to blaspheming the bible, or defiling the music of the spheres, not unlike the attitudes of the dyspeptic character in Richard Powers's *The Gold Bug Variations*. Mark Blaug (2001), among others, has pronounced the social study of economics an anathema; and below we shall take note of various scientists who have deemed it inconceivable that scientific numbers could constitute anything other than Nature braying in a very loud voice. Philip Kitcher (whom we shall encounter repeatedly) has waxed nostalgic that "Mertonian sociology of science was the first (and last) serious sociology of science" (2000, S38), and deplored that from his perspective, everything else since has been a disaster. People do seem inclined to retreat behind the firewalls when they detect someone venturing to explore the confused tendency throughout history to compare science to an economic process, or else engage in comparative cross-disciplinary empirical investigation of the relative stability of quantitative scientific measurement, or ask whether science could possibly have underwritten the widely revered "laws of supply and demand" which supposedly govern our modern marketplace of ideas, or question whether a statistical tradition like econometrics really deserves the empiricist reputation which it appears to enjoy outside of economics. In such instances, one is flagged: You can't get there from here.

Of course, no one is obliged to rejoice in any such combinatorial explosion of mix-and-match hybrid inquiry, just as no one can be expected to get effusive about hybrid corn or chi-chi designer cocktails. And perhaps most people are simply hewing to the prudent maxim that strong walls and well-insulated buffer zones make for friendly neighbors. Nevertheless, it has struck me that there is something distinctly odd about those interstices marked "There Be Dragons" on the academic disciplinary map, the crawl-spaces and half-basements and hidden stairwells that surround the conventional academic disciplines. As Steve Fuller has put it in a different context, "The intensification of analytic philosophy in the United States from the end of WWII to the end of the Cold War may have unwittingly instilled what the social critic Thorstein Veblen would have called a 'learned incapacity' to reflect on the social conditions of knowledge production" (2002a, 171). This incapacity is especially stark in a discipline which just recently has claimed for itself newfound expertise in the "economics of information." Consequently, this book sets out to explore that no-man's land at the borders of science and economics with attendant emotions pitched somewhere beyond the thrill of spelunking and the delectation of trespass. It has often been forcibly brought home to me that most people (Zamora Bonilla 2003; Leonard 2003), beyond paying obeisance to a vacuous "marketplace of ideas," really do not want to entertain the idea that science and economics are simultaneously yean and yield, or at least they have avoided the idea until recently.

The recriminations surrounding the areas reconnoitered herein have an identifiable source, something that has only recently been accorded serious attention by some perspicacious authors such as Wade Hands (2001) and Don Howard (2003). Contrary to popular impressions, political economy and what Hands calls "science theory" have enjoyed a protracted and intimate liaison; it is just that the affair has been kept surreptitious, perhaps a bit seedy, and maybe even equipped with plausible deniability, especially after the 1950s, as Howard makes clear. Philosophers of science before the Second World War had unabashedly committed to normative doctrines of what science was "good for"—think of John Dewey, or Otto Neurath, or Pierre Duhem, or F. S. C. Northrop—and openly linked them to their political and economic enthusiasms (Mirowski 2004); for their part, economists have always had direct access to favorite images of "science" not only to justify their own methodologies but also to provide templates for the very content of their models (Mirowski 1989b); policymakers have always had to deal with the conundrum that he who would take the prince's coin will perforce sing the prince's tune; those who design and build scientific measurement devices have always understood that even the act of measurement was costly, not to mention disruptive, and therefore measurement was always corrigible and calibrated relative to a larger budgetary framework. Earlier generations understood that scientific research was not "naturally" oriented toward any single goal or terminus. There is nothing new in all this. What was novel, and accounts for much of the modern disdain which greets the hybrid inquiries mentioned above, was the fervor with which all these things were descried and denatured in the second half of the twentieth century. It is true that the movement for a "value-free science" began in Germany in the early twentieth century (Proctor 1991), but it flourished, with a lag, in the United States. Analytic philosophy starting with Reichenbach (1938) declared that the context of discovery was irrelevant for the context of justification; pundits repeated ad nauseam that scientists could never be held responsible for however their discoveries were put to use;[1] thinkers such as Friedrich Hayek and Michael Polanyi insisted that the "attempt to rearrange science or society with some explicit theory of rationality in mind would disturb the delicate balance of thought, emotion, imagination and the historical conditions under which they were applied and would create chaos, not perfection" (Feyerabend 1978, 7). Not coincidentally, during the period of the largest expansion of military funding of all the sciences in history, public figures such as Vannevar Bush and Warren Weaver were trumpeting the virtues of "free science"; nominally free, that is, from the dictates of its paymasters, with the supplemental "linear model" of pure science ⇒ applied science ⇒ technology appended to placate the taxpayers. For their part, American neoclassical economists busily began to purge the history of economics from their curricula, the better to maintain the fiction that theirs was a timeless doctrine of disembodied "rational choice," cut adrift from all institutional specificity or, conveniently, direct inspiration of the physical sciences. Because it suited their own purposes, they also subscribed with alacrity to the "linear model." Politically pugnacious economists such as Milton Friedman and Kenneth Arrow threw their weight behind the supposed "positive/normative distinction" in their theories, while selling their services to politically committed clients, often under the aegis of military classification. Philosophers, together with statisticians and economists, began to pretend that elaborate statistical algorithms incorporating garbled components of Neyman-Pearson and Bayesian techniques, perhaps fortified with game theory as in sequential analysis, could somehow provide solutions to the value relativity of measurement and quantification, not to mention age-old problems of induction. Somewhere along the way, with the help of the logical positivists, "science" itself was getting conflated with mechanical induction, a conflation made more acceptable by the hypnotic flashing lights of those imposing mainframe computers upon which the algorithms were played out. All further tended to treat some generic thing called "mathematics" as if it were capable by itself of cutting the knot binding science and the economy.

This is not to assert that everyone with a modicum of intellectual pretensions withdrew altogether from the hybrid concerns located at the intersection of the *Geisteswissenschaften* and the *Naturwissenschaften*; indeed, in this book we identify and discuss many of the polymaths who influenced the twentieth-century science-economy problematic. It is rather that the previously pertinent disciplines (philosophy, economics, science policy . . .) in the American academy were thoroughly reconstituted in the period following the Second World War so as largely to exclude these concerns. The postwar phenomenon of "analytic philosophy" provides one instance of this pattern (Howard 2003; McCumber 2001; Mirowski 2004); the rise of American neoclassical economics is another (Mirowski 2002); the postwar construction of politics is still another (Purcell 1973; Amadae 2003); the heretofore neglected role of "operations research" in channeling trained natural scientists into a generic but well-funded theory of the command and control of social organizations is a fourth (Hughes and Hughes 2000; Kirby 2000; Mirowski 2002); the rise of a Mertonian sociology of science, constituted as a study of science purely from the outside looking in, as if through bulletproof glass and one-way mirrors, is a fifth (Hollinger 1996; Wang 1999; Turner 1999). That exfoliating science-economy hybrids were rooted out and sterilized across the academic board suggests that this was a systemic phenomenon, linked to the postwar state-military organization and the funding of science in the American context, and not some mere artifact of this or that disciplinary idiosyncrasy.

In this book, we do not plan to waste time bemoaning how brusquely the science-economics nexus was shoved out to the margins of discourse after the Second World War, but instead set out to explain and understand the ensuing state of affairs. After all, the relationship of economics to the organization of science continues to be marked by pitfalls and ironies. The scientific status of economics is often a matter for ridicule and disdain; but anyone familiar with the history of economics knows that just about every economic theory which has gained a substantial following has of necessity attached itself to some very specific conceptions of science, both in method and in content. Conversely, there is no natural science which has achieved a rude minimum of results without keeping at least one eye trained on the economic foundations of its activities, both in a practical sense (Who pays for research? *Cui bono?*) and in a manner that resonates with the economic common sense of its era (variational principles, conservation principles as no-free-lunch rules, "fitness" as individual success, Nature as rationally comprehensible). One polarity of the distinction does not merely "inform" the other; instead, they have always been mutually constituted. Therefore, it will not get us far to try pinning the blame for this artificial quarantine on a particular school of economics, or the ideas of one or two politicians, or the ambitions of this physicist or that biologist. Since this book argues that the Social and the Natural are often intertwined, prudence would dictate taking some caution when posing the question, What are the forces which argue for and militate against the kinds of research contained in this book?

There are a few hopeful developments which suggest that the cold-war deep freeze of any protracted examination of the science-economics nexus may be starting to thaw. These trends fall under three broad categories: (1) recent profound changes in the social structure and organization of science, which one can regard as a post–cold war regime change centered upon the imperative of commercialization, (2) the recognition, epitomized by Hands (2001), that older notions of "economic methodology" are moribund, and that the intellectual future resides in amalgamating natural science and economics themes into a general research program of the political economy of science in action; and (3) the increasingly strenuous competition between the budding specialty of "science studies" and a certain branch of American philosophy of science to claim expertise over inquiries such as those found in this book. After a brief glance at these developments, I shall give some indications of how this book can be read as a contribution to a field of inquiry which has yet to find a name, but may eventually find a home within science studies.

How Science Theory Is Being Forced to Come
to Terms with Economics

Privatized Science

The initial impetus behind this collection, as well as its companion volume
(Mirowski and Sent 2002), is a conviction that a number of profound alterations have been affecting science in the last two decades, and that we who
are caught up in the groundswell possess a most inadequate vocabulary with
which to understand them. Very roughly, as explained in that companion
volume, we are situated in the midst of a top-to-bottom transformation of
science organization and funding in the Western countries, starting from a
cold war regime to something we call a regime of globalized privatization. In
the rarefied precincts of science policy and the legal literature on intellectual
property this is neither an altogether novel nor a controversial thesis;[2] and
yet, being so all-pervasive, reaching into every recess of laboratory life and
encompassing such diverse phenomena as the dissolution of the individual
scientific author as the linchpin of inquiry and bearer of "credit," the legal
and conceptual reconstruction of intellectual property, the re-engineering of
the institution of the university and the reconfiguration of previous disciplinary prerogatives, the outbreak of the science wars and the consequent
loss of any sense of mutual reinforcement between the natural sciences, the
social sciences, and the humanities, the unreflective treatment of information as a commodified "thing" and its obverse phenomenon, which is a
contempt for the history of inquiry, and the ascendancy of postwar American neoclassical economics as the lingua franca of public justification of any
and all of the above—the high fences and minefields between the relevant
disciplines have stopped being merely a nuisance and become debilitating,
making us incapable of appreciating the breadth and scope of the changes
happening all around us.

The attempt to wean the university off its twentieth-century military
patrons and turn it into a cornucopia of "technology transfer" for economic
growth and regional development has had the unintended consequence of
reviving the entire question of the legitimacy of an "economics of science,"
for both economists and philosophers (Fuller 2002a; Zamora Bonilla 2003;
Kitcher 2001). Whereas previously "pure science" was deemed beyond the
purview of economic considerations, with the possible exception of Arro-
vian appeals for no-strings funding to subsidize the "public good" of in-
completely appropriated knowledge, now it has dawned on any number of
pivotal constituencies that the privatization of funding and the vast expansion of intellectual property might entail revisiting the question of the economic underpinnings of science. Predictably, some economists have jumped

into the fray with assertions that their same old "tools" could be applied to "science" in the same ways that they have been applied in the past to hamburgers and welfare checks (Stephan 1996; Shi 2001; Jensen and Thursby 2001; Leonard 2002), and some philosophers and science policy analysts have followed suit (Goldman, Kitcher, and Ziman in Mirowski and Sent 2002; Schmidt 1994; Zamora Bonilla 2002). However, most natural scientists themselves have been notably unwilling to find themselves situated on a par with temporary laborers, salesmen, and entrepreneurs, and have consequently been inclined to cast the net wider for what they consider a better way to understand their modern predicament. Perhaps this is not just a matter of the inevitable invidious pecking order between the natural and social scientists, or a misguided belief in class distinctions, or nostalgia for an erstwhile golden age, but something that should be taken more seriously as one symptom of a structural weakness of recent forays into a "new economics of science." New Economics of Science

There are a number of ways to question the relevance of postwar American neoclassical economics in helping to understand the vast reorganization of science occurring in the twenty-first century. Some have questioned the simple presupposition that "credit is seen as a substitute for money in scientific exchange" (Shi 2001, 28; see chapter 6 below); others complain that all the various neoclassical variations upon a decision-theory framework totally misapprehend the cognitive attributes of the successful scientist and have no plausible scientific basis in psychology (see chapters 5 and 10 below); while still others point out that the idea of a "free market" for ideas functions as a purely metaphorical construct with no objective correlatives which compare to the panoply of legal and social rules and norms of actual markets. The fact that I advocate an alternative theoretical account of the operation of markets (2002; see chapter 1 below) reinforces my own critical stance toward the ill-considered trope of the marketplace of ideas. Whatever the merit of each of these complaints, I believe that there will prove to be two primary obstacles to the pursuit of a vibrant and useful neoclassical economics of science. The first is the observation that neoclassical economics was itself patterned upon nineteenth-century energy mechanics (Mirowski 1989b), and even in its modern incarnations maintains a rather outdated notion of certain key scientific terms such as "equilibrium," "frictions," and even "model"; beginning in the second half of the twentieth century avant-garde natural scientists noticed this when they became acquainted with neoclassical economics, and this fact was often sufficient for them to lose all respect for the scientific ambitions of economics (Mirowski 2002, chapter 3; Waldrop 1992). Modern proponents of a neoclassical economics of science who protest that their exercises "owe nothing to physical modeling techniques" (Zamora Bonilla 2003, 839) need to learn a little history. Even modern attempts to import

Economics / Reorganizing Science

more *au courant* physical techniques into the economics of science such as spin glass models (Brock and Durlauf in Mirowski and Sent 2002) rarely overcome this aversion, since most physicists are not favorably impressed with having their quotidian research struggles compared to the behavior of a molecule on a lattice in a magnet. (Unlike economists, they only need to see the mathematics to understand its provenance.) In short, while portraying agents as natural physical phenomena may go a long way in conjuring valid scientific credentials and solid scientific legitimacy in the minds of the general public, it tends to be much less effective in recruiting and placating the scientific actors who daily construct and deploy those same mathematical models of natural physical phenomena.

Whatever one might think of the prospects for a rational mechanics of the social structures of science, it will turn out to be the second obstacle which most insistently prevents the application of orthodox neoclassical ideas to the contemporary problems of the interanimation of economics and science. For the hallmark of the neoclassical tradition is to search for the timeless, abstract, and fundamental laws of economic behavior, irrespective of cultural, geographical, and structural idiosyncrasies of human interaction. This accounts for the central place that such doctrines as utility maximization, the dominance of self-interest calculations in human nature, and the Nash equilibrium hold in the neoclassical canon. At first glance, such universal ambitions would seem to resonate with the idea of globalization in the economy and in science management, enforcing as it does greater uniformity in commodities, production, and retail trade. And yet, this renunciation of all differences that make a difference ultimately renders the tradition incapable of adequately dealing with historical change, and in particular with the precept that changing scientific organization and theories will eventually result as an unintended consequence in a transformed economics. There is something curiously poignant about an imperialistic economics, always looking for new frontiers to conquer, which stridently insists upon the essential stasis of its subject matter, when in fact its own conditions of existence are persistently being revised in tandem with those of the process of scientific research.[3]

For instance, recent avatars of a "new economics of science" such as Paul David have applied their generic game-theory model indifferently to the scientific revolution of the sixteenth century and to late-twentieth-century science (David 1998; David and Dasgupta 1994) to explain the "efficiency" of the organization of Western science. David argues for an optimal mix of secrecy and disclosure in the Renaissance court and in the modern research university, a thesis sure to win the endorsement of teachers of Western Civ everywhere. Yet David's vision of utopia is situated squarely back in the Ike Age, when Stanford grew from mediocrity to eminence through mass infusions of military funding and science management. Another paper of the same sort attempts to argue that there exists only one uniquely efficient way to set up intellectual property rights in a university context for all time (Jensen and Thursby 2001), conveniently ignoring how earlier neoclassicals had just as glibly defended the obverse cold war separation of university scientific research from commercial exploitation through a different distribution of property rights as "efficient," when doing so was politically expedient (Hounshell in Hughes and Hughes 2000). A third argues that economic self-interest throws up no obstacles to convergence to scientific truth, even though the exact obverse was a key tenet of the Mertonian sociology of science endorsed by the same author (Kitcher 1993). In these and a whole raft of other cases, neoclassical economics is primarily serving as a weapon of mass distraction, diverting attention from the causes and consequences of the vast contemporary reorganization of the scientific process, and not providing tools for understanding and discussing the emergent nature of science in the twenty-first century. It is instead a misleading caricature of an "effortless economy of science"—modern science as a set of self-sufficient and efficient social structures, perduring throughout human history, operating as the ultimate unmoved mover of that history, patterned upon the neoclassical image of the market.

Perhaps my attitude is a little too redolent of Pollyanna (although I must aver that I am not often accused of this personality trait), but it does seem to me that most scientists will eventually come to realize that the so-called new economy of science is serving as little more than the emperor's new drycleaner, and that confident appeals to the effortless economy of science in our brave new world—of wrenching career restructuring, of offices of technology transfer and research governance boards, of offshore outsourcing of laboratory work to needy Second and Third World countries, of interminably stretched-out employment periods as university unfaculty, the rise of ghost authorship of scientific papers, not to mention legal covenants over intellectual property the length of *War and Peace*—this notion of an effortless economy of science will come to appear a quaint aberration in the annals of intellectual discourse. Management consultants are already turning this neoclassical notion of a new economy of science into a chalice of hemlock: for instance, characterizing universities as "dumb organizations" and McDonald's franchises as more market-savvy "smart organizations" (Stewart 1997). Instead, people who care about the scientific enterprise will eventually want to know how we arrived at the modern state of affairs, which means they will want to know something about the set of conditions which gave rise to the temporary configuration and conduct of university science after the Second World War, as well as the dubious ways in which science was then portrayed as transcending market operations, which suggests in turn that they will be interested in the chapters below on "Science as an Economic Phenomenon."

Revamped Relationship of Philosophy to Economics

Once upon a time economics knew its place, and philosophy conspired to keep it there. This era, as already hinted, was located in the latter half of the twentieth century. During this Bronze Age, economists were very worried that they be highly regarded as scientists; philosophers deigned to assist them by pointing to the scriptures of the scientific method, generally extracted from the annals of their favorite science, physics. This service was performed out of sheer public-mindedness, an altruism thoroughly removed from political considerations or considerations of social context.[4] Economists, accustomed to mimicking physicists, and deferring to their betters, sought to incorporate all the ritual behaviors of axiomatization, covering-law models, quantification, quarantined contexts of discovery, inductive inference, falsification, normal science, hard cores and protective belts, and all the latest accoutrements. Some might complain that their recital of the catechism was less than fervid, and their ritual performance a tad mechanical, but nevertheless philosophers hastened the balm of scientific reason on its downhill course, and the economists in their inferior location dutifully scooped it up.

One of the benefits of recent scholarship in the history of the philosophy of science is that we now can see that there was little about this parable that rang true; and therefore, it really has become imperative to rethink the very idea of a professional field of "economic methodology." Wade Hands (2001) has made this case with great aplomb, so we need not explore the present predicament of the self-styled methodologist here. However, a quick glance at the content of the ways philosophers have used economics in the past does bear some relevance for the project of this volume. As Hands suggests, it might be better to approach the philosophy of science as having existed in a dialogue with economics. In particular, the philosophical holy trinity of Popper, Kuhn, and Lakatos has recently come under intense scrutiny in a secular trio of intellectual biographies (Hacohen 2000; Fuller 2000b; Kadvany 2001). While the books differ quite substantially in their historiographic stances and intentions, one thing that stands out quite starkly in all three is the insistence by the biographers on the central importance of the "political economy" (in the older sense of that term) of each philosopher of science in governing many of his doctrines concerning the prosecution of science, even though it also seems that each philosopher took pains to suppress or disguise those motivations from becoming too apparent in his published texts. It is worth dallying a moment over each figure, if only to set the stage for the different sort of relationship between philosophy, economics, and science advocated in this book.

Let us start with the case of the neoclassical economists' favorite philosopher, Karl Popper. Whatever his supposed contributions to the philosophy of physics (given that it was frequently conflated with the doctrines of the logical positivists that he said he opposed; and in any event, physicists did not pay much attention beyond perfunctory praise of falsification), it appears clear in retrospect that Popper's work is saturated with both Marxism and neoclassical economics. Popper was not shy of admitting it in certain contexts, as in his intellectual biography (1976, 113): "it had been in part a criticism of Marxism that had started me in 1919 on my way to *Logik der Forschuung*." The service that Hacohen provides is to situate Marxism as the central defining concern of Popper's early career. He reminds us that Popper's initial notoriety as a philosopher was due primarily to his books *The Poverty of Historicism* and *The Open Society and Its Enemies*, which can be read as extensions of the famed *Methodenstreit* between German historicists and Austrian subjectivist economists of the late nineteenth century (Hacohen 2000, 468). He demonstrates that Popper started his career as some version of interwar socialist, but upon encountering Friedrich Hayek during the war, and beholden to him for being rescued from the Antipodes and given refuge at the London School of Economics, moved rightward with alacrity and became a cold warrior, which was his major claim to fame in the immediate postwar period. It is important to remember that when Popper "bemoaned the sorry state of the social sciences in *The Poverty of Historicism* he excluded economics" (284); and that his later "situational analysis" was, as he conceded, "an attempt to generalize the method of economic theory (marginal utility analysis) so as to become applicable to the other social sciences" (1976, 117–18). So the postwar philosopher that the intelligentsia hated to love was an Austrian philosopher of science trumpeting the virtues of neoclassical economics and denouncing the vices of Marxism, all under the cover of extending the methods of the natural sciences to the social sciences. Popper's connection to Hayek is especially significant, as Thomas Uebel (2000) points out, since their shared attack on the Viennese positivist Otto Neurath and their loathing for his "scientific socialism" tended to wash out many of their other substantial intellectual differences, such as conflicting evaluations of the ultimate wisdom of a "social physics," or the indispensable role of "psychologism" in the social sciences. That according to his biographer Popper was not personally familiar with much social science writing, nor indeed had much patience with describing real social structures, given that he "paid no attention to institutions . . . When he spoke of observation, experiment and refutation, he made no distinction between the individual scientist and the community . . . He presupposed a Republic of Science but did not formulate a vision of it" (2000, 513), only makes more salient the thesis that what tended to set Popper apart from the general run of philosophers was his particular vision of the political economy of science, and not any specific analytical innovations or perceptive descriptions of day-to-day scientific operations. Indeed, the supposed prophet of critical rationalism characteristically never even considered whether it was possible for laypersons outside the science in question to criticize the agenda of the research program pursued by scientific leaders (Jarvie 2001). However much Popper sought to distance himself from the logical positivist movement, this basic image of a scientific method floating free of all social instantiation, ineffable and yet incongruously inaccessible to "totalitarian" societies, a special arena where ideas clashed and died but their proponents never suffered any consequences, was the key to understanding the relevance of Popper to the cold-war world.

Even more fascinating is John Kadvany's account of how a Marxist-inspired Hegelianism disguised as an improvement upon Popper came to supplant Popperian philosophy of science on its home ground at the London School of Economics, as well as in the hearts of many Europeans. Imre Lipsitz (Lakatos) began his career in Hungary as an avid Stalinist and (apparently) a strong externalist in the philosophy of the natural sciences, but fled after the disastrous Hungarian Revolution in November 1956 to England. There Lakatos was fascinated by the strategies by which ideas successfully come to power, and realized that Popper shared substantially more with Hegel than he would admit, such as an antifoundationalism, and an appreciation of error and its role in the progress of human knowledge. He came to realize, as Kadvany explains, that the "same kind of historicism" "implicit in the 'negative' progress made via the critical elimination of theories is, for Lakatos, Popper's Achilles Heel. This leaves open the technically sweet philosophical problem of historicizing Popper" (2001, 12). Lakatos set out to implement his insight in his PhD dissertation, *Proofs and Refutations*, a stunning display of virtuosity which argued that the complex process of mathematical proof cannot be modeled in a fixed formal language, at least in part because history had to be intentionally falsified for both pedagogical and philosophical purposes.

What at first seemed an elaboration of Popper's critical rationalism rapidly turned into a scathing critique of the master, however. Lakatos possessed a wicked sense of humor, and later characterized Popper's three main contributions as: "(1) a step backward from Duhem (the falsification criterion), (2) a step backward from Hume (the supposed solution to the problem of induction), and (3) *The Open Society* by one of its enemies" (in Motterlini 1999, 89–90). But more to the point, Lakatos was also skeptical of

Popper's latent neoclassical economics: "Popper . . . never discusses the ceteris paribus clause problem seriously. Anybody who has read anything about the methodology of economics knows that this clause is always discussed" (88).[5] However, as Kadvany argues, the Lakatosian Methodology of Scientific Research Programmes is itself a projection of a different branch of political economy: "Lakatos' covert Hegelianism within Popper's world demonstrates the virtuous role of intellectual dissemblance and cunning in the Hungarian Revolution" (2001, 301).

Lakatos, much more than Popper (and in contrast to Kuhn), was assiduously concerned with one vexed question: What it is that prevents reason from descent into demagoguery? As his friend and interlocutor Paul Feyerabend understood, "The so-called authority of the sciences, however, i.e., the use of research results as barriers to further research, relies on decisions whose correctness can only be checked by what the decisions eliminate—a typical feature of totalitarian thought" (1987, 158). Rather than evoke a Land of Cockaigne where the personal fallout from disputes was magically banished, where science bequeathed to its beneficent supporters only more marvelous consumer goods, and where markets were always efficient, Lakatos was concerned with a rather more drab social existence predicated upon powerful bureaucracies and Machiavellian agents, crossed with the monopolist's problem of overproduction—indeed, as Kadvany argues, something more closely representing the Hungary which he had fled. It was a world of staged falsifications in the public quest for vindication, manipulative élites and personality cults, dissembling and betrayal. In this world, pathologies could sometimes become virtues: histories could be falsified, élites were a necessary evil, it was sometimes prudent for criticism to be covert, and deliberate lies were not always straightforwardly mendacious (as in "rational reconstructions"). In contrast to earlier postwar stories, Lakatos urged a more skeptical political economy of science: "Scientific autonomy is not equivalent to the unconstrained funding and support of any scientific research" (2001, 224). Perhaps he was joking—and then again, perhaps not—when he said: "we are currently facing both an academic and a publication explosion. We therefore need a demarcation criterion in order to be able to 'burn' the right people and the right books" (in Motterlini 1999, 96).

This political economy of the commissar proved altogether too bleak and downbeat for American tastes; and therefore Lakatos complained that the new paymasters opted for what he called "a rather ad hoc footnote to Polanyi and Merton" (30), namely the characterization of normal science found in Thomas Kuhn. Early on, Paul Feyerabend recognized that Kuhn's *Structure of Scientific Revolutions* was an "ingenious defense of financial support without corresponding obligations" (1978, 99); but it has been the lively book by Steve Fuller (2000a) which has brought the political economy of the Kuhnian portrayal of science to widespread attention. Since this work of Fuller is considered at length in chapter 4, it may suffice here to note that the political economy of Kuhn was in practice just as authoritarian as that of Lakatos: "I was trying to explain how it could be that the most rigid of all disciplines, and in certain circumstances the most authoritarian, could also be the most creative of novelty" (Kuhn 2000, 308). Fuller juxtaposes Kuhn's revolutions to Pareto's theory of the circulation of élites (2000b, 166), but I think that particular comparison a little misleading. After all, Pareto's sociology was intended to account for the irrational surd of society left over after neoclassical rational choice had explained the fundamentals. Kuhn's aim was instead to assert the unintentional benefits of leaving normal science to its own devices, once the paychecks were cashed. But stripped of Lakatos's Hegelian historicism and any acknowledgment of the deadly politics of large bureaucracies, Kuhn's centerpiece of normal science corresponds most nearly to the rational choice image of operations research, something he himself spent the war engaged in.[6]

Operations research (OR) was a new field growing out of the Second World War. It was the major conduit bringing physical scientists into what would be considered the social sciences in the second half of the twentieth century, and it had intimate contacts with the rising American neoclassical orthodoxy in that period (Mirowski 2002, chapter 4). Operations research was the nascent science of command, control, communications, and information processing par excellence. It was initially applied to problems of military organization, which in the postwar context also meant the problems of science management, since the military had become the preeminent patron of scientific research, first in America and then elsewhere. Later it became applied equally to corporate settings (Kirby 2000), and had profound implications for fields seemingly as far apart as analytic philosophy, artificial intelligence, organizational theory, politics, and computer science. While the history of operations research as such is not discussed explicitly in this book (but see Mirowski 1999; 2004), in retrospect it nevertheless constitutes one of the threads that connect most of the topics that the book contains. For instance, the crusading aura of the operations researcher was based on the assumption that he would bring the tonic of quantification to fields and questions which had previously been sorely wanting in that dimension; and as such, he helped to foster the mistaken belief that quantification and precision measurement were methodologically stabilizing influences bestowing scientific credibility in their own right, entirely removed from the larger social dimension to science. The chapters in Part III on "Rigorous Quantitative Measurement" are intended to counteract such superficial understandings of the role of numbers in scientific research. Another calling card of postwar OR was a certain facility with statistical models, which was itself an artifact of the spread of probability concepts throughout physics in the first half of the twentieth century. Without such a broad-based proselytization across the academic board for the empiricist virtues of statistical procedures on the part of OR, it is indeed doubtful that econometrics would have had quite the impact that it did in the second half of the twentieth century. The chapters in Part IV which ask "Is Econometrics an Empirical Endeavor?" were written to demonstrate that statistical algorithms did not really solve many of the thorny problems of inductive inference as much as they shoved them under the rug, especially (but not exclusively) as they became used in postwar economics. Finally, OR was often retailed as the application of a generic "scientific method" to issues of war (and later peace); the reason, as explained in Mirowski 2002, was that physicists and other natural scientists wanted to be consulted on issues of command and control, but not to *become* social scientists; the myth of a portable scientific method served their interests well in that regard. It was their conjuration of a generic expertise in models of command and control which also underwrote their arrogation of special status for themselves as scientists situated beyond the reach of conventional social hierarchies and external demands to make their own activities accountable. (During the Second World War, American operations researchers enjoyed a unique and envied status of officer rank outside the command structure of the individual services.) And this brings us back full circle to the political economy portrayals of science considered in the section "Science as an Economic Phenomenon."

The historical protagonist (as opposed to the philosopher's ally) Thomas Kuhn assumes a different hue when situated in this context. It was becoming apparent that earlier attempts by figures such as Michael Polanyi to argue for the monastic quarantine of science from society, couched in a discourse of faith and tacit knowledge, would just not do the job in a postwar world predicated upon the military funding and organization of scientific research, based as it was on large, impersonal laboratories and the new phenomenon of science managers.[7] That job fell to a short book in which, notably, *none* of the examples were drawn from any science later than 1920 (Fuller 2000b, 74). *The Structure of Scientific Revolutions* is a book which argues that science has always operated in the same manner from the sixteenth century to the present, that cognitive competencies of individual scientists are pretty nearly on a par across the board so that their disagreements are fairly rare, that normal scientists voluntarily relinquish their intellectual fates to their authoritarian masters, that accountability equals control over the ability to rewrite your own collective history, that the optimal strategy in scientific research is to not rock the boat (but if you must, make sure beforehand that you have plenty of the right kind of allies), with "incommensurability" promoted up front as a warning for the layman to not even think of becoming embroiled in paradigmatic commitments he could never hope to come to comprehend. Therein lay the gist of Feyerabend's pointed diagnosis of "an ingenious defense of financial support." The true genius of the book is that it was written with sufficient recourse to the idiom of "revolution" to appeal to the generation of the 1960s, and in a style so guileless that it was assigned reading for subsequent generations of undergraduates.

It does not matter whether Thomas Kuhn the human being ever seriously set out to write an apologia for Big Science in the military modality; his book served that function nonetheless. Further, the doctrines described above resonated rather conveniently with the operations researcher's approach to the corporate organization, again intentionally or not. Scientists' individual preconceptions could be described by the fledgling field of cognitive science (Kuhn's duck-rabbit example); they made optimal calculations of their own individual self-interest and engaged in game playing which might be described as strategic in the novel idiom of game theory; normal science was an authoritarian hierarchy, rather like an army or a corporation; "revolution" was something to be harnessed and pacified (like those operations researchers in the seething Vietnam conflict); historical narratives were deemed little better than propaganda subordinate to considerations of power and influence; science produced output for its own sake in a context of generalized individual competition. Perhaps the only aspects of postwar OR that were missing were a penchant for quantification of paradigms (although Kuhn did write elsewhere on "quantification" itself as a scientific stratagem) and a recourse to probability and statistics to summarize the bold generalizations from individual case studies (that option was left to the Mertonians and their "scientometrics," a pale imitation of econometrics).

Contrary to popular convictions, the philosophy of science was saturated with the language and concerns of the dominant political economy in the postwar period; it is only now, with some historical distance and after the Fall of the Wall, that we can begin to perceive the extent of its influence. This has serious implications for the ambitions of a new generation of philosophers who seek to promote their own version of "social epistemology" (Schmidt 1994; Goldman 1999) as an antidote to the creeping painful irrelevance of contemporary philosophy of science (considered below); but it also has direct importance for what those less infatuated with academic philosophy can hope for in a seriously engaged economics of science. Contrary to those self-styled defenders of science, the world does not particularly need yet another reified picture of the imaginary operation of a perfect marketplace of ideas. Recent scholarship helps us understand that a useful economics of science will tend to live "in the cracks" between a self-confident economics, the pedagogical methodological self-image promulgated within the formal natural sciences, and a righteously prescriptive philosophy of science. The reason for this exile is the very tendencies we have identified above: where economists revel in atemporal models of social activity inspired by natural science, philosophers of science tend to surreptitiously retail thinly disguised political economy notions to each other and the larger populace; and the natural scientists sometimes fall back onto their supposed monopoly of a generic scientific method in order to better control their own nagging dependencies upon various constituencies within the university and upon the larger political economy, the better to be permitted to carry on their own research in ways they see fit. It goes without saying that in recent times all three groups have tended to treat history after the fashion of Big Brother, and as if that weren't bad enough, to treat each other with open contempt. The denizens of the Technology Transfer Office and their economist allies think they have found a better way out: simply privatize the process of research and let the best epistemologists win! The claims and counterclaims of each of these constituencies have thus turned out to be extremely opaque and unhelpful when it comes to understanding the patterns of the contemporary privatization of science identified above. Unless one is to be permitted to shift idiomatic bases with relative abandon, and to bring to bear the insights of one tradition upon the presuppositions of another, without holding inquiry hostage to the half-submerged value systems of any one of these groups, I seriously doubt we shall breach the impasse of modern science theory. That is the guiding principle of any inquiry which has to replace the older, moribund notion of "economic methodology," at least if there is to be something more than crass opportunism and pedantic special pleading for existing academic disciplinary boundaries. That is the standard to which this book tries to adhere.

Possible Alliances with Science Studies

The question remains of where such hybrid inquiries can find a home, and who, if anyone, will take them in and nurture them. This is a life-or-death issue for the history of economics in general (Weintraub 2002), as well as the hybrid studies discussed in this book. If we hew to our own precepts, it follows that at least in part, the answer will depend on when and how the modern university gets restructured.[8] While there do exist alternative sources of support for contemplation of the place of science in society, such as the popular media, politically motivated think tanks, contract research houses, and so on, it does nevertheless seem rather far-fetched to argue that the varieties of expertise envisioned for the studies championed herein could thrive outside a university setting. For instance, it would result in cognitive dissonance, not to mention existential nausea, for specialists in science theory to hang out their shingle offering themselves for hire as possessors of generic expertise in pronouncing upon the goals of scientific inquiry in a democratic society, since that would inescapably embroil them in advocacy for one particular constituency, a role that a science studies avatar might assume under only the most dire of circumstances.[9] The whole point of insisting that scientists and nonscientists are inseparable in their social influences is to come to comprehend which research programs get stabilized through processes of negotiation, recruitment, purchase, and realignment; and hence eventually to appreciate that their publicly stated objectives are frequently as much a *post hoc* rationalization of events as they were forces that helped bring them to fruition. In such instances, legitimacy is always an ongoing construction project; and the university is one of the few places in society where (in the past) tolerance of messy construction sites and this sort of ambiguity could be reasonably presumed. (However, the privatization of university science may eventually banish this as well.)

There are a few niches in the university currently open to providing a haven for this style of thought: sometimes they are dubbed "science studies units," sometimes centers for the sociology and history of science, less frequently programs in the interface of business and technology. Thus it would seem pertinent to ask whether the studies in this book could be reasonably supposed to fit comfortably under any of those rubrics. One problem with posing the question in this manner is that the nascent specialty of science studies has weathered some severe storms lately in the guise of the so-called science wars,[10] and the prognosis for its own place, especially within the American university, remains profoundly uncertain. This is not the appropriate venue to replay those old battles nor to rewrite the history of the conflict of the faculties: our only interest at present is to evaluate some modern tensions in science studies writ large, and to situate this book within that agonistic field. Another problem with our rhetorical question is the implicit need to define and characterize modern "science studies" for the newcomer; this is something which cannot be done justice in the space of the present introduction.[11] If I may be granted the indulgence, I propose instead to meditate for a moment on what I conceive to be a misguided conception of the field of science studies, namely that associated with the name of Philip Kitcher.

There seem to be two major rivals within the broad church of science studies seeking to provide forums for the discussion of political and economic forces and their impact upon the output of scientific research. The first is a subset of the scholars congregating within the "social studies of science" tent, primarily concerned with the regulation and arbitration of science and the disputes that tend to arise when other social actors get involved. Authors here would include Donald MacKenzie, Sheila Jasanoff,

Steve Shapin, Eveleen Richards, Corynne McSherry, Steve Turner, Trevor Pinch, and Andrew Pickering. These writers tend to engage in historical research, wear the badge of empiricists while acknowledging the pitfalls of selectivity of evidence, seek to explain processes of dispute resolution in terms of the "interests" of the parties involved, and insist that different social alignments can produce different scientific outcomes.[12] The second camp, and a sworn opponent of the first, is made up of those allied with the philosopher of science Philip Kitcher, although at various junctures the movement might be broadened to include those who march under the banner of "social epistemology," such as Alvin Goldman, David Hull, and Miriam Solomon.[13] This phalanx is united by the belief that one can provide abstract philosophical solutions to the political and economic woes which beset science, primarily by mounting a defense of what its members view as the obvious unique success of science as a social formation. Their characteristic trope is to transform some phenomenon which at first glance appears "irrational" into its opposite when repositioned through the instrumentality of some compact yet stylized "model" of behavior. By inclination, adherents of this view lean toward the rationalist end of the spectrum, although they do make use of some historical materials taken from others to justify their positions.

The intrepid reader will notice that a few of the chapters in this book seek to define my objectives by contrasting them with those of Philip Kitcher. From one perspective, this stands as a tribute to his work, since he is the *fin de siècle* philosopher who perceived long before his peers that the philosophy of science was inescapably a political undertaking, and as such, he has not hesitated to enter into controversies over issues that really mattered to contemporaries, such as the teaching of creationism, the legitimacy of sociobiology, the justification of the Human Genome Project, and so forth. But equally it serves as a warning that something about the makeup of the modern philosophy profession yearns to render it fundamentally conservative, in that Kitcher needs to be understood as a recognizable member of the group of philosophers identified above who retail neoclassical economics under elaborate disguise because they conceive it as an adequate characterization of the political economy of science. Once this is fully appreciated, then it follows that the chapters in this book (and not just the chapter explicitly concerned with Kitcher's writing) constitute one long argument that the way forward lies with the social-studies-of-science camp, and not with the Kitcher-style social epistemologists.

Kitcher, like so many other science warriors, seems to think that the not-so-hidden agenda behind science studies is to debunk, demystify, and delegitimize science, and perhaps Reason in general. This notion would be risible, were it not so grossly misleading: most scientists instinctively understand that they would have nothing to fear from any group prosecuting such an outlandish and silly agenda; while most science studies scholars are smart enough to realize that spending most of their waking hours studying science could not be justified under such motivations. Instead, Kitcher misses what seems to be the main division between science studies scholars and philosophers of science: the former wish to enumerate and explore all the ways in which science in action is imbricated in the societies in which it is embedded, whereas Kitcher has always wanted to assert some form of analytical separation between science and society;[14] in other words, Kitcher wants to shore up the tradition represented by Polanyi, Popper, and Kuhn. Kitcher's quest for a knockdown "demarcation principle" has assumed various formats over the course of his career but has only been made relatively explicit in his latest book, *Science, Truth and Democracy* (2001). There he restates his position as acknowledging that social structure has *something* to do with the way scientific research is carried out, but that in the majority of cases, the criteria for the success of science are effectively independent and separable from the value criteria by which individuals and societies gauge the conformity of science to their values and aspirations (124). This is nothing more than an "invisible hand" argument, as many have noted: science purportedly serves transcendent ends which are not and need not be the ends of the individuals engaged in their idiosyncratic pursuits. Furthermore, these ends are intrinsic goods in and of themselves, decoupled from the system of incentives and restrictions imposed by the paymasters of science. It is significant that Kitcher has never been able to definitively settle on the identity of these transcendent goods over the course of his career: they started out looking like formal notions of "truth," then mutated into the dependable identification of putative "natural kinds," and then into the "unification of explanation"; as of now, Kitcher seems to have retreated back to the logical empiricist default position of providing accurate predictions. But no matter: philosophers will forever wrangle about the true nature of science as a prelude to their dream of the final knockdown argument which will silence all doubt and opposition to their own favorite utopia. Kitcher's very real conundrum is that almost nobody today believes any longer that these abstract philosophical criteria of the success of science are sufficient to underwrite a separate, self-governing, and independent cloister of scientists supported by unlimited public funds: in other words, Golden Age philosophy of science is dead. Here is where our first thesis comes back into play.

During the cold war, when most science was primarily funded and organized by the military and the academic system was expanding, stories like those told by Polanyi, Popper, and Kuhn (and maybe Lakatos) were eminently *useful*. They asserted that the public should simply acquiesce in the kinds of science it got in return for its investment, because scientists were the only legitimate judges of their own activity, and in any event, the public could never fully come to comprehend how science worked. Scientists should not set out to challenge research programs in their own areas of specialization, but rather forge their identities and chart their personal progress within their preset parameters. The myriad ways in which this doctrine dovetailed with such outside structural impositions as security classifications, open versus closed publication outlets, activist science managers, handpicked peer review panels, and so forth should be obvious. Now, in the new regime of globalized privatization and flexible research specialization, all of that insistence upon the independent pristine constitution of the scientific sphere seems more than a little threadbare and outdated. Indeed, Kitcher's pressing problem is to somehow argue that the modern research structures, which are increasingly results-oriented in the shorter term, which stress bureaucratic accountability to outsiders, and which are less infatuated with the disciplinary power of professionalization, are nonetheless insignificant in their impact upon the true transcendental goals of science.

That is how Kitcher and the social epistemologists arrive at the seemingly discordant positions that modern science as a generic entity automatically serves a set of transcendental values and objectives independent of those imposed by society or held by individuals, and yet, incongruously, that something must be done to protect science from the inappropriate encroachments and corrupting demands of a societal nature. Kitcher phrases his question as follows: "What exactly is the goal of scientific inquiry in a democratic society? (Or, in economic terms, what precisely are we hoping that science will maximize?)" (2001, 145).[15] The answer to both questions from our present perspective is that they are both so ill posed as to be meaningless. The relationship of science to democracy is one of the most vexed and contested issues in the history of the twentieth century (Hollinger 1996; Purcell 1973; Ezrahi 1990; Wang 1999); the lesson seems to be that science neither is inherently democratic, nor does it necessarily thrive only in a democratic society. Furthermore, there is nothing palpable which science as a social formation exists to "maximize." However, these questions do reveal that Kitcher can only manage to conceptualize the interplay of science and society in quasi-economic and, moreover, strictly neoclassical terms. Hence, far from having the philosophy of science expand innovatively into novel questions of social organization and away from context-independent epistemic propositions of Legendary philosophy of science (as Kitcher sometimes likes to paint it), what we have instead is an awkward throwback to the crypto-neoclassical political economy models of science which have pervaded philosophy since the Second World War, as described above.

Kitcher's riposte to the science studies community can be found summarized in his latest book. Mimicking their language, he also avows that science is driven by "interests" (and who would want to deny that in the present atmosphere of corporate science?), but that these interests are merely individual biases which must be modeled as "preferences."[16] Preferences are not systematic or structural; and moreover, they merely serve to focus our attention. Hence interests just affect where we look for answers, not how we do research or what it is that we find there. And in Kitcher's latest incarnation, every question about possible pathologies of scientific research boils down to questions about "preferences" and what to do about them. Here Kitcher becomes all tangled up in the most awkward contradictions, exacerbated by his belief that he can incorporate political, moral, and economic theory into his philosophy of science without actually consulting their dauntingly voluminous literatures. (History as something that you actually had to document was abandoned long ago.)[17] Initially, Kitcher tries to equate collective social welfare with the aggregation of individual preferences under a democratic regime: surely he is not completely ignorant of the infamous Arrow impossibility results (1951), which suggest that the two are incompatible? It would appear that Kitcher likes to engage in talk about "freedom" and "morality," but deep down (like Polanyi, like Hayek, like Kuhn) he is paralyzed by the fear of what he calls "vulgar democracy," and perhaps religion as well.[18] His solution to this unbearable tension is to change the "preferences" of those individuals whom he deems untrustworthy, converting (brainwashing?) them into possession of what he calls "tutored preferences." So much for the shibboleth of freedom of thought. In case the carefully tutored citizens still do not qualify as sufficiently pliable for science, Kitcher then proceeds to invent an elaborate Shangri-La, one that conveniently comes fully equipped with an agora of ideal forms of deliberation concerning prospective scientific research programs, with votes on which programs should enjoy support (with what nature of franchise?) and a Supreme Court of experts to sort things out when they get a little testy. Curiously for one normally extolled as a clear writer, Kitcher then appears to think that piling on the neoclassical jargon will render this fancy more plausible: "[W]ith respect to each budgetary level, one identifies the set of possible distributions of resources among scientific projects compatible with the moral constraints on which the ideal deliberators agree, and picks from this set the option yielding maximum expected utility, where the utilities are generated from the collective wish list and the probabilities obtained from the experts" (121).

If this sounds akin to the kind of verbiage that was broadcast from RAND in the 1960s concerning the optimal choice of weapons systems by the Pentagon, then one would not be led too far astray concerning its intellectual lineage. Indeed, the application of decision theory terms to technoscientific options was one of the prime specialties of operations research in that era (Hounshell in Hughes and Hughes 2000) and designedly so: it draped a veil of political accountability over a process which was clearly disintegrating and rife with conflicting interests, Machiavellian manipulation, and backroom politics. As we have witnessed, philosophy of science itself has projected a pale reflection of the world according to the operations researcher since the Second World War; Kitcher's flaw is that his ingrained disdain for history leaves him incapable of realizing that the hired gun ethos of the operations researcher can be readily discerned in his own work. Kitcher, for all his vaunting ambition to innovate fresh topics for the philosophy of science, ends up being just another Kuhn, another Popper.[19]

Of course, if qualifying as being *à la mode* were the main virtue of science studies, then Kitcher's flaw would be a minor one; and indeed, this book would be equally culpable. The mortal sins of Kitcher's version of social epistemology are that it ends up being both irrelevant and tautologous. It is irrelevant in that his ideal world of "well-ordered science" has nothing whatsoever to do with the present predicaments of science—the runaway revisions of intellectual property, the frequent resort to litigation to solve scientific problems, the crisis of scientific publication, the disenfranchisement of university faculty from academic governance, the bankruptcy of ritual mechanized induction, the overemphasis on arcane mathematical expertise to validate relevance, the rationalization of teaching and lab work into temp McJobs, numerous popular crises of confidence in scientists as political actors—all this and more might as well be happening in another galaxy, far from Kitcher's ideal republic. Doubly vexed, Kitcher's social epistemology is also tautologous because of its circular notion of what it means to be a "tutored" legitimate agent participating in deliberations about science. If "having a legitimate voice" means getting a gold-plated PhD in the relevant discipline, then we are back to Polanyi's and Kuhn's original prescription that only holders of valid union cards (and then only those who publicly submit to the authority of the master) get to cast their vote for whether we get the Human Genome Project or the Texas Supercollider or a fortified Social Security system. Of course, by then your "tutored" vote is more or less a foregone conclusion. If, per contra, getting "tutored" only means that you need to know *something* about the sciences in question, then the prescription is unavailing, since there can be no settled prerequisite of everything one needs to know to participate.

If Kitcher had bothered to consult the philosophical literature on utilitarianism, he would have discovered that this idea of "cleansed" or suitably informed preferences is the Achilles heel of left-liberal neoclassical economics (Cowen 1993). The fundamental commitment of neoclassical models is to treat "preferences" as the independent unmoved movers of changes in market bundles. The mid-twentieth-century revision of the economic agent toward greater resemblance to an information processor (Mirowski 2002) raised the disturbing specter that if agents took action to change their own preferences through experience, learning, and interpersonal interaction, then the determinacy of economic equilibrium would evaporate. A whole sequence of attempts to avoid that consequence, from Nash equilibrium to schemes of mechanical induction to so-called rational expectations, has sought to endow the economic agent with some semblance of invariance, but Kitcher does not seem aware that his ideal Republic of Tutees doesn't even begin to address the problem. Not only do we lack any guarantee that *ex ante* intentions need not map into *ex post* evaluations, but the whole notion of "democracy" as giving the people what they want loses all cogency. As Cowen writes, "Fully informed preferences do not offer an Archimedean point for value theory in a world of imperfect information" (1993, 266).

This paradox, it seems to me, is one reason to opt instead for the tenuous existence between the disciplines that characterizes most of the essays in this book. Science studies does not aim to protect Reason, Progress, or all those other philosophical abstractions from the squadrons of subversion, safely storing them in some cool, dark Platonic cave. Neither does it argue that "social science" can provide us with all the pre-assigned answers we need in order to participate in an engaged political economy of science. If anything, the science studies community has been noticeably reticent in endorsing any brand of social theory as the philosopher's stone for decoding the behavior of scientists, their patrons, and their clients. Instead, its members follow the precept that a degree of familiarity with the science in question, combined with an appreciation for its history, a keen eye for the context in which it operates, and an attentiveness to the activities of its participants, tempered with a suspension of judgment over the final significance of any given theory or empirical finding, serve to adequately organize research into science in action and its repercussions in the larger society. Science studies is not out to found a City on a Hill; it would just like to find out if Celera really did give a boost to the public genome project or was merely a cynical move to profit from it. Science studies won't dream up an entirely different system of democracy; it will just address the interests behind the modern push to revamp intellectual property (Lessig 2001). Likewise, this book doesn't try to decide if neoclassical economics really is the application of "the scientific method" to the economy; but rather inquires whether the "laws of supply and demand" are capable of adequately organizing the set of social influences that bequeathed to us the Particle Data Group, the linear regression package for your PC, or indeed—the "laws" of supply and demand themselves.

Negotiating the Two-Way Crawl Spaces

I would not be entirely candid in this introduction if I did not mention that the science studies community has been more than a little wary of welcoming an economist into its midst. Given the sensitivity of its members to the diversity of the sciences and their imperialistic tendencies, they suspect that the only thing worse than economists pronouncing upon the folkways of science out of bone ignorance and boundless hubris is economists offering with their usual aplomb to "help out" science studies. Although it cuts against my own self-interest, in my saner moments I applaud their caution. The proof of the contributions of a political economy of science will come in the specifics, and not in any grand programmatic statements. Thus it may pay some dividends to briefly indicate the ways in which the final three sections of this book intersect with themes prevalent in the science studies literature.

Quantification

One of the most important conceptual issues in science studies is that many sciences seek to set themselves apart from the general run of human knowledge by their dependence upon mathematical expression, and especially by their reliance upon quantification in the process of empirical research. Justifications of the superior efficacy of quantification have been notoriously thin within the sciences, ranging from testimonials of faith in Platonism to Eugene Wigner's mystical evocation of an "unreasonable effectiveness of mathematics." Within science studies there has been some research into quantification and its usefulness in fending off challengers to the legitimacy of certain research programs (Porter 1995), and some interesting work on the meanings of "proof" as it is used by mathematicians (MacKenzie 2002), but very little on the social structures responsible for validating and revising the bedrock numbers which are asserted to anchor the major empirical and mathematical theories of our time. The purposes of chapters 7 and 8 are to provide a concertedly social account of how formal mathematics and the attribution of error interact to stabilize the numerical values of the physical constants, with the model of the process being compared explicitly to the operation of arbitrage in stabilizing prices. This is a version of the "economics of science" pitched far beyond the purview of anyone previously cited in this introduction, and perhaps of any previous philosopher of science, with the possible exceptions of Emile Meyerson and Charles Saunders Peirce.

Starting with a modicum of familiarity with mathematics, one rapidly comes to realize that many physical quantities would not exhibit fixed invariant numerical values: many are determinate only up to a monotonic (or other) transformation, are varying functions of an array of other values, or are artifacts of various scales. Chapter 7 discusses the history of the realization of this fact in empirical physics, and the attempt to save the Platonist thesis by recourse to a small set of key "dimensionless constants": the only quantitative evidence one might cite of Nature speaking in a loud and clear voice. What is an unending source of fascination to me is how scientists in action (in this case, physicists) have behaved in a much more methodologically relativist fashion than as conventionally portrayed by their supposed defenders in the science wars. That chapter reveals that the invariance and integrity of the rock-hard constants have continually been challenged and their variability entertained by physicists in good standing, without deleterious consequences for quantification. One intellectual source of strength of physics, contrary to Kuhn et al., is that physics has somehow maintained the possibility of doubting some of the most fundamental tenets of its received theories *within a certain framework of speculation*. Some more instances of this openness to rethinking the invariance of the invariants have popped up since chapter 7 was published in its original form.

One particularly fertile locus of sustained skepticism about the ultimate finality of quantification is the field of astrophysics and cosmology. In a recent instance, a team of scientists led by John K. Webb was led to speculate that some of the most fundamental physical constants, such as the speed of light (whose numerical value is assigned by definition, as explained below in chapter 8), might be changing slowly in magnitude along with the evolution of the universe (Glanz and Overbye 2001). Speculations like this are not as rare as one might think, as the chapters reveal. What is noteworthy is that the investigators were not immediately shouted down as heretics, even though the implications for the relationship between certain cherished subsets of physics might be dire and, further, were not explored by the original authors. Indeed, physicists have proven not only to have a capacity to entertain invariance with a light heart, but also to seriously propose inversions of the standard hierarchy of the various component physical theories (relativity, quantum mechanics, solid-state physics) which underwrite the quantitative invariants. Perhaps the fervor which seems to be invested in quantitative invariance is merely an artifact of a misplaced drive to find the unified Theory of Everything which physicists have taken as their holy grail for so long. One recent incident was described as follows in the *New York Times*:

> Last year Dr. [Robert] Laughlin and David Pines . . . published a manifesto declaring the "science of the past," which seeks to distill the richness of reality into a few single equations governing subatomic particles, was coming to an impasse. Many complex systems . . . appear

to be irreducible . . . Carrying the idea even further, some sold-state physicists are trying to show that the laws of relativity, long considered part of the bedrock of the physical world, are not platonic truths since time began. They may have emerged from the roiling of the vacuum of space, much as supply-and-demand and other "laws" of economics emerge from the bustle of the marketplace. (Johnson 2001, D1, D5)

(Here we see journalists jumping the gun: drawing morals for the laws of supply and demand from the latest hot topic in physics. More on this anon.) The article goes on to describe the work of Shoucheng Zhang, who developed a model of elementary particles bubbling up from a vacuum, suggesting that the bedrock of reality is not invariance, but chaos. The implications of this line of thought are broached in chapter 7 : the quantitative invariants are not some solid evidence of our access to the world, but rather artifacts of the way we have modeled phenomena.

The implications of this worldview are elaborated upon in chapter 8. There we follow the basic science studies precept to resist resting assured that the fundamental constants are indeed constant, but instead take an unprejudiced look, and then ask who and what are responsible for their presumed constancy. In that chapter we become acquainted with the severely underappreciated field of metrology, and discover that early-twentieth-century worries over social lacunae in enforcing the constancy of the physical constants provoked the designation of special agents and institutions whose job it was to enforce the constancy of the constants through explicit acknowledgment of the mathematical nature of their interdependence, and to impose the consistency of that interdependence by reassigning error estimates throughout the network structure of the constants. Furthermore, that chapter shows that we can deploy some of the analytical techniques of the metrologists to develop a comparative study of the treatment of quantification across various sciences. There we learn, among other things, that economics fails at stabilizing its supposed quantitative invariants to a degree that is orders of magnitude worse than in physics, or indeed psychology. These chapters give explicit examples of how one can move between the disciplines and undertake empirical research without pledging allegiance to any single one, as advocated in this introduction.

It seems to me that this social approach to the activity of quantification would appeal to the science studies community as broadly resonant with its goals and objectives. In support of that prognosis, the social approach is beginning to be put to use by science studies scholars like Trevor Pinch to counter ungrounded assertions that sociological factors never influence "solid" scientific results (in Labinger and Collins 2001, 223, 291). Yet the approach also has profound implications for economics. It raises the question: why does one science give markedly different results from another one? Below, I suggest that some of the main differences between physics and economics are not traceable (as the chestnut has it) to ontological differences in their subject matters, but to quantifiable differences in their social structures. Physics (until the very recent past) was an extremely self-assured science which left a fair amount of latitude for individuals to question seemingly fundamental models and assumptions. If someone took the trouble to make a coherent argument, that was often seen as sufficient justification for publication (witness the acceptance rate for articles in *Physical Reviews* of more than 80 percent, compared with 15 to 20 percent for the *American Economic Review*).[20] Of course controversy would still exist, and the orthodox would be tempted to peremptorily dismiss the discordant data, but special social structures—in this instance, the Particle Data Group and its Handbook of Constants—were set up to adjudicate differences. Economics, on the other hand, was rife with cold-war distrust of the competence of its own membership, and yet preternaturally opposed (by its theory of markets) to the idea that explicit social structures should be set up to adjudicate differences (such as differences in statistical estimates; see chapter 10). So instead, discipline was *imposed* in supposedly impartial but functionally arbitrary fashion, through restrictions on publication in sanctioned "orthodox" journal outlets. A few editors and their chosen referees arbitrarily decide what constitutes a good number, hiding behind the opaque operation of the editorial process. The result has been much less stability and integrity in the quality of the numbers produced by the economics discipline.

Statistics and Econometrics

The spread of statistics has been an especially active area of science studies over the last two decades (Daston 1988; Porter 1986; Hacking 1990; Mirowski 1997b). Primarily, the interest has centered on the diverse understandings of probability and randomness in the eighteenth and nineteenth centuries, although some perceptive work has also been done on the conflicting philosophical definitions of probability (Fine 1973). The chapters in part IV of this book tend to be more concerned with the ways in which probability and statistics were used in the twentieth century to help define scientific discourse, with heightened concern for the phenomenon of econometrics in postwar economics.

Chapter 9 is an extended meditation upon the widespread conviction that historical research would become "scientific" through the deployment of techniques like linear regression analysis and more direct recourse to hypothesis testing. When I first embarked upon my career as an economist, figures such as Robert Fogel, Douglas North, and Jeffrey Williamson were notorious for making outlandish claims about how "Cliometrics" (their neologism) would sweep old-fashioned historians onto the ash-heap of discarded doctrines. Some reflection on intervening events reveals that their predictions were not borne out (although it did garner for the first two a Nobel Prize); and indeed, the Cliometrics is in retreat in most modern neoclassical economics departments. It should have been apparent that history and neoclassical economics were like oil and water, or better yet, Courvoisier and Coca-Cola, but hindsight was always more self-assured than prediction. In any event, I became concerned to concoct a little historical exercise which would show precisely where Professor Fogel's magic elixir became little better than whitewash. Chapter 9 twice tells the story of an intriguing set of wagers by British brewers in the early nineteenth century: once in the standard Cliometric idiom, and then once more as old-fashioned historical narrative. The point of the exercise is to isolate how even something so seemingly straightforward as empirical predictive success (remember: Kitcher's transcendental desideratum of science!) can look wildly different depending upon the explanatory framework.

Chapter 10 bears an even more direct connection to science studies, although that community may be forgiven for having overlooked the chapter in its embryonic form in a somewhat outré outlet. The paper started out as an attempt to draw out some of the strategic implications which lay obscured in Harry Collins's classic *Changing Order* (1985). Collins had argued that pure replication was extremely rare in science as practiced: much of what passed for empirical support was in practice an extension of some empirical protocol into different domains or materials. My co-author Steve Sklivas and I decided (tongues in cheek) to play up the conflict inherent in the situation between an originator of an empirical claim and the researchers who sought to confirm or contest it. To that end, we portray the "choice" whether to challenge an empirical finding as a game, with major policy variables the "amount" of tacit information which the originator opts to share with the outside researcher, the rising costs of complete replication in all respects, the level of hostility perceived by the originator when approached by the supplicant, and the level of disinterest of scientific outlets in publishing successful replications. We showed that one of the most important regularities uncovered by science studies—the paucity of pure replication in science—could be regarded as having a social component, which would be highly difficult to expunge from science in action. Furthermore, we suggest that science harbors an inbuilt bias toward fostering "extensions" of empirical exercises, rather than replications, which contrasts with the conventional wisdom that replication is one of the foundation stones of the reliability of the "scientific method." But far from constituting yet another instance of the "economics of science" as a simple projection of the neoclassical orthodoxy, we then turn around and reveal that attempts by the *Journal of Political Economy* to alter this state of affairs were themselves unavailing; if anything, neoclassical economics suffers from a more debilitating case of replication aversion, at least when it comes to econometrics, than the other sciences.

Chapters 11 and 12 recount one significant challenge to the legitimacy of econometrics, as it were, from within the citadel of formal probability theory. In the 1960s Benoit Mandelbrot set out to challenge the standard characterization of the stochastic character of time series of prices as consisting of linear combinations of Gaussian processes, a major presupposition underlying much of the justification of linear regression analysis in econometrics. Mandelbrot insisted that distributions of changes of prices had "fat tails" inconsistent with Gaussian or "normal" (cute Orwellian name) distributions. The reactions to Mandelbrot by economists over the last three decades have illustrated the ways in which certain sciences maintain their commitments to certain restricted sets of empirical practices, especially after Mandelbrot himself went on to become a celebrity for his discovery and popularization of "fractals" (which chapter 12 argues owed something to his brush with economics). Here again physics and economics remain inextricable. Contrary to popular impressions, probability theory has never totally succeeded in taming randomness. Randomness refuses to be corralled so tidily. However, as in so much of history, the story does not sport a linear plot line or a simple resolution. In the interim, "fat tails" and chaotic models persist in a sort of demimonde of financial economics, especially popular with the exiled physicists who tend to reside in the high-tech research departments of banks and mutual funds, whereas Mandelbrot himself has backed away from his prior insistence that Levy stable distribution theory was both a simpler and a more natural stochastic description of economic data. The challenge to quotidian econometric inference, however, seems to have got lost in the shuffle; nothing is harder to expose to doubt than something which has earned the sobriquet "normal."

Chapters 13–16 at first glance may seem like old-fashioned history of economic thought to the median denizen of science studies, who may therefore be inclined to give them wide berth; I would hope that one consequence of this volume would be to induce the reader to suppress that inclination. Those chapters belong here because they synthesize many of the themes pioneered in the earlier chapters having to do with science, quantification, and econometric empiricism. For instance, one prerequisite of a belief in science as a "marketplace of ideas" is the presumption that all markets operate essentially alike; by contrast, one objective of the last three chapters is to call that commonplace wisdom into question. Indeed, part of the deep structure of the neoclassical mindset is the presumption that the Walrasian and Marshallian models are in some unspecified sense consistent and hence mutually supportive of the conviction that there subsist generic laws of The Market. This creed represses the historical evidence that the theoretical tradition of "Supply and Demand" explanations and the parallel tradition of neoclassical utility maximization were for a long time *rivals*. This fact is brought out in chapter 13 by tracing the antecedents to the supply and demand tradition, and pointing out that natural scientists such as Antoine-Augustin Cournot and Fleeming Jenkin promoted it as superior to the utilitarian school. The controversy over the scientific pretensions of Supply and Demand came to a head with the insufficiently appreciated work of William Thomas Thornton, who first argued that there could be no such thing as generic laws of The Market, but only regularities of certain classes of market formats. Further, far from being a toothless observation that diversity mattered, Thornton's insight was also deployed by him as a political defense of the legitimacy of trades unions, a move that made most of the political economy community sit up and take notice.[21]

Chapter 14 reveals that most of the major players in the establishment of British neoclassical economics developed their doctrines, at least in part, in direct response to Thornton. This had the further side effect of fostering that curious precept that the reprocessed energy physics which was the vinculum of the neoclassical model (Mirowski 1989b) somehow underwrote the use of geometric supply and demand diagrams. So that which had previously been separate and opposed was forced to cohabit, especially in the textbook of Alfred Marshall. Since Marshall set much of the pattern for neoclassical introductory textbook pedagogy down to the present, there we find the origins of the widespread belief in "laws of supply and demand," even among those for whom economic textbooks are an abomination.

Just because a doctrine attains textbook status doesn't mean it is correct, however. For instance, it was the early-twentieth-century American economics community which felt that Marshall had neglected fortifying supply and demand by forging the downstream links to quantitative empiricism, as well as adequate upstream links to the formal model of neoclassical utility optimization. This story continues with Henry Ludwell Moore in chapter 15, who was one of the first to apply the nascent Pearsonian theory of statistical inference to the fitting of demand curves to real data. Again defying the modern conventional wisdom, Moore was not trying to fortify the Marshallian program with his empirical forays, but rather regarded his work as a critique. Far from being an unalloyed success, his faltering project was bequeathed to two of the major players in the stabilization of the American neoclassical orthodoxy (see Mirowski 2002, chapter 5), Henry Schultz and Harold Hotelling.

The point of these chapters is not to ridicule the proponents, or treat them as bumbling precursors, but rather to demonstrate how hard it was to carry out the project of rendering the "laws of supply and demand" as something a bit more solid than *figures of speech*, and to fortify them with all the trappings of scientific legitimacy which the proponents felt were indispensable to their efforts. It wasn't enough that one could inscribe a geometric shape on a blackboard, or write down a few bits of mathematics which supposedly legitimated them. That may have been good enough to browbeat students, but not sufficient to win the allegiance of the scientifically trained. In the early twentieth century, the imperative to quantify was taken as the hallmark of true science; but eventually that didn't prove to be sufficient either. Much effort was then poured into the construction of specialized statistical techniques which were purpose-built to capture the answers to questions about the relationship of supply and demand to the neoclassical organon; but they didn't produce the sought-after parameter estimates either. The reason that each succeeding initiative to strengthen the link failed was that the Walrasian model and the tradition of supply and demand were analytically uncoupled—or to put this slightly more formally, the Sonnenschein, Mantel, and Debreu theorems developed in the 1970s revealed that Walrasian systems placed almost no restrictions on excess demand functions—so that the presumed dependence of the "laws of supply and demand" on the underlying "deep parameters" of individual utility maximization was a forlorn ambition. What this implies for the cogency of the supposed "laws" is an exercise left for the reader.

We end the book with a chapter which may seem to rest uneasily under the rubric of the history of supply and demand of Part V, or worse, seem incongruous in both style and substance in the book as a whole. I again plead with you, dear reader, to temporarily withhold judgment so that the chapter's place in the larger oeuvre might become clear. As with much else in this book, the original motivation was to understand the strengths and weaknesses of the neoclassical school through an exploration of the social processes which buttress its use and abuse. In this particular instance, I set out to address the commonplace (but I believe doomed) predisposition to dispute the neoclassical model as too "selfish" a portrayal of human nature. In the chapter I make use of some themes found in Jacques Derrida to argue that the attempt to counterpoise debased market motives with the "gift" and selflessness is a one-way ticket to intellectual dissolution. Those skeptical of the neoclassical program are misled in thinking that the major point at issue is the cognitive or moral philosophy of the agent—neoclassical arguments are too slippery to be pinned down there, and anyway I would insist that the fundamental strength of the neoclassical model derives rather from its attempts to embody popular images of scientific inquiry and content into what purports to be a description of social interaction. Although not explicitly spelled out in that chapter, this thesis has direct relevance to science studies as well. In the 1960s the sociologist of science Warren Hagstrom (1965) attempted to counter marketplace metaphors for science by positing instead that science constituted a "gift economy," not so different from the groups cited within chapter 16. For precisely the same reasons enumerated there, the attempt to make science "special" by supposing that it constitutes a distinct gift economy and therefore is the epitome of the polar opposite of market exchange only serves to open the door to the unconstrained application of rational choice models; once again we discover that the undecidability of the essence of selfishness works in favor of the neoclassical school, only this time in attempts to describe science as a social process. This goes some distance toward explaining the weakness of the older Mertonian sociology of science in providing an alternative social account of science in action, and leaves us with the suggestion that such an account can only be provided by an economics of science which does not keep other disciplines (and their theoretical contents) at arm's length.

This book seeks to create a space where we can get past the grand abstractions about Science, Truth, and Democracy and begin to talk about the ways that scientists live their lives on the ground today. If we are successful, we may just measure up to the standard already set by authors of fiction like Carter Scholz, who in his novel *Radiance* has found a language to evoke what it feels like to work in a weapons lab run by a government which is being exhorted to convert to "dual use." Here he imagines a conversation between two weapons scientists:

> "Think your man Leonardo didn't have to hold his gorge every day? . . . These are our allies boy."
> "They're thugs Dan. They're enemies of reason."
> "Common cause, Leo. You don't have to share a pew with them."
> "Common cause? What cause?"
> "Power, money, influence. Commonest causes there are. Who gives a shit what they believe?"
> "You remember when Schott won his Nobel? A year later he was pushing master race eugenics."
> "What are you getting at, Leo?"
> "Just because you're smart don't think that you can't be stupid."

1

Confessions of
an Aging
Enfant Terrible

How This Essay Works

Anyone who has kept up with literary theory over the past two decades would probably quail at the idea that simple, heartfelt *apologiae pro vitis suis* chronicle success in any walk of life, and would deny most emphatically that they play any pedagogical role in academe. I myself have been very much taken with some work done on the genre of the autobiography, subgenre vindication (Furbank 1993; Sturrock 1993). Briefly, and crudely, there are two classes of autobiography: let us call them the Academy Award Speech and the Adventures of a Self-Made Man. In the first, you are put at great pains to thank everyone from your kindergarten teacher to your shrink for their wonderful communal effort in bringing you to the brink of success and recognition; all hints of envy and struggle and despair and randomness are banished in a warm diffusion bath of responsibility and self-congratulation. Morals are of course drawn, but they inevitably verge on the platitudinous. Sitting through even one of such testimonials immediately makes clear that this genre will never be art. At best it can be of minor interest to those who will construct our narrative histories after we are gone.

And then there are autobiographies of the second class, those more substantial *Confessions*, from Augustine to Rousseau to de Quincey to Hobson to Verlaine to Richard Rorty: the ones that to varying degrees can be elevated to the status of art. Here the pattern is decidedly different. The *topos* is the story of someone fearlessly opting out of staid convention and the fellow feeling of mankind to wander in the wilderness and, with success, to return preaching strange and novel doctrines. Intrinsic to the narrative is the conviction that the author is self-made or self-taught (men write these much more often than women: feminists, take note!). "They are likely to tell us of some turn in their experience when they were thrown back on their own resources (like Descartes, alone in his stove-heated room) . . . rendering them unsociable for the moment, with a need one day to make their terms again with humankind . . . As a class, they have a tendency to megalomania . . . For all their self-castigation and earnest proclamations of indebtedness, [these] autobiographers are an arrogant and autarkic bunch" (Furbank 1993, 6).

Economists, it seems, inevitably find themselves torn between these two genres. Insofar as they are wont to be satisfied team players (not to mention eager to reinforce their reputations as dull and dismal souls), they should opt for the first narrative, pretending that there are uncontentious transpersonal rules and an orderly structure to their discipline, a functional meritocracy of incremental normal science. Yet however much this would seem to be the harsh imperative of academic etiquette (Hamermesh 1992), economists' own social theories tell them that this communal conception of social life is bunk, that everything law-governed springs directly from individual consciousness, that the lonely genius is the only real fount of innovation, and that aggressive self-promotion is the law of the jungle. The commonplace fallback of a competitive "marketplace of ideas" best captures this latter temptation among economists to apply their own theories to their own economistic lives, with the coda that the inevitable reintegration into the society of scholars comes in the stylized format of chastened, vanquished opponents humbly acknowledging the prophet's property and ideas as coin of the realm.

I couldn't possibly produce a plausible version of either narrative; I just can't summon sufficient faith in either genre, much less the requisite enthusiasm. Because I am not a product of a successful socialization into the economics profession, lots of things that economists say strike me as funny. The idea that we are paid according to our marginal productivity, for instance, is risible; the suggestion that an economy "overheats" is a richly wrought satire. The doctrine that the market maximizes the freedom of a set of agents identical in all relevant respects is a joke worthy of Nietzsche. At the University of Michigan, where I did my graduate degree, the people who worked in the econometric forecasting unit used to call tinkering with unsatisfactory predictions "adding the bump constants." These are fine as harmless entertainments, but turn to ashes in my mouth when I am forced to render an account of my own life.

I have resisted becoming integrated into the "normal science" practices of the discipline, and I know that this sedition has been one common thread connecting the diverse areas within which I have labored. Others sense this instinctively: I am frequently reprimanded in print for my style and tone;[1] some of my teachers in graduate school warned me ominously that I would not fit in; and fellow faculty at Yale cautioned graduate students to keep an assured clear distance from any of my projects while I was a visiting professor there. Economists from outside Notre Dame conspired to segregate me and other heterodox colleagues in a ghetto sequestered from a newly formed neoclassical department while I was there. Now, in retrospect, I can appreciate the kernel of wisdom in all this unsolicited advice. The ingrained stodginess of the social structures of science does serve certain cognitive functions. The most immediate is fostering the feeling of being a part of something larger than oneself. Asking me now to write on how I feel about economics journals is like asking a lamppost to write a memoir on dogs. But the alternate narrative portrayal of myself as a Nietzschean *Übermensch*, performing the magic trick of conjuring myself out of thin air, or even more incongruously, the idea that some of my writings have somehow become valorized in the marketplace of ideas, is just ludicrous. Anyone who had actually read any of my other stuff would immediately have detected an inauthentic note from page one.

One consequence of my scrambled sense of identity has been an attempt to understand myself as a product of my age by understanding economics as a product of the social conditions of its production. This may sound like an impossibly misplaced motivation, rather like trying to understand Mozart by studying Freemasonry, or to take the comparison down a notch, Charles Manson by studying the lyrics of the Beatles. Perhaps a surfeit of incredulous reactions will one day convince me of that fact. Yet until that day dawns, I will continue to be taken with the notion that philosophical discourse is a species of veiled autobiography, "the personal confession of its author and a kind of involuntary and unconscious memoir; also that the moral (or immoral) intentions in every philosophy constituted the real germ of life from which the whole plant had grown" (Nietzsche 1966, 13). Thus, when I read confident, imperious declarations by economists —for example, that children are consumer goods, or that countries in the Third World should be dumping grounds for toxic industrial wastes since life is cheap there, or that no sound economist would oppose NAFTA, or that some price completely reflects all relevant underlying fundamentals in the market, or that magnetic resonance imaging locates the seat of utility in the brain, or that no credible theorist could recommend anything but a Nash equilibrium as the essence of rationality in a solution concept—I do not see an occasion to dispute the validity of the economists' assumptions of their "models"; rather, for me, I see an opportunity to investigate the conditions which allow such classes of statements to pass muster, as a prelude to understanding what moral presuppositions I must evidently hold dear, given that I find them deeply disturbing. However unpopular it may be, I find it hard to understand economics as anything other than a subset of moral philosophy, even though this definition of "philosophy" awaits explication. Thus, by learning about economists and their peccadillos, I learn about myself; discovering how these things work helps me understand How I Work.

"I'm an economist. I don't think in historical terms."—Polish government official, on the erstwhile "MacNeil-Lehrer News Hour"

The separation of "is" from "ought," the positive from the normative, is of course the byword of our stridently secular discipline. I am perfectly well aware that political economy traces its lineage out of moral philosophy, essentially renouncing the terms of that earlier discourse in favor of the instrumentalist terminology of Science in order to assert its novel identity as "economics." For most of my colleagues, this reality dictates that the language and concepts of moral philosophy are an anathema, the province of confused claims and counterclaims. Although they might differ as to whether it happened in 1776 or 1838 or 1870 or 1944, at some juncture economics attained its status as a science and forswore moral philosophy.

My little epiphany, which occurred quite early in my career, was to decide that I should provisionally accept the economists' ukase regarding philosophy, and follow them part of the way into their kingdom of preferred legitimacy, namely Science. This did not mean for me, as it did for so many of them, starting off with a degree in physics or engineering or mathematics; nor did it imply direct recourse to the self-conscious philosophy of science or its bastard offspring in economics, "methodology." Rather, it meant following my own prior inclinations to learn some history of science and history of economics. In this quest, I was fortunate to be encouraged by a few open-minded individuals along the way: Warren Samuels, Gavin Wright, and Lawrence Sklar.

Because this sounds like such a prescription for disaster in modern economics, I want to stress that the whole thing was not the result of some decision-theory calculation on my part.

I was only dimly aware in the early 1970s that an interest in intellectual history was tantamount to career suicide in academic economics, though things certainly have got worse in the interim. I acted simply out of curiosity. I would never counsel anyone else to follow me in this respect, because that career path no longer exists. However intemperate, I have never been able to accept the definition of "economic science" prevalent among my colleagues. It has remained my practice down to the present day to do at least a third of all my reading well outside of economics, both in the natural sciences and in literature, and further, to sporadically read randomly, trusting my instincts and keeping copious notebooks in order to trace my way back to any particular node. In a world where it is cute to think that the only famous

Ricardo was the second banana on the "Lucy" show, but getting the Euler equation wrong is grounds for getting you booted from the profession, imputing rationality to my actions would be a shameless whitewash. Sometimes I wonder the extent to which my younger self was conscious of living in the material world.

Once I had gained a fair grounding in the history of physics (having also had a few courses in the area), I began to discern a repetitive set of invocations of Science among various economists, and then my ear became attuned to some of their ambivalences and ambages along the way. Luckily, I was living through an era in which belief in any context-independent Scientific Method was being unsentimentally deconstructed, so I did not have to take the various economists' characterizations at face value. I began to understand how their dependence upon Science was inextricably time bound, and further, the astounding degree to which these economists would persistently confuse imitation of the trappings of physics (or lately, biology) with privileged access to the ontological heart of the economy. I still marvel at the extent that economists openly pride themselves on living in the material world, when they are mostly surrounded by shadows in their own private cave.

Once I had become convinced of the pervasive character of this dependence upon diverse meanings of "science," I became more and more excited, like Borges in his Library of Babel; so many of the things about economics which had nettled and disturbed me now had a context and a frame, inviting detailed clarification through comparison of the history of the sciences. Just one product of this reconfiguration of the history of economics which has subsequently attained some notoriety is my argument (1989b) that the "Marginalist Revolution" of the 1870s was no discovery, but rather a fairly straightforward appropriation of the energetics movement of the mid-nineteenth century, with utility being the direct analogue of potential energy, prices the analogue of forces, and the budget constraint a deformed version of kinetic energy. While some readers misunderstood the message of *More Heat Than Light* as "economics copied physics and that's patently wrong," others have seen that I tried to explore what it is that makes certain metaphors and their attendant special mathematics work in some disciplines and fail miserably in others. Images of physics must be separated out from real physics; children's fairy tales about the scientific method must be distinguished from the historical practices of real scientists; images of a generic mathematical rigor must be distinguished from mathematical arguments in action. Other examples of the use (and misuse) of physical and biological concepts in diverse areas of economics were the subject of an inaugeral conference of my chair at Notre Dame, the proceedings of which have been published (1994b). The shock waves of the wartime genesis of the computational sciences and their consequences for the rise of the American neoclassical orthodoxy have been recounted in *Machine Dreams* (2002).

It has been difficult not to let this excavation of physical metaphors come to usurp my entire research life, since it has opened up so many new questions and areas of inquiry. Indeed, I am heartened to observe that some others have seen fit to take up the gauntlet, as is evident from Rob Leonard's exploration of the role of structuralism in game theory, Bruce Caldwell's inquiry into the role of the computer in the socialist calculation controversy, Geoff Hodgson's fine-grained explication of the metaphor of biological evolution in a number of economists, Roy Weintraub's demonstration of the importance of Alfred Lotka and E. B. Wilson for the evolution of the neoclassical stability literature, Michael White's unpacking of the meaning of equilibrium in Jevons, Abu Rizvi's connection of British psychophysics to modern doctrines on the nonrecoverability of neoclassical preferences, Tinne Kjeldsen's clarification of the rise of the Kuhn-Tucker theorem, Esther-Mirjam Sent's exploration of the importance of artificial intelligence for Tom Sargent's and Herbert Simon's peregrinations, and Paul Christensen's detailed exposition of the importance of Quesnay's training as a surgeon for his innovation of the concept of the circulation of value. But as Arjo Klamer has written in his contribution to the *Natural Images* volume, this work has yet to get much beyond the stage of "Look, Ma—a metaphor!" Certainly no one else has felt the force of this observation more than I. As someone who has gone on record as skeptical of the McCloskeyesque version of a "rhetorical program" in economics, I have come to appreciate how effortlessly this work might be shrugged off by a profession contemptuous of its own history, overtly hostile to philosophy, smug in the trappings of academic success, ready to absorb any intellectual challenge as an analytical special case, and quick to hurl accusations of the genetic fallacy at any of these scholars wishing to reopen consideration of the meanings of Science in practice. This standoff has nudged me ever closer to the discipline of "Science Studies," as the present volume attests.

Rather than simply retreat to the bailiwick of Science Studies (wherever that might be), the rival theoretical approach has prompted me to alter my behavior toward the economists. My own response has been to broaden the program by constructing specially targeted exercises for specific subsets of the economics profession. Often I have adopted the persona of the empiricist for the methodologists, the philosopher for the economic historians, the historian for the theorists, and the theorist for disaffected groups of antineoclassicals, such as the Institutionalists. Let me give one example of each. As to the first, I have been much concerned to address a common objection to *More Heat than Light*: perhaps mathematical theory has worked itself into various dead ends because of the original physics inspiration, but, goes this objection, one cannot ignore the rich history of empirical endeavors which provide the real backbone and continuity of the economics profession. Since one of the lessons I have drawn from comparisons with physics is that neoclassicals have been egregiously lax in their commitments to what is indeed conserved or invariant in their portrait of the economy, I confronted the econometricians on a related malaise which seems to have infected their own bailiwick of late. Using techniques from physical metrology (especially Birge ratios), in chapter 8 I show empirically that the quality of quantitative agreement in econometric estimates of numerical "constants" is far and away inferior to that of parallel endeavors in either physics or psychology. Rather than appeal to inchoate personal conceptions of "good science," we should try to look at track records. This, in an indirect way, calls into question the assumed existence of the consensual stable empirical base which lies at the center of econometric practice, as well as at the heart of this response to *More Heat*.

In chapter 9, I have tried to confront the conviction that Cliometrics has made the study of history Scientific in its own terms. I have sought to do so by writing a standard Cliometric paper on the rationality of wagers by brewers in nineteenth-century Britain, and then rewritten the same paper showing that the path-dependence of econometric estimation does not at all adequately constrain the historical narrative. In other words, by judicious choice of assumptions, I can depict the historical actors as rational or irrational as I please—only to then demonstrate that good old-fashioned archival digging serves to restrict the range of interpretation of the actors' behaviors much more perspicaciously than regression analysis does.

An instance of the ministering as historian to the economic theorists would be my recent work on game theory. We are fortunate to be alive at a time when the neoclassical orthodoxy has rapidly shifted its allegiance from Walrasian general equilibrium (I would suggest that Marshall was left behind long ago, spooned out only as thin gruel for weak minds in the principles course) to noncooperative game theory as the core doctrine of what is regarded as the hallmark of economic expertise. One finds during such tectonic shifts that major players feel impelled to comment upon epistemic ruptures, play up or play down the obsolescence of their predecessors, and gear up to rewrite the Whig histories. Regarding game theory, events have moved with such alacrity that no canonical story of the rise of game theory yet exists, though glimpses can be discerned here and there, such as in Robert Aumann's essay (1995) and Roger Myerson's revision of the canon (1999). What I have tried to do, along with a number of others, is intervene in this process at an early stage and make it a little bit harder to write that standard hagiography in which the hallowed progenitor has a number of inconvenient appendages amputated in the interests of a progressive narrative. In particular, we have excavated evidence (Mirowski, 2002) of some of the motivations and concerns of John von Neumann and Oskar Morgenstern, showing, for instance, that von Neumann was heavily influenced by twentieth-century physics (especially quantum mechanics), disliked neoclassical theory, and was never favorably disposed toward the solution concept of choice of the modern orthodoxy, the Nash equilibrium. Indeed, he anticipated the present fascination with the theory of automata by half a century. I am not so deluded as to think that these insights will substantially change the behavior of modern game theorists in their quest for the philosopher's stone of rationality, but they may make it more difficult for the theorists to present their burgeoning program as a natural outgrowth of the prior orthodoxy.

Finally, I must confess that there are a small number of self-consciously theoretical papers listed in my vita, though I do not hold that abstract genre, appropriated from the rhetoric of the physics journal, in very high regard. After all, forcing people to write in such an impoverished style is one of the major instruments by which historical consciousness is exiled and the aleatory character of science repressed. Although it may seem quixotic, I have felt compelled periodically to counteract the common impression that Institutionalist economics is hopelessly atheoretical (an impression studiously promulgated by the alumni of the Cowles Commission) by insisting that the mathematical character of the practices of economic actors (and *not* economists) needs a rational explanation, something lacking in every formal economic tradition of which I am aware. In pursuit of this goal I have cribbed together a few underutilized bits of mathematics, like abstract algebra, automata theory, and directed graphs, to argue that economic value is not intrinsic either in the commodity (as in classical political economy) or hard-wired in the psyche (as in neoclassicism), but is instead socially constructed by the postulation of mathematical invariants where none truly exist. I now see the intellectual roots of this tradition as essentially consisting of three main strands:

A. The thesis that there is no such thing as a generic "Market"; rather, there are numerous diverse forms of rules and behavior which could be used to facilitate trade. Hence what we would call an "economy" is really a patchwork of many market forms, imperfectly interlinked and integrated.[2] This vision was pioneered by the underappreciated economic writer William Thomas Thornton, in his classic *On Labour*, as part of a critique of the notion that there existed a single "Law of Supply and Demand."[3] This thesis was developed in a different direction (proposing a taxonomy of different legal classes of transactions) by the Institutionalist theorist John R. Commons.

B. There is an uneven literature in the twentieth century that explored the formalization of markets as algorithms. *Machine Dreams* cites John von Neumann as the primary inspiration, but there are many figures who might be associated with this position, ranging from some experimental economists such as Ross Miller and Charles Plott to a subset of mechanism design theorists such as Roy Radner to artificial intelligence specialists such as Michael Wellman.

C. The question of how "evolution" is to be formally modeled is also central to transcending constrained optimization as a Theory of Everything. This has been an abiding concern of Geoff Hodgson (1993), among others. Recently, Walter Fontana has made a cogent argument that the inability of mathematical models of evolution as motion over a fitness surface to capture phenomena central to evolution such as temporal irreversibility, "punctuated equilibrium," and neutral drift can be traced to the presumption of a Euclidean topology for the fitness surface.[4] This critique can be extended to economics, by observing that the seemingly innocent postulate of a Euclidean "commodity space" equally precludes serious modeling of evolution in economics. Briefly, if you can get to any commodity basket from any other basket with equal facility and no trade is irreversible, then evolutionary change in the methods and modalities of exchange is ruled out a priori. The precept that "there is no such thing as commodity space" turns out to be indispensable for a theory of market automata.

Drawing together these sources of inspiration (taken equally from within economics and from other natural sciences), we can briefly characterize a formal evolutionary economics which models individual market forms evolving in an environment of people. In this economics, specific market forms—say, a posted price market selling cantaloupes, a Dutch auction selling flounder, a double auction selling number 2 red wheat futures, and so on—are each modeled as formal automata, in the von Neumann sense. The rules and structures of the individual form are reduced to states, alphabets, and transition rules: the "software" of our economic world. Some market automata accept bids and asks as inputs, and calculate prices and quantities as outputs. (Others conduct more complicated computations with a wider range of inputs.) Different markets will constitute automata of differing computational complexity.[5] Some markets of greater complexity will be capable of "simulating" the operation of simpler markets: for instance, the futures market for number 2 wheat "simulates" the operation of the spot market for number 2 wheat as part of its standard operation. The hierarchy of complexity defines a transitive ordering: more complex markets can "simulate" the operation of less complex relatives, but not vice versa. Much as in von Neumann's theory of automata, markets "reproduce" by extruding copies of themselves; they are then "selected" for persistence by the human beings who make use of them and constitute the environment in which they grow and reproduce. The goals and objectives of individual humans are irreducibly diverse and not susceptible to reduction to a single index or mathematical ordering. The irreducible diversity of possible reasons for privileging one set of automata over another is the root cause of why the entire system does not collapse to a single dominant market format.[6] However, there exists an "arrow of time" in the process of market evolution, with market automata of a given level of complexity infrequently giving rise to a market automata "offspring" of greater complexity: this is von Neumann (*not* Darwinian) evolution. The source of mutation of market automata is traced to the human beings who are always trying to "bend" or "break" the rules; this source of randomness is actually beneficial for the evolutionary process, if kept within certain bounds.

The purpose of such models is not to identify equilibria, or any other such vestigial holdover from physics envy, but rather to give an impression of what it is like for an actor to try to read the meaning of a transaction where no single correct reading exists. Rather than persist in the hallowed Western tradition of regarding the mind as a machine, perhaps a renovated formal Institutional economics could come to portray the set of diverse market institutions as algorithmic, undergoing a process of evolution in which people and cultures constitute the shifting environments.

The titillating name of this chapter promises confessions, and I realize that I have only been writing little abstracts of my work until now, so here comes my effort to make good on the initial promise. While playing the outsider with each of these groups of economists in a kind of musical chairs is good fun, it really has addled my sense of audience. Always play-acting the other has made it difficult to have a very good idea to whom I am talking; sometimes I despair at identifying exactly whom I may be influencing and to what end. Do economists care any longer to understand the forces that propel them willy-nilly across the intellectual landscape? Has intellectual history become anything more than high-toned PR about the Next Big Thing sweeping like a sirocco out of the natural sciences close-hauled to attract funding in an age of downsizing, or an insignificant diversion in the *fin de siècle* science wars? (Horgan 1997). I fear in the modern climate it may be relegated to the sphere of science fiction infotainment, as with the movie *A Beautiful Mind*. In my private moments I envy Marx or Hayek or Keynes or (dare I say it?) Milton Friedman, because they had supreme confidence in where they wanted people to end up, and merely adjusted their scientific manner and modalities to get them there in the most efficacious geodesic. (What better way to understand Friedman's essay on methodology?) I, on the other hand, am still struggling to figure out what it is that moral philosophy is or should be, so that economics might endorse some light at the end of the tunnel. I am reasonably sure it will not consist of yet more baroque epicycles on utilitarianism or ponderous academic pronouncements on ethics or another exculpatory paean to Nature or empty exhortations toward Truth and Honesty; but beyond that, I am as much in the dark as the next Technocrat or Aesthete. Poverty decimates lives; but what are riches?

No Man Is an Island

I am far from being an enemy to the Writers of Fables, since I know very well that this Manner of Writing is not only Ancient, but very useful, I might say sacred, since it has been made use of by the inspired Writers themselves; but then to render the Fable worthy of being received into the Number of those which are truly valuable, it must naturally produce some useful Moral . . . but this of *Robinson Crusoe* . . . is designd against . . . publick good.—Charles Gildon

The format of the brief autobiography is inevitably allegorical. The writer is a Pilgrim, searching for somebody or something, deflected this way and that, struggling to maintain a narrative thread in a world of chaos and dissociation. Here, for me, is where all the tensions between Science and Art meet. I am enjoined to talk about myself, and all I can manage to do is hide behind my Science. Neoclassicism wants desperately to be a Science, and yet all it can do is talk in terms of allegories. Unlike some partisans of the rhetoric movement, I do not regard this as an occasion to flaunt my (nonexistent) mastery of classical Greek or Vladimir Propp's taxonomy of folktales, with a view to provoking economists to acknowledge that they are telling stories, culminating in a hearty round of self-congratulation that We Are All Artistes Now. Alasdair MacIntyre has argued that the only two moral personae available to the intellectual in an era of bureaucratic individualism are the Technocrat and the Aesthete; economists like me would seem doomed to waver between these poles. Some, such as Richard Rorty, think this dilemma can never be resolved; others like MacIntyre think the answer is a return to earlier Aristotelian conceptions of the moral life. I myself would like to enlist as an advocate of a third position, namely that the promises of Modernity have largely been illusions with respect to the great divide between Science and Art, Objectivity and Subjectivity, Nature and Society (Latour 1993). We spend so much of our intellectual efforts trying to reconcile one to the other, when in fact they may have never been separate in practice. Let me give just one indication of what I mean.

I have been trying to write a narrative of my own wanderings, an allegory of what I am, but this is embedded in a narrative of the history of my profession, an allegory of what economics is all about. Just as I have my literary precursors, neoclassicism has its own allegorical account of its true *telos*. This account can be found in nearly every textbook: it is the story of

Robinson Crusoe. In the middle of an indoctrination of the tyro into our science, we find this story, this artful narrative, of what it means to be a neoclassical rational actor. The isolated individual, alone confronting scarcity on his island with his scant endowments, deliberates as to the appropriate combination of goods to maximize his well-being, imposing order upon the primeval chaos of Nature. As I have intimated before, economists generally don't read, but they think they know this story cold. The English hosier in the eighteenth century and the American academic in the twentieth understand each other perfectly, describing the inherent transcendental logic of their own system as it spreads across the face of the globe.

But because economists don't read, they don't generally realize that Defoe's novel does not underwrite their convictions to any appreciable extent. The man who wrote the following might resist being dragooned into the neoclassical cause:

> The most covetous griping miser in the world would have been cured of the vice of covetousness, if he had been in my case; for I possessed infinitely more than I knew what to do with. I had no room for desire, except it was of things which I had not, and they were but trifles . . . I learned to look more on the bright side of my condition and less upon the dark side and to consider what I enjoyed rather than what I wanted; and this gave me sometimes such secret comforts that I cannot express them; and which I take notice of here, to put those discontented people in mind of it who cannot enjoy comfortably what God had given them because they see and covet something He has not given them. (Defoe [1719] 1941, 126–27)

Some such observation that stories often sprawl outside the conventional interpretation is itself not novel. The few economists who have not lost the habit of reading have periodically tried to embarrass the textbook Robinson in various ways. One notable attempt was a paper by Stephen Hymer in 1971 that reminded us of the repressed character of Friday in order to turn the novel into an allegory of Marxist primitive accumulation. But trading one economic Robinson for another does not quite get at the crux of the problem: that was rather the achievement of Michael White (1982).

As opposed to the conviction that there is one invariant Robinson in our culture, the epitome of Art imitating Science, White showed that there were numerous rereadings of Defoe's novel throughout history, and that the neoclassical textbook Robinson probably dated from the mid-nineteenth century, roughly contemporaneous with the rise of marginalism in the 1870s. We might go further and suggest not only that was Defoe's *Robinson Crusoe* misread at various junctures for various purposes, but that it has periodically been rewritten in order to codify each generation's revision of the myth. The version which neoclassicals seem inclined to favor most closely resembles that of Johann Heinrich Campe's *Robinson der Jüngere* (1779), which was written for children to exemplify certain bourgeois virtues. (So the Rational Economic Man is a German folk tale!) Indeed, the novel has been rewritten so many times since that there is even a special term for the genre in German, the *Robinsonade*. From Johann Wysse's *The Swiss Family Robinson* (1812) to Frederick Marryat's *Masterman Ready* (1841) to Jules Verne's *The Mysterious Island* (1874) to Jean Giraudoux's *Suzanne et le pacifique* (1922) to William Golding's *Lord of the Flies* (1954) to Michel Tournier's *Vendredi: ou Les limbes du Pacifique* (1967) to Marianne Wiggins's *John Dollar* (1989), the narrative archetype has been bent and reshaped in so many directions to fit so many changes in concurrent images of Nature and Society in so many cultural contexts that perhaps one might suggest there is no solid Crusoe there to misrepresent anymore.

Isn't this just one of the characteristics of Art, that it is ephemeral and insubstantial, contextual and interpretive, whereas Science is forever? I would like to suggest otherwise. It is no accident that Robinson Crusoe and the mathematics of constrained optimization are yoked together in the same text, for in general they have suffered the same fate. Just as Robinson has been creatively misread and wilfully revised, the physics of the field which represented Hard Science to the late-nineteenth-century Western mind has been creatively misread as economics and wilfully rewritten any number of times, from utility to ophelimity to revealed preferences to convex sets to neural nets, and so on. All that holds them together is a vague family resemblance (and here mathematics as the bearer of inexplicit analogy plays an important role) which does not depend upon anyone's really *knowing* the physics or understanding the history in order to participate in the tradition. All those involved can honestly think they understand that of which rationality consists and what economics is really about, without ever once having to confront the disturbing fact that their narrative is the most frightful hodgepodge of bits and bobs, a *bricolage* that cannot be readily subsumed or sorted into Science or Art, Nature or Society, Objectivity or Subjectivity, Positive or Normative. This pattern of concerted revisionism will undoubtedly continue so long as some alternative narrative does not swoop down out of nowhere (or more likely, out of physics) and relegate Robinson to the dark oblivion of complete and utter neglect. Contrary to popular opinion, John Nash has not brought that particular tablet down from the mount.

Where does that leave the poor autobiographer, the person trying to proffer a moral tale or two to those who follow in this curious, blinkered profession? Given that any overarching Method has disintegrated into lumps of clay in our hands, disinterested general advice would seem presumptuous, if not foolish. Given that Robinsonades are still so popular, one could end on a note of narrative closure: having wandered far and seen wondrous things, our wayfarer returns from his remote island to peaceful Indiana to regale the locals with tales of his adventures. But just as equilibrium is a deeply unsatisfying resting place, specifying the ends of autobiography is a prematurely deadening procedure. Perhaps it is better to end as Defoe did: "All these things, with some very surprising incidents in new adventures of my own, for ten years more, I may perhaps give a further account of hereafter."

Part Two
Science as an
Economic
Phenomenon

2

On Playing the Economics Card in the Philosophy of Science: Why It Didn't Work for Michael Polanyi

Caveat Emptor

In an era when epistemology is being caught in a renewed tug of war between "socialized" and "naturalized" poles, one of the most noteworthy developments of the last few years has been the self-conscious reintroduction of economic models and metaphors into the philosophy of science. This reintroduction has become manifest in a variety of ways, ranging from bald appeals to the "marketplace of ideas" to a revival of Millian tendency laws (Hands 1994a; 2001) to explicit appropriation of rational choice models (Kitcher 1993). The extent to which this phenomenon has been driven by political and cultural upheavals of the recent past, or the "science versus anti-science" culture wars of the *fin de siècle* academy, or even the extent to which it stands as a symptom of the rivalry between philosophy of science and the sociology of science, are not issues to be reiterated here. Rather, we propose to focus upon the remarkable dearth of historical self-consciousness which accompanies the conviction that this development is new or unprecedented, be it in the science studies literature, or within the community of the philosophers of science. In particular, we shall recount the narrative of Michael Polanyi, someone not often acknowledged as a philosopher, yet a landmark figure who sought to explain the efficacy of free inquiry in science by comparing it to the operation of a free market. While this comparison was implicit in many of his writings from the 1940s onward, he himself made it explicit in his essay "The Republic of Science: Its Political and Economic Theory" (1962; in Polanyi 1969). Polanyi's struggles with the market metaphor are worth recounting, if only because so many of his worries are getting replayed in the modern context: questions of the appropriate response to calls for the planning of science in an era of reduced funding and diminished expectations; questions as to the implications of a sociology of knowledge for the public understanding of science; questions about the meaning of objectivity in a world riven by self-interested constructions of the legitimacy and significance of science.

In this chapter, we do not intend to endorse Polanyi's own market metaphor so much as to spotlight the considerable depth of appreciation that he had for the problems involved. He came to the philosophy of science with both the background knowledge culled from an accomplished career in physical chemistry and a good working acquaintance with the relevant controversies in economics; indeed, he spent much of the 1930s and 1940s actively writing on economic issues related to the Great Depression and socialist planning (see chapter 3). Far from being an armchair theorist, he had himself suffered exile for his political activities—those of a classic Burkean and pro-market conservative—and had observed the political consequences of economic organization on science firsthand in his native Hungary, Weimar Germany, communist Russia, and capitalist England. He was personally acquainted with the major champions of a sociology of science in the persons of J. D. Bernal, Karl Mannheim, and his own brother Karl Polanyi. Moreover, in the 1960s he was regarded as one of the foremost thinkers responsible for the overthrow of positivist conceptions of science, often bracketed together with Kuhn, Toulmin, and Feyerabend (to his everlasting discomfort). Few modern philosophers have been as intellectually well prepared as he to develop an independent evaluation of the relevance of economics for an understanding of the scientific process. And yet, by the end of his career Polanyi felt that his market defense of unfettered science had been a dismal failure. His experience may serve as a salutary warning to the numerous modern philosophical enthusiasts for the market metaphor.

The implications of this story for the *fin de siècle* philosopher may just perhaps transcend any specific concern with Polanyi as a historical figure, or alternatively, a reprise of the chastened prognosis for applying economic theory to the cognitive or social organization of science. To explore this possibility, we close the chapter with a section comparing the understandings of that loaded term "freedom" on the part of three key figures: Polanyi, Thomas Kuhn, and Philip Kitcher. This comparison is intended to raise the possibility that profound or epochal changes in the philosophy of science are highly correlated with changes in the political philosophy (or political economy, if you will) which informs its practitioners. In other words, when it comes to arguing about science, heuristic images of the economy have always been lurking nearby, half in the shadow, usually at stage right.

The Enemies Within

Polanyi is best remembered, though barely, for his advocacy of the tacit character of much knowledge in scientific practice (Turner 1994; Holton 1995). This argument was widely, and correctly, regarded as an attack upon the project of an analytical philosophy of science to render the logic of justification transparent, reliable, and independent of context; but isolated from the rest of Polanyi's crusade, most commentators conclude that it makes little sense on its own. It may be that the fragmentation of intellectual life into isolated professional specialties is at fault here. Conflating Polanyi's conception of tacit knowledge with that of Ludwig Wittgenstein or Alasdair MacIntyre or Sidney Winter or even Harry Collins does it the disservice of making it both larger and smaller than it really was: larger, in that the conception was intended by Polanyi as subsidiary to his more encompassing comparison of science to a free market; and smaller, in that it involved a concerted attempt to reconcile the individual character of knowledge with its intrinsic social nature. Only by venturing outside the narrow ambit of professional philosophy of science do we discover the closest affinities of Polanyi's "tacit" knowledge with the project of his fellow *mitteleuropäisch* economist contemporary and political ally Friedrich von Hayek, who also set out to recast the interwar treatment of knowledge and freedom, only in his case with the aim of counteracting what he perceived to be dangerous tendencies in the theory of markets to venture down the road to serfdom.

Both Hayek and Polanyi emerged from their experience of the 1930s haunted by the conviction that both scientists and capitalists were obliviously vulnerable to movements advocating rationalization and subjugation to state planning, an eventuality which they believed would sap their vitality and stymie their progress. These movements were embodied in the British context in Bernal's "Social Relations of Science" section in the British Association (McGucken 1984), the turn taken by the Cambridge economics orthodoxy, and the growing strength of socialist parties. Far from being merely an external threat, Polanyi increasingly harbored the conviction that the ultimate source of this vulnerability lay within the communities of economists and scientists themselves. In effect, the inherited self-understandings of the market transactors and bench scientists were serving to undermine the social structures necessary for keeping markets and science in good working order. In a passage more reminiscent of Hayek, Polanyi wrote in his most popular volume, *Personal Knowledge*, "modern scientism fetters thought as cruelly as ever the church had done. It offers no scope for our most vital beliefs and forces us to disguise them in farcically inadequate terms" (1958, 265).

It seems that Polanyi sought the etiology of the malady he had identified in the essential instability of Cartesian doubt. While he acknowledged the necessity of doubt as a lever to emancipate scientific inquiry from religious dogma in the seventeenth century, the success of skepticism in eliminating religious authority had done nothing to abate the moral fervor which had accompanied it. Indeed, withering skepticism combined with moral enthusiasm tended to become fused together in the Enlightenment image of the scientist, who himself became the bearer of the rationalist ideal of the perfect secular society. This ideal was predicated upon an unrestrained autonomous individualism which could only flourish within an environment of absolute freedom and equality, a benchmark against which actual social relations could only appear as pale and inadequate approximations. This seemingly intractable and intolerable discrepancy then gave rise to an amoral individualism, asserting the rights of the truly free and creative individual as against the claims of a corrupt and hypocritical society, or, as Polanyi put it, "the chisel of nihilism driven by the hammer of social conscience" (1974, 44). While Polanyi asserted that this "moral inversion" assumed many forms, and deployed his diagnosis to attack a range of various intellectual movements which had provoked his ire, from Freudianism to Marxism to cybernetics, it is important to try getting past his unseemly and high-handed propensity to moralize and to extract the core of the implications for epistemology and economics, since it is these which governed his use of the market metaphor for science.

In a pair of analytical moves which seem not to have made much of an impression on Polanyi's admirers, Polanyi himself sought to indict the Viennese positivists in philosophy and the utilitarians in economics with being the vectors of "moral inversion" in their fields; and as such, wittingly or no, they were leading the way for the social planners who bore such contempt for freedom. Insofar as scientists tried to justify their activities on positivist grounds (or, as we shall see, as economists did on utilitarian grounds), they set up a field of cognitive dissonance so devastating that the only escape appeared to be the reimposition of rationality by a Romanticist transcendence, be it through revolution or capitulation to "nature." As Polanyi insisted, "the freedom of science cannot be defended today on the basis of a positivist conception of science . . . Totalitarianism is a much truer embodiment of such a program than a free society" (1974, 64). The task here was to understand how a quest to buttress individual rationality by fortifying it against rational doubt would end up making it impossible for an individual to exercise any agency at all.

Polanyi was convinced that no productive scientist wanted the kind of apodictic impersonal certainty that the positivists or their offspring had portrayed them as wanting. "To think of scientific workers cheerfully trying this and trying that, calmly changing course at each failure, is a caricature of a pursuit that consumes a man's whole person" ([1940] 1975, 60). Rather than impersonal *certainty*, what a scientist operating at the frontiers of the known desperately needed was personal *commitment*. In a working laboratory, he was fond of saying, one finds the laws of nature contradicted every hour (1946, 17); well before Kuhn or Collins or Cartwright, he pointed out that skepticism is trained on "the facts" more frequently in science than on "hypotheses" or theories or metaphysics. Without a personal commitment to the validity of a whole range of instruments, theories, and practices, no scientist would have any grounds upon which to discover novel entities or hypotheses and imagine their consequences. His deftly chosen example of Einstein's reactions to empirical disconfirmations of the theory of special relativity (Holton 1995) was calculated to shock his audience out of its complacency about the hardness of facts versus the nebulousness of metaphysical principles. He was also one of the first philosophers to go into some detail about how quantitative measurement error in laboratory science was being insufficiently comprehended by extant statistical doctrines, lessons which have been more suppressed than refuted in the interim (but hopefully not in Part III below).

The cumulative aim of all these observations was not to undermine empiricism as a philosophical doctrine so much as to demolish the positivist notion of "objectivity" as an impersonal reliance on facts to guide scientific inquiry. Polanyi regarded the positivist quest for foolproof algorithms for scientific inquiry as a prime example of Enlightenment moral fervor running rabidly out of control: in the interests of protecting personal freedom of inquiry and improving upon an imperfect quotidian reality, the positivists had neutralized all human agency and individuality, supposedly leaving behind nothing but a machine-like rationality. Few realize the role that Polanyi played in bringing arguments about the question of machine rationality to the fore in the third quarter of the last century: for instance, Alan Turing's famous paper on the "Turing test" was written in response to a debate with Polanyi on the issue held at Manchester in October 1949.[1] For Polanyi, the siren song of machine rationality was a fanfare for totalitarianism in science, since a process of inquiry which could be programmed could also be planned, and this played into the hands of the Bernalists and their calls for more relevance and accountability in science.

Here we are finally prepared to appreciate the true significance of Polanyi's tag line, "tacit knowledge." By insisting that the scientist knows more than he or she could ever explicitly recount, Polanyi was not appealing to *Zeitgeist* or "social facts" or anything remotely approaching a sociology of knowledge (more on this in the next section); and given his disdain for Freudianism, he was not gesturing toward the unconscious. Rather, for Polanyi the existence of tacit knowledge was a prerequisite to appreciating the indispensability of individual agency in successful science. The legitimacy of passionate commitment to entities or theories which were only imperfectly known and inadequately articulated was, he asserted, the only way that novelty and innovation could be incorporated into science; and moreover, it was the primary legitimate outlet for moral fervor in what was widely misunderstood as a highly rationalist "value-free" enterprise. Without open acknowledgment of the tacit component of knowledge, there could be no personal responsibility for the consequences of one's actions as a scientist. Unrestrained instrumentalism would lead to proliferation of cynical exercises consisting of barely concealed wish fulfillment; while conversely, robotic conformity to the letter of rigid rules would strangle all motivation to participate in the inquiry (1946, 27). Tacit knowledge was the sextant by means of which one was enabled to navigate between the Scylla of luxuriant extravagant speculation and the Charybdis of rote slavish imitation.

Yet tacit knowledge also served a political function, one which Polanyi acknowledged could be traced back to a Burkean conservatism (1958, 54), and which was used in a similar way by Hayek in his later economics. For Polanyi, tacit knowledge was not something inbred or picked up in passing, since that could not then account for the special progressive character of the scientific enterprise. Instead, the continuity of science should be traced to the ritual transmission of tacit knowledge across the generations. Such a conveyance of something which by definition could not be adequately codified and transmitted might seem an oxymoron, but Polanyi sought to turn this objection into a centerpiece of his definition of the scientific enterprise by associating it with the master-apprentice relationship through which the neophyte becomes initiated into the scientific community. Far from creating an "open society" which revels in unrestrained criticism, the politics of tacit knowledge dictate that criticism be muted and restrained by the process whereby one comes to understand in the first place how science is done. This socially cohesive function, and its kinship to Burkean tradition, were obvious to those who knew of Polanyi's opposition to utopian schemes of a leftist variety. However, this conception of tacit knowledge was also the linchpin of the argument that scientific research could not be centrally planned. Since tacit knowledge was intrinsically dispersed throughout the community, and could only be passed along piecemeal through a socialization process inculcating a particular personal commitment, there could never be any effective rationalization or codification of the process of research.

Perhaps it becomes clearer in hindsight why Polanyi's fiercest critics were the Popperians, even though their political positions vis-à-vis market organization were quite close to his. While the Popperians paid lip service to tradition, they were predisposed to a libertarian conception of "freedom from" any binding commitments to any social organization; it is noteworthy that this led many, including Popper himself, to defend the utilitarian tradition and neoclassical economics (Caldwell 1991). For Polanyi, by contrast, utilitarianism was the economic equivalent of positivism, since it produced a similar distortion of the ideal of human freedom. The fundamental flaw was its treatment of individual rationality as autonomous from all social commitments and determinations, predicated upon an individual knowledge-processing capacity that neither did nor ever could exist. In his opposition to utilitarian social theory, Polanyi was remarkably consistent throughout his career; he expressed it unequivocally in his early economic writings, as well as in his later epistemological work on science.[2] Since utilitarianism denied tacit knowledge, it produced a twisted conception of the real efficacy of market operations, which was not to maximize individual welfare, but rather to coordinate the dispersed and inchoate knowledge of the transactors.[3]

In effect, utilitarianism was the projection of the Enlightenment image of autonomous knowledge onto society, which then insisted upon the recasting of society in its own terms. The ideal of machine rationality had indeed been made quite explicit in the historical development of neoclassical economics, which concertedly imitated rational mechanics in its mathematics of utilitarianism (Mirowski 1989b). Although his opposition was partially rooted in hostility to an algorithmic rationality, Polanyi also believed that utilitarianism gave birth to a highly unstable politics, one wavering between defenses of the market grounded in a reductionist, deterministic Nature which bypassed all human agency and, in opposition, a reformist desire to recast all of society along more "efficient" lines.[4] Thus he remained adamantly opposed to all attempts to justify science along utilitarian ideals. Polanyi's recognition that the primary argument in favor of J. D. Bernal's science-planning movement had been the standard defense of the public funding of pure science— namely, the funding is a necessary means to achieve technological benefits— was what hardened his opposition to utilitarianism in all its manifestations, be they in economics, or in science policy, or in the philosophy of science.

Science and the Market Metaphor

The comparison of the social structures of science to the operation of a market, just as in the comparison of the transmission of cultural entities to natural selection, bears no necessary content or implications in and of itself. It is only with the unpacking of the metaphors within the home and target domains that one comes to realize the network of claims and assertions that are freighted within any such comparison. Michael Polanyi had been implicitly comparing the operations of science to the market since the later 1930s, although the comparison would invariably appear in some subordinate illustrative role, more rhetorical flourish than serious thesis.[5] Since he had been clarifying his own understanding of economics in one set of writings, and then his understanding of epistemology in another, later set of writings, it would have been premature throughout much of this period to spell out in detail just *what* it was about science that corresponded to just what he understood about markets. Over the course of the 1950s, however, the similarities between his convictions about the economy and his convictions about science were coming increasingly into focus in his own mind, but he kept them primarily to himself and a small circle of confidants.[6] This situation changed, however, about 1961.

The reasons for this change of heart are not completely transparent, but probably were bound up with the reactions to his major book *Personal Knowledge*, which had appeared in 1958, and a confrontation with Thomas Kuhn at Oxford in July 1961. In the book Polanyi had sometimes referred to his project as an "invitation to dogmatism" (268); and Kuhn had taken up the gauntlet in a paper which attempted to assimilate components of Polanyi's theses to his own discussions of "normal science" in his soon-to-appear *The Structure of Scientific Revolutions* ([1962] 1970, 44 n 1). Polanyi was not at all happy with Kuhn's interpretation of his work. As he wrote to Gerald Holton: "I criticized Tom Kuhn for not taking up the epistemological difficulties arising from the acknowledgment of dogmatism as he called it. *Personal Knowledge* was of course principally concerned with an attempt to answer this question."[7]

For modern avatars of an "economics of science," Polanyi's "Republic of Science" is a ringing manifesto, with all its talk of "invisible hands" (51) and scientific organization which "works according to economic principles similar to those by which the production of material goods is regulated" (49). Yet for those who bother to read the work with some care, the overriding impression is of someone taking away with a less obtrusive though still visible hand what he has just given with the other. Rather than seriously explore the ways in which economics characterizes market organization and operations, Polanyi instead hinted at a more general theory of coordination: "I am suggesting, in fact, that the coordinating functions of the market are but a special case of co-ordination by mutual adjustment. In the case of science, adjustment takes place by taking note of the published results of other scientists; while in the case of the market, mutual adjustment is mediated through a system of prices" (52). But of course the act of formal acknowledgment of published work does not look much like a price system— indeed, it is not at all clear that it has any of the properties of an ordering, outside of the odd citation or Nobel Prize—so the analogy begins to sputter even before it has left the ground. This became painfully apparent as Polanyi embarked upon his discussion of valuation in science, as a segue into his defense of scientific freedom.

He begins the discussion in a seemingly familiar way, portraying the scientist as making an optimal choice of problem given his "limited stock of intellectual and material resources." Yet, clearly apprehensive at the utilitarian drift, and unwilling to acknowledge what was by then the microeconomic orthodoxy, he immediately shifts the grounds of the valuation to "professional standards" and the "authority of scientific opinion." If these standards and this authority were merely algorithmic rules within which the individual choice had to be made, then one could treat them as a laundry list of utilitarian constraints; however, that would be an anathema to Polanyi. After some twists and turns (53–55), Polanyi decided to recast scientific valuation itself as a problem of *authority*, but a species of authority which does not encroach upon the necessary freedom to choose. Since "no single scientist has a sound understanding of more than a tiny fraction of the total domain of science," the legitimacy of any valuation was sorely in need of justification; Polanyi imagined that the problem could be solved if legitimacy of valuations would monotonically fall off as a function of the "distance" of the subject matter from that of the specialty of the scientist at ground zero of the gradient. If we imagine a collection of scientists arrayed on a grid of specializations, then their individual authorities would overlap; Polanyi then simply asserts that these overlapping valuations would also become reconciled into a transpersonal coherent professional opinion, though he does not specify precisely how this would come about.[8] Not only is this monolithic and internally coherent "scientific opinion" able to evaluate individual endeavors with pinpoint precision, but Polanyi then treats it as akin to utilitarianism in its posited ability to direct efficient resource allocation: "Such is in fact the principle which underlies the rational distribution of grants for the pursuit of research . . . So long as each allocation follows the guidance of scientific opinion, by giving preference to the most promising scientists and subjects, the distribution of grants will automatically yield the maximum advantage for the advancement of science as a whole" (57).

However much Polanyi's language parallels that of neoclassical economics, it should be apparent by this point that he has moved far away from its content. The "advancement of science" is not coterminous with the welfare of the individual scientists involved; their cognitive and computational capacities are not those of the utilitarian rational agent. Indeed, the advancement of science is not concerned with public welfare at all, which is the primary thesis of the second half of the article. Polanyi sought to displace utilitarianism by positing a kind of suprapersonal valuation function which is apparently reflexive, transitive, and complete, although how controversies, misunderstandings, and intransitivities are ironed out in the process of aggregation is nowhere explicated.[9] The orthodox market theory works in terms of competition and a transpersonal value index like money, a combination which (in theory) should allow individual actors to express their individually divergent valuations as a process of social valuation; but in Polanyi's case all the evaluative action happens *before* the resources get distributed and in the absence of any tokens of valuation. The fact that this scenario does not work in terms of a rationalist or instrumentalist valuation scheme is admitted later in the article: "The authority of science is essentially traditional" (66).

It is striking that Polanyi does not once make reference to the key concept of tacit knowledge anywhere in "The Republic of Science." Although tacit knowledge was treated as the centerpiece of his books both before and after the Republic of Science article appeared in 1962, here it is absent, replaced by the quasi-economistic language quoted above. In one sense this was unfortunate, since elaboration of the psychological character of tacit knowledge at least provided reasons (satisfying or no) for the necessity of a system of traditional authoritarian hierarchy. In their absence, and parachuted into the middle of a seemingly neoclassical market metaphor, the contradiction of a rigid authoritarian hierarchy superimposed on a "naturally" self-optimizing market could not be banished by any amount of citation to Burke and Paine. The man who once sneered at Bernal's glib appeal to "freedom as the understanding of necessity" ([1940] 1975, 23) had now come to resemble the thing he had once despised. But in another sense, the replacement of tacit knowledge by the market metaphor was probably intentional, the better to contrast one vision of the Good Society with a threatening rival. The rival vision, of course, belonged to Thomas Kuhn.

Kuhn, as is well known, traced some of his original inspiration to Gestalt psychology; Polanyi had credited many of his psychological doctrines to the Gestalt theorists. Kuhn had portrayed "normal science" as a regime of dogmatic belief; Polanyi had glossed his *Personal Knowledge* as an "invitation to dogmatism." Kuhn wrote about the functions of commitment on the part of the working scientist; commitment was the keystone of Polanyi's understanding of science. And yet, Polanyi wanted to put as much distance between himself and Kuhn's paradigms and revolutions as he could muster. But how? Since the disagreement was primarily over the appropriate *social theory* analogy, why not displace Kuhn's political metaphor with an economic one? After all, market conceptions of order were one class of locutions that Kuhn had never entertained; moreover, he had never shown much interest in the history of social theory. Polanyi, on the other hand, had been meditating about the nature of the merits of the market for three decades; the long apprenticeship had convinced him that the market metaphor was ideal to telegraph precisely the ways in which Kuhn had misrepresented the nature of personal freedom in his narrative. This explains the final section of the paper, expounding a vision of freedom which "has no bearing on the right of men to do as they please; but assures them the right to speak the truth as they know it."

In Polanyi's own mind, therefore, he was not hitching his wagon to any particular social science doctrine; rather, he thought of himself as expostulating a generic theory of the self-organization of free societies. This was made clear in the following passage: "It appears, at first sight, that I have assimilated the pursuit of science to the market. But the emphasis should be in the opposite direction. The self-co-ordination of independent scientists embodies a higher principle, a principle which is *reduced* to the mechanism of the market when applied to the production and distribution of material goods" (69). He didn't want a politics of science, or an economics of science in the modern sense (Zamora Bonilla 2003), and most definitively, not a sociology of science:[10] what Polanyi wanted was a society willingly subordinate to the scientific community, because that body was the finest instantiation of a politically unified corporate entity dedicated to consensual objectives, whereas in reality the state could only be a pale imitation for those who were not privileged to live the life of the scientist. The "Republic of Science" was quite literally that: *imperium in imperio*, a closed corporate entity situated within a larger commonwealth that was obligated to provide certain support services to it, but incapable of aspiring to the same level of clarity in objectives and political cohesion.

Harry Prosch, Polanyi's collaborator in the waning years of his career, reports that Polanyi believed his crusade for freedom a failure (1986, 203–4); and moreover, Prosch thinks that Polanyi's attempt to compare science to a market was a "basic error" (287). I concur. There was something fundamentally self-defeating about Polanyi's attempt to use the language of economics to gesture toward his own personal conception of market organization, even though he was fully aware that his personal image of a market was at odds with the orthodox view promulgated in economics. It should have been obvious to someone touting the dominance of a scientific consensus that if his market metaphor would be understood at all, it would be embraced as a neoclassical economics of science. Worse, by Polanyi's own criteria he could be accused of coming to resemble everything that he had denounced as characteristic of the "moral inversion" of the Enlightenment project: namely, by trumpeting the existence of ideal rational agents called "scientists" and setting them above the debased denizens of daily life, he facilitated political movements seeking to revamp that same society in his ideal image of the Republic of Science—a world of a single suprapersonal Valuation— even though Polanyi could never quite specify how that rational Republic really worked. The parallels to the Marxian silence on the structure of operational socialism were uncomfortably close. The road to serfdom is indeed paved with good intentions.

Should this diagnosis seem unduly harsh, one need only consult another major address that Polanyi delivered essentially at the same time, though significantly, one not reprinted in any of his essay collections. In the lecture "Science: Academic and Industrial" he reveals how a paean to liberty undergoes inversion to become an exclusionary taunt. As part of his campaign to uncouple the support of science from any of its allegedly utilitarian by-products, he makes one of the strongest distinctions between pure science and technology found anywhere in the literature on the philosophy and sociology of science. In effect, "technology" is associated with any research that is subject to any form of economic valuation, while pure science is entirely independent of any "change in the current relative value of things" (1961, 404). A world of such stark contrasts would be hard to capture in black and white, but Polanyi clearly signals his intention to resolve all hard cases unambiguously into one category or the other. The reason for this Solomonic judgment is that "pure science" and only pure science should inhabit the universities, while "industry" will need to pick up the tab for the rest. Not only are the money lenders to be driven from the temple; Polanyi then goes to the extraordinary length of assimilating the humanities to "technology," as a prelude to excluding them likewise.[11] One could scarcely imagine a more bald power play to exile all economic competitors of the natural sciences from public support in the universities on the a priori ground that only the natural science communities can deliver "progress," while simultaneously denying that they could be subject to any utilitarian cost-benefit calculus. Not only would the simple freedom of intellectuals to pursue their inquiries into topics of concern be curtailed, but the irony of a proposal to banish the philosophers and economists from academe by someone who had himself held a personal chair in "social studies" at Manchester from 1948 to 1958 could hardly be lost on his audience.

While there is little consensus on the exact meaning and reference of the term "scientism," I believe that a least common denominator has presented itself. Scientism here denotes the overweening confidence and chauvinism on the part of those inducted into a natural science that their own local culture represents everything noble, rational, and efficacious about the human race; and further, anything less than abject tribute and total capitulation to this position (which includes copious economic support) on the part of those without passports from the culture in question should be met with scorn, ridicule, and contempt. It is the chisel of naturalism driven by the hammer of self-interest.

The Road(s) to Freedom

The question of the shape and character of freedom of inquiry is a central problem for the economics of science in the early twenty-first century; it has also been a prime motive force in recent turning points in the philosophy of science. From a more detached perspective, this should not be surprising, given that the social organization of science in Western countries has undergone at least one wrenching change around the years of the Second World War, and is experiencing another regime shift at present, described in the Introduction. What is perhaps more noteworthy is that philosophers of science have not managed to develop a particularly rich lexicon with which to discuss the problem of freedom in science. If the topic arises, more often than not the philosophers find themselves slipping into economistic language and concepts to articulate their concerns. Since their appropriation of economics is often oblique and context dependent, not to mention fraught with pitfalls (because few philosophers of science are out-and-out enthusiasts for economics as a science), it might be instructive to spell out how three fairly similar philosophers—namely Michael Polanyi, Thomas Kuhn, and Philip Kitcher—grapple with the issue of freedom in science, and how they are ultimately distinguished by their divergent stances with regard to political economy.

Probably no one would deny that some modicum of freedom is necessary but not sufficient for having a flourishing, productive scientific community. However, if the appeal to freedom is not to be thoroughly vacuous, then the sorts of freedoms required have to be spelled out in more detail. The first casualty of the "free marketplace of ideas" or "invisible hand" doctrines is precisely this necessary enumeration of freedoms, since they trade on the impression that this enumeration in the context of a theory of spontaneous order has already happened elsewhere, most likely in economics. It is depressing for an economist to admit it, but outsiders should not take this for granted; disagreement over just this issue is one of the main reasons why there exist rival schools of economic thought. One of the merits of Polanyi as a philosopher is that he realized this, and moreover understood that the most frequent consequence of silence on this issue on the part of utilitarians was an inversion of the ideal of freedom. More specifically, ever since Mill, when utilitarians come to realize that their instrumentalist doctrines do not lead directly to a type of freedom worth fighting for, they suffer a Romanticist reaction to their rationalist precepts. The Romanticist retreat can take one of two forms: a pining for Revolution to break the impasse, or else a surrender to Nature which can reconcile freedom and necessity. Polanyi represents a valiant attempt to enumerate the requisite freedoms in a rationalist framework, whereas Kuhn takes the Romantic road to Revolution, and Kitcher counsels capitulation to Nature. The most remarkable feature of these three defenses of science is that each figure feels impelled to resort to economic language to justify his treatment of freedom in science.

Michael Polanyi was concerned to argue that personal freedom was both possible and indispensable for a viable science. However, like so many other thinkers, he discovered that this freedom had to be immediately hemmed in and qualified: truly unfettered creation is abhorrent to science, and each viable science constrains the inquirer at every turn. A utilitarian might want to express this as a constrained optimization problem, but as we have seen, Polanyi would regard that as a travesty of freedom. Instead, he identified freedom at the personal level with tacit knowledge. Employing a Hayekian conception of the market, he compared the diffuse coordination of individual understandings to the diffuse coordination of individual market demands into a global uniform valuation. The freedom for the individual scientist was not unconditional, but consisted of a willing subordination born of a moral commitment to a tradition handed down by generations of specialists in each area of inquiry. It was characteristic that Polanyi did not worry much about encroachments upon the personal freedom of individual scientists by the corporate body of scientists, even though he did admit that sometimes dogmatism did miscarry. Rather, his wary vigilance was always trained in the direction of the state. Just as the state was counterpoised to the market as the greatest threat to freedom in his favored version of economics, the state was also the greatest threat to freedom in science.

The crippling weakness of Polanyi's economics of science was the notable absence of symmetry implied by his conception of freedom. Within science, he asserted that a virtual "market" was in operation, allocating effort, attention, and funds. Blocking the utilitarian route, science was not conceived as engaging in trade with the rest of society because it didn't produce anything "useful"; thus it was the duty of the rest of society to fund science without demanding anything in return. Consequently, market operation was being negated in the sphere of the larger society, precisely where real markets were supposed to perform their coordination functions. A morbid suspicion of the state follows directly, because in the absence of market support science has no choice but to rely upon a conscious redistribution of resources from the society to itself, an allocational mechanism it had renounced within its own internal Republic—or had it? The more one scrutinized this Polanyite version of freedom, the more it looked like one kind of command economy being superimposed (or perhaps foisted) upon another. In a trope we shall encounter repeatedly, the nagging repressed question was: Why should the freedoms of yeoman members of society be sacrificed to the putative freedom of the Republic of Science, if not to the individual scientists themselves, especially if they did not seem all that free in the first place?

Thomas Kuhn is not often regarded as a theorist of freedom, although the centrality of "Revolutions" to his magnum opus should indicate otherwise. Kuhn showed almost no interest in the social sciences, but there is nonetheless a low-level utilitarian streak in his treatment of dogmatism and freedom. It comes in his attempt to provide a justification for "normal science," that unimaginative puzzle solving said to be the lot of almost all working scientists. Kuhn defended the rank dogmatism of textbooks and the restrictions on the freedoms of individual scientists on the ground that they were an economizing measure (Kuhn 1963). If there were unfettered freedom for each individual to follow his or her hunches wherever they might lead, then search of the virtual state space of possible explanations would be both unsystematic and unimaginably costly. The dreary grind of the normal scientist is the price of instilling some discipline in the search process, and, let it be said, balancing the costs against the benefits. As with all utilitarian schemes, this leads to an algorithmic rationality that can be stifling in the extreme; change may become all but impossible. As Kuhn wrote in *The Structure of Scientific Revolutions*: "Competition between the segments of the scientific community is the only historical process that ever actually results in the rejection of one previously accepted theory or in the adoption of another" ([1962] 1970, 8). Without a fully fledged market metaphor, Kuhn could not begin to imagine a mechanism internal to the "paradigm" which was capable of combining competition and cooperation. Kuhn's resolution to this impasse was to conjure a Romantic transvaluation of values brought about by the rupture of a Scientific Revolution. Even though Kuhn himself did not ground his description of revolutions in any social science authority, his treatment very much evokes a version of the political economy of development known as "modernization theory" which was popular at Harvard in the late 1950s and early 1960s.[12]

One reason why *The Structure of Scientific Revolutions* was popular in the 1960s was the inchoate equation of "freedom" with the throwing off of old élites; and a palpable feeling of liberation in the social sciences arose from a misreading of the book as a manual on "how to get yourself a paradigm and become a science." Yet the succession of revolutions with their incommensurate valuation schemes brought its own dilemmas. Like Polanyi, Kuhn believed that valuations and allocation schemes must be entirely internal to the scientific discipline; Kuhn never once condoned the idea that external pressures and demands could influence the content of normal science or the timing of revolutions. And as for influences running from science to society, Kuhn essentially adopted Polanyi's quarantine: "Science, when it affects socioeconomic development at all, does so through technology" (1977, 141). Science could not be held responsible for the separate sphere of technology; but Kuhn goes well beyond Polanyi in assuming that science has nothing to do with the layman's understanding of himself or of society. Therefore, the lay populace should simply acquiesce in the revolutions and upheavals that rock the sciences (admittedly infrequently), and continue their funding and obedience even through profound incidents of the transvaluation of values, because they were incapable of anything but a disinterested passive spectator's understanding of those values. Unfortunately, revolutions are rarely confined to their points of origin; and freedom to rebel would not be high on the list of treasured freedoms either within the paradigm or without. Kuhn gave no reason why members of society at large should wish to promote the freedom of scientists to undergo these paroxysms of transvaluation, certainly not when it made no difference to society at large (then why fund it anyway?) and not even when it made a profound difference (then why isn't society also "free" to contest this transvaluation of values, when society is underwriting it?).

This brings us to Philip Kitcher, who is distinguished from Kuhn in that much of his professional career has been spent on the battlements between science and society: the creationist controversy, the sociobiology debate, and in the 1990s, the Human Genome Project (1996). Kitcher has witnessed a much more intricate interpenetration of state, society, and science than Polanyi could ever have imagined; but in the interim, he has also witnessed the rise of an activist sociology of science within the science policy community, a development which openly challenges the prerogative of philosophers of science to have anything cogent to say about the social organization of science. In response, Kitcher aspires to reclaim the mantle of Kuhn from all those who wish to draw all sorts of relativist, historicist, and activist conclusions from the historical record, and indeed, to provide a theory of "rational dogmatism" in order to plat the appropriate demarcation between science and society (1993a, 7n). As he writes, "Philosophy of science should earn its way by trying to draw specific morals for the organization of scientific research" (1993a, 305). No longer can the role of the social structure of science be treated so breezily, or the dependence upon the larger society be treated as cavalierly as in Kuhn. But make no mistake: the ultimate aim was still to justify the privileged autonomy of science. What is striking about Kitcher's case is that in relative ignorance of Polanyi's dilemma (1993a, 320n), he apparently independently chose to have recourse to economics in order to resolve the problem of "optimum intolerance" both within and outside science.[13]

In common with Polanyi and Kuhn, Kitcher acknowledges that "deference to authority . . . enables individual scientists to pursue their epistemic projects more rapidly and makes feasible investigations that would be impossible for a single individual" (1993, 308). Yet in contrast to Polanyi and Kuhn, Kitcher sees nothing wrong with the strong reductionist approach that seeks to account for all aspects of social structure as the product of individual rational choice—no whiff of tacit knowledge here, nor any stab at a gestalt social psychology. This favorable predisposition to an algorithmic conception of knowledge, in conjunction with the commitment that philosophy of science be handmaiden to political power, essentially dictates that

Kitcher adopt a utilitarian stance. But this does not betoken a crude utilitarianism based solely on the "fruits of science"; Kitcher innovates on at least two fronts. On the first (which we cannot cover here, but see chapter 5), progress and "value" are defined in technical terms purely internal to the science; and on the second front, Kitcher openly appropriates neoclassical and game-theory mathematical models from economics to justify the division of cognitive labor. In a classic variation on the invisible hand, private vices are asserted to be public virtues: "While communities of isolated knowers who proceeded in ways commended by individualistic epistemologies would often be doomed to cognitive uniformity, social pressures and types of innovations often regarded as antipathetic to the progress of science will turn out to be helpful" (1993a, 345). Eschewing the insalubrious persona of the moralist (read: Polanyi), we are faced instead with the brisk ethos of the confident technocrat, describing how free competition ideally keeps vice in check: it is not from the benevolence of Kary Mullis that we get the test for phenylketonuria.

Nevertheless, it seems Polanyi was essentially correct in his diagnosis of the dangers of the utilitarian model. When one pays closer attention to the vintage of freedom which Kitcher's models provide, it is not the sort of freedom for which people would be willing to put their lives on the line. For example, with sufficient ingenuity, it would be quite easy to construct a comparable game-theory model where the whole freedom of access to information in science converges in gridlock because of the relative costs of self-interested behaviors.[14] This result is well known in the history of economics: for every orthodox neoclassical model M which demonstrates the self-equilibrating nature of the market, there is a model M' with assumptions only an epsilon different from M which demonstrates the necessary suboptimality of market operation. As Polanyi had predicted, the chasm between the utilitarian utopia and the debased reality pushes the adherent inexorably toward Romanticism, and in this case it is manifest in Kitcher's abandonment of freedom for the dictates of Nature.

Kitcher's program of a quasi-Darwinian Naturalism is well known in the philosophy of science community, and is contrasted to other forms of naturalism by Rosenberg (1996). All we suggest here is that a utilitarian defense of freedom along those lines can rapidly degenerate into its antithesis, as Polanyi warned. Indeed, this prognosis was realized in Kitcher's next book (2001), as argued in the Introduction. The authoritarianism that all our philosophers find in science threatens its dynamic innovation and progress; the authoritarianism they all expect to find in the outside world threatens its very existence. For Kuhn, the solution lay in revolutionary outbursts; for Kitcher, the solution can rather be found in a necessary *telos* that resides within the scientific process, of Nature coming to better know Itself.[15]

Kitcher is a sophisticated utilitarian: he realizes that it is a dubious proposition to ask society to fund pure science when the technological products of the quest are fraught on all sides with dashed hopes and unintended consequences. He is equally well aware that scientific progress can have all sorts of unpleasant side effects and externalities that impinge upon our cultural life and our very self-understandings.[16] But all of this and more are treated as mere second-order phenomena, turbulence in the wake of the juggernaut, because for a thoroughgoing Naturalist there is no freedom: "Grand rhetoric about human freedom seduces us into thinking that we must, quite literally, make ourselves . . . the conception was always incoherent. If the self that allegedly makes itself is already fully formed, then it does not, after all, *make* itself. To find our freedom, we have to start acknowledging that we are the people we are because of events that are beyond our control, even beyond our understanding" (Kitcher 1996, 283).

Far from being a rehash of ancient controversies over the possibility of free will, this position has immediate implications for the defense of the autonomy of pure science in the face of political challenges to its motives and its funding. The naturalist position guarantees, Kitcher basically believes, that the natural sciences will be successful in their objectives, a guarantee that cannot be matched in any other area of human endeavor. Our freedom is chimerical, as is the freedom of scientists. Hence the natural sciences are inherently privileged as deserving unquestioned and unqualified support from the rest of the populace, so long as they are left to their own devices to keep the organization of inquiry autonomous and running smoothly.

The only freedom which anyone possesses is to acquiesce in the Natural progression of things, or else to temporarily engage in futile resistance, obstructing the path of science in the interests of undependable social or moral convictions about its deleterious effects. The earlier utilitarian formulation—the posture of a policy-relevant optimum social organization of science—undermines itself: it can be shrugged off effortlessly in this more direct formulation. Thus Philip Kitcher served as the primary public defender of the Human Genome Project.[17] But once stated so baldly, we can see that this is not any sort of freedom worth having.

Science in a Free Society

One of the central problems in the philosophy of science is the role and meaning of freedom: freedom of inquiry within science, freedom from meddling in science by outsiders, freedom by outsiders to choose what science they will and will not support, freedom of outsiders from meddling in their lives by scientists. It is amazing (and for some, depressing) to observe the relatively low level of self-consciousness with which this problem has been approached by twentieth-century philosophers of science. Part of the problem can be traced to the tendency to reach for "invisible hand" explanations taken over from economics with little or no appreciation for the diversity of the theories and the attendant complexity of considerations in trying to make the diagnosis of successful self-coordination stick. It has been our contention that orthodox utilitarian theories of the invisible hand have been singularly unhelpful in limning the boundaries of freedom in science. One prognosis is that it is about time for philosophers of science to get over their instinctive contempt for the social sciences, if only by admitting that they have been dabbling in social theory all along.

If we surmount that first obstacle, then perhaps we can prepare to confront the second, more thorny part of the problem. Philosophers of science also need to bring one of their most repressed presuppositions out into the light of day. Is it in fact the constitutional mandate of philosophers of science to defend the unqualified autonomy of the social structure of the natural sciences vis-à-vis the society in which they are embedded, as well as all other intellectual disciplines, *no matter what the historical status of the science in question?* Or is there a more comprehensive program of inquiry, one broached by another admirer of Polanyi and Hayek, and yet treated as taboo by most philosophers of science? Could it instead be that "there is no reason why the research program *science* should not be subsumed under the research program *free society* and the competences changed and redefined accordingly"? (Feyerabend 1978, 100).

3
Economics, Science, and Knowledge: Polanyi versus Hayek

Philosophy of Science as Economics

It frequently happens lately that when I encounter strangers who may have some familiarity with my work, they ask me: Aren't you some species of philosopher of science, or do you consider yourself an economist? Leaving aside my own ambivalence about the state of the economics profession in the United States, I find myself increasingly responding that I see little to distinguish the concerns of the two disciplines at the dawn of the twenty-first century, and that a competent understanding of the one often requires a proficient understanding of the other. Indeed, it is a bland and complacent ignorance of the history and practices of the sciences that permits economists to make such outrageous statements about the capacities of agents to accumulate and process knowledge, just as it is the disdain for and ignorance of the history and practices of economists which leads philosophers to make such unwarranted statements about the "marketplace of ideas." But the situation is not uniformly one of mutual incomprehension and reciprocal ignorance, however much one can find instances of both. Some philosophers of science are coming to acknowledge that there just might be a pervasive political economy of epistemology, while some historians are beginning to uncover the numerous links between politics and beliefs about how science does (and sometimes doesn't) work.[1]

Another reason why the situation is not uniformly bleak is that there have been many figures in history who have straddled the divide between economics and the philosophy of science; it is only our own historical amnesia and narrow academic disciplinarity that prevent us from recognizing this fact. A few names that spring to mind in this regard are David Hume, William Whewell, John Stuart Mill, Auguste Comte, William Stanley Jevons, Charles Saunders Peirce, John Maynard Keynes, Nicholas Georgescu-Roegen—the list could go on and on. But in this essay I want to focus on the really remarkable concentration of figures who came out of Central Europe at the beginning of this century and whose work was indelibly marked by the political events of the time. A wider purview would encompass the political economy of the Vienna Circle,[2] the impact of such thinkers as Karl Menger Jr. and Oskar Morgenstern, and the clash of Karl Popper and Paul Feyerabend.[3] However, in the interests of tractability, but also timeliness, I will confine myself to only two figures: the Nobel prize winner Friedrich von Hayek and the physical chemist-turned-philosopher Michael Polanyi.

Hayek all economists have heard of, but Michael Polanyi is probably a different matter, although economists often have a glancing familiarity with Michael's brother Karl Polanyi, who wrote *The Great Transformation*. Michael Polanyi was born in 1891 in Budapest and died in Northampton, England, in 1976; and thus he was a near-contemporary of Hayek, born in 1899 in Vienna and living until 1992. However, his metric of nearness to Hayek can be defined in more than simple chronological terms. Both men made the long trek from their initial disciplines to philosophy in amazingly parallel trajectories. The break with their initial identities was made roughly simultaneously, in the 1930s, and for roughly the same reason, namely opposition to developments that they saw as exemplified by the regime in the Soviet Union. Both were deeply disturbed by intellectual trends in Britain at the time, where they were both in residence—Hayek at the London School of Economics, Polanyi at the University of Manchester. Both wrote books on macroeconomics; indeed, in some quarters the roster of Polanyi's disciplinary credentials reads: physical chemist, economist, philosopher.[4] But more importantly, the two knew each other personally and were intimately acquainted with each other's work, and for a good reason: both were essentially working on the same problems from the mid-1930s until the end of their careers. Although neither much acknowledged this in print, it was briefly the subject of an interview with Hayek in 1978:

> Buchanan: Let me ask you about your relationship, or did you know or how close were you, to Michael Polanyi? Did you know him very well?
> Hayek: Yes, he was for a few years my colleague on the Committee on Social Thought [at the University of Chicago], and there was an interesting relationship for a period of ten years when we happened to move from the same problem to the same problem. Our answers were not the same, but for this period we were always just thinking about the same problems. We had very interesting discussions with each other, and I liked him personally very much. I think, again, he is a somewhat neglected figure, much more—well, I think he suffered from the usual

thing; if you leave your proper subject, other people regard you as an amateur in what you are talking about. But he was in fact very competent. I would almost say he's the only non-economist that I knew who wrote a good book on economics.[5]

Two quick parenthetical comments help provide necessary background: First, it may sound as though the decade to which Hayek is referring occurred late in life, during his tenure at the University of Chicago, but the papers of Michael Polanyi at the University of Chicago suggest rather that the decade of closest contact between the two was the mid-1930s to mid-1940s, a fact that takes on extra significance when one realizes that it was the decade of Hayek's "transformation," as Bruce Caldwell calls it.[6] Secondly, Polanyi wrote two books on economics, so Hayek is implicitly rejecting the second of them with his back-handed compliment, as I will later explain.

There is an interesting story of neglected intellectual histories and tangled cross-currents of influence here, but I will not digress upon the knotted narrative, except insofar as it bears upon my purpose, which is to discuss the importance of the philosophy of science for an understanding of the nature and significance of the treatment of knowledge in economics. Hayek's primary warning against the pretensions of socialist planning was that human knowledge is intensely personal and irretrievably distributed throughout the population in such a manner that it would be impossible to collate, assimilate, and act upon it within the ambit of any collective entity which aspired to better or even match the coordination capacities of markets. This is the message which is developed beginning with his article "Economics and Knowledge" (1937) and on through his well-known "The Use of Knowledge in Society" (1945); it also animates the series of articles on "scientism" which were later collected as *The Counter-Revolution of Science*.[7] It is important to note that this is uniquely a claim about epistemology, individual and social; and further, that it was couched in an explicit discussion of the nature and character of scientific knowledge. Hence, in this sphere philosophy of science and political economy became fused into a single set of propositions.

In these reflections, I want to demonstrate that Michael Polanyi shared these same concerns with Hayek at exactly the same time; and furthermore, he held discussions with Hayek while Hayek was formulating his own positions. What is fascinating is that Polanyi ultimately arrived at different answers, as Hayek acknowledges: different answers concerning the institutional character of science, different perspectives on the personal character of knowledge, and different prognoses concerning the future of political economy. I personally think that Polanyi's answers were richer and better supported with subsidiary arguments than Hayek's, though that is certainly open to dispute. However, prosecuting the comparison will raise the issue of why Hayek has been lionized while Polanyi has largely been forgotten—except, of course, by a few philosophers.

How Michael Polanyi Became an Economist

Some biographical information on Polanyi is in order, if only to situate the events I shall cover in context, and to make up for the lack of any published biography. Michael Polanyi was the son of a Jewish civil engineer in Budapest who lost his fortune in 1899 but whose family maintained contact with a wide artistic and intellectual circle. He became a medical doctor in 1913 and served as a medical officer in the Austro-Hungarian army during the First World War, also taking a PhD in chemistry at the University of Budapest in 1917. He moved to Germany with the Hungarian uprising in 1919, and attained a position at the Kaiser Wilhelm Institute in the fall of 1920. He lived in Berlin from 1920 until 1933, becoming well known as an expert on the adsorption of gases and crystallography, and developing a circle of friends which included Alfred Einstein, Eugene Wigner, Leo Szilard, John von Neumann, and Max Born, among other illustrious scientists.[8] With the rise of the National Socialists to power in 1933, Polanyi accepted a chair in physical chemistry at the University of Manchester, which he held until 1948, when he exchanged it for a chair in social studies. This was the period of maximum overlap with Hayek, who held the Tooke Professorship in political economy at the London School of Economics from 1932 to 1949. After that the two drifted apart, with Hayek accepting a position at the University of Chicago in 1950 while Polanyi stayed at Manchester until accepting a research fellowship at Merton College Oxford in 1958.[9]

It was only after the move to Manchester that Polanyi became active in economics, with all his publications in that area falling within the period 1935–46; this in itself goes a long way toward explaining the close contact with Hayek. Why did Polanyi relinquish a stellar career in physical chemistry in exchange for a tenuous perch in a subject in which he had no standing or credibility? The answers range from the prosaic to the profound. The first is simply that the move from Berlin to Manchester made him profoundly unhappy, and as his friend Wigner writes, "I doubt he was ever again as happy as he had been in Berlin."[10] It does not appear that he ever felt as much at ease in the community of British chemists as he had in Berlin. The second reason was one shared by a raft of trained physical scientists who moved into economics in the 1930s: they were driven to distraction by the economic and social upheavals of the Great Depression, and felt that their scientific training might allow them to make a special contribution to solving its problems. The third reason was more specific to Polanyi: he made a trip to the Soviet Union in April 1935 at the invitation of some scientific confreres and was appalled at what he saw. As he tells us in *The Tacit Dimension*, he was shocked to the core when Bukharin told him that in a socialist regime there would no longer be anything called "pure science." This galvanized Polanyi to quickly pen his first book outside physical chemistry, *USSR Economics*, in 1936; it was the first serious critique of Soviet economic statistics published in the West. The fourth and final reason for his turn to economics was the set of developments in British science in the 1930s, variously known as the Social Relations of Science movement, the rise of the Association of Scientific Workers, and Bernalism.

The events of the science planning movement in Britain have yet to receive comprehensive study.[11] For our purposes it is enough to suggest that the British science planning movement of the 1930s and 1940s was easily as important as the rise of Keynesian economics, the "socialist calculation controversy," or the growth of the Communist Party in provoking what we now think of in retrospect as the Hayek Critique of socialist planning.[12]

This importance has been obscured by Hayek's subsequent references to Karl Popper as his staunch philosophical beacon, which have only served to muddy the waters. During the important gestation period for Hayek's transformation, he was in close contact with Polanyi about refuting the Social Relations of Science movement.[13] I quote from his letter to Polanyi dated 1 July 1941: "I attach very great importance to these pseudo-scientific arguments on social organization being effectively met and I am getting more and more alarmed by the effect of the propaganda of the Haldanes, Hogbens, Needhams, etc. I don't know whether you've seen the latest instance, C. H. Waddington's Pelican on the Scientific Attitude. I think this last specimen is really quite contemptible" (Michael Polanyi papers 4:5).

Polanyi himself had numerous motivations to be one of the first to jump into the fray with the "Bernalists": Bernal was one of the other premier crystallographers in Britain, but his collegial relations with Polanyi were not all that close; Bernal's *Social Functions of Science* (1939) had become a bestseller; and Polanyi was revulsed by Bernal's communist sympathies and praise of the Soviet Union, and distressed at the increasing evidence of Bernal's influence in journals such as *Nature*, in the British Association, and in the highest levels of government.[14]

Thus Michael Polanyi progressively opted for social theory in lieu of physical chemistry. In the decade 1935–45, this choice assumed three forms: (1) some early essays on the social structure of science, to be described shortly; (2) empirical work describing economic conditions in the Soviet Union; and (3) a project for cinematic treatment of economic theories for the purposes of popular education. The last may seem incongruous, but it was of major importance for Polanyi, since it was intended to counter what he considered economic fallacies spreading throughout the citizenry which would undermine the future of democracy. Ultimately he managed to get two films produced. The first, *The Workings of Money* (1938), already revealed some nascent Keynesian leanings.[15] Poalnyi's initial concentration upon the topic of money was no accident, however, given his initial agreement with Hayek that monetary disturbance was the primary cause of business fluctuations. Consequently, in the early 1940s Polanyi was a rare bird indeed: a respected natural scientist who voiced unremitting hostility to communism and criticized the Soviet Union, adamantly rejected all talk of planning of science or of the market, and yet stood relatively isolated as a strong supporter of Keynesian macroeconomics.

So why did Hayek persist in regarding Polanyi as an ally in the 1940s? The short answer is that the commonalities of the two overrode their differences. Their critique of the Soviet Union was essentially the same, even though Hayek did not engage in any empirical work on the topic. They both held liberty as the primary political virtue, to be defended above all others. There was also a practical consideration: until *The Road to Serfdom*, it was Polanyi, not Hayek, who was the more visible and publicly effective spokesman against the Left in Britain. It was Polanyi, for instance, whom the BBC recruited to debate the Marxist Julian Huxley on a series of radio programs. But most importantly, in February 1941 Hayek had just embarked upon his own crusade against Bernalism and the science planning movement with his first installment of *The Counter-Revolution of Science* in *Economica*, the house journal of the London School of Economics. Hayek's counterblast to "scientism" never quite managed to make it out of the realm of French nineteenth-century texts, so it was not at all clear to many readers precisely who the modern targets of his wrath might be; but their identity was made much clearer in some less accessible texts, such as his review of a collection of essays published by Polanyi in 1940: "The analysis of Professor Bernal's book in the essay on the 'Rights and Duties of Science' is perhaps the most illuminating discussion yet attempted of the psychological propensities which so frequently turn the man of science into an ardent advocate of central planning, and of the inconsistencies which this attitude involves."[16] Indeed, it was Polanyi and not Hayek who was situated at the axle of a vast wheel of controversy over political economy and science in Britain in the 1940s.[17] The spokes radiating outward from Polanyi led to the most amazing collection of natural scientists (such as Max Born) and literary figures (such as Arthur Koestler); but his ability to maintain intellectual engagement with diverse economic thinkers ranging from Hayek to J. R. Hicks to Karl Mannheim to his own brother Karl was nothing short of miraculous. In another context, his friend Wigner called him an "artist of encouragement," and that skill is revealed in the quality and candidness of expression that he evoked from his correspondents.[18]

Quite early in this process, before Hayek had demonstrated much of an interest in epistemology, we find Polanyi already foreshadowing his later positions on tacit knowledge in a note in *Philosophy of Science* in 1936.[19] He wrote there, "if at any time chemists would have been so ill-advised as to let themselves be frightened by physicists into abandoning all vague methods, and to restrict themselves to the field where exact laws (or what are supposed to be such by physicists) pertain, the development of chemistry would at that moment have stopped dead." Polanyi then suggested that the description of chemical substances had much more in common with "the art of commanding human behavior."

Nevertheless, Polanyi distinctly began to intellectually diverge from Hayek by the late 1940s if not before, around the same time that he essentially left economics behind to become a full-time philosopher. By most accounts his most significant books appeared after this period: *The Logic of Liberty* (1951), his magnum opus *Personal Knowledge* (1958), and *The Tacit Dimension* (1966). It is especially in these latter works that he carried on a lonely crusade against the logical empiricism and positivism which had come to dominate the philosophy of science in that era; yet for him all this was not simply an academic diversion, but part of a crusade to diagnose the modern malaise according to which science and morality were regarded as being at odds, and intellectual freedom seemed to lack all rational justification. Toward the end of his life, Polanyi felt that he had not been all that successful in his campaign.[20] Perhaps this was in part because he had earned the reputation of an incurable moralist and inveterate sermonizer by the 1960s; unlike Keynes, he was not a Cassandra whom people suffered gladly. Another possible explanation is that he tended to get bracketed with Thomas Kuhn in the 1960s and 1970s as someone who had uncovered the repressed irrationalist component of science. Neither author would have agreed with that interpretation, as we argue in chapters 2 and 4. Instead, here we outline how Hayek and Polanyi, starting from positions relatively close to one another, came to espouse epistemologies so diametrically opposed that it should make us reevaluate our own grasp of the case for freedom in the academy and in the marketplace.

Hayek vs. Polanyi on the Nature of Knowledge

Throughout most of the twentieth century, questions of economic planning have been intimately bound up with conceptions of what knowledge is or could be, and disputes over how it may or may not come to be known. Michael Polanyi felt the weight of these questions in the 1940s, and fairly quickly came to reject Hayek's epistemological stance as inadequate to the task at hand. He never opted to discuss Hayek's approach in his major books, but we can reconstruct his objections from reviews and correspondence. To begin with, he felt that the nostalgia for Burke and Acton would not suffice to provide foundations for modern philosophy or politics: "But is it certain that our disorders can be clearly defined in the words of an age so remote in its unsophisticated integrity? The attempt may entangle us in contradictions."[21] Far from being the standard scientistic fascination with the shock of the new, Polanyi's objection here was rather that Burke and Acton praised tradition, but what they had had in mind surely could no longer be commensurate with what "tradition" would mean in the 1940s; and furthermore, Hayek absolved himself from much that his own contemporaries would regard as stabilizing traditions—for instance specific religions, or Cartesian abstraction. The problem was that the content of "tradition" would appear to be as idiosyncratic and arbitrary as tyranny itself if it were not unpacked in rational discourse. This did not imply for Polanyi that all tradition must be reduced to rational stipulation; the one commitment he did persist in sharing with Hayek was acknowledgment of the inarticulate component of practice and a disdain for what Hayek called "constructivism." What Polanyi held against Hayek was that he was apparently not willing to describe the interplay between the inarticulate and rationalizable aspects of practice, be they in the marketplace or elsewhere, and therefore he had effectively reneged on the promise to theorize the role of knowledge in economics.

As one might expect, Hayek's crusade against "scientism" also made Polanyi nervous. Hayek's grasp of the natural sciences was tenuous, which created some problems, but what bothered Polanyi more was the tendency to indiscriminately accuse all scientists and engineers of narrow technical training and a predilection for mechanical rationalist prediction and control; anything that didn't fit their models wasn't worth knowing. Polanyi, as we have already indicated, had personally known a number of these scientists, including many who were professed socialists, and he could not bring himself to write them off in quite so imperious a manner. The solution was diagnosis and treatment, as was made clear in his review of Hayek's *Counter-Revolution of Science*:

> And yet one is tempted after all to caution Hayek the fighter in the name of Hayek the political thinker. In the other half of his book, where he examines the true scope of science in human affairs, he writes: "The most dangerous stage in the growth of civilization may well be that in which man . . . refuses to accept or submit to anything that he does not rationally understand" and "This may well prove a hurdle which man will repeatedly reach only to be thrown back into barbarism." If this be true then modern "scientism" is merely a waywardness, due to a deeper

and indeed total instability of reason at its present level of conscious-ness. It may appear then also that only by curing this basic disorder can we hope to prevail against the variety of delusions that have arisen and must continue to arise from it.[22]

The immediate need was to find out what, if anything, had gone wrong with modern science such that it induced reasonable people to propose infringe-ments upon liberty and the quality of life, and not, as Hayek was doing, to berate the scientists for their hubris. This is in fact the task to which Polanyi devoted the remainder of his career.

One would be remiss not to note that Polanyi had also come to distrust Hayek's economic theories. As he wrote, "He addressed an age obsessed by the fear of mass unemployment while turning an indifferent eye on this problem. This surely was a mistake."[23] In a roundabout way, this too was linked to Polanyi's conception of science. He believed that openness of information was central to the success of science, and that openness was imperative in the political sphere as well. He felt that people must be made aware of what was being expected of them in their roles as economic actors, and that the opacity of Hayek's theories was itself not conducive to this public function. Rightly or wrongly, he thought that "Keynesian theory is really quite simple—perhaps difficult to grasp at first, but once understood quite easy to handle. . . . It is a . . . veritable egg of Columbus."[24]

Therefore, Michael Polanyi essentially exited economics after 1947 in or-der to devote his time to construction of an epistemology which was suited to both twentieth-century science and twentieth-century market economies. To do justice to the products of his quest, and especially to his rather untidy text *Personal Knowledge*, is beyond my capabilities in this venue. Part of the problem is that the more Polanyi sought to elevate science as the paradigm human accomplishment, the more he fearlessly uncovered unsavory aspects of the process of scientific research, upsetting comfortable notions like pre-cision measurement, falsification, freedom from external authority, objec-tivity, open-mindedness, and the like. Rather than track down every obser-vation on the history of science or the distinct positions to which they gave rise, I shall here only provide a brief survey of the main points of his epistemological system, chosen with an eye toward comparison with the work of the later Hayek.

Methodological subjectivism was central to the way Michael Polanyi ap-proached most topics, and therefore it is no surprise that he wanted his epistemology to be rooted in individual cognition. Yet unlike so many other philosophers and social theorists who interpret a dependence on cognition to mean that mind must be reduced to the physiological functions of the brain, as a way station to final reduction to physics, Polanyi posited a hierarchy of phenomena, and in this view mind could not be reduced to brain. He had recourse to Gestalt psychology to lend some legitimacy to this notion; and later he even tried to add his own theory of the inarticulate control of the body as the paradigm of tacit knowledge. Since he believed that everyday modes of knowing were in principle no different from their scientific counterparts, what he intended was a general theory of the inarticulate component of knowledge.

Polanyi's chosen psychology led directly to his prescription of uninhibited liberty of thought, expression, and economic activity, unlike utilitarian psychology, which Polanyi believed served to encourage totalitarian tendencies. Whereas the utilitarian treats the individual as the unmoved first mover in a game where desires are fixed and modalities of gratifications transparent, Polanyi plumped for a situation where goals were surrounded by a penumbra of indeterminacy and most individuals could not articulate how they attained them in many instances; as he never tired of insisting, "we know more than we can say." Since this was true in science, the idea that scientific research could be directed into uniformly utilitarian paths was a travesty for Polanyi; and of course, the idea that economic activity could be planned was equally unacceptable. Liberty was thus a necessary prerequisite for progress in science and in the economy.

Still, no one could be expected to acquiesce in this position without understanding the answer to this question: "How can the combination of fragments of knowledge existing in different minds bring about results which, if they were brought about deliberately, would require a knowledge on the part of a directing mind which no single person could possess?"[25] Was it quantitative measurement, or the reduction of facts to impersonal observation language, or any other positivist conception of a "scientific method"? No, said Polanyi; none of these attempts to obliterate subjective differences between scientists could do the job. As one might expect, he attempted to found his case upon subjective commitment: "Unfettered intuitive speculation would lead to extravagant wishful conclusions; while rigorous fulfillment of any set of critical rules would completely paralyze discovery. The conflict can only be resolved through . . . scientific conscience . . . the tone of personal responsibility in which the scientist declares his ultimate aims . . . full initiation into the premises of science can be gained only by the few who possess the gifts for becoming independent scientists, and they usually achieve it only through close personal association with the intimate views and practice of a distinguished master."[26] Thus there was no mystery about the means by which the knowledge was transferred, though it might be difficult to render its content more fully explicit. Tradition was the counterweight to subjective freedom in science.

Polanyi found throughout later life that he often would be saying things about the processes of science which would provoke cries of outrage from those who regarded it as the summit of all human rationality, so he was forced to repeat that he also thought it was the paradigm of human achievement and remarkably effective in getting at the truth. One way he chose to put this in his paper "The Republic of Science" (1962) was to compare the self-organization of science to the self-coordination of a market.[27] In retrospect, we can see that Polanyi had implicitly been doing something like this since the 1940s, but when he at last made the point explicit, it was misconstrued by all as conforming to some neoclassical model, which it clearly did not. This much should have been apparent from his discussion of the subordination of one scientist's standing to the opinions of others, even though those others could never hope to be fully cognizant of all the specifics of the individual scientist's research. The same voluntary allegiance to authority was also supposed to extend to the layperson, who should freely acknowledge the superiority of the expert in this vast web of self-organized networks. This, then, was another stick with which to beat the Bernalists, since the prognosis was that the public should pretty much just let the scientists do what they wanted, and simultaneously defer to their superiority because of tacit knowledge whenever the polity came upon a question bearing upon their expertise. For Polanyi, the choice was stark: give the scientists free rein, or else relinquish all hope of a growth of knowledge.[28]

It is instructive to compare Polanyi's philosophy of science to Hayek's later development of his theory of the self-organization of complex orders. Hayek decided that he, too, must found his subjectivism upon some sort of psychological principles; but he set out in 1946 to construct his own system out of mid-nineteenth-century associationist psychology, and the result was published as *The Sensory Order* in 1952. Based upon some superseded neural theories from the turn of the century, the book attempted to portray the central nervous system as an apparatus of multiple classifications processing a stream of sensory input which are not themselves stored anywhere in the brain. For a subjectivist, physical stimuli need never directly map into fixed impressions, so "what psychology has to explain is . . . something which we experience whenever we learn anything about the external world . . . and which yet has no place in our scientific picture of the external world and is in no way explained by sciences dealing with the external world: Qualities. Whenever we study qualitative difference between experiences we are studying mental and not physical events, and much that we believe to know about the external world is, in fact, knowledge about ourselves."[29] But instead of the coordination of mental stimuli serving as a metaphor for the coordination taking place in the market, the reverse was true here, as Hayek himself later admitted, indicating that the point of departure was his model of the Austrian period of production in his *Pure Theory of Capital*: "I liked to compare this flow of 'representative' neural impulses, largely reflecting the structure of the world in which the central nervous system lives, to a stock of capital being nourished by inputs and giving a stream of outputs."[30] It is not clear that much more is going on here than an a priori belief in the efficacy of the market being projected upon the neural cortex in the guise of a metaphor, only then to be reflected back as an "explanation" of the efficacy of the market. Polanyi generally did not succumb to such circular arguments.

Of course, Hayek wished to draw a conclusion similar to Polanyi's to the effect that no one was capable of knowing enough of either the facts on the ground (since the mind did not deal in Machian "raw feels") or the rules of tacit inference in order to adequately plan the coordination. But again in contrast to Polanyi, who structured the argument along a telos, Hayek argued in a functionalist circle, the very thing Polanyi thought was the path of least resistance down the road to serfdom: "Like scientific theories, [rules of conduct] are preserved by proving themselves useful, but, in contrast to scientific theories, by a proof which no one needs to know, because the proof manifests itself in the resilience and progressive expansion of the order of society which makes it possible."[31] This divergence from Polanyi induced Hayek to back away from methodological individualism, to depend ever more heavily upon biological metaphors which were imperfectly understood, and to backpedal on his condemnation of scientism—all subjects of extensive commentary in the secondary literature on Hayek.[32]

The divergence from Polanyi could not be more distinct when we come to the politics. Hayek's move from the individual to the meta-level of social organism is at least in part due to how little can be promised to the individual economic agent in his system: he or she can't know the real meaning of price signals, can't count on the market rewarding economic effort along any conventional criteria of justice, can't pretend to comprehend the telos of the system as a whole since it can't be known, and certainly shouldn't place any credence in the pronouncements of experts. As Jeremy Shearmur has put it, Hayek "would seem to be a consequentialist whose subjective views and ideas about the philosophy of the social sciences imply that one cannot make out a consequentialist case for his own ideals."[33] This, of course, is why Hayekians are so suspicious of existing democracies and wish to restrict suffrage according to age, property, and other criteria. These suspicions are hardly compatible with Polanyi's efforts to buttress the role of experts, render the theory of the economy available to the populace through films, and have individuals subjectively acknowledge their allegiance to a system which they can see the point of, even if they don't fully understand where it is headed.

I have attempted in these reflections to argue that doctrines which pass as political economy are frequently thinly disguised *Methodenstreit* over images of science and what it is we are capable of knowing. Quoting Polanyi now, "the main influence of science on modern man has not been, as it is often supposed, through the advancement of technology; it has come, rather, through the imaginative effects of science on our world view."[34] So perhaps I can sum up the tensions between Polanyi and Hayek as a contest of genres, a battle for the soul of Romanticism. Polanyi, as usual, saw the connection: "The romantic movement of the 19th century mitigated the dilemma [of the divergence between appearance and reality] by claiming that the content of art is predominantly subjective, personal. Thus it does not imitate. It merely expresses our subjectively personal feelings. But the progressive sharpening of skeptical thought, leading to the wholesale questioning of traditional values, including the value of the individual person, espoused by the romantic movement, was presently to make any emphatic statements of man's deeper feelings sound trivial."[35] Hayek was a romantic writer, which is why he appeals so strongly to our *fin de siècle* sensibilities after languishing for so long among a small coterie of Austrian economists and conservative politicians. His oeuvre of his middle British period can be compared to a *roman à clef* which looks very much like Mary Shelley's *Frankenstein*. There is a mad scientist, and a monster, and a "constructivist" project which is bound to fail because no one can fully encompass the unintended consequences of treading on forbidden ground. All is set in a castle somewhere in eastern Europe, though the hero is British. The moral of the story is that there is knowledge which is intrinsically forbidden fruit; there are things which are better left unknown. The whole thing turns Gothic when we realize that there is plenty of room here for any number of sequels, all with roughly the same plot.

Michael Polanyi spent his entire life arguing that Romantic narratives like Hayek's are a symptom of a basic fallacy in how we think about science and the place of the subjective individual in the modem world. I sometimes get the feeling that Polanyi wanted to counter Romanticism with something like Milton's *Paradise Lost*, jazzed up for modern tastes, if not *Areopagitica*. I cannot assess the odds on such a revision of the canon—I can't predict how it would sell in the marketplace.

4
What's Kuhn Got to Do with It?

On Feeling Cheated by Kuhn

It is not a fate that you would wish upon anyone: to be feted and celebrated during one's lifetime as the author of one of the hundred most important books of the twentieth century, and yet close on the heels of one's demise, to become subjected to a bout of reconsideration and rejection that borders on the vindictive. Yet, singularly, that is what has happened to Thomas Kuhn and his (dare I say) paradigmatic work *The Structure of Scientific Revolutions* ([1962] 1970). Everyone all of a sudden seems miffed with Kuhn.[1] Stephen Weinberg accuses him of triggering the "revolt against reason" of the 1960s that has poisoned public understanding of science (1998); John Horgan (1996) portrays him as someone congenitally incapable of giving a coherent account of scientific progress; his students such as Kenneth Caneva (2000) bemoan their blindness to the flaws in his deceptively confident assertions about the role of criticism in theory change, or the role of history in understanding science. Participants at a symposium on "The Legacy of Thomas Kuhn" at the Dibner Institute in November 1997 groused that the best-known historian of science of the twentieth century didn't seem to possess the patience or inclination to work extensively with primary sources and archives. Even Steve Fuller engages in a little of this Kuhn bashing himself, writing in one place that *The Structure of Scientific Revolutions* has "a philosopher's sense of sociology, an historian's sense of philosophy, and a sociologist's sense of history" (32).[2]

What seems lacking amid all this flurried discontent is the realization that the upsurge of dissatisfaction should not be directed at the hapless scapegoat named Kuhn, but rather more justly at ourselves. Can anyone seriously maintain that we were duped or swindled by *The Structure of Scientific Revolutions*? After all, it was no one but we epigones who lit upon this most unlikely portion of the "International Encyclopaedia of Unified Science" and made it a best-seller. We were the ones who felt that first frisson of excitement in thinking that science was not the algorithmic sausage grinder of the positivists, but rather something more closely resembling the quotidian workplaces with which we were all familiar. And I blush to admit that it was especially we social scientists who grasped so feverishly at Kuhn's account of normal science and revolutions to lend some credence and legitimacy to our own intellectual traditions. It was none other than our own credulousness that led us to sniff around in the new specialization of the history of science because we apparently caught the whiff of something exhilarating in the pages of *The Structure of Scientific Revolutions*, and we alone who managed to overlook the strange contradictions that permeated the text and our reception of it.

Steve Fuller has been the first with the foresight to forsake the sterile self-pity of the disillusioned acolyte and ask the really penetrating questions concerning Kuhn's legacy; and for this alone we owe him hearty thanks. His book on Kuhn (2000b) helps us see just how odd a phenomenon the popularity of *The Structure of Scientific Revolutions* really was. How did it come to pass that someone who so regularly assailed any new intellectual alliance between the history and the philosophy of science could have ended up as its prophet and patron saint? Or, how did it come to be that an author who warmly preached the virtues of a hermeneutics of sympathy toward ancient superseded thinkers and their texts himself ended up so roundly and thoroughly ignoring his critics and repudiating his enthusiasts? How was it that someone so openly tone-deaf and disdainful toward the social sciences could come to be celebrated as having provided them with a major source of legitimation, even as having helped admit them to the "right" side of the demarcation criterion between Science and its Other? The ironies extend even unto the specific theses of the book. How did it come to pass that a caricature called "normal science," which surely did not exist before the late-nineteenth-century German industrialization of science (if even then), and was subsequently applied to a motley of incidents in the history of science, no one of which occurred later than 1930, came to be confused with a historically sensitive account of the sociology of science in the cold war era of Big Science? Or, coincidentally, how were we ever persuaded to focus so intently upon the "autonomy of science" precisely in the era and geographic location of the most aggressive expansion of state management and funding of scientific research in human history?

I agree wholeheartedly with Steve Fuller that Thomas Kuhn the man was not a cause but merely a symptom of some larger deformations of the philosophy, politics, and economics of science, especially those occurring in the postwar American context. That is why he compares Kuhn to the character Chance in Jerzy Kosinski's *Being There*, haplessly showered with credit for things he never did nor intended. Some reviewers of Fuller such as David Hollinger (2000) seem to resent being reminded that Kuhn's work was less a manifesto than a speculum serving back their own presuppositions. But Fuller does something even more subtle, in that he gives a reflexive "Kuhnian" reading of the career and writings of Thomas Kuhn, showing how his thought can be rendered more comprehensible by situating it within the context of his "masters"—and here James Conant is central—and his followers. Imre Lakatos once jokingly paraphrased Kuhn's message as "Do your master's thing, or your own if you can convert others, but not before then!" (in Motterlini 1999, 94). It seems that Kuhn really did manage the impossible, which was to "do his own thing" only after he had become the icon of thousands; by that time, it was too late. But Fuller's reading is Kuhnian in an even less disciplinary sense as well. Fuller will perhaps acknowledge that his is not a definitive historian's *history* of Thomas Kuhn, lacking in much of the standard armamentarium and chronological narrative line, although it should be said in his favor that he did spend some serious time in the Harvard archives. Rather, Fuller aims to write "philosophical history": that is, a broad-brush *explanation* of what may otherwise have appeared irrational or adventitious in standard narratives, with a view to prompting debate about the future of a particular line of inquiry.

I share Fuller's conviction that philosophical history is the project really worth our efforts, and so will confront his book accordingly on that level. I too worry about the present predicament and future prospects of science studies, which seems ever more intent upon withdrawing into *faux* playfulness and smug obscurity; and I fret over what has become of the profession of the history of science. The relationship of these prospects to the changing structure and functions of the university, first during the cold war and now in our brave new era of globalized privatization, is incontestably the major subtext to the saga of the rise and fall of Thomas Kuhn. But then there is also the question of what role the social sciences play in all this—on this issue I will diverge rather sharply from the line in Fuller's book, wherein the social sciences are praised for their propaedeutic qualities. It may seem odd coming from someone whose own intellectual identity is so thoroughly wrapped up with the social sciences, but I sincerely doubt that one can banish the ill effects of Kuhnian relativism by simply reversing Kuhn's own clear contempt for social science. It is my conviction that an even bigger dose of history, perhaps including a dollop of the history of American social science, is needed to appreciate and assess the regime of science organization and funding which pervades the post-Kuhnian landscape.

The Allure of Kuhn, and Its Discontents

Steve Fuller expends so much effort in uncovering the dark side of Kuhno-phrenia that I think he neglects to remind his audience (many of whom will by now have missed the experience altogether) of what it was like to become besotted with *The Structure of Scientific Revolutions* a little after it appeared in 1962. While it may appear incongruous now, Kuhn's book was regarded as a liberating experience by those looking for a respite from the unalloyed scientism of the immediate post-Sputnik years. It may be worthwhile to briefly revisit some of those themes that resonated so harmoniously with other cultural currents of the time, if only to contrast them with the deleterious effects which they may have had in the ensuing years.

The overarching theme that Kuhn never failed to foreground (and which constitutes the source of so much modern dissatisfaction) is the contrast between his reliance upon communal concepts and patterns of thought and the reductive psychological individualism of so much Anglo-American thought. This theme tended to give his writing a certain Continental flair, without, of course, his having to delve into any of the fine points of European treatment of social structures, much less the classic texts.[3] It is this apparent holism which draws the ire of so many Science Warriors intent upon blaming the excesses of the 1960s for all their woes, but I would instead point out that Kuhn's was a distinctly decontextualized and featureless portrait of the "oversocialized agent," one nicely attuned to the needs and demands of the American academy. The major way one could tell that scientific thought was said to be "socially conditioned" *à la* Kuhn was not by any appeal to tacit knowledge (that was the repressed Continental Polanyite wing of the anti-positivist reaction) but rather by an explicit rejection of the model of algorithmic decision theory which had come to dominate analytical philosophy of science in the postwar period, expediently tarring it with the ambivalent characterization of "normal science."[4] I believe it was this move, more than anything else, which rendered *The Structure of Scientific Revolutions* such a breath of fresh air for so many readers. (This point is crucial for understanding Kuhn's reception, and is unaccountably neglected by Fuller.) Because in the cold war mindset the act of insisting something wasn't algorithmic was tantamount to suggesting it was irrational, Kuhn sought to substitute one mechanistic scheme for another: namely, he resorted to the old Germanic social science modality of lockstep "stage theories" to provide meaning and form to something that resisted being reduced to law-governed component parts.[5]

Hence, there was a real sense in which *The Structure of Scientific Revolutions* was read as de-privileging the science of the 1960s, or at least the paint-by-numbers mechanical science of the postwar positivists. Sure, there were those mock-Foucauldian "radical ruptures" versus the uniform continuity so beloved by the "unity of science" movement; but there really were bits here and there redolent of a generalized social theory, albeit one with so few commitments as to vanish at the precise moment of its conjuration. This was a social theory that would *not* resemble the imitation mechanics of decision theory and neoclassical economics, a point which will assume some significance below. Nevertheless, it was not entirely fanciful in the 1960s to have read Kuhn as ushering in an era where science itself could be an academic topic of study in its own right, as opposed to an unquestioned basis for a uniform general pedagogy imposed upon the unwitting student. It was this largely unrealized promise of a future transvaluation of the values of the hierarchy of knowledge pivoting upon the natural sciences that lured historians of science in large numbers, and fostered a climate in which the "sociology of scientific knowledge" could take root here and there in the academy.

Steve Fuller's book on Kuhn has little patience with any of this. If I may paraphrase the argument, Fuller presents Kuhn as steeped in and shaped by a problematic first enunciated by James Conant in his multifarious roles as Harvard University president, Vannevar Bush's NDRC deputy in charge of the A-bomb, all-round governmental advisor and science manager, as well as pedagogue concerned with the future of American democracy and the threat of Soviet communism. The issue which motivated Conant, and latterly Kuhn, says Fuller, was how to reconcile the apocalyptic products and authoritarian processes of Big Science appearing everywhere in the twentieth century with their commitment to the superiority of democratic and egalitarian political structures; if you couldn't square that circle, then the entire cold war appeared as one dreary, hollow, cynical exercise, closer to John Le Carré than Alexandré Koyre.[6] One of the worries which beset the strategic community in the 1950s was that Soviet society was better configured to produce Big Science results on an assembly line than were the supposed *laissez-faire* conditions in the United States, and thus the Soviets would defeat the Americans in a technoscientific race.[7] Fuller argues that many of Kuhn's (and Conant's) doctrines were contrived to salve those worries and forge a science pedagogy that could thrive in cold war America.

In a nutshell, Fuller maintains that Conant and Kuhn concocted a "double truth" doctrine tailored to cold war exigencies and to the political conundrums they engendered. They began with the premise that Big Science was here to stay, and that continued support for the monster was preferable to starting afresh and trying to engineer a scientific community better suited to democratic needs and procedures. But the prescription was not to force the layperson to consciously accept this—to relinquish core democratic structures simply in the interests of defeating the Soviets through bigger and better Doomsday Machines was too repulsive a doctrine for any but the most Manichean to bear—but rather to develop one ideology for the layperson and another, distinctly separate pedagogy for the tyro scientist. The layperson was persuaded to accept an oversocialized account of the scientists so that they might believe (however wrongly) that dissension and disagreement were absent from legitimate science, and that Science exhibited a self-organizing structure and unified telos no matter what the setup. Further, it had become necessary to reify a strong distinction between pure and applied science in order to deny that the scientists bore any role or responsibility in the uses to which their discoveries were put; and indeed, the historical fact that military and industrial concerns were increasingly encroaching upon the prerogatives of the university since at least the 1880s was nowhere to perturb the equanimity of the hapless layperson. Instead, average citizens were exhorted to derive satisfaction from knowing that their tax dollars went to support who-knows-what classified research, which might eventually result in such boons to mankind as Teflon and the Internet. While the Harvard "general education" course sought to telegraph that Science deployed essentially the same "strategy and tactics" (Conant's terminology) from the seventeenth century to the present, and that your average student was simply too inept to successfully complete the simplest simulated tabletop experiment, the pedagogy for the tyro scientist banished any recognizable history altogether. According to that pedagogy the guild mentality of the postwar departmental organization was coming to reign supreme: budding physicists or chemists would simply take the legitimacy of what they were taught on blind faith, working the problem sets and filling in the lab notebooks, cranking the handles and crunching the numbers, dispensing with any awareness of the historical contingency or contested validity of delegated forms of scientific research. Ignorance of the cultural aspects of science would nurture docile and hard-working makers of thermonuclear bombs and Grand Unification Theories in short order, and with minimum fuss. Fuller makes much of Kuhn's Orwellian doctrine of the rewriting of the history books with each scientific revolution, but frankly, that was not so different from the other Orwellian doctrines kicking around RAND and other postwar institutions of higher learning during the cold war (such as the "impossibility" demonstrated by Kenneth Arrow of consistent democratic voting procedures, or Thomas Schelling's strategic doctrine that with atomic blackmail you could frighten your enemy into behaving rationally). Certainly there would in each case be a small community who were privy to the "real" situation—and for Kuhn, this would be the invisible college of professional historians of science—but they no longer had any critical function to fulfill, either within pedagogy or broad-based philosophical discussions of "whither science." Hence, Kuhn never supported the hybrid departments of the "history *and* philosophy of science" which sprang up in his wake, and have faltered in the interim.

I think there is much truth to Fuller's characterization of *The Structure of Scientific Revolutions* as a "noble lie" to shield science from political exposure in a democratic context and to protect its economic system of provisioning from demands for accountability; and I personally think it matters little whether Kuhn the man consciously intended to endorse the bulk of this package or not. After all, one virtue of Fuller's book is to show how dramatically and systematically the reception of Kuhn's work differed from the expectations of its author. Anyway, we tend to forget that it was the Viennese positivists and their American epigones who were by and large socialists and social planners; Kuhn fits in quite handily with anti-positivists such as Polanyi and Hayek and Merton as a defender of the élite status of science, one that entitled it to tribute in the form of unstinting funding and unqualified belief from outsiders.[8] If scientists such as Stephen Weinberg and Paul Gross seek to saddle poor Kuhn with the onus for the loss of faith in this particular catechism, it can only be because their own formative years were so sadly deficient in historical and philosophical training, and hence they seem incapable of appreciating that it was the end of the cold war that reopened all dossiers and voided all the agreements concerning the relationship of science to the state and to society, and of the scientist to his brethren. The irony is that the drab world of careerist normal scientists which Kuhn described and praised was the world which has since come to pass, and it is a world which would naturally want to heap calumny on his head.

Indeed, I should like to venture further than Fuller by suggesting that Conant was even more significant for the subsequent conceptions of science than he has suggested in this book. Not only was Conant the pioneer of an essentially ahistorical approach to the history of science, preaching *Realpolitik* as the only viable method to reconcile militarily regimented science with a free society, deploying contrived simulations of great moments in science in order to impose and police the distinction between internalist and externalist accounts, and insuring the meritocratic character of science by progressively bureaucratizing admissions to the university as well as the curriculum which would sort aspirants to a scientific career. Conant was also one of the main players in importing and developing the discipline of "operations research" into the United States in the Second World War, along with his fellow science managers Bush and Warren Weaver.[9] While I agree that the pedagogical aspirations of Conant were most directly played out in the shape assumed by Kuhn's *The Structure of Scientific Revolutions*, it was the managerial innovations of Conant and his comrades in the guise of "operations research" that are most salient for *Fuller's* diagnosis of the modern malaise of the history and philosophy of science.

Operations Research as Applied Social Epistemology

To a first approximation, "operations research" (OR) comprised a set of doctrines whose purpose was to more efficiently prosecute war through the better integration of men and the novel technological devices which had been developed by scientists during and after the Second World War. It has become standard in the historical literature to point out that many of these doctrines, which at first glance resemble later social science, were in fact innovated largely by physicists and natural scientists. Fuller (2000b, 201) reports that Kuhn himself worked on radar jamming and OR during the war, and this experience helped turn him away from physics and toward the history of science. While the specific content of OR is not so important in the present context, what is important is that it presaged a concertedly *interdisciplinary* approach to the understanding of social processes and their reactions to technological change. Especially through the intermediary of the computer, it ranged from experimental studies of the cognitive behavior of individuals to direct thermodynamic analogies treating the equilibrium configuration of groups of men. For the major significance of OR for Conant, Weaver, and other natural scientists was that it was a tentative solution to the problems thrown up by the wartime mobilization of science by the state. Physicists wanted to be paid by the military, but not to be *in* the military; physicists wanted to do social science for the military, but not to *be* social scientists; physicists wanted to give others orders, but not be *responsible* for the commands given. To enjoy these extraordinary immunities, the physicists and other natural scientists found themselves innovating new roles which would manage this awkward combination of engagement and aloofness from the chain of command. In effect, these natural scientists invented new mechanisms of control within the military hierarchy to better control their own agenda of research, which had itself come to be overwhelmingly funded by the military. Hence, the rise of Big Science and the innovation of OR went hand in hand in mid-century.

That OR doubled as a kind of theory of science policy is best illustrated by the circumstance that the whole "social planning of science" movement in Britain, the direct lineal predecessor of British sociology of science, overlapped with the luminaries of the British OR establishment then active. Patrick Blackett, J. D. Bernal, Conrad Waddington, and a host of others used their wartime experience to argue that science could be more rationally planned and funded for the benefit of mankind. The political overtones of this movement provoked a reaction in the form of a Society for the Freedom of Science led by Michael Polanyi and Friedrich von Hayek (McGuckin 1984). Since Kuhn was frequently accused of being the American Polanyi, we can again observe the close correlation between attitudes toward the postwar promise and prospects of OR and the rise of a particular version of the history of science. The OR connection to modern science studies is further revealed by the support by Waddington for the early incarnation of the Edinburgh Science Studies Unit.[10]

The reason this has bearing on the story in Fuller's book is that much that happened after *The Structure of Scientific Revolutions* is attributed to the baleful influence of Kuhn alone, when in fact it would be more historically accurate to approach *The Structure of Scientific Revolutions* as one small symptom situated within a much larger dynamic of the playing out of theories of science management and policy in the cold war era of Big Science. In effect, just as there were differential British and American versions of how science operated when it was "tacit" (Polanyi) and "normal" (Kuhn), there were also British and American versions of OR, corresponding to the British and American variants of science funding and management. The British version rapidly devolved into a left-wing sociology of science which had little direct bearing on day-to-day science management, whereas the American version got processed into Mertonian sociology of science and a neoclassical economics of technical change, both of which were subservient to an extensive infrastructure of science managers run by the military and (later) units such as the NSF and NIH. This explains a number of phenomena which Fuller treats as nearly inexplicable, including the curious relationship of sociology to political economy: "the political economy of science has been so verbally co-opted that Kuhn's sociological followers, be they Mertonian or SSK, have been able to cast several models of scientific activity in the discourse of political economy without either making links with the larger political and economic scene that sustains Big Science or even drawing much on the empirical and explanatory resources of political science and economics" (235).

Fuller has been misled by the absence of direct citations in coming to think that science studies bandies about economic terminology without touching base with economic content: the missing link is OR. Operations research inspired much of early science studies (either through advocacy or rejection), and operations research was a major instrument for the stabilization of the American orthodoxy in economics (Mirowski 2002). Even Thomas Kuhn himself participated in a conference on technological change sponsored by RAND, whose subtext was to argue out whether innovative weapons systems could be planned in detail before they were ever built (Nelson 1962; Hounshell in Hughes and Hughes 2000). Kuhn fit effortlessly into this community because, as Fuller notes, his model of normal science was eminently an industrial one, where "success can be measured by sheer output ... against a backdrop of a constant state of competition" (199). This was the cold war "double truth" doctrine all over again: outsiders would be continually reassured that scientists were the freest of free spirits and that scientific inquiry could never be planned or dictated, whereas those in the know were busy reprocessing physical mathematical models into social science doctrines whose major thrust was to justify very specific interventions in the funding and organization of science. In Britain the planning pretensions were a bit more out in the open, but were constrained by the happenstance that OR remained low-tech and disengaged from the computer: the result was a non-cognitive SSK largely decoupled from the political process. In compensation, it was philosophers of science who were fastened upon as the "enemy," with much effort devoted to debunking the existence of a context-free scientific method. In America, by contrast, OR went high-tech and morphed into systems analysis, retreating into a technocratic conception of planning which managed to evade any socialist taint or hostility to market allocation (Hughes and Hughes 2000). Philosophers of science there were most assuredly *not* the enemy (as they were not for Kuhn himself), since they had in the interim been largely co-opted into OR and decision theory. Willard Quine, Donald Davidson, Hans Reichenbach, Nicholas Rescher, and a whole roster of others all were consulting at RAND while they were forging postwar analytic philosophy (Mirowski 2004). It became a characteristic postwar trope to conflate cognition as intuitive statistics with a context-free "scientific method" in postwar America (Gigerenzer 2000). American science studies subsequently bifurcated into the history of science (including Mertonian sociology), with all the consequences of shortsightedness and irrelevance which Fuller has denounced, and the economics of technical change, itself an adjunct of OR.

Thus I would concur with Fuller that "a seemingly radical innovation that quickly acquires widespread currency probably serves some well-established interests which remain hidden" (372); I would just add that Fuller himself has only just begun to scratch the surface of Kuhn's "context of reception," and that when one digs a little deeper, one begins to appreciate just how resonantly in tune with the Zeitgeist Kuhn managed to be.

Older but Wiser

The above sketch tries to augment some of Fuller's own efforts to contextualize Kuhn; but it also has some implications for his own project of a socialized epistemology which he may not like. In both the last chapters of the Kuhn book and in other works (2000a; 2000c), Fuller has promoted the idea that the social sciences provide a dependable platform from which to launch a politically committed and social relevant discipline of science studies, one which will address many of the drawbacks of postwar history and philosophy of science which he has devoted many pages to document.[11]

In this quest, I believe he has overlooked the all-important historical fact that the kind of interdisciplinary inquiry, inflected by social science, into capital-S Science which he imagines as a resource for the future has already materialized in the postwar period, and it constitutes the core of the kind of history and philosophy of science which he so deplores. Not only did operations research give rise to the social studies of science movement, but it also shaped and promoted neoclassical economics, Parsonian sociology, analytic philosophy of science, structuralist anthropology, evolutionary game theory, and even the vintage of cognitive psychology that Fuller has especially endorsed as the future of science studies. What he has missed, I suggest, is that all these social science developments were not so easily separable from the physical analogies and models which constituted their conditions of existence, and that they were integral to the postwar structure of science management and planning within which they were situated. In a catch-phrase, there is little that is distinctively "social" about postwar social science (think of the conceptual dominance of statistics, or the fascination with methodological individualism, or the mechanics of modernization theory); and in any event those disciplines mainly constituted just another one of those "radical innovations" serving widespread interests which Fuller himself warned us against. If that indeed was the case, then where does Fuller believe the Archimedean point will be located against which he can leverage his critique of Big Science?

At various junctures Fuller presents his program of science evaluation as bearing resemblances to that of Karl Popper (394n); but I think he neglects to recall that the Popper of "critical realism" was also Popper the unabashed cold warrior, not to mention the Popper of "situational analysis," a crude attempt to exempt neoclassical economic theory from his otherwise falsificationist precepts (Caldwell 1991). I suspect that once Fuller's research agenda and policy prescriptions are fully spelled out (which they are not in his book on Kuhn, nor indeed elsewhere), his social epistemology will turn out to resemble nothing so much as the OR-inspired doctrines of the postwar period: in other words, it will be an "economics of science" not so different from a cognitively inspired version of neoclassical economics.[12] Maybe it will sport a little "bounded rationality" from Kahneman and Tversky or Herbert Simon, and maybe there will be stirred into the pot a little cost-benefit analysis from the consumer's point of view (Zamora Bonilla, 2003), and maybe there will even be room for some critical analysis of Pareto's theory of circulation of élites or Mancur Olsen's theory of the sclerosis of bureaucratic organizations; but these are all just offshoots of OR, and all trends that one can already discern within the precincts of the orthodox economics profession.[13] It is corporatist science planning in the name of rendering the research process more responsive and cost effective—and since there is no longer any political constituency attached to an abstract "societal welfare," much less to the medieval idea of the university, Fuller's proposal cashes out as the Taylorist prescriptions of hired consultants for the powerful, the well-organized, and the well-heeled.

But wouldn't it be distressing to discover that it wasn't just Kuhn's *The Structure of Scientific Revolutions*, or Quine's naturalism, or Merton's norms that turned out to be Cold War apologetics? That most of what passes for successful "social theory" in the Anglophone world is largely inseparable from the postwar organization and conceptual structure of the natural sciences? And that just because "most of what non-scientists need to know in order to make informed judgments about science falls under the rubric of history, philosophy and sociology of science, rather than the technical content of scientific subjects" (Fuller 1998, 10), this nevertheless is no reliable prescription for political action, but just reprises the cold war "double truth" doctrine in yet another guise? Wouldn't it end up being the *The Structure of Scientific Revolutions* for the MTV generation, or more to the point, the era of fully global privatized science? Wouldn't it be poetic justice to discover that Fuller, having established that Kuhn could not set the terms for the reception of his book nor control its ultimate message, found out he could no more transcend his context either?

5
The Economic
Consequences of
Philip Kitcher

Philip Kitcher's *The Advancement of Science* (1993a) is one of the landmark
texts of the philosophy of science in the 1990s, judging from its ubiquitous
and generally positive reviews. In part, this is due to Kitcher's own fame as
the popular spokesman for the profession; and in part, it is also due to his
having claimed to have staked out the "middle ground" between the Social
Studies of Knowledge (SSK) and *Social Epistemology* crowd on the one side
and the bulk of orthodox analytical philosophers of science on the other. Yet
the most striking thing about most of the reviews, in outlets ranging from
the *New York Times Book Review* to the *Journal of Philosophy*, is their evident
inability or unwillingness to evaluate the project as a whole; reactions to the
eighth and last chapter especially run the gamut from vague discomfort to
respectful incomprehension. It is the thesis of this chapter that it takes
an economist's perspective to adequately comprehend and evaluate what
Kitcher is trying to do, in particular because it has already been attempted in
economics decades ago. The bad news for Kitcher is that the parallel project
has essentially failed in the economists' estimation, and therefore the prognosis for Kitcher's somewhat revised version is not bright. However, in the
end, a narrow economist's perspective is not sufficient—it is a mistake to
think that one might readily separate out the "economic" content from the
rest of Kitcher's project—but only one necessary component of an evaluation of this attempt to tame the "social" in his social epistemology by evis-
cerating it. A second thesis is that one cannot adequately evaluate *The Advancement of Science* as an isolated document; rather, it must be situated in
the context of Kitcher's larger oeuvre both before and after the book. The
recourse to economic modes of discourse is intended to solve various problems for the discipline of the philosophy of science, problems whose salience

is most urgently astringent for someone like Kitcher. In insisting upon this thesis, we mean to demonstrate that Kitcher falls prey to problems of reflexivity as much as any "extreme" avatar of ssk, in that we are only applying his own prescriptions to his own project. As he himself has characterized the moral of his efforts, "we can ultimately calibrate informants, much as we calibrate instruments, so that all we claim to know comes to be based upon the exercise of individual judgment" (Kitcher 1994, 111).

An Invisible Hand in a Velvet Glove

Kitcher begins his book by pronouncing a eulogy over what he calls "legend." Legend was composed of varying proportions of noble scientists, noble goals, foolproof scientific methods, rapier-like rationality, unflinching objectivity, and truth. Legend may have departed philosophical circles, and many will mourn its passing, says Kitcher; but more importantly, someone must stand up to what he calls the "legend-bashers." Then he shifts tone to suggest that "philosophical reflections about science stand in relation to the complex practice of science much as economic theory does to the complicated and messy world of transactions of work, money, and goods" (10).[1] Is this modesty, or is it something else? To cite an author used to great effect by Kitcher in the past:

> I speak not to disprove what Brutus spoke,
> But here I am to speak what I do know.
> You all did love him once, not without cause:
> What cause withholds you then to mourn for him?
> O judgement! thou art led to brutish beasts,
> And men have lost their reason. Bear with me;
> My heart is there in the coffin with Caesar.
> And I must pause till it come back to me.

We need not pause for long over the narrative of the decline of legend and the role of Brutus (or Kuhn or Feyerabend or Latour) in its demise, so familiar to every historian and philosopher of science. The operant question for Kitcher is rather: who or what shall lay claim to the mantle of the dead legend? Could it really be sociology, or cognitive science, or economics, or ssk or (great ghost of Caesar!) some sort of generic cultural studies?

As with so many other things, this has become bound up and conflated in the minds of many with parallel cultural trends: political correctness, deconstruction, relativism, postmodernism, multiculturalism, and worse. When political circumstances such as the winding down of the cold war caught some physicists unawares, rapidly shriveling their financial support from government agencies, they in turn began to lash out at what they saw as the naysayers threatening their livelihood. Some went as far as to blame certain representatives of SSK for having killed the Texas superconducting supercollider. Congress and the press then got worked up over what they considered fraud and waste in science; suddenly, eminent scientists were being treated no better than grizzled Chicago ward-heelers. On their side, the scientists bemoaned their feeling of being trapped in an age of dross, soon after what many recalled wistfully as a golden one (Ziman 1994; Guston and Keniston 1994). Then the pundits and defenders of old-time values got into the act (Wolpert 1993; Gross and Leavitt 1994). In some quarters there arose the nagging suspicion that things were rapidly getting out of hand, both in and outside of academia, and that this strange brew of a sociology of science had more profound implications than the usual academic teapot tempests.

What was needed was a judicious defense of the legitimacy of science that would acknowledge the outpouring of SSK work and an attendant raft of historical studies that demonstrated the sheer contingency and indeterminacy of scientific practices and outputs. Such a defense would reassure the larger populace that science was fundamentally sound and that there existed some operational (and bureaucratically implementable) criteria for distinguishing good from bad science, tainted from pure science, real science from pseudoscience. Also, it would not hurt if the counsel for the defense were perceived as relatively liberal, unwilling to engage in some revanchist return to the good old days, uninterested in churning out another predictable book of virtues. Finally, if the defense were couched in the idiom of biological discourse, which had clearly displaced physics in much of the lay culture as paradigmatic of what was regarded as a progressive inquiry full of pragmatic promise for mankind, so much the better.

Enter Philip Kitcher. He tells us, "This is the book I have wanted to write since I began studying the history and philosophy of science" (vii). Yet what he wrote before is not irrelevant to the structure of this book. His brush with the creationist controversy in the wake of the creation curriculum trial in Arkansas in 1981 (Kitcher 1982) made him well aware of the problems of retailing existing philosophy of science as a resource in real-life political conflicts (Callebaut 1993, 194–95). His work on the philosophy of mathematics (1983) endowed him with an intellectual credibility and stature that are indispensable for anyone seeking to make broad generalizations about "modern science." His liberal credentials derive from his book (1985) critiquing the claims of sociobiologists such as E. O. Wilson and R. Alexander. His warnings there about the pitfalls of finding political meanings in nature would tend to foster the impression that there was someone who would not be blinded by the latest pop-biological or nouveau-eugenic analogy. In addition, his increasing visibility in the public sphere opened up the possibility

The Economic Consequences of Philip Kitcher   99

that here was a philosopher of science willing to engage in the hurly-burly of science policy debates and the hot-button issues of the day; in this capacity he has become one of the main advisors to the "ethical evaluation" of the Human Genome Project (Kitcher 2003).

Yet above all here was a *philosopher*, someone concerned to come to terms with the increasingly obvious trend toward the suicide of the field of the philosophy of science by means of progressive "naturalization": "Radical naturalism thus abandons the meliorative venture of Bacon and Descartes, letting epistemology fall into place as chapters of psychology, sociology, history of science" (Kitcher 1992, 96). Moreover, here was someone who thought of himself as resisting the postmodern disengagement from practical politics, unafraid of prosecuting a self-consciously normative program. In particular, Kitcher's proximity to Bruno Latour in the Department of Science Studies at the University of California at San Diego from 1988 to 1993 had a profound impact. Quoted in Callebaut (1993, 219), Kitcher compares Latour to Lear, who says, "I shall do such things / I know not what they are, but they shall be / The terror of the earth."[2]

The convergence of all these influences, mediated by Kitcher's long involvement with the philosophy of biology, culminated in *The Advancement of Science*. Kitcher begins by appealing to all those who would celebrate multiculturalism, diversity, and so on: the main problem with "legend," he suggests, is that it portrayed scientists (perhaps inadvertently) as rational robots, whereas he, in contrast, is concerned with "celebrating human cognitive variation" (68). However, the PC crowd should not get too excited about this, because this is evolutionary variation (or sometimes Bayesian variation), a prelude to some species of selection process (although not necessarily natural selection [300]) which occurs at the individual level in science: "I want to scotch at the outset the notion that universal methodology is doomed by variation in opinion" (86). Indeed, the purpose of the evolutionary analogies (which are first introduced in the form of a historical narrative *about* Darwin, but over the course of the book shade almost imperceptibly into something that could easily be regarded as a naturalized epistemology: more on this in the next sections) is explicitly to provide the primary argument for the unambiguous success of science, if not of a single generic scientific method. This purpose is brought into the open only at the end of the book: "social institutions within science might take advantage of our personal foibles to channel our efforts towards community goals rather than the epistemic ends we might set for ourselves as individuals" (351).

The economists (forever in danger of nodding off unless someone is mentioning markets) will perk up here: this is an invisible hand argument! Indeed, Kitcher knows this too, for he is aiming toward a narrative of spontaneous order arising out of the distasteful scramble for worldly goods and power uncovered by SSK. If Shapin and Schaffer maintain that science is nasty, British, and short, well, at least it delivers the goods. "The relevant issue is whether, given the actual social structures present in scientific communities, the input from asocial nature is sufficiently strong to keep consensus practice on track" (165). Here the economist, jolted from his torpor, calls a halt: just what kind of spontaneous order are we supposed to have here? Is this, for instance, a story like that found in Friedrich von Hayek, where an inherently incomplete and ill-defined knowledge is distributed efficaciously throughout the populace by means of market coordination? Well, no: Hayek despised the social engineering mentality, which Kitcher explicitly endorses as one of his motivations, and Hayek resists grounding the order in an algorithmic or calculational rationality.[3] In any event, as we shall shortly discover, there is no "market" at the heart of Kitcher's story. So our economist retorts: Or perhaps is it more like the natural order of Adam Smith? Well, again, no: unlike Smith, Kitcher nowhere discusses the pros and cons of the division of labor, in the sense of isolating the specific productive sources of differentiation and their dynamics. Moreover, Smith was not concerned with demonstrating any maximization going on anywhere.[4] Instead, Kitcher thinks his greatest contribution is to demonstrate how self-seeking agents maximizing their own psychological goals lead to impersonally reliable truth.

In other words, like so many others enamored of the dominant versions of cognitive science, Kitcher equates a naturalized epistemology with a grounding in some version of an individualistic psychology. "Epistemology should be *psychologistic*. Whether or not people are rational in their beliefs depends not simply on what beliefs they hold or how the propositions they believe are logically connected, but also on how their beliefs are *psychologically* connected" (184; also 201n). This point is absolutely central to an understanding of Kitcher's project in all its various ramifications. For instance, it was mentioned above that Kitcher was most concerned to demarcate pseudoscience from real science. Now the distinction all boils down to psychology (although delicacy in expression is the soul of discretion): "Pseudoscientists are those whose psychological lives are configured in a particular way" (196).[5]

Finally it all becomes clear to the economist: Kitcher is talking about neoclassical economics! Naturalism is diverted from sociology to become lodged in psychology (Hands 2001), but not psychology as the psychologists practice it;[6] nor is it psychology conceived as certain socially inclined cognitive scientists would wish it (Thagard 1993). Rather, Kitcher posits an ideal rational actor who, under the tutelage of eons of evolution, seeks the maximum personal advantage under the social constraints of the situation. Private vices become public virtues, and conflicting schemes are reconciled to a

Private vices become public virtues

Pareto optimal outcome, which he identifies with a "socialized epistemology." True to form, chapter 8 is taken up with various recognizably neoclassical models, constructed, so we are told, with the help of Michael Rothschild (vii).

I can just imagine some of my orthodox colleagues in economics feeling their pulse start to race. "Science like a market!" they exclaim. Hasn't Kitcher heard of Chicago-style "economics of information" or "rational expectations," or recent game theory? Is he aware that Charles Sanders Peirce was doing stuff like this more than a century ago (1879)? Why, there is even a fairly extensive modern literature on the "economics of science" (Mirowski and Sent 2002)! So Kitcher wants to demonstrate that science is efficient and progressive, does he? Move over, Philip; and out tumble all those economists, eager to deploy their rigorous "tools" on yet another social phenomenon. You want something, Doctor Pangloss? We've got it, in twenty-nine flavors and all at bargain rates.

Perhaps one of the most incongruous aspects of all this is that Kitcher has convinced himself that he is 'pioneering' something: "I think a lot of the things I did in my 1993 book were right. There were some interesting spin-offs about models for understanding social knowledge . . . that's been taken up by economists and other social scientists" (Kitcher, 2003, 59). When all along, in his advocacy of decision theory he has been an unwitting promoter of a subject with a great past and a tenuous future.

Golden Chains, Emerald Cities, and Ruby Slippers

"Yes, of course," replied Oz. "I am tired of being such a humbug. If I should go out of this Palace my people would soon discover I am not a Wizard, and then they should be vexed with me for having deceived them. So I have to stay shut up in these rooms all day, and it gets tiresome. I'd much rather go back to Kansas with you and be in a circus again."

The Advancement of Science is not a single book, and that is perhaps why so many readers familiar with Kitcher's other works find themselves consternated by its style and organization. More than one person has expressed exasperation at having chapter 2, on "Darwin's achievement," right up front, without any indication as to the role it is intended to play in the subsequent argument. I have heard proposals that the chapters should be rearranged to make more sense. I think most of this should be written off to the attempt by the book, really multiple "books," to address diverse audiences simultaneously, but it does not really succeed in that endeavor. One book, which would roughly encompass chapters 3 to 5, is more explicitly addressed to the community of contemporary philosophers of science, touching upon all the Golden Oldies of philosophy, such as realism, truth, and explanation. If that was all there was to the work, it would have remained confined within rather standard disciplinary modalities of discourse. Nevertheless, it does play some role in the argument, and therefore I shall pay it some brief attention.

Next, there are the parts of the book aimed more explicitly at the science studies community, primarily chapters 2, 6, and 7. I treat this group as separate, because it is now acknowledged that diplomatic relations between the philosophers of science and the historians of science have more or less broken down (Nickles 1995); while sociology of science is widely viewed with anxiety as an upstart challenger. The purpose of the second "book" is to establish Kitcher's credentials as an honest broker, pursuing the prudent path between Scylla and Charybdis, the "golden mean" between legend and the wild-eyed relativism of SSK. This attempt to set himself up as the arbiter between two unacceptable extremes is one of the major attractions of the book for all manner of readers; the important question that has languished is whether Kitcher in fact managed to occupy the intellectual center of the discourse; whether he can legitimately claim the mantle of mediator and conciliator. This is the topic of "Black Box and Pandora's Box," below.

Then there is Kitcher's chapter 8, which serves as capstone of his argument, even though it fits uncomfortably within the outlines of the other two "books." Chapter 8 is where Kitcher really overreaches, because that is where he explicitly brings in neoclassical economic models to exemplify his own conception of natural order. While other chapters engage in the commonplace analytical philosophical rhetoric of "$\langle T, M, A \rangle$ just in case T . . . T given M, A," chapter 8 is the only place where the reader encounters real mathematical models; this format creates some problems that will be surveyed below in "Caveat Emptor."

The first "book," consisting of chapters 3–5, is Kitcher's attempt to carry on a conversation with his immediate peer group about the central terms of the "philosophy of science." In these chapters, he would like to treat the goals and attributes of science as technical problems that have been raised by other philosophers, such as Laudan, Fine, van Frassen, Putnam, and Hempel. Not surprisingly, these are the arguments that have subsequently received the most detailed attention from philosophers of science. Some care is required in these sections for the general reader, since Kitcher's own positions on topics such as realism, truth, reference, and explanation are subtly differentiated from those conventionally taught and discussed; in some instances, his characterization of the positions of others would be open to dispute. Nevertheless, it would be inappropriate to engage the text at this level here, primarily because doing so would entail accepting a basic unspoken premise: philosophers of science are still in the vanguard of modern discussions of the goals and structure of science. If anything, what has happened in the last two decades is that philosophers of science have generally retreated from such discussions, withdrawing deep into specialized topics within individual sciences. In becoming specialists on Bell's Inequality or the units-of-selection controversy or the common knowledge problem in game theory, philosophers of science have generally abdicated responsibility for synoptic evaluations of "success" or "fruitfulness" to the scientists themselves. In their absence, it has fallen to the science policy community, the ssk theorists, historians of science, and the social epistemologists to attempt to set the agenda for talking about the ends and means of science. Kitcher, far from occupying the center here, is trying strenuously to recapture the high ground from these groups for the philosophers. For this reason, I will briefly glance at how Kitcher attempts to deploy truth, realism, and explanation to achieve his objectives.

Here we offer a quick caricature of Kitcher's *philosophical* project, based not only on *The Advancement of Science* but also on subsequent texts (Kitcher 1993c; 1994). Science is about the pursuit of "significant truth," itself constructed from a correspondence theory of truth in conjunction with a theory of reference potential. "Progress" is attainment of this truth, not simply or solely through increasingly better correspondence of theory to empirical statements but through improvement of any one of a constellation of elements that may be indicated by the blanket term "practices" (1993a, 31). Since practices are a vector of all manner of ideas, activities, and conventions, improvement along any axis, compared in a pairwise procedure, results in global progress of science.[7] These practices are not completely defined or encompassed within an a priori framework but are themselves to be explored in a "naturalistic" fashion. The attempt to build bridges to the burgeoning field of cognitive science is plainly evident here, as Kitcher effectively conflates practices with the psychological predispositions of individual actors. The final step is to allow for some diversity in these psychological predispositions, and hence in the practices, but still claim that the overall conception of progress persists unscathed. Only at this juncture do we encounter Kitcher's version of "social epistemology." It is postulated that each individual is endowed with the psychological capacities to judge whether and to what extent his or her beliefs and practices should be subordinated to other individual scientists; this is treated as a quasi-Bayesian rational choice problem. Since it is "rational" to delegate epistemic authority to others, the diversity is collapsed to a *consensus*, "something that represents the common elements of the individual practices and becomes part of the cross-generational system of transmission of scientific ideas" (31). Given Kitcher's predisposition in the 1990s to equate "explanation" with unification of schemata, one can then assert that science produces explanations, and that these explanations themselves exhibit progress.

Again, it would not be wise to carve up this framework at each of its joints; that job should be left to the philosophy profession (although a decade later, the job still goes begging). Rather, it would be more germane to see how Kitcher relied on various aspects of the structure to reprimand and upbraid those whom he regards as misguidedly repelled by the language of truth, progress, and realism. It is precisely through observation of his elaboration of his more narrowly defined philosophical theses while defending the advancement of science that we come to understand more clearly his deconstruction of a "social epistemology." These will be covered under the arbitrary rubrics of "justifications for realism," "the uses of reference," and "the meaning of success."

As part of his rhetoric of the honest broker, Kitcher constantly has recourse to the language of "minimalism," which has to do not so much with Philip Glass as it does with Newt Gingrich. In chapter 2 of his book, Kitcher refers to something that he calls "minimal Darwinism," which serves as his gloss for what was preserved through the subsequent vicissitudes of history. In "Contrasting Conceptions of Social Epistemology" (1994) he settles for a "minimal social epistemology." In "Knowledge, Society and History" (1993c) he argues for a "minimal reliabilism." I believe a case can be made that these amount to pretty much the same thing, namely a curious admixture of methodological individualism, descent with modification, vague notions of good government, and an argument for a "unified" approach to reality. As one interlocutor summed it up, "your work can be seen as a first installment of the program for how you should do this sort of human behavioral science based on evolution" (in Kitcher 2003, 57). Somehow, in his view, we have all evolved in such a way that however different our capacities and experiences, we all think we can judge each other's lives and actions, and in fact (says Kitcher) we do this all the time. By a kind of Kantian imperative, we should then recognize that others feel the same way about us; and therefore a generic minimal account of our actions should be possible. Further, if we have the personal capacity to judge each other's actions, we should (by extension) be able to judge each other's statements about the world; so there we have the best argument in favor of an independent reality.[8] If this sounds familiar to those who know the history of twentieth-century social theory as veering dangerously near to a crude sort of behavioralist functionalism, then they would begin to understand the extent to which Kitcher's "minimalism" is a deeply revanchist project, retailed as the lowest common denominator that any postmodern thinker should willingly accept. Indeed, Kitcher has written an entire article (1993b) upbraiding Stephen Jay Gould and Richard Lewontin for uncoupling evolutionary natural selection from simple functionalist arguments.[9] It makes one wonder whether Kitcher has ever seen *Rashomon* or read any Shakespearean literary criticism.

Kitcher the philosopher also believes that his system can adequately respond to earlier criticisms raised by those in science studies: that clashing thought systems exhibit so much theory dependence or incommensurability of conceptions as to give to cumulative progress narratives an air of implausibility. Kitcher (like the later Kuhn and others) regards this problem as primarily an artifact of the use of *language*, and proposes a theory of reference potentials to dispel the doubt. In a nutshell, someone might intend the term "dephlogisticated air" to refer to one list of attributes, while a second someone might intend the term "oxygen" to refer to a second, partially overlapping list of attributes; but science is progressive to the extent that the token attributes that "do the work" are the ones that make up the intersection of the two (96–105). If this is not simply to stand as a blatant tautology—for example, we remember Priestley as significant in the history of chemistry because we choose to reinterpret his terminology as referring to what we ourselves consider to have been successful (100 n 13)—then the meaning of "doing the work" and the role of intentionality therein must therefore need further explication.[10] Kitcher does not make it sufficiently clear that the problem is to be ultimately solved by his later economic models. Again, you and I may subjectively intend wildly different classes of phenomena in our respective reference potentials, but ultimately, rational subjugation to "authority" will result in the winnowing down of these potentials, as well as the lexicon itself, to their appropriate corresponding natural kinds. In Kitcher's world, excess freedom of interpretation is restricted in the same way that the marketplace restricts too many flavors and brands of toothpaste.

Kitcher proposes to handle the definition of scientific success in much the same manner, although this is only made apparent in another of his works (Kitcher 1994). There he confronts headlong the thesis that "success" is itself culturally relative, and variant explanatory schemas are often incommensurable because they are constructed to conform to local goals and standards. Kitcher responds to this challenge by essentially denying that goals can be incommensurate once one takes a broader view and translates the goals of one culture into that of another, or as he puts it, "it would appear possible to achieve a broader set of representations that would incorporate the Western biological views and the non-Western social understanding in a system that would preserve both sets of successes. Because there would be no internal inconsistency, there would be no challenge to the link between success and accuracy" (128). In other words, "success" of science is a human universal, and can be demonstrated as such once one finds the right language in which to express universally held goals. This dream of a generic aggregate "welfare function" is not novel; indeed, its Esperanto is mathematics; and it was the dream of the nineteenth-century British utilitarians and their twentieth-century cousins, the neoclassical economists.

How long will it take before the residents of Oz discover that Kitcher is not a Wizard, but just a reincarnation of Vilfredo Pareto?

Black Boxes and Pandora's Box

What hath Kitcher wrought? A neoclassical "economics of science" has been percolating around the edges of philosophy literature for some time now (Nicholas Rescher, W. W. Bartley, Art Diamond, Alvin Goldman, Howard Margolis, Gerard Radnitzsky); but given Kitcher's philosophical stature, the floodgates will surely open. More conventional economists' objections are discussed toward the end of this chapter. First, it is necessary to telegraph just how daunting this book appears from the vantage point of someone situated within science studies, a rhetorical point also noted by Hull (1994).

The structure of Kitcher's book is extremely curious, given its avowed intent. We are not told that this is a text located within the well-established tradition of evolutionary epistemology; that Kitcher would strenuously deny. Instead, we are treated to a capsule history of Darwinism in the second chapter, ostensibly a case history for later analysis. Now, I am by no means a Darwin scholar, nor a historian of biology; but I cannot shake the impression that this is philosopher's history, and not historian's history, in the sense that the richness of context and contingency so important to the "legend bashers" from Robert Young to Adrian Desmond and James Moore is missing here. In Kitcher's own proffered example, the supposed triumph of "minimal Darwinism" in the period 1860–1900 could be called into question in various subfields (evolutionary morphology, taxonomy, embryology) and by judicious choice of individuals ignored by Kitcher.[11] Others have made similar points before (Hodge 1989). It would be churlish to insist that all philosophers should equally earn their spurs in the history of science, especially since they have made such notable progress in this arena over the last two generations.[12] Nevertheless, there persists the question of intended audience. What are we to take from this chapter?

It seems that it is intended as much as empirical grist for subsequent philosophical chapters as it is to induct the reader into various evolutionary themes that will reappear later in *Advancement*. Rather unexpectedly, the topic of evolutionary biology—Is it the "subject" of an epistemological thesis about science? Is it a metaphor for what the practice of science is like?—takes some vertiginous turns midway through the book, variously serving as text, subtext, and pretext. The passage below appears in the seventh chapter, closely following an argument that the problem of induction is overcome by some primitive propensities to generalize:

As a consequence of our genotypes and our early developmental environments, human beings come initially to categorize the world in a particular way, to view certain kinds of things as dependent upon others, to generalize from single instances of especially salient types. Moreover, just as there is a propensity to form certain generalizations, so too is there a propensity to restrict those generalizations in particular ways when matters go awry. I suggest that this *primitive apparatus* works tolerably well in confronting the problems that our hominid ancestors encountered: it is relatively well designed for enabling primates with certain capacities and limitations to cope with a savannah environment and with the complexities of a prime society (241).

Could this really be the same Philip Kitcher who wrote *Vaulting Ambition* (1985)? What has happened in the interim? Here the history of science serves to disguise the transition from naturalized epistemology to evolutionary epistemology to a hard-core naturalism verging on sociobiology. This slide in the direction of a social Darwinism with a human face during the 1990s became even more apparent in Kitcher's later writings (Kitcher 1995).

I believe these multivalent uses of biology in fact signal a deeper problem in the text. Kitcher wants to take us from some putative generic psychological regularities to an "economistic" society built up from such interchangeable atoms, but he cannot assume that the reader will willingly follow him in this quest for at least two reasons: he is disinclined to make direct appeal to experimental psychological findings (292), substituting instead the "model of man" prevalent in neoclassical economics; and he needs to walk the fine line between on the one hand allowing for real variance in human cognitive capacities and predispositions and on the other asserting enough lawlike behavior therein to justify his subsequent rational choice models. The solution in *Advancement* consists of the periodic insertion of evolutionary language without unequivocal endorsement of more conventional versions of evolutionary epistemology. Kitcher has proven unwilling to accompany his fellow travelers all the way into the modern fad of "evolutionary psychology" (2003, 57).

What compounds the incongruity is that while Kitcher rings the changes upon many connotations of evolution, the economic analysis comes out of nowhere: no history, no context, no hint of consciousness that invoking economics as "scientific" implies including it as subject to the same vagaries of the practices of science accorded to physics and biology. The problem of reflexivity is often bruited about as a refutation of SSK; but Kitcher also suffers the same problem in spades. Thus the hard-core naturalism is doubly disguised: once in the confusion of the uncertain status of the Darwinian episode with which the book commences, and again in the resort to a seemingly "social" theory like economics to wind up the book.

There is another philosopher's book that also begins with the history of an episode in evolutionary biology and ends up with an invisible hand narrative for science, namely David Hull's *Science as a Process* (1988). It was Hull who innovated many of the themes that Kitcher claims as his own: "The mechanism that has evolved in science may not be all that 'rational,' but it is effective, and it has the same effect that advocates of science as a totally rational enterprise prefer. To put the goal of this book succinctly, it is to present an evolutionary account of the interrelationships between social and conceptual developments in science" (Hull 1988, 12). While the books by Hull and Kitcher have very similar objectives, the execution of those objectives does diverge in one significant way. Hull makes no bones about wanting to tell an invisible hand narrative, but not once does he make any reference to any form of academic economics. It is as if, for Hull, the biological metaphor of inclusive fitness was sufficient unto itself to define natural order in the social sphere.[13] Kitcher, on the other hand, is much more determined to refute the literature of ssk, and *for precisely that reason* trundles out the mathematical armamentarium of neoclassical economics. This is effectively made clear in his only substantive reference to Hull's book: "However, some proponents of evolutionary epistemology can be viewed as defending the rationality of science without assuming the rationality of scientists. See, for example, Hull 1988" (178n). Hull, it is true, feels uneasy with intentionality (1988, 468–76); but Kitcher seems to believe that the *only* way to underwrite the rationality of the entire scientific enterprise is by founding it on some means-end principle rooted in individual psychology.[14] Thus for Kitcher, scientists only get to be scientists because they "desire" truth (which he deems "epistemically pure"), whereas his avowed innovation is to allow them to want other things as well, like fame or worldly power (which, in order to telegraph his own position, are called "epistemically sullied"). However, the purpose of this huge detour through neoclassical economics is to get us exactly back to where Hull would have left us: "Moral: there are conditions under which the sullied do better than their epistemically pure cousins, even conditions under which they come as close as you please to the ideal" (351). In other words, some vaguely defined social structures (the unseemly word "market" never is allowed to intrude) may reconcile the incompatible desires of the actors so that they may achieve a social optimum.

There is another aspect of the text that suggests deep ambivalence. Chapter 8 marches us through various mathematical models of authority and self-interest, but it is not at all clear from the prose that they are really intended to show us "how science really works." Indeed, when one observes the number of instances in which Kitcher must resort openly to totally arbitrary restrictions upon the magnitudes of his "utilities" and "authority functions," he cannot be seriously regarded as presenting us with a general theory of science nor a general neoclassical model of the agent. Rather, it makes more sense to read the exercise as a "possibility argument": namely, it simply demonstrates that Pareto optima *could* arise in "sullied" circumstances, not necessarily that they must. However, then their relationship to the case studies is even more tenuous, since none of the models is illustrated by the historical narratives. For instance, one of Kitcher's theorems recapitulates the orthodox neoclassical result that you shouldn't "put all your eggs in one basket" (358–61). How is it that we then managed to get so close to "truth" given that the Hapsburgs didn't give Leibniz permission to come to the UK on the condition that he spend time teaching mathematics to Hobbes, or that Victoria did not offer some crown bauble for a rebuttal of Darwin's translation of "selection" as a natural force, or that the French Academy did not think to offer a prize for a demonstration that Darwin's biogeography was entirely consistent with Lamarckian principles?[15] The point is that at least Hull proffered us a tangible narrative where alpha males and other unsavory types bullied through their confused and irreconcilable differences to a new plane of understanding, whereas Kitcher simply thinks that the rhetorical strength of his models alone will convert the serried sullied actors uncovered by SSK into the epistemically pure paragons of his own historical narrative.

Unfortunately, as we have already suggested, this innovation is self-defeating. As any moderately critical economist will immediately apprehend, neoclassicals have long maintained that the project to extract such normative principles from their models has a long history of failure (Hands 1994a; 1994b). The reason why this may not be immediately evident to the reader, or indeed to Kitcher himself, is that he treats the economics as a black box, a box of tools to reveal the real state of affairs in science. The black-boxing of economics must be treated gingerly, since if the forces of the Legend-basher-bashers view sociology with disdain, then what are they going to think of economics? True to form, Kitcher launches a preemptive strike in chapter 1:

> Much traditional philosophy of science, in the style of some economic modeling, neglects grubby details and ascends to heights of abstraction at which considerable precision and elegance can be achieved. We should value precision and elegance, for its own sake . . . But, like ventures in microeconomics, formal philosophy of science inevitably attracts the criticism that it is entirely unrealistic, an aesthetically pleasing irrelevancy. To rebut such charges—or to concede them and to do better service to philosophy's legitimate normative project—we need to idealize the phenomena but to include in our treatment the features that critics emphasize. (10)

That's it: that's all we ever hear about the problems that might beset microeconomics for the rest of the book. These problems extend well beyond the methodologically individualist stance that is baldly asserted with absolutely no justification (303). The problems involve repeating mistakes that have been hashed over in the last fifty years of neoclassical theory (including its offshoots, such as "decision theory"), especially with regard to bridging the chasm between individual maximization and macrosocial phenomena. Economists will recognize these problems under the rubric of "microfoundations of macroeconomics" and will be reminded of the relative impotence of welfare economics. Thus, the impression that we are somehow dealing with a theory of "society" here is deeply misleading. The only way the fiction can be maintained is by black-boxing the economics.

Caveat emptor

The impression that neoclassical microeconomics or game theory could provide some magic wand to produce normative statements is a failing of most attempts by philosophers of science to bend it to their own purposes; it is not just a problem for Kitcher. Since Hands (1994a) has covered this issue so well, I shall skirt over it in favor of pointing out a few more technical and historical objections that might be raised by someone familiar with the economics; but then I wish to wind up by bringing the issues back home to the problem of reconciling the social to the natural.

My economic objections fall under four rough headings: (1) representative actor models (Kirman 1992); (2) strategic versus nonstrategic conceptions of the actor (Weintraub, ed., 1992); (3) static versus dynamic conceptions of market operation (Ingrao and Israel 1990); and (4) neoclassical economics as reprocessed nineteenth-century physics (Mirowski 1989b). All these controversies are in fact interlinked historically, but their import for Kitcher is sufficiently differentiated that they can briefly be treated separately.

The first asocial aspect of Kitcher's chapter 8 is his use of representative actor models. While economists now often acknowledge this issue (Binmore 1994, vii), it seems that philosophers still have difficulty seeing the point. While Kitcher's text seems to be describing sets of different types of people, as in relations of scientific authority to some "other" or differentials between the sullied and unsullied actors, when one looks hard at the mathematics, one discovers that the results are usually cast in terms of the psychology of a lone exemplary rational actor, with the consequences "blown up" to the level of society, or at best as a two-person game in which the cognitive capacities and interests of the individuals vary by a parameter or two. For instance, section 8.3 is a representative actor model, while Technical Discussion 1 is a two-person game; section 8.7 is a representative actor calculation (with other agents' characteristics taken as fixed); section 8.8 turns the problem into a game, but where players are surreptitiously made alike (323n); section

8.9 is a representative actor; section 8.10 is a two-person game; and so on. This is an old and disreputable practice in neoclassical economics, dating back to Alfred Marshall, and a trick whose results rarely survive aggregation. It is often found in economics textbooks as the Robinson Crusoe scenario we discussed in chapter 1—Friday, of course, is nowhere to be found—or else the "Edgeworth scenario," where two somewhat differentiated individuals are cloned repeatedly to populate a society. What seems particularly galling about this tactic is that Kitcher claims to have come to celebrate diversity, whereas his models work only in terms of a relatively dour uniformity. Furthermore, the tactic violates one of the first principles of evolutionary thought, as explained in Mayr (1982) and elsewhere: it substitutes "typological" thinking for population thinking.

The second asocial aspect of chapter 8 is the patently nonstrategic character of Kitcher's models. Again, the text presents us with crafty, sharp-eyed individuals looking to do each other down and grab the brass ring; but the mathematical models generally describe an individual mechanically maximizing some fixed function. In a sense, this divergence just recapitulates the history of neoclassicism, in which dissatisfaction with the passive, mechanical nature of similar models prompted John von Neumann and Oskar Morgenstern to promote the theory of games as an alternative in 1944. Kitcher does, as we have indicated, insert a few game-theory models in chapter 8, but the most distressing aspect of this to an economist is that he is never very explicit about the kinds of solution concepts he is imposing upon his two actors. It would seem from the text that he is using Nash equilibria implicitly, but more importantly, the version of Nash known as evolutionary stable strategies.[16]

Making this technique more explicit would raise much more than narrowly technical mathematical issues. First, it would reveal with stark clarity the repressed naturalism identified above. Briefly, people have a few advantages over animals, one of which being that they can tell multiple stories about their motives and rationalizations; as a consequence, there is no single solution concept that has come to be accepted as predominant in economists' versions of game theory. There exists among aficionados of such things something known as the "folk theorem," which states that just about anything can be rationalized as a Nash equilibrium in a repeated noncooperative game. Still more troublesome is the recent suggestion that even dominated strategies can easily persist in an evolutionary setup (L. Samuelson 1993). This has got to be bad news for Kitcher. The implications of the indeterminacy of Nash equilibria for science studies have already been spelled out, apparently unbeknown to our author. Once one explicitly commits to a specific game-theory solution concept, then it is child's play to subvert any given invisible hand story in science, as demonstrated in chapter 10.

The third asocial aspect of chapter 8 is the palpably static nature of most of Kitcher's models. In economics, theorists have come to appreciate the Sonnenschein-Mantel-Debreu results, which state that in general equilibrium, the standard restrictions on utility maximization place negligible restrictions on excess demand functions, rendering a serious dynamics of convergence to equilibrium most unlikely. In simpler terms, just because a maximum can be shown to exist does not mean that a system will converge upon it. In many ways the situation is even more dire for Kitcher, since he is so loath to pronounce the m-word, and indeed stands firm in his conviction that he does not need to utter it;[17] consequently it is not clear that there are any prices in his system to coordinate all individuals' estimates of their own private optimal strategies. To be sure, everyone is permitted to calculate what he or she believes is optimum behavior by solipsistically consulting private utility functions, but at least in neoclassical theory it is the prices that provide the interpersonal information and constraints. Outside of clairvoyance and telepathy, it is not clear how such a system would be coordinated in Kitcher's radically individualist vision of science. In many instances, and especially in the games, he skirts the point by treating utilities as interpersonally known. Kitcher's aversion to The Social Process That Dare Not Speak Its Name is presumably mollified by his advocacy of an ersatz evolutionary psychology, as discussed above. The paradox is that dissatisfaction with the lack of any plausible dynamics in neoclassical economics has led to a breakaway school of "evolutionary economics" (Hodgson 1993; Rutherford 1993), which looks nothing like Kitcher's models. Neoclassical economics and evolutionary epistemology may just eventually turn out to be oil and water, if we view their interaction from the economists' side of the fence. (But then again, maybe not: see Binmore 1994).

This point could be rephrased to be more user-friendly for historians of science. It is now widely acknowledged that "there is within science a marked difference from one end of a century to the other in what it takes to trust one's own data or to trust the results of others" (Holton 1994, 61). Kitcher believes that he has widened his notion of progress to include the evolution of such practices, but has neglected to notice that his mathematical models of "trust" essentially exclude any such possibility. The nature of the calculation of authority in his chapter 8 does not allow the development of social institutions to offset what are perceived as personal "errors" through time. The rise of meta-analysis in quantitative measurement is just one example of a social structure of science that cannot be encompassed within Kitcher's utilitarian framework (see chapter 8 below). Kitcher's models are incapable of seriously dealing with the process of the building of trust, hence his supposed "solution" to the formation of consensus (which, recall, is the major foundation in his system for defining "progress") cannot ever be brought into contact with real historical incidents in science. Therefore, the validity of the models in his chapter 8 *cannot* be postponed as a mere "empirical" issue, to be settled at some future date. Kitcher's own citation of the experimental tradition within cognitive science, such as the results obtained by Kahneman and Tversky on biases in probability estimates, should have served notice that his own Bayesian approach had little or no "naturalistic" basis; it certainly reveals that his feints in the direction of cognitive science are comparatively empty.

However, the most egregiously black-boxed aspect of Kitcher's recourse to neoclassical economics is his neglect in asking after the historical provenance of his preferred technique of utility maximization. History of science, so solicitously acknowledged when it comes to physics and biology, is exiled to the margins of the text when it comes to economics. For the sake of argument, suppose that the reason why the maximization of utility took hold in economics in the nineteenth century was that it was a thinly disguised recapitulation of the mathematical problem of finding an extremum of potential energy in rational mechanics. If this narrative holds water, then it implies that a motley collection of physicists and engineers managed to recast economics as a social physics, projecting the natural order of the inanimate world onto the marketplace. The irony of Kitcher's subsequently appropriating utility maximization to append a "social dimension" to a science like physics then becomes rich indeed. The hall of mirrors so reflects and ricochets a few basic metaphors from nature to society and back again that finding the exit into a truly naturalized epistemology will not be easy.

This indictment, that once we open up a few selected black boxes, it follows that Kitcher cannot even begin to adequately distinguish the social from the natural, much less subject them to quarantine, is not made lightly. It is precisely the thesis of Bruno Latour, Kitcher's *bête noire*, in the period from 1987 to 1993. It is a message that has never gotten through to Kitcher, judging from some of his comments made about Latour.[18] Kitcher's project to "rebut the notion that one can infer directly from the existence of social pressures and nonepistemic motivations the conclusion that science does not advance" (388) is fundamentally misguided, not because we can legitimately make such inferences (we can't), but rather because the dichotomies of social pressures and natural imperatives can only be maintained with the help of heavy-duty repression. Parodying the social contract literature, which itself has a tenacious foothold in economics, Latour has posed this paradox as the "Constitution of modernity" (1993, 32):

> *First paradox*: Nature is not our construction; it is transcendent and surpasses us infinitely.
> Society is our free construction; it is immanent to our action.

Second paradox: Nature is our artificial construction in the laboratory; it is immanent.

Society is not our construction; it is transcendent and surpasses us infinitely.

Constitution: First guarantee: even though we construct nature, nature is as if we did not construct it.

Second guarantee: even though we do not construct society, society is as if we did construct it.

Third guarantee: nature and society must remain absolutely distinct: the work of purification must remain absolutely distinct from the process of mediation.

It should now be apparent that the objective of Kitcher's book is to "purify" nature and society, to render unto Caesar that which is Caesar's, so that the mediation can go forward with renewed vigor.[19] However, the very project deconstructs itself, since it involves transfer of evolutionary metaphors from the biosphere to the realm of the generation and continuation of ideas, social metaphors of utility maximization (themselves recently ported across from energy physics) to the realm of physical phenomena. Indeed, Kitcher's meliorative naturalistic program of diagnosing the maladies of science has the avowedly bureaucratic objective of having philosophers impose a social order upon science so that nature can impose a cognitive order upon science. I think that there have been few such exemplary instances of precisely what Latour means by "mediation" as Kitcher's book. Further, the subsequent work of Kitcher tends to back away from this impossible ambition (2003, 59).

Kitcher has not given us an account of society, as I have argued above, but a convenient image of society that will undoubtedly be found acceptable by a broad spectrum of his target audience. After all, hordes of undergraduates still seem convinced that either the Marshallian cross or Walrasian general equilibrium theory proves that the market "works." Kitcher has not given us an account of nature either, since the kind of rich narrative found in much of the history of the physical sciences is also absent. Instead, we are tendered a reassuring image of nature that will undoubtedly be deemed acceptable by a broad spectrum of his target audience. Only by positing broad abstractions like nature and society can Kitcher divert our attention from the day-to-day work of creating what Latour has called "quasi-objects": the dollar as Natural invariant; the gene as social invariant. These quasi-objects don't need Kitcher to attest to their validity or underwrite their "progress"; their polysemy renders them resilient in the face of challenge.

6

Re-engineering
Scientific Credit in the
Era of the Globalized
Information Economy

Why is it that so many serious and sober thinkers seem to experience such trouble coming to grips with the social processes of science and their shifting relationship to the economic structures dedicated to their maintenance and encouragement? Esther-Mirjam Sent and I have just finished editing a historical survey of the various approaches to analysis of what one might call "the economics of science" (Mirowski and Sent 2002). The major lesson drawn from the exercise, at least for me, is that the range of social theories deployed by science policy analysts in the past has served mainly to divert their attention from the pressing problems and great transformations within contemporary science. If I had to summarize the experience of the last century, it seems to have consisted of one of two root options: one says that science operates just like a market, so don't worry and be happy; while the other insists that science is the antithesis of the market, and must be approached with the reverence appropriate to a mystery, altogether denying the grubby details of funding. What is even stranger about this situation is the way in which those who think of themselves as strenuously resisting the metaphor of a "marketplace of ideas," from Michael Polanyi to Paul David to John Ziman to the Paris "actor-network" school (all reprinted in Mirowski and Sent 2002), tend to collapse their analyses back into the language and modalities of market analysis to a greater or lesser extent,[1] thus rendering their crusades to protect science from the idols of the marketplace more than a little suspect.

There are perhaps two bad habits that this literature tends to slip into, which serve to prevent any really incisive research into the complex relationship of scientific research to economic structures and institutions. The first proposes some broad-brush characterization of capital-S Science as though it held sway as an invariant throughout three centuries or more of research. Nothing is more inimical to examining the social structures and day-to-day procedures of science than the tendency to treat it as a Platonic ideal, something which the field of science studies has criticized in the philosophy of science and in Mertonian sociology of science. Even worse is the widespread impression that Science produces as an output a generic "thing" which perdures through time, be it called "knowledge" or "information" or epistemic virtue. The second pitfall is to confuse the operation of markets with the models of neoclassical economic theory. Some of the most important social aspects of markets, such as the treatment of property rights and the attribution of valuations, are accorded such garbled accounts in neoclassical theory that much discussion about the economics of science degenerates into arguments about the technical minutiae of the models.[2] In the past, the social structures of science have indeed depended in critical ways upon the operations of markets, but this dependence has changed its character through time. The recent intersection of information technologies, intellectual property definitions, and the restructuring of university finances is merely the latest in a sequence of interactions between science and markets. Tiresome arguments about an ineffable "spontaneous order" and the imperviousness of truth to pecuniary corruption, and descriptions of equally inaccessible utilitarian welfare measures, just provide diversions from the real issue, which is understanding how the social structures of scientific disciplines and the social structures of markets interact.

In this chapter we shall ask: What has happened of late to some well-worn pathways to success in contemporary science? Since we can take the index of success in the market economy—namely, getting rich—as given and unproblematic, the inquiry will mostly explore what it now means for a scientist to assume the mantle of an author at the turn of the millennium, and ask how he or she exercises control of authorship so as to garner social recognition and support which then can be parlayed into some modest economic success. This inquiry will involve examining the perennially uneasy status of the author in the process of disseminating scientific findings, as well as equally imprecise notions of the "ownership" of scientific discoveries and their relationship to forms of intellectual property. Scientific credit has always been embedded in a more encompassing environment of property rights; the way forward comes in exploring how authorship has been made, not born. In this manner, perhaps we can begin to make some headway toward resolving the vexed issue of how contemporary science relates to the market. Furthermore, by posing the question in this way, we may begin to analyze recent *changes* in the social structure of science which may be the result of changes in the structure of the economy, revealing the ways in which the two are mutually constituted.

Authorship and the Nature of the Scientific Agent

Becoming an author might seem one of the most straightforward things in the world: write something down, submit it to some reputable outlet, get it accepted, and make sure your name gets published with it. Be it poetry or science, the simple equation of the person with the product would seem to constitute authorship. But appearances are deceiving, and the situation in science is fraught with complexities, as has been shown in some recent work by Mario Biagioli (1999; 2000a) and by the legal scholar James Boyle in his *Software, Shamans and Spleens* (1996). It will be our contention that these authors have identified one of the most salient alterations of the social structure of science in recent experience, namely that concerned with how scientific achievement is subject to identification, accounting, and validations.

One of the most persistent obstacles to a useful economics of science has been the conviction, widely shared, that there is *something*, frequently called "credit" or "proven creativity" or (more crudely) "fame," which acts more or less analogously to money in the social system of science, which serves to channel and rationalize the allocation of resources for scientific research. This entity is thought to stand as both prospective incentive and posterior index of proven value, although in science it has been common to bemoan that it is also distressingly intangible, sometimes shamefully languishing unrecognized, and often supposedly lodged within the murky cognitive recesses of what would be deemed in some ideal world the "relevant" scientific community. It is supposedly durable and inalienable once "earned," and therefore does not derive its valuation from the market, although it may be leveraged into various forms of explicit economic support. This, of course, is an old idea in some sense, but one which was elevated to a more central position in science policy in the arguments of the 1930s and 1940s over the social organization of science, and represented by the famous paper of Michael Polanyi, "The Republic of Science." It underpins the post-Kuhnian accounts of philosophers of science such as David Hull (1988) and Philip Kitcher.[3] For a while, it constituted the linchpin of the Mertonian school of the sociology of science. It can also be found serving as an adjunct principle in many theoretical texts, and resonates handily with the "cognitive turn" taken by much of modern microeconomics, especially recourse to notions of "reputation" and credibility in game theory.

It seems that numerous structural changes in the organization of science at the turn of the millennium have prompted at least a few observers to reconsider the coherence of this commonplace notion (Cohen 1995; Koertge 1990; Biagioli 1999; Biagioli 2000a). After all, whatever can "credit" mean when there are more than two hundred names (in alphabetical order) on a four-page article in *Physical Review Letters*?[4] But the problem is not solely or simply the pervasive growth of multi-authorship in all the sciences, nor merely some technological artifact of the inexorable rise of Big Science projects. Likewise, the problem extends well beyond what has been called the "Matthew effect" in the sociology of science, namely the fundamentally unfair process by which some people are just more gifted at the process of academic self-promotion, and frequently others mistake fame for responsibility. Where do ideas come from, in the final analysis? Who manages to capture the credit for a published result emanating from a hierarchically organized laboratory with literally hundreds of workers in subordinate and vulnerable roles early in their careers, and who really deserves it? What good is the "credit" of a few close insiders when some third party goes out and patents the genetic sequence—or, closer to home for economists, your nifty computer trading algorithm embodying your latest rational expectations model of derivatives pricing—which you believe you were first to decipher and codify? What happens to "credit" when corporate sponsors force university scientists to sign nondisclosure agreements or prior restraint clauses as a condition of funding? Is "credit" something that falls neatly within the realm of "ethics," or does it occupy some hazy third category beyond both the market and canons of virtue? As usual in America, quasi-judicial bodies have begun to issue dictates on "credit" to fill the void: for instance, the Office of Research Integrity of the U.S. Department of Health and Human Services has ruled that disputes over credit among collaborators on a joint project should not be treated as matters of "scientific misconduct." Things have clearly gone well beyond ceremonial appeals to "trust" the discipline's graybeards to dilute the iniquities of human ambition. Biagioli (1999) nicely captures the impasse with his account of the debate over the nature of authorship among the International Committee of Medical Journal Editors.

The central problem, as it appears to both Boyle and Biagioli, is that there have been at least three conflicting conceptions of scientific authorship at large in the culture, and of late these have had a tendency to get conflated in the legal and economic spheres, with grave consequences for science policy, especially in the context of what we have called the "globalized privatization regime" (Mirowski and Sent 2002). By this we mean various initiatives to both privatize and reorganize university-based science over the last two decades, mostly in America, but often as well in transnational contexts which mirror the reach of transnational corporations. The question in this context therefore becomes: What is the relationship of intellectual property defined in the sphere of the market to authorship realized in the sphere of scientific publication, and therefore to the phenomenon of scientific "credit," especially in the context of science funding and policy? Let us canvass these various alternative personas of the author, in preparation for diagnosing the predicament of credit in an economics of science.

Three Characters in Search of the Author

The Romantic Genius. One commonplace version of authorship revolves around an idea of personal originality, which Boyle suggests dates back to the persona of the Romantic author.[5] Here the Author is not defined by mastery of a prior set of rules, but instead by the Promethean transformation of genre and the skillful (and sometimes shocking) transgression of much that is taken for granted in the culture. Lest the reader reject out of hand the relevance of this Romantic persona for the modern scientist, let us pause to contemplate the standard treatment of such physicists as Richard Feynman or Stephen Hawking, or biologists such as Kary Mullis or Barbara McClintock.[6] The Romantic scientist is the staple of cultural images from Ibsen's *An Enemy of the People* to the latest installments of the PBS program *Nova*. What is less than clear about the Romantic author qua scientist is whether the ultimate objective of his or her personal quest is a consensual truth or perspective-free (and seemingly anti-Romantic) social consensus. Ever since Thomas Kuhn, a distinction has frequently been made between mundane science, which solves puzzles and never perturbs the prior beliefs or expectations of other scientists, and something else purportedly more "revolutionary," which aims to revise our fundamental understanding of an entire research program. Unless the innovation is immediately and universally embraced, "revolutionary" science will, of necessity, summon advocates and fuglemen resembling the Romantic author to champion its cause, at least as long as it is resisted by the more conservative majority.

There exists an established legal framework for the validation of one species of "credit" in the image of the Romantic author: it is called "copyright." Copyright was initially intended to promote originality in expression; it is centered upon the protection of form; it is not an attempt to make any sort of pronouncement about the content or legitimacy of claims being made in the text in question. As Boyle explains,[7] the distinction between form and content was one approach to reconciling the contradiction that the author could maintain some rights in his or her work, even though the act of communication necessarily implied offering up use of the ideas to others. It may seem perverse to try to engross and control the collective wisdom of the human race, but ever since Locke, it has struck many as eminently sensible that we should be able to own *ourselves*. Yet even here there is room for slippage: copyright need not be claimed by the person who wrote the text, and it is usually only granted for a fixed interval of time. The reason for this curious set of prohibitions, dating from 1709 in Britain and 1790 in the United States, and regularized in 1887 in the international sphere by the Berne Convention,[8] is a program to assist in protecting a "personality" whose identity is intimately related to his or her originality; this frequently derives from a Kantian tradition which treats the individual self as self-constructed. Until recently, there has been but one generic form of violation of copyright, and it is called "plagiarism": it involves harmful impersonation of another legally validated author.

The initial construction of copyright centered on the act of making a copy because it aimed to separate out control over the uses to which a text might be put from the simpler question of controlling the sale of reproductions of the author's original text for a delimited time. Justifications for copyright do differ across national contexts, but in the United States Constitution, article 1, section 8, the objective of the protection is explicitly stated to be "to promote the Progress of Science and useful Arts." This distinction has been eroded of late, especially with regard to first sale and fair use, as we shall discover below (Halbert 1999; Cohen 1998; Mann 1998; Litman 2001).

The Applied Tinkerer. A second form of authorship aims for a different reconciliation of tradition and innovation. Here the author is best regarded as a "tinkerer" who improves on an existing entity or process, or else applies it to a purpose previously overlooked. The key distinction is that tinkerers do not conjure up knowledge as an original expression of their personality; rather, they *find* something, publicly accessible to all, and make *improvements* to it. It is important to note that the tinkerer excogitates a novel use and does not simply "discover" an existing natural phenomenon. The logic of "credit" enters here, since a framework exists within which the tinkerer can recoup a portion of the benefits of the improvement when it is put to use by others.

There has existed a legal format for validating this species of "credit" as well, and it is called a patent. Legal precedent here is a bit tricky, but one dominant interpretation of patent law until recently is that patents should be restricted to *applications* and not granted for *ideas*. Again, a subtle distinction is promulgated between the thing or process in itself, which is in some sense rendered accessible to all merely by virtue of its existence, and the use of the thing or process, for which "credit" can be claimed and protected. Patents have a long history, but in the modern context they were initiated as a means of encouraging marketed implementations of novel inventions. However, throughout their history it seems they could easily be put to other unintended uses, such as controlling existing patterns of industry concentration and market structure. The legal reality of the patent, however, has undergone some radical revisions over the last few decades,[9] a point to which we shall return below; and this also will have implications for the notion of the scientific author. Nevertheless, the generic form of violation of patent is patent infringement—the unauthorized use of a process or thing.

This second image of the scientific author as tinkerer undergirds that most trenchant dichotomy of the cold war regime of science policy, namely "basic science" versus "applied science." The dichotomy posited a strong separation of roles between the generation of an idea and the application of an idea, or alternatively the uncovering of a fact and the use of a fact, and fostered the impression that there were two different sorts of "credit" at work. It was grounded in a very particular framework of science organization (Asner 2002), which was characterized by relatively weak intellectual property protection for the pure scientist in the university, combined with structural impediments to patenting imposed at the military and university levels. In the older cold war model, pure science supposedly terminated with publication in a journal. However, the separation was never as clean, either conceptually or in the practice of science, as was then widely portrayed. In Big Science, instrumentation and technological virtuosity could never be completely quarantined from theory and empirical test (Galison 1997); and that science would involve the discovery of some previously existent phenomenon, not an expression of the personality or originality of the discoverer, and that the discovery was itself predicated upon a preceding sequence of constructed or orchestrated phenomena handed down from other scientists, left everything but the most abstract paper-and-pencil exercises at least somewhat resembling the activities of the tinkerer.[10]

In the twentieth century, tensions between "finding" and "making" truth tended to get submerged into the division of social roles between "pure scientist" and engineer. In short, the scientist under the older mid-twentieth-century model was exhorted to abjure the patent format of authorship, in proportion to the extent that the scientist wished to preserve his or her integrity as a personal fount of intellectual novelty.

The Employee. And then there is a third species of author; or rather, there is a residual category which was supposed to encompass everyone excluded from the first two. These are the people who uncover rationally anticipated natural laws and regularities by following uncontroversial routinized procedures and build incrementally upon widely accepted doctrines. These are people who often work in large structured teams, who dependably meet the expectations of their superiors, and who follow career paths up bureaucratic structures. It may seem incongruous to refer to these people as "authors," since they neither express their individuality (as in copyright) nor necessarily improve processes (as in patent); but they nonetheless account for the bulk of all published science. They perform assays, obey laboratory protocols, monitor error attributions, conduct literature searches, negotiate with other researchers over access to materials, draft papers, submit grant applications, revise where instructed, and cooperate to get their team's work published. These are Kuhn's despised "normal scientists," the post-docs and lab technicians and grad students and bottle washers of the world.

The problem with this third type of authorship is that it does not conform very well to any prior image of the author prevalent in Western culture. Scientists in this category largely sacrifice their individuality and submerge their contribution within some larger communal whole. Their job is to discover transpersonal truths that should be accessible to any adequately prepared, sufficiently alert soul of sound, normal intelligence. Their charge is most emphatically *not* to infuse their findings with local color or personality. The phenomenon of interest should "speak for itself." Even if personal experience tells them otherwise, nothing of the specificity of their procedures and discoveries should appear in their public reports. They must subordinate their plans and aspirations to the will of their group; and texts must be written in such a way as to make the individual members of the group transparent, approaching irrelevance. In the marketplace, there is a stable legal model for this sort of person: they are called *employees*. But employees, by legal definition, have no legal claim on the fruits of their own labor.

Is there a sort of scientific "credit" which accrues to this uneasy form of authorship? There's the rub: yes and no. Yes, there is the appearance of an individual's name on published documents and formal presentations to scientific audiences; there is the derived phenomenon of the *curriculum vitae*; there are citations and memberships on professional and honorific boards; there is inclusion in various invisible colleges and closed communities; and all the rest. These journals, these boards, these committees are nominally charged with allocating and validating this species of credit. If it is permitted, there may be inclusion in one of the multi-author title pages mentioned above, although patterns of crediting authorship vary dramatically between individual sciences (Kling and McKim 2000). But simultaneously, no: there exists no legally sanctioned index for weighing the motley of claims affixed to a person's name, festoons of widely varying legitimacy and validity, claims that in any event are conferred in a context where the person's identity was effaced in the first place.[11] It should become apparent that "authorship" under such circumstances has always been a highly negotiated phenomenon; hence, naïve notions of responsibility must have come under revision and reconsideration. For instance, scientific journals and the committees do not want to be forced to adjudicate credit, much less responsibility for a written text (Davidoff 2001); and in most cases, they don't. We are talking about a world in which someone can be treated as a species of secular saint because he "made it clear he only wanted his name on manuscripts where he actually contributed."[12] A freestanding matrix of this elusive kind of "credit" could rarely bear the weight of all the social functions it is often asserted to perform; most pertinently, and in contrast to the two kinds of credit discussed earlier, it cannot be buttressed by any strong economic indices of valuation. Its sole legal prop is the employment contract.

Curiously enough, the abiding tensions between "making" and "finding" truth in conventional notions of science, which beset the realms of copyright and patents, are altogether absent here. There is no exercise of personal genius and there is no unfocused tinkering in this social role; there is simply only the following of orders and the implementation of routines. This is the ultimate meaning of Biagioli's assertion that "according to definitions of intellectual property, a scientist *qua* scientist is, literally, a nonauthor."[13]

Morte d'Author: An Inquest

So which version of "the author" is best adapted for understanding the predicament of the modern scientist? Which species of credit rings true in the twenty-first century? Historically, divergent versions of the author have been favored relative to the available alternatives under various different schemes of the organization of science; even now, in any given discipline, there will be found individual human beings who would acknowledge themselves more comfortably slotted under one or another of the above three rubrics. The phenomenology of multiple author-personas not only acknowledges a real division of labor in the laboratory: there exist good reasons for alternative templates of authorship to coexist in the history of science, since they reflect a persistent tension in Western thought between images of "authorship" and of "discovery." What cannot be settled *in principle* will temporarily be settled *in fact* as various policy choices are made about the nature and status of intellectual property.

We here follow Biagioli and Boyle in approaching the problem of the historical organization of science as the makeshift construction of some roles for an author suitable for subordination to systemic allocation and funding of science. As Biagioli (1999) writes: "Since the emergence of the experimental philosophy in the 17th century, the notion of the individual author was often constituted through the erasure of the instrument makers and laboratory technicians who, because of their low social status and credibility, were not perceived as true knowledge makers . . . Historically, then, the author has always been more of an efficient accounting device for intellectual property or scientific credit than an accurate descriptive tool of knowledge making practices."[14]

One of the more salient lessons of modern science studies is that the history of science organization is simultaneously a history of makeshift accommodations to the problem of accounting for knowledge making and a sequence of role models held up for the scientific author. These modes of existence have included monastic cloisters, birth into an aristocracy, court courtier, early modern letters patent, military corps of engineers, and national academies and societies with formal prize competitions; somewhat later innovations encompassed patent systems, copyright conventions, the German system of state-sponsored research universities, and modem corporate research laboratories. We cannot embark upon an account of the economic history of science in this venue[15] but only seek to insist that scientific authorship and scientific credit have been continually revised and refashioned in parallel with the evolution of economic history itself. The economy is not merely an external agency which funds (or not) a free-standing immortal but independently constituted science; they mutually inform and reform one another.

Our immediate concern is to characterize the modern situation with regard to the scientific author and the problem of attribution of credit. During the cold war regime, stretching from the 1950s to the 1980s, as an economic proposition it was taken for granted that the paradigm natural scientist was an author of type 3,[16] although the scientist might intermittently acquire copyright, and less frequently patents, in ancillary functions subordinate to his or her primary activities as a scientist and member of the university faculty. In the process of socialization, tyros were taught to believe that their identities as scientists in good standing dictated that they publicly renounce Romantic originality and commercial applications, at least in principle if not in practice. Scientists were first and foremost supported and socialized as employees of their universities. However, it should be acknowledged that vague and intangible notions of credit of type 3 were only loosely coupled to the economic structures that supported the research activities of many of these scientists, which were more securely grounded through their university affiliation in the military-university system of funding of research, and state funding of post-secondary training. Credit types 1 and 2 were essentially deemed irrelevant within the boundaries of this system. The celebration of the odd scientific media star or facile troubleshooting technocrat merely diverted attention from the standard mode of economic provisioning of the system. Biagioli summarizes this situation as one where the economies of scientific credit and those of the marketplace were being constituted in direct opposition to one another;[17] but we might amend this to read instead: the economies of science funding in America and scientific credit of type 3 were decoupled largely by construction, due to the exigencies of the cold war subordination of science to national and military imperatives (Mirowski 1999; 2002).

Yet however one defines it, we do agree with Biagioli that scientific credit of type 3 could never be practically quantified (*pace* "scientometrics") or subjected to algorithmic manipulation in this era; therefore there were no formal or legal institutions available to allocate and adjudicate and validate it, in direct contrast with types 1 and 2; and consequently, this species of "credit" could never perform any of the analytical functions which were presumed in the economics of science models of, for example, Philip Kitcher and David Hull and Paul David. There never on earth existed an integrated tacit global system of overlapping cognitive valuations as expostulated by a Michael Polanyi, and described in chapter 2 above. These evocations of virtual scientific credit systems were never more than *metaphors* inspired by market experience—but we would never equate that with being inconsequential. The absence of a validation scheme implies that the *curriculum vitae* never actually functioned as a non-market index of valuation in any decision-theory sense, precisely because there was no set of social institutions to operationalize its attribution and allocation and adjudication, in direct contrast to credit of types 1 and 2. Someone (the military, the government, the foundation, the university) was indeed footing the bill for the scientist, but there abided no dedicated social structures beyond the employee relationship itself to validate a system of credit attribution of credit type 3.

Bemoaned or not, the cold war system has largely disappeared in the interim, and we have now embarked upon a new regime of science organization. (This sequence of events is recounted in Mirowski and Sent 2002.) One far-reaching consequence of these political and economic changes is that not just credit of type 3 but all the credit options with their attendant author types have been undergoing profound revision, owing to a concerted contemporary re-engineering of all extant forms of intellectual property. Scientific authorship is not what it used to be, leaving many with severe identity crises. Scientists by and large did not propose or initiate this bit of social engineering, but they are certainly both enjoying and suffering its consequences. "Facts," formerly just one communal component of the heritage of a particular scholarly community, now find themselves subject to ownership; and that ownership is currently up for grabs. Much of this is happening without any express concern for the impact upon the structures *of* scientific research; in this instance, as in so many others, far from existing in glorious isolation, the very structure of science is imbricated with that of the society of which it is a part.

Re-engineering Intellectual Property

Much of the fascination with post–cold war information technologies is based on an assumption that the contemporary "enclosure of the cybercommons" is the pure product of technological determinism: first the computer, then perhaps the magnetic core memory, then the Internet, and finally the World Wide Web. This technology in turn has been said to have given us e-mail, then Napster, and now an economy based on "information" rather than bricks and mortar. Of course, such linear moral tales are ripe for the debunking, and scholars of science studies such as Donald MacKenzie and Trevor Pinch have often assumed the lead in undermining simple parables of the inexorable march of technology. However, in this particular instance it becomes important to understand how a set of seemingly unrelated trends often attributed to technological determinism have come together in the last two decades to bring about the debilitation, if not actually the death, of the scientific author. To a large extent these trends have been blamed on "the computer" as an unmoved mover, but in fact can be traced to more humdrum sorts of actors and their machinations.

There exists a large literature which argues that roughly since 1980, the notion of the author has been deformed beyond recognition because of sweeping amendments to the legal and social structures of copyright and patents (Boyle 1996; Lessig 1999; Wulff 2001; Litman 2001). Of course, this development has been pursued to different degrees in different national contexts, but the effect of globalization has been to spread the transformation with unprecedented haste across national borders. A second trend, accorded somewhat greater attention in science studies, has been the reengineering of the modern university in the post–cold war era.[18] Both trends are equally linked to the redoubled fascination with the role of "intellectual property" in the polity and the economy more generally. When these two trends are augmented with the more recent impact of the Internet, it seems that scientific credit, never so sturdily grounded in social and economic structures (as suggested above), is now in danger of becoming unmoored and unraveled altogether. Or to put it differently, when the economy of information undergoes profound deformations because of major realignments of the interests of powerful players, then the organization of scientific research gets caught in the backwash.

The Enclosure of the Cybercommons

The story begins with the separation of computer software from hardware as a commercial proposition. Many historians date this split from the late 1960s (Mahoney 1988; Campbell-Kelley 1995). The problem which was immediately encountered was that software had been treated as a minor accessory to the machine, open to amendment and often freely traded between users. If there were to be a commercial software industry, as opposed to simply congeries of itinerant consultant programmers, there had to be some legal way of asserting various forms of property rights over software code.[19] In the

United States, where much of this industry had its origins, the problem was exacerbated by some court rulings in the early 1970s which seemed to suggest that computer programs did not qualify for patents.[20] With some pressure from the fledgling software industry, this prohibition was reversed by legislation in 1980; but nevertheless, patents were still regarded by lawyers and industry insiders as particularly unsuited for software protection. Patent applications were too slow relative to the rate of innovation in software design; the U.S. Patent Office was unprepared and unwilling to subject computer code to detailed scrutiny; patents had a much shorter effective life (twenty years, in general) than was anticipated for legacy software; and patents were proving an unwieldy weapon to control copies of software and the downstream use of code. The result was that from roughly 1980 there was a concerted push to bend the institution of copyright to conform to the needs and wishes of the software industry. As one commentator put it: "the court has tortured the copyright law into an unrecognizable *sui generis* form of protection for software."[21]

The amendments to copyright were subtle and seemingly limited in the 1980s but gathered momentum in the 1990s, particularly with the "National Information Infrastructure Report" of 1995 and the Digital Millennium Copyright Act of 1998 (DMCA). The first push was to chip away at the "public domain" by postponing it: in 1976 the copyright term was extended to life plus fifty years for authors and seventy-five years for corporations, and with the Sonny Bono Term Extension Act of 1998 the term was extended again, to life plus seventy years for authors and ninety-five years for corporations. Unwilling to stop there, some firms like Bill Gates's Corbis Corporation maintain that when an image or document is digitized, a new copyright is created, even if the document was previously in the public domain. These extensions could not be construed as providing encouragement for *living* authors: they were transparently attempts by corporate owners of copyright to deny the importance of the "public domain" as a space where text was not subject to commodification.

There were other more important ways in which copyright, once applied to software, underwent further amendment and deformation. Because software providers wanted to prevent not only reuse of copies once the software was sold but also reverse engineering of source code to produce small differences in similar software, both court cases and legislation began to attack the doctrines of "fair use" (the right to copy passages for government-sanctioned personal use) and "first sale" (the principle that the copyright holder had no control over what the buyer did with the text once it was purchased). All sorts of scholastic arguments were mooted over what a "copy" really consisted of, to the point of suggesting that the mere fact of holding a document in the cached memory of a computer was sufficient to violate copyright. The software industry, in alliance with its new partners in telecommunications and the "content providers," pushed aggressively to extend control of software and digital content long after sale, and to eliminate any possible "fair use" of the information once purchased. Anything which could be construed as "loaning" intellectual property was progressively criminalized, a turn of events which began to undermine the ideal of a "library." The U.S. Copyright Office was cajoled into making unprecedented accommodation to the wishes of the software producers, for instance allowing the blocking out of "trade secrets" in the source code submitted for copyright protection. This provided a telling instance of how the previous bias of copyright toward protecting expression rather than the ideas themselves began to suffer under these various amendments. Indeed, in a series of famous cases where software producers were allowed to copyright the "look and feel" of an interface and not just the underlying source code, the idea of a legal text grew more insubstantial, and copyright began to resemble more and more sheer corporate protection of trade practices. The Uniform Computer Information Transactions Act (or UCITA) was crafted to transform digital information into a commodity resembling others, by legitimating clickwrap licenses without requiring consumers to know all the license terms before agreeing to them.[22] The Digital Millennium Copyright Act, if anything, has only exacerbated the perversion of copyright. Provisions which were intended to restrict access to decryption and reverse engineering of code have been turned by corporations such as Microsoft and the Secure Digital Music Initiative into tools for censoring publications of which they disapprove (Julie Cohen 2000; Pamela Samuelson 2001). The cumulative effect of these attempts to "strengthen" protection of intellectual property was to undermine the original distinction between form and content and, significantly, the Romantic role of the author as the original underlying rationale for the existence of copyright in the first place. And it was this new model of copyright protection, under the mantle of regularization of trade relations, which has begun to be foisted upon other countries through the World Intellectual Property Organization (WIPO), the Trade-Related Aspects of Intellectual Property Rights (TRIPS) Agreement of the World Trade Organization,[23] and other transnational organizations (Drahos 2002).

While the Romantic author was being effectively garroted by the tendrils of extended copyright, the software industry and its allies in pharmaceuticals and biotechnology also sought to expand the scope and ambit of the patent system, with such success that some now claim the patent system is in a serious crisis (Kahin 2001). It is interesting that the altered definition of what could be patented has occurred almost entirely in the courts, whereas the other question—who was allowed to patent what—was much more concertedly defined by Congress. This latter question expands the notion of who or what might serve as the author and therefore impinges more directly upon the reengineering of the American university.

Since the 1880s the U.S. Commissioner of Patents had adhered to what was called the "products of nature" doctrine, which stated that objects discovered "in nature" were not subject to patent. This was but one manifestation of the important distinction between legal protection of an *improvement* and the monopoly of something available for all to find, as discussed above. This doctrine was repudiated with regard to nonhuman living organisms in *Diamond v. Chakrabarty* (1980) and *Ex parte Allen* (1987) (Kevles 1998). The biotechnology community has received the greatest scrutiny with regard to its burgeoning patent dependence, going from patenting whole organisms to patenting sections of the genome, at least in part to get around the proscription against patenting human beings. More than 25,000 DNA-based patents alone were issued by the end of 2000; recently, warnings have been raised about the quality and relevance of the data listed in such patents (Cook-Deegan and McCormack 2001). Nevertheless, it was the intervention of software producers in this area of intellectual property that has further destabilized the original intent of patent law. In the 1980s patent case law suggested that while a discrete text of computer code was patentable, the mathematical algorithm underlying it was not (a distinction hewing to that between form and content). This distinction was eroded over the 1990s in such decisions as *Arrhythmia Research v. Corazonix Corp.* (1992). But it vanished in the now notorious decision *State Street Bank and Trust Co. v. Signature Financial Group* (1998).[24] This decision deemed that software designed solely to make financial calculations is patentable subject matter, overturning both the prohibition against patenting mathematical algorithms and the long-standing rule against patents on business methods and practices. It is not our intention here to speculate whether the U.S. Patent Office has in effect been "captured" by the constituencies it was supposed to regulate (Kahin 2001), but rather simply to point out again the extent to which a system which was constructed to encourage a particular kind of author (the "tinkerer") has been turned into yet another device for excluding users of entities like algorithms, which had previously been generally conceded to reside in the public domain. Hence the assertion by legal experts such as James Boyle, Jessica Litman, Julie Cohen, and Lawrence Lessig that we are living in the midst of another grand property grab, on a scale with the great enclosure movement of seventeenth-century England.

While this legal history is fascinating in and of itself, it only takes on heightened significance in the present context when juxtaposed with the other major trend of the last two decades, namely the project of reengineering of the post–cold war university from an ivory tower into an engine of economic growth and privatized flexible specialization.[25] The cutbacks and drawdowns that followed the end of the cold war prompted many governments to renege on their previous policies of generously funding higher education and the combined teaching-and-research model supported by such cold war innovations as the research contract, the grant overhead charge, the research assistantship, and military funding of basic research. Instead, especially in the United States, universities were exhorted to contribute with greater urgency to the "competitiveness" of the nation through a higher "pass-through" of research findings to commercial development; and following upon the success of areas such as Silicon Valley in California and Route 128 in Massachusetts, universities were also supposed to act as growth incubators in regional economic development. Faculty were exhorted to themselves become more entrepreneurial, if only to relieve some of the financial stringency affecting most universities. To provide encouragement for bolstering university-corporate ties, legislation like the Bayh-Dole Act and the Technology Transfer Commercialization Act offered universities the prospect of keeping the patent rights on research originally carried out with public funding, an option which had already been pioneered by the National Institutes of Health with select universities engaged in biotechnology research and the Information Processing Technologies Office at DARPA. Most research universities opened offices of technology transfer, with visions of sugarplums mesmerizing provosts and bursars.

The ultimate contradiction of this attempt to wean science and the universities off their cold war patrons was that just as scientists were to be encouraged to cease reliance upon being scientific authors of type 3—that is, to relinquish their overwhelming dependence upon the relatively unstructured and noneconomic formulas of academic-based "credit" in favor of more "solidly" based structures of credit such as patents (author type 2) and to a lesser extent copyright (author type 1)—the same types of credit they were enjoined to embrace were being severely undermined by the corporate interests with which they were supposed to forge their new research alliances. As we have seen, under the banner of strengthening intellectual property, the definitions of personalized authorship originally represented by copyright and patent were rapidly going the way of the buggy whip and the record player. What compounded the irony was that the commercial sectors most receptive to creating university-industry hybrids—pharmaceuticals, biotechnology, and information technologies—were precisely the sectors most responsible for the reconstruction of copyright and patent. Far from rejuvenating what had admittedly before been an imprecise and inaccurate system of attributing credit for scientific research, the new move to privatize and re-engineer university science had at its core a fundamental contradiction: *intellectual property in the larger society was no longer being structured primarily to foster personal innovation or incremental process improvement.*

The Romantic Genius and the Itinerant Tinkerer are no longer the primary inspirations or motivating personas behind copyright and patents. As author templates, their days are numbered. The formal system of intellectual property is increasingly uninterested in questions of responsibility and justice; in the interim, attribution of credit has become a minor consideration. Changes in intellectual property in the last two decades were rather primarily aimed at creating and engrossing intellectual property where it had not previously been dominant, and subsequently controlling and sequestering it for strategic corporate purposes in a globalized economy. No one was thinking about the implications for science when they set about protecting Mickey Mouse or Microsoft Windows or Nexium in the global arena; yet now do we reap the whirlwind.

That is the major thesis of this chapter. The movement to reengineer university science around more commercial pursuits through (among other initiatives) redirecting the process of attributing scientific credit toward more formal legal definitions of intellectual property, a movement pioneered in the United States but now advancing to varying degrees in most countries with well-developed academic research sectors, is based upon an egregiously incoherent premise, namely that any viable market-like social structure will miraculously take care of all problems of attribution and thus naturally facilitate any form of scientific research. The appropriate response to this logical error is not to disparage all markets as antithetical to science, but rather to acknowledge that some forms of funding and organization of credit promote certain kinds of creative or innovative activity, while other forms actively discourage them. Some forms of property smooth the process of disseminating and revising research results, whereas other forms of property restrict and control their dissemination and subsequent use. The confusion over how the parallel phenomena of scientific credit and intellectual property interact, and the consequences of their interaction, is prevalent among a class of commentators who force all scientific activity into simplistic models of generic economic processes, be they economists or modern philosophers.[26] We should instead shift our attention to the forms of authorship and employment that we expect will subsist under specific modern regimes of credit attribution, and not cold war vestiges under the sway of some imaginary intangible invisible college.

More than a decade of experience with the new regime of intellectual property has begun to reveal some of the pathologies of having the advocates for the *nouvelle vague* in the codification of intellectual artifacts call the tune for the academic scientist in the re-engineered entrepreneurial university. In the next section we survey a few of these cases, so as to illustrate our primary thesis that changes in definitions of intellectual property are already transforming how science is currently done, and not always for the better.

Losing Credit in Science

Many unintended consequences flow from the great transformation of copyright and patents in the last two decades; they range from the overarching to the highly local and specific. At the most abstract level, one might characterize the situations with regard to copyright and patent as follows. Copyright no longer exists to protect one person's expression for a limited time in the United States, and the global process of "harmonization" is spreading the practice to other countries. This erosion of a concern with personal forms of expression may initially seem relatively harmless to science, given that the median scientist is supposed to be relatively selfless and uninterested in stylistic niceties of expression. But it is the new uses into which copyright has been twisted which bear the most disturbing consequences for the future of scientific research. In brief, copyright now exists primarily to control the downstream uses of a text, and *not* to attribute responsibility or allocate credit for the creation of the text. Hence, modern copyright bears only the most tenuous relationship to the economic encouragement of authorship, and therefore the legal adjudication of scientific credit. Instead, if the social structure of scientific research revolves around the dissemination of the findings of other scientists, then modern copyright law seeks indirectly to revamp the entire social structure of science. After 1998, the very definition of a "copy" was revised to refer to anything that can appear on a computer, and copyright came to be aggressively deployed to regulate the "consumption" of copies so defined.[27]

Conversely, the demise of the "products of nature" doctrine along with the distinction in patent law between idea and application has led to a settler's rush to claim control over intellectual property, whether or not the applicant can be said to have "discovered" or "improved" the entity at issue. As *State Street Bank v. Signature Financial* showed, you don't have to be the progenitor of a calculation algorithm to assert proprietary rights over its use. The major implication of this development for scientific research is that intellectual property has become unmoored from any vernacular notion of "credit"; and furthermore, the distinction between the "tools" of research and the outputs of research has become profoundly blurred (Eisenberg 2001). This development becomes significant once one takes into account that patents above all are *strategic* instruments in a business context, and only secondarily are treated as substantial sources of revenue. It is well known that large corporations in the early twentieth century developed their ability to patent largely to stave off competitors' attempts to encroach upon their own markets, and not to any great extent to fund research into new products.[28] The same strategy threatens to become standard in science itself, with patents serving to block rival research groups from exploring the same research paths, especially as elaborate attempts are made to preserve secrecy and assert control through licensing agreements.

The level of abstraction of these generalizations concerning nascent trends in intellectual property renders empirical proof or disconfirmation difficult. After all, any particular controversy or conflict within science may easily be written off as an aberration, the unfortunate consequence of some personal foible or failure, and not a bellwether of future structural breakdowns.[29] Nevertheless, it is important to recognize that a number of recent "local," "parochial," or "technical" controversies in science organization of late assume a much more dire cast when situated within the larger context of transformed intellectual property in the era of globalized privatization. We shall examine these contretemps under three broad categories: the suppression of debate, the control of database access, and the subversion of the scientific journal.

Recent Suppressions of Criticism and Debate

Without attempting any generic characterization of science (like, say, the Popperian or Lakatosian), it would seem that one of the more significant functions of the social structures in a scientific discipline is to maintain a well-defined space for criticism and debate over ideas that the profession considers new or controversial or inadequately elaborated. The previous sentence is studded with weasel words because all controversy is restricted and channeled in any well-developed science; one must not reify an imaginary no-holds-barred situation as an effective ideal whenever one sets out to consider the effects of intellectual property upon science. The institution of "peer review" is itself a form of controlling criticism, in some instances verging on censorship (Chubin and Hackett 1990; Cicchetti 1991). Nevertheless, it is difficult to recount the narrative of any actual scientific discovery without at least acknowledging the forms in which criticism and debate came to shape the ultimate scientific consensus on the meaning and interpretation of the doctrines which were the outcome of the process. Criticism and debate can of course happen in many settings and take many forms; but again, one of the more important forums for debate is the archive of written documents associated with a particular discipline.

The mere fact that both patent and copyright have been reconfigured to exert more downstream control of texts suggests the potential for greater active repression and manipulation of debate in the scientific sphere. Of late, these have manifested themselves through a roundabout path. Much recent innovation by digital "content providers" has occurred in the field of technological restrictions placed upon users of digital information, such as click-wrap "end user licenses," copy prevention algorithms, and digital watermarks. It was realized early on that such devices could extend the control of the purveyor well beyond traditional definitions of the "copy." Fearful that many of these technological gatekeepers could be easily circumvented by sophisticated programmers, the software and content industries managed to have a provision written into the Digital Millennium Copyright Act of 1998 (DMCA) which criminalized any use of circumvention software to disable these devices, even for instances where the making of copies fell well within the bounds of what was permitted under existing copyright law.[30] Here it is important to distinguish between (a) outlawing circumvention which violated copyright; (b) outlawing all circumvention *tout court*; and (c) outlawing the production and use of any device for the purpose of circumvention. The WIPO World Copyright Treaty only suggested (a), but the DMCA went far beyond that in prohibiting all three.[31] By enabling content providers who had recourse to technological copy protection to criminalize the circumvention of clickwrap licenses, even in states where UCITA was not yet ratified, the DMCA permitted a backdoor extension of control of the end users of digital documents.

The possibility of exercising this sort of power through the DMCA did not long remain hypothetical. Microsoft, in response to criticism of its Kerebos software posted on the Web magazine *Slashdot*, posted its Kerebos specification on the Web with a clickwrap "end user license agreement" stating that it could not be disclosed without Microsoft's permission. This curious species of non-publication provoked numerous programmers to post directions on *Slashdot* for circumventing the clickwrap. Microsoft countered by invoking the DMCA and demanding the removal of all such postings from *Slashdot* (Julie Cohen 2000). To interpret any avoidance of some arbitrary clickwrap agreement as equivalent to violating copyright law, through the instrumentality of a ban on circumvention algorithms, reveals a rather stunning expansion of the ability of corporations to suppress public debate in the name of protecting intellectual property, extending even to prior restraints on speech. Whereas this initial incident involved professional software engineers writing their opinions in a public Web forum, similar preemptive use of the DMCA was soon extended to certain types of academic papers as well (Pamela Samuelson 2001).[32] Most of these early skirmishes surrounded explicit disclosures of software architecture and the decompilation of source code, but it is easy to see how the same techniques could be extended to the dissemination of archived experimental data or the sharing of algorithms which encode lab protocols or business practices; in extreme cases, one can envision tight control over who would qualify as an "authorized reader" of academic papers, with approval conditional upon a judgment about the intentions of the candidate to only make "constructive" use of the information and not engage in "destructive" criticism.

Many authors have dreamt of a world of coercive control over the responses of their readers, but the vast extension of the meaning of copyright protection fortifies those dreams with real legal muscle. For instance, many historical personages have tried to control scholarly use of their personal papers and archives by withholding reproduction rights, leaning upon an interpretation of copyright which would seem to have no discernible relationship to the original intent in the U.S. Constitution "to promote the Progress of Science and useful Arts." These figures could have kept the untoward aspects of their past activities secret by burning or otherwise selectively culling the papers under their control; but instead they have sought to fine-tune the interpretation of contentious events by selectively encouraging those whose opinions they support. (This has increasingly been the preferred method of burnishing a flickering reputation.) These authors undeservedly enjoy a reputation for openness and candor from having deposited their materials in a public archive, all the while exercising controls over intellectual property as stringent as those imposed by any corporation. This process perverts the Romantic author's ethos of self-definition in directions which were probably unanticipated by the inventors of copyright. Until now this means of suppressing criticism has been kept in check by the difficulty of judging before the fact whether a given researcher would report the evidence in a "constructive" way.[33] This problem of vetting researchers as candidates for research programs is endemic to all the sciences.

The desire to fortify prior restraint on criticism has now found one solution in a combination of copyright expansion and recourse to the Protection of Human Subjects clause (part 46) of title 45 of the U.S. Code of Federal Regulations. This is the rule mandating that any research institution which accepts federal funding should secure informed consent of human research subjects, with compliance monitored by institutional review boards. These rules were promulgated in 1981 in reaction to violations of human rights in certain high-profile medical experiments, such as the Tuskegee syphilis study and studies of radiation effects. However, most universities have extended the protections of part 46 to all research carried out at their institutions, no matter what the funding source, and irrespective of whether the topic of research is narrowly biomedical. Furthermore, in an especially imaginative extension of the definition of "human subject," the ambit of part 46 has recently been extended to any *researcher* who may become the topic of inquiry of another researcher, thus carrying the problem of logical self-reference to a whole new level. In particular, some historical researchers have recently been told to submit detailed questionnaires for review by the boards *and* their potential interviewees before receiving permission to conduct interviews (Shopes 2001).

While some analysts have worried about the chilling effect that this sort of control could have on the conduct of oral histories—a serious possibility—it has so far escaped notice how readily this development can be combined with the alterations in copyright identified above to produce something approaching Bentham's Panopticon with powerful scientist-entrepreneurs situated at its center. First, appealing to title 45, those wishing to find out about the research program of some well-established scientist (whether another member of the discipline or an outsider) can be forced by their "human subject" target to submit to arm's-length interrogation about their own motives, background, intentions, and beliefs. The scientist can then invoke some combination of clickwrap license and copyright to restrict access to his or her lab's research findings (including databases, algorithmic lab protocols, internal communications systems) by sharing them only with those who pass the interrogation. Lest the reader think this an absurdly paranoid scenario which no competent scientist would entertain, it will suffice to pick up any recent issue of *Science* and read about the problems that laboratory principal investigators have had with their staffs, which range from disputes over authorship of intellectual property to accusations by whistle-blowers of fraud or misconduct. To define the mass of computerized inscriptions generated by any lab as documents subject to downstream copyright controls, which would be the logical outcome of two decades of reengineered intellectual property, may just come to seem the "fair" and "impartial" and bloodlessly technological way to deal with all sorts of situations of immanent human conflict.

Database Access

The legal treatment of scientific databases as intellectual property arose as an issue relatively early in the process of refashioning intellectual property, in part because of a controversy between the European Union and the United States as to how to "harmonize" the legal treatment of databases across international borders. European and American approaches to copyright diverge somewhat: Europe, for instance, in stark contrast to the United States, leans on a strong "moral rights" doctrine and treats employees and not employers as legitimate "authors" who therefore are the initial owners of rights in the work they produce. Conversely, the American doctrine of "fair use" exemptions to copyright is largely foreign to the European intellectual property tradition. However, such divergences seemed to provoke little conflict in the international sphere until the European Union issued its Database Directive to member states in March 1996.[34] There exists a fair amount of speculation as to what inspired this directive. Some point to *Feist Publish-*

ing v. Rural Telephone Service (1991), in which the U.S. Supreme Court struck down copyright protection for the white pages listings of a telephone directory (as opposed to the yellow pages). This ruling suggested that copyright did not protect the data in databases. Others point to the fears of European content providers (which include some of the largest media conglomerates in the world) that American intellectual property innovations would allow American database providers to dominate the world through the Internet. Whatever the motivation, the EU directive counseled member states to extend new levels of protection specifically to digital databases.

The directive was noteworthy not only for its willful blurring of the traditional dichotomy between fact and expression in copyright law, but for the creation of new rights that had more or less been previously absent.[35] It strengthened dependence upon licensing, essentially dispensing with both fair use and first sale doctrines. It sanctioned legal protections for data which had previously been in the public domain or not covered by copyright provisions; and furthermore, it created a structure in which the fifteen-year protection window could be extended indefinitely, as long as the proprietor periodically augmented the database with "new content." Perhaps most significantly, it also stated that European legal protection would not be extended to database vendors on foreign soil, unless their home countries had enacted substantially the same level of protection. Given that the industry being protected was database vendors over the Internet, this was widely interpreted as a threat to other countries such as the United States to either "harmonize" or lose control over their databases. Indeed, initially the Clinton administration agreed, and various initiatives were proposed to legislate similar protections in America (Reichman and Uhlir 1999).

Interestingly enough, in stark contrast with the developments enumerated above, the American science community in the shape of the American Association for the Advancement of Science and the National Academy of Sciences rapidly mobilized to oppose this initiative.[36] Perhaps it was simply more obvious that some of the largest government-funded research projects in existence, such as GenBank of the Human Genome Project, the American Chemical Society's *Chemical Abstracts*, and the National Weather Service's Climatic Data Center, would immediately be transformed into for-profit database vendors. While it is true that the U.S. Congress had not yet passed database protections of the sort envisioned by the EU,[37] it was perhaps lacking in perspective to write that "So far [the scientific societies] have been successful, but database bills will be back, and victory in future rounds will depend on continued vigilance."[38] The database protection movement is not some isolated political feint by a small band of database entrepreneurs. It is just one more logical outcome of the policy to privatize academic research under the banner of intellectual property, and as such cannot long be thwarted in the face of the broad-based transformation of copyright and patent described above.

The original premise of most intellectual property legislation in the United States from the Bayh-Dole Act onward has been that government-funded research need not be reserved for the public commonweal, but instead should be commercialized as rapidly as possible. The tendency of intellectual property law during the digital revolution has been to treat the outputs of academic research primarily as *things* and not as free speech; nowhere would this conception seem more apposite than in the case of big communal databases such as GenBank or the physical and chemical properties databases of the National Institute of Standards and Technology. There have, of course, been some reservations expressed about how the patenting of genomes has served to degrade the quality of the data being made available (Cook-Deegan and McCormack 2001); but the logic of the intellectual property movement goes well beyond such qualms about the short-term effects of secrecy. The implication of revamping both copyright and patent law is that scientific research cannot long persist as a protected sphere outside the normal commercial provision of digital information, because government policy long ago dictated that the two be integrated; and the issue of special protection of databases is merely the most salient example of how that inconsistency keeps being revisited. Database protection will be fortified either by direct legislation or by indirect means, and scientists will find they simply have to adjust to the new regime of data provision.

Indeed, the biotechnology industry has already gone much further in this direction than most people realize. Fears about the inadvertent unauthorized use of existing databases have resulted in new preemptive measures to exert control over scientific data in the format of "pass-through" rights that place numerous restrictions upon data usage even after they may have become incorporated into other more comprehensive databases. One especially innovative variant of this attempt to exert downstream control is the "material transfer agreement" or MTA, a legal call-back provision granting an option to license any patent rights from subsequent discoveries made with the help of tools or data provided as a part of the agreement (Eisenberg 2001; Rai and Eisenberg 2001). What began as a method of exerting some downstream control over academic labs by corporate entities is now used by academic research groups to assert rights over the findings of other research groups. Once intellectual property opened up the possibility of downstream control, the inputs to scientific research became enmeshed in a tangle of contested assertions of credit and recompense.

Recall that both copyright and patent were makeshift responses to the problem that "knowledge" is only worthwhile if it is made available to others to contemplate and use, but some form of credit and control should be ceded to the "author" in order to encourage the further pursuit and advancement of knowledge. Further, science should be "open" to the extent that it welcomes criticism, but at the same time the province of a closed community who make it their business to specialize in the problems of interpreting and elaborating on that class of questions. Of course, there is no universal optimal solution to these conflicting objectives, so specialized credit structures were constructed for relatively circumscribed purposes, and relatively discrete communities, especially regarding the treatment of intellectual property. However, privatization of the research process works in curious and unanticipated ways, and will subsequently have repercussions upon the political framework within which science is forced to press to preserve certain prerogatives. Bluntly, the polity may come to believe that it can engross something resembling the ownership rights that have been seen as being ceded to corporate sponsors in the scramble for intellectual property rights. And in a subtle twist, it may be in the interests of corporate sectors to act as silent partners in such movements.

The contradictions of intellectual property surfaced in an amendment appended in 1998 by Senator Richard Shelby of Alabama to a massive congressional appropriations bill (Hilts 1999). This amendment stated that anyone could submit a request to the U.S. government under the Freedom of Information Act to get all of the data produced pursuant to any published academic study funded by federal support. The amendment combined an appeal to transparency in government, a tacit acquiescence in an older "public good" rationale for public support of science, and a more up-to-date conviction that if you pay for it in the marketplace of ideas, then you should be able to exercise some ownership rights. Of course, there was no particular constituency of concerned Citizens for Science for the People behind this bill; rather, it was promoted by various corporate and lobbying interests seeking access to lab notebooks, e-mail, raw data, and even rosters of experimental subjects of academic researchers who had published studies perceived as "unfriendly" by the industries involved. For instance, R. J. Reynolds wanted to review data on familiarity with Joe Camel by six-year-olds; power companies wanted the data from a study by the Harvard School of Public Health on long-term impacts of pollution; gun owners want access to data concerning accidental homicides in the home. Corporate researchers could then easily subject the raw data to reinterpretation, and corporate lawyers could more readily harass researchers deemed unreliable, especially in situations involving expert testimony. From one perspective, this legislation is just another instance of extending intellectual property rights to databases, a practice already pioneered by the software industry; but from another, somewhat more jaundiced perspective, the legislation was yet another expression of the assault on university research protocols by corporate interests (corporations accepting federal subsidies for proprietary research were left untouched by the amendment).

If the economics of science could ever see its way through to erect a moratorium on appeals to the virtual Panglossian marketplace of ideas, then it might actually help clarify what otherwise threatens to be an extremely confused controversy. The U.S. National Institutes of Health, for example, have opted to oppose the rule on simple cost grounds: they assert that it would be too burdensome to collect and warehouse raw data. However, this issue is not primarily one of costs, or "transactions costs": rather, it is a larger dispute over how science is to be conducted, and in which parties the rights to control over the research process will be vested. An earlier version of the economics of science would support the Shelby amendment's construction that science was engaged in producing a *thing*; but that would wildly misconstrue what was at stake. Different institutional packages of rights and credit allocation procedures result in different kinds of research. Under the proposed regime, the role and status of the scientist would be further reduced to that of data provider and numbers cruncher, whereas the functions of analysis and synthesis would further devolve to specialists for hire; with all the biases against accepting federal funding, ambitious researchers would be hustled all the more rapidly into the sector of corporate contract research. If this rule were to be upheld, then in the name of the "public interest" it would go a long way toward bringing about the final dissolution of an independent university sector of research capabilities funded by public money: a prospect many would regard with something closer to glee than despair.

What Is a "Journal" in the Era of Globalized Privatization?

A third set of examples of the new regime of intellectual property involves the impacts of commercial secrecy and research oversight upon the structure and content of academic journals. One of the few studies to empirically examine this problem (Blumenthal et al. 1996a) reports that 82 percent of companies in the life sciences which sponsor academic research in their survey had imposed confidentiality requirements in pursuit of the assessment and filing of patent applications, and 47 percent admitted to imposing gag rules beyond the time needed to file a patent. The most common complaint on the part of corporations was that university administrations often obstructed their desire to conclude agreements with individual researchers; and in 34 percent of cases, the companies admitted to having disputes with their academic contractors over intellectual property.[39]

If anything, the identity of the "author" in biomedical science has been further eroded in the interim. The pharmaceutical industry has discovered that its clinical trials can be run more cheaply and quickly by "contract research organizations" (CROs), or private firms that produce studies on demand. In 2000 CROs captured 60 percent of all research grants from pharmaceutical companies, compared with 40 percent going to academic units.[40] Part of the cost savings comes from redistributing authorship and control over trial design and data access between the CRO and the commissioning firm; who the nominal authors are and the nature of their affiliations have themselves become such contentious issues that the International Committee of Medical Journal Editors recently sought to impose disclosure requirements upon the *authors* of submitted articles (Guterman 2001). When credit and responsibility are at issue, gatekeepers try to fall back upon supposedly stable older personas of the "author" to restore some decorum.

Now, what might be the attitude of the researchers familiar with these constraints and practices toward the value of the published literature in their own specialty? They might conclude that the information inscribed in their academic journals was inevitably delayed, inordinately vetted and censored, freighted with hidden agendas, and written with an eye toward the effect that publication might have upon commercial competitors. In other words, researchers might come to see the information in such channels as *degraded*, albeit in a manner for which they might feel competent to compensate to a certain degree. Of course, it is common knowledge in science studies that almost no journal article in the history of science has ever provided ample enough documentation to actually replicate an experiment or spell out every step in a mathematical proof (hemmed in by certain costs of documentation); but we are concerned here with the unintended consequences of a particular set of constraints whose biases are common knowledge among the readership. Might not familiarity, while not breeding contempt exactly, give rise to a certain blasé attitude with respect to the outlet? Once widespread, wouldn't this skepticism (some might say cynicism) concerning the role and status of CROs allow for the possibility that corporations might then engage ghostwriters employed by third-party contract houses to produce manuscripts-to-order for the outlet, to which favored recipients of contracts with burnished reputations might append their names? After all, what more is a scientific author than the *employee* of one organized research collective or another, chosen as its "authorial representative"? One can appreciate that we might find ourselves enmeshed in a sort of Gresham's Law of privatized research, which could turn staid and dull academic journals into purveyors of glossy infomercials, where the whole point of the exercise would be to make the reader unable to tell where the articles stopped and the advertising began.

Conclusion

As James Boyle has written,

> Intellectual property policy has consistently undervalued the public domain, over-emphasized the threats and under-emphasized the opportunities presented by new technologies, ignored the extent to which information goods are actually bundled with more excludable phenomena, exaggerated the role incentives have in producing innovation while minimizing their negative effect.[41]

Once academic scientists were exhorted to come down out of their ivory towers and join in the commercialization of their endeavors, they too became caught up in this systemic trend; now the social structures of science will reap the consequences, if nothing is done to insist upon serious distinctions between science and the market.

Part Three
Rigorous Quantitative Measurement as a Social Phenomenon

7

Looking for
Those Natural
Numbers:
Dimensionless
Constants and the
Idea of Natural
Measurement

When I was bound apprentice, and learned to use my hands,
Folk never talked of measures that came from foreign lands:
Now I'm a British Workman, too old to go to school;
So whether the chisel or file I hold, I'll stick to my three-foot rule.
Some talk of millimetres, and some of kilogrammes,
And some of decilitres, to measure beer and drams;
But I'm a British Workman, too old to go to school,
So by pounds I'll eat, and by quarts I'll drink, and
I'll work by my three-foot rule.
A party of astronomers went measuring the earth,
And forty million metres they took to be its girth;
Five hundred million inches, though, go through from pole to pole;
So let's stick to inches, feet and yards, and the good old three-foot rule.
—W. M. Rankine, "The Three-Foot Rule," *Songs and Fables*, 1874

In an extremely perceptive volume on the economic history of metrology,
Witold Kula writes that "the right to determine measures is an attribute of
authority in all advanced societies" (1986, 18). This statement might seem
misplaced in the context of modern society: after all, the hallmark of legitimate measurement in a scientific context would seem to be *World Metric
Standards for Engineering* (Kverneland 1978), the paradigm of a dictionary
for a neutral, noncoercive language community. In Orwell's *1984* the Minis-
try of Truth might wield its arbitrary authority by changing the specification
of the imperial gallon from one year to the next, along with rewriting
history; but surely in the history of physics there is no discernible connection between measurement and social constructions of authority. Or
is there?

The purpose of this chapter is to carry recent research into the social context of science further into the heart of the commonplace notion that "as science has developed, the domain of quantity has everywhere encroached upon that of quality, till the process of scientific inquiry seems to have become simply the measurement and registration of quantities, combined with a mathematical discussion of the numbers thus obtained" (Maxwell 1870, 419). Interest in the history of science community has recently turned toward the problem of a history of experiment and the role of conceptions of empiricism.[1] But in many cases it seems to have stopped short of the actual practice of creating measurement scales and manipulating them, probably because "it is notoriously difficult to see how societal context can affect in any essential way how someone solves a mathematical problem or makes a measurement" (Wise 1988, 78). Measurement, however, presents many of the problems already familiar from the interpretation of literary texts: the recourse to mathematics does not intrinsically adjudicate or banish disputes in the relevant language community. The very idea that mathematics could have some such influence is central to the story told in this paper.

Although it will not be a major theme of this narrative, one could read it as support for the Durkheim-Mauss-Douglas thesis that the categories of things often reproduce the classifications of men (Bloor 1982). This reading is rendered possible by the observation that measurement conventions—the assignment of fixed numbers to phenomenal attributes—themselves are radically underdetermined and require active and persistent intervention in order to stabilize and enforce standards of practice. One way this has been broached in the metrology literature is through what has been called the "Zanzibar Effect" (Petley 1985, 8–9), named after the (probably apocryphal) story of a ship's captain who fired a gun every day at noon according to a clock that had been set by comparison with the timepieces in a shop of a watchmaker in Zanzibar, who set his clocks by the report of the gun at noon. . . .

Far from being some rhetorical flourish superimposed on what would in any event lead to isomorphic results, the recondite areas of metrology and the treatment of "dimensionless constants" are the arenas in which battles over the function of numbers in scientific discourse have been fought; moreover, they have in certain instances influenced the content of the evolution of physical theory, or at least the research programs of some very eminent physicists. Yet metrology and dimensionless constants have themselves undergone profound structural revisions over the last two centuries. While all the characters in our narrative clearly believed that the Book of Nature was written in mathematical language, the point at issue was whether the

Book could speak to us of its own accord or, rather, the reader played an intrinsic hermeneutical role in deciphering its complex text.

From Anthropometrics to the Manufactured Article

It comes as a bit of a shock to realize just how recently the systems of measurement that we take for granted assumed their modern form. Witold Kula (1986, 115) asserts that there have been three major waves of metrological standardization in the history of Europe—the Carolingian, the Renaissance, and the one beginning with the French Revolution. Before the last, systems of measurement of such fundamental attributes as weight and land area were parochial and geographically fragmented, but also incoherent in the sense that they could not be compositionally combined and extended in simple algebraic operations. The size of a bushel of grain would depend directly on who determined the standard, and units such as the ell and the foot were predicated on specific somatic proportions, which obviously were not identical among individuals. This inconsistency was not automatically perceived as a transgression of logic, since justice might demand differential treatment. For instance, the spice merchant's pound was smaller than the butcher's pound; the bushel would be heaped for grain of poor quality; the *seterée* of barren soil would be larger than the *seterée* of fertile soil;[2] and so forth. The unit of measure did not separate out the abstract notion of quantity from other sensuous characteristics and therefore (from our point of view) could not legitimately be added or multiplied. Indeed, in many peasant areas not only were the "units" incommensurable across individuals, but even for the same individual anthropometric units could not be divided into fractions. Clearly these systems of measurement did not qualify for the first requirement of the algebra of a group: there was no mathematical identity element.[3]

What was needed from the vantage point of the Enlightenment was an entire system of measures that were transpersonal, fixed for all time, and therefore possessing such an identity element. Kula, from his Marxist position, comments that "for a society to be able to adopt measures of pure convention, two important conditions have first to be satisfied: there must prevail a de facto equality of men before the law, and there must be accomplished the process of alienation of the commodity" (Kula 1986, 122). Whether or not this notion has some validity, that was not the way the metric system was either conceived or justified. Instead, the idea of the founders of the metric system was to remove it as far from any anthropometric taint as possible, to extract the act of measurement from the realm of man and situate it securely in the realm of nature. As is well known, the basis of the metric system, the meter, was decreed by a French statute dated 18 Germinal, An III (7 April 1795), to be one ten-millionth of the earth's meridian passing through Paris. The object of this great act of hubris (Kula 1986, 243) was to assert by example that the only legitimate units were those to be found by any suitably prepared student in nature itself; disputes about the accuracy of measures were to be seemingly extricated from the discourse of the inanimate. Of course, there was the residual irony of the necessity of a political revolution as a prerequisite to the imposition of such an allegedly self-evident scheme; and not just in the case of the French Revolution, either. The metric system tended to follow the barrel of a gun, only becoming instituted in Germany in 1868, Austria in 1871, Russia in 1918, China in 1947, and of course never in the United States.

However, the act of the political authority grounding the system of measurement in nature did not necessarily solve the Zanzibar problem, in the sense that while secular authorities had sworn off further tampering with the meter, doubts could just as easily arise concerning the integrity and stability of the natural unit chosen. It seems that organized inquiry into these doubts was the product of two historically linked trends: the mid–nineteenth-century energetics movement and the subsequent slow development of the theory of dimensional analysis. But further, for much of the nineteenth century the doubts seem to be almost entirely located in one European country, namely Great Britain.[4] Serious historical research will be required to discover if this dynamic did not play itself out in other cultural contexts as well, but the predominance of British citizens in this part of the subsequent narrative is a coincidence that demands some comment. I would suggest that it is an artifact of the historically specific pattern of the spread of the metric system, and Britain's unusual exclusion from that pattern.

Talleyrand's original proposal in 1790 for the adoption of a new basic standard *pris dans la nature* intended that the work would be undertaken jointly by the French National Assembly and the English Parliament and Royal Society; but of course hostilities intervened, and by the time Albion had soundly defeated Napoleon, there was no attraction to adopting the metric system with its revolutionary heritage (Heilbron 1990). As more European countries were assimilated to the standard, Britain grew metrologically isolated; but xenophobia, cultural pride, and some trepidation about the costs of conversion all blocked attempts to switch over to the metric system in 1862, 1897, 1904, 1911, and 1952. It is possible that the quotidian necessity of translating experimental results from the awkward English system into the Continental equivalents for purposes of comparison was something more than a nuisance; it brought home the sheer contingency of metrological practices in a way that would not have happened in any of the other advanced scientific centers of that age. Besides, for a British citizen to doubt the integrity of the meter was not an affront to nature: it was merely an affront to the French (Halsey 1920, chapter 1).

The role of the energetics movement in the narrative of the "fundamental constants" begins with the Scot William Macquorn Rankine (1820–72). In 1855 Rankine proposed to found a new science, which he called "energetics," for the purpose of both realizing the promise of the unification of physics (which many at the time thought would be the fruit of enunciating the law of the conservation of energy; Mirowski 1989b, chapter 2) and more closely linking the formalisms of physics with natural sense data. Rankine felt that the success of mechanics had misled those impressed with its efficacy, enticing them to import mechanical hypotheses into other branches of physics by positing conjectural "motions" in theories of heat, light, and so forth. He hinted that these motions would never be accessible to confirmation by means of direct sense data. "Instead of supposing the various classes of physical phenomena to be constituted, in an occult way, of modifications of motion and force, let us distinguish the properties which those classes possess in common with each other, and so define more extensive classes denoted by suitable terms" (Rankine 1881, 213). The remainder of the paper constructed taxonomies of variable and invariant properties of a generalized energetic transformation in such a way that the modern reader detects an early quest for the algebraic group structure that would underlie all the various formalisms of the different subsets of physics. But more important, Rankine's concern with the fact that energy would assume many varied but similar forms, owing to the plurality of its measures in different contexts, led him to expend particular effort on reconciling the *dimensions* of energy with each manifestation.

Rankine's most direct influence was on James Clerk Maxwell (Maxwell 1965, 2:259). Maxwell inherited both Rankine's enthusiasm for energetics as a philosophical doctrine (2:760) and his concern with dimensional analysis. His own further contribution was to combine both with a concern for metrology. In particular, he began the convention of designating any length as L, any mass as M, and any time measure as T. The dimensions of energy would always have to be ML^2 / T^2, and this gave valuable indications of the appropriate formalisms to be used in any "conversion" of energy between different phenomena. Maxwell disseminated the rudiments of dimensional theory in his popular writings and in his *Theory of Heat* (1871, 235, 261).[5] In his presidential address to section A of the British Association for the Advancement of Science in 1870, he suggested:

> If we examine the coins, or the weights and measures of a civilized country, we find a uniformity, which is produced by careful adjustment to standards made and provided by the State. The degree of uniformity

of these national standards is the measure of the spirit of justice in a nation. . . . Yet, after all, the dimensions of our earth and its time of rotation, though, relatively to our present means of comparison, very permanent, are not so by any physical necessity. . . . If, then, we wish to obtain standards of length, time and mass which shall be absolutely permanent, we must seek them not in the dimensions, or the motion, or the mass of our planet, but in the wave-length, the period of vibration, and the absolute mass of these imperishable and unalterable and perfectly similar molecules. (Maxwell 1870, 421)

An orderly system of weights and measures was of the utmost importance to Maxwell; indeed, his discovery that the ratio of electrostatic to electrodynamic charge was the same as the velocity of light (Maxwell 1965, 1:569), leading to his electromagnetic theory of light, was a vindication of Rankine's program of orderly analogy predicated on close attention to dimensional conformity.

But the more one knew about energy, the less confident one grew about the natural grounding of the metric system in the figure of the Earth. Not only were there problems of heat radiation, there was also the friction of the tides and other forms of the slow degradation of the earth's motion. In the British mind, an orderly state was not founded on the invariance of the aggregate, such as the *Volk* or the *Geist* or any other such communal notions; instead, natural law doctrines had to be traced to the invariants present in the individual. Measurement would be sufficiently guaranteed only if the components that made up energy—mass, length, and time—were themselves traced to the smallest atoms:

Atoms have been compared by Sir J. Herschel to manufactured articles on account of their uniformity. . . . [In many cases] the whole of the value of the object arises from its exact conformity to a given standard. Weights and measures belong to this class, and the existence of many well-adjusted material standards of weight and measure in any country furnishes evidence of a system of law regulating the transactions of the inhabitants and enjoining in all professed measures a conformity to the national standard. (Maxwell 1965, 2:483–84)

Hence there grew up a British tradition of metrology that commenced with an attack on French dominance: as Maxwell put it, "the French standards, though originally formed to represent certain natural quantities, must be now considered as arbitrary standards" (1871, 79). The attack assumed the form of a search for a better grounding of measurement in nature to ensure a superior conformity to a "national standard"; again quoting Maxwell, "the whole system of civilised life may be fitly symbolised by a foot rule, a set of weights, and a clock" (1871, 75). For an Englishman steeped in his Edmund Burke and Adam Smith, the French spirit of justice left something to be desired. As one textbook put it, "Whether we are to measure time, space, density, mass, weight, energy or any other physical quantity, we must refer to some concrete standard, some actual object, which if once lost and irrevocable, all our measures lose their absolute meaning" (Jevons [1874] 1905, 305). Because Maxwell's atoms bore the stamp of the manufactured article, they were sufficient bulwark against the loss of absolute meaning. The advocacy of finding nature's yardstick in the atom was salubrious to the British temperament; and Maxwell's own work indicated that the vibrations of those atoms could provide the invariant; all the rest would simply be bookkeeping.[6]

The next metrological step was taken by George Johnstone Stoney (1826–1911) in 1881. Under the influence of Maxwell, he agreed wholeheartedly with the project of grounding measurement in the atoms of nature; but, he asked, why feel constrained by length, time, and mass as primitive concepts? "It has been usual to regard the units of length, time and mass as fundamental, and the rest as derived; but there is nothing to prevent our regarding any three independent members of the series as fundamental, and deriving the others from them. It is the aim of the present paper to point out that Nature provides us with three such units; and that if we take these as our fundamental units instead of choosing them arbitrarily, we shall bring our quantitative expressions into a more convenient, and doubtless a more intimate, relation with Nature as it actually exists" (Stoney 1881, 384).

The coziness of increased intimacy seemed harmless, yet the shift in premise was subtle; it would prove to have far-reaching implications. Rankine and Maxwell thought that energy was the primary entity uniting all of physics, and that its constituents (in mechanics, length, time, and mass) were therefore transparently the fundamental dimensions of any system of measurement. Stoney turned this around by suggesting that all measurements should be directly denominated by the *constants* identified by accepted theories of electromagnetism, mechanics, and "the chemical bond"—expressing more intimately, as it were, the unity of all physical theory. Of course, the set of constants chosen as units must ultimately be a permutation of the prior three dimensions of length, time, and mass, in order that they be related to existing experimental practice. The attraction of what might at first blush seem a redundant translation was that nature could speak in a clear and undistorted voice.

Clearly in homage to Maxwell, Stoney chose as his first unit the above-mentioned ratio of electrostatic to electrodynamic units, which also had the dimension of the velocity of light in a vacuum, or L/T. His second unit was the Newtonian gravitational constant, which had the dimension L^3/MT^2.

To bring in chemistry as well, Stoney chose for his third unit the "quantity of electricity in a chemical bond," which he believed was a constant and had the dimension *LM*. The third choice was soon rendered obsolete by further developments in physics (although Stoney's later term "the electron" for something like that unit was destined to live on); but the first two choices were significant in a way that Stoney did not even discuss. The gravitational constant was a global invariant, as far as anyone knew; after 1905 the speed of light would also be accorded that status. When Maxwell alighted on the vibrations of his atoms as his standard, their constancy was more an issue of empiricism and metaphor than one having any particular theoretical justification. Really, they were little better than the meridian of the earth, which he had just scorned, because the solid theoretical explanation of invariance was still lacking. But if one chose for units the constants that had been identified and explained by the most fundamental theories of physics, then indeed nature would be providing a set of dimensional units that had been copied directly from the invariant language in which nature spoke. It would be as if a bookkeeper had finally seen beyond the veil of money into the real world of fundamental values, no longer having to worry about inflation, arbitrary depreciation, and the like. These would be "physical units deserving of the title of a Natural Series of Physical Units" (Stoney 1881, 389).

Raising the issue of the place of electricity in the scheme of natural units broaches the subsidiary topic of the worldwide determination of electromagnetic standards, a process gaining momentum just as Stoney wrote. The setting of practical electrical standards was a German and not a British initiative, largely because the Germans had captured leadership in the burgeoning electrical implements industry in the latter half of the nineteenth century. Beginning with Gauss's introduction of units of measurement of magnetism based on length, time, and mass in 1832 and extending through the metrological work of Weber, Kohlrausch, and the members of the Physikalisch-Technische Reichsanstalt (Cahan 1989), Germans were in the forefront of defining the metrological standards for the electrical industry. In 1881 the International Electrical Congress arrived at an agreement for an absolute system based on the ohm (resistance), the volt (electromotive force), and the ampere (current). Even at this level of standardization, nationalistic rivalries created problems (Lundgreen 1986, 36, 56–57; Cahan 1989, 27), and it took three more congresses, the last in 1908, to iron out the numerous differences. Even then, two slightly different sets of international standards coexisted until 1942 (Cohen, Crowe, and Dumond 1957, 9).

One might ask how it came to be that international agreement on electrical measurement could have been arrived at, given that the metric system met such resistance. The answer is that industrial standardization in that particular arena was not merely convenient but actually imperative if there was going to be any international commerce in things ranging from light bulbs to electric trams. Political pressure came not only directly from man- ufacturers but also indirectly from the need to endow specific national bureaus of standards with powers of testing and enforcement and the sov- ereign ability to negotiate international standards.[7] The rise of national bureaus at the end of the nineteenth century injected a further political note into the creation and enforcement of practical units of measurement from that time forward; it also had an impact on the program of natural measure- ment growing out of the energetics movement mentioned above. A period of contention and cacophony with regard to metrological standards could not but bring home the pervasiveness of "non-natural" considerations in the development of a system of units; moreover, the entire center of gravity of both the energetics movement (Wilhelm Ostwald, Georg Helm, et al.) and the push for practical standardization had shifted to the German context by the turn of the century. As a consequence, the concern over a natural set of constants also migrated to the German community around the same time. Yet as it crossed the border it assumed different nuances, not fully explained by pragmatic concerns.

This incipient promise of pure numbers—constants free of the mundane fetters of space and time, and indifferent and invariant to whatever con- tingent metrological system was used to express them—marks the next stage of evolution of the quest for natural measurement. At this stage the concep- tion of the quest itself underwent a bifurcation: the Anglophone tradition, which created something called "dimensional analysis" as a self-contained formalist metalanguage (Rucker 1889; Buckingham 1914; Bridgman 1931), and the German tradition, for which it became an active tool for construct- ing physical theory.

From Industrial Standards to Extraterrestrial Standards

The effect of cultural milieu on the notion of natural measurement becomes somewhat clearer when the British and German cases are contrasted. Ger- many by the late nineteenth century had become the preeminent European industrial power, but the industrial and bookkeeping attitude toward mea- surement did not seem to animate the academic "German mandarins" of physics. It is well known that late-nineteenth-century German culture was relatively hostile to the mechanistic and atomistic worldview of the British, stressing organicist metaphors in social theory (Pribram 1983, chapters 14– 15) and intuition or *Anschauung* in physical theory (Miller 1986, chapter 4). German philosophy was concerned with the problem of "historism," which Ringer (1969, 340) described as dealing "primarily with the difficulty of rescuing timeless truths and values from the flux of history." Even the problem of measurement was regarded through historicist lenses, with (for example) Werner Sombart equating the rise of capitalism and modern science as of a piece with the rise of double-entry bookkeeping.

More than one commentator has seen Max Weber's quest for a value-free science as a reaction to the widespread attitude in Germany that subjective values and intuition permeated all forms of inquiry; Weber would admit that such considerations did instruct the choice of topics of research, but he did not allow that they could infect the individual "facts." It has also been observed that the structure of the German professorate as a privileged class in the pay of the state both insulated its members from experience with industrial endeavor and politicized them to the extent that the validity of various forms of instrumentalist rationality was continually being brought into question (Ringer 1969).

In this environment the notion of a transhistorical standard of measurement struck a different chord. Instead of being regarded as a bookkeeping convention, it was rather thought to serve as a method of transcending such problems as creeping historicism and skepticism regarding empiricism, and it could simultaneously provide an active device for constructing new theories. The best example of this sort of attitude is found in the life and work of Max Planck. The theme that runs throughout his writings is the need for science to provide principles that would "possess absolute, universal validity, independently of all human agency" (Planck 1949, 14). It seems that the historicism besetting German social attitudes severely disturbed Planck; resorting to language similar to that of the many critics of scientific rationality, he allowed that the very act of measurement was intrinsically historical and therefore essentially suspect: "All our measurements are relative. The material that goes into our instruments varies according to its geographic source; their construction depends upon the skill of the designer and toolmaker; their manipulation is contingent on the special purposes pursued by the experimenter. Our task is to find, in all these factors and data, the absolute, the universally valid, the invariant, that is hidden in them" (Planck 1949, 47).

This is where the notion of the fundamental constants of measurement came into play. "Our view of the world must be purged progressively of all anthropomorphic elements. Consequently we have no right to admit into the physical world-view any concepts based in any way on human mensuration" (Planck 1931, 53; Heilbron 1986, 52). Unlike the British, who merely wanted retrospectively to reread the Book of Nature in its original language, Planck wanted actively to purge science of doubt by erasing all taint of humankind. This goal receives its strongest statement in the lecture he gave at Leiden in 1908. There he held out the promise of a unified science that all physicists, with or without human senses, would come to agree on; the hallmark of that physics was the existence of such fundamental constants as

Boltzmann's k and his own radiation law constant, as well as the gravitational constant and the speed of light. "With their help we have the possibility of establishing units of length, time, mass and temperature, which necessarily retain their significance for all cultures, even unearthly and non-human ones" (quoted from Heilbron 1986, 48).

That this otherworldly conception could have a real payoff in the here and now has been argued in great detail by Martin Klein (1977). Even before Planck's derivation of the famous black-body law, he had tried to construct a system of universal units out of the gravitational constant, the speed of light, and two coefficients found in Wein's earlier proposed black-body conjecture. By 1900 Planck had suggested a new modified law to fit the data, but from his own point of view it had no theoretical justification or scientific validity, for the reasons stated above. Klein argues that the "justification" of the black-body law (1900), which introduced the famous Planck constant, was incoherent in various respects—not the least because no other physicist seemed to believe the argument for the next five years, and Planck himself described it thirty years later as an "act of desperation." Nevertheless, he was led to invent some counterintuitive "energy elements," extend Boltzmann's description of molecules to describe imaginary oscillators, and introduce the new constant, h—all because he believed that Boltzmann's k was a natural and direct measure for the atom. To trace all processes back to the absolute constants (h was not yet in that category, since Planck published nothing further on it until 1906) was the ultimate goal of scientific inquiry for the reasons outlined above, so the jerry-built "derivation" must be correct.

Thus science for the extraterrestrials could serve as a heuristic to discover new and important physical laws; but above all it could serve as a bulwark against hoi polloi who felt no compunctions in deriding the vaunted expertise and social position of the mandarinate. It is important to note that the following digression in Planck's *Scientific Autobiography* occurs in the context of a discussion of absolute moral values: "There must exist in science, too, absolutely correct and final maxims, just as there are absolute values in ethics. Moreover, and this is the main thing, these very propositions, maxims and values are the most important and worthwhile goals of every endeavor. In the realm of exact science, there are the values of the *absolute constants*, such as the elementary quantum of electricity, or the elementary quantum of action, and many others. These constants always prove to be the same, regardless of the method used for measuring them" (Planck 1949, 77–78).

At this juncture, both the terminology and the significance of the terms "absolute constant" and "fundamental constant" and "dimension" began to vary drastically with the user, so it will repay the effort to develop a quick and dirty taxonomy to distinguish the historical actors.[8] The term "dimension" had originally referred to the three orientations in space; but once the notion that time might be included as a dimension was also entertained, the connotation of the term shifted to the set of axes in a heterogeneous vector space that might span the space of physical lawlike statements. It was at about the time of Maxwell and Stoney that this transformation in attitude started prompting synonymous use of the terms "dimensions" and "fundamental units of measurement." With this change in the vernacular it subsequently became possible to entertain a yet more extreme version of the same argument—namely, that dimension could be dispensed with altogether.

In retrospect, we can distinguish at least three sorts of physical constants, which were often confused in subsequent debates. The first class of constants are the candidates for "natural units of measurement" identified by physical theories and easily reproducible because of their appearance in numerous physical contexts—such as the gravitational constant, G, the speed of light, c, Planck's constant, h, and the unit of electrical charge, e. These constants, because they are built up from the fundamental generators of length, mass, time, and so forth, could serve as the basis for the group of dimensions for all previous measurement governed by the theories in question. The second class of constants consists of the true "dimensionless" constants—that is, numbers determined from experiment, where all dimensional quantities cancel out. For instance, the ratio of the mass of the proton to the mass of the electron is roughly 1840, which is a pure, dimensionless number. The third class of constants consists of those purely instrumental factors that permit the conversion from one measurement scale to another. Examples of such constants are the 32° that must be added to the Centigrade scale to convert to Fahrenheit, or the Avogadro number 6.02×10^{23} to convert from a gram mole to molecules.

That many physical laws were expressed as products of powers of the first class of fundamental units (for example, the dimension of c is LT^{-1}, while the dimension of h is the same as that of "action" $ML^2\,T^{-1}$) led to the realization that it was precisely that class of laws which would remain invariant to changes in the arbitrary scales in which the units were measured (Campbell 1957, 372). That realization, in turn, led in the Anglo-American context to the quasi-mathematical discipline of "dimensional analysis" (Buckingham 1914; Bridgman 1931; Campbell [1920] 1957). The purpose of this discipline was to aid the theorist in such activities as checking that proposed equations were dimensionally homogeneous, or placing restrictions on the arguments of an arbitrary function that was projected to be the prototype of a novel natural law.

While "dimensional analysis" was intended to be a tool for constructing physical theories, it was not supposed to perform the cosmic heuristic function that Planck championed, as can be seen in the highly critical stance adopted by both Campbell ([1920], 1957, 395–96) and Bridgman (1931, 100) toward Planck's absolute units. Campbell claimed that one should not accord the same privilege to the notion of a "dimensionless constant" such as π, which was the result of a ratio of two magnitudes of the same fundamental type measured in the same units, as to an "absolute" constant such as c (the speed of light) or G (the gravitational constant), which remained invariant only if all component units of differing types were simultaneously scaled to preserve invariance. Both Campbell and Bridgman rejected the idea that there was any cosmic necessity in Planck's units, Bridgman because he was skeptical of the centrality of Planck's constant, h, and Campbell because he saw a surfeit of arbitrary choices still inherent in the units. In particular, Campbell turned Planck's assertion on its head by insisting that any constants chosen would be conditional on the theories that had generated them, and this was an argument against basing the whole structure of measurement on what was potentially a transient situation. For Campbell, even length, time, and mass were not given by nature but rather historically conditioned by ease of measurement in the historical evolution of physics (although no actual historical documentation was provided to back this up).

It is noteworthy that this instrumentalist approach to "dimensional analysis" has never realized its early promise or played a large role in physical theory, whereas those who took a more metaphysical approach to measurement continued in the forefront of innovation. Another figure in this latter approach, concerned with all three classes of fundamental units, was Albert Einstein.[9] Einstein's early work on the multiple derivation of Avogadro's number—a constant expressing the unity of molecular phenomena—is well known, as is the importance of legitimate invariance of measurement in widely separated reference frames for the theory of relativity. Einstein made some relatively insignificant use of dimensional analysis in an early paper (Einstein 1911) with regard to the specific heats of solids. But more interestingly, he was not averse to engaging in Planckian speculations about the meaning and significance of dimensionless constants in physical theory. Like Planck, Einstein viewed the human element of any physical theory as essentially arbitrary, something that should be purged on realization of the final true theory. Only he did Planck one better in appealing to the ultimate extraterrestrial: "With the question of universal constants, you have broached one of the most interesting questions that may be asked at all. There are two kinds of constants: apparent ones and real ones. The apparent ones are simply the outcome of the introduction of arbitrary units, but are eliminable. The real [true] ones are genuine numbers which God had to choose arbitrarily, as it were, when He deigned to create the world. My opinion now is—stated briefly—that the constants of the second type do not exist and their apparent existence is caused by the fact that we have not penetrated deeply enough. I therefore believe that such numbers can only be of a rational type, as for instance π or e" (Einstein to Ilse Rosenthal-Schneider, 11 May 1945, quoted in Rosenthal-Schneider 1980, 33–34).[10]

The divergence from the British "dimensional analysis" tradition is clear, with the insistence that certain constants have something more than conventional significance, and the conflation of the terminology of dimensionless constants applying to something like π, along with other constants such as Planck's h. But there was also something new added by Einstein, the idea that natural constants must have some sort of restricted magnitude on purely a priori grounds, as well as a dimensional configuration that would span the space of physical laws. For Einstein, nature had to be "rational" (a double meaning that may itself prove a source of confusion in the above quote), which meant among other things that true physical constants would not assume arbitrary values other than those already encountered and privileged in pure mathematics. One indication of this phenomenon in the past was the progressive reduction of a large set of physical constants to a smaller derived set, a trend many at that time expected to continue indefinitely with the development of physics (Rosenthal-Schneider 1980, 57). In a further variation on the notion of the unity of science, Einstein expected that the order of magnitude of the remaining true constants should hover about unity, which would provide some justification for the claim that they "did not exist." However much he predicated such vague notions on aesthetic principles, there lurked in the background the problem of how to recognize a purely natural rationality, adroit yet inhuman and extraterrestrial, which would prefer the numeral one to 10^{79}; and moreover, one so sublime that it might eventually validate the dissolution of all natural constants. (If the authority that was supposed to sanction the constants already should prove sufficiently alien and omnisicient, what was to prevent it from declaring them all null and void?)

Here the metaphysical problem of a search for natural numbers encountered another stumbling block: the palpable irrationality of such bizarre numbers as 6.626176×10^{-34} J Hz^{-1}, 6.6720×10^{-11} N m^2 kg^{-2}, and 2.997924580×10^8 m s^{-1}. What had been initially sought as the objective signifier of nature's absolute integrity now seemed more like a reproach to the claim of transcendental understanding. In reaction to this strange otherness, the tenor of discussion of the "dimensionless constants" again took another sharp turn, one aimed at returning to the anthropomorphic justification for the constants. But such a drastic reorientation again demanded a discontinuity in cultural context. In our present narrative, it meant a return to Britain.

The Long Road Back to Anthropometrics

Until the 1920s it was recognized that when it came to nature's numbers, "the continental authors laid greater stress upon the *units*, while the English authors laid more stress on the *dimensions* of physical quantities" (Lewis 1925, 747). There were also, as I have argued, differences in the attitude toward what the search for natural numbers was all about, as well as what must appear in retrospect as profound differences in the fruits of the search for innovations in physics. The Anglophone conception of a method of depicting the formal aspects of physical theory—or, as Bridgman put it, "an analysis of an analysis"—really did not get very far, largely because it attempted to cut itself loose from any commitment to any particular construction of nature. Again quoting Bridgman: "With no clear conception of a dimensional constant or when to expect its appearance, hesitancy is natural in applying the method" (1931, 88). The Germans, on the other hand, were not averse to seeing the constants rooted in some transcendental authority and therefore boldly went where no physicist had gone before.

The whole characteristic British attitude toward nature's numbers began to undergo another sea change starting in the 1930s, and it appears we are still experiencing the implications (which makes evaluation all the more difficult). The first notable revision of the tradition which asserted that "Nature is measured with her own gauge" came with the maturity of Sir Arthur Stanley Eddington. For the last fifteen years of his life he was almost exclusively engaged in elaborating what he variously called his "relativity theory of protons and electrons," the "group structure of physical science," and sometimes just the "fundamental theory." Although his prestigious position at Cambridge and his immensely successful popular books on physics seemed to ensure his intellectual stature, the reaction of the physics community to this project was almost exclusively derisive. Einstein wrote, "Eddington made many ingenious suggestions, but I have not followed them all up. I find that he was as a rule curiously uncritical towards his own ideas" (quoted in Rosenthal-Schneider 1980, 40). Wolfgang Pauli wrote to Bohr that it was "rubbish" (Ruger 1988, 389). Schrödinger, although sympathetic to some elements of the program, pointed out serious errors in Eddington's derivations (Ruger 1988, 391–92; W. Moore 1989, 326–29). Yet however much this program is now considered a case of misbegotten theory, I think it has been overlooked how much it altered the frame of discourse about natural numbers, opening up the option for at least a subset of modern physics to return to the original conception of measurement as inherently anthropomorphic and thus grounded in an irreducibly human authority.

Eddington's project has been sympathetically summarized in the principle that "all . . . the exact values of the pure numbers that are constants of science, may be deduced by logical reasoning from qualitative assertions, without making any use of quantitative data derived from observation" (Whitaker 1951, 3; Kilminster 1994). In a sense, this was the next logical step in the progression that began by grounding the constants of nature in the earth, then exiling them to a distant heaven, and then dissolving all dimensions into a single homogeneous number—all in the name of a final, irrefutable justification of quantitative empiricism. We have already seen that the rather curious magnitudes of the modern constants were a source of disquiet in the early twentieth century; the apparent gulf between quantum mechanics and the theory of relativity boded ill for seeing the constants as somehow connected in a fundamental, unified system. Eddington was originally drawn into the whole question of dimensionless constants by a concern over the apparent disjuncture between relativity and quantum theory: "Current quantum theory neglects the curvature of space, and therefore falls into error either way: Either it postulates that a light reference object is used and wrongly neglects its uncertainty of position and velocity, or it postulates a heavy reference object and wrongly neglects the resulting curvature of space" (Eddington 1936, 179).

Eddington wanted to argue that the atomic structure of matter was a consequence of the existence of a curved finite space in the theory of general relativity, using an analogy between curved space-time and the wave equation to arrive at quantized energy levels. In a manner of speaking, he chose to treat the Einstein universe like an atom, in order to reveal the relationship between the gravitational constant, Planck's constant, and the masses of the proton and the electron. Thus Eddington set out to give two descriptions of a system of N particles: the first, in terms of a closed curved space of radius R, in which mutual gravitational attraction is exactly balanced by mutual repulsion because of the cosmical constant in Einstein's then current version of general relativity; the second, in terms of a radiationless quantized system in its ground state, making particular use of Pauli's exclusion principle. The two solutions, he claimed, would give a relationship between N, R, the gravitational constant G, and Planck's constant. Using Dirac's wave equation, he made a heuristic argument that electron mass should have the rough form $\sqrt{N/R}$, and therefore $\sqrt{N/R} = mc^2/e^2$ (where e is the electron charge). Combining this with the equation $NGm_p/c^2 = (1/2)\,\pi\,R^2$ (with m_p representing proton mass), he asserted that one could calculate both N and R in an a priori manner (Whittaker 1945, 139). The resulting value of R appeared to agree with the known radius of the universe at that time; but the key insight from Eddington's point of view was the interpretation of the value of N. In a separate argument he suggested that since according to relativity theory all measurement involved four entities, measurement should be thought of as involving quadruple wave functions. In a spherical space the number of independent wave functions with the requisite relativistic properties would be $N = (3/2) \times 136 \times 2^{256}$; and lo and behold, this was roughly equivalent to the calculated value of N above. Thus Eddington dubbed N the "cosmical number" or "the number of protons in the universe"; but perhaps better, it was the ultimate natural constant from which all the other constants sprang.

It is important to see that Eddington wanted to combine Planck's project of grounding all measurement in units based on the fundamental constants with a theory that would explain the rough magnitudes of those constants. The basis of the measurement system would be the three arbitrary units of length, time, and mass, the ratio of the mass of the proton to the electron $\sim$ 1840, the fine structure constant $\sim$137, the "force ratio" e^2 / GMm $\sim$2.3 $\times$ 10^{39}, and the "ratio of the curvature of space-time to the wavelength of the mean Schrödinger wave" $\sim$1.2 $\times$ 10^{39} (Eddington 1935, 231–32). At that point he asked "whether the above ratios can be assigned arbitrarily or whether they were inevitable"; and he answered the question by asserting that "the unification of different branches of science reduces the number of fundamental constants" (233). Since Eddington saw the fine structure constant explained by the number of possible permutations of wave functions mentioned above (= 136; the extra integer took a bit of waffling), the other constants should all be functions of the cosmical number. For instance, the ratio of proton to electron masses was claimed to be of the order of $(h/2\pi c)$ $\times$ $(\sqrt{N/R})$; the force ratio was nearly $\sqrt{3N/\pi}$; and the last ratio was of order $\sqrt{(N/30)}$ (249–52).

Eddington's linchpin, the cosmical number, ran into problems almost immediately. For instance, Schrödinger warned him in correspondence that in the heuristic argument about mc^2 above, the correct power of N would be the cube root, undermining the metrological coincidence (Ruger 1988, 391–92; W. Moore 1989, 327). Moreover, Eddington's theory of the nucleus was very nearly obsolete on its appearance and could not account for such recent discoveries as Yukawa's meson. Nevertheless, Eddington did not give up on finding the appropriate formalism that would link the constants of quantum mechanics and relativistic cosmology. But more important, in his popular writings he mounted a far-reaching reinterpretation of the meaning of measurement. In a position he called "selective subjectivism," he insisted that "because a man works in a laboratory it does not follow that he is not an incorrigible metaphysician" (Eddington 1939, 33); and that consequently led to an argument that "not only the laws of nature but the constants of nature can be deduced from epistemological considerations, so that we can have *a priori* knowledge of them" (58). Rather than regard such idealism as the destruction of physics, Eddington believed that it was the ultimate deliverance of physical measurement from the vagaries of history and circumstance, as well as the explanation of the existence of the dimensionless constants of nature. It seemed somewhat a play on words, but what Eddington meant by "subjectivism" was the pure justification of the certainty of natural measurement. Thus "the constants of nature (apart from arbitrary units) are numbers introduced by our subjective outlook, whose values can be calculated *a priori* and stand for all time. For that reason my personal conclusion is that there is no more danger that the velocity of light or the constant of gravitation will change with time than that the circumference-diameter ratio π will change with time." (78)

The physics community looked askance at Eddington's theory and reacted with revulsion to this language of "subjectivism"; but it should not be inferred that his work was therefore uninfluential, particularly with regard to the ongoing reconceptualization of the dimensionless constants. Instead of presuming that natural measures were an arbitrary language bequeathed to us by a wholly alien nature, which by its very character could give no guarantees about the stability of measurement—not to mention the epistemological conundrums associated with the question of how we could ever become fluent in such a language—Eddington wanted to plumb the grammar of this language and relate it to the circumstance of our use of it.[11] The imprimatur on the Book of Nature would thus no longer be traced to other worlds: indeed, the extension of physics into cosmology tended to render that option rather less attractive. Instead, the validity of measurement would be acknowledged as a derived phenomenon, a function of the unification of physical theory.

In a heretical reading of the energetics movement which had given rise to the quest for natural measurement in the first place, Eddington reinterpreted the bookkeeping metaphor in a way that was to apply to fundamental constants as well as to such invariants as the conservation of energy:

> The famous laws of conservation and energy . . . *are mathematical identities*. Violation of them is unthinkable. Perhaps I can best indicate their nature by an analogy. An aged college Bursar once dwelt secluded in his rooms devoting himself entirely to accounts. He realised the intellectual and other activities of the college only as they presented themselves in the bills. He vaguely conjectured an objective reality back of it all—some sort of parallel to the real college—though he could only picture it in terms of the pounds, shillings and pence which made up what he would call "the commonsense college of everyday experience." The method of account-keeping had become inveterate habit handed down from generations of hermit-like bursars; he accepted the form of the accounts as being part of the nature of things. But he was of a scientific turn and he wanted to learn more about the college. One day in looking over the books he discovered a remarkable law. For every

item on the credit side an equal item appeared somewhere else on the debit side. "Ha!" said the Bursar, "I have discovered one of the great laws controlling the college. It is a perfect and exact law of the real world. Credit must be called plus and debit minus." And so we have the law of conservation of £.s.d. (237–38; emphasis in original)

This idea, that the invariants supposedly found in nature were instead an artifact of our mode of organizing empirical inquiry, was an increasingly popular notion among philosophers in the 1930s, as can be witnessed from the reactions to Eddington, as well as to the earlier Meyerson ([1908] 1962). Nonetheless, the problem of authority was still not settled for good, if only because reason was rarely sufficient to enforce invariance.

Ironically, this freedom immediately led to a doctrine that Eddington could not accept: that the constants of physics were not constant at all. Among other responses, it prompted Paul Dirac to write in a letter to *Nature*:

The fundamental constants of physics . . . provide for a set of absolute units for measurement of distance, time, mass, etc. There are, however, more of these constants than are necessary for this purpose, with the result that certain dimensionless numbers can be extracted from them. The significance of these numbers has excited much interest in recent times, and Eddington has set up a theory for calculating most of them purely deductively. Eddington's arguments are not always rigorous, and while they give one the feeling that they are probably substantially correct in the case of the smaller numbers . . . the larger numbers, namely the ratio of electric force to gravitational force between the electron and proton, which is about 10^{39}, and the ratio of the mass of the universe to the mass of the proton, which is about 10^{73}, are so enormous as to make one think that some entirely different type of explanation is needed for them. (Dirac 1937, 323)

Hence under the influence of Eddington, Dirac also subscribed to the project of natural measurement; but in a relatively minor shift of the premises, he felt that the magnitude of the large, dimensionless constants should not be linked to the number of particles in the universe but rather to the age of the universe, thus avoiding Eddington's cosmic constant. The implications, however, were staggering and unprecedented: for one thing, the gravitational constant appeared constant only because we had not used the appropriate units. In an appropriate measurement scheme, gravitation should "weaken" over time, proportionately to t^{-1}. Further, all large, dimensionless numbers were proposed to be simple functions of time. What is significant for our present purposes is that this suggestion was not exiled to the margins of discourse but subsequently taken quite seriously by Chandrasekhar (1937), Kothari (1938), Jordan (1939; 1949), and a host of others. Some took to developing alternative theories of gravity that also allowed for variations in G over time (Norman 1986).

One significant further innovation found in the work of Dirac and elsewhere was the importance of the *overdetermination* of fundamental constants in physical theories, which would later become a mainstay of the metrological literature (Cohen, Crowe, and Dumond 1957, 104). Because the constants appear so often and in many overlapping combinations with one another in the theories, the specification of the magnitudes of a small subset will fix the magnitudes of all the others. Multiple determinations of the magnitudes then become feasible, and the issue of the consistency of the various implied magnitudes becomes transformed. If no single magnitude is privileged, then choice of the "correct" magnitudes cannot be purely deterministic but must be intrinsically stochastic, conforming only to certain systematic checks of consistency. In only slightly metaphorical language, the problem becomes one of "arbitrage."[12]

Far from having the stabilizing effect envisioned by Eddington, speculations concerning the linkage of the natural "constants" seemed to undermine any previous connotation of the word, not to mention fostering the almost Hegelian inversion of the original project of the quest for natural units. Of course, many read Dirac's challenge as a mandate to go forth and empirically test the constancy of the natural constants; but here the original conundrums at the heart of the project doubled back on themselves. We are back at the Zanzibar problem: "If we cannot find some basic units for our system of measurement whose constancy in space-time is assured, it may be a meaningless question to ask whether or not the constants may vary with time" (Petley 1985, 36; Ohanian 1977). For instance, if time is measured by the frequency in cesium atoms, and length by the wavelength of krypton-86, then length and time are constant by definition and cannot be used to measure changes in the gravitational constant (Barrow and Tippler 1986, 242). Using the krypton-86 wavelength to define the meter also effectively defines Planck's constant as fixed (Petley 1985, 39). While many scholars (e.g., Norman 1986) take the position that these sorts of considerations have all been reasonably accounted for, there are still grounds for questioning the empirical status of the constancy of the constants (Barrow and Tippler 1986, 238). For instance, the cosmological theories of Kaluza and Klein, which have (temporarily?) come back into vogue in the guise of string theory, allow for time variation of fundamental constants in extra compactified dimensions that would appear to be invariant only in our phenomenological three dimensions.

Another indication of the postmodernist mind-set with regard to the fundamental constants, one that takes its cue from the introduction of stochastic considerations mentioned above, is a recent attempt to invert the time-honored theme that the magnitudes of these constants have some sort of transcendental significance, and to regard them instead as purely random, arraying them on a histogram and discussing their stochastic distribution (Frieden 1986). Arguing only that the distribution should be invariant to changes of system of units and invariant to multiplicative inversion, empirical and theoretical considerations both point to a simple, uniform distribution in logarithms, or $f(x) \sim a/x$. Eschewing the higher aspirations of the previous physicists in our narrative, Frieden calls this exercise "a kind of obtuse unified theory of physics; obtuse because it results from lumping together all disparate physical phenomena as if the details of each didn't matter" (899).

While the eventual implications of all this work are certainly up in the air, it seems safe to say that something profoundly curious has occurred to the original project of constructing the ultimate rational measurement system out of purely natural components supplied by nature. In effect, the Eddington program of "subjectivism" does live on in the "anthropic principle" (Carr and Rees 1979; Barrow and Tippler 1986) that much of the universe's structure as represented by the magnitude of the dimensionless constants can and should be accounted for by the existence of carbon-based observers, such as ourselves, who have required an appreciable length of time to evolve to our present state of consciousness. However, our present narrative does take issue with a theme found throughout Barrow and Tippler (1986) that treats much of the work I have described as simply anticipating the anthropic principle. On the contrary, the cultural motivations that have driven the quest for the pure system of measurement have been historically diverse, with many—Planck among them—wishing to rid physics of all anthropic taint. Further, since such cultural motivations are not icing on the cake but rather inform the very structure of some of the physics they have inspired, we may be excused if we see the modern anthropic school as a reflection of cultural trends in our own time which entertain the possibility that there are no real deterministic laws of physics (Deutsch 1986)—the full fruit of Eddington's original advocacy of "subjectivism."

Again, this school of thought has not won widespread acceptance among physicists; but again, that is not the point. The "anthropic" enthusiasts are essentially the major heirs of the tradition of theory concerned with the fundamental, dimensionless constants and the belief in a natural set of units that would provide the final validation of measurement. As one skeptical observer puts it: "Most scientists feel, intuitively, that there must be some natural units against which all other measurements may be expressed. However, different natural units might well be appropriate to different disciplines . . . scientists have a tendency to make their measurement with respect to some local unit" (Petley 1985, 29); mostly, it is the enthusiasts of "anthropic principles" and metrologists who are left to worry about the gulf between desire and practice.

8
A Visible Hand
in the Marketplace
of Ideas: Precision
Measurement as
Arbitrage

Initiates into the social studies of science in the 1990s could easily be forgiven if they tended to equate the "social" with the "economic." Marxist analyses of science date back to the "Hessen thesis," if not earlier. Representatives of various earlier sociologies of science have more or less self-consciously used the metaphor of a "marketplace of ideas" as their starting point; while representatives of a more postmodernist bent, from Latour and Woolgar to Pierre Bourdieu, have reveled in the language of the market and the accumulation of credit in their debunking exercises (McClellan 1996; Hands 2001). As discussed in the Introduction and chapter 5, there are now signs that more conventional analytic philosophers of science such as Radnitzky (Radnitzky and Bernholz 1987), Goldman (1992), and Kitcher (1993a) are appropriating mathematical models from neoclassical economics to reach some accommodation with (or better, neutralize) what they regard as outlandish constructivist accounts of science. All this newfound enthusiasm for economics among those who thought only a few short years ago that it should be safely quarantined on the far side of the demarcation divide is a phenomenon that deserves close scrutiny by philosophers and historians alike.[1] Having criticized the more commonplace appeals to market metaphors in previous chapters, I shall here begin from the observation that if economic analogies in science studies are to have any bite, to count as something more than coffee-room chatter, it would be wiser not to start with *rough qualitative* analogies in the manner of the above but rather with *quantitative* ones, which at least have the advantage that their mathematical character would be more likely to draw support.

The crucial issue, as with all such exercises, is to identify a plausible starting point in science for economic comparisons. This chapter suggests that we pursue the analogy to the heart of the image of scientific enterprise—namely, to the precision measurement of physical constants. Curiously enough, all of the authors cited above have neglected the one literature where economic reasoning abounds: that of the treatment of error in inductive inference. It so happens that all modern accounts of the stabilization of quantitative error possess an economic account of rationality at their core; the purpose of this chapter is to propose an alternative account based on rival economic concepts. The reason why we explore this option here, rather than in a journal of metrology or statistics or analytic philosophy, is that this theory of scientific practice is explicitly intended to resonate with modern social studies of science, especially the recent work of Alder, Shapin and Schaffer, Gooday, Galison, and Porter. As such, it encompasses (1) an explicit mathematical model of the stabilization of constants in a quantitative science, (2) a framework for the writing of a history of practice with regard to quantitative measurement error, (3) resources for the comparative sociology of scientific disciplines, and (4) a platform for the critique of "accounting" or "economics" as a discrete theory of social life. Individual components of this program have been elaborated upon elsewhere.[2] The purpose of this chapter is to provide an introduction, synthesis, and overview of items (1) to (3).

The Assignment of Number as a Process of Give and Take

It is striking just how quickly the paradigmatic exemplars of rationality in our culture, the physicists and the economists, ascend to ethereal realms of mysticism whenever they take it upon themselves to discuss the role of mathematics within their disciplines. Appeals are ubiquitous to an "unreasonable effectiveness of mathematics," to a partially obscured Book of Nature written in mathematical dialect, to an inborn utilitarian calculus, to a magic language more transparent than any vernacular and to a conflation of number and the phenomenon that somehow manages to escape crass numerology. Number and mathematics in these narratives are endowed with transcendental epistemic significance, which is subsequently used to explain the effortlessly maintained acceleration of empirical progress in the successful sciences. The problem with this mode of argumentation is that it grasps at legitimation from the wrong end of the stick, from the side of abstract formalism rather than the side of *error* accounts.

From Pierre Duhem and C. S. Peirce onward, some philosophers have realized that the key to understanding the assignment of number is to focus on the problems of accommodation to error in a world where there is no prospect of its complete extirpation. In the early twentieth century, this concern was tamed by being absorbed into the theory of probability and reduced to an instrumental concern of the discipline of statistics. The two dominant accounts of the treatment of error in the twentieth century, the theory of Neyman-Pearson hypothesis testing and the Bayesian theory of subjectivist probability assignment, constitute the scaffolding upon which all modern empirical activity in all the quantitative sciences is draped, propagated throughout the disciplinary landscape from its original incubator in operations research. It is therefore no accident that many contemporary accounts of the rationality of science should take one or the other of these stories as their point of departure.[3] What has been neglected in the interim, however, is that each of these two grand metanarratives is itself based on a core notion of economic rationality: a metaphor for the tradeoffs and compromises encountered in everyday practice.

The version of Neyman-Pearson found in the plethora of undergraduate statistics texts is a garbled and distorted version of the original doctrine (Gigerenzer and Murray 1987); and there is substantial evidence that its progenitors did not agree on its content (Mayo 1985; 1992). But for our purposes it will suffice to recall the major components of the doctrine. It presumes the ability to specify two rival quantitative hypotheses before the fact of data collection; to assign probability distributions to a unique variable under both rival hypotheses; and to define regions of acceptance or rejection of the null hypothesis as a function of the power of the test statistic. Neyman in particular motivated the last step by explicit reference to the costs and benefits of acceptance or rejection of the null; and this economic reasoning has been ensconced in the tradition by reference to loss functions, optimal estimators, and the like. The pervasive dissatisfaction with the Neyman-Pearson organon among philosophers and statistical theorists (Howson and Urbach 1989; Gigerenzer and Murray 1987) derives from observations that economistic calculation as an a priori categorical imperative does not seem to capture the actual behavior of scientific researchers, even when they themselves believe they are faithful adherents of the Neyman-Pearson doctrine.

The Bayesian doctrine, while clearly in the ascendant in terms of attracting adherents, also has its own version of economic rationality and its own peculiar drawbacks. While it allows that probability assignments might be individually idiosyncratic and even inconsistent at times, this doctrine depends on some version of the "Dutch book" argument to assert that personal probabilities ultimately obey the Kolmogorov axioms (de Finetti 1974). According to this argument the inconsistent actor is to be "punished" by some external agent who makes a sequence of bets with the first party that pay off with probability one, thus transforming personal inconsistency into a hemorrhaging "money pump." The role of the virtual economy here is clear: to police the otherwise unexplained diversity of opinion. The drawback is that in science, as opposed to the racetrack, it is not clear how the Dutch book is supposed to work and who is to play the role of the venal bookie. When combined with complaints about the a priori need to restrict individual prior probabilities and the freedom of actors to update their conditionalized priors as they like, it would seem that these economic arguments are not sufficient to clinch the determinacy of error in the way imagined by avid Bayesians (Earman 1992; Kahneman, Slovic, and Tversky 1982).

A further reason to be skeptical of both these accounts, at least within the social studies of science community, is their willful methodologically individualist character. The Neyman-Pearson doctrine imagines a frequentist theory of probability underwriting a mechanical decision process fully implementable by any isolated self-contained individual inquirer. The Bayesian model is often retailed as being founded on a utilitarian or "rational choice" conception of individual action. It is precisely this orientation, which seeks to ground rationality in the epistemic capacities and inclinations of isolated individuals, that has encouraged recourse to economic metaphors: some sort of "invisible hand" must then reconcile these marooned Robinson Crusoes of science, and the discipline most willing to supply such notions has been neoclassical economics.

Because scholars in more recent manifestations of science studies may be more disinclined than most to endorse such invisible hand explanations, it would seem that the time is ripe to rethink the treatment of quantitative measurement in the history and sociology of science. We shall therefore begin our sketch by drawing on a relatively recent literature in economics that conceptualizes the social constitution of value as the outcome of a process of arbitrage within the institutional constraints of a monetary system and a set of external definitions of the identity of commodities. This literature treats the market as an evolving network, thus resonating with certain versions of the philosophy of science (discussed in chapter 1) as well as certain connectivist themes in complexity theory (Farmer 1991). For obvious reasons, the mathematical component of the economic theory cannot be developed in detail here; citations are provided for the curious.[4] Rather, I shall provide a brief description in the vernacular, using diagrams, of the analogy between commodity exchange and the assignment of quantitative error, and follow with the relevant central theorem before moving on in subsequent sections to sketch the uses to which the theorem may be put in science studies.

The governing trope of my account in both the economic and the measurement cases is one of enforcing numerical invariance through arbitrage. In the marketplace, the prices of most commodities can be stated in terms of prices of other commodities; in physics, most constants can be defined by other constants. The key variable in the market situation is *profit*; in scientific measurement it is *error*. In markets, exchange is deemed arbitrage-free when any sequence of trades between commodities, however circuitous, always ends up with identical numerical relative prices of the initial and final commodities. One can think of this as the transitivity of value relations: knowing the going rates of corn for gold, gold for oil, oil for beef, and beef for silver means the going rate of corn for silver can be directly inferred without actually consulting the marketplace. In parallel, a set of physical constants is *consistent* (arbitrage-free) when any sequence of measurements, however circuitous, always gives the same numerical value for the resultant implied physical constant. One can think of this as the transitivity of measurement relations through successive theories. The root phenomenological problem both in markets and in physical science is that the numbers are never really arbitrage-free (actual prices are never mutually consistent; actual measurements never completely transitive), and therefore the algebraic systems that they embody do not strictly possess invariants. The absence of invariance in both instances is initially comprehended as *error*: Did we make a mistake at any node of the calculation? Was the valuation in a particular market in some ill-specified way "wrong"? Are the theories in fact in conflict? Was the experimental setup somehow at fault? Within a certain indeterminate range of quantitative discrepancy, actors are willing simply to ignore the problem of consistency: in arbitrage, it is within the band of "transaction costs"; in precision measurement, it is outside the band of "significant figures." But there is more to it than that, since a major part of the problem is to foster interpersonal agreement as to where the band lies.

It is noteworthy that the arbitrageur always claims to halt the dark threat of infinite regress at the "fundamentals"—the underlying real determinants of value—while an experimentalist claims to halt the threat of infinite regress at nature. One of the triumphs of the science studies literature, and particularly the work of Harry Collins (1985), has been to undermine this account and show in actual circumstances how the "experimenter's regress" is short-circuited in practice. The parallel development in financial economics has been to show that "the fundamentals" are effectively bypassed in the course of closing a deal (Bernstein 1992). The advantage of the economics literature is that it shows how this closure can be achieved in a quantitative manner, whereas Collins has so far confined his commentary to the qualitative phenomenon. Important in extending this formal analogy to physics is the convention that all physical constants be treated as though they were ratio combinations of other, derived, physical constants. A fact rarely commented on is that many of our present constants do exhibit this character: for instance, the Josephson frequency-voltage quotient is $2e/h$, the fine structure constant is $\mu_0 c e^2 / 2h$, the electron specific charge is e/m_e, the Boltzmann constant is R/N_A, and so forth. I shall make use of this algebraic curiosity in figure 1, below.

There is, however, one extremely critical way that the market analogy *does not* fully carry over into the process of physical measurement. In the marketplace there is an entire class of transactors who are on the lookout for price inconsistencies, because the unit magnitude of those divergences is realized in the form of money profit. This is often stated as a truism: no \$50 bills will be found lying on the sidewalk. In physics, the unit magnitude of divergences is denominated in errors; however in that sphere we shall not presume that anyone is motivated to accumulate error units for their own sake. Therefore, while one could imagine a "laissez-faire" situation in which transactors police price consistency in a marketplace out of nothing more than venal self-interest, it is highly unlikely that such a situation would ever arise in physical measurement. Far from crippling the effectiveness of the analogy between market and measurement, this divergence is responsible for our first empirical finding: that historically, arbitrage emerged much later in the process of physical measurement than in the evolution of the marketplace, and that its emergence required the imposition of an "artificial" actor whose whole purpose was to develop a set of error accounts. This persona was the invention of a real historical figure, the physicist Raymond Birge.

The theory of arbitrage that undergirds this account is based on the work of Ellerman (1984) on the formalization of "market graphs." A *directed graph* $\xi = [\xi^0, \xi_1, t, h]$ is a set of ξ^0 nodes numbered 1, . . . , N, a set of ξ_1 arcs or darts numbered 1, . . . , L, and head and tail functions which indicate that arc k is directed from tail node $t(j)$ to head node $h(j)$. A "path" from node $j = 1$ to $j = n$ is an unbroken sequence of arcs connected at their heads or tails that extends from node j^1 to node j^n. A graph is called "connected" if a path exists between any two arbitrary nodes. When we endow graphs with economic significance, we associate each generic commodity with a single node and associate each arc with a permitted exchange. In order to discuss prices, each arc is assigned a nonzero rational number r_k, here called a "rate." One unit of the commodity at the tail node can be exchanged for r_k units of the commodity at the head node.

In the arbitrage theory of physical constants, we instead assign nodes to physical entities that are supposed to exhibit some fixed quantitative attribute: it could be the electron charge, or the Planck quantum of action, or the Avogadro number. A truncated graph of a selective subset of physical constants is illustrated in figure 1. The arcs here represent theories that connect the entities in fixed quantitative relationships: for example, the BCS theory of superconductivity links the electron charge and the Planck quan-

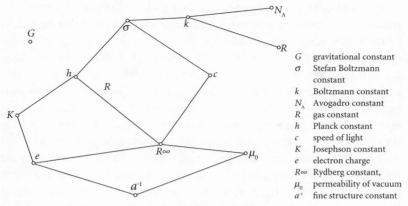

Figure 1. A simplified graph of some physical constants.

G	gravitational constant
σ	Stefan Boltzmann constant
k	Boltzmann constant
N_A	Avogadro constant
R	gas constant
h	Planck constant
c	speed of light
K	Josephson constant
e	electron charge
$R\infty$	Rydberg constant,
μ_0	permeability of vacuum
a^{-1}	fine structure constant

tum through the Josephson effect, while the permeability of the vacuum and the speed of light are linked through spectroscopy and the Rydberg constant. The role of the graph both in economics and in measurement theory is to stress that no value can ratify itself (no self-loops) and to demonstrate that a specific node can be reached only along a subset of all possible paths. Market graphs must be connected for successful arbitrage to take place; measurement graphs must be connected for successful error arbitrage to take place. The gravitational constant is portrayed as an isolated node in figure 1 because it is the least well connected of the physical constants; as a consequence, the gravitational constant has the least successful history of error stabilization of all the fundamental physical constants (Petley 1985, 11). Disciplines that posit quantitative constants which are entirely decoupled from one another cannot institute effective structures of error control and attribution.

Why can an individual measurement not ratify itself? Quite simply, because no single laboratory can simultaneously fix the values of all the constants used in measuring other constants. The danger of self-ratifying constants is called by Petley (8–9) the "Zanzibar effect" (see chapter 7). Another way to think about this is to approach it as a concrete elaboration of the analytical insight by Latour (1987) that inscriptions must pass through other labs and enroll other workers to become black-boxed. Here, at the most basic level, the analogue of money becomes the fundamental yet arbitrary standard of length, time, mass, and charge. Metrology thus stands to the physical sciences as central banking stands to market economies.

It is the purpose of this theory to illustrate how the introduction of money and standards, in conjunction with other social structures, renders the system of "rates" an algebraic group or, in this case, the multiplicative group of nonzero rationals. It is indispensable to this portrait that the existence of the money or standards is a necessary prerequisite for movement along a path to be reversible: here, if a path traverses an arc in the opposite direction, the rate is treated as the reciprocal r_k^{-1}. Reversibility is induced because many actual trades cannot be reversed (the BMW lost substantial blue book value the minute it was driven off the lot), and many physical measurements cannot be unproblematically inverted (remember, we cannot ourselves generate all the quantitative values needed). Let us define a composite path as the product of the relevant rates over each segment of the path, namely $r[\alpha]$ $= \Pi_\alpha r_k$. Under these circumstances, we will be able to assign a number ($\mathbf{p}$ for price, $\mathbf{c}$ for constant) to each node as a function of the rates associated with the graph. The triple $[\xi, r, \mathbf{p}]$ is called a market graph in economics; I propose that in physics we call the triple $[\xi, r, \mathbf{c}]$ a "measurement graph."

The main conditions for the formal existence of such a graph are that (1) there are no self-loops at any node (no self-measure stabilizes itself); (2) the graph ξ must be connected (theories must use each other's variables); and (3) any circuit, either of exchange or measurement, beginning and ending at the same node results in a composite rate $r[\alpha] = 1$ (this is the desideratum of consistency). Under these conditions, Ellerman proves the following theorem:

Cournot-Kirchoff Arbitrage Theorem. Let $[\xi, r, \mathbf{p}]$ be a market graph with $r[\alpha]:\xi_1 \to T$, taking values in any group T. Then the following conditions are equivalent:

1. There is a price system P derived from the rate system r.
2. The exchange rate system r is path-independent.
3. The exchange rate system is arbitrage-free.

The theorem may be restated for the theory of measurement graphs $[\xi, r, \mathbf{c}]$ as:

1. There is a system of physical constants C derived from the theoretical rate system r.
2. Quantitative measurements in the theoretical rate system r are path-independent.
3. Measurements in the theoretical rate system r are error-free.

The advantage of the arbitrage approach to the phenomena of both markets and the measurement of physical constants is that it provides a structural framework within which one can argue that both phenomena are made, not discovered. Even with the vast social technologies of money, banks, and accounting, prices do not "naturally" conform to the Cournot-Kirchoff theorem: prices are rife with inconsistencies and therefore informational anomalies. One way this is made manifest is through the existence of arbitrage opportunities; and the way a "consistent" system of prices is approximated is through the activities of the arbitrageurs. Likewise, even with the vast laboratory resources of SI units, the National Institute of Standards and Technology, and the persistent interventions of metrologists, the measured physical constants do not "naturally" conform to the Cournot-Kirchoff theorem; at any moment in time the reported constants are rife with inconsistencies and therefore informational anomalies. One way this is made manifest is through inconsistencies uncovered by meta-analysis; and I shall argue in the next section that the Raymond Birges of the world are their arbitrageurs. Thus the history of error would have to trace the joint evolution of the self-seeking arbitrageur and the institutions that render new versions of arbitrage conceivable and achievable. The narrative in section 2 was constructed with just such an outline in mind.

A Natural History of Quantitative Error

Until very recently, the history of the fundamental physical constants was in a state of deplorable neglect. Depending on the source, one might have got the impression that some of our more hallowed constants were quickly identified and measured in the seventeenth century, close upon the heels of structured experimentation; or perhaps that they were quite securely nailed down by the spread of precision instrumentation and an Enlightenment "quantifying spirit" in the eighteenth century; or surely, that they were codified as an uncontentious compendium of reliable numbers in the industrialized standardization of the nineteenth century. Hence it must come as a bit of a shock to read the assessment of Raymond Birge, a major figure in the natural history of the physical constants, in a retrospective on the state of play in the *1920s:*

> A distinguished scientist would obtain a value of some such constant, which he believed more accurate than any previously found. He would make such a claim in a published paper, and thereafter, for some longer or shorter period, his value would be generally accepted and used throughout the scientific world. . . . In that case there was only one exhaustive investigation. Another situation tended to develop when research workers residing in two or more countries were involved. If, for instance, a distinguished German scientist obtained one value, and a distinguished French scientist another value of the same constant, one usually found the German value used subsequently in German papers and texts, and the French value in French papers and texts. . . . Another unfortunate aspect of the situation, as I found it, was that the generally adopted value of each constant was chosen quite independently of the value of other, often related constants, so that no *consis-*

tent set of values of the general constants existed. . . . There have even been instances of two *different* values of an auxiliary constant (the velocity of light) used in the *same* equation. (Birge 1957, 40–41; emphasis in original)

This certainly does not resonate with many of our commonplace notions of the special character and status of physics, ranging from the bracing regimen of quantification, to the relentlessly impersonal ethos of scientific knowledge, to the quest for clarity and consistency in the painstaking reproduction of the physical phenomenon. There is a simple explanation for this yawning gap between image and actuality. Everyone who has sought to write a history of the physical sciences has done so in the terms used by their subjects: precision, accuracy, replicability.[5] Yet this language is curiously ahistorical, in that each generation tends to claim some such virtue as an attainable goal and then, essentially by fiat, claims to have attained its own version of it.

But how to write a more sophisticated history of error? Are there not so many potential ways things can go wrong in all empirical endeavor that any attempt to present them in an organized or systematized manner can only come to grief? Not if one consults any standard textbook or practitioner's account of the modern status of the physical constants (Petley 1985, 10). There we learn that all uncertainty about the legitimacy of the values of the constants may be divided into two categories: (1) random error and (2) systematic error, which corresponds to the modern distinction made between "precision"—the closeness with which measurements agree with one another—and "accuracy"—the closeness of measurements to their "true" value. The distinction, as one might expect, has something to do with the canons of statistics versus discrepancies between theory and evidence. Ideally, in the former category there exists an irremediable element of variance that cannot be completely banished, though it can be neutralized by statistical techniques like ordinary least squares; the latter category is conversely something that could be eliminated by dint of the diligence of the experimentalist or the theorist, again ideally in the limit. When systematic error has been vanquished, the conventional index of success is the finding that all that remains is a Gaussian distribution of reported results, justified by reputedly uncontentious limit theorems, which in turn yields to readily understood estimation techniques.

Giora Hon (1989, 476 et seq.) finds this all quite useless for the historian of error, if not positively misleading for the practitioner. He insists that "the dichotomy between systematic and random errors does not focus on the source of the error; rather, it examines the nature of the error by applying a mathematical criterion." In the sense that the distinction tells us nothing interesting about the potential sources of error, or indeed about the practices used for either eradicating or accommodating the error, he is certainly correct. There is also the further consideration that methods for justifying and ascertaining the Gaussian status of random error are preponderantly groundless by the standards of *fin-de-siècle* probability theory.[6] Yet contrary to Hon, there is a grain of truth in the distinction, which may provide the beginnings of an analysis of a history of error. The distinction between random and systematic error, taught in every introductory laboratory practicum, is a fair description of how the actors practically constitute the meaning of error and then allocate it to various "causes" as a prelude to rendering it harmless. The analogy, which is explicitly acknowledged in such standard terminology as "error budgets," is to the allocation of profits to various sequences of transactions. In this way of thinking, precision is to arbitrage as accuracy is to the actual final pattern of realized exchanges.

Let us begin our brief retrospective history with any practitioner's survey of suitably ancient fundamental physical constants—such as that found in, say, Petley (1985). On page 228 we find a table of the major laboratory measurements of the gravitational constant. Beginning in 1798 and until the 1870s these are few and far between. Petley reports standard deviations back to the beginning, starting with Cavendish in 1798 and Reich in 1837. Or take the determinations of the velocity of light on pages 56–57. Values there date back to Römer in 1676, but again they are few before the 1870s, with no standard deviations reported before then. Without wishing to impugn Petley's tables (for, after all, his first interest is in metrology, not history), the few occasions when standard deviations are reported before the 1870s are dubious. For instance, recourse to his cited texts reveals that whereas extreme values of relevant variables are reported, individual observations are not; all we are tendered is a "best" or "mean" value. Therefore no legitimate statistical "error" is reported, nor can one be extracted from these early experimental reports. A similar problem arises with Römer's determination of the speed of light, once the historical context is taken into account (van Helden 1983). Indeed, it would be extremely difficult to form any independent opinion concerning the nature or extent of quantitative errors in any of these texts, for while we are tendered the seeming minutiae of endlessly described apparatus, the delicate "corrections" and attentions required, and protestations of the diligent patience of the experimenter, it would be effectively impossible to compare the outcomes to roughly contemporary experiments, much less to modern determinations of the "same" constant.[7] So the distinction between precision and accuracy cannot be carried back into the earlier history of the physical constants—at least not before 1870 or so.

If there is one thing which sets apart the eighteenth-century notion of error from the complex of practices that came afterward, it is that error was almost always associated exclusively with the virtues (or shortcomings) of the individual experimenter. As one contemporary put it: "Everything Sir Isaac Newton handled became Demonstration" (quoted in Gooding, Pinch, and Schaffer 1989, 99). The central icon of the process of measurement inherited from the Enlightenment is that of the experimenter as engaged in an unmediated, asocial encounter with nature, even though this assumptions contradicts all the social technologies involved with the institution of an "experimental form of life" (Shapin and Schaffer 1985). "The historical rhetoric of solitude typically signified a series of normatively patterned disengagements from specific institutions or sectors of society . . . solitude was often an intensely public pose, intended to express an evaluation of the society from which the isolate represented himself to be disengaged" (Shapin 1991, 195). When the savant returned from his private communion with nature, his own virtue and reputation were thought to be the primary guarantors of truth or error. His act of communion, like the faith that often underwrote it, possessed a private, ineffable, mystical dimension that would not bear too close scrutiny, especially given the tensions between science and religion. Thus physical inquiry was a "calling" to which many responded but for whom few were chosen by nature to bestow her secrets. "Great exactitude and a spirit of order—these are the principal requirements of the physicist who devotes himself to these sorts of observations" (Cotte quoted in Frängsmyr, Heilbron, and Rider, eds., 1990, 166). Error itself was regarded as too amorphous and polymorphous to display any structural order in its multifarious manifestations. The central point is that this ethos of exactitude is a matter of vigilance and sensibility—rarely a communal phenomenon and not inherent in the observations themselves. From our present perspective, the conflation of error with personal virtue is an artifact of the necessarily *asocial* character of measurement in the early modern era: in other words, quantitative constants were not yet treated as connected one with another, and therefore could not be policed.

This extreme personification of error explains many of the curious aspects of eighteenth-century experimental reports and protocol statements that so perturb more modern observers, often expressed in such comments as "Precision and reliability, in fact, did not trouble early eighteenth-century natural philosophers" (T. Feldman, quoted in Frängsmyr, Heilbron, and Rider, eds., 1990, 148); "In eighteenth-century quantitative science no need was felt for a theory of errors as a vehicle for the discussion of discrepancies between data and the proposed laws describing them" (Tiling 1973, 56); or "The physicists and chemists of the eighteenth century, unlike the astronomers and mathematicians, did not find it imperative to make use of very great accuracy in their measurements" (Daumas 1963, 430). For instance, there was a tendency to report not more than one or perhaps two trials of experiments, even while openly admitting that they were extracted from a much larger sequence of trials. As Newton once wrote of his optical investigations: "The historicall narration of these experiments would make a discourse too tedious & confused & therefore I shall lay down the *Doctrine* first and then, for its examination, give you an instance or two of the *Experiments*, as a specimen of the rest" (quoted in Gooding, Pinch, and Schaffer 1989, 68).

The doctrine of *experimentum crucis* was itself an artifact of this asocial regime, intended to convey efficiently the distilled insight of the savant in illustrating the discovery, which would be validated by witnesses of impeccable credentials. The extirpation of error was something best done alone and in private, although of course disputes in public could not be altogether avoided. Hence we observe a special social practice attuned to operate in a fundamentally asocial structure of quantitative measurement.

The watershed in our prospective history of error was the deconstruction of the convention that the lone individual was morally and intellectually responsible for its extirpation. The new history of "objectivity" has made us aware of the extreme confusion and lack of specificity in our own uses of the term; it has also stressed the profound changes in the early nineteenth century of the various referents of the status of the objective (Daston 1992). The rise of the aperspectival connotation of objectivity in the early nineteenth century was intimately bound up with changes in the social structures of science, as well as with the reconstitution of the category of quantitative error. The expansion of scientific communities tended to undermine earlier presumptions of personal acquaintance and contact with a small number of competent researchers in any single area. As the experimenter came increasingly to depend critically on the results of strangers for quantitative inputs and inspirations, the ideal of the interchangeable observer and the "view from nowhere" came to dominate the earlier moral economy of the laboratory. In place of simply conveying what was known about a measurement, it became incumbent on experimental reports to somehow convey what was *not* known (Olesko 1991, 139). But of equal importance, the network of theoretical terms began to attain a critical state of connectedness, whereby "identical" numbers might be reached by several methods. All of this had far-reaching implications for the conceptualization of error.

Three manifestations of this depersonalization of measurement led jointly, over the course of the nineteenth century, to the systematization of quantitative error: the spread of ordinary least squares as a research technique for the reduction of data; the promulgation of the notion of a "personal equation" of error; and the drive toward metrological standards. With respect to a history of error, it should become apparent that the concerted construction and maintenance of invariant standards and the circulation of representatives among laboratories certainly helped to break down the earlier reliance on an unmediated personal confrontation with nature, as well as to bring home the significance of personal frailty in the reproduction of such basic entities as the units of mass, time, and length. Charles Babbage's proposal for a compendium of the "constants of Nature" in 1856 was merely the first glimmer of a realization that the contemporaneous codification of standards in trade among nations might also be prudent, if not inescapable, among laboratories.

Hence by 1870 the problem of transpersonal error in precision laboratory measurement was no longer avoidable; it is only at this point in history that the distinction between systematic and random error was regularly made explicit, and the derivative distinction between precision and accuracy thus became uncontentious. This shift was instantiated in many activities and aspects of physical science. First, as noted in our discussion of Petley (1985) above, after about 1870 we actually start to get multiple readings of precision measurements commonly reported in individual published papers, so that the authors (or for that matter we historians) can calculate standard errors of estimated physical constants of a specific vintage. Graphical presentation of experimental results becomes a standard rhetorical trope, attesting to an ethic of candidness with regard to error. This same period witnessed the rise of the physics teaching laboratory in the British and American pedagogical contexts (Gooday 1990; Olesko 1988); and much of what was taught within the practicum was the correct protocol to separate out systematic from random error to the extent then thought possible.

The next landmark in this prospective history of error is the work of the hero of modern metrology (but not yet of any recent histories of physics) Raymond Thayer Birge (Helmholz 1990; Petley 1985, 153; Cohen, Crowe, and Dumond 1957, 105). His major achievement was single-handedly to create the role of the meta-analyst in atomic physics and therefore to make more explicit what had until his efforts been merely latent: the ineluctable social character of error and thus precision. While primarily remembered for his discovery of the isotope carbon 13, Birge's main contributions to physics were his talent for reevaluating the experimental reports of others, his appreciation of the (almost Peircian) implications of statistical practices, and his bold willingness to challenge some of his most famous contemporaries in experimental physics. His critical review of the physical constants (Birge 1929) was the first to examine the relationship of the entire constellation of numbers (as then understood) to the errors reported by their individual assayers. His reconsideration of the relevance of least squares in estimating structural relations between constants and across experimenters (Birge 1932) led to the graphical analysis of error bars and what are now called Birge ratios and Birge-Bond diagrams (Petley 1985, 296, 304). Birge ratios compared standard errors between experimenters' reports with errors reported within individual experiments, while Birge-Bond ratios became used in a statistical technique of fitting the "best" configuration of individual constants, given some imposed constraints. Birge ratios will occupy pride of place in the section entitled "Quantitative Indexes of the Social Construction of Error," below.

While these might appear to be dry, technical considerations, in practice they brought to light the deeper problems of defining errors of measurement. As Cohen, Crowe, and Dumond (1957, 104) admitted, it is not generally the concern of the individual experimentalist "to enquire how *consistent* the overdetermined set is. . . . Aside from the exercise of vigilance in the experiments themselves, this test of consistency is in fact the only safeguard we possess against systematic errors." The distinction between systematic and random error had been initially intended to demarcate those discrepancies that were the responsibility of the analyst from those residua to be tamed by statistics; but once statistical constructions of error became ensconced, they tended to usurp the causal character of the "systematic" residual. As Birge himself noted: "We never know the *true* errors of individual measurements. We know only their deviations from some calculated average value. Hence we can only state an estimate of probable error . . . and a corresponding estimate of the odds to be attached to the stated measure of uncertainty" (Birge 1957, 61). But in such a regime the physical constants became the product of averages of averages of averages—the Russian doll as an act of measurement, with personal responsibility for the extirpation of error grown ever more diffuse and difficult to isolate with each subsequent revelation. "But although my original object was thus merely to bring about *consistency* in the field, I have, as a result of such detailed recalculation, occasionally come across serious errors in the published reduction of the data. . . . Naturally I am both surprised and shocked at such discoveries, and I am often placed in a most embarrassing position. But the only point I am making now is that it seems necessary, in all serious work of a critical nature, to take nothing for granted. In fact, the great complaint of everyone who attempts to do such work is that the average investigator—to be sure, under pressure from the editor—fails to include sufficient detailed observational material in his published paper to make even possible a valid recalculation of his results" (Birge 1945, 64).

In this regime it made more sense for someone not embroiled in any specific experimental protocol or laboratory to oversee the work of averaging, to provide an external review of possible systematic errors, a critical view of the publishing practices of the relevant outlets, and a survey of all potential interconnections. This of course just rephrases the point made above about the absence of any plausible construction of laissez-faire based on individual self-interest. As Birge observed, "It is really difficult for one who has not worked in the field to visualize the maze of interconnections that exists between the general physical constants" (Birge 1945, 63). What was missing was the person who would sketch out the measurement graph, inspect it for connectedness, and gauge the discrepancies along its multiple paths. Hence Birge's innovation of the persona of the meta-analyst—or better, the "scientific arbitrageur"—and the relatively open acknowledgment of the social character of the final numbers inscribed in the reference tables.

Birge's genius was to realize that far from being a glorified anthologist, the meta-analyst had the job of actively supervising the attribution of error throughout the interconnected network of constants (as in figure 1), doggedly imposing consistency in the teeth of error. In his survey of 1929, he suggested that the metrologist begin with those constants least dependent on all the others and most "solid" in his estimation, selecting a path through the subsequent constants that was predicated on fairly accepted conversion factors and auxiliary constants, compounding the least statistical error along the way. This might end up being a thankless task, given the need to deflate egos not accustomed to having their laboratories turned upside down by outsiders. In this regard Birge was brazen, reserving especially sharp criticism for Robert Millikan's oil drop experiment, among others.[8] But even this procedure did not result in a unique set of final values, prompting Birge in the 1930s to research further techniques for minimizing overall statistical error, as well as expository techniques such as plotting error bars and calculating Birge ratios to render error more explicit. Yet the more attention was lavished on error, the more apparent it became that the distinction between systematic and random error was persistently compromised. In one of the major fruits of meta-analysis, the exposure to the light of day of the estimation of random error opened up the possibility that there might be yet further systematic patterns to such previous attributions.

The story of Millikan's determinations of the charge of the electron (e) provides one illustration of the conundrum. Birge, working *only* from published data, made a number of criticisms of the reported value of e, which he claimed was "accepted without question by everyone, [with] no one else even attempt[ing] similar work of comparable precision" (Birge 1957, 43). Initially noting an inconsistency between values of e derived from x-ray crystal diffraction and Millikan's oil drops, he tended to attribute the discrepancy to use of an incorrect auxiliary constant for the viscosity of air. Further digging revealed that Millikan had also used discrepant units of voltage, and that he had derived a slope estimate from a freehand plot and not least squares, thus revealing that his "error" estimate was relatively subjective and not dependent on statistical calculation. Recourse to Millikan's laboratory notebooks, an option not open to Birge, has revealed even more discrepancies in patterns in the treatment of error. As described by Holton (1978), Millikan's earliest published work on water droplets assigned subjective ratings of validity to braces of observations. By the time of the oil drop experiments, Millikan had learned the hard lesson of impersonal statistical rhetoric in his writing; but it did not appreciably alter his private behavior in the laboratory. There he regularly dismissed events that would have implied nonintegral units of charge, not including them in his final error estimates. Holton regards this tendency as illustrating the theory dependence of observation, since if free quarks were thought to exist, then one would be on the lookout for fractional charges. While quarks could not have been imagined before the fact, the existence of fractional charges was advocated by the Austrian contemporary Felix Ehrenhaft, who, although going so far as to reprocess Millikan's published data, did not have his own findings taken into account by Birge and others. From our own vantage point, this episode highlights not so much older Kuhnian notions of incommensurability as much as the pervasive adulteration of reports of "random" error by unspecified systematic components. All Birge's meticulous care and concern over air viscosity and international voltage units could still have been for naught, swamped by the systematic effect of unreported selection on the part of the original investigators.

The ultimate implication of the modern explicit rendering of error practices is to realize that the uniform approach of the physical constants to some invariant asymptote is itself a myth. Not to suggest that Birge ever doubted the palpable reality of the physical constants, he certainly developed nevertheless a shrewd appreciation for anomalies in the patterns of error attributions toward the end of his life (Birge 1957, 51): "The tendency of a series of experimental results, at a certain epoch, to group themselves around a certain value raises a very interesting psychological question." That question, rephrased in modern terms, is: To what extent does the experimenter fight the systematics until he or she gets the "right" answer? This is now known as the problem of "intellectual phase locking" or (following Allan Franklin) the "bandwagon effect." Before the advent of meta-analysis and its calculation of Birge ratios, and the whole panoply of error analysis, this problem could never even have been isolated in the act of quantitative measurement of physical constants, so in that sense it is a problem characteristic of the late twentieth century. But from an alternative perspective, it is the same old problem of the sociology of knowledge—namely, how findings come to be stabilized in a community of inquirers.

The bandwagon effect is common knowledge among practicing metrologists (Youden 1972; Langenberg and Taylor 1971; Petley 1985; Rosenfeld 1975, 581; Franklin 1990, 135); and it should be made better known among historians and philosophers of science. Briefly, it is the tendency of individual estimates of physical constants plotted chronologically to bunch together in certain eras, then to jump outside previous error bound estimates, only to cluster within the new range for another indeterminate length of time. This behavior violates almost every assumption buttressing the use of statistics in assessing measurement error; however, it is entirely consistent with the practical blurring of the distinction between systematic and random error described above. Practicing metrologists have commented on this: "One has to remember that some errors are random for one person and systematic for another. . . . It is not possible for one person to perform every single experiment to prepare his own determination of something. One has to take other people's results. So if one uses those results and they are the same all the time, they are systematic to this particular investigation" (Vigouroux, quoted in Langenberg and Taylor 1971, 524). Yet combining this observation with the knowledge that everyone's results are jointly and severally dependent on everyone else's in a simultaneous manner, we can imagine a situation where very small changes somewhere in the web of estimated constants can shift the entire structure discretely and discontinuously. And far from being a hypothetical possibility, metrologists are also aware that this shift has actually occurred in the past and, more important, do not find it daunting or distressing that it has. "No cry of anguish was heard from the general scientific community when it was discovered in 1967, as a result of the Josephson effect measurement of $2e/h$, that many of the previously accepted values of the constants would have to be changed between 20 and 100 ppm (four to five times their assigned [standard] errors)" (Taylor, quoted in ibid., 496).

In summary, this historical sketch of the estimation of the physical constants has been one of more and more elaborate institutions and social structures for producing and allocating quantitative error. Meta-analysis is itself a thriving industry. For example, the Particle Data Group at Berkeley—the final arbiter of numerical characteristics of subatomic particles—throws out roughly 40 percent of all experimental reports before reporting a preferred estimate of a measured constant (Rosenfeld 1975, 578). Many laboratories engaged in precision work now internalize this process by producing their own "error budgets," allocating error bars to individual components of any multi-tiered experiment (Mackenzie 1990, 267; Cartwright 1989, 68).[9] Just as economists have long wondered why large firms often internalize various functions that might potentially have been performed by "the market," a looming problem in science studies will be to plumb the reasons why some laboratories in the age of Big Science now manage to perform some of their meta-analysis in-house.

It is no accident that the bureaucratization of error audits spreads in tandem with the bureaucratization of scientific inquiry. For instance, the Defense Department is at present the largest employer of metrologists in the United States; the ohm now follows the barrel of the gun (O'Connell 1993). Political worries about the appearance of accountability and fraud in the era of Big Science have threatened to superimpose yet another layer of oversight on the existing error attribution process, only this time at the level of congressional subcommittee investigations or judicial intervention. *Science* magazine and the Sunday tabloids now endeavor to take sides in public accusations of shoddy laboratory protocols. Sociologists and risk analysts have even been getting into the act of late, subjecting the "subjective" probability estimates of measurement error to the traditions of decision science (Henrion and Fischoff 1986). There is no end in sight to the evolution of novel social processes of intervention in the interests of stabilizing error.

Quantitative Indexes of the Social Construction of Error

One of the advantages of a mathematical description of the economics of error arbitrage is that it not only suggests a diachronic account of the history of error but also provides a synchronic set of indexes of the status of error arbitrage both within and between sciences. The quantitative measure of greatest simplicity in this tradition is the one already pioneered by the meta-analysts—namely, the Birge ratio. The purpose of the Birge ratio is to provide a quick diagnostic comparison of the consistency of a field's own assessment of its success in taming error with the assessment of the outsider examining its published reports—in other words, the relative magnitude of internal and external consistency of measurements (Petley 1985, 304). Suppose that in some empirical endeavor of interest each experiment reports an estimated value X_i of some relevant constant and an estimated standard error σ_i. Let us collate a number N of individual published experiments in the particular science claiming to estimate the same constant, construct the mean of their estimates $\bar{X}$, and use that to define a value of the external error consistency as:

$$\sigma_E = \left[\sum_{i=1}^{N} (X_i - \bar{X})^2 / \sigma_i^2 \right] \left[(N-1) \sum_{i=1}^{N} (1 / \sigma_i^2) \right]^{-1}$$

If one then defines as σ^* the sum of the reciprocals of the individually estimated standard errors, then the Birge ratio is defined by $B = \sigma_E / \sigma^*$. When $B = 1$, the assessment of error bars within experiments could readily account for the distribution of errors in the network of constants of estimates of X between experiments; or in our economic language, error is being successfully arbitraged between constants. However, if B is very much greater than unity, then one or more experiments have severely under-

Table 1. Birge Ratios for Physical Constants

Constant	Dates	B	N[a]
Speed of light	1875–1958	1.42	27
Gravitational	1798–1983	1.38	14
Magnetic moment proton	1949–67	1.44	7
Fine structure[b]		2.95	24
Fine structure[c]		1.26	14
Muon lifetime	1957–80	3.28	10
Charged pion mass	1957–80	2.23	10
Lambda mass	1957–80	4.34	10
Lambda lifetime	1957–80	2.72	27
Sigma lifetime	1957–80	1.62	16
Omega mass	1957–80	0.86	11

Sources: Upper panel Henrion and Fischoff 1986, 794; lower panel Hedges 1987, 447.
[a] Number of studies estimating value of constant.
[b] "High accuracy" measurements of inverse fine structure constant. No dates given.
[c] "Low accuracy" measurements of inverse fine structure constant.

estimated the uncertainty surrounding the value of X, or else the presumption of joint independence between experimental determinations may be violated. In either case the meta-analyst uses the diagnostic to search out sources of inter-experimenter inconsistency. In our economic terminology, there are profits to be made by eliminating some experiments or else by re-estimating the magnitude of some of the network of constants or, most drastically, by reconfiguring the entire theoretical network.[10]

Metrologists regularly make use of Birge ratios in their daily endeavors; it is my contention that Birge ratios should also be a part of the tool kit of the sociologist of science. To show how they might be used in science studies, I shall reproduce a few collections of Birge ratios reported in greater detail elsewhere and then draw out a few social implications of their relative magnitudes. The fields chosen for comparison are modern physics, modern experimental psychology, and modern neoclassical economics.

In Table 1 we have two samples of Birge ratios, one for the fundamental physical constants over longer periods and one for some more recent sub-atomic constants over much shorter periods. What first jumps out at the novice is that most Birge ratios in physics exceed unity. This result would seem counterintuitive, except for the considerations already broached above. To recap, inconsistencies always exist in any densely connected network of quantitative constants, and no individual experimenter can effectively personally allocate the error across the net. Moreover, quantitative error itself has changed in epistemic significance over longer stretches of time, in no small part because of historical changes in institutions, so no single inter-

Table 2. Birge Ratios for Psychological Measurements

Subject	B	N
Sex/spatial perception	1.64	62
Sex/spatial visualization	1.27	81
Sex/verbal ability	4.09	11
Sex/field articulation	1.75	14
Open ed./reading	5.87	19
Open ed./math achievement	2.73	17
Open ed./school attitude	2.16	11
Open ed./self-concept	1.39	18

Source: Hedges 1987, 449.

pretation could be legitimately attached to reported error over time. And then, more recently, there is the bandwagon effect, which would tend to violate the independence of experimenter reports presumed by the Birge ratio. In economic terms, arbitrage opportunities are always present in precision measurement; it is only a question of their greater or lesser magnitude. Thus Birge ratios should be considered a comparative device, indicating rough orders of magnitude of quantitative disagreement.

Our second brace of Birge ratios (table 2), compiled by a psychologist, reports results for a set of quantities deemed legitimate constants by the relevant experimental community. Again we observe that the preponderance of Birge ratios exceeds unity. While a few ratios are above four, by and large one might claim that the magnitude of "agreement" in psychology was roughly comparable to that in physics, which was indeed the interpretation of the compiler of the statistics (Hedges 1987). Before psychologists embark on a round of hearty self-congratulations, however, it is imperative to recall that many things can account for low Birge ratios, and that one should not confuse low ratios with unqualified empirical success. Nevertheless, this finding is significant for science studies, since it does call into question an often implicit hierarchical ranking of the sciences.

Table 3 reports Birge ratios from some of my own work on the empirical practices of post-1945 neoclassical economists. (The underlying data and sources are documented in an appendix that is available on request.) It should be stressed at the outset that these "constants" are not the product of controlled experimentation, but rather the output of econometric statistical packages. The relationship of econometrics to controlled experimentation has been a contentious issue throughout its brief history; but many economists believe that their statistical devices are an adequate substitute for controlled experimentation.[11] Here let us take those beliefs as a given, simply so as to be able to report on their own practices with regard to the attribution

A Visible Hand in the Marketplace of Ideas   189

Table 3. Birge Ratios for Economics

Model	N	Years	Birge
U.S. money demand elasticity	9	1971–88	49.66
UK money demand elasticity	7	1971–91	73.34
Purchasing power parity, 1920s FF/$	6	1973–88	3.14
U.S. import income elasticity	14	1974–90	29.87
U.S. import price elasticity	10	1974–90	5.49
U.S. export income elasticity	13	1963–90	24.90
U.S. export price elasticity	9	1963–90	4.89
Employment-output elasticity, U.S. mfg.	6	1967–74	22.70
Male labor supply	5	1971–76	1.26
Welfare spell length and race	5	1986–92	2.23

Source: Available on request.

and arbitrage of error. We observe that Birge ratios in economics are orders of magnitude above those generally found in physics and psychology, if we accept the values reported in tables 1 and 2. It seems that there may exist a myriad of unexploited opportunities for error arbitrage within the community of neoclassical empirical economists.

This seeming divergence of the amount of agreement among physicists, psychologists, and economists has many causes, most of which can be traced to their divergent histories. Clearly justice cannot be done to that inquiry here; the theory of error arbitrage presented herein is intended as a prelude to a research program in science studies, not its culmination. However, there is one very salient reason for this pattern that is germane to the thesis of this chapter. As I have argued, it is very unlikely that a laissez-faire pattern of arbitrage would successfully stabilize the empirical measurement of quantitative constants, because no one is personally motivated to accumulate the results of arbitrage—namely, the error units themselves. This is the most striking way in which the conventional market differs from the process of error arbitrage. The primary reason why both physics and psychology display distinctly lower Birge ratios than economics does is that *they have institutionally acknowledged that fact*: at some juncture in the twentieth century, both managed to institute disciplinary structures of meta-analysis both to foster and to enforce the reconciliation of error attributions on the part of individual experimentalists. Physicists have their particle data groups, and psychologists have a special journal and the subdiscipline of meta-analysis. The empirical economists have nothing comparable.

Here is where the history and sociology of science reenter the metanarrative with a vengeance. Why do economists not acknowledge the problem of which the astronomical Birge ratios are a symptom? The short answer is that neoclassical economics is a peculiar species of social theory that has its own special problems of reflexivity. The standard Walrasian general equilibrium tradition is a theory that claims to describe how a market works to reconcile individual desires and activities as if by an invisible hand, without the intervention of any conscious external agency. Many, though not all, neoclassical economists thus imbibe a deep skepticism toward the claims of government to be capable of allocating resources according to any standards of efficiency or welfare. Indeed, some psychological researchers have claimed that one result of socialization in the economics profession is a pronounced antipathy toward social cooperation (Frank, Gilovich, and Regan 1993). Economists, not surprisingly, have also been among the most serious advocates of applying their theory reflexively to themselves, regarding their discipline as a "free market of ideas" (Hands 1994c). Thus any movement to set up an agency devoted to meta-analysis has been blocked by a vocal coalition as the encroachment of Big Brother on their academic freedom, an attitude very different from that which prevails in physics and psychology. In other words, because of their social ideology, neoclassical economists (or at a minimum, their econometric practitioners) remained mired in the asocial structures of measurement which physics experienced in the seventeenth century.

I shall close this survey on what may seem a note of irony. In this chapter I claim that a model of arbitrage taken from one version of economics could help us better understand the process of stabilizing quantitative measurement in all the sciences. Yet upon deployment and elaboration of this model, it was discovered that economics itself was an extreme outlier in the lack of agreement in its attempts at precision measurement and attempts at stabilization of its quantitative empirical practices. Is there not here also some sort of reflexive problem? Not if we insist that the theory of arbitrage (which, by the way, is not an integral part of the neoclassical school) is a generic theory governing the imposition of an algebraic structure on a heterogeneous network. The reason why economic metaphors seem so helpful in understanding the theory of arbitrage is probably a historical accident: the theory evolved first in the economic sphere and only later was applied to other realms of quantitative activity. That the theory can be turned into an auto-critique of economics, rather than represent another imperial triumph by the most imperious of the social sciences, should stand as one of the strongest arguments in its favor. It may also illustrate one component of an economics of science which does not depend for its theoretical inspiration upon orthodox neoclassical theory.

Part Four
Is Econometrics an Empirical Endeavor?

9
Brewing, Betting, and Rationality in London, 1822–1844: What Econometrics Can and Cannot Tell Us about the Historical Actors

Why Beer Should Interest Economic Historians as Well as Joe Sixpack

It has been inadequately noted just how much changing fashion in neoclassical economics has prompted the ebb and flow in the fascination that economic historians have with particular industries (Cannadine 1984). For instance, now that the orthodoxy has shifted to an image of the economic agent as information processor (Mirowski 2002), it becomes possible to recast the "Industrial Revolution" as the advent of the "knowledge economy" (Mokyr 2002). An earlier vintage of economic historian, perhaps more familiar with the practical workaday physics and chemistry of commodity production, and more concerned with the institutional structures of capitalism, looked to what now might be considered more prosaic industries, such as brewing (Mathias 1959), to explain the causes and consequences of British growth.

As it so happens, there are some very good reasons to look to breweries for exemplars of technological and institutional innovations characterizing the British industrial revolution. On the institutional side, it is fairly clear that under the force of circumstances, brewing was one of the earliest sectors to innovate many of the organizational structures we now associate with the large-scale corporation. Because of the nature of their product and the exigencies of the excise, breweries were induced to keep track of many far-flung purchases and sales of relatively small magnitudes, as well as to concentrate upon supervision of the network of tied pubs. Hence we find in brewing one of the earliest well-articulated accounting systems, including attempts to systematically attribute desegregated costs to activities, of any British industry in this era. Moreover, we also find one of the earliest appearances of a centralized hierarchical management structure, often associated with the railroads by Alfred Chandler and other business historians. On the technological front, it would be a mistake to regard brewing as a backward or unprogressive industry. As Mathias explains, breweries were in the forefront of combining the new physics of heat with problems in chemistry and biology; they were also among the earliest to adapt the steam engine to their production requirements. While it has become commonplace to assert that the steam engine owed very little to the science of physics (Cardwell 1971), it is a Mancunian brewer, James Joule, who is often given credit for the founding of thermodynamics upon the "discovery" of the conservation of energy. Indeed, his apparatus was an only slightly modified device in common use in breweries of the time (Mirowski 1989b, 40–43). For all these reasons, British breweries should be considered among the most forward-looking and rationalized firms of the British industrial revolution.

It should then come as no surprise that given British breweries' record of early rationalizing innovations in these spheres, their surviving business archives are among the best of any records dating from the eighteenth century and the early nineteenth. And of those, one of the most comprehensive and detailed business archives in the whole of British eighteenth- and early-nineteenth-century economic history is that of the brewing firm Truman, Hanbury and Buxton, housed at the Greater London Record Office. It is one symptom of the biases of the Cliometric approach to history (which harbors a muted suspicion toward business records) that this trove has remained largely ignored in the literature of British economic history, with the exception of some few direct comments by Peter Mathias in his magisterial history of eighteenth-century British brewing, the survey history of British brewing by Gourvish and Wilson (1994), and a largely uninformative vanity history published by the firm of Truman's itself (Anonymous 1959).

A very sketchy outline of the firm's history will help set the stage for our subsequent econometric inquiry. The Black Eagle Street brewhouse predated the involvement of the Truman family, which apparently began when Joseph Truman senior acquired it in 1679. His son Benjamin Truman so expanded the brewery that in 1760 it was the third-largest in London. After Benjamin's death in 1780, James Grant (d. 1788) conducted the business, although ownership was held in trust for Benjamin's great-grandsons Henry (1777–1847) and John Truman Villebois. In 1789 Sampson Hanbury (1769–1835) acquired James Grant's share; he managed the business until roughly 1827. His nephew, Thomas Fowell Buxton (1786–1845), joined the firm in 1811, immediately installing the firm's first Boulton and Watt steam engine; while Thomas and Robert Pryor (1778–1839), proprietors of the recently absorbed Proctor's brewhouse, were made partners in 1816. In 1821 Robert Hanbury (1798–1884) was made a restricted second-class partner, though he was increasingly responsible for the day-to-day operation of the business. By dint of aggressive acquisitions and expansion, Truman's became London's second-largest brewer by 1820, at which juncture Thomas Butts Aveling (1783–1837), the head clerk of the concern, married a Truman granddaughter; he became a restricted partner in 1825. In 1830 the beer duty was abolished, making it much easier to start up a pub; contemporaneously, urban tastes shifted from porter to lighter ales. The other big Victorian breweries— Barclay Perkins, Whitbread, Meaux Read—were slow to adjust to the new circumstances; but Truman's directors were more sure-footed, and by 1850 the firm managed to become London's (and Britain's) largest integrated conglomerate of breweries, pubs, and extender of small-scale commercial credits. Truman's continued to grow and prosper and absorb other breweries until the twentieth century.

The immediate motivation for our present interest is a fascinating memo book in the Truman archives (B / THB / C / 242) at the Greater London Record Office entitled "Précis of Hops & Barley, 1822–1880."[1] One early custom of the British brewing industry was the periodic formal closing of the account books at what was called a "Rest Dinner" for the partners and head clerks. These were openly festive occasions, where prodigious quantities of the company product were consumed, and talk regularly turned to the agricultural vicissitudes of the two main ingredients of beer, barley (used to make malt) and hops (a flower used to stabilize and preserve the beer).[2] Since in the early nineteenth century malt and hops alone accounted for more than 60 percent of the cost of production, the fluctuations of hops and barley prices weighed much on the minds of the partners as they closed their books on another year. What set the Truman partners apart from other brewers is that they attempted to separate out their market prediction skills from other skills of management and organization with regard to their primary inputs. On the first quarto sheet of this memo book, a clerk wrote: "At our Rest Dinner in July 1822 whilst we were speculating on the probable prices of Barley & Hops for the coming Season, it was suggested and agreed to that at our future Annual, Rest Dinners each of us should put down in writing what we considered would be the price of Barley and Hops on the first Monday in January in the ensuing year . . . [Here the ground rules for the public report of the price were spelled out] . . . A Sweepstakes of one Sovereign each in Barley and Hops by each individual & those who were nearest the actual prices of the day to be the Winner." What follows is a continuous record of the prices wagered by each partner, the subsequent actual price, and the declared winner or winners for the years 1822–46. The partners must have understood the principle of extrapolation from prior trends, since inside the front cover, someone in a different hand had inscribed information from newspapers on prices of wheat and barley, along with comments on the state of the weather, for the years 1790–1837 (though the exact timing of this inscription cannot be discerned). One gets the impression that the competition was keen and spirited, for although the sum wagered was small for people of these means, a loose sheet included in the volume reveals that someone else, in yet a third hand, had drawn up an extensive table of actual and winning prices for the years 1822–40, with remarks on the spread of realized prices about the actual price, and an abstract of who among the partners had won for each wager on hops and barley a specified number of times. Given that what we have in this book is a time series of consistent bets on a relatively generic input price for a production process of which all the bettors had at least some control and oversight, this is a remarkable document.

One imagines that an imaginary representative Cliometrician, especially one of a rational expectations bent, would already be inwardly relishing the possibilities; and since until recently one often encountered many such real characters in the economics profession, that constitutes part of the motivation of our exercise. So much of modern Cliometric history, under the tutelage of orthodox neoclassicism, is taken up with questions of the supposed "rationality" of the historical actors or the "efficiency" of the market in a specific setting that it would seem almost natural to situate this archival treasure in that frame. However, the problem faced by many Cliometricians, be they concerned with the supposed efficiency of medieval open-field agriculture or the rebuttal of widespread impressions of the decline of late Victorian entrepreneurial capacity, is that the evidence is always at three or four removes from the original construction of the theoretical model. Much Cliometric work is predicated upon index numbers, often manufactured for other purposes, which inadequately capture the controversy at hand; or when the inquiry does deal with prices, there are no assurances that the data are representative of the exact sorts of market information faced by the actors. In particular, quantitative evidence is often cast in modern definitions presuming modern theories with little or no concern shown for the mentalities or capabilities characteristic of the denizens of the historical era in question. Even in the rational expectations literature of the 1970s and 1980s, when contemporaneous data were supposedly of so much higher quality than the data dealt with by historians, "tests" of the rational expectations hypothesis mostly made use of mean forecasts, and did not track the actual behavior of living, breathing individuals facing rational numbers. This persistent recurrence of aggregation over predictors is offered unapologetically, even though one of the supposed attractions of the orthodoxy is its solid grounding in methodological individualism. When recourse to survey data is had, there is generally no way to track the same individual through time or to ascertain who knows what, when, and how much about the presumed identity of the object of prediction or purchase. I myself have never seen a rational expectations test where real individuals have a chance to track two economic variates simultaneously through time (outside the racetrack or other leisure contexts), except perhaps in the experimental economics literature. So what we have here is an extremely rare bit of evidence.

Therefore, let us turn first to the sort of Cliometric exercise that a historian trained in a conventional economics department might be inclined to construct, patterned upon the practices of orthodox economics journals; and only then, afterward, return to the real history, the rough-textured narrative of these people's lives.

Econometrics and Rationality

The standard statistical procedure for addressing the question of the "rationality" of actors' expectations in a market where explicit forecasts have been recorded in a timely manner is to begin by comparing the forecasts and the realized values, here of actual prices. The initial low-tech approach, which has decided advantages in terms of intuitive appeal, is simply to plot the values of specified wagered price against actual realized price for each participant in the brewery Rest Dinner. At this early stage, it becomes apparent that some bettors had a harder time than others tracking the turns in prices: Thomas Buxton seems to have possessed the curiously useless ability to lead price movements of hops by a full year; Robert Pryor appears by contrast to have overestimated the price swings of hops; Tom Aveling, on the other hand, seems overly sanguine with regard to the smoothness of barley prices. In a quick geometric manner, we come to observe that different actors have distinct "signatures" in their betting behaviors, signatures which may very well be specific to a particular commodity without carrying over to a complementary commodity. Since the subtext of so much orthodox neoclassical theory is the quest to telegraph that people are fundamentally the "same" in their rational economic behavior, while supposedly simultaneously respecting their idiosyncrasies, it is salutary to get some rough empirical feel for the extent to which people have persistent marked differences in behavior which could potentially be turned to profit.

Undoubtedly our representative Cliometrician would be champing at the bit here, convinced that these casual observations lack the one attribute that Cliometrics has brought to the discipline, namely its self-consciously scientific approach. To a Cliometrician the point of the entire exercise should be to quantify and to "test" hypotheses, the better to bridge the gulf between the *Geisteswissenschaften* and the *Naturwissenschaften*. As one famous Cliometrician has written, "historians do not really have a choice of using or not using behavioral models . . . The real choice is whether those models will be implicit, vague, incomplete and internally inconsistent, as Cliometricians contend is frequently the case in traditional historical research, or whether the models will be explicit, with all relevant assumptions clearly stated, and formulated in such a manner as to be subject to rigorous empirical verification."[3] But a contemporary Cliometrician would not rest satisfied with these research guidelines, for just any behavioral "model" wouldn't do in the current climate; to write legitimate "economic history," one would further need to have recourse to a model which is sanctioned by the current theoretical orthodoxy in economics departments. It is this requirement, rather than any generic numeracy or familiarity with statistical technique, which has frightened off the vast bulk of practicing historians. But let us accept these constraints for the nonce, and see where this species of scientific history will lead us.

"Rationality," while not well and thoroughly documented within departments of economics, has in the recent past come to signify for neoclassicals some convex combination of no-arbitrage conditions, an "efficient markets" hypothesis, rational expectations, and whatever restrictions might be imposed by the canons of probability and the underlying price theory. This packet of doctrines has given rise to an accompanying set of statistical procedures, which in the 1980s diffused throughout the applied economics literature to such an extent that one might readily characterize it, with justice, as creating a *distinct genre* of journal article.[4] In 2003 two of the main advocates of this genre were awarded the Bank of Sweden (misleadingly dubbed "Nobel") prize in economics. The curious can consult a very nice survey article which covers many of the relevant statistical points (Jeong and Maddala 1991). It would seem, therefore, we have the makings of an exemplary Cliometric paper, bringing together a brace of accepted econometric techniques, an eminently orthodox theoretical model, and some antiquarian data, in order to now pose the inevitable question, "Were the Actors Rational?" We shall proceed to do just that in this section, although at a somewhat more leisurely pace than in the standard journal literature, to draw out the implications of this exercise for economic history and for "scientific empiricism" in general. The fruit of being a bit more explicit about the process of Cliometric research is to be able to insist that inductive research, like so much else in human history, is inexorably path-dependent.

The standard initial step in this literature is to calculate the difference between the predicted and actual prices, in order to discern whether there are any systematic patterns in errors of prediction. The justification for highlighting this variable is usually traced either to the rational expectations doctrine or to the efficient markets hypothesis: if errors are persistently made in a context where they can translate into immediate monetary gain or loss, then "rationality" would dictate that the actor either (a) change his or

Table 4. Bet Prices on Hops and Barley

Name	Bet Price, Hops		Bet Price, Barley	
	Mean	Stand. Dev.	Mean	Stand. Dev.
J. Villebois	−11.00	43.31	−2.40	6.83
H. Villebois	−8.62	37.37	−1.81	7.07
S. Hanbury	−18.76	51.12	−2.34	7.22
T. Buxton	−9.09	39.44	−0.79	5.77
T. Avelig	51.42	57.11	1.71	6.11
R. Hanbury	5.48	39.36	−1.88	6.15
R. Pryor	29.88	87.89	−1.79	6.64
E. Buxton	−5.00	17.81	3.45	5.97
A. Pryor	8.33	29.85	2.60	7.08

her behavior or (b) be eliminated from play by market penalties. Sometimes this justification is conflated with the postulate that the actors have the same model of the economy as the neoclassical analyst, a postulate to which we shall return shortly. In practice, one begins by examining the divergence of bets from realized prices, with the stipulation that these divergences should exhibit a mean of zero and be roughly uncorrelated through time for rational actors. In table 4, we present means and standard deviations of each actor's "errors" in bets made at the Truman rest dinners.

Once again we note some personal signatures of individual behavior. Some members of the partnership consistently underestimate the level of agricultural prices: the Villebois brothers, Sampson Hanbury, and Thomas Buxton. Others consistently overestimate their movements, like Tom Avelig, while still others show more mixed results. Everyone remains within one standard deviation of zero, which is the expected value at "rationality"; but for many, this is only because the spread of their errors is so large in the first place. Based on the time series plots of the errors (not included here), it seems highly likely that there is some temporal dependence and probably autocorrelation in many cases: for instance, with Richard Hanbury's barley bets. Another question, not often broached in the orthodox literature, is whether the divergences of each individual from the actual price are themselves correlated; in this instance it turns out that they are, with positive correlation coefficients in the 0.5 to 0.7 range. So these men, the proprietors of the most successful brewery in London in their era, were neither spot on target nor wildly wrong; in some ways they acted alike, but in others they displayed a tenacious individuality. The evidence so far is ambiguous. But we still have yet to deploy our formidable econometric armamentarium.

The next step would be to recast the hypothesis of rationality as one in

Table 5. Brewer Error Equations, 1822–1846

Barley

J. Villebois
$$\text{Price} = 27.7 + 0.25 \text{ JVILL} \qquad R^2 = .07$$
$$\quad\;\;\; (3.09) \quad (1.00) \qquad\qquad t = -2.86 \; n = 15$$

H. Villebois
$$\text{Price} = 27.5 + 0.27 \text{ HVILL} \qquad R^2 = .09$$
$$\quad\;\;\; (4.35) \quad (1.53) \qquad\qquad t = -4.13 \; n = 24$$

S. Hanbury
$$\text{Price} = 29.79 + 0.20 \text{ SHANB} \qquad R^2 = .07$$
$$\quad\;\;\; (2.68) \quad (0.62) \qquad\qquad t = -2.50 \; n = 13$$

T. Buxton
$$\text{Price} = 18.45 + 0.51 \text{ TBUXT} \qquad R^2 = .18$$
$$\quad\;\;\; (2.08) \quad (2.12) \qquad\qquad t = -2.00 \; n = 22$$

T. Aveling
$$\text{Price} = 22.11 + 0.37 \text{ TAVEL} \qquad R^2 = .07$$
$$\quad\;\;\; (1.56) \quad (1.01) \qquad\qquad t = -1.69 \; n = 14$$

R. Hanbury*
$$\text{Price} = 1.04 \text{ RHANB} \qquad R^2 = .07$$
$$\quad\;\;\; (30.79) \qquad\qquad t = 1.35 \; n = 25$$

R. Pryor
$$\text{Price} = 23.57 + 0.38 \text{ RPRYO} \qquad R^2 = .13$$
$$\quad\;\;\; (2.60) \quad (1.52) \qquad\qquad t = -2.44 \; n = 17$$

E. Buxton
$$\text{Price} = 1.09 \text{ EBUXT} \qquad R^2 = .52$$
$$\quad\;\;\; (23.62) \qquad\qquad t = 2.14 \; n = 12$$

A. Pryor*
$$\text{Price} = 1.07 \text{ APRYO} \qquad R^2 = .40$$
$$\quad\;\;\; (18.22) \qquad\qquad t = 1.20 \; n = 10$$

Hops

J. Villebois
$$\text{Price} = 53.17 + 0.71 \text{ JVILL} \qquad R^2 = .71$$
$$\quad\;\;\; (2.47) \quad (5.77) \qquad\qquad t = -2.25 \; n = 15$$

H. Villebois
$$\text{Price} = 29.02 + 0.86 \text{ HVILL} - 0.255\epsilon_{t-1} \qquad R^2 = .77$$
$$\quad\;\;\; (1.83) \quad (8.91) \qquad\qquad\qquad\qquad t = -1.36 \; n = 24$$

S. Hanbury*
$$\text{Price} = 1.12 \text{ SHANB} \qquad R^2 = .57$$
$$\quad\;\;\; (12.53) \qquad\qquad t = 1.36 \; n = 1$$

T. Buxton
$$\text{Price} = 34.85 + 0.83 \text{ TBUXT} \qquad R^2 = .75$$
$$\quad\;\;\; (1.93) \quad (7.83) \qquad\qquad t = -1.60 \; n = 22$$

T. Aveling
$$\text{Price} = 0.74 \text{ TAVEL} \qquad R^2 = .57$$
$$\quad\;\;\; (12.97) \qquad\qquad t = -4.35 \; n = 14$$

R. Hanbury
$$\text{Price} = 43.37 + 0.70 \text{ RHANB} \qquad R^2 = .84$$
$$\quad\;\;\; (3.64) \quad (11.10) \qquad\qquad t = -4.68 \; n = 25$$

R. Pryor
$$\text{Price} = 75.41 + 0.43 \text{ RPRYO} \qquad R^2 = .79$$
$$\quad\;\;\; (5.62) \quad (7.57) \qquad\qquad t = -9.82 \; n = 17$$

E. Buxton
$$\text{Price} = 24.90 + 0.86 \text{ EBUXT} - 0.51\epsilon_{t-1} \qquad R^2 = .96$$
$$\quad\;\;\; (2.64) \quad (19.69) \qquad\qquad\qquad\qquad t = -2.99 \; n = 12$$

A. Pryor*
$$\text{Price} = 0.91 \text{ APRYO} \qquad R^2 = .81$$
$$\quad\;\;\; (17.40) \qquad\qquad t = -1.60 \; n = 10$$

Asterisk (*) denotes candidate for "rational expectations." The t-statistic in parentheses refers to the estimated coefficient. The t-statistic under the R^2 reports the results of a test of the null hypothesis that the coefficient on each individual's bet variable = 1.0, that is, is unbiased.

which there is no systematic error in betting to conform to a regression model of a generic "rational" expectation. The standard practice is to posit a simple linear equation like:

$$\text{Actual Price} = \alpha + \beta \, \text{Bet} + \epsilon, \tag{1}$$

where $\epsilon \sim N(0, \sigma^2)$ and expected values in the case of rationality are $\alpha = 0$ and $\beta = 1$. The problem with this seemingly straightforward procedure is that while the null hypothesis is initially portrayed as reasonably sharp, the alternative hypothesis is in practice inordinately diffuse. This problem is paradigmatic of what is wrong with the entire rhetoric of "testing" in Neyman-Pearson econometrics, as we shall discuss below. Here the Cliometrician may opt to assume as a mandate the objective of presenting the "best" simple time series description of error behavior for each individual bettor which is as "close" to the above equation as possible; that is what is most frequently done in the literature, and that is what we present in table 5.

The joint restrictions on α and β may seem fairly stringent, and that impression is initially borne out by the results in our table. For the barley bets, only Robert Hanbury and Arthur Pryor pass the test with flying colors ; Edward Buxton does not simply because the estimated error variance is low enough to make it more likely according to the t-test that his $\beta > 1$. As for the hops betting, only Sampson Hanbury and Arthur Pryor pass the unbiasedness test. One does get a sense from the R^2 and residual diagnostics that barley prices were much harder to track than hops prices in this period. Thus if we halted our exercise right here, we would be left with the rather disconcerting conclusion that there was only one confirmed consistent *homo economicus* at the Truman breweries in this period, and further, as we shall see shortly, he was not a principal owner, nor even a partner in good standing.

But everyone knows that our dogged Cliometrician would not stop there: and should not. For no econometrician worth his or her salt takes the time and trouble to construct a data set, frame a hypothesis, and deploy statistical skills merely to ask a single one-shot yes-or-no question of the data. At the very least, it would seem reasonable to begin exploring why the result turned out as it did; and it would take superhuman self-denial not to be on the lookout for any auxiliary hypotheses which might readily overturn an unexpected result. In this case, our Cliometrician, a partisan of the neoclassical model, would most likely be distressed with the rather poor showing of our brewers, who after all were just about as successful in their economic calling as one could be in the nineteenth century, and, instead cast about for explanations which would preserve their "rationality."

One standard response of the disappointed econometrician is to look to the residuals for various diagnostic problems. But we have already encompassed that procedure in our local search for the "best" time series representation of equation (1). Indeed that is why both Henry Villebois and Edward Buxton have a first-order autocorrelation correction in their hops bet equations. However, even this description is not ultimately decisive, since no exhaustive search was performed in the time domain. Another option might be to explicitly model the error divergences in the time domain as VAR processes. For instance, if we designate the divergence of Robert Hanbury as DRH, then his barley bet errors can be modeled by the following vector autoregression, with t-statistics in brackets:

$$\text{DRH} = -2.80\,[1.42] - 0.45\,\text{DRH}_{-1}\,[2.36] + 0.38\,\epsilon_{-1}\,[2.08]. \qquad (2)$$

Various other individual divergences have similar autoregressive representations. But our Cliometrician would clearly not like the way this "diagnostic" was trending, since it is generally conceded in the rational expectations literature that temporal structure in errors of prediction is not congruent with the efficient markets hypothesis; someone should be punishing these people for their errors by making arbitrage profits from them. Indeed, our Cliometrician would probably choose not to report the above equation, since it contradicts the result reported in table 5 that Robert Hanbury was "rational" in his barley bets. If the Cliometrician instead tried to brush off the incongruity by suggesting that these bets were only a harmless game, whereas real business was business, that would effectively undercut any justification for writing the paper in the first place. Other possible "corrections" to estimates of equation (1) will be discussed shortly.

There are some other classes of econometric tests which are claimed to have a bearing upon the question of rationality: for instance, the entire "variance bounds" literature (discussed in Mirowski 1988). Very crudely, the idea behind a variance bounds test is that people's predictions of prices and other economic variates should actually be *smoother* than the realized series, predominantly because of random shocks which could in no way be foreseen beforehand. If, conversely, people's anticipations were seen to fluctuate more extremely than the historical realizations, this would call their rationality into question. Thus our Cliometrician might choose to rephrase the question away from the first moments of the bets, as in table 5, and toward their second moments; and the results are reported in table 6.

These results would surely perk up the flagging spirits of our Cliometrician. For here we not only pick up most of the same "rational actors" who were identified in table 5, but we have now also extended the evidence for "rationality" to ten out of eighteen cases. Of course, there are still a few blots on the record: just three people—Sampson Hanbury, Edward Buxton, and Arthur Pryor—qualify as consistently rational actors, and then there is the notable result that variance bounds seem easier to pass with barley than with hops. We have already commented that barley was apparently a more diffi-

Table 6. Variance Bounds Test

| Name | Var (P) > Var (Bet)? | |
	Hops	Barley
J. Villebois	no	no
H. Villebois	yes	no
S. Hanbury	yes	yes
T. Buxton	no	yes
T. Aveling	no	yes
R. Hanbury	no	yes
R. Pryor	no	no
E. Buxton	yes	yes
A. Pryor	yes	yes

cult agricultural price to predict, hence by definition its realized variance would tend to be large. Nevertheless, it is a good bet that our Cliometrician would stop here, write up these tabular results, and ship the whole thing off to the *Journal of Economic History*.

Yet the further addition of auxiliary hypotheses and the implied criticism of the practice of econometrics need not halt here. The most common reaction among those familiar with the variance bounds and unbiasedness literatures would be to recognize that the widespread rejections of rationality found elsewhere have led to a revanchist literature which finally settled upon generic non-stationarity of economic variates as the main reason for doubting all the above tests. This revisionism has led to a series of techniques for detecting what is now called "cointegration" of time series.[5] The idea behind cointegration is that if the time series which is to be predicted has a unit-root representation (namely $X_t = X_{t-1} + \epsilon_t$) then standard time series regression results are invalid, with OLS estimators biased downward. These observations have given rise to a large econometric literature concerning the estimation of presence of unit roots and subsequent estimation of whether two such unit root series are "cointegrated"; intuitively, whether the difference of the two time series might itself be represented as a unit root process, such that neither series wanders "too far" from the other. In some of the macro literature, tests for cointegration are often used synonymously with tests for "rationality"; though as some more judicious commentators have noted (Jeong and Maddala 1991, 432), this characterization of rational behavior does not even approach the level of concrete specification found in the unbiasedness tests above.

Notwithstanding these caveats, suppose our Cliometrician wishes to become known as second to none in keeping up with the snazziest developments in econometrics (or at least those thought snazzy by a previous generation). She therefore subjects the actual barley and actual hops prices to the augmented Dickey-Fuller test (Dickey, Jansen, and Thornton 1991) for the presence of unit roots. What she finds is that if the specification does not include a constant term, then neither price series has a unit root; but if a constant term is appended, then both do now appear to have a unit root representation. Since there is no theory-driven "estimation" going on here, in the sense that the Cliometrician has complete freedom to specify the shape of the "rational" representation, we predict a choice of the one most supportive of the non-stationary interpretation. The next step is to apply the same procedure to the time series of bets; but here the Cliometrician encounters the problem that most of the bets series are appreciably shorter than even those of the actual prices. However, since the bets by Robert Hanbury extend throughout the entire sample period, we can apply the Dickey-Fuller test there, and discover much the same results. Finally, the Dickey-Fuller test is run on the difference between the two series, with the curious outcome for hops that in contrast with the above cases, the unit root appears when the constant is absent. Our Cliometrician would probably report these results as supporting the hypothesis of rationality—again, probably without filling in all the details about the twists and turns of specification choices made along the way. Or perhaps these would be included in an appendix, but then the editor would want to remove them from the published version, because they are boring, and as we all know, resources are scarce.

I, myself, have not reported the cointegration "tests" here because they have a very tenuous claim to be sanctioned as legitimate in this context. First, they don't generally meet the standards of an orthodox test for rationality unless the expected values of prices minus bets are zero (unbiasedness) and the forecasting errors $P_t - B_t$ exhibit no serial correlation. In the case of Robert Hanbury, we have already demonstrated that neither condition holds for hops, and the latter condition is violated for barley. But there is a more profound econometric objection. The literature on cointegration arose in areas where very long time series were being used to test market efficiency, and the objection was then very legitimately raised that few economists would expect the relevant time series to be stationary over such long stretches of time. Indeed, the question of non-stationarity may only be legitimately posed in a statistical sense when time series data points number in the hundreds, and better yet the thousands. This problem has also arisen in the chaos literature (see chapter 12 below), where researchers have given up trying to answer whether economic series are chaotic because of a critical conceptual problem specific to economics: econometricians can get thousands of readings of financial asset prices, but only if they are willing to take them minute by minute (in which case the "deterministic" structure which

Table 7. Brewers' Wager Status

Name	Barley				Hops			
	N	Wins	Expec. Wins	W/E	N	Wins	Expec. Wins	W/E
J. Villebois	15	1	2.16	0.46	15	2	2.16	0.92
H. Villebois	24	5	4.0	1.25	24	3	4	0.75
S. Hanbury	13	4	1.85	2.16*	13	2	1.85	1.08
T. Buxton	22	5	3.5	1.42	22	4	3.5	1.14
T. Aveling	14	2	2	1.0	14	2	2	1.0
R. Hanbury	25	8	4.33	1.84	25	9	4.33	2.07*
R. Pryor	17	3	2.5	1.2	17	5	2.5	2.0
E. Buxton	12	2	2.47	0.74	12	4	2.47	1.61
A. Pryor	10	1	2.16	0.46	10	0	2.16	0.0

might be discovered there is inherently not very interesting), or else over very long time frames—say, monthly prices over centuries (in which case almost no one is willing to claim that the price actually refers to the "same thing"). In our humble little example, precisely what makes the data set so ideal for testing "rationality"—it refers to a consistent set of actual individuals making their bets on clearly identified generic commodities in a repeatable manner—also renders it impossible to ask any serious questions about non-stationarity. Therefore I doubt whether the cointegration tests have any meaning at all in this context.

So that, if I have not overlooked anything, is pretty much what a standard econometric paper based upon these archival materials would look like, should a Cliometrician have actually exploited this unusual source. However, luckily for us, there is one further significant bit of evidence which should be extracted from the archive and brought to bear on the econometric exercise. We know from the "Rest" books who was declared the winner of each wager by the gathered worthies. Now, if we assume that each player had an equal chance of winning in each bet in which he took part, and standardize for their times participating, we can compare the expected number of wins with actual experience.[6] This information is presented in table 7, with the last column expressing the ratio of actual wins to the expected number, as defined above. The expected value of this ratio should be unity, with excessive losers tending to zero and outstanding winners achieving two or above. The outcome was that Sampson Hanbury was far and away the most successful wagerer on barley, while Robert Hanbury and, to a slightly lesser extent, Robert Pryor were the most successful in wagering on hops.

This final table brings us to the second major thesis of this chapter: were the Cliometrician to write the paper we have outlined above, he or she would have made the elemental mistake of confusing neoclassical notions of rationality with economic success. For those who were far and away the best at winning wagers did not show up as "rational" in most of the econometric tests deployed; or to put it somewhat differently, the mechanical rationality characteristic of rational expectations has little or no relationship to the strategic rationality of outsmarting your economic competitors. Indeed, the whole point of rational expectations is to render other economic actors faceless and irrelevant, and to deny in the determination of present choice any role to history (even if only the pale and tepid version of history as the time series of past realizations).[7] But Sampson and Robert Hanbury were smarter than that, which is probably why they sequentially served as (in effect) the chief executive officers of the partnership (as revealed by the memo books B / THB / A / 129 and B / THB / B / 120). There is the further oddity that precisely when one of this duo is identified as "rational" by the initial regression analysis, it is the other who manages to dominate in cumulative wins. So in this very specific sense, if we had just stuck to the Cliometrics, we would have negated the historical content of this interesting episode, blurring the economically relevant differences of the actors in the name of "testing a well-defined hypothesis."

But there is another, deeper lesson to our exercise. The reason why the sequence of tests was spelled out in such detail above was to begin to reveal at the outset of the econometric inquiry the sequence of choices that the historian will face along the way. It is now well understood in the philosophy of science community that no one obeys the standard Neyman-Pearson sequence of "posit H_0 and H_A first; get the data; choose the uniformly most powerful procedure; then run the test," because such behavior would be irrational.[8] Instead, one always does "exploratory data analysis" (if one looks upon the practice favorably) or "data mining" (if one frowns upon it), because hypothesis formation and data construction are inextricable and always and everywhere contaminated.[9] What our Cliometric exercise shows is that in such a world, with enough persistence, I can get any outcome that I want from the econometrics. Depending upon which sequence of results excerpted from my personal econometric forage that I choose to report, and of how much freedom of auxiliary hypotheses I choose to take advantage, I can make any member of the Truman partnership appear as "rational" or "irrational" as I please. Our Cliometrician, now sputtering with indignation, would likely interject here: "What about Arthur Pryor? He consistently passed all rationality tests throughout!" I need only respond, if the Cliometrician has had a reasonable grounding in Neyman-Pearson theory, that none of the t-statistics or other test statistics are legitimate (and indeed are biased upward) because I have violated the first precept: Thou shalt not alter the specification to fit the data. Indeed, it is well known among statisticians that if one merely reverses which hypothesis is designated the null and which the alternative, then the outcome of Neyman-Pearson hypothesis testing can often be easily reversed.

The point I wish to make is that Cliometricians have foisted a false set of claims upon economic history. Under the banner of "science," they told their colleagues that by quantifying history, subjecting it to the regimen of neo-classical theory, and exposing all historical narratives to statistical tests, they would curtail the fancy of the mere literary historian, imposing the steely discipline of hard facts. But of course nothing of the sort has happened. Rather, the hegemony of neoclassicism has tended to recast any interesting economic question in a concertedly ahistorical manner, and then the application of econometrics in the hands of a skilled practitioner has merely given us back, in a less accessible but wantonly anachronistic format, whatever the Cliometrician sought to find in the data in the first place. Even so committed a neoclassical as Robert Solow admits this fact (in Parker 1986). If anything, the narrowing of the discourse to an audience of a few souls sufficiently tooled to see the point of the exercise has substantially increased the freedom of flights of fancy, rather than restricted it. Most generalist intellectuals curious about history were driven away decades ago. That is the plight of Cliometrics at the start of the millennium.

I should now like to bid our imaginary Cliometrician adieu, retell the story of the Truman partners in the supposedly antiquated "literary" format, and suggest that the hermeneutic and archival skills of the historian are far more likely to restrict the narrative than anything the Cliometricians might snatch out of their econometric bag of tricks.

The Semiotics of a Truman Rest Dinner

Any time a deal is cut, or an association is formed, it takes place in a rich context of intended meanings and unintended consequences, of tacit knowledge of the players and their peccadillos. It is the elaboration of that rich context which makes for a good narrative, a good story. This is not to say that quantitative evidence is downgraded; here it is very interesting to use our data to define divergences and look for "signatures" in each of the actors. Indeed, we find the actors themselves drawing up elaborate summaries of winners and losers, commenting upon the spread of bets and actual prices, and speculating upon causal regularities with weather and the like. But the first rule of hermeneutics is to try putting yourself in the historical actors' shoes: What could they have known and intended? What might we possibly find out about it?

From some work in the history of science which straddles intellectual history and economic history (Daston 1989), we learn that it would be a mistake to situate the betting activity of the Truman partners in a framework of formal probability and inductive inference. Much of the mathematics of probability was still in a highly unstable state in the early nineteenth century, to such an extent that even in situations in which probability was acknowledged to be relevant, such as in lotteries and insurance, it was not put into computational practice until very late in the century. Therefore, to phrase the question of rationality as one of stochastic unbiasedness or consistency is to start off on the wrong foot. Instead, it would be better to regard the betting activity at the Rest Dinners as a form of vigorous communication by other means. But in that case, what could this practice of wagering with such insignificant sums have to do with the business? We need to get better acquainted with the actors to answer that question.

We should start with the partnership in 1811. At that juncture the share valuations were divided as follows: Henry and John Villebois, £101,595 apiece; Sampson Hanbury, £88,343; Thomas Fowell Buxton, just brought on board with £26,503 (B / THB / B / 5 / 9). The Villebois brothers behaved much as Martin Weiner (and Adam Smith) have described old, inherited money: they cared little about business, preferring fox hunting, gambling, and country life. Sampson Hanbury was the Quaker made good, starting small by running the business for the Villebois brothers, cementing a relationship with the Gurney banking family by marriage, and increasing his fortunes in tandem with those of the brewery. But he had no children, and sought to construct some sort of continuity by bringing in his nephew Buxton. Thomas Buxton is the most famous of our cast of characters, the only one to make it into the *Dictionary of National Biography* and to have a memoir published.[10]

Buxton was a terribly earnest young Quaker who initially threw himself assiduously into his work at the brewery from 1808 to roughly 1815. Indeed, some of his exhortations concerning business practices would warm the cockles of the modern orthodox economist.[11] But this unbending moralist was not temperamentally well suited to the day-to-day running of a brewery; and soon his energies were progressively diverted elsewhere, first to running a Spitalfields Benevolent Society and then in 1818 to a successful candidacy as MP for Weymouth. His claim to fame was as a major campaigner for the abolition of slavery; after 1820 he was no longer able to give much attention to the brewery, moving from Hampstead to Cromer. The lack of interest in business was apparent to many visitors to the family; for instance, the Baron Rothschild once told his son, Edward Buxton, to stick to brewing (Buxton 1849, 344).

So Truman's was still faced with the dilemma so common to British family firms: How to ensure the smooth continuity of management of a successful business? In 1816 Robert Pryor was admitted as a partner with the absorption of Proctor's Brewhouse; but he seemed never to be really admitted to the inner circle. His accession may also have been something of a political move, to cement a relationship with a family of maltsters in Hertfordshire (Anonymous 1959, 31). An obvious replacement for Thomas Buxton was another Hanbury nephew, Robert, admitted to partnership in 1821. Tom Aveling, the head clerk made good, was admitted to second-class partnership in 1825, though he was always the poorest by far of the group, and treated in brewery documents more like a salaried underling than an equal. Thomas Buxton did manage to get his son Edward made a partner by 1836; but Robert Pryor's similar attempt on the part of his brother Arthur was opposed by Robert Hanbury, who thought Arthur constitutionally unsuitable for business.[12]

By 1836 the status of the partnership shares (B / THB / B / 519) stood as follows:

J. Villebois	126,500
H. Villebois	126,500
T. Buxton	88,000
R. Pryor	74,250
T. Aveling	24,750
R. Hanbury	55,000
E. Buxton	22,000

By this time Robert Hanbury was effectively running the business, but there were still many unresolved tensions as to the future disposition of the business and its ownership. These broke open with the death of Henry Villebois in 1847; the contempt of the insiders for the outsiders is expressed in a remarkable letter preserved in the Truman archives (B / THB / G / 10A / 5) from E. Buxton to Robert Hanbury concerning the son of Henry Villebois:

> Many thanks for your letter. I fully acknowledge the great difficulty of dealing with H. V., whether we decide in favour of excluding him or accepting him back. But I earnestly desire that we may all be led by a spirit of wisdom, justice and mercy. Some of your arguments have much force, but there are others, with which I cannot agree . . . Again you say that it has been "the greatest possible blot and disgrace to be connected with the V. Family." This may be true or it may not, but we knew their character when we consented to join them in business. If we "are ashamed of working for such," our *best* remedy is to retire ourselves from the concern. Being once a partner, H. V. has as much right to spend his gains in fox hunting as I have to spend mine in a contested election, or you yours in beautiful watercolours.

Now that we are aware of some of the context, we can begin to reinterpret the meaning of the hops and barley wagers. They were indeed fundamentally about the ability of each individual to predict the costs of the business, but more than that, they were about signaling who should be running the business. The Villebois, with their ineffectual bets, were expressing their preference to relish their status of the wealthy landed gentry, knowing little about agriculture or brewing and caring less. Thomas Buxton, who did have some knowledge, was far too distracted by the momentous political events of the day, and so his wagers wildly overshot actual movements. Tom Aveling, however close he was to the day-to-day purchases, was trying to prove his mettle not as a contender but as a team player, making relatively safe and unimaginative bets. The real battle of wits was between the Hanburys and the challengers to their position: the younger Edward Buxton and the Pryors. It is crucial to remember that Arthur Pryor—our neoclassical *homo economicus*—was only acknowledged as a full partner with the death of his brother, achieving by inheritance what he could not attain by talent.

Why couldn't the partners assess the capabilities of hops and barley knowledge more directly, perhaps by letting the rivals speculate on their prices? This probably had to do with the scruples of Sampson Hanbury, who "did not like to be concerned in any speculation in hops, as all such purchasing was on the joint account of the brewery" (in Mathias 1959, 530). How much better for the health of the firm to have a public joust, with negligible stakes, in full view of all the relevant actors, even if some of those actors were not seriously in the running. Hence it was of utmost significance that the Hanburys came out on top as the most strategically savvy of the bettors; and it must have been doubly satisfying to have Robert Hanbury's poor opinion of Arthur Pryor reinforced by his dismal showing. One final bit of evidence supporting this interpretation is that when the succession degenerated into legal squabbles upon the death of the Villebois after 1847, the practice of betting at Rest Dinners ceased altogether.

Therefore, what might initially seem a simple expression of prowess in projecting input costs was understood by the players as a restrained expression of the competition for control and dominance of the firm. Outside the orthodox mindset, it is possible to reconceptualize many, perhaps even most, "economic transactions" as forms of communication or the veiled exercise of dominance. There may be circumstances when such an interpretation is strained or tendentious, but the only point to be made here is that at the very least, it provides a much more robust narrative for writing history—and is implicitly held much more closely to the sources—than one which proleptically reassures us that the past was never a foreign country and that on no account could rationality have reasons dictated as much by the heart as by the pocketbook.

10

Why
Econometricians
Don't Replicate
(Although They
Do Reproduce)

Replication and the Complete Bayesian

In a series of articles proposing an eclectic, Bayesian approach to econometric model building, Dale Poirier (1988a, 222) has called for a "shifting [of] attention economics from the fascination with corroboration and falsification in isolated data sets to the more scientifically compelling issue of replication across multiple data sets." This concept of replication is of profound importance for the Bayesian econometrician; or indeed for the Bayesian philosopher of science (Howson and Urbach 1989), since its role is to provide the objective linchpin binding together the various researchers and their prior subjectivist definitions of causality and inference. As Poirier (1988a, 220–21) puts it: "Replication [is] the process by which predictive performance of a law is evaluated in a series of data confrontations. Obviously, such confrontations should be limited to those data environments for which the law is applicable ... If the "background" variables involved in these conditions are numerous and/or difficult to quantify and observe, then the empirical counterparts of those conditions can be viewed as probabilistic in nature, i.e., they give the probability of the law being applicable to the data environment with characteristics identified by the background variables."

This analytical leap—from a recognition that laws never apply in all circumstances without restrictions on relevance and scope, to the higher plane of expressing those restrictions as a probability density function or a likelihood function over variables in an externally given data environment—seems a vulnerable, or at least an incongruous, move for a subjectivist theorist. After all, where does the likelihood function for the applicability of a "law" come from? There is a body of literature which calls into question whether all relevant background or auxiliary variables could ever be sufficiently specified so that they demarcate the domain of a newly discovered law; in philosophy literature, this is called the Duhem-Quine thesis. Moreover, if the law is already of a stochastic character, doubt would rapidly surface that such "relevance" uncertainty conforms to the conventional Kolmgorov axioms of probability. (For instance, exhaustive partition of all eventualities would seem ruled out by the very nature of the problem.)[1] Thus we believe that this approach to the question of replication misses many of the most interesting aspects of the problem. In its place, we propose to bring different resources to the problem of econometric model selection which do not depend as heavily upon the stochastic formalism as they do upon two other considerations: empirical evidence about the actual practices of econometricians and economic journals, and the technique of game theory.

While we agree wholeheartedly with Poirier's message that "the performance of theories over many data confrontations" is the key to understanding econometric model selection (Poirier 1988b, 137), it is the ideal of replication which first requires much more careful examination. If replication does not serve as an automatic regulative principle in science in action, then it cannot provide the foundations of a Bayesian theory of model selection predicated solely upon objective data.

Since the issue of the meaning of replication would seem to be a problem for *all* schools of econometrics, some might wonder why we have chosen to pick on the Bayesians in our attempt to set the stage for the question of replication. Bayesian econometricians are already a beleaguered bunch, and therefore sympathy might demand that we confront instead their more numerous counterparts in classical statistics; but we decline that option here because that would lead us into a mare's nest of problems concerning realism versus anti-realism versus instrumentalism, the differing attitudes towards the meaning of "empiricism," the problem that Neyman-Pearson strictures are not rigidly observed in actual practice, and so on. In particular, we believe that a great virtue of the Bayesians is that they do not generally attempt such ad hoc immunization strategies as a tortured distinction between replication of a researcher's "findings" and replication of the (supposedly independent) "phenomenon." Thus we prefer to restrict our observations to a subjectivist framework in a game theory setting precisely because doing so isolates and highlights the practices we wish to discuss (and not because the present author is a confirmed subjectivist—or even a card-carrying neoclassical!).

Conveniently for our purposes, the pathbreaking empirical work on replication practices among econometricians has already been reported in an article by Dewald, Thursby, and Anderson (1986). In that article, the authors devised an approach specifically aimed at the criterion that an acceptable regression model should be replicable by other researchers if it is indeed to meet the most basic standards of scientific research. In a prodigious undertaking, the authors requested programs and data sets from the authors of all the empirical articles published in the *Journal of Money, Credit and Banking* (*JMCB*), broken into two subsets: (a) those published from 1980 to June 1982, before the initiation of the *JMCB* project; and (b) all articles submitted or under review from July 1982 onward. Their results were noteworthy, to say the least. First, 66 percent of authors of class (a) articles and 28 percent in class (b) were unable or unwilling to comply with the requests. Second, of the fifty-four instances in which requested materials were supplied, only eight of the submissions were sufficiently problem-free to permit attempted replication. And finally, only *two* of the articles, 1.3 percent of the total, were found susceptible of replication in their entirety. Although these authors do not say as much in so many words, it is clear that this estimate is well outside the bounds of any confidence intervals around the conventional norm of replication.

The question which we wish to pose in this chapter is: How should advocates of Bayesian learning models, and indeed anyone interested in the state of economic science, interpret these results? The authors of this study make some efforts to portray their findings as evidence of "market failure," suggesting that the "benefits of reduced frequency of errors on empirical articles share many of the characteristics of public goods" (Dewald, Thursby, and Anderson 1986, 589). We suggest that this transfer of a standard economic model into the realm of a "marketplace of ideas" for econometric practices should be subjected to careful scrutiny. First, there is the problem of specifying precisely what is being replicated, and therefore what should play the role of the "good" in the public goods analogy. The most narrow interpretation would insist that the mere mathematical processing of the data—say, just the running of the regression equation—is the object of replication, but many comments in the work of Dewald and his colleagues belie that interpretation. A broader construction of replication would include the operations by which the data themselves were collected, collated, and processed. This is a much more plausible way to interpret the subject of Dewald's research; yet this interpretation begins to blur the objectivity of what it is that is to be replicated, since it involves numerous social and subjective aspects of research, bordering on issues of model choice which are to be held in quarantine in the Bayesian scheme of things. With only a slightly broader construction, one can observe that the referent of the "good" in this analogy tends toward a vague concept of reliability or "truth value" of an entire research program, rather than some easily identifiable product or object.

However, our objections to the public goods analogy run deeper than questions surrounding the definition of the good purveyed. We also suggest that many characteristics of the replication process do not conform to the conventional definition of the public good. Public goods are generally defined as commodities which are nonrival and nonexclusive, or as one authority puts it: "A good is nonrival or nondivisible when a *unit* of the good can be consumed by one individual without detracting, in the slightest, from the consumption opportunities still available to others from the *same* unit . . . Goods whose benefits can be withheld costlessly by the owner or provider display excludable benefits . . . nonexcludability is the crucial factor in determining which goods must be publicly provided" (Cornes and Sandler 1986, 6).

Our objections to this description of econometric research, described in detail in the next section, are that (1) the mode of the "consumption" of econometric results by readers does directly influence the benefits of those results for other readers; and (2) one of the main findings of Dewald, Thursby, and Anderson (1986) was precisely that some of the benefits of econometric research are "excludable" in the sense described above. To understand how this situation exists in science, let us reconsider the definition of replication.

The Nature of Replication

It is a commonplace that the replicability of experiments is the single most important attribute which distinguishes scientific from nonscientific research. As with much else of the "received view" of the structure of scientific inquiry, this dictum has been subjected to critical scrutiny in the post-1960 history and philosophy of science. The entire issue of replication was called into question by means of an empirical observation: namely, in the history of science, it is rare to find actual replications; and in many of the paradigm instances they were never even tried.[2] If science was truly governed by the norm of replication, then why was replication not regularly observed?

The first reaction to this anomaly was to claim something akin to the idea that "marginal returns" to replication fell off rapidly, such that although the option always existed, the actual practice was rarely observed (Popper 1965, 240). While this was an interesting idea, it was soon pointed out that without amplification, this definition of returns was little better than a tautology, and in any event, it violated Popper's own ideas about the impossibility of an inductive logic.[3] A more promising line of inquiry has been initiated by Collins (1985) and Hesse in McMullin (1988). They found it necessary to approach the problem from two perspectives: (1) a reevaluation of the unobtrusive presupposition that "replication" is a standardized and mechanical procedure freely accessible to anyone who desires to engage in it; and (2) an analysis of the fact that the *choice* to replicate or not replicate is embedded in a social context which indisputably influences the outcome.

In the following pages we provide a brief primer of these issues for economists; the reader is encouraged to consult Collins (1985), Latour (1987), Markus (1987), Coleman (1987), and Pinch (1985) for illustrative material specifically from the history of the natural sciences.

The indispensable prerequisite for understanding the replication process is an appreciation of just how difficult it is under the best of circumstances to achieve "perfect replication." Perfect replication should reproduce every aspect of the original experiment; clearly, this is simply impossible. No one can achieve the same spacetime coordinate, the same apparatus, the same path of inquiry, and so forth; nor would anyone ever want to do so, because perfect replication, if successful, could not by its very nature add one iota to our knowledge. Instead, the activity we call "replication" is hedged about by numerous heuristics which we might suggest define "asymptotically satisfactory replication": time invariance of the experiment, independence of outcome from the personality of the investigator, near identical tacit background knowledge, the independence of seemingly irrelevant alternatives, and many others. Yet try as we might to justify all these heuristics after the fact, there is no way in any "frontier" research effort (and, we might add, particularly in economics) that we can be sure they are all true a priori. Indeed, the struggle to replicate an experiment is simultaneously a struggle to *define* what is relevant in constructing the asymptotically identical experiment.

Let us draw some examples from Dewald, Thursby, and Anderson (1986) to illustrate this problem. One might expect that once the data and programs were provided by the original investigators to the JMCB project, the definition of successful replication would have been straightforward from that point onward: it would just be the exact numerical reproduction of the estimated regression coefficients, t-statistics, and so forth. But as the researchers of the JMCB project discovered to their dismay, at one time or another many of the heuristics of asymptotically satisfactory replication were violated. Time invariance was compromised by the updating and revision of data sets which rendered the exact figures used in the original study difficult to recover. Independence from the investigators' personality was violated by the need of the JMCB project to contact the original investigators in order to clarify various implicit research tactics and to understand the possible causes of divergent results (see Dewald, Thursby, and Anderson 1986, 593). The location of the experimenter, far from being irrelevant, actually created difficulties for the JMCB project, as instanced by their frustration in failing to reproduce the Harvard-MPS model on Ohio State University's IBM mainframe. The independence of seemingly irrelevant alternatives was violated by such minor considerations as differences in computer hardware and software, and even more disturbingly, differences in the precision of rounding in algorithms and subroutines, even within purportedly the same statistical package (Dewald, Thursby, and Anderson 1986, 594n).

The point of these horror stories is not to place blame, but rather to demonstrate that econometric research is in this respect little different from any other species of experimental research: it confronts all of the same problems encountered in the search for gravity waves, quarks, and the gas laser. The problem of true scientific replication is that it is a struggle to constitute a sufficient degree of identity "in the phenomena" so that a result may be agreed upon by the relevant scientific community. "Results" do not come from a mechanical search procedure, as every good econometrician knows, but are the product of a tremendous quantity of work and negotiation and reconceptualization. In a word, our starting point is the simple but crucial proposition that scientific research is a social process (see, for example, Cunningham 1988; Latour 1987).

This is where the scholarly journals enter the process. The average scientific report is not written with explicit acknowledgment that science requires persistent negotiation. On the contrary, the impersonal stylistic format of problem, model, results is calculated to make it appear as if the results could transparently present themselves with no temporal dependence, no intrusion of the investigators' personality, in an atmosphere of obvious tacit knowledge and an unproblematic shared literature, with only the relevant considerations telegraphed in a neutral observation language. The average scientific paper must be written as if "interpretation" could be entirely divorced from "description"; and indeed, as if any competent reader could have performed the exact same experiment. While this democracy of the laboratory is laudable, it is also generally false (Markus 1987; Latour 1987). The reason why most people believe, however misguidedly, that the primary characteristic of science is the replicability of experiments is not that it is encountered daily, but rather that the scholarly journal presents experimental reports as if such were the case. "Replication" is an ideal of science; rarely is it an activity of scientific practice.

If they do not replicate, what, then, do scientists do? A short, flip answer would be that they generally "reproduce": that is, they convince each other and build on previous results. This is hardly sufficient as a general theory of science, but we are not that ambitious in this chapter. Instead, here we propose to build a reasonably general model of the choice of research strategies, starting from some insights by Collins (1985). We posit that each scientist, after a period of training and apprenticeship, enters into the social arena of research equipped with some general research heuristics, including prior knowledge of the profound ambiguities of empirical endeavor. In particular, we posit, each scientist realizes that asymptotically satisfactory replication is very difficult to achieve because of the reasons broached above. In short, asymptotically satisfactory replication is costly to carry out. In our example of the JMCB project, the replicators encountered insuperable difficulties even with the assistance of a National Science Foundation grant.

Situated in this context, the prospective empirical practitioners face a choice: he or she can either seek to *overturn* an existing empirical result, or else opt to *lend confirmation* to an already existing empirical program. We shall call the first option "replication." It is inherently costly, extremely tricky, and risky, because there is only one way it can be perceived by the originator of the experiment. The originator often perceives attempts at replication as hostile, in the sense that nothing new is to be learned from perfect replication, and the only apparent intention is therefore to falsify the original experimental report. The perceptions of the originator as to whether the intentions of the new entrant to the empirical arena are hostile are of paramount importance, not because of sordid motives or faked data but because, as we have already seen, a modicum of empathy and coopera- tion are indispensable to an adequate understanding of the previous experi- mental apparatus, the operative research heuristics, and the presumed tacit background knowledge.

There is no such thing as free, independent access to such highly specific information; it is not sold on any market (but that could be changing under the current privatization of some areas of science); it certainly is not to be explicitly found in the text of the journal article or report. Yet without it, new entrants could so misconstrue the original empirical report that they could fool themselves (but not a third party) that they had succeeded in overturning the original finding. Hence, a potential replicator faces two obstacles: the originator may release a small amount of information con- cerning how the initial results were obtained, thereby raising the costs of attempted replication; and there is the risk of confirming the originator's results. This latter outcome is a complete failure for the new entrant, because no journal wants to republish an already published paper: nothing further accrues to the replicator from pure replication.

The second option faced by the new entrant, that of lending confirmation to an existing empirical set of results, is much more attractive: we shall call it either "extension" or "reproduction." Here most aspects of experimenter behavior are different from those under the first option, mainly because the new entrant has no need or desire to understand the original result in all its details. The aim of a "reproducer" is to extend existing empirical results into new domains or contexts divergent from those reported by the originator, consciously altering the apparatus, the variables, the circumstances surrounding the result, the time frame, and any other aspect of the experimental set-up which may or may not be central to the original problem situation. This is of course Kuhn's "normal science," the dotting of i's and the crossing of t's so prevalent in the modern scientific milieu, the paradigm of the doctoral thesis. One reason it is so prevalent is that it is transparently in everyone's interest. The originator is moved to cooperate because extension of the primary result lends validity and importance to the initial research finding. The new entrant finds the task made easy because the costs are lower, encouragements are ubiquitous (grants, etc.), and the journals are predisposed to accept the new findings whether they are thought to limit the significance of the original report or to expand them. The journals must regard this work as a legitimate contribution to the literature because it cites reports already published, legitimizing past editorial choices, and because its limited novelty renders it easier to evaluate.

Thus, from the point of view of a new entrant to empirical scientific research, replication must appear more costly and less rewarding than a strategy of extending and reproducing an original empirical result. Replication is an inherently difficult procedure for the reasons discussed above, and if successful, has all manner of unattractive consequences. The new entrant could simply prove the originator right, which turns out to be a waste of time for all concerned; or else prove the originator wrong, which creates further problems for the reporting process. A successful disconfirmation always implicitly calls into question the refereeing competence of the journal, and also makes inordinate demands upon journal editors to adjudicate the inevitable controversy which ensues between originator and replicator about the nature of asymptotically satisfactory replication. Confrontations of this sort are often ended only by recourse to third parties and further costly processes, if they can ever be settled conclusively at all. The payoff to replicators is intrinsically low: this is not an assumption, but rather an intrinsic feature of the social structure of science.

Hence we suggest that previous attempts by economists to discuss replication by using such analytical devices as the isolated public good and the Bayesian external constraint upon prior subjective distributions be placed within a more flexible analytical frame: one that sees research as a game between different classes of players—originators, replicators, reproducers, and journals. The description of science in game-theory terms can already be found in the philosophy of science literature (Cunningham 1988; Kitcher 1993); we see no reason why it should not also be applied to the research area that gave birth to game-theory techniques, namely economics. Looking at the process of econometric research using game-theory models possesses at least one advantage over previous discussions of econometric method: instead of dead-end appeals to vague and unspecified "loss functions," this strategy would force us to seriously consider the costs and benefits of existing econometric practices; it might even provoke further *empirical* work on the actual practices of econometricians.

In our model, costs rise the closer the proposed research design is to the original, and payoffs to replication are low. All players understand these realities, which brings us to the heart of the incentives problem in science: attempts to replicate are almost always perceived as hostile by journal editors and the originator of the result; whereas attempts to "reproduce" are generally perceived as responsible extensions whose intent is to develop scientific knowledge. Hence, whenever an established researcher is confronted with a new entrant whose intentions are not immediately made clear through some structured research institution (such as the relationship between dissertation advisor and doctoral student), then the major signal as to whether the proposed activity constitutes "replication" or "reproduction" is derived from the relative closeness of the proposed project to the original experiment. As for the new entrant, he or she faces a complex strategic problem characteristic of game-theory models.

Given this configuration of the game, it should come as no surprise that in equilibrium there exist very few replications in science, although there exist plenty of extensions of existing results. This pattern can begin to explain the paucity of disconfirmations in econometric literature, as well as the obvious hesitancy with which many members of the *JMCB* sample responded to the request for everything needed to replicate their econometric results. With the assistance of a more formal model, we should be able to begin weighing the relative importance of the various determinants of this equilibrium.

A Model of Replication and Reproduction

In this model we have an originator O, who has a paper about to be published, a potential replicator R, who may or may not attempt to replicate O's work, and n potential extenders denoted by $i = 1, \ldots, n$ who may or may not attempt to extend O's paper. First O decides how much information (I) to provide on how his results were obtained. We represent I as a non-negative real number. O is constrained by the journal editor to provide at least $\bar{I}$. After observing I, player R decides whether to attempt replication ($x = 1$) or not ($x = 0$) and players $1, \ldots, n$ decide whether to extend ($y_i = 1$) or not ($y_i = 0$), $i = 1, \ldots, n$.

$$Y = \sum_{i=1}^{n} y_i$$

is the number of actual extenders. This describes the players and sequence of actions in our game.

The amount of information I determines the cost $C_o(I)$ incurred by O in reporting the result, as well as the costs $C_R(I)$ incurred by players R and $i = 1, \ldots, n$ should they attempt to replicate and the costs $C_E(I)$ incurred should they attempt to extend.[4] If R does attempt replication there is some probability (θ) of overturning O's results which is known to both O and R and for simplicity is assumed to be independent of I. The probability of confirmation is then $1 - \theta$. If O's results are overturned R receives a positive payoff and O receives a negative payoff while confirmation gives both a zero payoff. Let W be player R's positive expected payoff if he attempts replication. If i decides to extend he receives positive payoff V, and O receives a positive payoff also. We see that O wishes to encourage extension and discourage replication in his choice of I.[5]

The benefits accruing to the originator are solely a function of the activities of the potential replicator and potential extenders. The activities of the potential extenders may be summarized by Y. Hence player O's benefits are represented by the function $U_o(x, Y)$. O's total payoff is then given by $U_o(x, Y) - C_o(I)$. R's and i's total payoffs are given by $U_R(x, I)$ and $U_i(Y_i, I)$, as follows:

$$U_R(x, I) = \begin{cases} 0 & \text{if } x = 0 \\ W - C_R(I) & \text{if } x = 1 \end{cases}$$

$$U_i(Y_i, I) = \begin{cases} 0 & \text{if } Y_i = 0 \\ V - C_E(I) & \text{if } Y_i = 1 \end{cases}$$

$$i = 1, \ldots, n$$

We make the following assumptions:

$$U_O(0, Y) \geq U_O(1, Y) \text{ for all } Y \qquad (\text{A1})$$
$$U_O(x, Y) < U_O(x, Y + 1) \text{ for all } x, Y \qquad (\text{A2})$$
$$C_O \text{ is an increasing function of } I \qquad (\text{A3})$$
$$C_R \text{ and } C_E \text{ are decreasing functions of } I. \qquad (\text{A4})$$
$$C_R(I) > C_E(I) \text{ for all } I \geq 0. \qquad (\text{A5})$$
$$W \leq V \qquad (\text{A6})$$

We normalize by setting $U_O(0, 0) = 0$.

(A1) and (A2) simply restate that O receives a negative payoff from attempted replication and positive payoff from extension, reasons for which were given above. By its very nature greater information is costly to communicate and results in lower costs of replication and extension, giving us (A3) and (A4). As was discussed above, (A5) and (A6) state that replication is a more costly and less rewarding activity than extension.

Now that we have described the payoff structure, we complete our description of this game by identifying the players' strategies. O's strategy is simply $I \in [\bar{I}, +\infty)$. Player R's strategy is a mapping h, which determines whether R replicates or not as a function of I; $h: [\bar{I}, +\infty) \rightarrow \{0, 1\}$. Similarly, player i's strategy is function f_i, which determines whether to extend or not depending on I; $f_i: [\bar{I}, +\infty) \rightarrow \{0, 1\}$ $i = 1, \ldots, n$. We make the usual common knowledge assumption that all players know the structure of the game.

We employ the notion of subgame perfection as our solution concept. Simply put we solve the problem backwards excluding the possibility for any noncredible threats.

Let C_R^{-1} and C_E^{-1} be the inverse functions of C_R and C_E, and define I_R and I_E as in equations (1) and (2), below.

$$I_R = C_R^{-1}(W) \qquad (1)$$
$$I_E = C_E^{-1}(V) \qquad (2)$$

Proposition 1 below gives the unique subgame perfect equilibrium strategies for the potential replicator and extenders and shows that replication (extension) occurs only if the amount of information provided, I, is above the threshold level $I_R, (I_E) > \bar{I}$

Proposition 1

$\hat{f}_i: -1, \ldots, n$ and $\hat{h}$ are subgame perfect equilibrium strategies if and only if:[6]

$$\hat{f}_i(I) = \begin{cases} 1 & \text{if } I \geq I_E \\ 0 & \text{if } I < I_E \end{cases}$$

and[7]

$$\hat{h}(I) = \begin{cases} 1 & \text{if } I \geq I_R \\ 0 & \text{if } I < I_R \end{cases}$$

When $I \geq I_E$ each potential extender's payoff from choosing $y_i = 1$ is positive and zero from choosing $y_i = 0$ and similarly for the player R. This proves *Proposition 1*.

Proposition 2

The level of information at which extension occurs is lower than for replication, i.e. $I_R > I_E$.

We obtain the following inequalities from (A5) and (A6), $I_R = C_R^{-1}(W)$ $C_E^{-1}(W) \geq C_E^{-1}(V) = I_E$, proving *Proposition 2*. *Proposition 3* states the main result.

Proposition 3

Let $\hat{I}$ be player O's subgame perfect equilibrium strategy.

$$\text{If } \bar{I} \geq I_E \text{ then } \hat{I} = \bar{I} \tag{3}$$
$$\text{If } \bar{I} < I_E \text{ and } U_O(0, n) \geq C_O(I_E) - C_O(\bar{I}) \text{ then } \hat{I} = I_E \tag{4}$$
$$\text{If } \bar{I} < I_E \text{ and } U_O(0, n) < C_O(I_E) - C_O(\bar{I}) \text{ then } \hat{I} = \bar{I}. \tag{5}$$

The only reason for O ever to provide information beyond $\bar{I}$ is to encourage the potential extenders. Increasing I from I_E to I_R only results in higher information costs, and increasing I beyond I_R encourages replication. Both effects lower O's payoff. Hence $I = max\{\bar{I}, I_E\}$. (3) then follows since $\check{I} \geq \bar{I}$. Now consider $I < I_E$, increasing I on $[\bar{I}, I_E)$ only increases O's costs resulting in a lower payoff for O. Hence $\hat{I} \in \{\bar{I}, I_E\}$. Recall that $U_O(0, 0) = 0$. (4) and (5) then follow easily, completing the proof of *Proposition 3*.

Proposition 3 informs us that replication never occurs in equilibrium unless editors are very tough and set $\bar{I}$ at or above I_R. Presuming that $\bar{I}$ is set below I_R we will never observe replication since there will not be enough information provided. If $\bar{I}$ is at or above I_E then we will see extension and if it is below I_E then we may or may not observe extension depending on the sizes of $U_O(0, n)$ and $C_O(I_E) - C_O(\bar{I})$. $U_O(0, n)$ is increasing in n. So the higher n is, the more likely that enough information will be provided for extension to occur. $C_O(I_E) - C_O(\bar{I})$ is decreasing in V and $\bar{I}$. So the higher V and $\bar{I}$ are, the more likely that we will observe extension. Hence we only observe no research activity when n, V, and $\bar{I}$ are sufficiently low.

Some Further Observations on Economics Journals

Our model demonstrates that replication generally will not be an observed activity unless the journals set their information requirement $\bar{I}$ high enough to sufficiently encourage replicators. In a seeming extrapolation of the policy conclusions of this model, the solution would appear simply to have journal editors "get tough"; and indeed, this appears to have been the response of the editors of the *American Economic Review* to the publication of Dewald, Thursby, and Anderson (1986). In their editorial statement preceding the article, they assert their requirement that "the data used in the analysis are clearly and precisely documented, [and] are readily available to any researcher for purposes of replication, and where details of computations sufficient to permit replications are provided." While we agree in principle with this statement, we think our model predicts that such exhortations generally will prove ineffectual in altering the equilibrium realization of replications.

The reasons for such a prediction are simple. Although we did not model the journal editors as separate players in our game, it is not surprising that those editors may be confronted with incentives which do not encourage setting the required information level $\bar{I}$ high enough to provoke frequent replication. First, we have seen that the provision of I is costly to the originator of an empirical report; to set $\bar{I}$ high enough to place all readers on an equal footing with the originator would demand massive tomes of documentation and would be a great waste of resources, because it would be attempting to duplicate what the entire social structure of science already exists to do, namely inculcate a new entrant with sufficient tacit background knowledge to be able to attempt replication. The originator wants to provide just enough information to draw in "reproducers" as new entrants, but not more owing to the costs of provision. The journal editors, on the other hand, would like to set $\bar{I}$ high enough to make their journal well respected, but not so high that it would drive away all new originator articles into other journals or other outlets, leaving their journal to publish only less prestigious and cheaper-to-document extender articles. (This omits the entire issue of degrading the readability of texts that are already unreadable, and mostly unread.) The journal editors cannot escape the bare facts of their social existence: there are few good results so transparently reported that they may be easily replicated (for the reasons discussed above), and yet if they raise the costs of reporting too high, they run the risk of unintentionally lowering the quality of the journal.

It is possible to bring further empirical evidence to these theoretical predictions. In a note to the *Journal of Political Economy*, Feige (1975) claimed that there had been too much encouragement of what we have called "reproducers" and not enough encouragement of "replicators," and called upon the *Journal of Political Economy* to change its editorial policy. The editors responded: "It would be extremely expensive—in editorial and referee time above all—to deal with carefully formulated research proposals and then with final products . . . We believe that the true remedy is to resort to the powerful force of competition" (Feige 1975, 1295). Yet contrary to this belief that there already existed sufficient competition and to their credit, the editors of the *Journal of Political Economy* said that they would initiate a special section of the journal entitled "Confirmations and Contradictions" to encourage replicator submissions.

It is interesting that the early contributors to "Confirmations and Contradictions" understood the distinction which we have made between replicators and reproducers. Ronald Ehrenberg, in a response in the issue of April 1977, even uses the terms replication and extension. However, the history of "Confirmations and Contradictions" over the eleven years of the experiment bears out the predictions of our model. In table 8 we list all published submissions to "Confirmations and Contradictions" from 1976 to 1987,

Table 8. Accepted Submissions to "Confirmations and Contradictions,"
Journal of Political Economy, 1976–1987

Author	(vol): pages	Econometrics?	Attempted Replication?	Successful Replication?
N. Cardwell & M. Hopkins	(85): 211–15	yes	not reported	
S. Long & R. Settle	(85): 409–23	yes	no	
A. King	(85): 425–31	yes	no	
H. Rosen & D. Fullerton	(85): 433–40	yes	no	
P. Linneman	(86): 535–38	no		
K. Mohabbat & E. Simos	(86): 539–41	yes	no	
W. Hansen et al.	(86): 729–41	yes	no	
J. Stone	(86): 959–62	yes	yes	yes
F. McCormick	(87): 411–22	yes	no	
T. Hannan	(87): 891–95	yes	no	
G. Scully	(87): 1139–43	yes	no	
B. Lindgren & C. Stuart	(88): 412–27	yes	no	
J. Long	(88): 620–29	yes	no	
J. Meerman	(88): 1242–48	no		
D. Clark	(88): 1249–54	yes	no	
V. Daly & G, Hadjimatheou	(89): 596–99	yes	no	
R. Reinhard	(89): 1251–60	yes	no	
M. Sumner & R. Ward	(89): 1261–65	yes	no	
K. Rosen	(90): 191–200	yes	no	
M. Friedman & A. Schwartz	(90): 201–12	yes	no	
D. Leimer & S. Lesnoy	(90): 606–42	yes	yes	no
R. Burkhauser & J. Turner	(90): 643–46	yes	no	
A. Martin & G. Psacharopoulos	(90): 827–53	yes	no	
P. Geary & J. Kennan	(90): 854–71	yes	no	
P. Volcker	(90): 854–71	yes	yes	no
C. Carter et al.	(91): 319–31	yes	no	
R. Arnould & L. Nichols	(91): 332–40	yes	no	
G. Calvo & D. Peel	(91): 880–87	no		
F. Lui	(91): 1067–74	yes	no	
G. Fane	(92): 329–33	no		
W. McManus	(93): 417–25	yes	no	
T. Muris	(94): 884–89	no		
I. Heravi	(94): 1120	no		
A. Lewbel	(95): 211–15	yes	yes	no
J. Barron et al.	(95): 632–40	yes	no	
C. Nelson	(95): 641–46	yes	yes	no

noting whether the note attempted any econometric estimation, whether this estimation attempted to replicate the article being critiqued, and finally, whether the attempted replication of the original econometric equations was successful.

The first notable finding is that "Confirmations and Contradictions" has not been used primarily to provoke or encourage replication activity, in contrast to the original suggestion of Feige. Of the thirty-six notes which have appeared in this special section over eleven years, only 14 percent have reported attempting to replicate the econometric exercises of the articles which they have subjected to critique. Of those five attempted replications, only *one* apparently succeeded in replicating the original results. While the replication success rate here is somewhat better than that reported by Dewald and his colleagues, it is hardly enough to inspire confidence, and of course there is the problem of the extremely small and self-selected sample.

The predictions of our model can help us to understand this outcome. The incentives for researchers are skewed heavily toward reproduction and extension of original results, and this is borne out by the ratio of six extender notes for every attempted replicator in a section of a journal explicitly dedicated to encouraging replicators. Moreover, the five instances of observed replicator activity carried out by Stone, Leimer and Lesnoy, Volcker, Lewbel, and Nelson can be explained by unusually low costs due to their locations. The one successful replication carried out by J. Stone was made possible by access to data on labor intensities provided by his employer, the Bureau of Labor Statistics. As for the four unsuccessful attempts, Leimer and Lesnoy were employees of the Social Security Administration, the very agency supplying the data to the author of the article they critiqued; Paul Volcker had the resources of the Federal Reserve System at his disposal; Lewbel's data were entirely taken from national income accounts in the *Survey of Current Business*; while Nelson's were exclusively taken from *Business Statistics*. The last two replications become more comprehensible when one observes that the "models" being estimated were in fact simple single-variable Autoregressive Moving Average equations.[8] Hence, even the best intentions of the editors of a reputable journal such as the *Journal of Political Economy* have not been sufficient to offset what must be understood as a structural regularity in the process of scientific research. The activity of replication (as opposed to reproduction) remains an ideal notable in the rarity of its realization. As such, it does not serve much of any regulative principle in the process of econometric research; and it is doubtful that it serves as a benchmark for any Bayesian learning process.

If the members of a discipline decided that they really wanted a sustainable higher level of replicator activity, then we predict that they would encourage a more profound and far-reaching reconstruction of the incentive structures of science, and not just some "jawboning" or isolated attempts to raise the costs for the originators of pioneering scientific findings. Among other issues, such an effort would involve changing the incentive structure of empirical research; it might involve subsidies to replicators (much like the *JMCB* National Science Foundation grant) to offset the cost differentials between replication and reproduction; it also might just involve going around the entire structure of costs and benefits by requiring apprentice empiricists (perhaps at the graduate student level) to attempt replication of one or more articles in the same way that they are now required to do theses. (Of course, this might drive tyros away from empiricism, but that's another issue.) Finally, such a far-reaching effort might entail a serious reconceptualization of what econometricians claim to be doing with regard to their statistical practices (see Mirowski 1989e; 1989c; 1990d).

11
From Mandelbrot to
Chaos in
Economic Theory

Can Economic Theorists Admit That History Matters?

There was a time not so long ago that some scientists believed they were living in the midst of a profound rupture between older and emergent notions of scientific explanation (Prigogine 1980; Prigogine and Stengers 1984; Ford 1983; Gleick 1987; Mandelbrot 1987). The very meanings of order and chaos, the deterministic and the stochastic, were reconceptualized in the 1980s. Some economists, understandably, did not want to be left in the lurch, and turned their prodigious efforts to assimilating some of the new doctrines and mathematical techniques. But so far, what this movement lacks is historical perspective. While it was easy to be swept up in the enthusiasm of the moment for what is unquestionably one of the more significant intellectual innovations of the twentieth century, that still does not absolve the economist from asking some very basic questions: Why should this particular set of ideas or mathematical formalisms be well suited to economic discourse? What is it about this new mathematics that will necessarily improve economics? What accounts for this rush to appropriate new techniques? How will they change the way economics is done? Despite the appearance of numerous survey articles these questions were not adequately addressed (Baumol and Benhabib 1989; Brock and Malliaris 1989; Kelsey 1988).

The reason these questions languish is that they are inherently historical rather than narrowly technical. Since most economists cannot be presumed to have a firm background in the histories of physics or of economics, and such a background cannot be provided in the space of a few pages, most of the statements made here about these histories will not be documented, although the reader is directed to some of the author's writings (Mirowski 1988; Mirowski 1989c; Mirowski 1989b; Mirowski 1990b; Mirowski 1989d) for the corroborating evidence. Here we set the stage for the narratives in the subsequent sections of this chapter, which will document the historical relationship (or, more to the point, the lack of a relationship) between Benoit Mandelbrot's work in economics and the later work of such authors as J. Grandmont, R. Day, J. Benhabib, W. Brock, J. Scheinkman, W. Barnett, P. Chen, and others who have sought to import the insights of chaos theory into economics. The purpose of this narrative is to illustrate the major thesis of this chapter, namely that economists have not sufficiently thought through the implications of the chaos literature for their discipline with adequate depth and rigor, because they are not yet ready to admit freely that history matters at all levels of discourse.

The intense attraction which the chaos literature exerted in the 1980s upon modern mathematical economics can be readily explained by the history of their discipline. Mathematical economics is essentially coextensive with the school of neoclassical economic theory; and neoclassical theory was directly copied from mid-nineteenth-century energy physics (Mirowski 1989b, chapter 5; Mirowski 1990b). The purpose of that transfer of metaphor, which equated "preferences" or "utility" to a field of potential energy, was multileveled: at the grossest level, imitation of physics was thought to render economic discourse intrinsically "scientific"; at another level, constrained optimization over a conservative vector field was thought to embody the deterministic ideal of all scientific explanation prevalent at the time; at yet a third level, some believed that energy was the intermediate term which allowed the reduction of the social to physical law, from psychic energy down to mechanical motion. Hence mathematical economics, and more specifically its neoclassical incarnation, has a long history of imitating the physical sciences. What is more important for our present concerns is the problems which such imitation has raised over the past century.

First, while neoclassical economics attempted to partake of the ideal of deterministic explanation, it was nowhere as successful in this endeavor as its exemplar, physics. This weakness can be directly traced to a persistent tergiversation over what, precisely, was conserved in the economic system (Mirowski 1989b, chapters 5–7; Mirowski 1989d; Northrop 1941). Without an analogous conservation principle, neoclassical economics was blocked from following physics into the realm of a serious formal dynamics, including the formal structure of Hamiltonians,[1] and instead retreated into the spurious pseudo-dynamics of *ceteris paribus* conditions. This inability to emulate the core of the ideal of deterministic explanation tarnished the entire program of imitating physics.

Second, the absence of a legitimate dynamics also compromised the ideal of a scientific empiricism (Mirowski 1989c; Mirowski 1989a; Mirowski 1990d). What could it mean to attempt to fit neoclassical relations to time series evidence when the fundamental determinants of neoclassical equilibrium displayed no necessary stability from one moment to the next? Indeed, most prominent first- and second-generation neoclassicals were hostile to attempts to import such techniques as least squares estimation into economics; and the earliest efforts in this area were pioneered by individuals skeptical of neoclassical theory (Mirowski 1989a; Mirowski 1990d). Such disputes over the meaning of scientific activity also compromised the claims of neoclassical theory to have attained "scientific" status.

Third, there was the problem that physics continued to evolve rapidly after the mid-nineteenth century, whereas the neoclassical research program tended to remain mired in its original, nineteenth-century orientation. In particular, from James Clerk Maxwell onward, physics increasingly incorporated stochastic ideas into physical explanations, whereas neoclassical economics did not (Porter 1986). This progressive abandonment of the ideal of deterministic explanation has been summarized felicitously by Ilya Prigogine (Prigogine 1980, 187): "In the nineteenth century, there was a profusion of controversy between 'energeticists' and 'atomists,' the former claiming the second law [of thermodynamics] destroys the mechanical conception of the universe, the latter that the second law should be reconciled with dynamics at the price of some 'additional assumptions' such as probabilistic arguments. What this means exactly can now be seen more clearly. The 'price' is not small because it involves a far-reaching modification of the structure of dynamics." Now, it is true that neoclassical economics finally admitted some aspects of stochastic concepts into its ambit with the rise of "econometrics" (and somewhat further with the "rational expectations hypothesis") (Mirowski 1989c, 631); but the curious aspect of this development is that the stochastic terms were merely appended to the existing constrained optimization formulas, and were not part and parcel of a fundamental reconceptualization of economic theory, unlike the parallel events in physics. Moreover, as we shall observe below, these stochastic "shocks" had little or no theoretical justification, but themselves seemed only an excuse to maintain the pure deterministic ideal of explanation in the face of massive disconfirming evidence. As one prominent neoclassical put the case: "[Neoclassical economists] naturally tended to think of models in which things settle down to a unique position independently of initial conditions. Technically speaking, we theorists hoped not to introduce *hysteresis* phenomena into our model, as the Bible does when it says, 'We pass this way only once' and, in so saying, takes the subject out of the realm of science and into the realm of genuine history" (Samuelson 1970, 184–85).

Now, into this unsatisfactory situation we witness the intrusion of the further development of chaos theory in physics. The allure of this development for neoclassical economists is readily apparent: it seems to outsiders that there is now a "technical" solution to many of the most irritating and endemic problems of neoclassical theory over the last century. Here it *seems* that the most rigid determinism is reconciled with the pervasive appearance of random phenomena. Here again it *seems* that the previous lack of a substantive dynamics may be repaired with only a little more sophisticated mathematics. Here it *seems* that the formalism of strange attractors may promise law-governed behavior independent of historical location. Here it *seems* there is a remedy for the palpable failure of half a century of econometric endeavor. Further, the remedy merely involves a simple extrapolation of the original tendencies of neoclassical theory, since it requires further direct imitation of theories generated within the physics community. In summary, chaos theory appeared in the 1980s as if it just might be the salvation of the neoclassical research program.

Contrary to these impressions, nothing was further from the truth.

Mandelbrot on the Irrelevance of Modern Econometrics

Benoit Mandelbrot wrote a number of stunningly original papers in economics from roughly 1962 to 1972; and then he went on to become famous elsewhere. Although Gleick (Gleick 1987, 81–118) writes as though Mandelbrot's economic ideas had a great impact upon the profession, the simple historical fact is that they have been by and large ignored, with some few exceptions (Blattberg and Sargent 1971; Fama 1965b; Fama 1965a; McFarland and Sung 1982; Meyer and Glauber 1964) which seem to have been subsequently abandoned by their authors. Moreover, while it can be claimed that Mandelbrot's work on economics was an important influence on his later innovations concerning "fractals," which did make him famous, one can find no indication in the existing literature of how the connections might have been made. Hence we observe the curious fact that economists conceived of an enthusiasm for the chaos literature a decade or more after this literature may be said to have had its roots in economics, and yet they betrayed no interest in or curiosity about those roots. (The honorable exception is Sent 1998.)

Mandelbrot the persona is at least as fascinating as Mandelbrot the theorist. His primary identity is as a mathematician, although on occasion mathematicians have insisted that what he does is not *really* mathematics (Gleick 1987, 114). He himself has said, "Very often when I listen to the list of my previous jobs I wonder if I exist. The intersection of such sets is surely empty" (Gleick 1987, 86). He is often voluble concerning the view that he could never have accomplished his work in any conventional academic discipline or department, and that he was extremely fortunate to have worked for IBM, where he was allowed to follow his instincts. And he admits, "Economics is very far from what I planned to tackle as a scholar" (Albers and Alexanderson 1987, 214).

Four special traits of Mandelbrot and his work are central to an understanding of the episode from 1962 to 1972. The first is that Mandelbrot has been a perpetual outsider in almost every intellectual context; and especially outside the hidebound distinctions between disciplines in the modern university. There is a clear connection in this respect between his ideas and his life, as he himself has noted: "As I allowed myself to drift, I soon came to view the normal unpredictability of life as contributing layers or strata of experience that are valuable, demand no apology, and add up to a unique combination" (Albers and Alexanderson 1987, 208). No rational maximizer, he. Second, in an attitude refreshingly unorthodox for a mathematician, Mandelbrot dismisses Bourbakist formalism, and thinks the fetish for axiomatization has largely run its course: "To a student, the reduction to axioms is largely a matter of satisfying the teacher" (Albers and Alexanderson 1987, 216). Clearly, such a person would not be taken with the work of a Kenneth Arrow or a Gerard Debreu. Third, Mandelbrot is a partisan of reviving a specifically geometric intuition in mathematics, to the extent of there being a profound phenomenological approach in all of his work (and not just the economics) (Mandelbrot 1972, 261). Any research program that regularly displays a certain methodological disdain for visual evidence would certainly find this attitude quaint, at best. And fourth, Mandelbrot has persistently ridiculed the physics envy of neoclassical economists; and the irony that much statistical theory originated in social theory has not been lost on him: "It is not true that differences in development between sciences are related to, and therefore excused by, differences of 'age' as measured by the earliest systematic investigation of the different topics. Indeed, probability theory saw its first triumphs in physics, but it had been born elsewhere, in the study of problems raised by economic-psychological choice . . . Even as late as 1912, statistical social science could still be presented as a model to be followed by statistical physics" (Mandelbrot 1987, 120).

Mandelbrot's early work in physics, geology, economics, and meteorology has all been part of a larger, partially hidden agenda, one revealed in his "Premature Fractal Manifesto," written in 1964 but published only much later (Mandelbrot 1987). In that work he argued that his efforts should be regarded in the vanguard of a "second stage of indeterminism," one that he suggested with his usual modesty was a broad cultural phenomenon. The first stage of indeterminism was an attempt to introduce probability theory into such areas as physics and economics by partitioning off the causal deterministic aspects from the stochastic disturbances, in effect subordinating the latter to the former. The key to the plausibility of this first stage was a resort to the classical central limit theorem, which allowed those so inclined to cling to their previous deterministic worldviews. The second stage would be marked by an exploration of those areas where the classical central limit theorem failed to hold. These would be in the "less-developed sciences," the intellectual slums of deterministic science: weather prediction, turbulence, tensile strength and fractures, and of course economics. Much of this widening of the circle of exemplars resonated with the "holism versus reductionism" debate which was endemic to social theory, and which Mandelbrot thought was merely symptomatic of a larger problem: "in studying economic records, it may very well be preferable to avoid the temptation to attack periods of crisis separately" (Mandelbrot 1987, 124). It didn't look like Kansas, Toto; and it certainly didn't look like rational expectations.

Mandelbrot was drawn into the whole question of prices in economics by a colleague's speculating about whether "filter rules" wouldn't provide an optimal stock market investment strategy. A filter rule calibrated at ρ% is a device that monitors a share price continuously, records all local maxima and minima, and activates a buy signal at the moment when the price first reaches a local minimum plus ρ%, and conversely activates a sell signal when price first reaches a local maximum minus ρ%. Mandelbrot decided that filter rules could not dominate any other strategy, and that the problem lay where no neoclassical economist would look for it: price changes were geometrically conceptualized as continuous, generally through modeling them as continuous functions, but in the real world they were not. "Even on days when price variation seems reasonably continuous, its continuity is the result of deliberate action by a market specialist . . . The specialist creates bargains reserved to friends, while most customers have to buy at the next higher price" (Mandelbrot 1982, 102). In many instances, even insider trading does not experience continuous prices, which is why it is not foolproof. Rule changes such as stop-trading orders, "circuit-breakers," and the like are simply de facto admissions of this state of affairs.

This insight set Mandelbrot down the path of actually *looking* at time series of prices; and what he saw did not at all accord with the orthodox economic stories. First, as just mentioned, price records were punctuated by large discontinuous changes. "The only reason for assuming continuity is that many sciences tend, knowingly or not, to copy the procedures that prove successful in Newtonian physics . . . But prices are different: mechanics involves nothing comparable" (Mandelbrot 1983, 335). Second, large changes tended to "bunch" together: this contradicted the Gaussian smoothing property which would be inherent in existing stochastic models of prices. Third, as a corollary of the first two attributes, root mean square deviations did not seem to stabilize as the record grew longer. All of this implied that prices should not be modeled as analogous to Brownian motion, as had been the practice since Bachelier (Cootner 1964) (and generally still is). But further, price changes did exhibit the previously unnoticed attribute that their geo-metric appearance seemed unchanged by changes in time scale. In particular, for any arbitrary time lag d, be it daily, weekly, monthly, or yearly, $\log P (t + d) - \log P(t)$ seemed to be distributed independently of d, except for a scale factor. This implied a hyperbolic distribution of price changes, at least for the tails of the distribution. One observes that Mandelbrot was congenitally predisposed to notice all this, given his "geometric" intuition and his phe-nomenological approach.

But there was another, fortuitous element to Mandelbrot's preparation. His teacher, Paul Lévy, had demonstrated that the central limit theorem was much more complicated than had been previously suspected (Lévy 1925). Briefly, he showed that the Gaussian or "normal" distribution was only one of a family of "stable" distributions; the log of the characteristic function for the stable Lévy (sometimes called "stable Paretian" in the economic litera-ture of the 1960s) family of distributions is (Hall 1981):

$$\log f(t) = \log \int_{-\infty}^{\infty} e^{iut} \, dP(\bar{u} < u) =$$
$$i\delta t - \gamma |t|^{\alpha} [1 - i\beta \mathrm{sgn}(t) \omega(t,\alpha)]$$

where δ is any real number, $\gamma > 0$, $|\beta| \leq 1$,

$$\omega(t,\alpha) = \begin{cases} \tan(\alpha\pi/2) & \text{if } \alpha \neq 1 \\ -(2/\pi)\log|t| & \text{if } \alpha = 1 \end{cases}$$

and

$$\mathrm{sgn}(t) = \begin{cases} 1 & \text{if } t > 0 \\ 0 & \text{if } t = 0 \\ -1 & \text{if } t < 0. \end{cases}$$

When the parameters $\alpha = 2$, $\delta = \mu$, and $\gamma = \sigma^2/2$ (β is a skewness param-eter; when $\beta = 0$, the distribution is symmetric), then the resulting charac-teristic function is Gaussian (Gnedenko and Kolmogorov 1954, chapter 7; Zolotarev 1986). Lévy showed that the only possible limiting distribution for sums of independent, identically distributed random variables was a stable Lévy distribution. The conventional central limit theorem, which is a special case of the above, restricts the outcome to normality by imposing the condi-tion that each of the constituent random variables has finite variance.

Here, miraculously, a connection fell into place. Mandelbrot had been looking at distributions of price changes that were not Gaussian because they had too many outliers, a problem referred to in some previous litera-ture as the problem of "fat tails" (Mirowski 1989e). It just so happened that the tails of all non-Gaussian stable Lévy distributions resembled an asymp-totic form of "Pareto's Law," namely $P(\bar{u} > u^*) \rightarrow [u^*/V]^{-\alpha}$ as $u \rightarrow \infty$. Mandelbrot was familiar with the literature in economics on the Pareto law for incomes and had himself published on that topic (Mandelbrot 1961; Mandelbrot 1962). He now began to suspect that such hyperbolic distributions were endemic to economic variates, and that fact would have profound consequences for how one thought about the economy.

Lévy stable distribution theory was, however, no piece of cake. For instance, explicit expressions (excluding series expansion approximations) for the density functions of the family of distributions were known only in three cases: the Gaussian, the Cauchy ($\alpha = 1$, $\beta = 0$), and what was sometimes explicitly called the Lévy distribution ($\alpha = 1/2$, $\beta = 1$, $\delta = 0$, $\gamma = 1$). In the other cases, which were precisely the ones Mandelbrot suspected were characteristic of economic variates (where $1 > \alpha > 2$), since there existed no analytical density function (given the caveats above) one was prevented from making any statements about the sampling behavior of estimators; nor could one write down an analytic expression for an estimator. Further, variances were infinite, so any estimator could not depend on any moments higher than the first. Mandelbrot took to plotting the cumulative sample density of $\{\log P(t + d) - \log P(t)\}$ to estimate the magnitude of α by making use of the asymptotic Pareto law result mentioned above (Mandelbrot 1963). Although there was no way of gauging the confidence intervals, α did seem to consistently clock in at less than two, a result seconded by Eugene Fama (Fama 1963; Fama 1965). Whatever else one might say about this work, "It can be said without exaggeration that the problem of constructing statistical estimators of stable laws entered into mathematical statistics due to the work of Mandelbrot" (Zolotarev 1986, 217).

Any lesser intellect might rest content with this finding, perhaps testing for Lévy stable distributions in a thousand different guises, improvising small variations on this theme and padding the vita. But Mandelbrot wanted to push further; to see how the finding *connected* with everything else, writ large. "When working in economics, I was similarly dying to be allowed to make it known in my research papers that my methods were part of a general philosophy, of a certain approach to irregularity and chaos, and that they also mattered in physics. Invariably, the referees asked me to take these statements out" (Albers and Alexanderson 1987, 222). There was, for instance, the problem of what the existence of infinite variance *meant*. It did not mean that the values of observed prices were infinite; nor did it mean that sample moments of all orders were not themselves finite. All it meant was that sample variances grew unpredictably and without bound with increase in sample size. Then there was the problem of the widespread habit of enforcing a bound on sample variances by automatically regarding the processes as non-stationary, and detrending or otherwise "pre-whitening" to produce a finite variance.[2]

Here is where Mandelbrot's philosophical position began to set him apart from others. He regarded this practice as backsliding, letting the old tropis-matic predispositions for a partitioning of a deterministic core and a subor-dinate stochastic explanation (Mandelbrot 1967b, 396–97) dominate the inquiry. More than once he suggested that a resort to the hypothesis of non-stationarity was nonscientific (Mandelbrot 1972, 266), in that it relin-quished the search for a truly general law; at the very least it violated the principle of parsimonious explanation in the context of a phenomenological description. "It is well known that photography is simplest when an object is at an infinite distance from the camera. Therefore, even if the actual distance is known to be finite, the photographer ought to set the distance at in-finity if that distance exceeds some finite threshold" (Mandelbrot 1967b, 399). Increasingly, Mandelbrot was led to think about what it would mean for something to appear non-stationary but in fact to have built-in low-frequency dependence.

Thus Mandelbrot entered the next phase of his economics research, which he later distinguished as the difference between "Noah" and "Joseph" effects; it is my impression that no economist accompanied him beyond this point. The Noah effect was the extreme non-Gaussian character of the marginal distribution of prices: the name was intended to conjure up the abrupt flash floods that came out of nowhere and swept away all in their wake. The Joseph effect was the existence of very long-run temporal dependence, inde-pendent of the nature of the marginal distribution: the name was intended to refer to the Biblical seven lean years and seven fat years. The Joseph effect was evident whenever observers thought they saw "cycles" in economic time series which would fail to remain stable as the series lengthened. These two effects were separate and separable, but they did have one connection in Mandelbrot's way of thinking: time series with long dependence would exhibit a characteristic spectrum, a hyperbolic spectral density $S'(f) \sim f^{\alpha-2}$ with $1 < \alpha < 2$. By direct analogy with the previous case, a pure Gaussian spectral density would have $\alpha = 2$ (that is, the spectrum would be flat, "white noise"); a situation with a $\alpha < 2$ was dubbed (perhaps unfortunately) "fractional Gaussian noise." Again, note well that all these processes are purely stationary.

Infinite variance was certainly bad enough; but now the purely general case was mind-numbing: "Were all [economic time] series to have an in-finite variance, one might have been able to save linearity while replacing all Gaussian distributions by stable Paretian [i.e., Lévy] distributions. But we must also allow for coordinate series with finite variance and an H-spectrum [of fractional Gaussian noise] . . . No linear model I can think of allows for such coexistence, and I have become resigned to give up linearity for the sake of coexistence . . . [Two time series] can be identical in the long run even if the structures are vastly different, one having an H-spectrum and a finite variance, while the other has infinite variance and—in effect—has a white spectrum" (Mandelbrot 1969, 86, 88). This was the first time in history that someone had developed a taxonomy for all the possible cases which would cover the "typical spectral shape" of an economic time series. Yet it was not a taxonomy without rhyme or reason: the great preponderance of cases encompassed either infinite variance or infinite intertemporal dependence; Gaussian white noise was just the most special of cases. To anticipate our narrative below: whereas the Gaussian case corresponded to the Euclidean world of integer dimension, the rest of the cases corresponded to fractal-dimensioned processes. But these were precisely the sorts of speculations regularly expurgated by journal editors.

While one can repair to the sequence of journal articles from 1962 to 1973 to survey the technical issues, there is no text where Mandelbrot actually drew out all the implications of his program for neoclassical economic theory and for orthodox econometrics. (This only happened in a belated, and it must be noted, not completely straightforward way, in Mandelbrot 1997.) Indeed, after 1972 one gets the impression that he just lost interest in economics (or perhaps the reactions of neoclassical economists just grew tedious);[3] and in any event, insights he had gained into the relationships between fractal dimensions and random processes were finding all sorts of fruitful applications in physics, meteorology, and computer graphics. Nevertheless, one can glean from his papers a bill of indictments against orthodox economics that is more profoundly coherent than most others drawn up in the twentieth century.

To begin at the beginning, recall that the "marginalist revolution" of the 1870s was derived from direct imitation of the energy formalism of nineteenth-century physics (Mirowski 1988; Mirowski 1989b); the name itself reveals that value was predicated upon continuous and reversible fields of force that gave rise to continuous and reversible functions with prices as their main arguments. The entire project of smooth substitution and constrained maximization is compromised by Mandelbrot's initial observation: empirical time series of prices are not continuous functions. "But prices are different: mechanics involves nothing comparable, and gives no guidance on this account" (Mandelbrot 1983, 335). In this context, one is not making reference to a few discontinuities here and there, like that dinosaur the "kinked demand curve"; instead, the whole penchant for differentiable functions is where the program goes off the rails. To discuss many of these random processes, Mandelbrot often finds that he must resort to functions which are nowhere differentiable, such as Weierstrass functions and Cantor dusts. As usual, the neoclassicals were using the wrong mathematics for the wrong reasons (Mirowski 1986; Mirowski 1990b).

The Marshallian "law" of supply and demand is most certainly the primary victim of this reconceptualization. I have argued (Mirowski 1988, chapter 4) that the central analytical device of the Marshallian system is the division of all economic phenomena into differing time frames, which are then ranked according to their relative inertia. Yet as Mandelbrot observes, "It is astonishing that the hypothesis of independence of weekly changes can be consistently carried so far, showing no discernable discontinuity between long-term adjustments to follow supply and demand, which would be the subject matter of economics, and the short-term fluctuations" (Mandelbrot 1967b, 406). The primary insight of Mandelbrot's empirical work is that distributions of prices are approximately scale-invariant: it just doesn't matter from the stochastic point of view if you look at them minute by minute or year by year. That scale invariance suggests that the Marshallian distinction between short run and long run is an analytical mistake.

But the Noah and Joseph effects chamfer even deeper than that, cutting to the very heart of the neoclassical worldview. The notion of efficient markets is bound up with the possibility of arbitrage: that is, a class of rational trades that serve to stabilize the price by bringing it closer to the "fundamentals." To put it another way, perfect arbitrage should "whiten" the spectral density, as often asserted by the rational expectations school. But in the presence of the Joseph effect—that is, very long dependence in prices—"there exists indeed a class of important cases where useful implementation of arbitraging is *impossible*" (Mandelbrot 1971, 225). The idea is really quite simple, although it can be expressed as formally as one might wish. Suppose price changes are discontinuous and exhibit long dependence. The arbitrageur is trying to "get rid" of sharp discontinuities (the Noah effect), but since changes are intrinsically discontinuous, he can almost always never quite "catch up." With anything less than a perfect infinite anticipatory horizon, his actions have systematic consequences far down the line (the Joseph effect) that no one can foresee, and so he ends up increasing the variance of the overall time series. (Mandelbrot doesn't mention it, but Bayesian "learning" schemes are also compromised in this context, since we have already noted that long dependence can give the impression of periodic cycles which just aren't there.) Various combinations of the Noah and Joseph effects (or indeed some markets where pure white noise reigns) will produce different consequences for the actions of the arbitrageurs. "Those closest to efficiency are of two kinds: some in which anticipatory horizon is infinite, and others where 'market noise' is so overwhelming that prediction is impossible and the assumption of efficiency cannot be disproved!" (Mandelbrot 1971, 233). Paradoxically, incremental improvements in foresight could result in price variation that is less smooth. A few perceptive souls caught a glimpse of what this would mean for finance departments: "Since no rational man with a quadratic utility function would invest in stocks, most normative work on utility approaches to speculative markets is obsolete" (Cootner 1964, 196–97). (Notice the date of that quote—1964!)

Of course, the main implications of Mandelbrot's work revolve around issues of inference, information, and the meaning of rationality in a world that diverges from smooth Normality. Neoclassical theorists like to talk in terms of "economizing" with respect to information, to have inference governed by "loss functions" and the like. One of the profound implications of the Mandelbrot program is that the constrained maximization version of rational behavior is often meaningless when confronting a Lévy stable stochastic environment. Take, for instance, a sample from a Cauchy distribution. The distribution of the sample mean (the expected value of the distribution does not exist) in this case is identical to the distribution of each individual item in the sample (Feller 1971, 51). Hence calculation of the sample average is superfluous; and indeed, collecting more information is futile (Tintner and Sengupta 1972, 23). Since augmentation of the data set never improves the performance of the estimator, the whole notion of "economizing" on information is nugatory. To a great extent this is also true with other Lévy stable distributions, since augmentation of a sample does not result in convergence of sample statistics to higher moments; and many consistent estimators of first moments actually do not make use of all the component sample elements (Taylor 1974).

The upshot is that almost every technique of orthodox econometrics is useless and would probably have to be discarded. First and most obviously, one loses the Gauss-Markhov theorem, and with it least squares; in the presence of Lévy stable distributions, least squares is a defective estimator because it gives too much weight to outliers and is too heavily sample-dependent (Taylor 1974, 170; Mandelbrot 1963b, 410). ARIMA estimation would also have to be jettisoned, because in the presence of the Joseph effect fractional Gaussian noise is technically ARMA $(0, \infty)$; and most sample statistics depend upon the assumptions that $p < \infty$ and $q < \infty$. "When the Arma approach is viewed as analogous to fitting of curves by broken lines, and when it is recognized that such curve fitting does not warrant being called 'modelling,' there is nothing in the approach to warrant criticism (or interest?)" (Mandelbrot and Taqqu 1979, 25). Spectral analysis is also heavily compromised, because the technique is an attempt to decompose a time series into a sum of periodic harmonic components. The thrust of the Joseph effect is that the separate periodicities have no actual existence, but are merely an artifact of infinite long dependence (Mandelbrot 1972, 268). Hence, while spectral analysis might be useful in trying to diagnose the presence of long dependence, there may be nothing actually to *estimate*.

If Mandelbrot is right, and all the econometric idols need to be smashed, then how is it possible that so many practitioners have been so grossly misled for so very long? Perhaps Mandelbrot's most disquieting thesis is that their own flawed practices served to deceive them: "One very common approach is to note that large price changes are usually traceable to well-determined 'causes' that should be eliminated before one attempts a stochastic model of the remainder. Such preliminary censorship obviously brings any distribution closer to the Gaussian . . . the distinction between the causal and random areas is sharp in the Gaussian case and very diffuse in the stable Paretian case" (Mandelbrot 1963b, 403, 415).

The very practice of fitting linear models, particularly those involving trended variables, acted to filter out low-frequency variance and outliers, thus effectively "pre-whitening" the data. "Normal" distributions weren't normal at all; they were just artifacts of the shotgun wedding of deterministic theory with "random shocks." In a stable Lévy world, linear transforms of stochastic processes could look deterministic and vice versa: in a sense, a preoccupation with "theory" would obstruct the ability to "see" the full range of stochastic possibilities. This was a very wry twist on the orthodox interpretation of the victors in the "measurement without theory" controversy (Mirowski 1989a).

This project was of the most thoroughgoing indeterminism; one which could brook no compromise or make no peace with the neoclassical research program, a program which was, after all, nothing more than a bowdlerized, nineteenth-century imitation of physics. "Broadly speaking, a pattern is scientifically significant and is felt to have chances of being repeated, only if in some sense its 'likelihood' of having occurred by chance is very small . . . But, when one works in a field where the background noise is Paretian, one must realize that one faces a burden of proof that is closer to that of history and autobiography than that of physics. . . . some stochastic models . . . dispense with any kind of built-in causal structure, and yet generate paths in which both the unskilled and the skilled eye distinguish the kind of detail that is usually associated with causal relations . . . these structures should be considered as *perceptual illusion*" (Mandelbrot 1963a, 433–34).

Fractal Bridges over Troubled Waters

The reactions of econometricians and finance economists to Mandelbrot's critique deserve a separate narrative, which we intend to provide below in chapter 12. However, before doing so, there are some direct bridges between the work on Lévy stable distributions and fractals which may prove of interest to those concerned with the chaos literature. These areas of continuity between the earlier and later work may be found in the governing role of chance, the geometry of the irregular, and the analytic importance of hyperbolic distributions.

The interesting characteristic of Lévy stable distributions, as revealed by Lévy's work on central limit theorems, was their self-similarity relative to scale.[4] As Mandelbrot has often said in lecture, "A process that has no scale has the scale of the observer"; or, as he observed in *The Fractal Geometry of Nature* (Mandelbrot 1983, 18), "The notion that a numerical result should depend on the relation of object to observer is in the spirit of the physics of this century," but not at all, we hasten to add, in the spirit of the nineteenth century. In that sense, a time series of prices looks like a coastline: it appears to be very irregular, but however close you get, it also looks roughly the same. A coastline also looks as if it might be generated by some sort of stochastic process; but the problem here is that the standard Gaussian or random walk processes are not able to adequately simulate the geometry. In an effort to describe the degree of irregularity, suppose we define a number $d(S)$ such that:

$$d(S) = \lim_{\varepsilon \to \infty} \ln M(\varepsilon)/\ln(1/\varepsilon)$$

where $M(\epsilon)$ is the minimum number of N-dimensional cubes needed to cover a subset S of space containing such an irregular curve. For small ϵ, this implies that $M(\epsilon) \sim K^{-d}$, where K is some arbitrary constant; Mandelbrot originally called $d(S)$ the "fractal dimension" of the curve.[5] If one is dealing with a self-similar curve, then a graph of $\ln M / \ln \epsilon$ against $[\ln \epsilon]^{-1}$ would be linear with slope d. This is precisely the estimation technique that Mandelbrot had been using on his time series of prices; and here was the link between the geometry of the irregular and Lévy stable stochastic processes. Just as the Gaussian distribution was only a special case of the more general Lévy stable class of distributions with an integer exponent, conventional geometry was only a special case with integer exponent of a much more general geometry, called fractal geometry. As Mandelbrot had earlier claimed that the stable distribution exponent α for price changes was a fraction between 1 and 2, he now claimed that nature abounded with the geometry of fractional dimensions, far beyond anything suspected in the heavenly city of the Greek geometers. The norm of Nature was not the smooth celestial orbits of the planets, or the music of the spheres, but rather the roiling turbulence of Heraclitus's brook. Even the distribution of intervals in music was closer to fractal noise than to being Gaussian. Moreover, "the probability distribution characteristic of fractals is hyperbolic" (Mandelbrot 1983, 422), just as one might say that the probability distribution characteristic of the Euclidean world is the Gaussian.

At this juncture we leave the specific writings of Mandelbrot, since the uses found for fractal geometry extended beyond his own interests in mathematics, hydrology, meteorology, and geology (Barenblatt 1996). The application most relevant to a modern neoclassical economist is in the area closest to his own heart: namely, the physics of energy and motion. More relevant to our overarching thesis is the impact of Mandelbrot's marriage of geometry and probability theory upon problems of Hamiltonian dynamics in physics, since it is that literature, and *not* Mandelbrot's economic writings, which in the 1980s spurred the mimetic impulse among modern neoclassical economists.

The story of the breakdown of determinism in Hamiltonian dynamics has been well told by Prigogine and others (Prigogine 1980; Prigogine 1984; Ford 1983; Earman 1986; McCauley 1993), and so we shall not repeat it here. While textbooks and classroom expositions of Hamiltonians made it seem as though in the general case Hamiltonians had determinate analytical solutions, it was a growing embarrassment that they had an "incurable disease unmentionable in polite society" (Ford 1983, 40), namely no well-behaved constants of motion other than H itself. The breakthrough came when physicists stopped looking for deterministic invariants and began looking at geometric patterns in phase space.[6] What they found was a wholly different kind of order amid the chaos, the phenomenon of self-similarity at different geometric scales. This suggested that many phase-space portraits of dynamical systems exhibited fractal geometries; and this in turn was taken as an indication that a wholly different approach must be taken to describing the evolution of mechanical systems.

It is at this point that economists tend to lose their way, so it is imperative to make it clear how on just this juncture all the strands of our narrative converge. Neoclassical microeconomics is predicated upon the metaphor and formalism of potential energy which is the heart and soul of the Laplacean daemon in physics, the deterministic worldview. However, neoclassicals never partook of the successes of that worldview, namely, a Hamiltonian dynamics in their core doctrine of Walrasian general equilibrium, however much they prognosticated that a viable dynamics was just around the corner.[7] Mandelbrot essentially proposed to relinquish all hope of determinism by renouncing the quest for any mechanistic dynamics in favor of a thoroughgoing stochastic approach in economics, but since this renunciation would have inherently contradicted neoclassical theory, it was rejected by the majority of economists. In the 1980s physicists found the Hamiltonian approach wanting, but used it as a benchmark and as a springboard for reconceptualizing the nature of dynamics. Now some neoclassical economists, with no sign of self-awareness that one can't persist in legitimate imitation of the physics if one never had the solid analytical structure of the Hamiltonian to start with, rushed headlong to embrace the new mathematical technology largely, one fears, because of its popularity among the physicists. A brief consideration of the modern chaos literature will reveal that a little physics is a dangerous thing.

Many introductory texts such as Devaney (1986) and surveys for economists such as Kelsey (1988) and Baumol and Benhabib (1989) begin with the simple tent map $x_{t+1} = \phi\, x_t\, (1 - x_t)$ on the unit interval [0, 1], and show how raising the forcing parameter ϕ causes period-doubling and the onset of chaos; then the reader is led to the more general map $f: \mathbb{R} \rightarrow \mathbb{R}$ and, by a detour through the Sarkovskii theorem,[8] to the result that if f has a periodic point of period three, then f has periodic points of all other periods (Devaney 1986, 60–68). While this logical sequence is responsible mathematical pedagogy (and a great toy if you have access to computer graphics), it has been disastrous for economists, because it gives the impression that somehow this is what chaos is all about, not to mention giving rise to the temptation to generate all sorts of single-variable matchbook models where a single recursive difference equation is somehow supposed to "account" for the apparently stochastic behavior of stock prices, macro fluctuations, monetary disturbances, and every other scourge known to mankind. The issue of conceptualizing chaos in physics is much more complex than these little mathematical exercises.

More advanced texts in physics acknowledge that the problem of extracting seemingly stochastic behavior from seemingly deterministic processes is much older than the present chaos craze, dating back at least to the work of Henri Poincaré (Lichtenberg and Liebman 1983; Prigogine 1980; McCauley 1993). Over the last century, physicists have come to believe that there are many qualitatively different kinds of stochastic output, which should be distinguished by the sort of process that generates them. For instance, it has long been known that well-behaved Hamiltonians could themselves give rise to apparently stochastic trajectories, but this has nothing to do with the mathematical niceties mentioned in the paragraph above.

In what follows, it may be useful for economists to be made better aware of the difference between fractal structure in maps and chaotic flows (Ruelle 1989, 25). In maps, as in the simple tent map above, a plot of the motion of the system is discrete, and there are no restrictions upon the continuity of the motion described. However, the dynamics of physical systems are generally cast as problems of motion in phase space, which must conform to requirements of continuity in motion (Schuster 1989, 107). Although the terminology in this arena has not yet stabilized, we shall reserve the terms "chaos" and "phase space" exclusively for flows because we are here concerned with the relation of neoclassicism to the treatment of dynamics in physics. Thus the "degrees of freedom" of an economic model will be defined as the N parameters required to fully specify the motion of the system

Table 9. The Categories of a Stochastic Dynamics

	Degrees of Freedom	
	1, 2	3 or more
conservative (integrable) system	resonance	mixing, c-systems Arnold diffusion
dissipative system	no stochastic behavior	strange attractor:true "chaos"

minus the p independent constraints on the system. This convention is at extreme variance with almost every other discussion of "chaos" in economics, which generally starts with examples of maps and not flows (Barnett, Berndt, and White 1988; Barnett and Chen 1988; Baumol and Benhabib 1989; Kelsey 1988).[9]

The most important distinctions to be made from the present point of view are those which divide *conservative* from *dissipative* systems, and distinctions between low and high numbers of degrees of freedom in the particular dynamical problem. The various permutations of these categories are presented above in table 9, to stress the differing kinds of seemingly random behavior that may arise in a deterministic context.

One can observe from this table that the terminology of "chaos" has already been sadly abused in the literature, since it should only legitimately be attached to dissipative systems of flows (and then, not to all of them): namely, systems that "lose available energy" or wind down owing to friction, heat loss, or some other cause and hence evolve in an irreversible manner. *The mere appearance of stochastic behavior in a deterministic system does not depend upon the presence of "chaos."* Mandelbrot, as usual, was right: irregularity and randomness are everywhere; it is only we who have chosen to avert our eyes from them.

Already, the very notion of "determinism" has suffered a serious setback in these instances, since it is widely acknowledged that conservative systems stand as the epitome of the deterministic ideal. But this is more than a terminological or philosophical quibble; it cuts to the very quick of the neoclassical fervor to imitate the physics. It is important to recall that Hamiltonian dynamics only apply to conservative or integrable systems, whereas true "chaos" is confined to those situations where Hamiltonians are not applicable or solvable. The reason for this distinction is that the stochastic motion that one observes in Hamiltonian dynamics is exhibited over the entire parameter range (Lichtenberg and Liebman 1983, 422), whereas the distinguishing characteristic of the phase space of dissipative systems is the simultaneous presence of regular trajectories and regions of stochasticity. In other words, only dissipative systems display such phenomena as a "transition to chaos" conditional upon some forcing parameter. Only intrinsically dissipative systems can exhibit a strange attractor in phase space, because trajectories can't be "attracted" in a conservative system. It is the dissipation which serves to lower the "dimension" of the geometric characterization of trajectories in phase space.

Physicists needed something to ground their analysis in these situations where Hamiltonians couldn't work, and they found it in the entirely different kind of invariant other than energy conservation: namely, the geometric self-similarity of the attractors in phase space, that is, in their "fractal" character. It was not just another version of mechanism or a neat bit of math to get them over the hump (so to speak); it was an entirely different way of attacking a long-standing problem.[10]

It is critical to see that physicists have used their prior theory to divide the world into regions of invariance and regions of change: thus they know in which situations one might expect to find a strange attractor, and more importantly, have prior theoretical expectations about which variables should be governed by low-dimensional attractors. Unfortunately, neoclassical microeconomists possess no parallel expertise or theoretical resources, and therefore are whistling in the dark when it comes to claiming that any economic phenomenon is or even might be "chaotic." First, they possess *no legitimate Hamiltonian dynamics*. The reason for this is that neoclassicals have never made up their mind about what precisely should be conserved in their theoretical system (Mirowski 1989b; Northrop 1941). It then follows that neoclassicals have *no theoretical rationale* for claiming that any economic system or phenomenon is dissipative, and hence no legitimate rationale for even looking for strange attractors.[11] Indeed in the neoclassical case, one might argue, it is more likely that conservative preference fields are the paradigm of reversible phenomena and hence should give rise to mixing or Arnold diffusion, where stochastic behavior is pervasive and "order" is entirely absent.

Second, neoclassical economists have no arguments to place some bounds upon any *expected degrees of freedom* in any of their models. Since the number of goods and actors in true general equilibrium models is unbounded (especially if one resorts to the Arrow-Debreu ruse of defining physical goods at different temporal locations as different commodities), they have no analogue to the physicists' a priori knowledge of the relevant number of spatial dimensions and so on. Often this issue is finessed by arbitrarily restricting models to a single actor, or two goods, or two periods, as if degrees of freedom were not a central criterion for assisting in evaluating a model. Hence the neoclassicals have ignored the crucial distinctions in table 9 because they have no idea which restrictions should be placed on the sorts of random phenomena to be detected in the social sphere. Do price fluctuations more closely resemble mixing sorts of turbulence, or are they rather more like resonance? No matter how mathematically sophisticated they might seem to an untutored outsider, neoclassical general equilibrium models leave too many degrees of freedom dangling, and therefore place no intelligible restrictions upon economic explanation.

The prime implication of these lapses of explanatory practice is that all claims that chaos theory will somehow "reconcile randomness and determinism in economics" are spurious. The flaws show up in different ways, depending on whether the statements are made by a neoclassical economic theorist or else by an economist more concerned with econometric practices. On the neoclassical side, the flaws often appear in the context of a claim that some small recursive model "demonstrates" how random output can be endogenous to the economic system, and then perhaps some further moralizing as to how this might disprove rational expectations or reveal the legitimacy of government intervention or Keynesianism. In fact such models have nothing coherent to say about the actual economy, since the incoherence of a neoclassical dynamics is neither rectified nor clarified by the introduction of nonlinear mathematics. If anything, chaotic models might serve to reveal the futility of the neoclassical research project, if the models were ever seriously entertained (but see chapter 12), but this development betokens the abandonment of determinism, not any sort of reconciliation.

The case of the econometrically oriented economist turned out to be much more interesting. Here we find researchers who view the chaos literature in a much more sophisticated manner, as a source of possible empirical techniques which may or may not have any direct connection to the existing neoclassical research program. These authors championed the use of such techniques as estimation of Liapunov exponents or the dimension of strange attractors in economic time series by means of the Grassberger-Procaccia method (Grassberger and Procaccia 1983; Schuster 1989). Yet even here the confusion over the correct meaning of "randomness" is evident. The crucial question, often skirted nervously, is what should we expect to find out from such procedures. What can we say about "intrinsic" versus "extrinsic" randomness? Some say we should expect both: "In economics, however, it seems inevitable that we will have random terms in our equations. If for no other reason, this will be because economic activity is affected by biological and meteorological phenomena. These systems will almost certainly be chaotic in nature. As far as economics is concerned they will appear as random terms in our equations" (Kelsey 1988, 12). Others suspect that that road leads to perdition, and therefore try to opt out of the problem: "For the purposes of this article we will avoid the deep questions of philosophy and define 'random process' to be a process whose [fractal strange attractor] dimension is 'high.' A 'deterministic process' is a process with 'low dimension'" (Brock and Sayers 1988, 74).

But this "deep philosophical" problem is not to be shunted off onto the despised band of philosophers and methodologists so easily; there is an *impasse* here born of an unthinking mimesis of the physicists. Both approaches to conceptualizing the distinction between order and randomness are equally incoherent. Contrary to Brock (in Brock and Sayers 1988), the dimensionality of strange attractors does not exhaust the universe of forms of randomness, as explained above. Contrary to Kelsey (1988), mixing chaotic processes with other stochastic processes renders both unrecoverable, and hence the distinction meaningless.

The inability to divide the world into types of stochastic phenomena described in table 9 now comes home to roost, in that different forms of randomness have become hopelessly tangled. As Grassberger and Procaccia (1983, 190) remind us, the estimated Liapunov exponents may get at the "stretching" in phase space, but they have nothing to say about "folding," which is one of the main criteria of differentiation of types of stochastic behavior. And even worse, Liapunov exponents cannot even be defined in the presence of other sorts of "noise." As for the Grassberger-Procaccia method of using the correlation integral to arrive at an estimate of the dimension of a strange attractor, it is a technique severely compromised by the presence of "noise" precisely because the fine geometric detail of a self-similar attractor is "fuzzed" out by extraneous shocks. All of this does not bother the physicists much, since their theories tell them when to expect each particular eventuality, and they can intervene in an experiment to take each into account. Economists wedded to finding an unspecific "deterministic" explanation adopting a quasi-phenomenological approach to economic time series are not so well equipped or well prepared. All the possible "types" of randomness are lumped together, and the net result is a wash. This, rather than any recalcitrance of the data, explains such disappointing results as those found by Brock (1986) and Brock and Sayers (1988), and others discussed in the next chapter.

Chaos Comes to Economics

It seems to me that the most sophisticated economists concerned with the chaos literature rapidly soured on the vaunted promise that chaos research would reconcile determinism and randomness in neoclassical economics, something I had predicted back in 1990. For instance, the tone of Baumol and Benhabib (1989) is notably muted. Or, in Brock and Malliaris (1989, 322) we find the downbeat prognostication that "it is an irresolvable question whether macroeconomic fluctuations are generated by high dimensional chaos or infinite dimensional, i.e., stochastic processes." What has been missed in the interim is that this was exactly the point of Mandelbrot's earlier work in economics, and has been a theme of his work since his "Premature Fractal Manifesto." Once one is open to the pervasiveness of seemingly random phenomena, then it becomes possible to see the observer as inextricably bound up with the phenomena. Is economic life random or deterministic? Is the glass half full or half empty? The much-trumpeted thesis that chaotic models "save" deterministic law is itself a bit of wishful thinking, when one observes from such mathematical work as that of Bamsley and Demko (1985) that Julia sets and other fractal shapes, while properly viewed as the result of a deterministic process, have the equally valid interpretation as the limit of a random process.

This chapter does not argue, it should be made clear, that the chaos literature had no substantial implications for economics. Quite the contrary. The seeming ubiquity of Lévy stable distributions of economic variates such as prices and incomes suggests that fractal attractors in phase space may ultimately have some import for economic explanation. After all, as Mandelbrot (1983, 422) has written, "the probability distribution characteristic of fractals is hyperbolic." Economic variates have often been noted to display forms of self-similarity as regards time scale, but no one (outside of a curious group of "Econophysicists" not discussed here; but see Burda et al. 2003) has known what to make of the observation (Rose 1986). Further, as Mandelbrot has often claimed, the Grassberger-Procaccia procedure of plotting the log of the correlation integral against log of "distance" really differs very little from Mandelbrot's original procedure of plotting the log of price differences against the log of lags, so there is some hope for this procedure to be used as a taxonomic device, *as long as it is subordinate to a coherent economic theory*. This theory will have to allow for randomness not as error or perturbation, but as constituting the very substrate of economic experience in a manner never dreamed of by the advocates of rational expectations. It will also affect the type of mathematics used in economic explanations, in a manner parallel to that predicted by a famous physicist: "Without this infinite precision, the continuum becomes, physically speaking, meaningless . . . Newtonian dynamics has twice foundered on assumptions that something was infinite when in fact it was not: the speed of light, c, and the reciprocal of Planck's constant $1/h$ . . . Complexity theory now reveals a third tacitly assumed infinity in classical dynamics, namely the assumption of infinite computational and observational precision . . . Perhaps the most striking feature of this reformulation is that all physical variables will be quantized" (Ford 1983, 46–47).

However, what the chaos literature ultimately did not do is augment or save neoclassical economic theory. Mandelbrot's heritage is not a mere matter of "stylized facts" that neoclassicals may choose to ignore when it suits them (Brock and Malliaris 1989, 322). On the contrary, if followed to their bitter conclusions, chaos models would render orthodox theory meaningless, which is why I predicted that they would prove as hot a potato as Mandelbrot's original work. Neoclassical theory exists to paint a portrait of a deterministic, lawlike *order* in the economic sphere, independent of the machinations and beliefs of the economic actors. The chaos literature instead reveals the curious symbiosis of randomness and determinism (Bondi 1983), the blurring of the boundaries between order and chaos. We may finally have arrived at the critical juncture in human intellectual history where our images of the natural world are so very anomic and frightening that economists can no longer seek to imitate modern physics, since doing so would undermine their role and function in social life.

12

Mandelbrot's
Economics after a
Quarter-Century

Introduction

Many academic fields have had the distinctive pleasure and honor of experiencing Benoit Mandelbrot "wandering in and out" (his words) of their well-defined preserves; but few have realized that at least when it came to fractals, the first field to enjoy this experience was not physics but rather economics.[1] As we have described in chapter 11, starting in 1960 and extending through 1972, Mandelbrot wrote a series of seminal articles on the interpretation of Pareto's Law of income distribution, the statistical properties of time series of prices, the martingale hypothesis with regard to asset prices, and the various implications of these stochastic properties for conventional ideas of arbitrage. After that point, Mandelbrot exited from economics, and thereafter became famous for his championing of fractal geometry in the physical sciences. It is hard to impress upon a general audience how very extraordinary this seems in hindsight. It has been relatively common for natural scientists, and especially physicists, to transfer to economics; but it is unprecedented for someone to begin by publishing in economics, only to decamp to the natural sciences to find fame and fortune—not to mention resisting the temptation to parlay that success in the natural sciences into credibility in economics. Here, I will provide a survey of the response to Mandelbrot's economic work within the economics profession since its publication.

Mandelbrot's work has experienced two discrete surges of interest in economics, once in the late 1960s and again in the late 1980s. In the first instance, it was perceived as a frontal assault upon both econometrics and theories of asset pricing then dominant; by the early 1970s it became common wisdom that this critique could safely be ignored. But in the late 1980s Mandelbrot's name became widely associated with chaos theory in nonlinear dynamics, and many economists became fascinated with chaos in economics, thus indirectly prompting a renewed consideration of his work. Mandelbrot reacted by repackaging his earlier work for economists, augmented with some further commentary (1997). Nevertheless, by the mid-1990s chaos theory had gone the way of stable Paretian distributions in economics, with the orthodox wisdom now widely holding that "chaos" could not be found in economic models or economic time series. Further, one could also find a renewed series of articles criticizing the earlier work on stable distributions. One might regard these two incidents as inappropriate subjects for a review essay, except for the possibility, raised by the published record, that neither incident was an open-and-shut case of Popperian bold conjecture and astringent refutation. Indeed, I had predicted in 1990 that the neoclassical orthodoxy, hereafter referred to as "neoclassical economics," would find chaos theory and nonlinear dynamics indigestible, insalubrious, and inconsistent with its entire approach to economics; and I take no pleasure now in reporting my success in this prediction. Rather, the task before us now is to document how this happened and to provide a roadmap and a cautionary tale for those interested in the fractal character of economic data. In my opinion, Mandelbrot's economics still holds appreciable unrealized promise which has been temporarily obscured by disciplinary inertia and some curious empirical practices. It has been further exploited in the fledgling community of physicists employed within the finance sector (Pimbly 1997; Burda et al. 2003); but this application has further served to make Mandelbrot's themes appear unsavory for economists.

From Pareto's Law to Stable Distributions

One of the first mathematical curiosities to catch Mandelbrot's attention, along with Zipf's Law in linguistics, was the so-called Pareto's Law of income distribution. Far from possessing the full-blown status of a "law" in economics, this was rather an observation by the *fin de siècle* economist Vilfredo Pareto that income distributions across a wide range of European contexts seemed to be distributed along the following curve: $\text{Log } N = A - \alpha \log x$, where N is the number of households with incomes greater than x, and A and α are parameters.[2] Pareto's observation had occupied an uneasy place in economics when Mandelbrot took up its explanation in a series of papers from 1960 to 1962, with some economists maintaining that it fitted the data poorly, others that it needed some sort of microeconomic justification. Mandelbrot, because of his familiarity with the work of Paul Lévy, instead saw fit to stress that the phenomenon of "fat tails" in the distribution of income indicated the presence of stable distributions other than the Gaussian, especially when α was estimated as $1 < \alpha < 2$. It also marked the beginning of his fascination with self-similar processes, and the plotting of cumulative distributions on log-log diagrams to estimate fractional dimensions. At essentially the same time, Mandelbrot saw the possibility of extending his insight to the distributions of prices of other goods (since, for an economist, income is simply the price of human effort). When he began to look at time series of share prices for evidence of stable distributions, only then did economists take notice.

Two papers in 1963 especially drew an immediate response. Previously, economists had been modeling time series of stock prices as "random walks" or standard Brownian motion; but Mandelbrot insisted that the empirical record did not resemble that found in conventional diffusion physics. Price records were punctuated by huge discontinuous changes, which often tended to bunch together, violating the Gaussian smoothing tendency. As he wrote later, "The only reason for assuming continuity is that many sciences tend, knowingly or not, to copy the procedures that prove successful in Newtonian physics . . . But prices are different: mechanics involves nothing comparable."[3] Root mean square deviations did not seem to stabilize as price records grew longer, and furthermore, Mandelbrot thought that the geometric shape of the series appeared unchanged whether the time scale was weekly, monthly, or yearly. His proposed hypothesis was to reconceptualize the marginal distribution of price changes as one of the class of stable Lévy distributions, or as he called it at that time, "stable Paretian."

Since the Gaussian distribution, which had been previously favored by economists, was one member of the class of stable Lévy distributions, this proposal might initially seem a harmless minor revision of previous economic doctrines; but Mandelbrot (1963a, 432) realized from the start that this was not the case. For all densities outside the Gaussian, stable Lévy distributions with $1 < \alpha < 2$ had infinite moments outside the first moment; and worse, with the exception of the Gaussian and Cauchy distributions, closed form analytic density functions could not even be written down. Almost every statistical practice of the econometricians in the 1960s would have been compromised or undermined with this amendment: ordinary least squares, the workhorse of econometrics in the 1960s, would be deemed a defective estimator because it gave too much weight to outliers. Correlation exercises in the time domain, such as spectral analysis or ARIMA models, would lose their statistical rationale. Maximum likelihood procedures were effectively stymied. However, the stochastic implications for economic models were even worse. The idea of "economizing" on information, so very central to neoclassical economics, was rendered ludicrous in a stable Lévy world. The very concept of spreading risk through diversification of the portfolio—the centerpiece of neoclassical portfolio theory from Markowitz onward—was progressively neutralized the further away the stable Lévy parameter α of the price distribution fell below 2, the value which indicated a Gaussian distribution (Samuelson 1972, 861–76).

It is important for the history to observe that the dire consequences and deleterious character of Mandelbrot's hypothesis for most of orthodox economics were not immediately apparent to most economists. His initial argument from Occam's razor—that Lévy stable distributions were the more general case of the central limit theorem used to justify Gaussian formalisms, and therefore should be accorded commensurate explanatory legitimacy—initially carried the day with some prominent economists. It was thus acknowledged: "There can be little doubt that Mandelbrot's hypotheses are the most revolutionary development in the theory of speculative prices since Bachelier's initial (1990) work" (Cootner 1964, 195). For instance, Eugene Fama built his early career at Chicago championing the ideas of Mandelbrot; Thomas Sargent endorsed an estimator more robust to the presence of Lévy stable distributions than least squares; Paul Samuelson explored the consequences of the new approach.[4] Nevertheless, some perceptive critics sounded the tocsin over Mandelbrot's hypothesis: "Since no rational man with a quadratic utility function would invest in stocks, most normative work on utility approaches to speculative markets is obsolete . . . Almost without exception, past econometric work is meaningless. Surely, before consigning centuries of work to the ashpile, we should like to have some assurance that all our work is truly useless" (Cootner 1964, 196–7, 337).

The earliest resistance to Mandelbrot's economics did not come from statisticians or econometricians, primarily because there was so very little in the way of statistical theory to bring to bear upon stable distributions in the 1960s. Indeed, "It can be said without exaggeration that the problem of constructing statistical estimators of stable laws entered into mathematical statistics due to the work of Mandelbrot" (Zolotarev 1986, 217). Rather, those who were galvanized into initially making a response were the neoclassical economic theorists. What Mandelbrot had brought to consciousness was a looming crisis over the correct method of incorporating probabalistic considerations into the purely deterministic neoclassical model of price formation. Although most of the discussion of his work was carried out under the rubric of "speculative prices," the problem ran much deeper.[5] In the early twentieth century, there had been substantial opposition to any rapprochement between neoclassical pricing theory and stochastic considerations. But by the 1940s, a new generation at the Cowles Commission had worked out a compromise: the stochastic appearance of economic time series would be modeled by the superimposition of white noise upon deterministic neoclassical equations; while "uncertainty" or risk would be modeled by some version of expected utility theory based upon perfect knowledge of a linear quadratic objective function. Randomness and instability were thus portrayed as "external" to the operation of the market, "shocks" impinging upon a mechanically deterministic (and usually linear) system. The neo-classicals, as usual, thought they were taking their cue from the physicists: "Just as Ehrenfest and other physicists had to add probability to the causal systems of physics in order to get around the time-reversibility feature of classical mechanics that was so inconsistent with the time asymmetry of the second law of thermodynamics, so we must, in the interests of realism, add stochastic or probability disturbances to our economic and biological causal systems" (Samuelson 1972).

Unfortunately, the literature treating time series of asset prices as though they were random walks, usually prompted by examples from thermody-namics, was threatening to unravel the nascent compromise. One possible implication of the random walk literature was that there was no determinis-tic process underlying price movements; another was that there was little or nothing there for the econometricians to estimate. In other words, this literature called into question the very lawlike character of the economy upon which the neoclassicals had staked their reputations.[6] Mandelbrot's intervention at this juncture, stressing infinite variance and inability to dis-criminate between disparate statistical descriptions of price time series, only exacerbated a festering situation. The overwhelming response that Man-delbrot's hypothesis could not be true assumed at least two forms in the mid-1960s: some clamored for a better bridge between statistical and theo-retical versions of the hypothesis so that a concerted program of empirical testing could ensue; while others sought to "prove" that the stochastic ap-pearance of prices was actually consistent with neoclassical theory, perhaps relying on some other stochastic hypothesis to rival that of Mandelbrot. The first program was obligingly initiated by Mandelbrot himself and Fama, the latter by Paul Samuelson.

It is unfortunate that in some retrospective accounts (e.g. Niehans 1990, 441) Mandelbrot and Samuelson are yoked as joint progenitors of the "mar-tingale" theory of asset prices, since Mandelbrot (1966) clearly proposed it first as one possible formalization of the stable Paretian hypothesis, and Samuelson instead responded by inventing the "efficient markets hypothe-sis." That Mandelbrot's approach to the issue was orthogonal to that of Samuelson can be readily discerned from Mandelbrot's "Premature Fractal Manifesto" (1987), issued (but not published) at the same time. In it Man-delbrot distinguishes two stages of indeterminism in the history of the sci-ences: in one, "the additional information provided by statistics is an im-portant but detailed correction, an 'error term,' a 'fluctuation around an equilibrium state' "; in the other, the classical central limit theorem fails to hold, and one cannot generally expect a reduction of fluctuations to deter-ministic causes, or even a well-defined partition between the deterministic and indeterministic components (1987, 120–22).[7] Undoubtedly Mandelbrot did not appreciate the extent to which economics had not yet managed to enter the first stage, much less entertain serious consideration of the second. At least physicists had realized that a deterministic microdescription of the dynamics of something as complicated as the molecules of a gas was well beyond the analytic capacities of their system, and had therefore innovated the phenomenological approach to the macrosystem in thermodynamics. However, most of the neoclassical economists whom Mandelbrot encountered at Harvard were still working with single-actor representative agent deterministic models, and aggregating up to market-level phenomena with little justification. This indeed was also the approach of Samuelson to martingales, *pace* the quote above.

There was another marked difference between the approaches of Samuelson and Mandelbrot, which would have more consequences further down the line. Mandelbrot proposed his martingale model to explain why some generic "fundamentals" might themselves sport stable Lévy distributions, and therefore why broader limit theorem considerations could possibly account for the ubiquity of stable distributions of price changes. Samuelson, on the other hand, couched his result in terms which suggested that random price changes "proved" the market was efficient, irrespective of the second and higher moments of the marginal distribution of those changes. While Mandelbrot wished to endow the empirical stable distributions with some theoretical significance, Samuelson wanted to circumvent the stable distributions and tame the seeming randomness of the price record. It goes without saying that it was Samuelson's version of the martingale which was taken up by the economics profession; and for that reason, economists were disconcerted when "it was realized around 1975 that the martingale model implied that asset prices should be less volatile than they apparently were" (LeRoy 1989, 1586).

In this respect, as in so many others, Mandelbrot had already anticipated this possibility. In two papers (1969; 1972) one can observe his concern shifting to dependence in the time domain, and especially to long dependence, such as $1/f$ noise and fractionally integrated noise. Econometricians and advocates of the newly popular Box-Jenkins approach to time series seemed to only consider "high frequency" variance like serial correlation and Markov dependence, in consonance with the prior philosophy that local linear effects could approximate any phenomenon. Mandelbrot once more insisted that the phenomenology of the "typical spectral shape" of an economic time series did not conform to this paradigm, and suggested that economists also consider "long dependence" or low-frequency variance, especially because of the seeming ubiquity of non-periodic cycles in economic variates. "The main alternative description I know assumes behavior to be wholly non-stationary. If such were really the case, the possibility of a rational description would be negated" (Mandelbrot 1972, 266). In his still-underappreciated article from 1969 he gives a taxonomy of all possible combinations of time series with either Gaussian or stable Lévy marginal distributions in conjunction with pure independence or long dependence; and concludes that in many instances the Gaussian–long dependence combination may look very much like the stable Lévy-independent series. Given this phenomenological similarity, and especially given the econometricians' habit of pre-whitening and otherwise trimming their data sets in the interest of rendering them more user-friendly, he ends up very skeptical about the use of ARIMA models as descriptions of economic phenomena.

In these last papers, one can observe Mandelbrot's increasing insistence upon the general applicability of his methods in the natural sciences—he had by this stage begun to proselytize for fractal geometry—which might be taken to signal his frustrations with economics. While one cannot discount his preferences for fresh faces and a change of scene, there were also some "push" factors which explain that Mandelbrot's last economics publication dates from 1972 (again, until 1997). A case can be made that the turning point in the receptivity of the economics profession for Mandelbrot's ideas came in 1970; however, the vectors of change were numerous, and can only be mentioned here in a cursory fashion. One important event was the demise of econometrics of the Cowles structural estimation variety, which one could date from the conference in November 1969 on the evaluation of large-scale econometric models (Hickman, ed., 1972). Two papers were especially distressing: one by Philip Howrey demonstrating that the Wharton model could not account for the general shape of business cycles from an examination of its linear filter characteristics; and the other by Ronald Cooper showing that simplistic ARIMA models could out-predict many of the large complex econometric models of the United States. More than one commentator was prompted to wonder what economists had achieved in two decades of expensive statistical research. The reputation of econometrics suffered a stain which it has yet to erase within the profession (although it was never banished from the core graduate curriculum). More importantly, the large macro models were intimately associated with Keynesian economics, which suffered disgrace in the oil crisis of 1973 and its aftermath. The reaction to all these tribulations became known as the "rational expectations" movement; and it is no accident that many of its major proponents have already surfaced in our narrative: Thomas Sargent, Eugene Fama, and Paul Samuelson. It may seem odd or incongruous to outsiders, but the thrust of rational expectations theorizing was to redouble the commitment to deterministic neoclassical economics with a representative agent, combined with the Samuelsonian interpretation of martingales as characteristic of completely efficient markets, and a penchant for ARIMA time series models (Sent 1998). The rejection of everything that Mandelbrot stood for was nearly complete: stable distributions, long dependence, the impossibility of complete arbitrage, the statistical indistinguishability of wildly divergent stochastic characterizations of economic time series, the phenomenological (thermodynamic) approach to modeling, and the second stage of scientific indeterminism.

The year 1970 is an even more precise watershed with regard to Mandelbrot's work. It was the year of Peter Clark's PhD thesis at Harvard, which argued that the fat tails in distributions of economic variates could be better modeled by a subordinate stochastic process than by stable Lévy distributions. Taking a suggestion from Mandelbrot and Taylor (1967), Clark imagined that the support for the distribution of time series was not properly specified, in the sense that "economic time" did not flow smoothly during the trading week. In this scheme, if price $P(T(t))$ is "subordinated" to a directing process $T(t)$ which is itself stochastic and independent of $X(T)$, then the resulting time-varying mixtures of standard Gaussian processes would result in a more leptokurtic observed process. This practice of approximating seemingly stable Lévy distributions by time-varying variances of standard Gaussian processes would become the hallmark of economic orthodoxy in the next decade. In addition, 1970 is the year of Eugene Fama's important survey of the efficient markets hypothesis (Fama 1991), which signaled his break with a decade of support for the Mandelbrot hypothesis. Thomas Sargent also simply dropped any reference to stable Lévy distributions from this point onward and neglected to mention that all his subsequent work would have been vitiated by their prevalence.[8] Blattberg and others (Blattberg and Gonedes 1974) followed suit by recanting their enthusiasm for stable Lévy distributions. Christopher Sims (1971) and Clive Granger (Granger and Orr 1972), two econometricians who would become important in the rational expectations movement, went public with their disdain for stable distributions, preferring some variant of autoregressive heteroskedasticity instead. The profession acknowledged its preference for this format of "explanation" when Granger and Robert Engle were awarded the Bank of Sweden Prize in 2003.

By and large Mandelbrot did not choose to counter these trends, although there are a few published instances where his impatience with the woodenness of the economic orthodoxy did peek through. One is his published response to Clark (Mandelbrot 1973, 157–58): "This paper raises again an issue of scientific judgement I have often encountered: either Clark and numerous other critics are sensible in their belief that infinite variance per se is a feature so undesirable that, in order to paper it over, the economist should welcome a finite-variance formulation, even when it is marred by otherwise undesirable features; or I am sensible in my belief that stability in Paul Lévy's sense is a feature both convenient mathematically and illuminating of reality . . . I believe that scientific model making is not primarily a matter of curve fitting. Ordinarily if one fits different distinct aspects of the phenomenon separately, the best fits are both mutually incompatible, and unmanageable outside their domain of origin." Or, more recently (Mandelbrot 1989b, 12):

> security and commodity prices had been in the early 60's the topic of the first descriptive account that was later to be counted as fractal. It is a widespread assumption that price is a continuous and differentiable function of time. We claimed not only that it is not obvious and not only that it is contrary to the evidence, but that it is in fact contrary to what should be. The reason is that competitive price should respond in part to changes in anticipation, which can be subject to arbitrarily large discontinuities . . . Our study of prices kept eliciting the comments already mentioned in the context of hydrology, the third one being phrased as "Your models look fine, but how do you relate them to economic theory?" In moments of irritation, we are quoted as responding, "There is, as yet, no explanation of these findings; in fact, no explanation could reasonably be expected to come from existing economic theory."[9]

In my opinion, much of this frustration was amply justified, especially in the 1970s. Most empirical studies had demonstrated that marginal distributions of price changes or stock returns were too leptokurtic to be Gaussian, and that estimates of the stable Lévy parameter α (by the standards of the day) reliably fell in the range between one and two (Fama 1963; 1965a). The studies which challenged this finding such as in Blattberg and Gonedes 1974, Clark 1973, and Hsu, Miller, and Wichern 1974 did so by positing some other fat-tailed alternative and asserting with little direct evidence that it fit some data better than a stable Lévy distribution. At that time no one challenged the Mandelbrot hypothesis on its home ground: that limit theorem considerations privileged the stable Lévy description, and that earlier studies which had supported random walks had achieved most of their fit by prewhitening, detrending, and other forms of censorship of variance. In sum, the economics profession dropped the Mandelbrot hypothesis largely for reasons other than empirical adequacy and concise simplicity. What lends primary support to this statement is that the rival or alternative hypotheses concerning leptokurtic distributions never made inroads into day-to-day econometric practice, which remained blithely satisfied with Gaussian distributions. The only discernible purpose of the negative studies was to "refute" Mandelbrot.

From the mid-1970s until the mid-1990s, one found no further substantial mention of the Mandelbrot hypothesis in the orthodox economics literature or in econometrics texts. Rather, questions of the nature of distributions of economic time series had been kept alive in journals read by statisticians, or else in journals more narrowly targeted at business school faculty.[10] At present, there are so many journals solely devoted to the statistical examination of financial time series that it may be nearly impossible to encompass all this work in a single survey; or worse, there is the suspicion that the same share price data have been pored over numerous times, vitiating any rational sampling theory. However, there has been substantial progress in the development of statistical procedures for estimating stable law parameter (see, for surveys, Akgiray and Lamoureux 1989; Knight 1993; and Zolotarev 1986), and for that reason there are now some rather more substantial controversies than one found in the 1970s over the empirical prevalence of Lévy stable distributions.

As computational capacity has got cheaper, it has become possible to run tests on vast banks of time series of individual share prices, futures prices, and exchange rates. Indeed, one could argue that this is the more appropriate venue for tests of the Mandelbrot hypothesis, since prior work using single index numbers or other aggregates was bedeviled by a range of extraneous considerations. Nevertheless, it would be fair to say that most of these more recent statistical exercises are hostile to the Mandelbrot hypothesis, although the authors would admit that the verdict is at best mixed and at worst pyrrhic.[11] The attempts to test for presence of stable Lévy distributions have taken four forms, although as one of the authors admits, "there is not much theory of statistical inference for stable laws" (Akgiray and Lamoureux 1989, 85). The first approach is to use a regression-based procedure (Koutrouvelis, 1980) to estimate the parameter α. Here the verdict is clear: all work admits that estimates fall in the interval from 1.5 to 1.9, and rarely are within some bootstrap standard errors of 2, which would be the value indicating Gaussian processes. The second approach is based upon Mandelbrot's own stress upon the self-similarity of time series, and asks if the distribution is stable under addition by summing daily (or higher-frequency) changes to form "weekly" or "monthly" samples. The consensus here is that price changes are not purely stable under addition along the time axis, but that estimates of α tend to rise as the time frame lengthens. The third approach tries to focus on the tails of the distribution, especially since the above alternatives are conditional upon the other stable distribution parameters (stable Lévy distributions have four-parameter characteristic functions, unlike the two parameters for the Gaussian). This is the least clear of all the approaches, but it seems to find that empirical tails are significantly thinner than those characteristic of stable distributions. Finally, the fourth approach compares empirical estimates for kurtosis and higher moments to simulated values for various stable distributions (because technically the moments above the first do not exist for $1 < \alpha < 2$); here again, the finding is that kurtosis and the sixth moment are much smaller than expected for empirical samples.

The interpretation of these results is still very much up in the air. In none of these cases is there anything remotely similar to a Neyman-Pearson hypothesis test, for reasons already mooted. The stability under addition tests is compromised by the observation that it only can address the issue of addition of completely identical stable distributions in all four parameters; but many would concede that share price returns are substantially skewed to varying degrees—the upward trend in α could potentially be explained by this fact alone. As for the issue of the insufficiently fat tails, few have mentioned that the various institutions and market makers of the stock exchange explicitly intervene in daily operation to impose price-change limits; and indeed, mechanical circuit breakers imposed in the United States after the crash of October 1987 have only made this more explicit. Finally, the moments tests are clouded not only by these particular problems, but also by the lack of any standardized tables for simulated moments for the full four-parameter distributions. Any forms of de-trending or pre-whitening, often deployed without comment, would themselves produce many of the results reported.

But criticisms of the tests mentioned above run even deeper. First, the choice of variable of interest has not been sufficiently standardized across experimental design. Mandelbrot himself consciously chose the first difference of price time series $(P(t) - P(t-1))$, because he wanted to stress the stable Lévy property of stability under addition. Other economists were not satisfied that this variable adequately represented what the market participants were after, and so they proposed proportional returns $[P(t) - P(t-1) + d(t)] / P(t) = P^*(t)$, (where $d(t)$ is dividends, stock splits, etc.) or even log returns $(\log P^*(t))$. Worse, many of the studies above use none of these variables, but rather proportional changes $(P(t) / P(t - 1))$ or log proportional changes. The need for some theoretical discipline here is evident. Second, the resort to the bootstrap is questionable, since there exists no proof of the validity of bootstrap methods with stable parameters. Third, and most dire, proponents of these negative results rarely carry their logic out to its bitter end: if indeed stable distributions are an incorrect characterization of price time series, then by inference so too is the Gaussian. Since there is no known model is portfolio analysis which presumes anything other than stable or Gaussian returns, this self-denying ordinance is a foray into true terra incognita.

At this point, we should acknowledge that in the view of most orthodox finance economists there is a widespread alternative hypothesis which was nurtured within the orthodox econometric tradition and could account for the above results. This tradition began with Clark (1973) and with Barr Rosenberg's Berkeley thesis (1972), continues with Engle's Auto Regressive Conditional Heteroskedastic (ARCH) model, and culminates in the Generalized ARCH or GARCH model (Bollerslev, Chou, and Kramer 1992). These models, very much in the subordinated stochastic process mold, treat noise as basically Gaussian, but amended to have a changing second moment, usually through some kind of familiar distributed lag or ARMA structure. These models can mime many hallmarks of stable distributions, such as fat tails, the clustering of volatility, the presence of autocorrelation when one strips the signs from returns time series, and so forth (de Vries 1991). What has not yet been noted is that many of the progenitors of this technique had explicitly cited Mandelbrot's hypothesis as one that they wished to displace or render obsolete. While GARCH has been the state of the art in orthodox finance until recently, again one finds that the reasons for this dominance are not all that clear-cut. In the first place, the actual GARCH structure is not suggested by any specific consensus model of asset pricing, nor indeed by any neoclassical pricing model. Moreover, when one comes to understand conventional GARCH estimation, it becomes apparent that it consists of little more than fitting local linear approximations to moving averages of past volatility, in the general spirit of ARIMA time series models: it is the analogue to the overfitting of any mathematical function with a sufficient number of free parameters. But finally, the one thing which GARCH might have trouble with is non-local or "long" dependence in variance, and indeed this has been admitted by some of its most ardent supporters.[12] Therefore, the model has not been a stunning empirical success. It is difficult to account for its widespread acceptance, except for the fact that it was widely perceived as the only alternative to Mandelbrot's hypothesis which was less threatening to standard econometric practices.

In sum, Mandelbrot's proposal of stable distributions as being singularly apposite for economic time series has enjoyed something less than unalloyed enthusiasm among economists, although its virtues have kept it alive as an underground hit among the cognoscenti. If anything, it is now undergoing a revival of sorts among the econophysics movement. Nevertheless, this has not been the major topic with which Mandelbrot's name has achieved recognition with the vast bulk of economists. That, rather, has been chaos theory.

Chaos and Fractal Dimensions in Economics

Mandelbrot has never shown any interest in the presence or absence of deterministic chaotic dynamics in economics, though again, this may just be a function of the early date at which he departed the discipline. However, the cultural fascination with chaos theory in the 1980s and its subsequent fallout in economics would be the first thing the average economist would probably associate with the name Benoit Mandelbrot. The reason, I suspect, is fairly straightforward. While the implications of stable Lévy distributions for the issue of determinism versus randomness have never seemed particularly clear-cut or pressing for economists, the advent of chaotic dynamics in physics and biology has effectively brought home the urgency of the Second Stage of Indeterminism. It may not be apparent to outsiders, but one of the endemic controversies that haunts economics is whether market economies are dynamically unstable inherently, or, per contra, episodes of instability that have occurred can be attributed to external shocks (Boldrin and Woodford in Benhabib 1992). Earlier econometric models were predicated upon a prior belief in a stable lawlike economic structure subjected to external Gaussian noise, but these models had great difficulty reproducing the observed stochastic patterns of empirical economic time series, as we have noted above. Things changed when it was no longer possible to simply equate stability of the economy with a non-explosive deterministic difference equation model. While Mandelbrot's original empirical critique had only marginal impact, the real change of attitude in economics followed the lead of physical scientists who demonstrated their willingness to entertain a greater degree of randomness in their human-scale, law-governed processes.

In retrospect, one can see how Mandelbrot found his way from economics to fractal geometry. His insistence upon Pareto distributions led fairly naturally to a concern over random walks and martingales; and this, in turn, led him to look more closely at the geometric properties of the time series of prices, which we would now characterize as fractal. Realizing that Lévy stable marginal distributions could also have novel consequences for stochastic processes in the time domain, he moved on to consider long dependence and fractional Brownian motion, as with his work on Hurst processes and the range-scale statistic. His interest in self-similarity and recursive structures led fairly directly to symbolic dynamics. Nevertheless, it fell to others to forge the more direct links between fractal geometric structures in phase space and neglected aspects of both conservative and dissipative dynamical systems. For neoclassical economic theorists, however, it was the revolution in dynamical systems which caught them unawares, and made them sit up and take notice of fractals.

The motives of the neoclassical orthodoxy have a long and only recently resurrected history, to which we can only justify indirect reference here.[13] Suffice it to say that neoclassical price theory has a surprising resemblance to nineteenth-century static classical mechanics because of the conditions of its invention; commensurate success in imitating a Hamiltonian dynamics has proved elusive in the interim. Thus one would expect that many orthodox neoclassical theorists would pay closer attention to developments in analytical dynamics than in other areas of natural science, and indeed, that has been the case in the postwar period. Notably, most of the economists who later became prominent in the evaluation of chaos in economics, such as William Brock, José Scheinkman, and Jess Benhabib, had spent their early careers trying to adapt Hamiltonians and optimal control models to economic purposes. However, the impact of chaotic dynamics upon economics was very different from its impact in the physical sciences. Because of the curious predicament of neoclassical economics—bereft of a consensus dynamics, heavily dependent upon a nineteenth-century determinist stance, lacking clear empirical support, burdened by the politics of market instability—chaos theory was deemed potentially dangerous, possibly capable of undermining the entire orthodox theoretical tradition, and therefore the conventional wisdom as of 2004 is that there has been no evidence of "chaos" found in economics. Hence, albeit in a more oblique manner, there has also been a repudiation of Mandelbrot's legacy in this area. Nevertheless, it is the thesis of the rest of this chapter that this repudiation is nearly as ill-grounded as that of Lévy stable distributions, even though substantially more effort has been devoted to research in this area.

The crude narrative of events would go something like this. In the mid-1980s, even before the cultural fascination with chaos unleashed by Gleick's popular best-seller, a few individuals like Richard Day and Jean Grandmont realized that they could embarrass the orthodox preoccupation with stable equilibria by rewriting some matchbook economic models to demonstrate tent map-like behavior. Unlike Lorenz's famous climate model, none of these models ever sufficiently approximated a level of specificity to satisfy many economists that they were "realistic"; their purpose was primarily didactic. They were intended to show that random-looking outputs could be derived from simple deterministic structures, and that previous stress on stable equilibria was conceptually flawed. In sharp contrast with the physical sciences, chaotic dynamics have never been analytically derived from a standard micro model in economics, because there has never been a widely accepted dynamics.

Indeed, this derivation would have been impossible in any event, since neoclassical economics has no well-established theoretical tradition of dissipative systems.[14] Hence, once the novelty of the matchbook models had worn off, a small set of orthodox economists (including Brock, Benhabib, LeBaron, and Scheinkman) decided to transform the tenor of the question. What, they asked, would it imply for econometrics to suggest that empirical economic time series had been generated by a chaotic dynamic process?

The intellectual trendsetter in this movement was William Brock; his definitive move was to focus single-mindedly upon the Grassberger-Procaccia correlation integral. While physical scientists were inclined to have recourse to a much larger array of techniques to detect chaos—period doubling transitions relative to forcing parameters, Lyapunov exponents, comparison of differing dimension measures, qualitative arguments concerning phase space—Brock and the economists have much more doggedly pursued the correlation integral approach to estimating the correlation dimension in the context of a Takens embedding procedure. What is noteworthy is the abrupt *volte-face*: many of these individuals changed overnight from the purest of theorists to free-spirited empiricists, looking for some ill-specified structure in a Poincaré section of phase space without the slightest a priori restrictions. But their approach was even more extreme than a straightforward empiricist one—Brock set the pattern in economics for using the correlation integral (CI) without having to mention fractal geometry at all.

How was this accomplished? Brock's innovation was to ignore the usual interpretation of the CI as an estimate of the exponent gauging the self-similarity of a geometrical object, and instead reinterpret it as analogous to a characteristic function in the case of independent, identically distributed random variables (Brock, Hsieh, and LeBaron 1991, 18 et seq.). In such a case, as the embedding dimension was increased the CI of an m-dimensional vector should look like the m-product of the CIs of the component substrings. Combining this presumption about the CI with some heavy reliance upon ergodicity assumptions to assert smoothness as the time series record grows to infinity, Brock constructed what he would subsequently call the "BDS statistic," which would allow for conventional Neyman-Pearson hypothesis tests of a null hypothesis of "pure randomness" of an empirical time series. Since this test is often referred to in the literature as a "test for chaos," it is important to note how Brock repeatedly refused to become embroiled in any of the disputes over the meaning of chaos in the natural sciences. His high church agnosticism merely posited two polar opposites: "high dimensional estimates," which he equated with the "randomness" of his null hypothesis, and a "low dimension process," which remained unspecified, except for being equated with "the number of effective dynamical modes or numbers of degrees of freedom that ultimately generate the motion" (Brock, Hsieh, and LeBaron 2). It would have been much better to retail the BDS statistic as a test for asymptotic absence of structure in a stationary ergodic situation in the face of a nonspecific alternative; but doing so would have highlighted that it was rooted in a rather narrow hypothesis of randomness, and in fact had little or nothing to do with chaos.[15] For instance, natural scientists would generally be loath to put commensurate stress on ergodicity, if only because they recognize transients when a process is "off the attractor" or other forms of bifurcations and transition to chaos

(Bausor 1994). Most of this gets completely lost in subsequent commentaries in economics.

By the later 1980s interest in chaos had heated up to the point where there were perhaps too many potential entrants to research, but prior developments had essentially split economists into two camps: on the one hand, an unorganized array of individuals deploying varying combinations of Grassberger-Procaccia plots, Lyapunov exponents, and phase portraits on various economic time series; on the other hand, Brock, Scheinkman, Benhabib, and their students, systematically employing the BDS statistic and some of the collateral machinery found in the natural sciences upon macro time series of orthodox interest. Although it would require a more comprehensive survey to underwrite a definitive history, the first group generally was favorably inclined toward "finding" chaos in their time series, whereas the second was more dubious about claiming success, if not inclined against chaos a priori. For instance, Benhabib (1992) announced that evidence was "weak" for "low dimensional deterministic chaos" in the quarterly U.S. unemployment rate, real GNP, gross private domestic investment, and an index of industrial production. The published paper was curious in that Benhabib did not bother to report all the actual low dimension Grassberger-Procaccia estimates and positive Lyapunov exponent estimates, but rather spent much effort giving non-chaotic reasons why such estimates might show up. Similarly, Scheinkman and LeBaron (1989) reported dimension estimates of about 5–6 for stock price returns, but again spent much of their article inventing other explanations for the result. It is worthwhile to note that the BDS test rarely accepted the null hypothesis of pure randomness in economic data; but the Brock, Scheinkman, and Benhabib group took to developing a locution in their research reports which suggested that they had found "nonlinear structure" but no "low dimensional chaos" in their data. No other science had developed such a distinction at that point, so this particular squeak of the weasel was unique to this group of economists.

The next turn of events was complex, and awaits its historian. Two collateral developments now came into play which cannot be adequately described here: (1) a number of our major players in economics were brought face to face with some real physicists at the Santa Fe Institute;[16] and (2) some more orthodox econometricians were induced to turn their own attentions to chaos, in part because it dawned on them that chaos theory might call into question many of their practices as well. Briefly, the economists visiting Santa Fe learned that some mavens of chaos in physics, like Doyne Farmer and Jim Crutchfield, had become less enthusiastic about what they considered chaos in dynamical dissipative systems and had instead moved into areas like computational complexity, genetic algorithms, and artificial life. This hardened the Brock, Scheinkman, and Benhabib economists in their prior convictions that chaos was not essential to their interpretation of economic phenomena. On the other hand, after Brock had turned the correlation integral into the BDS statistic and treated it as a stand-alone naïve empiricist procedure, the econometricians came along and complained about two sets of issues: that the alternative of a purely stochastic (although perhaps nonlinear) time series model was not being accorded adequate attention; and that physicists were not conducting their search for dimension estimates at the level of sophistication demanded by the Neyman-Pearson approach already found in econometrics. In other words, having misunderstood or misconstrued the way physicists went about searching for chaos, econometricians were now going to tell physicists how to go about doing their job properly.

The high-profile econometricians to attack the correlation integral were James Ramsey (in a series of papers collected in Benhabib 1992 and Liu and Granger 1992) and Clive Granger (in Liu and Granger 1992). The points at issue were numerous but could be summarized as follows. First, they claimed that the Grassberger-Procaccia method was not a legitimate statistical inference procedure, but too much like an eyeball approach. Here Ramsey and Yuan proposed explicit introduction of regression analysis, allowing a whole range of collateral techniques already developed within conventional econometrics to be brought to bear. Second, even after this amendment, estimates of the correlation dimension were biased downward in small samples. Third, Ramsey and Yuan showed that bias increased as the embedding dimension increased, and variance of estimates also increased as embedding dimension increased. Fourth (though this was known previously), it was pointed out that Lyapunov exponent estimates were degraded in the presence of external noise, while the effect of noise on the CI was not insubstantial. Fifth, the output of auto-regressive processes would often give low dimension estimates. It should be stressed that much of this critique was based upon the presumption that the CI was intended as a tool of orthodox statistical inference, a proposition popularized by Brock but not generally prevalent in physics.

At this point, from roughly 1990 onward, the comments of Brock and his collaborators turned unremittingly negative toward any possibility of finding chaos in economics. In a whole series of essays which essentially reproduce the same party line, it was argued *in principle* that one should not find chaos in economics, and then only in a more qualified and hedged manner that chaos has not been empirically found in fact (Brock 1991; Jaditz and Sayers 1993; LeBaron 1994; Scheinkman 1990). The authors treat the articles of the other (generally non-neoclassical) class of economists as essentially irrelevant, merely citing one another. One then found some respected natural scientists uncritically repeating their verdict (Ruelle 1994). If one might summarize their case not unfairly, it is that given enough freedom of proposing auxiliary hypotheses, one can explain away almost any finding of a positive Lyapunov exponent or low-dimensional Grassberger-Procaccia plot.

I have no doubt that there are major problems with trumpeting a positive Lyapunov exponent or Grassberger-Procaccia slope of 2 or 3 as a "discovery" of chaos; but Brock, Scheinkman, Benhabib, and their allies have so misrepresented the question, that their crusade to eradicate chaos from the economy has done the discipline of economics a real disservice. Let us begin to sort out the issues with a statement from one of their papers (in Benhabib 1992, 396): "In physics and chemistry, the simple dichotomy of 'either an attractor, or the data are merely (high dimensional) noise' has been considered to be appropriate. But this is not the case in economics. The extended and maintained hypothesis must include as alternatives the options that the data came from ARIMA or nonlinear stochastic processes." And one from Brock, Hsieh, and LeBaron 1992, 182: "When talking to economists, especially in the US, we have found that the burden of proof is on the scientist who is trying to establish evidence of low-dimensional deterministic chaos in economic time series . . . On the other hand, when talking to some groups of natural scientists . . . we have found the burden of proof is on a scientist to demonstrate that the time series under scrutiny is *not* low-dimensional deterministic chaos."

What is it about the natural sciences that makes them treat this issue so very differently from the economists? We might suggest a number of answers. First, and most importantly, physics started with *good reasons grounded in theory* for suspecting the presence of an attractor, and physicists used their a priori knowledge to learn more about the character of the attractor. They already had a good idea of the constitution of the relevant phase space because they had an agreed-upon theory of dynamics. Armed with such foreknowledge, they could decide whether they were faced with a conservative or dissipative situation, which placed further restrictions upon the object in phase space. They had prior beliefs about whether a system was on the attractor or off it, and about the number of degrees of freedom they were facing. This alone explains why the spectacle of the econometricians upbraiding the physicists for their statistical practices was injudicious, if not embarrassing.

Second, it has been disingenuous of Brock and his group not to admit at the outset that the neoclassical orthodoxy had a vested interest in neutralizing chaotic descriptions of the economy. There is no such commensurate bias in physics. Thus, when one of these commentators suggests that "arbitrage, substitution and intertemporal smoothing" should block the appearance of chaotic dynamics (Brock 1991, 258), or another states flatly that "none of these developments are far enough along to bring about a change in the way economic practitioners proceed" (Scheinkman 1990, 46), then what we are faced with is not reasoned argument but prejudice. An equally admissible hypothesis is that orthodox neoclassical theory, given its dependence upon perfect foresight or rational expectations, is being put at risk (Evans, Honkapohja, and Sargent 1993). The standard rational expectations argument that "if there is forecastable structure in stock returns, it must be difficult for traders to discover it" (Brock, Hsieh, and LeBaron 26) could easily be turned against these economists. Indeed, by the usual "no free lunch" theorems, one would expect that those discovering structure in stock returns or other economic series would refrain from publication and sell their knowledge to the private sector, while those convinced that there was no such structure would remain in academia, loudly protesting that there was no structure to be found. Since that is precisely what we do find (Ridley 1993), these supposed arguments from economic principles are unavailing.

Third, the incursion of Neyman-Pearson hypothesis testing was a disaster for this research program. Neyman-Pearson is not a reasonable framework for inductive learning, especially since one can usually reverse one of its verdicts merely by reversing the identities of the null and alternative hypotheses. Therefore, the choice of null for the BDS statistic is itself primary evidence for the hostility of the Brock, Scheinkman, and Benhabib group toward the appearance of chaotic behavior in economic time series. Neyman-Pearson is really only applicable when one has two clear-cut, well-defined, and uncontentious alternative hypotheses. Physicists do not place such heavy emphasis on size and power of tests, partly because they have experimental protocols which they can vary, but also because they understand that there are many more effective ways of asking questions of the data in an exploratory mode.

This leads directly to the most commonly heard lament of the group: that conditions of data availability are the main difference between the physicists and the economists. They assert that there will "never" be a sufficient amount of data for any given economic variable to test for chaos, because sampling at very high frequencies and very long time frames should be ruled out a priori. The high-frequency samples of share prices, say minute by minute or tick by tick, should be ruled out, they insist, because market microstructure effects such as bid-ask bounce, end-of-the-day or end-of-the-week effects, and so forth are not admissible phenomena when searching for chaotic dynamics. On the other hand, they eschew time series extended over centuries, because they believe that there is too much change to justify their dependence upon stationarity. I believe this is one of the clearest instances of invoking auxiliary hypotheses simply to explain away possible chaotic evidence. In the entire history of econometrics up to this point, no one had raised such a data "impossibility result" against any other empirical finding, though it should apply with equal force to the near complete range of postwar econometrics. Time frames matter in economics, and empirical protocols should take that into account. Furthermore, it becomes clear that this objection is not taken seriously in economics, because when similar "impossibility results" were raised in physics—namely, that certain characterizations were inaccessible when position or momentum terms were "too small"—they prompted a drastic revision of physical theory in the form of quantum mechanics.

The most striking aspect of the claim that chaos has not been "found" in economic time series is the collateral claim that ARCH or GARCH models are "good enough" characterizations for all practical purposes (Jaditz and Sayers 1993; Brock, Hsieh, and LeBaron 1991, 107). We have already encountered this class of models earlier in this chapter, where we learned that both their theoretical justifications and the quality of their fit left much to be desired. It should be added here that the BDS test almost always rejects IID white noise residuals from GARCH models (Brock, Hsieh, and LeBaron 1991, 96). Thus, conveniently for our narrative, we come full circle. The very same inferior econometric models used to refute Mandelbrot in stable Lévy distributions are also being used to refute the legacy of Mandelbrot in chaos theory.

In sum, advocates of neoclassical economic orthodoxy have been subjected to two invitations to the second stage of indeterminism in science and have been left reeling, all the while protesting insistently that nothing much has changed. In the wake of such disappointments, they have the temerity to claim that "the typical economist has a strong prior belief that economic phenomena in general and price series in particular ought to be modeled as stochastic processes rather than deterministic processes" (Jaditz and Sayers 1993, 746). As we have documented, it was Benoit Mandelbrot, and not a typical economist, who was arguing that issues such as long dependence, variance bunching, and the fractal appearance of time paths be approached from a thoroughgoing stochastic viewpoint.

The question of "deterministic vs. stochastic models" in this literature is a red herring, largely an artifact of efforts by the economics profession to maintain the appearance of having retained the orthodox neoclassical theory of individual constrained optimization. In fact, Mandelbrot's point all along was that the world never looked much like the polar opposites of smooth determinism or white noise which had underpinned the first, and inadequate, stage of indeterminism in science. Most phenomena fall somewhere in between, such that they might be equally well characterized by a more sophisticated stochastic process or chaotic dynamics. If this is equally true of the weather and the economy, then the real question is: What is the best practical approach to model these phenomena? In economics, Mandelbrot's phenomenological approach has yet to be given a serious chance.

Part Five
Episodes from
the History
of the "Laws
of Supply and
Demand"

13
The Collected Economic Works of William Thomas Thornton: An Introduction and Justification

Why Put Together a Collected Economic Works of William Thomas Thornton?

Upon proposing this project to a number of our friends and acquaintances, the most frequent reaction we encountered was: William *Who*? This is hardly a propitious start for a program to increase historical sophistication and an appreciation of the traditions which conspired to bequeath us modern economics. Whereas other scholars have given us wonderful editions of the complete works of Adam Smith, David Ricardo, Karl Marx, and John Maynard Keynes, which have immeasurably enhanced our appreciation of their endeavors and contexts, it would not ever impinge upon the consciousness of most economists to consider William Thomas Thornton (1813–80) for commensurate treatment. Since the present author is not much of an antiquarian, nor does he harbor an especially fond fixation upon the more obscure corners of Victorian British history, nor does he especially wish to tilt at windmills, it is clearly incumbent upon him to explain why you, the reader, should take this project seriously, and perhaps even become acquainted with Thornton's ideas.

Among specialists in the history of Victorian social and economic thought, Thornton is widely regarded as little more than a bit player, perhaps like Rosencrantz or Guildenstern in *Hamlet*. The comparison is more apt than they might at first concede. In the play, Rosencrantz and Guildenstern are reputed to be close friends of Hamlet, but they are summoned by Hamlet's nemesis in an effort to penetrate his odd behavior and cryptic utterances. They are subsequently treated rather rudely by both sides in the larger dramatic conflict, to such an extent that they are often confused and conflated with one another.[1] Hamlet then stage-manages a play within the play, which Rosencrantz and Guildenstern protest is not a credible performance. Hamlet treats them with stiff cordiality when he is in their presence, but conspires to send them to their deaths at the hands of the English, unwittingly bearing their own death sentence as a message from the prince, a demise which (in the opinion of many critics) is even more senseless and tragic than the trademark Shakespearean bloodbath at the conclusion of the play. In the end, the huge chess game of duplicity and feints is all for naught, since all the jockeying for political advantage in Denmark merely clears the way for the ruthless invader Fortinbras to assume the throne and bring down the curtain on a century or more of royal rule. Only in the last century did we come to realize that interpretation of the play need not dwell so insistently upon the vicissitudes of Hamlet himself, and that some more subtle bathos inheres in the experience of Rosencrantz and Guildenstern as pawns in a larger game for which they never enlisted and could never adequately comprehend (Stoppard 1967).

Lest we be accused of speaking in riddles in the manner of Hamlet, let us describe Thornton's fate in more prosaic terms. William Thornton is treated in the orthodox history of economic thought literature, if at all, as the person who created the occasion for John Stuart Mill's celebrated "recantation of the wages-fund doctrine," a doctrinal revision of near eschatological significance for his contemporaries which we shall treat in some detail below. This crisis in English classical political economy, it is often said, was triggered by the publication of the first edition of Thornton's book *On Labour* (1869). What is notable about modern accounts of this incident is the cavalier disdain assumed by all toward Thornton and his role. In our experience, almost no modern commentator (with one or two honorable exceptions to be noted below) has deemed that Thornton's ideas merited serious scrutiny, then or now. Because of this conviction, they expend no effort to explicate his writings in any sympathetic detail, instead concentrating all their hermeneutic powers upon such revered figures as John Stuart Mill or Alfred Marshall. To offset the impression that we generalize about this contempt hastily and unwarrantedly, let us sample some of the calumny which has been heaped upon Thornton's head.

George Stigler sniffed that Thornton's *On Labour* was "absurd" (1965, 9). Krishna Bharadwaj opined that his arguments "were rather confusing and weak" (1978b, 260). William Breit accused Thornton of "fatuous" examples and "flimsy criticism" (1967, 519, 521). Lujo Brentano once wrote, "Mr. Thornton's chapter "On the Origins of Trades Unions" bears the same relation to the real origin of Trades-Unions as Rousseau's *Contrat Social* to the historical origins of States" (1870, clxv). The economist Robert Ekelund finds himself unable to repress his roiling scorn, launching into a barrage of *ad hominem* accusations: "Thornton's purpose appears not to be a scientific

search for truth, but rather to find an argument that will support his precon-
ceived political conclusions"; he "was inappropriately applying the method
of the natural sciences to the social sciences"; "there is no textual evidence
that Thornton ever understood Mill's simple but serviceable theory"; and
his book could not be considered "anything more than an unsophisticated
stab in the dark" (Ekelund and Thommesen 1989). Evelyn Forget, in a somewhat more cautious mood, asserts with confidence that Thornton's "contribution does not reach the same level of analytical sophistication as does
Mill's or Longe's" and that his "economic analysis did not transcend the level
of popular debate of the era" (1991, 207, 215). From this litany of disdain—
and we have by no means exhausted its breadth—one would infer that
Thornton would not deserve even the attention it would take to do a serious
job of refutation.

Yet here we encounter one of the first of a sequence of paradoxes which
seem to hover about the historical personage of William Thomas Thornton.
If he really was such an intellectual lightweight, a literary leper, a sad specimen of someone who couldn't think his way out of his own inkwell, then
why was it that so many of the acknowledged giants of nineteenth-century
political economy took him so very seriously? It is indeed wondrous to see
how the modern paragons of scientific logic and sober orthodoxy squirm in
the presence of contemporaneous testimonials to his intellectual acuity and
conceptual consequence—that is, if they even deign to acknowledge their
existence. For instance, John Stuart Mill, in promoting the intellectual merits of *On Labour*, wrote, "The present work, though popular and attractive
in style, is strictly scientific in its principles and reasonings" ([1869] 1967,
633). J. E. Cairnes acknowledged Thornton's impetus to his own work: "the
one living writer [for] whose abilities and acquirements I feel high respect,
and [with] whose practical aims I not unfrequently sympathize . . . I trust I
have profited by the example he has set me of courtesy towards opponents"
(1874, 1–2). The *Economist* opined, "This is a book all true economists
should welcome." An anonymous reviewer in the *Examiner* of 4 November
1871 called Thornton's book so "revolutionary in its effects that it rendered
obsolete all existing economical works." An essayist in *Westminster Review* of
July 1869 wrote, "Admirable as the work is in itself, embodying the results of
a lifetime of disinterested study, and full of new lights on obscure questions
of economical science, it has done the most service perhaps by calling im-
peratively upon every man of note to revise and test his opinions upon this
momentous subject. . . . for though there is a good deal in his scientific
reasoning to which exception may be taken . . . we cannot fail to recognise in
his work the result of independent thought, high moral aim, and a generous
intrepidity in a noble cause" (37). The *British Quarterly Review* enthused,
"His style is at once popular and precise; so perfectly clear and sparkling that

his readers can follow him with ease through subtle and complicated discussions . . . Mr. Thornton makes us realize that the conclusions of the economist both need the perpetual verification of experience, and, in fact, receive it; while he questions anew those formulas which, by reason of their very excellence as abbreviations of an enormous multitude of particular facts, are liable to lose their meaning when, like algebraic symbols, they are applied to long and complicated problems" (1869, 448). A less starry-eyed reviewer in the *Athanaeum* was still prompted to admit, "He is given to digression, and uses everywhere from twice to ten times as many words as are needed to set forth his meaning; nevertheless, it may, on the whole, be doubted whether any considerable economic work of equal merit has appeared since the first publication of Mr. Mill's Political Economy" (1869, 275). There were other Victorian contemporaries who attained more exalted academic positions than Thornton—one thinks of Henry Fawcett at Cambridge, John Elliot Cairnes at University College, or Bonamy Price at Oxford—who in their cautious orthodoxy and placid commonplaces never achieved a vanishing fraction of the attention and (more importantly) scrutiny which was lavished upon Thornton. Of course, not all commentators would equally attest to his analytical perspicaciousness or resort to unchecked praise; but the enervated levels of rhetoric, pro and con, did suggest that something rather more significant had occurred than the inept frothings of a developmentally challenged intellect.

But that is only the most obvious paradox. To repress or disparage the judgment of those long dead is one thing; but to condemn the living is quite another. If Thornton really was the inconsequential character that so many make him out to have been, then he must enjoy the dubious distinction of being the single most discussed minor character in the modern archives of the history of economics. A survey of just the primary English-language journals dealing in history of economic thought reveals more than ten articles concerned with Thornton over the decade of the 1990s. The incongruous spectacle of repeated attempts by diverse scholars to either explain away his writings or simply thrust him unceremoniously back into his grave (one fears endless reruns of *Night of the Living Economists*) itself calls into question whether he is indubitably irrelevant. Recently, the growing secondary literature on Thornton has provoked the redoubtable Robert Ekelund to an academic frenzy, prompting him to call Thornton an "idiot" who "should receive a grade of "F" (with strongly worded advice to return to the pursuit of poetry and sociology)," to insist that his "(in)famous arguments were worse than nonsense," and to extend his disparagement to modern writers who study Thornton (1997; Ekelund and Thornton 2001). Lecturing skulls in graveyards, especially those belonging to persons supposedly deemed Fools when alive, is not calculated to foster confidence in the Royal

House of economic orthodoxy. Perhaps something really is rotten in the state of Trademark.

This brings us back full circle to our perceived need for a readily accessible *Collected Works* of William Thomas Thornton. It seems that his writings, but especially his book *On Labour*, touched a pervasive chord for many writers in that crucial period of the 1860s and 1870s in Britain: that is, right when British classical political economy began to be superseded by what has become known in retrospect as "neoclassical" economic theory. Indeed, we shall argue that Thornton's book played a major role in the actual configuration of events which led up to the initial statements of the fledgling doctrine by such figures as Fleeming Jenkin, William Stanley Jevons, Francis Ysidro Edgeworth, and Alfred Marshall. The importance of the controversy swirling about Thornton in the 1860s and 1870s has still not been adequately appreciated by historians, at least in part because of the inaccessibility of his works and the lack of a convenient summary of reactions by his contemporaries. Thornton the gadfly was in a large measure responsible for the condensation of the specifically British form of microeconomics prevalent around the end of the nineteenth century. This British version of price theory remains the foundation of "introductory economics" in countless university courses down to the present.

Second, Thornton was also relevant because of his influence upon the rise of political trade unionism in Britain and its changing relationship to academic political economy, something which has gone relatively unnoticed in the literature of the social history of the labor movement. Again, we attribute much of this neglect to the lack of a convenient compendium of his writings. There was a period when much of social history was concerned with searching for the influence (or more pertinently, explaining the lack of influence) of Marxist doctrines upon working-class politics in Britain. A newer generation of scholars has initiated an inquiry into the relevance of middle-class reformist movements in the normalization of union activity (Finn 1993); and it is our opinion that Thornton should be considered one of the major intellectual resources for those movements in Britain in the critical period of the legal legitimation of union activity.

Third, there is the question of Thornton's relevance to modern understandings of economic theory. It is our view that recent controversies over his significance may derive some salience from larger-scale transformations within our *fin de siècle* theoretical orthodoxy of neoclassical economics. In effect, new questions opened up by the modern projects of game theory, experimental economics, computational economics, and evolutionary processes foster a situation in which Thornton can be read in a new, perhaps more user-friendly light. Historians of economics of an earlier generation were generally partisans of a Marshallian mode of price theory—a thesis we shall elaborate upon below—and this implied a jaundiced view of Thornton. One of the most important events of the last forty years has been a progressive repudiation and sloughing off of the Marshallian approach by neoclassical high theory, especially as a result of demonstrations that market supply and demand functions *cannot* generally be derived from more rigorous specifications of neoclassical general equilibrium models.[2] Dramatic transformations in the modern understanding of the so-called law of supply and demand within the orthodoxy of economics cannot but prompt reevaluations of the nineteenth-century traditions which attempted to wed such laws to the neoclassical organon of optimizing utility subject to constraints (see chapter 14). Here is where a reconsideration of Thornton's significance for modern economics becomes relevant. Thornton famously insisted that there were no such things as "laws of supply and demand," even though invocation of such laws had become conventional wisdom in the British classical tradition of his era; yet far from preaching paralysis, he insisted that one could still make fruitful theoretical statements about the operation of the economy in their absence. In this opinion he was rebutted most vigorously by various economic theorists, most effectively Alfred Marshall, who forged an alliance between utilitarianism and a revised conception of the laws. Now that Marshall's hundred years of solicitude have been torn asunder (however much some Marshallian holdouts may persist in denying it), it is interesting to trace the filiation back to where the choice was made, and explore the first few steps on the road not taken. Hence, Thornton assumes a new relevance for a generation searching for precursors who might be read as sharing its own concerns.

Fourth, we offer these texts and our interpretation of them as a small contribution to a larger dispute over the future of the history of economic thought. Since the end of the Second World War, the economics profession has precipitously withdrawn its support for scholarship in the history of economics (Weintraub 2002). The motivations have been many and complex, but one reaction of those remaining scholars engaged in the enterprise has been to become more narrowly focused, specializing in perhaps one or two "great men" and subjecting the same canonical texts to repeated microscopic readings, as though that extra modicum of bunkered attention might finally arrive at the "correct" interpretation, the one which vindicates the prejudices of the modern profession, to stand unchallenged for all time. I think there has been no surer prescription for utter irrelevance and oblivion. To phrase my objection in a language we hope these historians can understand, we believe this sort of history has entered a region of sharply diminishing returns. One possible antidote would be to widen the context, expand the roster of players, augment the body of archival evidence, and appeal to traditions of scholarship which have been ostracized by the anti-historical biases of the economics profession. One particularly apposite example of these alternatives applies to an incident central to the career of William Thomas Thornton, namely John Stuart Mill's so-called recantation of the wages fund doctrine. This incident has been a big favorite of the "close reading" camp of historians for years, since it constitutes a major challenge to their project of presenting the last two centuries of economics as a single, homogeneous narrative of continuous progress. Perhaps the most extreme exponent of this practice, Samuel Hollander, is therefore forced to admit that Mill's "retraction of support from the wages fund doctrine constitutes one of the most difficult problems in the history of economics" (1985, 409). Yet no amount of compiling quotes from Mill's published texts on the part of Hollander, nor anyone else, has served to illuminate this incident in a satisfactory manner. We shall instead assert that only when we shift our perspective to adopt Thornton's point of view, and then entertain the notion that much of our own heritage of understanding is a function of what the immediate contemporaries made of Thornton, can much of the intractable and problematic character of the incident be dissolved.

A fifth reason for revisiting Thornton is to establish his place in the conversation concerning the British role in India, and indeed in the economics of colonial rule in the era of high imperialism (Zastoupil 1994). Although we do not attempt to discuss this facet of his work in this chapter, for many historians it may loom at least as large as the other considerations above.

For all these reasons, we have undertaken to present in a convenient format the *Collected Economic Works* of William Thomas Thornton.

A Brief History of the "Law" of Supply and Demand from Year Zero to Cournot

There is a surfeit of writing in the history of economics which seeks to discover the Marshallian laws of demand and supply in numerous texts all the way back to Aristotle, if not before. While the topic of what happens to price and quantity in various market situations was a subject of interested commentary as far back as the beginnings of recorded history, it makes a mockery of the history to simultaneously assert that there is some Platonic economic essence of "supply and demand" which remained intact through the millennia;[3] and worse, that Alfred Marshall did little more than provide a textbook codification of what everyone already implicitly knew. This genre of writing, which Richard Rorty has dubbed "doxography," exists primarily to smother curiosity and stifle any sophisticated appreciation of how we arrived at our present predicaments; it certainly makes it all but impossible to understand the role of William Thornton in the history of British classical political economy.

The indispensable prerequisite for comprehending the very idea that there could exist such a thing as a "law" or "laws" of supply and demand is to acknowledge that the phrase did not refer to any single concept or phenomenon over time: rather, it was repeatedly recast in conjunction with some rather critical variables over the course of the history of economic thought. The conditioning variables to which we shall make passing reference are: transformations in the economic history of diverse market structures; relationships to notions of "science" and scientific explanation; the strength of conviction in the unity of human social experience and the fundamental identity of human cognitive structures; the role of geometry and mathematics in British science and economic expression; and the pivotal importance of theories of value, and especially the critical difference between "classical" or substance theories of value (Mirowski 1989b) and neoclassical or "field" theories of value. In brief, notions of supply and demand were continuously adjusted to conform to some matrix of these variables, and this process continues down to the present day. One simply cannot comprehend Adam Smith, Antoine Cournot, William Thornton, Fleeming Jenkin, William Stanley Jevons, Alfred Marshall, Henry Schultz, or Werner Hildenbrand without taking each of these factors into account; this has been one of the glaring weaknesses of previous historical narratives from Joseph Schumpeter to Mark Blaug to John Creedy.

Joseph Schumpeter once asserted that the laws of supply and demand "proved unbelievably hard to discover" (1954, 602). Perhaps the reason why the trek was so arduous was not any failing on the part of those who ventured down that trail ; rather, it was a necessary consequence of Schumpeter's project to squeeze something so promiscuous and profoundly variable onto the Procrustean bed of a single brace of "laws" grounding the totality of economic analysis. Because the famous Marshallian scissors still serve as the golden arches over the entranceway into orthodox economics, the geometrical Checkpoint Charlie of Economics 101, it may seem almost perverse to insist that these ideas are neither obvious nor well-defined in such a way that they could readily be extended back to the dawn of economic analysis. Perverse or not, it remains the truth, a truth intimately bound up with William Thornton's role in the history of economics.

The Constitution of Subsistence Markets

We shall embark upon our narrative in the late seventeenth century, since this is the context most relevant to the history of British conceptions of supply and demand, and latterly to the writings of Thornton. The single most significant fact to notice about economic writers in this era is that they did not uniformly presume all markets to be fundamentally alike, either in form or in function; certain markets identified by the specific commodity and geographic provenance were felt to obey alternative principles of legitimate operation, and thus to require alternative explanations. Land markets were heavily informed by kinship procedures and distinctions, which in practice could lend appreciable flexibility to land measurement (chapter 7); household items would be negotiated ad hoc with itinerant peddlers; in some instances, labor obligations partook of a customary character. In the same sense in which numerical measurements were not globally invariant nor cosmopolitan, neither were markets. The market for bread in urban centers was always acknowledged as operating according to distinct sets of principles. The very notion of an impersonal and standardized market was a relatively circumscribed phenomenon, and for good reasons: outside a few metropoles, units of measurement and legal relations were anthropomorphic and narrowly local, most people had great difficulty with even simple forms of calculation, and consequently sellers were as likely to alter the character or physical constitution of the commodity offered as to adjust the money price in the face of altered circumstances of what we would now call scarcity. Standardization, monetary and metrological, was plainly a function of the spread of political hegemony; few contemporaries would have associated it with the spread of a generic "market" or disembodied "division of labor." Because most trade was ineluctably local and personalized, the most common mental model of exchange was one of "fair trade," which is why the earliest attempts to portray a generic market function are derived from moral and political philosophy. The European fascination with the "just price" had appreciable justification in the actual configuration of lived economic experience.

To indulge briefly in bald generalization, the dynamism of the Western polities in the seventeenth century had profound consequences for these patchy, disconnected, and fundamentally heterogeneous markets, and for the patterns of thought which underwrote their operations. Without getting into the controversy over whether notions of natural science induced ambitions of market standardization or vice versa (Hadden 1994), clearly models of fair trading were giving way to something altogether more general and mechanistic at the end of the century. Fairs and itinerant peddlers went into decline, and were being replaced by all manner of other forms of structured retail activities, especially in large and burgeoning cities. Standardization of weights and measures became a rallying cry for reformers, who used the state to impose it from above; merchants increased their reliance on the judiciary to settle disputes about the terms of trade and discharge of obligations; the maintenance of double-entry accounts became the *sine qua non* of the prosperous merchant, and even the proto-industrialist. The model of idiosyncratic, personalized fair trade was being displaced by another model, one with higher turnover, greater interaction with strangers, layered abstractions for the gauging of success, and limited manipulation of the constitution of the goods sold. The spread of standardization and price-regulated markets proceeded hand in glove, although this change did not resemble the "spontaneous order" so beloved of those who would rather recount fairy tales about virtual origins than study actual history. In order to render the market more impersonal and mechanical, it was thought necessary to relegate it to a limned and well-policed space, so that supervision could insure that an increased dependence upon price-regulated adjustment did not backfire and undermine the state which had set it in motion in the first place.

The shift from "fair" to "price-regulated" trade did not proceed along a uniform front, either geographically or across commodities. Neither was the substitution without friction; much of the literature of the "moral economy" of spontaneous revolts documents the clash of the two (Thompson 1993, 200–207). Although a synoptic history of this "great transformation" is still notable primarily by its absence, one cannot read the contemporary literature discussing markets without noting that a fair proportion of writers felt that the market for bread warranted special care and attention because of its distinctive features, and that British attitudes and analysis diverged sharply from those prevalent across the Channel in France. Initially, both England and France engaged in elaborate intervention and regulation of the production and sale of bread, regarded as "subsistence," particularly in urban settings; the fear was that intermittent crises of subsistence could not be adequately contained by a price-regulating market structure, and therefore required vigilance and overt control. However, by the eighteenth century England and France had diverged in their approach to the problem of bread markets. In England, the Assize of Bread was allowed to lapse; forestalling, regrating, and engrossing were essentially decriminalized (Webb and Webb 1904; Barnes 1930). In 1795 England suffered the worst grain shortage of the entire century, and yet there was no renewal of targeted market controls. If there was any attempt to offset crises of subsistence, it took the form of policies like Speenhamland: rather than stipulate the correct operation of the market, relief was scaled to the local price of bread. In effect, the British did not subject the operation of the bread market to close scrutiny, trusting Nature and their convenient insularity to effect most of the required alterations in the machinery of trade. This would have subtle consequences among the British for their subsequent conceptual picture of commerce.

The situation in France was altogether different. Grain police and micro-management of grain market operations were a hallowed tradition, only to be redoubled in the eighteenth century (Kaplan 1976; 1984). The French also had their champions of trust in Nature: the Physiocrats made it one of their crusades to revoke this doctrine of supervision of grain sales. In 1763 their followers managed to lift most market controls, but the result was political and economic disaster, and the system of close market scrutiny was re-imposed in 1770. Upon the accession of Louis XVI, A. R. J. Turgot was appointed controller general of finances, and he immediately ordered the grain police abolished once again. Serious dearth beset France in 1775, and yet in the teeth of hunger Turgot tried to force through further market liberalizations, only to be sacked for his efforts in 1776. The sequence of dearths of subsistence is still widely credited as one of the triggers of the French Revolution. Beyond the political consequences, this plague turned out to be the defining moment in the development of French political economy. Every attempt to come to grips with price theory in France, from Turgot to Galiani to Lavoisier to Canard to Say, was in one way or another a struggle to come to terms with the distressing sequence of failures to under-stand how the bread market worked. Every evocation of the "naturalness" of the commerce found itself compelled to confront this particular market, and to explain the utter disarray of the grain police in their efforts to render markets fair and transparent.

Modern commentators often attribute the failure of the grain police to the hubris of the Enlightenment project of rational planning; they pass over in silence the failures of the attendant market liberalizations. These super-ficial reactions ignore one of the more important common denominators of the Physiocrats and the grain police: both had more or less the same under-standing of how grain markets worked. Both would cite an array of forces under the dual rubrics of demand and supply to organize their causal ac-counts of price movements; the difference was that the grain police believed they were not countermanding or suppressing these forces, but instead rendering them more transparent and aboveboard, so that justice and equity would be better served. This was the motivation behind such strictures as a restriction of all commerce to a public marketplace, prohibitions on resale, forced offer of inventory within three market days (or risk seizure and sale by grain police), and explicit public encouragement of higgling and bargain-ing. In practice, the grain police were seeking to render demand and supply visible and accessible to all, so that there would be no hint of corruption or exploitation in its justice and operation. By *imposing* a specific means of clearing the market and *defining* demand and supply in terms of palpable quantities and clearly posted prices, it was the French regulatory tradition which first made it possible to even conceive of a market as a Natural configuration which equilibrated a relatively decontextualized set of price-quantity relationships focused upon the activities of buying and selling. It is because of this development that the tradition of treating demand and supply as *functions* was first nurtured in France, and found its initial expression in French political economy.

The Impact of Enlightenment Natural Philosophy

Since most histories of the sciences tend to restrict themselves to a single line of inquiry or distinct subset of subject matter, it has been difficult in the past to recognize the essential commonalities across disciplines of the movement of ideas and technologies in specific historical eras and geographic contexts. Of late, this situation has been remedied to some extent, with historians of the natural sciences paying more attention to the social sciences, and some historians of the social sciences achieving greater acquaintance with the literatures of the natural sciences. There are two signal themes from this interdisciplinary endeavor which bear direct relevance for the history of price theory. The first, which we cannot adequately summarize here, identifies the seventeenth- and eighteenth-century predilection for explaining trade as motion, and the explanation of motion in turn as the transmission and exchange of a unified "substance" which inheres in all massy bodies (Mirowski 1989b, chapter 2). The upshot of this structure of explanation is that it was "second nature" to depict market trade as being controlled by some embodied substance inherent in all commodities, be it *blé* for the Physiocrats or embodied labor in the British context.

The second theme has recently been adumbrated by Norton Wise (1993). He argues that much of Enlightenment thought was unified by the idea and the technology of the "balance," ranging from the calorimeter to the treatment of *vis viva*, from the products of fermentation to the manipulation of probabilities, and from animal health to the balance sheet. Although the centrality of the icon of balance was pervasive in European thought, the French were the acknowledged virtuosi of the balancing act. Vis viva was balanced in mechanics; caloric was balanced in the calorimeter; debit and credit were counterbalanced in the balance sheet. Nevertheless, there existed a noticeable equivocation on the correct application of the balance in various scientific contexts. On the one hand, "balance" might denote deterministic harmonic fluctuations about a predefined equilibrium position, themselves attributed to external perturbations of a second order of significance; here, classical mechanics provided the model. In this case the laws governing the equilibrium and the perturbations were essentially identical. On the other hand, "balance" might connote a canceling out of numerous accidental disturbances to a system, where the aggregate of disturbances would be presumed to have no special bias in any particular direction; the exemplar here was testimony in legal settings. In this version, the disturbances might originate from causes having nothing to do with the laws governing the central tendency. This ability to shift back and forth in explanatory resources when explicating balance would have direct implications in elaborating the concepts of supply and demand.

There is a collateral theme from the history of science which also deserves a glance. It is a commonplace in the history of mathematics that by the eighteenth century, styles of mathematical expression had diverged in pronounced ways between England and France. The British tended to hew to their Newtonian heritage, preferring geometric arguments and the rather awkward notation of fluxions, whereas the French tended to favor algebra and the Leibniz notation. Of course one could be translated into the other, but persistent biases in matters of perceived rigor and elegance of expression tended to have real consequences in terms of the areas of mathematics which exemplified these standards and thus were deemed to warrant concerted attention. The British would stress the timeless quality of Euclid's *Elements*, the French Descartes's analytical geometry and Lagrange's celestial mechanics. The British fondness for geometric curves and the French penchant for functions would extend even to the presentation of data in scientific reports, although few outside the history of science have come to appreciate just how rare it actually was until well into the nineteenth century to present observations as points plotted on graphs or freehand curves (Tiling 1975).

The Debut of the Discourse of Supply and Demand

William Thweatt (1983) has performed the invaluable service of compiling an inventory of the uses in English of terminology of supply and demand in early classical political economy, and has come up with a number of unexpected findings. It seems in the seventeenth century "supply" was rarely used as a noun, and never in conjunction with "demand." Prices were instead situated in a context of scarcity and plenty, or "quantity in proportion to vent." It is only in the early eighteenth century that one finds prices being related to "quantity in proportion to Demand," notably in the work of an author steeped in French discourse, namely John Law. This language of proportionality echoes early discussions of rational mechanics in English, and points toward incipient metaphors of balance. The political economist who deserves the laurels for the introduction of the terminology of "supply and demand" is the underappreciated Sir James Steuart in 1767;[4] however, the personage who most often garners the credit for promulgating the discourse of demand and supply is Adam Smith in his *The Wealth of Nations*. Since it is Smith rather than Steuart who is the touchstone for much which follows, we will briefly examine his usage of the terms.

Whatever else Smith may have intended, he was by no stretch of the imagination an advocate of the later Marshallian organon of supply and demand. Smith discusses his theory of price in book 1, chapter 7, of *The Wealth of Nations*, in which he distinguishes the phenomena of "natural price" and "market price." Natural price, determined by natural cost considerations, was of course the primary analytical concept and in the literature of the history of economic thought is often referred to as Smith's "adding-up" theory. Market price denoted observable, day-to-day price quotations, which were said to be determined by "supply and demand." There is no question that Smith believed that market price was superimposed upon yet subordinate to natural price, although his discussion of both their determinants and interactions left much to be desired. Market price was said to be propelled by the *ratio* of supply to demand: a common enough locution before Smith, but also one which would readily conjure Newtonian affiliations for Smith's audience. The quarantine of market from natural determinants was achieved through the use of the natural science metaphor of "gravitation": market price would "gravitate" toward natural price over time. However, this recourse embroiled Smith in the trademark Enlightenment equivocation over whether market price was the playing out of law-governed harmonic motions or instead the canceling out of externally acausal accidents described above. This equivocation itself is responsible for a fair number of the non-Marshallian features of Smith's discussion: no notion of price-quantity schedules, no law of one price outside of natural price, no dictum that the market must be cleared. A major consideration for Smith's characterization of market versus natural price is the ability to reserve participation in the market, a theme which will assume ever greater significance in our narrative: "The market price will sink more or less below the natural price . . . according as it happens to be more or less important to them to get immediately rid of the commodity" ([1776] 1976, 65).

The French predicament is also a significant subtext of Smith's discussion of price. He praises the Physiocrats in book 4, chapter 9, thanks to whom "the agriculture of France has been delivered of several of the oppressions which it before labored under" (199). At the very least, this statement was premature when it was written, given the history recounted above. Book 4, chapter 5, is scathingly dismissive of those who believe that the bread market requires state intervention: "famine has never arisen from any other cause but the violence of government attempting, by improper means, to remedy the inconveniences of a dearth" (33); "popular fear of engrossing and forestalling may be compared to the popular terrors and suspicions of witchcraft" (41). It was far and away easier to compose such statements in the 1770s, comfortably ensconced in Edinburgh, than to be precariously perched in Paris; but there was also the differential willingness to ignore all the various details of the specific market operation, since they were all deemed the outcome of an inexorable Natural process.

Most aspects of Smith's brief foray into demand and supply would have been recognized as standard operating procedure in Enlightenment discourse. Natural price was to be regarded as an expression of enduring substance—and many pounced upon Smith's brief comments on the labor content of commodities—whereas market price (and therefore supply and demand) could be relegated to the realm of the temporary balance. For instance, Lavoisier could write in 1786: "One may compare the increase in price that accompanies the [grain] shortage to the fevers of illness; the fevers are nothing other than the effort that nature makes to re-establish in the animal oeconomy the order that has been troubled" (in Wise 1993, 220). Yet there remained differences of emphasis and concern, and when the French read Smith, they were not entirely convinced. Perhaps he was thought a little too cavalier about the operation of supply and demand; perhaps he did not quite grasp what the French meant by balance; perhaps the section on labor costs was unseemly; perhaps Smith displayed a tin ear when it came to an understanding of (early) modern science. At a minimum, the French would feel with acute displeasure the deficit of system in his presentation. This deficit would be a complaint of even his major French supporters, Germain Garnier and Jean-Baptiste Say. The differences started small, but gained force and gravitas over time. These differences matter, because the concept of supply and demand was more the province of the French economic community than the British, at least until the advent of late British classical political economy.

France at the turn of the century was replete with Enlightenment balancing acts. Nicolas-François Canard's prize essay in 1801 marked the birth of mathematical political economy in France, and stood as the only work of political economy that Cournot read before setting out to compose his own *Recherches*. Canard, an engineer, initiated the French practice of fully and unapologetically disengaging market price from natural price, and in explicit analogy with the balance beam, wrote down an equation of forces which determined price under nonspecific circumstances. Here the sellers and buyers were accorded a single function each, with price as the shared variable; psychological need is identified as the ultimate source of each function; equilibrium is equated with the balance of those forces. Unfortunately, all specification of the sequence of actions by which equilibrium is brought about is absent, in a clear analogy with d'Alembert's principle in mechanics.

Jean-Baptiste Say attracted much more attention and commentary than Canard, and although he was opposed to mathematical expression of political economy, he resembles Canard more than he diverges from him. Say objects to the idea of natural price in Smith, collapsing all lawlike regularities to market price determined solely by supply and demand. "Demand and supply are opposite extremes of the beam, whence depend the scales of dearness and cheapness; the price is the point of equilibrium, where the momentum of one ceases, and that of the other begins . . . the rise of price is in direct ratio of the demand, and inverse ratio to the supply" (1830, 232). Say's lack of facility with mathematics did not prevent him from attempting to mold his doctrine into a geometrical format in his *Cours complet d'economie politique practique*. The only diagram in the entire work is a triangle, which was intended to represent the number of "fortunes" which (who?) were able to purchase the given commodity at a price represented on the vertical axis (1852, 358; Forget 1994). The relationship to "balance" was more visual than analytical—the figure resembled nothing so much as a fulcrum—and although it made little sense, even with the help of Say's commentary, it did capture the French ambition to develop a theory of supply and demand in critical dialogue with Smith's text which would unify all of political economy and help it to ascend to scientific status through explication of the natural operation of market pricing. Government intervention is denounced in no uncertain terms, and the bread market was cited as one of the relevant examples (362).

Antoine-Augustin Cournot is a landmark figure in our narrative, and not just because he was the one author identified by Marshall as the source of his own inspiration in price theory. Since a geometric portrayal of supply and demand curves can be found in Cournot's *Recherches* (1838), his work is often used to suggest a long and continuous history for the mathematical theory of demand and supply; but such inferences are premature and critically flawed. There exists one very perceptive study of Cournot's oeuvre in French (Menard 1976), but because it languishes untranslated into English, appreciation of Cournot's career has been stunted in the Anglophone world. While Cournot is a recognizable member of the sequence of economic authors in the French engineering tradition (Etner 1987), it is necessary to understand why he was largely ignored in his own country, and why it was that his stock began to rise only at the end of the century in Britain, long after his demise.

Cournot, unlike Canard and Say, possessed a very strong background in mathematics and physics by the standards of his contemporaries; he also demonstrated a deep concern for the pedagogical relationship of geometry to algebra, something which paved the way for later appreciation in the British context. However, he was largely innocent of any previous literature of political economy, which permitted him to venture some rather unorthodox opinions once he came to write his *Recherches*; it was these opinions which rendered him virtually invisible to his Francophone economist contemporaries. The paramount fact of his career, and the source of embarrassment to all who wish to elevate him to precursor status, is that this text met with resounding failure in its intended audience, so much so that Cournot himself repudiated his earlier economic doctrines later in his life (de Ville and Menard 1989). He had failed by the very criteria for which he had hoped to proselytize: his early ideas were deemed poor applied mathematics, and an inadequate codification of Reason.

Cournot begins his 1838 text by considering what about exchange could and could not be considered amenable to mathematical treatment; it is significant that he explicitly identifies that favored concept of Francophone political economy, *utilité*, as falling into the unsuitable category. After a glance at the problem of money, Cournot than confronts the trademark distinction between natural and market prices: "Here, as in astronomy, it is necessary to recognize *secular* variations, which are independent of *periodic* variations" ([1838] 1971, 28). Like his predecessors, Cournot opts to restrict the analysis entirely to short-run or "periodic" phenomena, without any further justification. But that should not be confused with observable prices, as we learn in his chapter 4, "De la loi de débit."[5] Cournot tells us that he intends his curve to correspond to realized sales—and not, we must insist, virtual unfulfilled desires. He then invokes "the single axiom . . . that each one seeks to derive the greatest possible value from his goods or his labor" (44). This axiom is pivotal, since it justifies recourse to the calculus for Cournot.

At this point we are introduced to the central analytical device of the book: "Let us admit therefore that the sales or annual demand D is, for each article, a particular function F(p) of the price p of such article. To know the form of this function would be to know what we call the *loi de débit*" (47). It will now be necessary to quote *in extenso*:

> Since so many moral causes capable neither of enumeration nor measurement affect the law of sales, it is plain we should no more expect this law to be expressible by an algebraic formula than the law of mortality . . . Observation must therefore be depended on for furnishing the means for drawing up, between proper limits, a table of the corresponding values of D and p; after which, by familiar interpolation of graphical techniques, an empirical formula or curve can be given to represent the function; and solutions can be extended into numerical applications. But even if this objective were unattainable (on account of the difficulty of obtaining observations of sufficient number and accuracy, and also because of progressive variations which the law must undergo in a country not yet at the stationary state), it would nevertheless not be improper to introduce the unknown law of demand into

analytical schemes, by means of an undetermined symbol . . . Thus without knowing the law of the decrease of capillary forces, and starting from the principle that these forces are insensible at sensible distances, mathematicians have demonstrated the general laws of the phenomenon of capillarity, and these laws have been confirmed by observation. (47–48)

The nonspecific reference is to Laplace's work of 1805–7 on capillary action (Grattan-Guinness 1990, 442–49); Cournot's mentor Poisson had also been involved in elaborations of the theory. Thus it was all the more damning that Cournot suppressed the comparison after raising it, since Laplace had physical (and not just mathematical) reasons for positing the undetermined capillary function in his theory, and these underwrote the application of various integrals and other mathematical devices. Further, when subjected to experiment, the results were mixed, and this caused Laplace himself to doubt the legitimacy of his analysis. Those cognoscenti familiar with the case would tend to doubt its relevance; and everyone else would simply be passively dazzled by the references to the physical sciences.

It is very difficult to imagine that Cournot himself was unaware of the disanalogies with his economic model. Hard upon the above quote, Cournot posited that his $F(p)$ function was continuous; this was justified by the assumption of a large number of consumers in a thick market (50). Since continuity was a requirement for every mathematical manipulation that followed, Cournot uncharacteristically devoted it much consideration, acknowledging that there might be "exceptions," but conjuring them away with the comment that "just as friction wears down roughnesses and softens outlines, so the wear of commerce tends to suppress these exceptional cases" (51). To pile ignomy on top of unreliability, he then posits that "the price of an article may vary notably in the course of a year, and strictly speaking, the law of sales may also vary in the same interval, if the country experiences a movement of progress or decadence," and therefore "the curve which represents the function F must itself be an average of all the curves which would represent this function" (52). In the midst of this litany of excuses, the all-important negative slope of the function F is inserted as an unmotivated assumption. Time frames, assertions of continuity and regularity, statistical means and individual instances, realizations versus virtual realities, renunciations of mental causes with appeals to human nature, all become hopelessly jumbled in the headlong rush to concoct a function, *any function*, which might be manipulated in the manner of physics: that is, subjected to an optimization procedure. Is it any wonder that Cournot ends this section with the disturbing concession, "We may admit that it is impossible to determine the function $F(p)$ for each article" (53), all the while proposing that economic agents are going to use this function in order to inform their own behavior?

In their unseemly rush to award laurels, modern economists overlook that Cournot's was legitimately deemed a sorry performance, a sad set of *non sequiturs* understandably shunned by Cournot's contemporaries. It is a travesty of history to suggest that Cournot "discovered" anything other than the forever resplendent rhetorical power of physical analogy, let alone the "law of demand." The incongruous imposition of "already completed" price arbitrage on a putative variable state of the thickness of the market and strength of competition is difficult to swallow. The law of one price was only plausible in the case of monopoly, which explains why Cournot's next chapter begins with that topic; and the analysis works solely in terms of the single curve. Since the curve purportedly depended upon "the kind of utility of the article, on the nature of services it can render or the enjoyments it can procure, on the habits and customs of the people, on the average wealth, and on the scale which wealth is distributed" (47), and none of these held out the promise of any stability or invariance, it would have been wishful thinking to regard the function $F(p)$ as anything other than a will-o-the-wisp, much less as continuous with first and second derivatives.

We do not mean to suggest that the majority of Cournot's peers thrust the volume away in disgust over the dubious character of its formal arguments (although Joseph Bertrand's review of 1883 could be cited as one instance). Indeed, it is more likely that they were put off by the text's politics, that is, if they managed to reach the last chapter. There Cournot explicitly set his work in opposition to "the school of Adam Smith," which "with a view to removing the barriers between nation and nation, has always argued from the uncontestable increase in wealth, which has been the invariable result of the removal of barriers" to international trade (160). Cournot's argument was that the extension of the sway of markets could either raise or lower incomes relative to the pre-trade status quo. This alone would have been sufficient to alienate the author from the orthodoxy of French political economy.

No historian other than Claude Menard has paid any attention to Cournot's career after the *Recherches*, which extended for another four decades and numerous books, including two more on political economy. Somehow it is deemed legitimate to ignore the later books because they had no impact on contemporaries; but by those standards, neither should we take a second look at the *Recherches*. The young Cournot relied heavily upon a belief in the inexorable spread of the market and of rationality (with the metric system as its embodiment) to rationalize his own project of a mathematical political economy. He thought that as markets grew thicker and more competitive, and people increasingly rational, it would become legitimate to rely upon the law of large numbers to treat participants as homogeneous, markets as frictionless, and hence F(p) as continuous and well behaved. Menard explicitly links this belief to a common engineering mentality prevalent in that era. However, later in life Cournot grew disenchanted with trends he thought he had observed—the relative failure of the spread of the metric system, lack of progress toward greater competition, and scant evidence of rationality among the masses. These observations provoked a growing philosophical conviction that economics should strive to look more like biology than rational mechanics. For just these reasons, Cournot's later works on political economy contain no mathematical content, and thus no law of sales. It was on just these grounds that Cournot rejected Walras's *Elements* (Walras 1965, letter 294).

British Treatments of Supply and Demand in the Nineteenth Century before Thornton

The discourse of laws of supply and demand was noticeably slower to catch on in Britain than in France. Indeed, as Thweatt (1983, 289) demonstrates, after Steuart and Smith there were no substantial discussions for a quarter-century. The silence was broken by Thomas Malthus's pamphlet *The High Price of Provisions* in 1800 and Henry Thornton—no relation to William Thomas—and James Mill in 1802. But soon thereafter, the number of texts escalates rapidly, with numerous mentions of "supply and demand" in Parliamentary debates by 1810. The primary camp which appears to have adopted the terminology as its own was the "Philosophical Radicals," who included Francis Homer, Henry Brougham, and Richard Torrens (Halevy 1972). It is safe to say that by the end of the Napoleonic Wars the laws of supply and demand were common currency in the British context; but there are many curious and counterintuitive aspects of this sea change which have yet to attract major scrutiny.

The first incongruous aspect of the rise of supply and demand theory in Britain is that this discourse gains purchase right in the period of the genesis and development of the Ricardian orthodoxy in British classical political economy. David Ricardo's hostility to supply and demand as generic explanations of price and quantity in his *Principles* of 1817 and elsewhere are well known, and need not be reiterated here. Thus it is all the more noteworthy that many of the proponents of supply and demand theories were engaged in close contact with Ricardo and grappled with his notions of a scientific political economy during their genesis, all the more reason why classical political economy should never be treated as a monolithic doctrine. Second, it is also well known that the primary context for these debates was disputes over the corn laws and the "high price of provisions." Hence, just as in France (although later in time), it was the vexed question of special treatment to be accorded to the bread or grain markets which called forth the conceptual clarification of notions of supply and demand. Third, this similarity in the conditions of genesis is no mere coincidence, since it was precisely those figures most heavily influenced by French writers and French ideas, especially Malthus, Horner, and Mill Sr. (Halevy 1972, 270), who promoted the primacy of supply and demand in the construction of a scientific political economy. Nevertheless, once the doctrine recrossed the Channel, it tended to assume a different tenor and tone; and this specific historical manifestation requires description in some depth in order to begin to grasp the impact of Thornton's work in the later 1860s. We shall sketch the outlines of such a description by briefly relating the conceptions of supply and demand proposed by a number of key texts in the period, from Thomas Robert Malthus to John Stuart Mill.

From a historiographic distance, Thomas Malthus's *The High Price of Provisions* would resemble a rather standard broadside against those who would seek to regulate bread markets, such as one would find in that era in France. Britain had just suffered a terrible dearth of grain in 1795, and even though harvests had subsequently recovered, prices were still high by historical standards. Malthus's pen was mobilized by his observation that "Many men of sense have joined in the universal cry of the common people, that there must be roguery somewhere; and the general indignation has fallen upon the monopolizers, forestallers and regraters" (1986, 6). The problem for Malthus was that a sophisticated understanding of the laws of political economy was absent: "When any commodity is scarce, its natural price is necessarily forgotten, and its actual price is regulated by the excess of demand over supply." In times of crisis people needed an understanding of the short-term workings of markets; appeals to long-run natural determinants were essentially unavailing. Parson Malthus could not restrain himself from also blaming the Poor Laws and Speenhamland; but the paramount message was that the operation of the market, here explicitly equated with the balance of demand and supply, was not at fault. One observes that even in the British context, the advantages of downgrading the importance of the theory of "natural" price relative to some lawlike supply and demand doctrines were becoming apparent to a few key figures.

It is now frequently forgotten that Jeremy Bentham entered this fray on the opposing side in his *Defence of a Maximum* (1801), supporting temporary price controls on corn. Such heresy, especially among the clique of Radicals, cried out for a response; and James Mill responded to the call in 1804 in his essay on the trade in corn. His major weapon against market intervention was the assertion that "the demand will always be proportioned to the supply, however great that supply may be" (1966, 56). In 1805 Mill was the first to acknowledge J.-B. Say and his "loi de débouches" as a theoretical and political ally. In 1806 Mill wrote an elaborate review of Sir James Steuart's *Principles*—the first systematic treatise to extensively use the language of supply and demand—as a pretext to discuss the corn trade. Mill subsequently developed a close personal relationship with Say, serving as his intermediary with the British luminaries of political economy and facilitating correspondence with Bentham, Malthus, and Ricardo, among others. By 1820 their personal and intellectual careers were so intertwined that Mill Sr. arranged for his adolescent son John Stuart Mill to reside with Say during his first visit to Paris (Bain 1882, 190; Anna Mill 1960). Thus it was not unexpected that when Mill Sr. produced his own *Elements of Political Economy* in 1821, asking in chapter 3 "What Determines the Quantity in Which Commodities Exchange for One Another?" the answer should have been "the principle of supply and demand, in the first instance" (1966, 255). With Mill, the doctrine of price determined by supply and demand and the doctrine that a general glut was impossible became yoked together, so that mere assertion of "laws" of demand and supply were taken as shorthand for a belief that markets always operated, problem free, for the benefit of the common weal.

Hence, by the 1820s, at least in the hands of the "Millians" (as they were then called), "supply and demand" became a sort of litmus test to divine the soundness of someone's position on political economy. The assertion that grain markets always correctly represented the state of scarcity reigning in any given situation shaded over into a dogma that markets would never allow the existence of overproduction in general (although disproportionalities between industries might make for temporary disruption), and therefore all unemployment was merely a matter of frictions, temporary imbalances, or external interference with the wage mechanism. This was a defining moment in British classical political economy: French concern over the specific problems of a grain market with its own characteristic rules and practices, provoking a French liberal backlash against attempts to regulate and regularize subsistence markets, slowly transmuted into a British belief that all markets exhibited the same generic mechanisms described by "laws" of supply and demand, and therefore constituted the primary explanation of why free markets for labor could not result in pervasive unemployment or impoverishment of the workforce.

Consequently, by the 1820s the language of supply and demand was coming to be deployed as a shorthand in England for a very specific political position (Groenewegen 1973, 509): in Parliamentary debates, for instance, it signaled opposition to subsistence aid to the poor or any organized interference in the wage labor nexus. The transformation was swift: in little more than two decades, supply and demand went from a tentative hypothesis to a proposition so well established that one violated it only under the most dire of circumstances. One observes it used unselfconsciously in speeches from the floor, like that of the marquis of Landsdowne in 1822: "That it is mischievous to interfere with the regular course of supply and demand in the market was a principle no less generally recognized; but, so singular was the situation of Ireland, that this great principle of political economy must be violated" (in Fetter 1980, 59). This was the orthodox use of supply and demand which Charles Dickens savaged in 1854 in his novel *Hard Times*: "For the first time in her life Louisa had come into one of the dwellings of the Coketown hands . . . She knew them in crowds passing to and from their nests, like ants or beetles. But she knew from her reading infinitely more of the ways of the toiling insects than of these toiling men and women. Something to be worked so much and paid so much, and there ended; something to be infallibly settled by the laws of supply and demand; something that blundered into those laws and floundered into difficulty; something that was a little pinched when wheat was dear and overate themselves when wheat was cheap; . . . something that occasionally rose like the sea, and did some harm and waste (chiefly to itself), and fell again; this she knew the Coketown hands to be" ([1854] 1961, 160).

However, the stronger were the links forged between the British discourse of demand and supply and this construction of the political lessons of political economy, the less precise were the specifications of what the imperious "laws" actually implied or ruled out. "Laws" they might very well be, but it was noticeable that British political economists expended appreciably less effort than their French counterparts in shoring up their expression with mathematics or empirical data. Perhaps this oversight might be attributed to the uneasy coexistence of the discourse of demand and supply with the stated tenets of the dominant Ricardian school; perhaps the relative quarantine of British political economists from trained engineers and natural sciences (in contrast to the situation of the French) could also have played a role. In any event, the configuration of forces did have the result of producing a much less coherent and sustained discussion of demand and supply in Britain from roughly 1820 to 1870, a period punctuated by periodic unresolved controversies over the meaning and significance of demand and supply.

Especially in the 1820s and 1830s, one cannot but notice a proliferation of positions vis-à-vis the theory of supply and demand. As de Quincey once noted, "that one desperate enormity of vicious logic which takes place in the ordinary application to price of the relation between supply and demand has secured more arguments dispersed through speeches, books, journals than a long life could fully expose" (1897, 118). In the interests of brevity, we shall identify three major categories.[6] First, there were the hard-core Ricardians who sought to defend the central doctrinal primacy of the labor theory of value; this group would include J. R. McCulloch, popularizers such as Jane Marcet, Ricardo himself, and later Thomas de Quincey. Natural price as a cost of production was deemed by them the preeminent theoretical device; the accidental and imponderable aspects of the day-to-day operation of markets were to be disposed of under the rubric of supply and demand. This group, understandably, bore the least stake, and thus exerted the least effort, in trying to stabilize the precise theoretical referent of the terminology of supply and demand. "You must, however, recollect that it is the cost of production of a commodity which constitutes its exchangeable value; the proportion of supply and demand should be considered as only accidentally affecting it" (Marcet [1816] 1827, 417). "Variations of demand and supply occasion corresponding variations of price; but it is essential to remark that these valuations are temporary only. The cost of production is the grand regulator of price—the centre of all those transitory and evanescent oscillations on the one side and the other . . . wherever industry is unrestricted and competition allowed to operate, the average price of the various products of art and industry coincides with the cost of production" (McCulloch 1864 [1825], 252, 257). "It is a metaphysical impossibility that Supply and Demand, the relation of which is briefly expressed by the term "market value," could ever affect price except by a *secondary* force" (de Quincey 1897, 121).

Then there was a second camp seeking to occupy something like a middle ground: unwilling to wholly repudiate the labor theory in its guise as a "cost of production" approach, but seeking to downgrade it to something resembling a special case of the more general laws of supply and demand. The best representatives of this group were Malthus and his sympathizers such as Longfield and Scrope; but the tent was sufficiently large to encompass the rather more venturesome Mills, the antipodean William Hearn, and Ricardian sometime fellow travelers like Torrens. This was the group that frequently sought to engage Say on his own ground, often flirting to a greater or lesser extent with "utility" as an ur-principle of value, and less frequently looking to French liberals for political inspiration. As Mill Jr. wrote, "The principle, that value is proportional to cost of production, being consequently inapplicable, we must revert to a principle anterior to that of cost of production, and from which this last flows as a consequence,—namely, the principle of demand and supply" (1897, 13). One implication of this inversion of importance was that the theory of supply and demand should, in principle, enjoy explication of the conditions under which it would operate freely and the environments in which it would dominate cost of production; yet precious few of the authors in this second group ultimately devoted much effort to that task. Nevertheless, their rallying cry, this figure-ground reversal as regards the labor theory of "natural price," combined with the supply and demand locution, would soon prove their downfall, since the need to broaden the supply and demand tent, all the while doggedly maintaining agnosticism on what was "natural" about natural price, tended to rob this crew of all conceptual precision or political efficacy. It is no surprise that this bloated and disorganized middle ground would be where William Thornton would choose to mount his attack in the 1860s upon political economy, its confusions on price, and its strictures on wages.

Finally, there did exist a third group of writers rooted primarily in the natural sciences, outsiders to the Ricardian orthodoxy, who had no interest in defending past verities or recent French fashions. They too sought "laws" of the economy; in their no-nonsense instrumental world, the language of "supply and demand" would serve as well as any other to demarcate their quest. However, all notions of reconciliation with the classical labor doctrine were dismissed as futile. These writers are sometimes identified in the modern literature as the "Whewell group" of political economists (Henderson 1996)—Edward Rogers, William Whewell, Dionysius Lardner—although by all rights, Fleeming Jenkin would fit neatly into this category as well. Although they may look very modern in retrospect, they had almost no lasting impact upon their contemporaries in Britain. Partly, this was because the demand and supply organon was deployed in their writings more as a tool of critique of the other rival groups than as engine of analysis, at least until the 1870s; and in part, their influence was confounded by widespread hostility to algebraic models in the British context.

Because it was the second, largest group that provided the prime milieu and target for Thornton's later work, it may prove worthwhile to take a closer look at a few of the key texts which constituted the mid-nineteenth-century orthodoxy concerning the theory of supply and demand. The leitmotiv of this literature is the repeated accusations launched at others of dire confusions over the deployment of the laws of supply and demand, and endless reiteration of the desperate need for sound definitions, although each subsequent proposal never seemed more satisfying than its predecessors. Malthus, for one, could never make others understand just what he meant by the laws of demand and supply. In his *Principles of Political Economy* (1820) he appeals to Turgot and Say but still feels he must enter a note of caution: "The terms Demand and Supply are so familiar to the ear of every reader . . . [yet] are by no means applied with precision" ([1820] 1966, 36). Paradoxically, everyday usage is held as the arbiter: "[When] society has been divided, in common language, into buyers and sellers, demand may be defined to be the will combined with the power to purchase, and supply, the production of commodities with intention to sell them" (37). What one member of the pair giveth, the other immediately taketh away: "existing market prices are, at the moment they are fixed, determined upon a principle quite distinct from cost of production, and that these prices are in reality almost always different from what they would have been if this cost had regulated them . . . the great principle of Demand and Supply is called into action to determine what Adam Smith calls natural as well as market prices" (45–46). Perhaps one can share Ricardo's vexation with this passage, reproduced in his notes on Malthus: "The author forgets Adam Smith's definition of natural price, or else he would not say that Demand and Supply could determine natural price."

Malthus cluttered up the end of his career with screeds assailing others for the inadequacies of their definitions, surely the very last refuge of the pedant. As is frequently the case, the guns were turned on those closest to his own position: "the most culpable confusion of terms which Mr. Mill has fallen into, is in relation to demand and supply; and as he has a more original and appropriate claim to this error than any other English writer . . . the notice of it is particularly called for" (1827, 44). This prefaced a rambling critique of the surfeit of meanings of demand then prevalent in political economy, only to end up with Malthus's preferred specification(s): "two distinct meanings: one, in regard to the extent, or the quantity of commodities purchased; and the other, in regard to the intensity, or sacrifice which the demanders are willing and able to make in order to satisfy their wants" (244). To preserve a semblance of continuity, this "intensity" was further equated with the labor commanded by the commodity.

No one could rest content with this; everyone felt impelled to propose some variation upon it. Poulette Scrope wrote: "the value (or selling price) of an article at any time and place is determined by the proportion of the demand to the supply at that time and place . . . The extent of the Demand for a thing depends upon the intensity of desire for its possession among a larger or smaller group of persons, and likewise upon the means of purchasing it . . . The supply of goods is determined by the circumstances that affect their production, and is subject to greater variations than the demand" ([1833] 1969, 185–87). Mountifort Longfield took the dramatic step of attempting to restrict its meaning in the interest of rendering the definition more general: "that portion of any commodity which any one possesses and does not intend to consume is supply; the disposition to give something in exchange for it is demand. . . . if the quantity of the article to be sold is more than sufficient to supply all those who are willing to pay the natural price for it, the competition among the sellers . . . will sink the price until the supply comes equal to the effective demand . . . In this case the equality between the Demand and the Supply is produced not by diminishing the supply, but by the increased demand consequent upon a diminution of price" (1834, 45, 49). Perhaps one can conjure some empathy with the frustration of the author of *Observations on Certain Verbal Disputes* . . ., who complained: "If the degree of demand can itself be altered by the degree of supply, what information is given us by saying, that something depends upon the balance of forces (as it were) between the two?" (in V. Smith 1951, 253).

The writings of John Stuart Mill must have appeared as welcome terra firma amidst an endless Sargasso Sea of shifting definitions. In his youthful work *Some Unsettled Questions in Political Economy* (written 1829–30), Mill had already set about judiciously distancing himself from the hard-core Ricardian position, but equally so from his father's advocacy of Say. It is noteworthy that this positioning took place within the context of one of the first extended commentaries on supply and demand in English not explicitly devoted to either the corn trade or the wages question. Mill's first essay is concerned rather with the theory of international trade—not insignificantly one of the exceptions to the primacy of natural price in Ricardo's system— whereas the second essay tends to mitigate the insistence by Say upon the ironclad impossibility of a general glut. Mill here insists upon a construction of his version of supply and demand as predicated upon market clearing: "Whatever be the commodity—the supply in any market being given, there is some price at which the whole of the supply will find purchasers, and no more. That, whatever it be, is the price at which, by the effect of competition the commodity will be sold" (1897, 13). Nevertheless, the precision promised by this point of satiation was still treated as eluding the effective grasp of the science of political economy: "The result of our most fortunate inquiries will seldom assume a very definite form: it will be more frequently a genus than an individual: we shall seldom be able to accurately measure its dimensions, or to express it precisely in numbers. It is not unlikely, however, that an artificial science might be formed, which should promote the practical discovery of political truth" (70).

Such circumspection, while laudable in an essay, has no place in a textbook; and thus Mill's *Principles of Political Economy* approached the problem of price in an aggressively confident manner. His unfortunate assertion that "there is nothing in the laws of Value which remains for the present or any future writer to clear up" (1965, 456) has oft been quoted as a masterpiece of imprescience; but few seem to have realized the extent to which Mill so qualified Ricardo's cost of production strictures that the "theory" of supply and demand became the de facto doctrinal core of his political economy, or as he put it in an important emendation of the phrase from his earlier essay, "we must revert to a law of value anterior to cost of production and more fundamental, the law of demand and supply" (1965, 583). Much of this doctrinal hubris, this drastic innovation retailed as doctrinal faithfulness to Ricardo plus some unalloyed common sense, has been praised in retrospect as an anticipation of the Marshallian orthodoxy of a half-century later:[7] "Thus we see that the idea of a *ratio*, as between demand and supply, is out of place . . . the proper mathematical analogy is that of an *equation*. Demand

and supply, the quantity demanded and the quantity supplied, will be made equal. If unequal at any moment, competition equalizes them, and the manner in which this is done is by adjustment of the value" (1965, 467). Yet it is important to take note of the ways in which Mill's doctrine was less forward-looking than profoundly conservative (Packe 1954, 312). Mill only cited two authors in his discussion of the theory of supply and demand: de Quincey and Say. Say is credited with a "clear exposition" (466) of the theory, whereas de Quincey is upbraided for not realizing the extent to which the doctrine remains fully supportive of the Ricardian tradition. For those familiar with Say and de Quincey, these two statements would in essence imply a contradiction, something often encountered in Mill's ex cathedra mode. The sense of misplaced concreteness undoubtedly derived from Mill's desire to uphold the Ricardian catechism that "production" [read: substance] was the root determinant of value, with exchange operations treated as secondary perturbations superimposed upon the fundamental relationships, to such an extent that the two could be dealt with as analytically separable. Thus Mill could still insist that supply and demand constituted "the Law of Value, with respect to commodities not susceptible of being multiplied at pleasure" (468), but then genuflect toward Ricardo by adding, "the value of things which can be increased in quantity at pleasure, does not depend (except accidentally, and during the time necessary for production to adjust itself) upon demand and supply; on the contrary, demand and supply depend upon it" (475). Here, as in many other instances, Mill was simultaneously retailing the two alternative Enlightenment conceptions of balance, with no attempt to distinguish or differentiate them. Were divergences from the theoretically correct price due to accidents not covered in the theory but averaged out in large numbers? Or a set of determinants fundamentally separate from the law of normal price? Or the same lawlike determinants as account for the normal price, just operating on a meta-level, such as perturbations around equilibrium?

In Mill's *Principles*, the theory of supply and demand was both delimited and confirmed in its previous doctrinal commitments. In their prior incarnations, the "laws" of demand and supply were never intended to encompass every possible market phenomenon under every conceivable circumstance; and here Mill's version was no different. He notoriously exempted supply and demand from what would become the paradigm case of catallactics in the neoclassical era, namely the case of the isolated individual purchasing goods for private use. Said Mill, "Purchases for private use, even by people in business, are not always made on business principles" (460). Since psychological motives were not deemed sufficiently regular to underpin economic laws, Mill proposed that the laws of supply and demand might not capture pricing behavior in retail markets, but would be best exemplified in wholesale markets, where "values and prices are determined by competition alone." Thus the notion was promulgated that it was men of business who were the most capable and trustworthy representatives, conduits and mouthpieces for the inanimate forces of production; only they were driven by impersonal dictates of competition, which overrode all specifics of the actual organization and structure of the marketplace. Rather than a description of a process, competition tended to be conflated with the "axiom" that "there cannot be for the same article, of the same quality, two prices in the same market." For Cournot, the *loi de débit* would be most transparently expressed in the case of monopoly, since it was only then that one would expect the one-price rule to hold; whereas for Mill, the fullness of competition in the guise of the one-price rule was the only regime under which there might obtain a "law" of demand at all. Not only did this invert the usual understanding of the significance of price dispersion in a market: it also began a long tradition of repressing distinctive market processes under various rubrics of degrees of "competition" (Dennis 1977).

There was another way in which real existing markets were acknowledged as diverse: foreigners might be exempt from the idealization of "economic man" and full competition to a greater or lesser degree. "In political economy . . . empirical laws of human nature are tacitly assumed by English thinkers, which are calculated only for Great Britain and the United States. Among other things, an intensity of competition is constantly supposed, which, as a general mercantile fact, exists in no country in the world except in those two . . . Yet those who know the habits of the Continent of Europe are aware how apparently small a motive often outweighs the desire of money-getting, even in the operations which have money-getting as their direct object" (*Collected Works* 8:906). We can thus observe that the boundaries of the set of markets to which the "laws" of supply and demand would pertain were conveniently imprecise and highly variable; this fact will shortly prove relevant to Mill's own attempts to defend these laws against critics, as well as in understanding the ways in which he diverged from the subsequent neoclassical doctrine.

Mill's textbook bears responsibility for another, rather dismal doctrine in the history of Anglophone economics. Mill took up the prior political valence of popular appeals to supply and demand and hardened it into a rigid dictum about the impotence of workers to do anything about the level of their own wages, which he himself popularized under the label of the "wages-fund." In books I and II of the *Principles*, the wages fund is described in the context of a stationary economy: wages "depend mainly on the demand and supply of labour; or as is often expressed, on the proportion between population and capital . . . nothing can permanently alter general wages, except an increase or diminution of capital itself (always meaning by the term the funds of all sorts devoted to the payment of labour) compared with the quantity of labour offering itself to be hired." In book III this notion has become indissolubly linked to the primacy of supply and demand as a causal explanation of price: "there are commodities of which, though capable of being increased to a great, or even an unlimited extent, the value never depends upon anything but demand and supply. This is the case, in particular, with the commodity Labour" (1965, 469). In books IV and V, a more fluid and dynamic perspective is taken, whereby the working class as a whole might eventually improve its lot through population control, education, and Mill's favorite Golden Mean of "Co-operation" between Labour and Capital; but after all was said and done, there was very little hope held out for the worker in his or her own lifetime.

Mill's tendency to change his mind about political economy under the influence of Harriet Taylor after 1848 has been the subject of much commentary (Packe 1954, 313; Hayek 1951). Nevertheless, it does appear that Mill suffered reservations about how the doctrine of the wages fund was being used, especially after Henry Fawcett's article in the *Westminster Review* in 1860 on strikes. These reservations, in conjunction with the links between the wages fund, the condemnation of the economic impact of trades unions, and the burgeoning significance of the demand and supply doctrine as an explanation of price, set the stage for the momentous intervention of William Thomas Thornton in the 1860s.

The Life of William Thomas Thornton

One reason why Thornton has been neglected in the historical literature is that his station in life, not to mention his publications before *On Labour*, made him a most unlikely candidate for having a lasting impact upon the evolution of British political economy. To a certain extent, his obscurity has masked his role behind the scenes in the evolution of British political economy in the 1860s and 1870s, over and above his publications.

According to the *Dictionary of National Biography*, William Thomas Thornton was born in Burnham, Buckinghamshire, on February 14, 1813. William was the youngest son of Sophie Zohrab, the daughter of a Persian merchant, Paul Zohrab, who had settled in Turkey, and Thomas Thornton, a man involved with international commerce from an early age. Thomas Thornton was perhaps best known for his book *Turkey Past and Present.* (1807), a detailed description of the social, political, and military institutions of the Ottoman Empire. Most of Thomas Thornton's familiarity with the Levant derived from his many years of residence in Constantinople and the surrounding region, pursuing British mercantile interests.

Unfortunately for the young William, his father died on March 28, 1814, on the eve of a voyage to Alexandria to assume the position of counsel to the Levant Company. While this left William bereft of a father at a tender age, after settling in the Moravian community at Ockbrook and reaching majority he received a wide-ranging education abroad. Most notable are his three years' residence with the auditor general of Malta, William Thomas's cousin Sir William Henry Thornton (1786–1859), and his work in Constantinople from 1830 to 1835 on the staff of the consul general. This extensive experience abroad may have influenced Thornton's espousal of more cultural relativist positions later in his writings, in contrast with the more insular run of British political economists.

Upon his return to Britain, in August 1836 William Thornton obtained a junior clerkship with the examiner's office in the East India House, then at the height of its power and prestige. According to his own testimony, his preferment was due to the intervention of Sir James Carnac, then chairman of the East India Company. In December 1837 Thornton was transferred to the marine branch of the secretary's office. Again by his own testimony, the duties of the office were not onerous, permitting him to prepare for his début as an author. *Over-population and Its Remedy* (1846) was his anti-Malthusian tract, which inverted the conventional wisdom in maintaining that "the original cause of overpopulation is almost invariably misery." At this early stage in his career one can observe a nascent fascination with the wages fund doctrine. He accepted that wages were determined by the ratio between the "fund" and the population of laborers but questioned the extent to which the denominator conformed to simple stories of immiseration. In this work Thornton first stated his lifelong theme that the cultural experience of being lifted out of poverty would not render the subject feckless and lazy and profligate, but rather was the most generally assured method of fostering a set of behaviors which would maintain prosperity. His indictment of Malthus therein was that he "overlooked or undervalued the tendency which the possession of property has to engender prudence, and seems, indeed, to have thought that the quality is rarely to be found among members of the labouring class, except under the pressure of misery" (270). Thornton instead believed that there might exist a low-level trap in economic development, according to which the hardscrabble struggle for existence would actually lower living standards. He also revealed a skepticism toward the benevolent progress of natural forces, something that would subsequently grow in importance, noting situations where workers "are too numerous to earn a competent subsistence for themselves and their families, competition takes place amongst them: each, in his anxiety to obtain employment, offers to accept lower wages than he requires for his comfortable maintenance . . . Neither has this state any tendency to correct itself. Whatever point populations may attain, it can with equal ease at least maintain itself there" (3–4).

However, in 1846 Thornton felt compelled to couch his assault on the Malthusian consensus in terms which left the orthodox concepts of supply and demand unquestioned. This tentativeness is revealed in passing in his commentary on the Poor Laws: "It cannot be denied that in this instance the rate of wages was in part determined by the price of provisions, but this can only happen where the circumstances which naturally regulate the price of labour are arbitrarily interfered with. When the money price of labour is suffered to adjust itself according to the proportions between the supply and the demand, it will remain unaffected by any variations in the price of provisions or of other commodities" (227). Initially closer to Malthus than to Ricardo on questions of price theory, Thornton was situated somewhere in that large second group identified above, consisting of those inclined to elevate supply and demand to leading roles in political economy, but with the proviso that there was plenty of room for concerted action on the part of the state and of the actors to lift the poorest members of society out of penury. In this regard, he resembled no major contemporary figure in the British context so much as John Stuart Mill.

This resemblance raises the very important issue, perversely avoided by most historians of economic thought but openly acknowledged by general historians (Packe 1954, 387), of the close and prolonged personal relationship between William Thomas and Mill Jr. As he relates in his memoir, Thornton knew Mill by sight at the India House, but he had no occasion to have a conversation with him until he sent him a copy of his *Over-population* in 1846. As he told it, "A day or two afterwards he came into my room to thank me for it; and during the half-hour's conversation that thereupon ensued, sprang up, full grown at birth, an intimate friendship, of which I feel that I am not unduly boasting in declaring it to have been equally sincere and fervent on both sides. From that time for the next ten or twelve years, a day seldom passed without, if I did not go into his room, his coming into mine, often telling me as he entered that he had nothing particular to say; but that, having a few minutes to spare, he thought we might as well have a little talk" (1873a, 34–35). This working relationship developed into a close friendship which was enriched by discussions of many philosophical, intellectual, and economic issues, described primarily in Thornton's eulogy to Mill. Indeed, in many ways Thornton owed his elevation in intellectual stature to his friendship with Mill. For instance, we know that in 1850 Mill wrote to the editor of the *Westminster Review* proposing Thornton as a contributor (1972, 47). As Mill once wrote to Cairnes, "Thornton is a person I particularly respect and like. In perfect candour, sincerity and singleness of mind few men come near him" (in O'Brien 1943, 274). As Mill proceeded to vouch for him, others began to take him more seriously. In 1856, when Mill was promoted to examiner at the India Office, he made it a condition of his acceptance that Thornton be appointed assistant examiner of public works. Yet as time wore on, much more than mere intellectual issues bound the two together.

In times of personal crisis or distress, one would often turn for assistance to the other. In Thornton's case, his perennial ill-health was periodically the cause for alarm. Once when Thornton suffered from nervous exhaustion that kept him away from his position for over a year in 1857, Mill carried his workload at the India Office so that Thornton would not lose his position (Thornton 1873a, 35). This intervention undoubtedly saved Thornton's career in more ways than one, since it coincided with the transfer of the East India Company's administrative functions to the India Office, after the Sepoy Rebellion and the conveying of the company's territories to the Crown. Upon recovery, Thornton was appointed secretary of the newly constituted Department of Public Works. For his part J. S. Mill, immobilized by his bereavement over the death of his wife, entrusted to Thornton the task of placing Harriet Taylor's obituary in London newspapers:[8]

> Hotel d'Europe, Avignon
> Nov. 9, 1858
>
> My Dear Thornton—The hopes with which I commenced this journey have been fatally frustrated. My wife, the companion of all my feelings, the prompter of all my best thoughts, the guide of all my actions, is gone! She was taken ill at this place with a violent attack of bronchitis or pulmonary conjestion—the medical men here could do nothing for her, & before the physician at Nice who saved her life once could arrive, all was over.
>
> It is doubtful if I shall ever be fit for anything public or private, again. The spring of my life is broken. But I shall best fulfil her wishes by not giving up the attempt to do something useful, and I am not quite alone. I have with me her daughter, the one person besides myself who most loved her & whom she most loved, & we help each other to bear what is inevitable. I am sure of your sympathy, but if you knew what she was you would feel how little sympathy can do.
>
> We return straight to England but shall be detained here for some days longer & I beg of you the kind office of inserting the inclosed notice twice in the Times & once in the Post, Herald & Daily News & in the principal weekly papers. Believe me my dear Thornton, very sincerely yours, J. S. Mill

Thornton was the right person for this job, given that he was an intimate of Harriet Taylor's circle as well as Mill's. For instance, it was he, along with

Arthur Ley, who was a trustee of the estate of John Taylor, the long-suffering first husband of Harriet Taylor (Packe 1954, 382).

If anything, after Mill bought a cottage in Avignon to be near his wife's grave, Thornton and Mill grew closer. Although Mill retired from the India Office in 1858 and was frequently absent from London, Thornton was always treated as a welcome guest. It was Thornton who was entreated to visit Mill and Harriet's daughter Helen Taylor in Avignon, and Thornton who provided others in the early 1860s with reports on Mill's emotional status (Elliot 1910, 1:261–62). Mill, when writing to Thornton from Avignon as late as 1869, makes reference to "your room" as being refurbished (*Collected Works* 16, letter 1380).

It is my view that much of Thornton's subsequent literary output, from 1848 until roughly 1870, in the field of political economy (but most emphatically *not* his poetic or philosophical writings!) should be regarded as the product of a prolonged discussion, shading imperceptibly over into collaboration, with Mill. John Stuart Mill had few close friends; and fewer still whom he regarded comfortably as intellectual equals. This dialogue in and of itself should constitute just cause for a substantial reevaluation of Thornton's writings. One of the early fruits of this long relationship was Thornton's tract *A Plea for Peasant Proprietors* (1848). As mentioned in his first edition of *Principles*, Mill was greatly concerned over the plight of the laboring peasantry in England and Ireland. Thornton's *Over-population* had argued that the settlement of "wastelands" by small peasant proprietors would constitute one plausible remedy for the Irish famine, and Mill praised this analysis in his *Principles* (1965, 997–99), calling it "honourably distinguished from most others which have recently been published [this in 1849], by its rational treatment of the great questions affecting the economical condition of the labouring classes." Sharp criticism by others of the thesis that small landholdings would be economically viable (e.g., Anonymous 1847), and that population growth would simply wipe out any temporary gains, prompted Thornton to redouble his efforts toward a program for Irish resettlement, and a vindication of the social and economic consequences of a wide distribution of smallholders. Mill read the proofs for this second book, and there is reason to think much of his stamp is imprinted upon it.[9]

Nevertheless, the *Plea* would seem in retrospect Thornton's least satisfactory economic work. There is a penchant for excessive minutiae and the retail of anecdote as a replacement for concerted marshaling of evidence in all of Thornton's writings, yet here these vices tend to overwhelm his other virtues. For instance, that certain forms of smallholdings seemed to flourish on the Channel Islands would seem to bear little relevance for the larger agricultural infrastructures of Ireland or England, a point which appears to have eluded Thornton. Likewise, isolated national statistics of average agricultural production per acre did not begin to confront the issue of whether scale economies in agriculture were as pervasive as they appeared to be. Furthermore, Thornton did indulge a weakness for writing "conjectural history," a tendency already noted by Brentano, and in the *Plea* given free rein in the treatment of Irish history as well as ancient Greece. It is worthwhile to note, however, that an entire chapter was given over to the effects of peasant proprietorship in France. It seems that Thornton was here for the first time forced to confront the vexing French problem of explaining why the freely operating grain markets there were not able to stem the tide of subsistence crises; owing to his extensive experience with other cultures, Thornton could not accept the conventional wisdom that the problem could be traced to the absence of large-scale capitalist agriculture and the atavism of *morcellement*.

Outside of Mill and his small circle of confidants in the 1850s, it would seem that Thornton was not deemed a major thinker or accorded much respect among the literati of the day. The *Plea* was essentially ignored in the periodical press, even though Mill in the second edition of his *Principles* called it "the standard work on that side of the question"; and there followed a notable hiatus in Thornton's output in political economy, beginning in 1854 and lasting roughly a decade. Some of this might have been attributable to the illness and disruptions to the India Office mentioned above; but part of the explanation must lie in Thornton's advocacy of what were regarded as lost causes, as well as perceived flaws in his own personality. To put it bluntly, there were few others like Mill who treasured Thornton's tenaciousness in argument and his deficiency in the civilities associated with a certain stratum of the leisure classes in Victorian Britain. Our primary evidence of this latter character trait comes from the minutes and records of the Political Economy Club.

From 1847 until his death, Thornton was an active member in the Political Economy Club of England. This was a monthly conclave of influential scholars and business people, founded by David Ricardo and sustained by his followers, to address the major issues affecting the new science of political economy. The meetings consisted of an evening of supper and an after-port discussion of a question posed by one of the members. Thornton's entrée into this august conclave undoubtedly was owed to Mill's intervention. In the thirty-three years that Thornton was a member of the club, he formally presented questions on fifteen occasions (Political Economy Club 1921). These questions give us a very good indicator of Thornton's enthusiasms; but they also provide us a fair calendar of the years in which Thornton was actively engaged in political economy. We reproduce the full schedule of these questions below, divided into three discrete phases.

February 3, 1848. Is the system of letting small pieces of land to agricultural labourers, commonly called the allotment system, open to any valid objection, as a means of improving the condition of those labourers?

June 6, 1850. What reason is there for believing that the recent approximations toward Free Trade in food, have affected the ability of the country to bear the burthen of the National Debt?

May 1, 1851. Is not the Ricardo theory of Rent unnecessarily artificial, and might not another be devised less complicated, yet equally accurate and more comprehensive?

June 5, 1851. Instead of being true, as is frequently asserted, that taxation presses with disproportionate weight on the poor, would it not rather appear that no taxes, other than Protective duties, can permanently diminish the income of the labouring classes?

February 1, 1852. Can it, in any circumstances whatever, be advantageous to raise the money required for public expenditure, by means of a loan, instead of immediate taxation?

June 2, 1853. What is the most correct definition of Capital?

May 4, 1854. Are Copy-right and Patent-right founded on justice, or merely on sufferance, and are not those terms really misnomers?

December 7, 1854. What is the foundation of the Tenant Right of Ulster?

June 5, 1862. Can any Income Tax, and, *a fortiori*, an uniform Income Tax, be otherwise than at variance with the just principals of Taxation?

July 1, 1864. What would be the effect on Literary Produce and Literary Producers of a total abolition of Copyright?

December 7, 1866. What is the meaning of Supply, and what of Demand? Is it correct to say that supply and demand determine price? If not, in what manner is it that supply and demand affect price?

February 6, 1874. Is it possible for the construction of a Railway, the purposes for which are purely commercial, and which cannot by the most judicious management be made to yield profit at the current average rate on its cost, to have been other than a bad investment of a portion of the National Capital?

May 7, 1875. Political Economy being commonly regarded as the Science which treats of National Wealth, in what sense should the word Wealth be understood when used in politico-economical discussions?

June 7, 1878. Is there really such a thing as Economic Law? If so, how far should Economic Law be defined, and what specimens of it can be adduced?

July 4, 1879. Is it possible, and if possible, would it be desirable, to establish and maintain Bimetalism in India, without regard to the monetary arrangements of any other country?

From the materials surviving from the Political Economy Club, it seems safe to infer that Thornton was not one of the social favorites at these gatherings. Leslie Stephen was one of the least tolerant, reporting, "I am suffering the torments of the damned from that god-forgotten Thornton, who is boring on about supply and demand . . . He is not a bad fellow, but just now I hate him like poison."[10] Another of Thornton's frequent sparring partners was William Newmarch.[11] An extract of a letter from L. H. Courtney to Sir Louis Mallet describes the setting of one argument:

> Dear Mallet,
> I share your regrets at the apparent decline of decorum at the Political Economy Club. Last Friday the breaches of manners were sadly conspicuous. One officer must not find fault with another, but the truth is that our treasurer is habitually too contemptuous of views other than his own—not infrequently wider than his own—and this characteristic does not abate as the years pass. With his rough disdain and Thornton's tendency to querulous irritability there must be occasional splutterings, and the only way of keeping them down is for you and other members to attend as often as convenient to discountenance them by quietly maintaining the rules of debate.[12]

On another occasion, Sir J. Macdonnel tagged Thornton a "disruptive revolutionary influence," but nevertheless a "useful solvent [who] had the art of putting questions disconcerting to the dogmatic spirit, and he had a vision, temperate of a world that was to come—more questions than he himself could answer" (1921, 344).

It is difficult to imagine that such a cantankerous fellow with such unseemly enthusiasms would have been suffered so stoically by the members of the club without the obvious and repeated endorsement of Mill. In the first phase of Thornton's career, his questions reveal a concern with agricultural issues which derived from an essentially anti-Ricardian stance, well in line with his earliest publications. This stance would not have endeared him to the members of the club, and there is no evidence that he succeeded in winning any of them over to his position through his efforts. In 1853–54 Thornton branched out into issues of capital theory and intellectual property rights, although he would never write about these subjects specifically. Instead, it is hard to escape the impression that Thornton grew rather disappointed with political economy; for instance, his participation in the Political Economy Club experiences a hiatus of eight years beginning in 1855. In its place, in the mid-1850s he turned to poetry, publishing "The Siege of Silestria" in 1854, *Zohrab and Other Poems* in 1854, and *Modern Manicheism, Labour's Utopia and Other Poems* in 1857. One of these poems, written in 1854 in the form of an epistle to Mill, confesses his disaffection with political economy:

> Dear Mill, whose friendship's kindly emphasis
> Approved my first work, and encouraged this.
> Scarce will you ask, why, from old studies turned,
> My name unknown, a pension yet unearned.
> Problems abstruse and tough, no more I try,
> Of dark Political Economy.
> Digging no more in serious dissertation
> To trace the source of "Over-population,"
> Nor publishing what hidden treasure lies
> Deep in the soil of "Peasant Properties."

Unfortunately, Thornton's Muse fared no better with poesy, even given the Victorian predilections for iambic pentameter, heroic couplets, and deliciously awkward rhymes like "try" and "Economy." (I particularly relish his habit of footnoting his poems to "explain" his egregiously obscure allusions. Here we can savor the trademark practices of later modernists such as T. S. Eliot *avant la lettre*.) One reviewer of his later translations from Horace accused Thornton of a deficient ear and a want of metrical grasp, while backhandedly complimenting his seventeenth-century quaintness (Ellis 1878). It seems safe to observe that Thornton's poetical works would not have cemented his intellectual reputation for future generations. Hence, at the age of forty, that fearsome watershed in many lives, there was very little to indicate that Thornton would ever amount to much more than a competent bureaucrat in colonial government service.

The situation was changed dramatically in the mid-1860s, for reasons that we have been unable to fully divine. While we know of no particular landmarks dating from that era in Thornton's personal life, there is reason to suspect the hand of Mill in encouraging Thornton to return to political economy. He resumed attendance at the Political Economy Club in 1862, and a prodigious stream of publications on wages, unions, and the treatment of labor in political economy commenced in 1864. In part this was a response to British political initiatives of the 1860s to gain the suffrage for workingmen and legal legitimacy for trades unions (see below); and in equal part it must have been sparked by Thornton's conviction that there was something fundamentally flawed about the conventional wisdom concerning price theory, a wisdom, it must be noted, best exemplified by his friend's own *Principles of Political Economy*. In that text, Mill's abstract treatment of demand and supply did not correspond very well to the newly added passages, such as the following from the 1862 edition, where he intended to signal a much more favorable inclination toward certain forms of union organization:

> [D]emand and supply are not physical agencies, which thrust a fixed amount of wages into a labourer's hand without the participation of his own will and actions. The market rate is not fixed for him by some self-acting instrument, but is the result of bargaining between human beings . . . those who do not "higgle" will long continue to pay more than the market prices for their purchases. Still more might poor labourers who have to do with rich employers, remain long without the amount of wages which the demand for their labour would justify, unless, in the vernacular phrase, they stood out for it; and how can they stand out for terms without organized concert? What chance would any labourer have who struck singly for an advance of wages?. . . . I do not hesitate to say that associations of labourers, of a nature similar to trades unions, far from being a hindrance to the free market of labour, are the necessary instrumentality of that free market. (Mill 1965, 932)

Here in a nutshell was the position that Thornton chose to critically examine and elaborate upon in the *Fortnightly Review* over the course of the 1860s, and then republish together as the first edition of his epoch-making book *On Labour* (1869). Since 1844, Mill had been desirous of repudiating the "hard, abstract mode" of treating the "labour question" (*Collected Works* 13:645); by the early 1860s he was endorsing a pamphlet by Thomas Dunning, *Trades Unions and Strikes*, which argued that only by combination could workmen negotiate on a basis of equality with employers. Essentially, Thornton set out to expound in greater detail Mill's position vis-à-vis the benefits of union organization, but fairly quickly concluded that if this doctrine were to hold, revision of the "laws" of supply and demand would be required to restore a semblance of consistency to Mill's position. In 1866, both in the *Fortnightly* and at the meetings of the Political Economy Club, Thornton first aired this conclusion.[13] It was the pained reactions to his presentation in 1866 which provoked the disparaging comments from other Clubmen about the deficiencies in Thornton's character which we quoted above. Nevertheless, at least among the cognoscenti, and the readers of Mill's preferred outlet the *Fortnightly*, Thornton's heresies were familiar, dating at least from 1866.

Let us be quite clear about this. Thornton's positions on supply and demand and the legitimacy of trades unions were known to Mill at least from 1866, and perhaps before, largely because he helped thrash them out in concert with his friend Thornton. Both Mill and Cairnes gave Thornton comments on the manuscript before the book was published.

Presumably, Mill facilitated this early exposure to other prominent political economists to assay their reactions, and it took his intervention to pave the way for immediate reviews in the *Fortnightly* and other publications. But there is more. Research at the British Library has uncovered evidence that Mill had some involvement in the actual publication of *On Labour*. Mill was indeed more sensitive than Thornton about the politics of changing economic opinion, as revealed by his comment in a letter to Cairnes in 1869: "It is very amusing in this and other cases to see how the tyros in Political Economy think themselves bound to give no quarter to heresies, being afraid to make any concessions which their masters make" (*Collected Works* 16, letter 1418). As the following review notes of a Macmillan editor indicate, Mill was fully cognizant that the book was being positioned to provoke a controversy:

> Review of On Labour Manuscript:
> I have thought about the Thornton Book. The following considerations sum to the point.
> Mill's testimonial could not very well be made known on the surface of the book. Even if it could, just now it would not be so very effective, though it might become so. Thornton's book is not of the size or caliber to be a standard work or a text-book. It has already been published in the F[ortnightly].R[eview]., and the students of economic questions who would otherwise have bought it are now familiar with it.
> On the other hand is the very weighty fact that the subject will shortly be *the* subject of the day—and will probably continue so for a considerable time to come; and everything bearing on it will be brought. And Thornton is an authority in economics, as the author of the "Plea for Peasant Proprietors." It will be a *risk*, decidedly, I think-though the book is one which would look well in your list.[14]

We shall describe the intellectual content of *On Labour* below; for the nonce we restrict our attention to how this situation has been treated in the historical literature. It is our contention that historians, following the lead of some subsequent commentators such as Cairnes, have reified the appearance of *On Labour* and J. S. Mill's review in the *Fortnightly Review* in 1869 as the earth-shattering fissure in the homelands of British classical political economy, the Recantation of the Wages Fund Doctrine. In this construct, Thornton is relegated to the marginal status of Rosencrantz (or is it Guildenstern?), passive observer of Hamlet's solo deconstruction of Denmark.[15] To their credit, Evelyn Forget (1992) and Mark Donoghue (1997) have both smelled something rotten, and have suggested alternative (Copenhagen?)

interpretations. Forget asserts that "Mill's recantation was not motivated by internal inconsistencies, but was a calculated political act" (32). Donoghue goes further, suggesting that Mill never regarded himself as recanting something so grand as "the wages-fund doctrine." We shall propose a third interpretation, buttressed by our new evidence, which restores Thornton to his rightful role as an independent and active agent, uniting Forget and Donoghue in something resembling a convex combination.

In fact, neither Mill nor Thornton initially regarded the theses of *On Labour* as anything other than tangentially concerned with "the wages-fund." Indeed, in the first edition of *On Labour*, the wages fund was mentioned only in a footnote.[16] Instead, the objective was to flesh out the argument broached in Mill's 1862 edition of the *Principles*: supply and demand for labor were neither mechanical nor inevitable in wage determination; the steadfastness of will and bargaining behavior of masters and men mattered; unions could help offset an asymmetry of bargaining power in the wage relationship; and unions could serve longer-term goals of education and social improvement of the lot of the working class. On every point, Mill and Thornton were in full concert. Both also thought that workingmen were vulnerable to pernicious and wrong-headed analysis of their predicament by contemporary socialists, although they might have differed as to who the socialists were in their rogue's gallery of error. Both felt the need for a text which would codify what they both anticipated would be the orthodox case that unions were a necessary complement to the operation of the market, once a society reached a certain level of development. When Mill was in London, the two regularly discussed these issues; when he was in Avignon, their letters reveal that these were the overriding shared concerns.

Nevertheless, Thornton could never be considered a stalking horse for Mill. That he was his own man is what endeared him to Mill—let us not forget, the author of *On Liberty* as well as *Principles of Political Economy*. The author of *On Liberty* argued that truth was not found in consensus, but derived from the process of individual dissent. So Thornton was encouraged to set out on his own path to determine what he believed exactly would have to be given up to prosecute the case outlined in the previous paragraph. Mill thought that a revised understanding of supply and demand would suffice to make the case; Thornton, notoriously, believed rather that the laws of supply and demand would have to be given up. Mill, the serene proponent of common sense, believed "that what is true in the abstract, is always true in the concrete with proper *allowances*" (*Collected Works* 14:326). Thornton the iconoclast sought rather to base the case for unions on the bare minimum of theoretical presumptions: in effect, just the axiom of self-interest and a few symmetry principles.[17] In contrast with Mill, he signaled an unwillingness to depend upon Mill's or any other version of utilitarianism to ground his account. That Mill was fully aware of this well before the appearance of *On Liberty* can be gleaned from a letter to Thornton dated 19 October 1867:

> I have just finished reading your Chapter in the Fortnightly & I put down my observations while my mind is full of its contents. In execution I think it excellent & of good augury for the success of the book . . . I expect that the subsequent chapters will be equally well executed & that I shall agree with all or most of your practical conclusions. But in its principles the chapter does not carry me with it. I find in it what I always find where a standard is assumed of so-called justice distinct from general utility . . . Not only do I not admit any standard of right which does not derive its sole authority from utility, but I remark that in such cases an adversary could always find some other maxim of justice equal in authority but leading to opposite conclusions. . . . I have stated strongly the fault I find with your Chapter. It would take me a considerable space to set out all the good I find in it. To mention only one thing, the book will be very servicable in carrying on what may be called the emancipation of pol. economy—its liberation from the kind of doctrines of the old school (now taken up by well to do people) which treat what they call economical laws, demand and supply for instance, as if they were laws of inanimate matter, not amenable to the will of the human beings from whose feelings, interests, & principles of action they proceed. This is one of the queer mental confusions which will be wondered at by & by & you are helping very much in the good work of clearing it up. (*Collected Works* 16, letter 1150)

This explains why, in a seeming paradox, both Forget and Donoghue could actually be right. Mill could orchestrate an endorsement of Thornton's *On Labour* both behind the scenes and in print, because he thought the political objectives were fundamentally sound, and moreover, the need for a synoptic text treating the theory of unionism was imminent. Yet simultaneously, he could disagree with Thornton's rejection of his version of price theory and his utilitarianism, and still cheerfully endorse the book, because he himself did not think he was "renouncing" much of anything—it was those epigones, those "tyros of Political Economy" who had turned the doctrine of supply and demand into a wicked device, a "hard, abstract" object to prod and torment the working classes with its dismal prognostications. Of course no one, including Thornton's most loyal follower Cairnes, was impelled to share his view; and by and large the self-identified orthodoxy did not.[18] Instead, Mill's endorsement of Thornton was treated initially as a gracious but somewhat inexplicable gesture to an old friend; and then later, as a moment of deplorable weakness which in a few decades brought down the whole jerry-built structure of British classical political economy.

Mill did not live to experience the latter collapse, but he did manage to enter a demurrer regarding one of the culprits behind it.[19] The very idea that there was something so dramatic as a "recantation of the wages-fund" was a construct of those who came after, such as Cairnes, Taussig, and Jacob Hollander. It was these late classical political economists who feared that their world was turned upside down; it was the fledgling neoclassicals like Jevons who donned their white hats and put it right again, thus supporting the recantation narrative. These ruptures are important for the student to remember, especially after Marshall sought to impose a bland façade of continuity over the whole episode by imposing a separate peace and inventing a fanciful history of price theory out of whole cloth.

Having insisted upon a proper understanding of the motives and role of Mill, we now return to the life of Thornton. *On Labour* and the subsequent furore provoked by its bold theses rendered Thornton something of a celebrity in political economy circles. The book was rapidly translated into Russian, German, and Italian; his *Plea* was reprinted in 1874; now not only the *Fortnightly* but the *Cornhill* and the *Contemporary Review* were happy to publish his occasional pieces; and Macmillan even sanctioned a second edition of *On Labour* (prodigiously expanded) in 1870, a year after the first. In 1873 Thornton was presented with one of those peculiarly British distinctions, a "Companion of the Order of Bath," upon the recommendation of the duke of Argyll. More importantly, in the critical decade of the 1870s Thornton was the writer one just had to confront if one had any hope of gaining one's spurs in English political economy. J. E. Cairnes's book *Some Leading Principles of Political Economy* (1874) was one long wrangle with Thornton. Fleeming Jenkin's classic papers on supply and demand were intended primarily to upbraid Thornton. Jevons, with Jenkin serving as intermediary, was also responding to Thornton in his *Theory of Political Economy*. Edgeworth's *Mathematical Psychics* was the ultimate utilitarian riposte to Thornton's disdain for utilitarianism. And last but not least, Marshall without Thornton is like the Prince . . . well, one readily gets the drift. (For more of this argument, see chapter 14.)

It is instructive to take the measure of those whom Thornton deems worthy to answer in the last decade before his death. Cairnes here holds pride of place, precisely because he was so very close to Mill; and that does help to explain why each of the two accorded such ample courtesy and attention to the other. Longe is acknowledged after the fact, only to be written off as irrelevant. Mill is repeatedly revisited as a fount of authority and touchstone of dissension, even after his death. The new breed of utilitarians, by contrast, did not warrant individual confrontation; instead, Thornton sought to deal with them *en masse* in his broadside "Anti-utilitarianism" (1870, republished in 1873 in his *Old-Fashioned Ethics*). And that exhausts his reference set within political economy. This failure to acknowledge others was not due to lack of acquaintance or opportunity; indeed, Thornton became very active in the Political Economy Club in the mid-1870s, proposing such impertinent questions as "Is there really such a thing as Economic Law? If so, how far should Economic Law be defined, and what specimens of it can be adduced?" However, it seems that Thornton did not regard his fellow members as rising to the lofty standard of discussion he had grown accustomed to with Mill. He would rather turn his critical attention as an author to someone like Thomas Huxley, whose "naturalism" was the most diametrically opposed to his own position.[20]

In the mid-1870s Thornton returned to what was clearly his first love, the specifics of land tenure systems, irrigation works, and other artifacts of the bureaucratic levers of control and economic development. In his last substantial book, *Indian Public Works* (1875), he put on display the economic specifics which had absorbed much of his working life; in this respect he diverged from Mill, who largely excluded explicit acknowledgment of his India House work from his writings (Zastoupil 1994). Thornton's book tracked the controversies over Indian railroads, ship canals, telegraph wires, and educational establishments as the nitty-gritty of providing infrastructure in which markets operate, something which underlay much of Thornton's theoretical approach to markets. Among its virtues, it surveys the late classical case for the legitimate undertaking of public works, suggesting that market rates of return may be an inadequate guide for choice of projects in poorer or less developed countries: there, the second-round effects of drawing out "idle capital" might more than offset the costs of what initially appear to be unpromising projects. Thornton was very critical of the "Dalhousie plan" which sought to draw private investment into railway construction through investor guarantees: the result, he claimed, was a cost per mile far above that experienced in direct government construction. The book was not entirely disengaged from Thornton's previous preoccupations, however; in it, for instance, he recommended that the Indian government consider various cooperative schemes to deal with problems of motivating and supervising labor (1875b, 90).

By all accounts, William Thornton lived out his last years in Cadogan Place near Sloane Street enjoying the respect of his India House colleagues and the joys of classical Latin literature, publishing a volume of *Word for Word from Horace* in 1878. Judging from his personal estate of roughly eight thousand pounds, he also enjoyed the modest prosperity of a colonial bureaucrat of middling rank.

William Thomas Thornton died on June 17, 1880, and according to his desires was buried in a wicker coffin in an unbricked grave. He was survived by his wife, Elizabeth Evelyn Thornton (1818–1903), and a son, Edward

Zohrab Thornton. While it appears that some of his heirs shared in his penchant for classical literature, sadly none felt impelled to perpetuate or preserve his views on political economy.

The British Trades Unions Movement as a Context for the Rupture in British Political Economy

While historians of economic thought have been busy rooting about asking who should be charged with having killed the wages fund, it seems that they have overlooked a phenomenon much more relevant for the evolution of political economy in the 1870s, namely, the political movements which served to legitimate trades unions in Britain. Sir John Hicks once wrote: "The sixty years from 1870 to 1930 were in Britain the time of the rise of the Labour Movement; thus it was not surprising that the British post-classics (Marshall, Edgeworth, and Pigou in particular) should have had labour problems very much on their minds" (1983, 71). Yet far from passively reacting to a new-found empirical development—"I say, don't you think it's high time we looked at these union chaps!"—the British neoclassical movement was instead provoked by the earlier political problem of trades unionism. Hicks's timing was off, at least by a decade.

The saga of the demise of Chartism, the rise of the new model unions, and the foundation of the International Working Men's Association and the Trades Unions Congress has been often told. We direct the reader to a number of fine histories of this development for an appreciation of the context for the rise of neoclassical economics in the 1870s.[21] Some have asserted that "Political economy suffered a sharp decline in prestige and influence in Britain after 1870" (Mason 1980, 565); and one of the most compelling reasons for the slide was that numerous representatives of classical political economy persisted in their mantra that unions could not "permanently" alter wages nor benefit society, all the while that unions were growing in strength and numbers as a political force. The demise of classical political economy in Britain was intimately bound up with the various political and economic reform movements of the 1860s and 1870s, something overlooked by those doggedly intent on operating only in the rarefied realm of pure ideas.

After the failure of the Owenite and Chartist movements in the 1830s and 1840s, a number of "new model" unions took form in the later 1850s, at first limited to particular trades, and favoring the better-paid and -educated strata of the labor hierarchy. Foremost among these were the Amalgamated Society of Engineers (ASE) and the Amalgamated Society of Joiners and Carpenters, two unions which would provide much of Thornton's stock of exemplars. The ASE experienced rather stunning expansion, from eleven thousand members and an annual income of 22,000 pounds in 1851 to twenty thousand members and 52,000 pounds in 1860; and by the time of Thornton's attention, 33,000 members and 83,000 pounds in 1866 (Howell 1890). This occurred during a period of pronounced expansion of employment of engineers, growing from 75,000 in 1841 to 130,000 in 1851 and 198,000 in 1861 (Lee 1979). More importantly, it had become apparent to those closest to the industry that the ASE had managed to raise average wages of the engineers. Even after a generation or more of Cliometrics, there exists very little in the way of solid quantitative data which allows us to get specifically at this issue; however, the earlier work of Arthur Bowley did allow some generalizations to be made (Bowley and Wood 1905; 1906). Although the data really only commence in 1860, it appears the ASE managed to persistently raise the standard wage rates in a number of areas in England, and this in an era of falling prices. Bowley and Wood also provide some evidence that wages paid to nonunionized trades in unionized firms tended to rise in tandem with elevated standard union rates. At least before 1873, the period most germane to Thornton's claims, it was difficult to argue that the ASE had produced deleterious effects upon the growth of the firms where unionization had taken hold. Therefore, the first and most immediate challenge to the time-honored laws of political economy derived from the success of the new model unions.

The unions, while often claiming to restrict themselves to parochial bread-and-butter concerns, were in fact in the vanguard of various broader-based political movements to redress political inequities. The most salient example was the relationship of union agitation to the Reform League in the early 1860s, which culminated in the Reform Act of 1867, extending manhood suffrage and doubling the electorate. That the extension of the suffrage and the legitimation of unions were often regarded as a single spreading conspiracy from the vantage point of the British Right is best instantiated by the dyspeptic writings of that favorite of the first generation of neoclassicals, Herbert Spencer: "And if there needs a demonstration that representative equality is an insufficient safeguard for freedom, we have it in the trades unions already referred to; which, purely democratic as is their organization, yet exercise over their members a tyranny that is almost Neapolitan in its rigour and unscrupulousness . . . Hence the great mass of the new borough-electors must be expected to act simultaneously, on the word of command being issued from a central council of united trades" (1872, 378–79). One measure of the hairline fractures which such middle-class reform movements were inflicting on political economy was that John Stuart Mill, the great self-proclaimed "socialist," did not join the league, whereas his follower Cairnes did. Margot Finn argues that the mobilization around the extension of suffrage acted to move the goalposts for other middle-class reform initiatives: "Determined both to pre-empt the escalation of class sentiment incited by the Reform League speakers and to seize the initiative of reform from the Tory government, bourgeois liberals now offered working-class radicals new varieties of liberal argument that conceded, albeit reluctantly, the very legitimacy of abstract political rights . . . [and] the efficacy of trade unions as political agents . . . the escalation of class-consciousness under the aegis of the Reform League encouraged an efflorescence of bourgeois radical agitation in which left-wing liberals endorsed lines of political argument that they had earlier denounced as socialist delusions of the working class" (1993, 249, 252). This interplay of political reform and trades union legitimation is a necessary backdrop for the publication of *On Labour*.

The perceived link between unions and reform agitation conjured the prospect of a state backlash right on the threshold of the successful extension of the franchise. Using as a pretext the "Sheffield outrages" of 1866 and the case of *Hornby v. Close* in 1867—a Queen's Bench ruling which suggested that unions could not prosecute thieves for their stolen funds since they organized strikes in restraint of trade, which violated common law—the government announced the formation in 1867 of a Royal Commission to look into all aspects of trades unions. The outcome of the inquiry was by no means a foregone conclusion, inducing both sides to sharpen their nibs and occupy strategic positions in the *Quarterlies* and the *Reviews*, which should signal that the dispute over the legal and economic legitimacy of unionism had reached a fever pitch precisely in the period when Thornton composed *On Labour*.

At this juncture, classical political economy was retrieved from the realm of mere apologetics to become a tool for stripping the trades unions of all legal protection. The language of the "immutable laws of political economy" took on an especially ominous heft and virulent tone in the mid-1860s; and most of the heavy lifting was carried out by the particular "laws" of supply and demand. For example, the *Times* of 27 November 1867 regarded the effulgence of labor activism as an effort to subvert the laws of political economy (Finn 1993, 245). Henry Fawcett wrote: "If trades unions are permitted to prevent this free passage of labour from one employment to another, wages may permanently maintain an artificial advance; but trades unions can only exert such an influence by resorting to a social tyranny, which is in every sense illegal and unjustifiable." In a comparison which would shortly assume deeper significance, one P. H. Rathbone wrote in 1867, "let it be understood that labour is only a commodity (like fish); that employer and employed stand in relation to each other merely as buyer and seller of the commodity; and that the laws of political economy, rightly understood, are as much the laws of Providence as the laws of gravitation" (in Clements 1961, 96). Frederic Harrison, a Comtist and a member of the

Royal Commission of 1867, captured some of the frustrations of the time when he complained about those who "even suggest an Act of Parliament to suppress all [union] associations whatever. It is like the Vatican raving at newspapers and railways" (1908, 299). For their part, some unionists were quite fed up with constantly being chided about these supposedly ironclad "laws." While they were rarely direct participants in the debates among the high theorists, reports of their exasperated disdain for the imperious laws were commonplace. As one David Chadwick reported in 1860, he "much regretted to find that some of the leading members of Trades Unions, attempted to deny the existence and operation of the *law* of political economy in regard to Supply and Demand governing the *price* of labour."

We also tend to forget that this antagonism was the context for the composition of Karl Marx's *Capital* in the early 1860s. Marx's first public statement of his theory of wages came in an address before the General Council of the First International Working Men's Association in June 1865, published posthumously as *Value, Price and Profit*. The objects of Marx's scorn on that occasion were figures within the International who had made use of Mill's wages fund doctrines to argue that unions who achieved wage increases merely hurt other segments of the working class. Marx, good Ricardian that he was, felt that he could wave away supply and demand as a mere accessory to a theory of value: "You would be altogether mistaken in fancying that the value of labour or of any other commodity whatever is ultimately fixed by demand and supply. Supply and demand regulate nothing but the temporary *fluctuations* of market prices. They will explain to you why the market price of a commodity rises above or below its *value*, but they can never account for that *value* itself" (1935, 26).[22] Of course his innovation was to deny that "labour" (as opposed to labor power) was a commodity at all.

There is a literature which debates the relative consequence of Thornton and Mill in this agonistic field of labor mobilization and political proselytization of the 1860s and 1870s (Clements 1961; Biagini 1987; Pelling 1963, 63); this is neither the place nor the time to intervene in that debate. Nevertheless, there are two things to note about the immediate aftermath to the publication of *On Labour*. First, after the report of the Royal Commission in 1869, Parliament passed the Trades Unions Act of 1871, the Conspiracy and the Protection of Property Act of 1875, and the Trade Union Amendment Act of 1876, the effect of which was legal acknowledgment of the full legitimacy of trades union organizations. This legitimation placed classical political economy in the awkward situation of condemning as an unnatural abomination a political entity and economic framework which was clearly here to stay, and moreover, one which enjoyed the support of a large proportion of the voting polity as having salutary benefits. This untenable situation could not persist indefinitely. Second, by roughly 1880, conventional wisdom among the literati had performed an about-face, wherefor it became commonplace to deride those supposedly inviolate laws of supply and demand as defunct. Trades unions sympathizers did it: "To-day the old orthodox Economy—the Gospel, or Sophism, of Supply and Demand, absolute freedom for Individual Exertion—all this is ancient history . . . [Socialist unionism] has killed that old Targum about Supply and Demand—the plain English of which was—'May the devil take the weakest!' " (Harrison 1908, 410). But pillars of the establishment, such as presidents of section F of the British Association for the Advancement of Science, also did it: " 'The recognized principles of political economy' or 'the immutable laws of supply and demand' were phrases that occurred as readily to a journalist in the sixties as 'the exploded doctrine of laissez faire' does to the leader writer of today" (in Smyth 1962, 127).

In our view, Thornton's *On Labour* simply brought to a head the contradictions inherent in the classical theory of value and distribution when juxtaposed with the political realities of escalating worker organization across Europe. The effect of these contradictions was to induce a brief and concentrated period of theoretical innovation in political economy unmatched by almost any other period in British history. While much of this innovation would be couched in the language of supply and demand, it is important to acknowledge that in the two decades until 1890 there were several other approaches to resolving the contradictions, and that only in Marshallian retrospect were they all reduced to a single orthodoxy, known by the neologism "neoclassical economics." These alternatives can be arrayed according to their relationship to the prior multiple interpretations of supply and demand outlined above.

To begin, there was the hard-core Ricardian response, best exemplified in Marx's *Capital*. In this narrative supply and demand still played no fundamental role, and the doctrine that lasting wage increases by trades unions were economically possible was reified in the dichotomy between "labor" and "labor power." For Marx, trades unions were not an end in themselves, but merely a necessary way station for a proletariat seeking to usurp political power from the bourgeoisie (Marx 1974). By contrast, the "engineering" group derived from the Whewell orientation assumed the technocratic position that supply and demand constituted the sum total of economic theory applicable to this controversy; yet a suitably disinterested perspective would admit that unions violated no particular "natural" equilibrium, since the interests of capital and labor were naturally antagonistic. This position had its own special piquancy, since it was the British labor aristocracy of engineers who had pioneered the structure of the new model unions. Fleeming Jenkin ventured this interpretation in his article "Trade-Unions: How Far Legitimate?" (1868), written, it should be noted, *before* the more widely known "Graphic Representation of the Laws of Supply and Demand." In the earlier article he wrote that "simple restriction of the extension of trade is not *per se* an evil, and none of the pleas against trade-unions founded upon it will hold water" ([1887] 1931, 33). Combination for the purposes of bargaining could permanently raise wages, but only at a cost to the larger community. "Admitting that total abolition [of unions] is out of the question as impolitic, undeserved and impossible, we must insist that the great power granted to bodies of workmen shall be administered upon stringent regulations" ([1887] 1931, 67). From an Olympian height, unions performed no necessary or logical function; they were simply a fact of existence, rather like the mechanical imperfections of steel beams or chemical imperfections of copper wire which every engineer had to take into account (Smith and Wise 1989, chapters 19–20). Supply and demand theory could incorporate unions just as well as any other relevant structural parameter—once supply and demand were adequately formalized, an unfortunate detail awaiting rectification.

If these two positions constitute the polar extremes of approaches to supply and demand, it was the great muddled middle—the forced alliance of the classical and demand and supply perspectives—which dominated the controversy. It may seem odd to lump together such figures as J. E. Cairnes and W. S. Jevons in this group, but their similarities do tend to overcome their standard distinctions: Cairnes as the last orthodox champion of British classicism, Jevons as the parvenu herald of the nascent neoclassical position. The reason the two belong together is that they both wished to have their cake and eat it too: they strove to preserve something very like the wages fund story, but also insist that wages were natural phenomena set by supply and demand; they wanted to accord a certain grudging legitimacy to trades unions, and allow that they had effectively raised wages, but insist that this legitimacy and efficacy had nothing to do with economic laws, which were still being violated and besmirched by the existence of unions; they felt that Thornton was onto something in focusing on the structure of the bargaining situation and previous inadequacies in demand theory, but that when all was adequately explained it would be seen that Thornton had exaggerated some minor special cases way out of proportion. For both, their dicta concerning supply and demand and trades unions ended up being a terrible hotchpotch, distinguished primarily by their desire to upbraid and discipline the reprobate Thornton.[23]

We shall merely indicate what a vertiginous experience it must have been for a stalwart trades unionist to read the prognostications of the sober representatives of political economy in the 1870s and 1880s. After denying that the content of political economy sufficiently underpins the prescription of *laissez faire* (1871), Cairnes proceeded to assert that "there is a law of market price, as there is a law of normal price, as there is a law of wages, of profit, of rent, as there are laws of the winds and tides and seasons, and of the phenomena of external nature" (1874, 98). Although no sane economist is thought to ever have fully believed in the doctrine of the wages fund (182), trades unions were nonetheless deemed utterly incapable of enlarging the wages fund (218). Finally, "combination, whether employed by capitalists or by labourers, may succeed in controlling for a time the price of labour, is utterly powerless in the hands of either, to effect a permanent alteration in the market rate of wages as determined by supply and demand" (235). Likewise, for Jevons the wages fund was transparently false, and "Practically, the whole question resolves itself into a complex case of the laws of supply and demand" ([1882] 1894, 95). However, when Jevons got down to the task of specifying the details of his price theory, an explicit description of these laws of supply and demand was notable predominantly by its absence (White 1989c; 2003). As for unions, they were a curse and a fraud, since "whosoever tries to raise his own wages . . . attempts to levy contributions from other people. It is simply a case of private taxation" (1894, 106). Contrary to all contemporary belief, "the supposed conflict of labour with capital is a delusion. The real conflict is between producers and consumers" (101). Nevertheless, "Even when we can clearly perceive that the action of a "corner" or trade union is pernicious, it does not necessary follow that the State would do well to intervene. In some cases evils are best left to work their own remedy" (32). In a bizarre variant on Marx, Jevons seems to have believed that union organization would simply degenerate and wither away (129). Mill's belief in the civilizing effects of union organization upon the workers was derided as just so much rank ignorance of the teachings of science. "Human nature is one of the last things which can be called 'pliable.' Granite rocks may be more easily moulded than the poor savages which hide among them" (Jevons 1890, 290).

The 1860s and 1870s were the silly season of the political economy of British labor, marked by hysterical denial of obvious political realities and a shortage of logical analysis; observers avoided discussing actual unions and their actual functions, regarding them either as little better than abstract spanners in the clockwork market or, alternatively, as concrete embodiments of Christian charity. Purblindness had as much to do with the diminished reputation of political economy in Britain as did its dreaded dismalness. An appreciation of this fact will help to explain why it was Thornton's *On Labour* which came for many of his contemporaries to represent the locus of calm, dispassionate economic analysis of unions; the central tendency of political realism; the Golden Mean among rival value theories, incommensurate pretensions to scientific status, diverse attitudes toward empiricism, and lurking threats of socialism. Thornton's book garnered the attention it did because it appeared to occupy the elusive center: that is, at least until Marshall's *Principles* burst upon the scene.

Perhaps now we possess some inkling of the context in which John Hicks's heroes—Jenkin, Marshall, Edgeworth, Pigou—were all so very exercised to repeatedly address the problem of the "indeterminacy of wages" and the "correct" understanding of demand and supply. Their convergence upon this issue was no mere coincidence.

What Did Thornton Do?

As broached above, Thornton's dominant purpose in writing *On Labour* was to elaborate upon Mill's mature position that wages were the product of intentional activity and bargaining, that unions leveled the field in this respect for workers, and that far from hobbling the operation of a free market, they offered a fine example of the means by which the evolution of markets encouraged civilized improvement over time. Where Thornton departed from Mill is that he regarded the doctrine of supply and demand as hopelessly confused, and worse, a major hindrance to the prosecution of Mill's political brief in favor of the legitimacy of trades unions. Thornton's contemporaries certainly found this his most compelling and contentious theme, for although it accounted for a very small proportion of the text in the first edition—basically chapter 1 of book II—it drew more criticism and commentary than the rest of the text combined. Having hit this obviously exposed nerve, Thornton responded by doubling the length of the chapter in his second edition.[24] For long afterward, Thornton's overarching position regarding the virtues and vices of unions was neglected in favor of his strictures regarding supply and demand. To avoid repeating this habit, let us first survey the architecture of the volume, and then return to the problem of supply and demand in greater detail.

The first book of *On Labour* is concerned to argue that because of a flawed theory of pricing, political economists had misapprehended the fundamental function of trades unions. Labor was appreciably different from any other commodity because—under the rules of bargaining and closure specific to British practice—it was offered unreservedly in the market, whereas other commodities were not. If shoes went unsold, or if buyers made unsatisfactory bids, the shoes could be put aside by the seller for another day. If the commodity was perishable, like fish, special kinds of auctions could be arranged to move the product with dispatch and thus address the bargaining imbalance. But labor by its very nature could not be reserved—labor unsold simply evaporates, never again to be put on the market. Because of this, and because it is predominantly the poor who labor and the rich who provide capital, the purveyors of labor find it difficult to use the most important device available to all other participants in the marketplace for higgling the terms of trade in their own favor. Note well, this is a structural regularity which leads to a procedural asymmetry: it is not a complaint about injustice, nor is it an argument about a state of ideal equality. Moreover, owing to the class interests of the buyers of labor, there were no special market institutions to redress the imbalance. Without some form of concerted intervention, this asymmetry between buyers and sellers would persist indefinitely. The economic functions of trades unions were primarily two: to restore symmetry to the commodity labor by allowing labor to be reserved in effect (if not in fact) when buyers made unsatisfactory bids; and to elevate labor to a plane of bargaining equality with the more powerful and already locally coordinated body of employers.

There were a number of minor additional functions which trades unions might also perform, although Thornton was rather less sanguine about their abilities to do so: unions might administer pensions, disability insurance, and strike funds; they might actively seek to alter the market institutions and practices which coordinated the pricing of labor (after the style of the fish merchants); they might help legislate the conditions of work on the shop floor and arbitrate individual disputes between masters and men; they just might help bring about self-improvement through the encouragement of education and the bracing experience of self-government and self-reliance. But Thornton was not some starry-eyed apologist for unions; his contemporaries recognized this as one of his chief virtues. For instance, he opined that most of the latter auxiliary functions might be better performed by the state. He allowed that unions were often corrupt; that the costs of union organization might be burdensome to those within and without the union; that strikes often hurt the workers concerned more than they helped, at least in the short run; that they might throw up obstacles to the mobility of resources. Unions, in his view, were a "necessary evil," at best an intermediate expedient on the road to some better future form of work organization. Indeed, "the great object of this treatise is to show, that whatever unionism may be able to do for working men, industrial co-operation can do still more" (*302–3). In this regard Thornton was not so very different from Mill, Cairnes, and many of his contemporaries, who placed their millenarian faith in cooperatives, profit sharing, and some vague form of industrial democracy to address the larger questions surrounding the future of the troubled adversarial relationship between labor and capital.[25]

The most striking novelty to be found in Thornton's work is that whereas he openly accepted the principle of universal selfishness as the starting point for analysis, he abjured all appeals to "Nature" and "natural law" to ground his theory. The ambition of constructing a natural science of society was a chimera for Thornton. He applied this belief evenhandedly to his patron and friend Mill, to the old-fashioned detractors of unions, and to the social-ists. It begins, of course, with the theory of price, but it does not stop there. To the political economists he throws down the gauntlet: "Price is scarcely ever mentioned without provoking a reference to the 'inexorable,' the 'im-mutable,' the 'eternal' laws by which it is governed; the laws which, accord-ing to my friend Professor Fawcett, are 'as certain in their operation as those which control physical nature.' It is no small gain to have discovered that no such despotic laws do or can exist; that, inasmuch as the sole function of scientific law is to predict the invariable recurrence of the same effects from the same causes, and as there can be no invariability where—as in the case of price—one of the most efficient causes is that ever-changing chame-leon, human character or disposition, price cannot possibly be subject to law" (*82).

Yet the socialists were warned they also must take their medicine un-sugared. There are no abstract principles upon which workers might base their claims for improvement, Thornton warned. No one has a right to a job, or a "living wage," or claims upon the means of production, or "original rights" to the fruits of his labor, or realization of his God-given potential for happiness. John Locke and David Hume were painted as part of the prob-lem, not part of the solution. There is nothing "natural" which serves to allocate "responsibility" to labor and capital: "Your employer's profits are not the product of your labour in any sense in which your wages are not equally the product of his capital."[26] There exist no principles of justice which insist that employers not combine against the interests of their work-ers, said Thornton; they owe no economic obligation to society for having been born with the proverbial silver spoon. Thornton was a theorist of the symmetry imposed upon market process, not of equality of status or oppor-tunity or of original position in the manner of Rawls. To Mill's discomfort, he became an anti-Millian; but it has escaped attention that he also was an anti-Marxist before the fact.

It is interesting to speculate on the extent to which Thornton can be read in retrospect as a representative of a "Darwinian" approach to political economy antithetical to that innovated by Herbert Spencer and others. Thornton certainly devoted more than passing consideration to the argu-ments for and against Darwinian evolution.[27] Whereas Spencer was the theorist of a *telos* of development, a Victorian scientism which sought to reduce utilitarianism to a few physical laws, Thornton was the prophet of irreducible diversity of human ingenuity: of market forms, of legal forms of property, of human motives, of economic outcomes. In this, he felt he was seconding Mill's opinion that there existed different categories of markets (in Mill's case, wholesale versus retail) which would in principle require differing explanatory strategies. Thornton described a world where structures cobbled together initially to meet one purpose might end up subserving another one, entirely unforeseen. He privileged competition as a causal principle, but warned that the outcome is never unique. "There is never any such 'stable equilibrium' as that of which the teachers of political economy dream" (*48n). Spencer regarded man as a machine, a conceit which underwrites the ambitions of a unified science of man; whereas Thornton regarded this to be a delusion prevalent among those who aimed to turn Darwinism into just another version of Cartesian philosophy: "Professor Huxley . . . goes on to avow his belief that the human body, like every other living body, is a machine, all the operations of which will sooner or later be explained by physical principles, insomuch as we shall eventually arrive at a mechanical equivalent of consciousness, even as we have already arrived at a mechanical equivalent of heat" (1873b, 169). This, perhaps to a greater degree than any other consideration, explains why Thornton was impervious to the charms of the new model mechanical version of utilitarianism which was being taken up by Jevons, Edgeworth (Mirowski, ed., 1994a), and the younger Marshall (1994).

Indeed, the dispute over supply and demand and the legitimacy of trades unions was to a notable extent reinforced by and overlapped the controversy over the meaning of Darwinism. Here we refer not to any simplistic and erroneous equation of the ideology of rapacious capitalism with "social Darwinism" (Bowler 1988, 156–65), but rather the more specific point that the major players in the union controversy were understood to also have substantial intellectual stakes in interpreting theories of evolution. Herbert Spencer of course popularized the term "evolution" as a biological analogue to utilitarian self-improvement, giving it a very Lamarckian cast (Bowler, 1988, 39–40). Fleeming Jenkin is well known in the literature of the history of biology as an early critic of Darwinian selection.[28] Cairnes sought to explain Thornton's attack on what he considered the "demand" side of orthodox explanations of the wage by positing that the "supply" side, by which he meant the population principle, had been situated beyond the pale of dispute by Darwin: Malthus's theory "has of late been powerfully helped forward by the influence of Mr. Darwin's work, in which the obnoxious principle . . . was shown to be merely a particular instance of a law pervading all organic existence" (1874, 157). Jevons believed that one of Mill's most grievous faults was that "the whole tone of Mill's moral and political writings is totally opposed to the teaching of Darwin and Spencer . . . He might be defined as the last great philosophic writer conspicuous for his ignorance of the principles of evolution" (1890, 290, 289). One would surmise that Thornton's somewhat similar anti-Spencerian stance would have equally earned his contempt. Alfred Marshall, notoriously, sought to relocate the mecca of the economist into biology, but what this meant in practice was a warmed-over Spencerianism (Groenewegen 1995, 167); for instance, he proved unable to grasp the significance of Weissman's disconfirmation of the inheritance of acquired characters (484).

Whatever Thornton's exact relationship to Victorian biology, he did make one statement of principle in the second edition of *On Labour* which earned him the obloquy of future generations, as well as loss of some measure of Mill's favor. In Mill's famous review essay of Thornton's book in the *Fortnightly* of May and June 1869, he took exception to Thornton's attack on the theory of supply and demand, insisting that if one conceded special cases in which the analysis did not apply (as Mill had repeatedly done previously), then Thornton's strictures should only have counseled amendment, not full-scale repudiation. Inexplicably, Thornton, an intemperate debater at the best of times, felt impelled to strike back, adding the following passage to the second edition: "a scientific law admits of no exception whatever, one single exception sufficing completely as a thousand to deprive it of all legal character. If one single instance could be found, or conceived, in which water failed to seek its own level, that water seeks its own level would cease to be a scientific law" (*67). It is incomprehensible that any reader of Mill's *Logic*, which contains an elaborate defense of tendency laws, and a proviso of their special application to political economy, should have made such a bald statement and hoped to get away with it. Whatever prompted Thornton to make such a rash and fundamentally false statement, it certainly gave welcome hostage to the clutch of younger economists eager to reprimand the older generation on its weak understanding of the nature of science, and diverted the controversy back in a direction that Thornton had originally tried to avoid.

Thus the real significance of Thornton's masterpiece lies in his attempt to rid political economy of its unhealthy dependence upon natural law, and yet simultaneously produce a theoretically grounded economics that could make strong and controversial policy prescriptions about one of the most politically charged issues of the day. In that light, contemporaries were correct to focus their attentions upon book II, chapter 1, which serves as the pivot of this argument. Since everyone from Jenkin to Negishi to Ekelund who sets out to indict Thornton of various "confusions" begins by denying this very first premise, it is important to register his rhetorical question: "what is it that determines price? Assuredly neither inherent utility nor cost of production has the smallest effect on it" (*136). In the question of isolating the causes of realized price, "Our best chance of finding this out is by considering carefully all that happens when a sale takes place" (*76). To that end, Thornton proposes a series of examples of specific markets: Dutch versus English auctions for herring (56); two horse fairs with face-to-face negotiations (59); a shopkeeper selling gloves at various posted prices (64).

The point of each of these differing bargaining situations is to suggest that a generic law of supply and demand cannot adequately explain how it could be that under essentially the same circumstances, with the "same" goods and the "same" transactors, realized prices *may* turn out to be different, depending upon the sequence of bargaining and the nature of the closing rules. Some imprecision does haunt the discussion, given that Thornton both challenges Mill's "definitions" of supply and demand and then posits in his examples that "demand" is greater or less than "supply" for purposes of exposition.

What provokes later readers more than anything else to accuse Thornton of inconsistency and muddle is his denials that the laws of supply and demand exist, juxtaposed with his use of the terminology of supply and demand to discuss specific cases. Therefore, it behooves us to clarify what Thornton believed about price theory. First, when engaging with other theorists, but mainly Mill, Thornton tries to use their conceptions of supply and demand to demonstrate that standard conclusions need not be drawn from their premises. This is the rhetorical device of temporarily entertaining your opponents' premises and respecting their preferred terminology. Secondly, and beyond this first device, Thornton reluctantly sanctions the use of the terminology of supply and demand to refer to specific quantities of goods formally offered in a well-defined spot market, and explicit bids tendered in the same market. However, in Thornton's view *these quantities do not regulate price*. This is because in most well-organized markets—and, following Mill, this probably excludes most retail markets—dealers continually privately harbor estimates of magnitudes of bids or quantities which might be tendered in the near but nonspecific future. Because all markets exhibit the phenomenon of "reservation" to a greater or lesser extent, the relationship between flow bids and asks on the one hand and order backlogs and inventories on the other is inescapable. All actual behavior is predicated upon these beliefs, which Thornton calls "prospective demand and supply." However, there is no fixed mathematical relationship between the solid quantities which appear in a spot market and the psychological estimates which constitute prospective supply and demand. "The competition which [a dealer] apprehends is that of a variety of men anxious to sell, or believing themselves under the necessity of selling, very different proportions of their actual stocks, and that within very different periods of time—a competition of men of every gradation of experience, shrewdness, and neediness; who, in the first place, estimate the future probabilities of the market for very different periods; in the second, would form very different estimates, even for the same period; and in the third, would be influenced very differently by the same estimate. Surely such competition can in no intelligible sense be said to *depend* upon prospective supply and demand" (*80). The irreducible diversity of the participants, as made manifest in their widely divergent linkage of observable quantities to their own private expectations and their resulting behavior of reserving some portion of their stocks from immediate bid or offer, prevents "supply and demand" from dictating a single outcome as to price and quantity in any given market.

This constitutes the core of Thornton's theory of price. "Plainly, then, it is competition, and competition alone, that regulates price; but what regulates competition? . . . if by regulating be meant the laying down of rules or prescribing a course which competition in any given circumstances must follow, the simple answer is Nothing. There is no regularity about competition—competition is not regulated at all" (*79–80). Was this nihilism, or the abdication of all pretense to scientific explanation, as modern commentators moan? No indeed, although it must be said that at this exact juncture Thornton leaves off his analysis of commodities in general to concentrate his attention upon labor, thus abandoning the analysis just where he ought to have driven it home. From the remainder of the book, it might be easy to extrapolate that Thornton was left paralyzed, unable to propose anything further about the nature of competition and its bounding of realized price. But if that had been the case, then nothing he said about the effects of unions would have been predicated on what had gone before. Instead, the next obvious thesis concerning price theory for Thornton was that although competition was not regulated by any natural laws of psychology or cost, competition could be hemmed in and regulated by the specific market structures which came over time to be associated with particular commodities in certain cultural settings. Patently, if trades unions could raise wages, then something about the market had been altered to regulate competition.

It was only in the late twentieth century that each of Thornton's theses on price theory was vindicated, ironically enough through the prosecution of a research tradition which was initially generated to reprimand Thornton for his heresy. Although this is not the place to make the case in detail, we can briefly indicate how the argument would run. First, utilitarian psychology has been proven incapable of underwriting deterministic laws of supply and demand. This is the lesson of the Sonnenschein-Mantel-Debreu proofs of the indeterminacy of excess demand functions in a full system of neoclassical general equilibrium.[29] The point can be made in a much less technical fashion: if Walrasian general equilibrium cannot guarantee uniqueness and stability of equilibrium except under wildly unrealistic circumstances, then even with a supposedly generic market mechanism, these economic "laws" don't operate in general the way their neoclassical advocates suggest. Thornton said that supply and demand do not lead to unique pairs of price and quantity; and so does Hugo Sonnenschein. Second, a generation of research on decision theory has produced one very pronounced empirical generalization: people don't generally conform to the so-called laws of probability in their formation of expectations. The utter bankruptcy of the Bayesian tradition in finding itself asserting that everyone must form identical probability assignments to be "rational" only reveals the fundamental soundness of Thornton's insistence upon the irreducible diversity of traders' cognitive capacities and economic expectations. Third, suppose for the moment that we abandon the pure modern neoclassical approach, but instead preserve the idea that there still exists some kind of function relating demand price to quantity demanded of some suitable aggregation of market traders. Even in this relatively unprepossessing case, Thornton was still correct in asserting that the "equation" of a supply and a demand function will not itself determine price. Since this last point may be unfamiliar to most economists, it may be worthwhile to sketch the argument in some detail.

The postwar rise of "experimental economics" has had a salutary effect on the community of economic theorists by driving home two points: first, that individuals do not conform to the neoclassical characterization of rational choice in controlled laboratory circumstances; second, that the form of market institutions matters, and while some kinds of structures (primarily double-sided auctions) conform to neoclassical predicted price and quantity equilibria when costs and reservation prices (that is, preset supply and demand curves) are given exogenously, other alternative sorts of market structures do not (Holt in Kagel and Roth 1995, 371 et seq.). For some economists, such as Vernon Smith, this second observation suggests that the profession should seek solace in something he calls the "Hayek hypothesis": namely, that markets somehow "work" independently of the cognitive states of the agents (1991, 221 et seq.). For Smith the Marshallian, "working" means converging to the equilibrium identified by the pre-given supply and demand curves; he neglects to consider that success is restricted to a small subset of possible market formations. The situation has been better clarified by the recent papers of Gode and Sunder (1993, 1997), wherein it is demonstrated that *it is the market rules alone* which explain eventual convergence or nonconvergence to equilibrium pre-identified by supply-and-demand price and quantity pairs, since this convergence will happen even with brainless automata making random bids and asks in the environment most favorable to the neoclassical model (that is, the double-auction market). In other words, if for the sake of argument stable Marshallian curves are presumed to exist a priori, then any predictable regularities are attributable solely to the form of institutional market rules: auction setup, closing rules, bid-improvement rules, the ability to withdraw posted offers, the enforcement of budget constraints. *Markets are not an expression of individual rationality*. In general, price and quantity pairs for the same good in the same market fall within a probabilistic range rather than collapse to a single point, unless this condition is itself imposed by some sort of clearinghouse mechanism. Among other interesting corollaries, in most cases the supposed "law of one price" fails to hold even within a single market period, if recontracting is disallowed. All of this can be found in Thornton's writing of more than a century ago.

We might venture further to suggest that there is no longer any good reason, other than irrational, sentimental attachment to a hallowed analytical tradition (which has recently, rather inconveniently, been cut adrift from its moorings in utilitarianism), to believe that platonic supply and demand curves really do exist, somehow independent of the contingencies of time, chance, and price distributions transmitted from other, similarly constituted markets. One cannot have it both ways: lawlike functions predicated upon individual free choice, and the unfettered interdependence of markets. This chapter reveals that those curves are cultural vestiges of the nineteenth century, a period when hard sciences like physics were thought to uncover rock-solid deterministic functions which could be readily subjected to the differential calculus for purposes of manipulation and control. This too can be gleaned from Thornton.

Thus ends the case for entertaining Thornton as a serious economic thinker, one that differs from those previously made in his favor. Thornton was not a partisan of hysteresis phenomena, nor was he Brian Arthur without the urn model. The problem faced by these and other authors who seek to recast Thornton's claims in more modern language is that the neoclassical framework is not only awkward, but thoroughly antithetical to the ideas Thornton was striving to express. This incompatibility is no accident, given that much of the Marshallian variant of the neoclassical program was generated expressly for the purpose of denying the cogency and legitimacy of Thornton's claims. In the language required to capture Thornton's intentions, the portrait of active agents and passive economic environments consisting of generic markets undergoes a gestalt reversal: one must envision a multiplicity of market institutions, which had generations of experience with the eccentricities of particular commodities and cultures, hemming in the output of price and quantity pairs through their individual operations and therefore accounting for much of the predictability of the essentially random actions of the economic agents. This is the format of economic theory endorsed in chapter 1.

The observation that modern economics obstructs hermeneutic understanding extends to the one neoclassical economist who has accorded Thornton the benefit of serious and close reading, Takashi Negishi (1986). He correctly points out that the attempt to subsume Thornton as a special case of supply and demand where the two curves coincide for some portion of their range, begun by Jenkin in 1870 after a reading of Mill's review of the preceding year, is fundamentally incorrect, and was rejected by Thornton himself in the second edition of *On Labour*. However, he then proceeds to interpret Thornton as discussing a situation of "disequilibrium," one perhaps due to a situation of imperfect competition. This interpretation is easily countered with a quote from *On Labour*: "There is never any such stable equilibrium as that of which the teachers of political economy dream" (*48n). Thornton did not believe the proposition that an equilibrium of supply and demand really existed, but was thwarted by some unfortunate "false trading" before the fact: rather, he thought supply and demand curves were an unfortunate figment of the imaginations of political economists, which could be disproved by temporarily entertaining their premises and showing that they could not withstand the consideration of actual behaviors observed in the marketplace. Negishi's insistence upon the former reading is all the more puzzling because in a footnote he reveals that he is aware of the correct alternative reading: "Thornton's point is not so much that different institutions (bid forms) generate different prices as that under some institutional condition the price is not determined by the equality of demand and supply" (1986, 572n). Our only explanation of this puzzle is that Negishi shares with the rest of the neoclassical profession the deep conviction that if all markets don't operate in a generic fashion, subject to a single set of laws, all hope of a science of economics is lost. In an era dominated by physics this belief would be more plausible than in an era dominated by biology.

The practice of Thornton exegesis has since been driven to bedlam, primarily by the strident efforts of Robert Ekelund. First, Ekelund took Negishi to task for imposing a Walrasian framework upon Thornton; but he then proceeded to ignore the textual evidence and loudly proclaim that no sympathetic reading of Thornton was conceivable. For instance, given the evidence presented in this volume, it is unconscionable to argue that there is "no textual evidence that Thornton ever understood Mill's simple but serviceable theory" (Ekelund and Thommesen 1989, 577). Thornton would have been truly offended at being accused of being a Comtist (571n); and no contemporary British political economist in good standing, one suspects, would have maintained that he "demonstrated little or no knowledge of supply and demand theory." Ekelund's attempt to recast the whole issue in terms of Vickrey's model of auctions (1961) is a solecism which far exceeds any residual Whiggism which Negishi might have displayed, if only because Thornton explicitly denied that traders could carry out the probabilistic calculations required in Vickrey's model; and in any event, Thornton also explicitly rejected utility as an explanatory concept. Ekelund's accusation that Thornton did not grasp the difference between a theory and an application presumes that there exists a canonical handbook of Economic Method with which he should have been familiar. This last accusation is particularly anachronistic, since the very *genre* of handbooks of economic methodology in English were jump-started by those who were recoiling from the controversy which Mill and Thornton precipitated (Blaug 1992, chapter 3). Cairnes's *Logical Method of Political Economy* (1875) and John Neville Keynes's *Scope and Method of Political Economy* cannot be understood without understanding the backdrop of controversy swirling around Thornton. Keynes himself innovated the standard modern response to Thornton: if you know enough mathematics, then all critique can be deflected into "technical" issues: "Amongst the characteristic direct advantages of mathematical analysis and diagrammatic representation is the fact that the significance of *continuity* in the variations of phenomena is brought into prominence. This remark applies pre-eminently to the diagrammatic treatment of the law of supply and demand. Such a treatment affords, for example, the simplest means of dealing with the ingenious criticisms to which Mr. Thornton has subjected this law. He adduces cases which at first sight look like exceptions overturning this law altogether; but the method of diagrams at once shews them to be extreme or limiting cases due to a break in the continuity either of demand and supply. They are accounted for, and their true signification easily apprehended" (1917, 262). Once again, we might suggest that the mere escalation of mathematical formalism is no *prima facie* evidence of progress in economics (Niehans 1990), but rather simply one technique among many to recast, reconceptualize, and co-opt intellectual criticism; and if all else fails, to misrepresent and ignore it altogether. Perhaps this explains why Ekelund remains incapable of addressing any of the above reconsiderations of the actual theoretical arguments of William Thomas Thornton on his own terms, resorting in desperation to ever-more fervid recitations of the catechism.[30]

The real problem which Thornton the historical figure presents to modern economists is this: To what extent must they acknowledge the legitimacy of a tradition whose explanatory principles violate every basic presupposition of their own hallowed tradition? The question parallels one that they pose concerning the economic agent: To what extent must the economist simply tell the agent what the economist believes the agent is doing, and how far can the economist credit the agent with holding a legitimate account of the causes of his or her own activity?

14

Smooth Operator:
How Marshall's
Demand and Supply
Curves Made Neo-
classicism Safe for
Public Consumption
but Unfit for Science

Natura non uncta deficit

Occasions dedicated to the commemoration of landmarks such as Marshall's *Principles* (like the Cambridge meeting for which this chapter was originally written) are most appropriate times for weighing and evaluating the significance of classic texts for our own situation, as well as reviewing the assessments of the intervening years. The problem with Marshall is that many of those intervening *pronunciamentos* are, shall we say, of a peculiarly "wet" character when it comes to his theoretical achievements. Marshall's students began this habit by introducing a note of lubricity into their assessments. Keynes has the famous passage where he attributes to an unnamed reviewer delight in the "humanising which the dismal science received at his hands," only to follow it with the warning that "the lack of emphasis and of strong light and shade, the sedulous rubbing away of rough edges and salients and projections, until what is most novel can appear as trite, allows the reader to pass too easily through. Like a duck leaving water, he can escape from this douche with scarce a wetting" (Pigou 1925, 47–48). The asperges continued with Langford Price's *Memoirs*, which among other things expressed dismay at Marshall's prediction that in a few years Pigou would be "known as the greatest economist since Adam Smith."[1]

Upon venturing outside the immediate circle of Marshall's Cambridge, things become even more damp. Schumpeter, for instance, normally quick off the mark to praise any neoclassical theorist, calls the period after 1885 "the Marshallian Age" but qualifies the remark profoundly with the caveat: "abroad, Marshall's work never succeeded as had A. Smith's . . . the economists of all countries who were open to economic theory at all had by 1890 evolved or accepted systems that, however inferior in technique, were substantially like Marshall's in fundamental ideas" (Schumpeter 1954, 833–34). The disdain of Walras for Marshall's theoretical prowess is well known (Walras 1965, letter 1123); I think less often noticed is Edgeworth's drier irony toward the Marshallian organon, found, for instance, in his entry in Palgrave on "Supply-Curves."

Marshall has not fared better with more modern commentators outside the University of Chicago orbit. Frisch (1950, 495) began his paper on the Marshallian theory of value with the moist preamble: "Like all human work, Alfred Marshall's theory of value had its definite shortcomings." Whitaker, who has spent much of his life improving our access to and understanding of Marshall's writings, detected the mugginess: "there is an awkwardness and hesitancy about Marshall's efforts at mathematical economics that argues against his ever having breathed freely on the pinnacles of abstraction" (Whitaker, ed., 1975, 5). Hicks, upon reading Whitaker's collection of Marshall's early writings, noted that "we can see the outline of an early Marshall who is really pre-Jevons, and much more like Mill than he is like Jevons. Consumer's rent, to take a leading example, begins as the difference between value in use and value in exchange, much as in Mill: it is, initially, a sum of 'money' not of 'utility.' It only takes on the latter form when Marshall goes Jevonian, perhaps not until 1880. It might have saved later writers a lot of trouble if this transmogrification had not taken place" (Hicks 1983, 336). The view from across the waters was not much kinder: "Marshall was so afraid of being unrealistic that he merely ends up being fuzzy and confusing—and confused" (Samuelson 1972, 24), and as Samuelson mellowed with age, "After the Anglo-Saxon world had come to digest the contributions of Leon Walras, Knut Wicksell and Irving Fisher, it is realized that Alfred Marshall's reputation—deservedly great—was overrated in the 1900–30 period. If the world excessively overvalued Marshall, Oxbridge outrageously treasured his writings" (Samuelson in Feiwel 1989, 125–26). But Oxbridge did not pull its punches either: "[Marshall] worked out his short period for forward movements with great lucidity and then he filled the book with tear gas, so that no one would notice that he had fudged the whole of the rest of the argument" (Robinson 1973, 259). "Marshall had a foxy way of salving his conscience by mentioning exceptions, but doing so in such a way that his pupils could continue to believe in the rule" (Robinson 1979, 169). I think we can agree that these are not the sort of pleasantries which one might expect to be directed at the progenitor of what, after all, is still the standard introductory textbook pedagogy in orthodox neoclassical economics departments. Now, not everyone would douse Marshall so relentlessly; I have already mentioned the erstwhile fondness for him in the near neighborhood of the shores of

Lake Michigan, normally drenched in intermittent lake effect. He also seems to have been the favorite of numerous neoclassical economists of older generations who were disaffected in various ways with some of the more jarring and awkward aspects of the neo-Walrasian synthesis, such as its intractably static character, its unapologetic abstraction, and its banishment of the entrepreneur (and perhaps even the trade coordinator and the firm). In other words, the Marshallian heritage was still the subject of live controversy a century later, with some claiming that his is the only legitimate line of neoclassical theory, a sort of social physics with a human face; whereas others disparaged his version of neoclassicism as only suitable for the care and watering of undergraduates. Since the 1980s, the rise to dominance of Nash game theory has tended to eclipse his relevance to a greater degree.

I propose to clarify Marshall's importance for the history of neoclassical theory by concentrating on the checkered history of the apparatus of the curves of demand and supply. The problem, as in so many of the narratives of the history of economic thought, is the absence of a coherent conceptualization of the incidence of continuity and discontinuity within and between research programs. Alfred Marshall loses some of his reputation for idiosyncrasy only when situated within the larger context of problems in British natural science (Wise and Smith 1989) and Cambridge mathematics (Richards 1988; Warwick 2003) in the Victorian period. His achievement is brought into focus by making a sharp distinction between neoclassical economics, which constituted a profound "epistemological rupture" with the previous classical theory of value, and the curves of demand and supply, which in some respects did not, as observed in chapter 13. Hence Marshall was not really responsible for invention of the curves of demand and supply, but he did attempt to reconcile them with the impending "Marginalist Revolution," which surely accounts for his fame. However, this reading leaves open the possibility that the "Laws of Demand and Supply" were not really central to neoclassical theory but were rather superficial appendages, and hence became expendable once the scientific core of the program reasserted itself after the Second World War (Mirowski 2002).

This reinterpretation of the legacy of Marshall will itself be conducted within the narrative frame of this section's history of supply and demand. We shall begin with a bird's eye view of the meaning of supply and demand in the half-century before 1890; then move on to further discuss the work of the neglected William Thornton and the sorely maltreated Fleeming Jenkin. From there we shall consider the work of Stanley Jevons, whose *Theory of Political Economy* marks the rupture with classical political economy; and then finally evaluate the contribution of Marshall as one who wished to smooth over the rift.

Decontextualizing Price and Quantity

One of the most important benefits of the great flowering of the profession of the history of science in recent culture has been the prompting of the progressive realization that the structure of explanation across such diverse disciplines as physics and economics bears closer family resemblance than previously suspected. Two very significant shared metaphors for our present purposes are: [A] the image of the conserved embodied substance (Mirowski 1989b, chapters 2, 4); and [B] the image of equilibrium as the balance of forces (Wise and Smith 1989; Wise 1993). In the sphere of natural philosophy, the notion of the conserved substance dates at least from Descartes's treatment of motion as an embodied entity passed from one body to another; it also makes its appearance in the theory of heat in the guise of the "caloric," in electricity as flows of an electrical "fluid," and so forth. On the other hand, the ideal of balance was pervasive in Enlightenment discourse, from the law of the lever to Lavoisier's chemical equations, Hutton's and Playfair's geology, and Condillac's treatment of algebra. These two generic metaphors could be mixed and matched in various permutations and contexts; but it is not our intention to demonstrate here their appearance in natural science. It will suffice to note that anyone who dealt in one or both metaphors would immediately be recognized as engaging in the formal discourse of explanation characteristic of the natural sciences in that period. Indeed, the metaphors of the embodied substance and the balance of forces were the primary loci for the mathematization of the disciplines cited.

What has only recently been noticed is that these same two metaphors constituted the core of value theory in classical political economy as well. The "natural" ground of value in the classical period always assumed the format of [A, B], whether the embodied substance was called *blé*, "corn," or "labor." The stable natural determinants of value behind the blooming, buzzing, phenomenological confusion of money prices were treated as if they were generated in "production," conserved in "exchange," and destroyed in "consumption."[2] "Natural price" was the direct expression of this underlying determinism. However, the observed "market price" was often thought to diverge from this underlying natural state; and it was at this point that the alternative metaphor of balance of forces was brought into play. "Competition" in almost every case was conceptualized as the collision of opposed forces, which in the political liberty of the well-governed state resulted in the eventual convergence or "gravitation" of market to natural price.

I use the terminology of "metaphor" here because there did not exist full identity of the [A, B] structure from one writer to the next. In particular, Wise and Smith (1989) have done us the service of insisting that the classical political economists were particularly unfettered in their use of the metaphor of balance, rhetorically sliding between two radically different constructions of the meaning of opposing forces in the arena of market prices. On the one hand, the classical political economists frequently portrayed market price as a deterministic oscillation around a central natural value. This is, of course, the full "gravitation" metaphor; the causes of the fluctuations are predominantly the same as the causes of natural price in the first place; the image is modeled upon the harmonic oscillations used to approximate solutions to the three-body problem in Newtonian mechanics. On the other hand, competition was also portrayed as taming the numerous "accidental" disturbances to market price which could not be analytically encompassed because their motives were deemed outside the realm of economic (or even rational) explanation. In this version, the opposing disturbances were regarded as roughly symmetrical; hence an average of market prices would be expected to indicate the true natural price. The rhetorical freedom grew out of the structure of the coupled [A, B] metaphors: [A], the natural value substance, provided the anchor for the system, while different versions of [B] allowed various authors to exercise their imagination in absorbing as much (or as little) of the dynamics of social interaction in the marketplace as they wished.

While much of this must sound familiar to the reader of chapter 13, it is imperative to sort out these structural metaphors because of extreme confusion prevalent in the literature about what does and does not constitute an anticipation of the subsequent neoclassical research program.[3] The operation of "supply and demand" as opposing forces in the marketplace which result in an "equilibrium" in the presence of a healthy atmosphere of competition is indeed the gist of metaphor [B], and as such it is an integral part of the research program of *classical* political economy. The opposed forces are identified with the opposed interests of the two sides of the market, and their interplay is expected to result in convergence to the underlying natural value determinants *in both versions*, be it deterministic oscillation or the canceling-out of numerous disturbing factors. Supply and demand as an argument became central and indispensable to the structure of classical political economy, because it was the *locus* of temporal and dynamic reasoning in value theory. This intrinsically dynamic cast of classical "supply and demand" will shortly play an important role in our narrative.

One important bit of evidence for the thesis that "supply and demand" was a peculiarly classical notion is that the language of "supply and demand" was pervasive in nineteenth-century political economy. But tracking the mere appearance of the words, which after all would qualify any parrot as an economist, are not sufficient to understand the subsequent role of Marshall in the history of economic thought. It will behoove us to pay close attention to the changing face of supply and demand over the nineteenth century if we are to understand the vexed issue of the putative "continuity" of classical and neoclassical economic theory. Here the rhetorical wavering concerning the exact meaning of supply and demand comes into play: I want to suggest that the analytical underdetermination of the supply and demand metaphor [B] was crucially responsible for the internal breakdown of the substance metaphor [A] over the course of the century, and that this happened through the progressive decontextualization of price and quantity from other classes of oscillations or disturbances which had previously been lumped together under the rubric of supply and demand. In a nutshell, reducing supply and demand to deterministic functions of price and quantity led to a situation where natural price could no longer be equated with their equilibrium, destroying the entire analytical structure. What Marshall did was not so much preserve the structure as propose to shore up a dilapidated, jerry-built metaphor [B] upon a new natural determinant, the recently borrowed physics model of constrained optimization over a conservative vector field (Mirowski 1989b). But since the problems of convergence and temporal dynamics were not strengthened or fortified by this amendment, the entire structure remains to this day precariously perched upon sand (Mirowski 1989d). In other words, not only are the Marshallian scissors superfluous to neoclassical value theory; they give rise to intractable contradictions within that framework—contradictions wrought by Marshall's own particular contribution to the neoclassical research program. This goes some way toward explaining all the "wet" quotes that preface this paper: scissors cut paper, but paper wraps stone, and stone blunts scissors; only water dissolves all three.

From Smith to Mill

It is important to recall that in the era whose boundaries are marked by Smith and John Stuart Mill, which was described in chapter 13, one could readily cite the "firmly established doctrine that the value of all commodities depends on the supply and demand," and in the same breath also assert an embodied substance theory of value. Hence, in Jane Marcet's little textbook for children published in 1827, one would find on page 314 that "the proportion of the supply to the demand . . . regulates *market price*"; and yet find on page 317 this statement: "You must, however, recollect that it is the cost of production of a commodity which constitutes its exchangeable value; the proportion of supply and demand should be considered as only accidentally affecting it." This view is most certainly derived from Ricardo; but one can also find it in McCulloch, who in 1825 argued that "buying and selling are in commerce, what action and reaction are in physics, always *equal and contrary*" (McCulloch 1825, 135); and yet also that the "average real value of all sorts of commodities will be precisely proportioned to, or coincident with, the common and average quantities of labour required for their production" (224).

It seems that in the early nineteenth century one could simply assume that a reference to supply and demand would be understood as a synecdoche, the part which stood for the whole metaphorical complex. C. F. Bastable, looking back from the end of the century, claimed in an address to section F of the British Association for the Advancement of Science in 1894 that " 'the recognized principles of political economy' or 'the immutable laws of supply and demand' were phrases that occurred as readily to a journalist in the sixties as 'the exploded doctrine of laissez faire' does to the leader-writer of today" (in Smyth 1962, 127). This can be observed not only in political economy, but also in literature; for instance, in Dickens's *Hard Times* (1854): "But she knew from her reading infinitely more of the ways of toiling insects than of these toiling men and women. Something to be worked so much and paid so much, and there ended; something to be infallibly settled by the laws of supply and demand; something that blundered against those laws and floundered into difficulty" (Dickens [1854] 1971, 160). It also seems that to a certain extent, the usage reflected the self-images of the period in that the fundamental natural determinants of price were almost taken for granted, whereas the transitory accidents of the market were subject to deliberate planned response. This can be observed in the 1820s in the instructions of Owens and Son of Manchester to their partner in Philadelphia to apportion their cotton purchases to price fluctuations according to an explicit price-quantity schedule (Clapp 1962); or in the wagers of the major brewing families of London over the prices of hops and barley in the prospective harvest.[4] Supply and demand in this context would thus refer simultaneously to underlying natural forces and to schedule-like adjustments in the face of inevitable accident and unforeseen circumstance.

What was good enough for quotidian discourse was not good enough for science, however. The [A, B] metaphoric complex which was used with great frequency in the early nineteenth century did not seem to be resulting in a quantitative model as it had done in other fields; even though words which suggested mathematical structures such as "proportion" and "equality" kept surfacing with regularity. Hence it was not so very unusual that a number of mathematically inclined individuals such as William Whewell and Antoine-Augustin Cournot sought to formalize the imprecise vernacular in the third and fourth decades of the century. The consequences of their activities, until recently treated as some sort of unproblematic foreshadowing of later neoclassical theory, actually were nothing of the sort.

The reason was that the mere fact of formalizing supply and demand according to nineteenth-century canons of scientific reasoning caused them to become decontextualized from their underlying metaphorical basis. Partly because of its psychological overtones, "demand" began to lose any connection with natural price; but more profoundly, the condition of the *clearing of a market* began to assume much greater significance than it did in the context of classical theory. In a substance theory of value, market clearing at a point in time bore little relevance to natural price, primarily because the underlying determinants of value were conceptualized as persisting through time, independently of contingent market activity (Mirowski 1989b, chapters 4–5). But to formalize supply and demand as functions in equilibrium inadvertently raised the touchy issue of what was to be considered invariant in the process of exchange; through the stress on market clearing, the mathematics itself riveted attention on the underlying determinants of the curves and their temporal integrity.

What appears to have happened in the 1820s and 1830s is that the drive to construct formal models of supply and demand implicitly gave rise to a third connotation of those terms. Neither the purely deterministic oscillations around natural price nor the average taken over an arbitrary set of imponderable accidents was the path chosen for mathematical formalization (although models of both were already available in the physical sciences). Instead, a third, coy option materialized, which was to model supply and demand themselves as deterministic functions with little or no reference to natural price or value theory; to abjure any serious attempt to justify the stability of the functional forms, thus leaving room to readmit the language of "accident" if desired; and to associate equilibrium with the occurrence of market clearing at a point in time, which was purportedly identical with the intersection of the demand and supply functions in an abstract price-quantity space. This was the prime legacy of Cournot and Whewell and the engineering tradition discussed in chapter 13, and not the "mathematical statements of price flexibility, demand elasticity, and the Giffen paradox" (Henderson 1973).

Whewell's method of achieving this innovation was relatively straightforward: just redefine demand to mean a fixed sum of money irrevocably devoted to the purchase of the commodity in question. Why should a fixed sum be fixedly devoted to a particular purchase? The requirements of mathematical formalization loomed larger than the canons of logic in this instance:[5] "*Supply* is of itself a quantity and offers us no difficulty in measuring it theoretically: but *demand* is of a more intangible and fugitive nature. It consists originally of moral elements as well as physical: of the vehemence of desire, and the urgency of need which men have, as well as the extent of their means . . . [Tooke] supposed (merely as a means of reducing the question to calculation) that men set aside a *certain sum* to purchase a given article, and that sum measures the *demand* . . . Now this mode of beginning the reasoning answers extremely well the purpose of avoiding all indefiniteness" (Whewell [1829] 1971, 9–10). The structure of the argument then became: the demand curve in price-quantity space was formalized as a rectangular hyperbola (as a consequence of the fixity of expenditure), while supply at a point in time would be conceptualized as equal to a constant quantity; their intersection would identify equilibrium price. Whewell felt compelled to acknowledge that the "approximation is a very loose and inaccurate one," but also to make some gesture toward linking this curious construction of the meaning of supply and demand to the classical value framework, which was nowhere to be found in the mathematics: "Price is determined by the conflict of supply and demand; price is also determined by the cost of production, in which latter expression demand is not mentioned: how then do these agree? In answer to this it is to be observed, that the former is the immediate, the latter the permanent, determinant of price" (12). This superimposition of time frames in the text without expression in the mathematics was illegitimate, as Whewell must have known, since he repudiated it in his very next paper: "In order however that solutions of this nature may have any value, it is requisite that the principles, of which we estimate the operation, should include *all* the *predominant* causes which really influence the result . . . The quantities which we neglect must be of an inferior order to those which we take into account; otherwise we obtain no approximation at all. We may with some utility make the theory of *tides* a question of equilibrium, but our labour would be utterly misspent if we should attempt to consider such a principle a theory of *waves*. It appears to be by no means clear that the irregular fluctuations and transitory currents by which the elements of wealth seek their natural level may be neglected in the investigation of the primary laws of their distribution" ([1831] 1971, 13). The comparison held particular poignancy for Whewell, since his main mathematical claim to fame was his treatment of the theory of tides (Becher 1971). It was a commonplace in the nineteenth century to compare supply and demand to the ripples of disturbance upon the surface of a body of water; but Whewell understood that doing so conflated the two versions of the [B] metaphor, namely periodic wave motion and random disturbance. Since Whewell did not accept the classical substance theory of value, he knew there was no legitimate mathematical approximation to wave motion around equilibrium; and because there was also no legitimate mathematics of random shocks at that time, he had no alternative but to repudiate his own model of supply and demand.[6]

Cournot's *Researches into the Mathematical Principles of the Theory of Wealth* (1838) is another example of the same decontextualization process being worked out in a slightly different cultural arena. Cournot is often credited with innovation of the curves of demand and supply; and indeed, there is a graph of downward-sloping loi de débit and an upward-sloping function in the price-quantity plane (Cournot [1838] 1897, 92). But just as with Whewell, attention to detail will reveal that the grounds for formalization were equally precarious and vacillating. It is frequently overlooked that Cournot was explicitly anti-utilitarian, viewing such notions as "ill-suited for the foundation of a scientific theory" (10). He refused to give any justification whatsoever for his "law of sales," other than to hint that its continuity (required for differentiation) was due to a sufficiently large number of customers. At least Whewell had the common sense to posit a fixed sum of money devoted to specific purchases, whereas there is no reason at all to accept Cournot's assertion of a differentiable function deterministically relating price to quantity. Mathematics is not intrinsically self-justifying; and mathematical expression is not adequately fortified by ambiguous evocations of "science." The reason for the groundless professions of faith in Cournot was probably the problem of straddling the two previous connotations of supply and demand: "the price of an article may vary notably in the course of a year. And strictly speaking, the law of sales may also vary in the same interval, if the country experiences a movement of progress or decadence. For greater accuracy . . . the curve which represents the function F [should] be itself an average of all the curves which would represent this function at different times of year" (52). Were supply and demand law-governed or not? Cut adrift from any particular theory of value, Cournot and all the mathematics in the world were incapable of answering the question, so he chose rather to avoid it by means of baseless retreat to the previous metaphor of random imponderable disturbances. The prospect grew downright forlorn once the pervasive interdependence of markets was acknowledged (127).

And yet, the drive to formalize supply and demand continued unabated throughout the European context, mainly through the efforts of engineers and others acquainted with increasing abstraction from context in mathematical physics in the mid-nineteenth century. Jules Dupuit in 1844 also inscribed a downward-sloping function relating price to quantity to solve various practical problems of pricing public tolls and taxes. However formidable this may have looked as geometry, even Dupuit had to acknowledge that it was hopeless as science: "Suppose that we have two columns of figures showing the number of articles consumed according to each market price from zero, at which consumption is largest, right up to the price which causes all consumption to cease. This series of relationships is not known for any commodity, and it can even be said that it will never be known since it depends on the volatile will of human beings; it is today no longer what it was yesterday. It is thus of no avail to try to determine this relationship exactly by experience or by groping experiment" (Dupuit [1844] 1952, 103).

Given the lack of enthusiasm on the part of many early leaders of this movement, we may be prompted to ask why the drive to formalization maintained its momentum throughout the nineteenth century. Above all, I would suggest that the very obscurity of what supply and demand referred to (in the sense that the three different connotations of the terms coexisted peacefully throughout the mid-century), combined with their credentials as a central theme in classical political economy, made the doctrine of supply and demand extremely adaptable and acceptable. Everyone knew that there were two sides to every exchange, and like Tweedledum and Tweedledee, supply and demand were good enough placeholders for the indefatigable opponents in the marketplace. But there was also another consideration, that supply and demand seemed intrinsically quantitative, and therefore held out the bright promise of mathematical formalization to those so inclined. But formalization meant forcibly imposing deterministic functions upon the price-quantity plane, precisely in an area where classical political economy did not anticipate any such "scientific" laws. This in turn had all sorts of unsavory consequences: it abstracted price away from the classical substance theory of value; created great confusion about the relevant time frames in a doctrine which had previously been used to account for the dynamics of adjustment; surreptitiously began to reinterpret equilibrium in the marketplace as market clearing at a point in time; and, not least, led to some embarrassing statements about the appropriate empirical referent of this dubious "science." If not for its increasing political use, as described in chapter 13, it would be much harder to comprehend its purchase upon the nineteenth-century analytical imagination.

The situation was not a happy one, and it was not helped by John Stuart Mill's attempt to make the laws of value complete and uncontentious by fiat. While he merely ratified Whewell's and Cournot's line that "the proper mathematical analogy is that of an equation" (Mill [1848] 1899, 432), he did not follow them into the thickets of mathematical formalization. By contrast with them, Mill attempted to reconcile supply and demand terminology with the thrust of classical political economy and with his "three categories" of the law of value, relegating supply and demand to the case where production could be expanded at increased cost (428), and subordinating the whole to the classical natural price (439). But this was merely a slapdash expedient; and it was William Thornton's frontal attack upon the analytical structure of supply and demand in 1869 which brought matters to a head.

Thornton and Jenkin and Jevons

William Thomas Thornton (1813–80) is one of the more important figures in the history of English political economy, although he is rarely accorded the attention he deserves in histories of the subject. Often mentioned as the person responsible for Mill's recantation of the wages fund doctrine, it is my contention that he should be credited with motivating (directly or indirectly) most of the major exponents of the neoclassical movement in England, including of course Alfred Marshall. His attack on Mill's version of supply and demand was noted by MacLeod, approvingly, by Jenkin as the starting point for his own work on wages and trade unions, by Jevons in both his *Theory of Political Economy* and his posthumous *Principles*, and by Marshall in his review of Jevons's *Theory* (Black 1977, 143) and his essay of 1876 on Mill's theory of value: "Mr. Thornton's work is not free from faults: but he has not received his due meed of gratitude for having led men to a point of view from which the practical importance of the theory of market values is clearly seen" (Whitaker 1975, 2:263). But beyond these vague and unspecific acknowledgments, I should like to argue that Thornton sagely put his finger on what was incoherent about the mid-century evolution of the doctrine of supply and demand, and that his insight set in train the following concatenation of events. First it provoked the engineer Fleeming Jenkin to reformulate the orthodox mid-century interpretation of supply and demand in a geometrical format resonant with the state of mathematical education in Victorian Britain; this in turn so rattled William Stanley Jevons that he, in mortal fear of being scooped as the progenitor of a mathematical political economy, rushed to pen *The Theory of Political Economy* in 1870 to assert his own version of the theory of value; and then Marshall, reading Thornton, Jenkin, and Jevons in near proximity after these events, believed he had found all the components of a reconciliation of supply and demand (and therefore, in the specific sense discussed above, classical political economy) with the newer doctrine of the marginal utility theory of value.

Thornton marks a turning point in the history of economic thought because he systematically attacked both components of the [A, B] metaphor. He simply dismissed the embodied substance theory of value as "that pure abstraction of the mind" (Thornton 1870b, 45). He then devoted the bulk of his attention to the [B] component of the theory, first spelling out with admirable succinctness the decontextualization of supply and demand in the price-quantity plane (50), only then to demolish thoroughly any claim for its status as a "law." Indeed, the best way to understand Thornton's onslaught is to recognize that he rejected the entire tradition of western value theory, which strove to ground economic value in natural invariants (Mirowski 1989b, chapter 4): "Price is scarcely ever mentioned without provoking a reference to the 'inexorable,' the 'immutable,' the 'eternal' laws by which it is governed; the laws which, according to my friend Professor Fawcett, are 'as certain in their operation as those which control physical nature.' It is no small gain to have discovered that no such despotic laws do or can exist; that, inasmuch as the sole function of scientific law is to predict the invariable recurrence of the same effects from the same causes, and as there can be no invariability where—as in the case of price—one of the most efficient causes is that ever-changing chameleon, human character or disposition, price cannot possibly be subject to law" (Thornton 1870b, 82).

Thornton's basic arguments in his masterwork *On Labour* were summarized in chapter 13. The overarching theme of his critique is that no real market transactor is stupid enough or passive enough simply to acquiesce in the abstract market-clearing price (63n, 73). Indeed, the institutional structure of the diverse formats of market organization is the most important determinant of market prices; Thornton bolsters this assertion by comparing the Dutch and English auctions, which result in different "equilibria," even given the same objective circumstances, same transactors, and so on (56 et seq.). For these and other reasons, demand should not be conceptualized as a single-valued function of price (60). One of the most important aspects of a specific market format is the temporal pattern of price setting; that market clearing takes time inherently violates the presumption that the entire target stock will be sold at a unique price (64–65). Here in a single gesture Thornton demonstrated the incoherence of writing demand and supply as decontextualized functions of price, either at a point in time or as some "average," and then asserting that they could be the basis of a serious dynamical theory of price. Far from being a fusty antiquarian issue, the controversy is still relevant to the modern neoclassical fascination with the "law of one price" (Mirowski 1986, chapters 4, 6).

For Thornton, even the connotation of supply and demand as a congeries of random but offsetting influences held no promise, since "the variations of demand from week to week, and from day to day, would defy all calculation" (Thornton 1870b, 66n). The notion of the two sides of the market as personifications of opposing forces in the Newtonian mode was also forlorn: "There is no regularity about competition—competition is not regulated at all" (80). Nevertheless, if one were a committed utilitarian, a few throwaway phrases could be read as offering a slender palm of conciliation: "The upper of these limits [of price] is marked by the utility, real or supposed, of time commodity to the customer; the lower by its utility to the dealer" (76). These phrases would shortly loom all out of proportion to their place in the text, especially for Jevons and for Marshall.

As if this were not radical enough to roust the political economists, Thornton proceeded to apply the lessons of his critique to one of the most burning issues of the day: the role and efficacy of trade unions. If the institutional structure of the market were one of the most salient determinants of the resulting price, and it were also the case that labor time was an unusual commodity in that it could not be readily reserved by the seller, then the existence of trade unions would permanently alter the price of labor by allowing it to be treated on a footing with other commodities: "Labourers may by combining acquire an influence which, if exercised with moderation and discretion, employers will be willing rather to propitiate than to oppose . . . the fact of an increase in the rate of remuneration having been artificially caused, furnishes no reason why in the great majority of cases that increase should not be lasting" (320). Thornton's deconstruction of the distinction between artificial and natural, so very crucial to the self-image of political economy as a science, demanded a response; it was swift in coming. While some rejoinders, like that of Mill in the *Fortnightly Review* in 1869, were relatively ineffectual, those written by souls trained in the natural sciences were more concertedly mobilized to reassert the primacy of the natural. The key to this revanchist movement was displacement of the discourse in the direction of *geometry*. While geometric diagrams for supply and demand were not unknown on the Continent, they did not make their début in England until this juncture. The reasons for this timing are many and varied—much of the French discussion took place in the *grandes écoles* among civil engineers; mathematics in early-nineteenth-century France was more advanced than that in England; French physical science was more comfortable than English science with phenomenological description—but the privileged position of geometry in English Victorian culture now came to the fore.

By mid-century, geometry had come to represent the paradigm of both necessary and self-evident truth in British pedagogy, and not only in such relatively uncontroversial areas as surveying and the physics of motion: "The transcendental truth mathematics was believed to describe had long stood as an exemplar of the perfect truth to which the human intellect aspired. It was a particularly central issue in theology . . . In the 1860s and 1870s, the cultural context of geometrical development was still the unitary view of truth articulated by men like Herschel and Whewell" (Richards 1988, 104, 103). In such a milieu, simply to restate the recently decontextualized supply and demand relations in geometric form could *by itself* serve as a powerful response to the brash challenge of a Thornton. This was not because "mathematics renders assumptions and logical steps more transparent" or any other such silly homily; but rather because the displacement of discussion into a geometric discourse could subtly reassert the supposedly timeless or "natural" character of the supply and demand relationship and present it as a self-evident, abstract truth. Geometry entered English political economy at precisely the point where images of natural order were put at risk; it was the cultural significance of the geometry that mattered, not its precise form. The impression that one could build price theory up from basics in the image of Euclid was much more important than commitment to any particular proposed formalization. One can observe this in the three models promulgated by Jenkin, Jevons, and Marshall.

Jenkin's response to Thornton was constructed by a method which resembled the earlier work by Cournot. In his article of 1870, "The Graphic Representation of the Laws of Supply and Demand, and their Application to Labour,"[7] it is Thornton who is repeatedly reprimanded with geometry, but not, we might observe, with actual market observation. Much like Cournot, Jenkin rested content to posit continuous curves in the price-quantity plane without any satisfactory justification for their stability, continuity, or integrity. One observes this most directly when he denies Thornton's analysis of the Dutch and English auctions by insisting that his ideas must be expressed with demand and supply curves, a proposition against which, as we have seen, Thornton would have most strenuously demurred.

Jenkin begins and ends the essay by invoking natural law: "The laws of price are as immutable as the laws of mechanics" (Jenkin 1887, 93) and indeed should be constructed in their very image. The laws of both supply and demand are asserted to be grounded in psychology, but at the very outset the quest for natural laws goes awry: "The law thus stated assumes that each man knows his own mind, that is to say, how much of each commodity he will then and there sell or buy at each price, and that the condition of his mind shall not vary . . . But, in practice men's minds do not remain constant for five minutes together" (78–79). Costs of production are brought in as another candidate for determining the shape and slope of the supply curve, and "in the long run, the price of the manufactured article is chiefly determined by the cost of its production" (89), but the exact relationship to psychology is left unexplored. And finally, the political threat to the status quo is deflected by means of the assertion that "the cost of production of labour determines wages, but is itself determined by men's expectation of comfort" (102), but if workmen should combine in trade unions, they will only succeed in reducing employment and the production of wealth.

While much in this article anticipates Marshall (even down to identical niceties of phrasing), I do not think it at all accurate that Jenkin gives the "first clear statement in English writing of the concept of supply and demand as functions of price" (Black 1987, 1007). The baseless bravado of inscribing decontextualized demand and supply schedules had a long history in the nineteenth century, as did vague justifications nodding in the direction of psychology and costs. Moreover, the penchant for sheepishly admitting the spuriousness of the natural law character of the curves was also simply one more variation on a well-worn theme. The only real novelty was pedagogical stress upon the actual geometry; but this was not trivial.

William Stanley Jevons certainly did not think it trivial. In 1868 Jenkin sent Jevons his earlier article on trade unions, and Jevons responded with a copy of the précis of his theory of value which had appeared in the *Journal of the Royal Statistical Society*. Significantly, Jenkin was then prompted to pen a letter to Jevons disputing his "fluxion theory of exchange" (Black 1977, 3:166 et seq.). Jenkin's objection seemed to be that price ratios would not be determinate in a bilateral exchange predicated upon different utility functions, given fixed endowments of the goods to be traded. (Edgeworth made precisely this same point thirteen years later.) Then Jenkin proceeded to compose his 1870 paper *Graphic Representation*, described above, *abjuring all dependence upon mathematical specifications of utility*. When Jevons happened upon a copy of this paper, "in wh[ich] no reference was made to my previous," he was shocked and galvanized into action: "Partly in consequence of this I was led to write and published the Theory in 1871" (166).

Why would Jevons feel threatened or preempted by Jenkin's paper, especially when Jenkin made no use of the constrained maximization of utility and Jevons (eventually) had no supply and demand curves in his *Theory of Political Economy*? An answer, which transcends the simplistic reaction that both works must have been a part of the same neoclassical research program, has been initiated by White (1989c); but now we may situate this *curiosum* in the larger cultural context. Above all, Jevons felt threatened by Jenkin because both were engaged in the project of constructing a *mathematical* political economy that would subsume what both were calling "the laws of supply and demand." Both allowed that "demand" should be grounded in utility or psychology; and both were advocates of the natural law character of price determination. Both were concerned that Thornton's challenge should be answered. Finally, both were determined to redirect economic discourse into a geometrical mode. But even so, they differed on almost everything else, and that goes some distance in explaining Jevons's sudden mobilization to write his *Theory of Political Economy*.

Superficial similarities in geometry and terminology did not mask profound differences between the two in their approaches. For Jenkin, the "laws of supply and demand" referred directly to the theory of price setting embodied in the price-quantity diagram, whereas for Jevons, the "laws" bore a connotation alien to modern usage. In Jevons's mind, scientific laws "were a set of observation statements or propositions devoid of theoretical content" (White 1989c, 428); one observed this in his *Principles of Science* and also in his later attack upon Thornton, whose writings, he asserted, were "based upon a misapprehension of the nature of these so-called laws. They are in no sense ultimate, natural or invariable laws, but are only expressions of the general course of phenomena exhibited in commerce when there are many buyers and many sellers. They are laws of aggregate supply and demand, but an aggregate is a sum of separate quantities, so that the natural law in order to be manifested in the aggregate must be manifested in the elementary quantities" (Jevons 1905, 57). Hence Jevons believed that the true natural law character of prices could only be revealed by total reduction of all phenomena to individual utility, which meant a more direct imitation of physics: "Utility . . . is the alpha and omega of the science, as light is of optics or sound of acoustics" (6). But whereas Jenkin merely wanted laws of supply and demand to resemble those of mechanics in some vague appeal to balance, Jevons proposed literally to reduce empirical supply and demand to the laws of energetics: "The notion of value is to our science what that of energy is to mechanics" (50; Mirowski 1989b, chapter 5). This explains such otherwise cryptic comments as: "A mere quantity of goods does not constitute supply until it is offered for sale—that is to say, until the quantity is connected with a mental feeling" (Jevons 1905, 55).

Although there are minor resemblances in their appeals to geometry, supply and demand did not mean much of the same thing for Jenkin and Jevons. The only "scissors" to be found in the *Theory of Political Economy* (Jevons [1871] 1970, 140) are not identified as a supply and demand diagram, because they represent two utility curves for the same trading body. Jevons's contempt for any reconciliation of supply and demand with cost of production theories is well known (Jevons 1905, 63); this would have been another source of friction with Jenkin. But most importantly, the subsidiary status of the laws of supply and demand were further diminished in Jevons's opinion by doubts concerning their empirical integrity, doubts absent in the paper by Jenkin:

> It would be a matter of great importance, if it were practicable, to ascertain statistically the exact law of the variation of price of the more important commodities. Assuming the demand to be constant, in the sense that there is a constant population of purchasers with fixed tastes, we should make the supply of the commodity . . . the variable, and then ascertain the changes of price, the variant. . . . The laws will not be laws of any generality; they will, in fact, be little more than compendious statements of numerical results . . . But it may seem rather needless to consider what these laws should be, inasmuch as we have not got them, and have no present prospects of getting them. . . . The difficulties in the way of such empirical determination of laws are so formidable that I entertain little hope of successful investigations being made for many years to come . . . there are complicated reactions among the variations of separate markets which defy statistical analysis. Many years ago, about the years 1861–62, I spent a good deal of labour in endeavouring to arrive at a rough determination of the laws of price of a few commodities specifically selected for that purpose. (146–47)

Thus neoclassical price theory, the theory of constrained optimization over a conservative vector field, was for Jevons an avenue of escape from the fruitless dialogue over the supposed laws of supply and demand from Whewell to Mill to Thornton to Jenkin. While one might attempt to fit a curve (but *not* demand and supply curves) to some collection of numbers such as the King-Davenant corn price data (Jevons, 1970, 18–83), the exercise would yield no added insight into the scientific causes of price movements, which were exhaustively described by the theory of utility and energy. Jevons, ever the lone wolf, was proposing to do away with most prior existing connotations of supply and demand: with lawlike oscillations around the embodied substance (*nota bene*: his dismissal of the labor theory of value comes directly after his discussion of the King-Davenant data in *Theory of Political Economy*); with counterpoised and offsetting random disturbance; and with decontextualized schedules floating in aggregate price-quantity space. Jevons's innovation of neoclassical price theory was intended to be a rival to the nineteenth-century tradition of supply and demand functions which we have sketched in this chapter, and not its culmination, as has been suggested by many historians of economic thought who have taken their cue from Alfred Marshall.

Marshall (Finally)

Never again will a Mrs. Trimmer, a Mrs. Marcet, or a Miss Martineau earn a goodly reputation by throwing [the principles of economics] into the form of a catechism or of simple tales. —Marshall in Pigou 1925, 296

If the reader can forgive the circumlocution of the discussion so far, the time has arrived to render unto Marshall the things that are Marshall's. It seems that much of what passes as Marshallian in the modern economics literature is not in fact traceable to Marshall; and further, much that is now deemed "Marshallian" has little or no logical connection to the core program of neoclassical price theory as it was innovated in the 1870s. I do not intend this to be understood in the conventional antiquarian sense that one claims to find ever-earlier "precursors" of some doctrine, or else quibbles over whether "Mr. X" was *really* an "Xian." Instead, it should now become clear that the supply and demand organon had little to do with the formal structure of neoclassical price theory; and neither was Marshall responsible for any substantive theoretical innovation in the theory of value.

Marshall is best understood as one more figure in the mathematical and engineering tradition of Cournot and Jenkin (Warwick 2003). His early manuscript, "Essay on Value," contains his first foray into geometric curves of demand and supply, but also evinces little interest in what lay behind the curves (Bharadwaj 1978b). Variations in demand are simply associated with variations in the number of buyers (Whitaker 1975, 1:122), even though this association displays rather less rigor than Whewell's attempt to derive the slope from a fixed sum of expenditure. Similarities of language, particularly in attributing supply to ill-defined cost-of-production considerations which converge to classical doctrine in the long run, merely echo Mill and Jenkin. All of this would be second nature to anyone steeped in Cournot, Jenkin, and the rest. Many others in Marshall's own lifetime noticed as much, and to them he violently insisted that he had not read Jenkin before making his own "discoveries."[8] As has often been noted, it was only after reading Jevons's *Theory of Political Economy* and becoming a lukewarm convert to the energetics revolution that Marshall made any attempt to justify the slope and structure of the demand curve through what remained, at best, a sort of half-hearted utilitarianism.[9] A more technical evaluation of the jerry-built structure of the constant marginal utility of money, the notion of consumer's surplus, the treatment of production, and much else Marshallian can be found in Mirowski (1989b, chapter 6).

There is a plethora of reasons why the Marshallian demand and supply functions are inconsistent with neoclassical theory; the simplest way to make the case is to examine any modern advanced text of neoclassical general equilibrium and notice that they are essentially absent.[10] Another, more involved, method is to realize that the sum total of Marshall's "innovations" undermines the very meaning of equilibrium which was brought over from physics at the inception of the neoclassical school. The mid-nineteenth-century notion of equilibrium as embodied in the mathematics of the field describes a situation which is conservative and path-independent. All of Marshall's literary attempts to infuse realism into supply and demand involved the introduction of differential time frames, path dependence, and irreversible change. Now, one might fervently believe that social life is closer to biological evolution than the fall of a stone, but one should then renounce neoclassical value theory as a consequence, and not somehow pretend that the mathematics of constrained optimization in the appendices had any logical connection to the notoriously evanescent geometry in the main text. Moreover, as Wicksteed claimed long ago, the two curves do not strictly "live" in the same price-quantity plane from a consistent neoclassical vantage point; but then again, mere mathematical consistency was never a Marshallian strong point.

Even Marshall's penchant for seeing biological metaphors in his curves had no foundation in the mathematics. The supposed applications of Taylor's Theorem to the webbing between a duck's appendages within biology was a figment of his imagination (Marshall [1920] 1947, 841–42), as was the purported connection between differentiable functions and smooth evolution. The recourse to biological metaphors was itself an opportunistic maneuver, grounded more in the contingent circumstances of British academe than in the structure of the argument. In an incident in 1877 which deserves greater attention from historians of economics, the statistician and eugenicist Francis Galton spearheaded a drive to oust section F (Statistics and Political Economy) from the British Association for the Advancement of Science on the grounds that the economists were not comporting themselves in a scientific manner. In his presidential address to section F (in Smyth 1962) in 1878, J. K. Ingram countered that political economy resembled biology in many respects, and therefore should be accorded the same courtesy as the field in which Galton enjoyed his primary identity. Marshall's subsequent fascination with biological metaphor not only served to blunt the criticism that neoclassical economics was an improper bowdlerisation of physics, but also smoothed over the incongruity that a brace of curves originally intended to decontextualize price and quantity was now supposedly the vehicle for the reintroduction of context.

The (perhaps unpopular) point to be made here is that Marshall should not be regarded as a discoverer of anything, nor an original theorist of any stripe in the light of the history of neoclassical theory; he was, as the quotation above suggests, first and foremost a textbook writer, a popularizer and synthesizer of contradictory doctrines. The appropriate points of comparison are Jane Marcet, Henry Fawcett, and Harriet Martineau rather than Walras, Jevons, and Edgeworth. Marshall marks the watershed in the pedagogy of English economics, away from the Socratic dialogue or narrative parable and toward an imitation of science as he (and many of his academic contemporaries) understood it. The hallmark of this new genre was geometry; and the rest was the usual textbook practice of presenting the jumbled motley of the discourse of a profession as if it were unified, internally consistent, and profoundly self-assured, not to mention resonant with the larger cultural currents of the day.

Geometry was the shibboleth which attracted Marshall to the demand and supply tradition; and it was geometry with which neoclassical theory was watered to make it palatable for English tastes. Marshall signaled his predilection in his otherwise grudging review of Jevons's *Theory*: "We owe several valuable suggestions to the many investigations in which skilled mathematicians, English and continental, have applied their favourite method to the treatment of economical problems. But all that has been important in their reasonings and results has, with scarcely an exception, been capable of being described in ordinary language: While the language of diagrams, or, as Professor Fleeming Jenkin calls it, of graphical representation, could have expressed them as tersely and as clearly as that of the mathematics. The latter method . . . is not intelligible to all readers. The book before us would be improved if the mathematics were omitted, but the diagrams retained" (Black 1977, 7:146). What was true in 1870 was still true in 1880, except for

Marshall's private admission that the smooth surfaces of the geometry often served merely as a pedagogical device:

> I think there is room for question whether utilitarians are right in assuming that the end of action is the sum of the happiness of individuals rather than the vigorous life of the whole. As regards the application of practical rather than analytical reasoning in economics, I have not such decided views as you suppose. When tackling a new problem, I generally use analysis, because it is handier: and in the book which I am just going to begin to write I shall retain (in footnotes) a little mathematical analysis for questions which I can't reduce under the grasp of curves. But partly because curves require a special training, partly because they bear more obviously on the science of statistics—I intend never to use analysis when I can use geometry . . . My experience of the exact treatment of supply and demand in inference has been disappointing. The intricacies of the question are so numerous, the difficulties connected with the time element so great, that I have never got any curves relating to it which have satisfied me for many months after I first drew them.[11]

But geometry itself did not render either neoclassicism or the supply and demand organon an empirical or statistical proposition; indeed, as we observe in chapter 15 below, when scholars such as Henry Moore began to fit geometrical curves to real data, Marshall actively discouraged their work. Since geometry did not and could not solve any of the knotty problems in political economy, the question arises: Why the strident insistence upon its central place in the curriculum? We have already touched upon the place of geometry in Victorian Britain as the epitome of self-evident truth and clarity in thought; but the situation at Cambridge was even more peculiar. As another Wrangler reminisced: "In patriotic duty bound, the Cambridge of Newton adhered to Newton's fluxions, to Newton's geometry, to the very text of Newton's *Principia*: in my own Tripos of 1881 we were expected to know any lemma in that great work by its number alone, as if it were one of the commandments or the 100th Psalm. Thus English mathematics were isolated: Cambridge became a school that was self-supporting, self-content, almost marooned in its limitations" (Forsyth 1935, 167). Marshall, second Wrangler in 1865, was a product of this system, which valued rational mechanics over mathematical breadth, down-to-earth geometry over continental analysis, and regimented conformity in puzzle solving and humble prostration before timeless truths over originality. Marshall would have recognized the physics which inspired the novel neoclassical theory, but only just; he certainly was unprepared to innovate along those lines, unlike an Edgeworth (vastly more familiar with advanced mathematics and the continental literature) or a Pareto. Edgeworth saw his counterpart with great clarity: "He would prune whatever was ambitious in mathematical expression or mechanical analogy" (in Pigou 1925, 68). It was this persona of the dour schoolmaster, pruning shears in one hand and scissors in the other, which brought about the textbook reconciliation of the classical trope of supply and demand with the neoclassical image of free-floating energy in commodity space.

15
Problems in
the Paternity of
Econometrics:
Henry Ludwell
Moore

The statistical study of demand is a new field in economics and may be said to be the creation of only one man: Professor Henry L. Moore. —Schultz 1938, 63

[Moore's] name is indissolubly associated with the rise of modern econometrics. —Schumpeter 1954, 876

Oh, Dad, Poor Dad

One very common rhetorical trope of the historian of economic thought is the intellectual genealogy, the search for origins, the attribution of paternity.[1] To become associated with the birth of an intellectual discipline which later proves to flourish and engender further offspring is, of course, one of the premier rewards of science; for many, that alone is sufficient justification for the activities of the historian in rooting out intellectual filiation to its source. Such concerns, however, are not what motivate this chapter.

Paternity suits also play other roles in the social structures of intellectual disciplines, something that numerous historians and philosophers of science have reiterated: capsule biographies of seminal scientists are an inspiration for initiates to the discipline; their reputed procedures are paradigms for later sanctioned research practices; a single figure serves to unify through personification what may have been several scattered unconnected observations; and the persona that we construct for each figure is a sort of speculum, revealing the discipline's image of itself and its place in the constellation of intellectual discourse. For all these reasons, much of what passes as imputed paternity does not qualify as real genealogy, in the sense that concern with larger biographical context is frequently absent, often consciously so (Mirowski 1983), and in many instances the prospective father undergoes a fair amount of cosmetic surgery (if not selective amputation) before assuming the mantle of paterfamilias.

In this chapter we are concerned with the genealogy of something called "econometrics" and its supposed sire, Henry Ludwell Moore. There is much that is incongruous, queer, and artificial about this particular paternity case in the history of economic thought, ranging from an extreme amorphousness of the definition of the offspring to the palpable uneasiness of historians such as George Stigler, Carl Christ, Joseph Schumpeter, and Norman Kaye when confronting the historical persona of Henry Ludwell Moore. When those historians proceed to Moore's most prominent pupil, Henry Schultz, one can almost hear the sighs of relief: here at last is someone who finally got it right. On the contrary, I am not at all sure that Schultz was an improvement upon Moore, mainly because the two had so few points in common with regard to their mastery of the "science" which they so admired, their conceptions of the nature and limits of legitimate explanation, and their beliefs concerning the possibilities of economic explanation that they were, in effect, nonintersecting sets. But if Moore was not the father of "econometrics" or "statistical economics," then what does that imply about the attempts of so many historians to make their paternity suit stick?

"It is not easy to deliminate [sic] econometrics from quantitative economics, statistical economics, and mathematical economics" (Tintner 1953, 31). Indeed it is not at all easy to delimit and distinguish each historically; but such subtle distinctions are the crux of the problem in understanding both Henry Moore and the rise of the discipline of "econometrics." The story that I have been suggesting in this volume concerning supply and demand theories is that mathematical economics began with the importation of mathematical metaphors from mid-nineteenth-century physics; that particular vintage of physics was purely deterministic and had no stochastic aspect. An economics which made reference to stochastic ideas was a later phenomenon, primarily associated with opposition to neoclassical economic theory in the later nineteenth century and the early twentieth, especially in the guises of the historicist program of Wilhelm Lexis and the institutionalist program of Wesley Clair Mitchell and associates. The response to this threat to neoclassical economics, from which vantage point Moore was perceived as just one more challenger, was the melding (but emphatically not the reconciliation) of deterministic and stochastic themes in the 1930s and 1940s into a mélange subsequently dubbed "econometrics," particularly by scholars affiliated with the Cowles Foundation and the fledgling Econometrics Society (Mirowski 1989c). That Moore could be commandeered as the father of a movement which rejected his approach and which he almost certainly would have repudiated is just another instance of the social function of the paternity suit: better to construct a formal façade of One Big Happy Family than to confront the question of the intellectual coherence of modern econometric practices.

The Saga of Henry Ludwell Moore (1869–1958)

Henry Moore was a member of that generation of fledgling American scholars who traveled to Europe to round out their education, aspiring to a level of sophistication which was absent in the American academic scene of that period. Just before taking a PhD in economics from Johns Hopkins in 1896, he attended lectures at the University of Vienna and later took courses in mathematical statistics from Karl Pearson at the University of London. He was apparently fluent in German, French, and Italian, given the evidence of his far-flung correspondence and catholic reading. He was in contact with most of the premier mathematical economists of the day, including Walras, Pareto, Edgeworth, and Bortkiewicz; his first lectures as an instructor at Johns Hopkins in 1896 were on "the application of mathematics to political economy." His early debt to J. B. Clark is apparent in his first published writings on the wage theory of von Thilnen (H. L. Moore 1894) as well as in his later concern to test the theory that wages are apportioned according to the marginal productivity of the laborer (H. L. Moore 1906, 1911). So far, it appears we have here one of the earliest partisans of the neoclassical school of economics in America.

This impression is, at best, only partially correct. If there was an economist whose influence dominated all others in the mind of Henry Moore, it was, curiously enough, Antoine-Augustin Cournot. Moore apparently conceived an enthusiastic appreciation of Cournot in the first few years of the twentieth century, to the extent of writing an exegesis of his work for the American audience (H. L. Moore 1905a) and proposing to find a publisher for Cournot's intellectual autobiography (Walras 1965, 3, letter 1549). In his later writings (e.g., 1914, 86; 1922, 8; 1929, 4) he rarely missed a chance to praise Cournot, even while bypassing Walras, Pareto, and Edgeworth or perhaps gracing them with less enthusiastic references.

Since Cournot is often misidentified in histories of economic thought as the progenitor of the neoclassical demand curve, it may help to apply some distinctions to Cournot to bring Moore into better focus. As I have argued in chapters 13 and 14, Cournot's loi de débit or "law of sales" diverges in significant ways from the neoclassical demand curve of later vintage. First, and most importantly, Cournot does not derive the curve from the constrained maximization of utility; indeed he does not derive the curve at all, but rather posits it as an unexplained phenomenological regularity, rather of the same character as Newton's inverse-square law of attraction. "Since so many moral causes capable of neither enumeration nor measurement affect the loi de débit . . . [o]bservation must therefore be depended on for furnishing the means of drawing up between proper limits a table of the corresponding values of D and p; after which, by the well-known methods of interpolation or by graphic processes, an empiric formula or a curve can be made to represent the function in question" (Cournot [1838] 1897, 47–48).

But Cournot was not simply or exclusively an economic writer; he was much better known in his own day as a philosopher, in particular as a philosopher of probabilities and chance. He wrote in his *Essai sur les fondements de la connaissance* of 1851 that "in general, any scientific theory, conceived in order to bind together a certain number of facts found by observation, can be likened to the curve which one draws according to a mathematical definition, imposing on it the condition that it pass by a certain number of points given in advance" (quoted in Floss 1941, 17). Indeed Moore was drawn to quote a passage from Cournot's "Exposition de la théorie des chances et probabilités" where the natural laws of physics and of society were to be united by a single method of induction, that of statistics (H. L. Moore 1908, 4). Yet it is not often realized that Cournot did not actually apply his touted statistical method to his very own "law of sales" because of the great difficulty of deciding what constituted a significant correlation in a situation where the complex interdependence of social variables in the economic sphere could not begin to be untangled (Ménard 1980, 531). Cournot opined in the "Essai" that "the acts of living, intelligent and moral beings are in no way explicable, and there are good reasons to believe that they will never be explicable, in terms of mechanics and geometry" (in Floss 1941, 65).

The importance of situating Cournot in the nineteenth-century landscape is to bring into sharper focus how very much he set the research agenda for Henry Moore. The predominant influence was philosophical: Cournot had seen probability as the great unifying concept of the natural and social sciences; probability was not a subjective phenomenon but rather the result of combining long chains of causal deterministic structures which had developed independently of one another. Cournot's pioneering application of the mathematics of early rational mechanics to political economy merely opened the way to the formalization of those long causal chains as a prelude to the application of inductive—that is, statistical—procedures. Others, such as Walras, Pareto, and Marshall, sought to extend the formalist and rationalist aspect of Cournot, as Moore was well aware. Early in his career, before he began his statistical studies, he even wrote, "not only does Cournot not expound the law of diminishing utility with the corollary as to money, but his entire omission of the subject constitutes one of the defects of his great masterpiece" (H. L. Moore 1905b, 347). But as time went on, Moore reversed this initial evaluation and increasingly came round to Cournot's full-fledged position, namely that the reduction of mind to mechanics was an error.

In 1902 Moore moved from Smith College to Columbia University, where in 1906 he became a professor of political economy.[2] It was only in 1906 that he actually began in his research to employ economic data in correlation exercises; his paper in the *Quarterly Journal of Economics* of 1908 finds him in the role of proselytizer to the discipline, cannily arguing for a "statistical complement of pure economics," where pure economics meant the tradition of Jevons, Walras, and Pareto. Yet even at this early stage Moore showed signs of veering away from the orthodox neoclassical positions, especially with respect to the rather outdated notions of "science" found in the texts of those writers. For instance, the paper of 1908 has references to William James, John Dewey, and the philosophical movement of pragmatism, which was later to become the house doctrine of Mitchell's institutionalist movement (Mirowski 1988, chapter 7). Moore's reading equated pragmatism with Cournot's earlier doctrine of the essence of science as being pragmatic curve-fitting. Further, when it came to discussing Pareto, it was the infamous Pareto law of incomes, rather than the abstract price theory, which came in for particular praise: "Professor Pareto's law of income is a purely empirical law, for whose origin Pareto has not offered an explanation. His procedure has been similar to the procedure in physical science in which such laws as those of Boyle, Gay-Lussac, and Avogadro were at first established as purely empirical results. But just as one of the most fertile and characteristic developments of physics since the early work of Clerk Maxwell has been the rational deduction of those and similar laws from a molecular theory, so likewise has a movement appeared in economics in which an attempt is made to derive from the principles of pure economics the laws established by empirical methods" (H. L. Moore 1908, 28). This doctrine, minus the bridges built to "pure" or neoclassical economics, later became one of the hallmarks of the Columbia/NBER approach to economics: the insistence on the primacy of empirical regularities, the citation of statistical mechanics as evidence of a novel stochastic approach and a more modern epistemology of science, and the subordination of mathematical formalism to a pragmatic problem-driven approach to research methods. This position was repeated essentially verbatim nearly twenty years later by another Columbia economist, Frederick Mills.[3]

However, pragmatism did not mean a disdain for mathematical economics. Moore was rightfully proud of his own mastery of neoclassical theory and its implications and significance, which he was convinced should not be overstated. For instance, in a letter to his colleague Edwin Seligman, Moore wrote, "It was a surprise to me to find what extremely elementary teaching is done by Pantaleoni and Benini at the University of Rome. The level is not higher than an undergraduate standard. . . . Barone, however, makes ridiculous claims for the mathematical method. Results are stated as having been discovered by that method which I learned from Professor Clark fifteen or more years ago."[4]

In the years from 1906 to 1911 Moore set out to provide empirical evidence for the productivity theory of wages he had absorbed from J. B. Clark and to demonstrate the efficacy of the "statistical complement." Articles by Moore appeared in the *Political Science Quarterly*, the *Economic Journal*, and the *Journal of the Royal Statistical Society* and were republished in revised form in his first book, *Laws of Wages* (1911). Moore's "efficiency theory of wages" was an attempt to link biological characteristics of workers to the structure of wages, an attempt prompted by the work of Karl Pearson on biometric distributions of characters and attributes. Moore prepared two frequency distributions from wages data, one using Pearson's method of moments, the other a modified normal distribution; their differences, he claimed, demonstrated that wage distributions more closely resembled distributions of "attributes" than of output or time worked (for none of which he possessed the explicit data). In a separate exercise using French data he also attempted to see, by calculating a correlation coefficient across departments, whether wages of unskilled laborers were determined by costs of subsistence; he found no relationship of cause and effect, because the correlation coefficient was only 0.306 (1911, 32). Further correlation coefficients were calculated to relate wages to strike activity and capital investment. Moore's conclusions were predominantly conservative, claiming that "these inductive findings . . . reinforce the belief that, so far as the welfare of the laborer is concerned, concentration of industry is no ground for the socialization of industry" (1911, 194). All in all, by today's standards it was rather a modest exercise; but for its time it was the first systematic attempt to construct a statistical hurdle for existing economic theory in such a way that some competing hypotheses might potentially be rejected.

Given Moore's patience in explaining in painful detail every step of his procedure, his politically conservative results, his respectful attitude toward the orthodox marginalist economics, his advocacy of mathematical and statistical methods, and his characteristic modesty about the permanent truth of his conclusions, he had every right to expect a favorable response from the members of the economics profession who were predisposed toward those categories. Precisely for that reason he was all the more taken aback by the response he got from some of the key mathematical neoclassical economists.

First, there was the review of *Laws of Wages* by Edgeworth that was particularly critical of the efficiency wage chapter, swatting Moore's work aside with such choice aperçus as "Not only has he employed a steam-engine to crack a nut; but the nut is blind" and "The thinness of his conclusion is disguised by adventitious involutions. The general reader fails to recognize the familiar properties of the normal law, owing to certain peculiarities in our author's presentation of the subject; much as the candidates at a certain elementary mathematical examination who had become primed with propositions about 'triangles' were staggered by a paper in which the questions related to 'right lines joining any three points' " (Edgeworth 1912, 70).

But those who read the published exchange only saw half the story. Moore also received a letter from Alfred Marshall, dated 5 June 1912, which would have unnerved any recipient:

> I will be frank. I have had your book on Laws of Wages in a prominent place near my writing chair ever since it arrived, intending to read it when the opportunity came. It has not come; and I fear it will never come. For what dips I have made into the book made me believe that it proceeds on lines which I had deliberately decided not to follow many years ago; even before mathematics had ceased to be a familiar language to me. My reasons for it are mainly two: (1) No important economic chain of events seems to [*sic*] likely be associated with any one cause so predominantly that a study of the concomitant variation of the two can be made as well by mathematics, as by a comparison of a curve representing these two elements with a larger number of other curves representing the other operative causes: the "ceteris paribus" clause—though formally adequate seems to me impracticable. (2) Nearly a half of the whole operative economic causes have refused as yet to be tabulated statistically.
>
> I have worked at the comparative diagrammatic method . . . persistently: and each of the last forty years has confirmed in me the belief that your method is not likely to have practical fruit for a long while. I am extremely glad you (& I hope others) are working on it; it may do good practical work in your lifetime; but I feel sure it will not in mine.[5]

And then, as if that would not be sufficient to demolish any reasonably robust ego, Marshall opted for overkill. In a postscript to this letter he ventured that he had "plucked up" his "courage to perhaps a point where it should be called rash, or even impudent, audacity" by enclosing a private letter from Edgeworth to Marshall, which was clearly never meant to be seen by anyone else, and most certainly not by Moore. It was dated 16 January 1912, and read:

> Moore is a nightmare to me. I know I must write to him and I am afraid. I do not doubt he is of great ability; nor that his work will be of great service to economics. But his whole work is one prolonged dancing on what has been the most tender of my beloved corns since 1875.

As I think you know, the use of economic statistical talk in pairs of the extreme free traders and extreme protectionists in the USA set the corn growing. I think I have spent more time studying this particular source of fallacies than any one that ever lived. And I am a red hot fanatic about it. . . .

So you will bear in mind that all these pictures and decimals and learned terms are intended to prepare the way for a future generation of workers, who can put all the faith I have just mentioned, into a group of mathematical machines & turn the handles. But neither our statistics nor our mathematics is ready for this work. We are like the first assailants of a fortified position, our corpses will fill the trenches so that Moore can get on. . . .

He seems to me to have only proved that there was some sort of causal connection in cases in which no one would doubt that there was one: & to have reached results not really as helpful practically as those which I could have got by looking at the world with wide open eyes for a few minutes. . . . Here are two elements which probably bear some causal connection either as father & son, or as brothers and cousins. Now if you assume that neither of these has [any] causal relations with any other changing element, they may be simply put into a statistico-mathematical machine & the result worked out to n places or decimals. But of course this is mere play. In fact there may be many other causal relations: & therefore any results in reference to the real world may have errors not of .5 or .7 per cent, but of 50 or 70 per cent.

Such scorn could not have come at a more vulnerable moment. Moore had been casting about for support for his statistical program of economic research since 1907. For instance, he had solicited Walras for his opinion of statistical tests of "pure economics" in 1908 (Walras 1965, letter 1685); he never received an answer, perhaps because Walras was never that much enamored of statistics (Ménard 1980, 534–35), or perhaps because the self-pity of those convinced of their unjustly neglected genius rarely has room for sympathy for another, different species of neglected genius. As Moore wrote to Henry Schultz in another context: "On the 23rd of June 1903 Walras was deeply affected so he recalled how frequently his effort to get a just consideration of his work had proved futile. I did my utmost to restore his dragging spirit and used as one of my arguments my opinion that it would take 50 years for a [? method] so new, so difficult, so in conflict with prevailing schools to make its way to a point where it would be placed at its true value. His spirit bounded at once. You are entirely right he said, even to the number of years and he referred to a similar remark by Laplace about Laplace's own theories."[6]

As time went on and those who could reasonably have been expected to be Moore's allies seemed from his vantage point to desert him and even vilify him in his hour of need, Moore came increasingly to identify with this fatalistic posture; he never struck back at his tormentors but only further buried himself in the advancement of the project of what he regarded as a scientific stochastic economics. He took a drastic cut in pay in the academic year 1909–10 to free up more time for research, a move he later came to regret.[7] Nevertheless the slurs did have one pronounced effect: Moore clearly began to sour on the core propositions of neoclassical value theory. It is primarily this phenomenon which sets him apart from Schultz and the rest of the econometrics movement.

It seems that in this period Moore began to make a distinction between the mathematical economics of utility and other alternative forms of mathematical formalism. This distinction showed up first in his lecture notes. In one place he discussed "Edgeworth's attempts to get a Mechanique sociale to correspond with Lagrange's Mechanique Analytique"; in another he lectured on "economic utilitarianism in their [sic] historical relations and interaction."[8] The notes for the latter read:

> (1) Utilitarianism—a science of ethics originally—is made a psychology. Economists tacitly assume in their theory of utility that what the older economists preached we ought to do, we do. They assume that whenever a choice is made, the individual makes the choice because to him the act would afford greater utility. (a) ignores "absolute utilities." (b) ignores influence of impulse in action.
>   (2) Wherever psychological questions are considered they tend to be considered under the tacit assumption of a static state. (a) Marshall's estimate of consumer's rent. . . . (b) Menger's estimate of [?] of consumption of two commodities a mere adding up of their respective utilities. (c) fallacy of Menger's in estimating value of production goods.

This critique continued in his lectures on the "mathematical treatment of belief and the mathematical treatment of pleasure and pain." He cited Venn and Patten to the effect that the theory of probabilities did not generally apply to the psychology of belief, and hence theorists such as Marshall who resorted to probability theory as a vehicle to incorporate future estimations of pleasure and pain into their utilitarian theory were mistaken. To an increasing extent Moore suspected that the mathematical program of stochastic economics bore no necessary connection to the mathematical program of neoclassical price theory.

Hints of reservations first made their appearance in print in Moore's next book, *Economic Cycles: Their Law and Cause* (1914). This, the most famous of his books, is also the most unjustly maligned: "He apparently had no idea of the identification problem" (Christ 1985, 43); "The present day economist would complain to Moore that he was mixing up supply and demand relationships . . . it did not yield the demand function of economic theory" (Stigler 1962, 13); "it seems evident that Moore assumed the exogenous changes in supply would trace out the demand curve" (Epstein 1987, 16). This is History According to the Cowles Commission Worldview: Moore supposedly intended to estimate Marshallian demand curves, but because he left out the supply functions and did not understand problems of simultaneous estimation, he ended up erroneously claiming to have found an upward-sloping demand curve for pig iron.

But that is not the way Moore would have seen it at all. Having been badly burned by Marshall, he was in no mood to estimate Marshallian demand curves. Indeed *Economic Cycles* bristles with contempt for Marshallian theory: "the doctrine of the uniformity of the demand function is an idol of the static state—of the method of caeteris paribus—which has stood in the way of the successful treatment of concrete dynamic problems. . . . The fruitfulness of the statistical theory of correlation stands in significant contrast to the vast barrenness of the method that has just been described" (H. L. Moore 1914, 64, 67). Moore's primary objection was that theorists such as Marshall and Edgeworth had dealt superficially in the language and rhetoric of science but had abused its structure. Since Moore is so roundly misrepresented, it is worthwhile to quote him at length on this issue:

In the closing quarter of the last century great hopes were entertained by economists with regard to the capacity of economics to be made an "exact science." According to the view of the foremost theorists, the development of the doctrines of utility and value had lain [*sic*] the foundation of scientific economics in exact concepts, and it would be possible to erect upon the new foundation a firm structure of interrelated parts which, in definiteness and cogency, would be suggestive of the severe beauty of the mathematicophysical sciences. But this expectation has not been realized. . . .

It was assumed gratuitously that economics was to be modeled on the simpler mathematical, physical sciences, and this assumption created a prejudice at the outset both in selecting the data to be investigated and in conceiving the types of laws that were to be the object of research. Economics was to be a "calculus of pleasure and pain," a "mechanics of utility," a "social mechanics," a "physique sociale." . . . The biased point of view implied in these descriptions led to an undue stressing of those aspects of science which seemed to bear out the pretentious metaphors. One would naturally suppose from this manner of conceiving the science that the economic theorists would at once

have entered upon their task with the methods that had proved themselves useful in the physical sciences. But this they did not do. They
seemed to identify the method of the physical sciences with experimentation, and since, as they held, scientific experimentation is impossible
in social life, a special method had to be devised. This invention was a
disguised form of the classical caeteris paribus, the method of the static
state. (1914, 84–85)

Perhaps this critique might be rendered a bit clearer by recourse to the
narrative found in Mirowski 1989b, chapter 5. The theory of the constrained
optimization of utility was appropriated from the nineteenth-century physics of energy, but its use had a number of deleterious effects on economic
theory. First, it locked the profession into an awkward metaphorical psychology of utilitarianism and diverted attention from empirically accessible
economic variables. Second, the appropriation was incomplete, since without simultaneous adoption of the relevant conservation principles, the resulting mathematical structure was bereft of the analogous dynamics found
in rational mechanics. Instead of admitting this flaw to be fatal to a scientific
theory, the neoclassicals had attempted to paper over the hole with the
ceteris paribus condition; but all that did was restrict all statements to a
completely nonspecific static state, rendering all change arbitrary and analytically intractable and therefore all empiricism irredeemably impotent.
Thus, ironically, the neoclassicals were praising science extravagantly while
obstructing all attempts at empirical inquiry.

What Moore was doing in *Economic Cycles* was proposing an alternative
program of mathematical economics, a rival to neoclassicism. The program
was predicated on his earlier advocacy of his version of pragmatism, namely
that "for most of the problems of actual life, it is unnecessary to face the
complex possible interrelation of phenomena contemplated in the [neo-
classical] theoretical treatment" (1914, 82). His method of circumventing the
existing ersatz social physics was to ground his theory in actual physics;
or, as he wrote, "the control of phenomena dependent upon a cycle presupposes that the cycle is itself a real phenomenon with a natural cause"
(1914, 18).

The process of explanation in economic cycles consisted of a number of
discrete steps. First, using the most sophisticated time series techniques
of his day, such as Fourier decomposition and the Schuster periodogram,
Moore searched for the "natural" origin of fixed periodicities and believed
that he had discovered them in an eight-year cycle of rainfall. The next step
was to demonstrate a causal link between periodic fluctuations in rainfall
and in crop yields. Here what he was aiming at was something like cross-
spectral analysis (which did not as yet exist); for this purpose he invented a

statistic which he called the "K coefficient."[9] Convinced that he had demonstrated an adequate connection between rainfall and yields per acre, he next set out to find some Cournot-style "statistical laws of demand." Here he regressed percentage changes in the prices of hay, oats, and potatoes on a cubic polynomial in the percentage changes in yields per acre, obtaining downward-sloping functions. Finally, he regressed percentage changes in the price of pig iron on percentage change in its production, obtaining what he called "a new type of demand curve," one which sloped upward (H. L. Moore 1914, 110–16). Because of the widespread acceptance of the History According to the Cowles Commission Worldview, it is critical to note Moore's admission that "in all likelihood it will be said that what we have achieved is not exactly what the partisans of the method of caeteris paribus proposed" (1914, 87).

The reason why this was not neoclassicism is that it had nothing to do with the underlying determinants of neoclassical price theory and in fact resembled rather more the later stochastic aggregative exercises of Keynesian macroeconomics. In Moore's theory, periodic rainfall drove periodic fluctuations in crop yields, which in turn drove the entire aggregate volume of trade. Because contractions in output in the producer goods sector (his notorious upward-sloping "demand curve") implied falling prices, Moore thought he could round out the picture by linking falling producer goods output and prices to falling employment, falling agricultural demand, and thus a general fall in prices (1914, 114–16). Because feedbacks were kept to a minimum (admittedly more by fiat than by logic), one could regard this structure as simply Wold-recursive, with the "first cause" arising in the exogenous natural world. It was, quite simply, the first structural model of the macroeconomy, empirically implemented by statistical techniques.

Roughly the next ten years of Moore's professional existence were spent subjecting each of the links in his cycle theory to ever finer scrutiny. Forecasting the yield and price of cotton (1917) was expressly intended to improve the specification of the connection between weather and crop yield; only as a sideline did it revamp the way the Department of Agriculture produced its crop forecasts. "Generating economic cycles" (1923) took the mandate of driving explanation back to fully natural causes to ever greater lengths; as he wrote there, "However ingenious may be the mathematical methods that are used to isolate periodicities, there will always be a healthy skepticism as to the reality of the cycles unless true causes are adduced. Mere empirical regularities are always suspect" (11). Since Moore's earlier work had met with much skepticism concerning the strict periodicity of rainfall (15), in this volume he attempted to locate the cause of his eight-year cycles in the transit of Venus—that is, the interval of time between successive conjunctions of the sun, Venus, and the Earth. Not satisfied merely to collect instances of eight-year cycles, he then collected citations on recent advances in solar physics and cathode rays to suggest that solar emissions may ionize gases even at such long distances and that those gaseous ions might serve as nuclei for the condensation of water vapor (117).

No historian in the interim has given measured consideration to just how serious Moore was about the natural determination of fluctuations. He was much more knowledgeable in the scientific literature of his time than any of his peers; his writings are liberally sprinkled with quotes from Fourier, Duhem, Lodge, Clerk Maxwell, Poynting, Stokes, and Arrhenius, not to mention lesser-known writers in *Proceedings of the National Academy of Sciences*, *Transactions of the Royal Society*, and *Philosophical Magazine*. When he was engaged in statistical exercises, he employed the best practices of the time, which meant he was not a credulous virtuoso of the one-note ordinary least squares regression, as were so many of those who came later. Indeed, as late as 1936 Edwin Bidwell Wilson could write in a letter: "I know of no study subsequent to that of Moore which has approached his command of statistical techniques."[10] Moreover, Moore had respected precursors in all the lines of inquiry which constituted his cycle theory: even the weather connection had been pioneered by the physicist Poynting (1884) and William Stanley Jevons (H. L. Moore 1923, 111). So why was his Venus theory regarded by all as embarrassing (Stigler 1962, 11)?

It is not obvious that an appeal to the weather to justify the existence of macroeconomic disruption is a breach of intellectual decorum. After all, thirty years later Koopmans in an unpublished memo to the Cowles researchers rated weather the most important "source of randomness" in the economy, above biological vectors, human error, fads, labor unions, and other spanners in the works.[11] Further, the correlation between rainfall and macroeconomic indicators persists down to the present day (Hendry 1980, 395). No, the taboo behavior which exiles weather theories such as Jevons's sunspots or Moore's transit of Venus to the margins of discourse is symptomatic of a sociological problem specific to neoclassical economics (Mirowski 1988, chapter 3).

In an economic theory patterned upon the physics of inanimate objects, coordination of economic endeavor is implied to have come about "naturally"; that is one of the prominent functions of the physics metaphor. Immediately a problem arises as to how one should encompass the possibility of systemic disruption within this discourse; for the natural character of coordination to be preserved, the disturbing causes or "shocks" must also be of "natural" provenance. It is a short step to indictment of the weather as an eminently natural but external perturbation. But here is where the rhetorical considerations of the theory loom in importance: there exists the temptation to ground the weather in its natural physical determinants, and especially in astronomical phenomena, as one can observe with Jevons and Moore. This is an anathema to the neoclassical program, not because it is either true or false in some sense but rather because the resulting causal explanation smacks too much of astrology. It would not matter if "scientific proof" of celestial determinants of terrestrial phenomena were forthcoming: the problem is cultural. Astrology is taboo because it represents in the minds of many the paradigm pseudo-science (Wallis 1979); this in itself is a function of the cultural history of astronomy and physics; and since neoclassicism copied physics to guarantee its scientific status in the first place, flirting with anything that even remotely looked like astrology threatened to unravel the entire research program. Hence the double bind created by the cultural imperatives of scientificity dictated that Moore's theory could be only reviled, not seriously entertained.

Yet Moore's position by the 1920s was different. Having little attachment to the neoclassical program, he was free to ignore its rhetorical dictates. In place of the indirect metaphorical reference made in the neoclassical theory of the constrained optimization of utility, he derived the justification for his research program from direct linkage to existing physics and astronomy. This is not to say that criticism could not be made of his handling of the specifically statistical and mathematical issues (Wright 1924; Ingraham 1923); that would merely be the expected "normal science" response. I believe that Moore was taken aback instead by the ridicule directed at him in the popular press, derived from the taint of astrology, and by the accusations from colleagues that he misunderstood "theory." Even his friend John Maurice Clark seemed to misunderstand him: "at present I admit I'm baffled when a student fishes for a demand schedule, and pulls up something that turns out to have more claims to be called a supply schedule; and still more when you suggest that the distinction is merely a matter of what you choose to call it."[12] In any event the widespread rebukes led to the third and final phase of Moore's research, that which culminated in his proclaiming a new "synthetic economics."

In the early 1920s Moore decided to relinquish Cournot's position that the demand curve could be treated as a purely phenomenological matter. However, again, this did not mean capitulation to neoclassical price theory; rather, it meant that the time had arrived for the explicit derivation of the functional form of the demand curve without recourse to utility maximization. In 1922 Moore claimed that the simplest possible demand curve would be one where the "elasticity of demand" was a linear function of the quantity sold, which after integration gave $\log p = \alpha \log q + \beta q + \log$ (constant). Later he wrote out the conditions for a dynamic or "moving" equilibrium as opposed to the static equilibrium of neoclassical economics (1926b). The demand curves were constructed using the derivation of 1922 and abjuring any linkage to utility; Moore maintained that his equations were dynamic because the variables were written as ratios relative to trend, as they had been in most of his previous empirical work. At this juncture he did relent and posit parallel supply functions, derived from production functions through the marginal productivity conditions and written in terms of trend ratios. Most significantly, he regarded the resulting set of equations as able to account for nonperiodic fluctuations: "Economic oscillations, other than periodic oscillations or cycles properly so-called, are the consequences of statical forces compelling the economic system towards a moving general equilibrium" (1926b, 29). While he did not say so explicitly, this structure was intended to round out the empirical theory of macroeconomic fluctuations: any fluctuations of an empirical economic variable could be decomposed into its periodic components, traced to weather cycles, and its nonperiodic components, construed as evidence of stabilizing forces counteracting displacements from a moving equilibrium itself determined by external physical forces such as technology and population growth.

Moore was proud of the resulting theoretical edifice, which he was convinced was a profound advance upon neoclassical theory. Because it was a mathematical theory of general equilibrium which started from empirical reality, encompassing both change and stochastic disturbance, he dubbed it "synthetic economics" (H. L. Moore 1929). It was not Marshallian; he was quite clear on that score (1929, 8). It also avoided the sterility of Walras's and Pareto's versions of pure economics (29). *Synthetic Economics* did not contain an actual statistical estimation of the entire system; perhaps Moore felt he had already pointed the way in that direction, or perhaps he drew back from mentioning once more the need to trace the periodic movements back to Venus as a necessary complement to the nonperiodic oscillations attributed to the convergence to equilibrium in the model. Nevertheless, because there is no explicit statistical component in this last phase, it is roundly ignored by all those only interested in Moore as the "father" of econometrics.

At this point a number of external influences converged to bring Moore's research project to an end. As early as 1917 he had written to his chairman, Edwin Seligman, that he had "been in the position of a lonely pioneer in the midst of a threatening storm, fearing that his house will come down about his head and his small possessions be swept from him."[13] Something like that subsequently happened: his research position was stripped from him in the fall of 1918, in exchange for designating him the chair of the department of economics and sociology at Barnard; his teaching load was increased, and worse, he was required to abandon teaching mathematical and statistical economics for courses in sociology and the history of feminism.[14] There also seems to have been some growing friction with Wesley Clair Mitchell, whose work on business cycles had been much more successful within the profession and who had spurned Moore's weather theory and the use of periodograms in economic analysis (Mitchell 1927, 259–60). Moore, never one to stand up well to adversity, fell prey to severe attacks of colitis in the 1920s and suffered something akin to a nervous breakdown in November 1927.[15] He retired from Columbia in April 1929 at fifty-nine, just before the publication of *Synthetic Economics*; from then until his death in 1958 he took part in no further academic activities, published nothing further, and neither accepted nor declined the honor of being elected one of the first fellows of the newly formed Econometrics Society in 1933.

There is a coda to this story, one not found in any of the previous histories of Moore's economic contributions. It seems that the experience of teaching sociology was taken much more seriously by Moore than one might initially suspect; his papers show that he wrestled mightily trying to understand the place of his synthetic economics in an even larger theory of social action. For instance, in April 1924 he began to write a paper on Pareto entitled "Fascism: A Sociological Interpretation." After his retirement he embarked upon one final book, to be called either *The Good Life in a Progressive Democracy* or *Order and Unity of Society and the Theory of Social Equilibrium*. Large portions of the manuscript were finished, but then in the 1940s Moore decided that no part of the work was to be published.[16] One can only concur with Moore's judgment here: its publication would not have helped his already battered reputation; moreover, the work is neither a deep nor a sensitive attempt to bring psychological motivation within the ambit of his synthetic economics. However, it does further illustrate two theses of this chapter: that a utilitarian basis for mathematical economics is firmly rejected; and that Moore had an epistemology very different from that of his successors:

> The present essay is an answer to the question with which the final chapter of Synthetic economics closes. . . . The criterion of truth we showed to be: in the case of economic certainties, logical consistency with definitively formulated axioms, postulates and conventions; in the case of economic possibilities, relative frequency of occurrence in empirical data; in the case of economic dreams, conformity with our sentiments, wishes and interests. . . . In the former essay, after having shown how the combination of economic certainties and economic possibilities supplies the means of forecasting and control of economic phenomena, we asked the question: Control with reference to what? The answer given by contemporary societies is, we suggested, generally clothed in some myth, dream or fantasy rationalizing the will to power and wealth on the part of a smaller or larger group within the society.[17]

Eine kleine Schultzmusik

To complement my argument that Henry Moore needs to be taken a bit more seriously in his own context, the dictates of symmetry demand that some indication be given why Henry Schultz might be regarded with something less than unadulterated homage. Schultz was a Pole who emigrated to the United States in 1907, took an A.B. from CCNY in 1916, and then began his studies under Moore at Columbia. After serving in the army in the First World War, he resumed his studies at the London School of Economics and University College under Arthur Bowley and Karl Pearson, returning to take his PhD from Columbia in 1925. He often professed his gratitude and appreciation of Moore's work in print (Schultz 1928, viii; 1933), and this has led many historians and economists to infer that they were partisans of the same research program, namely the one that resulted in modern "econometrics." However, their work was profoundly divergent, in such a manner that what makes Schultz different also makes him much less interesting.[18]

During his time at Columbia and at the precursor of the Brookings Institution, Schultz had conceived a strong aversion to the school of institutionalist economics; and as part of this reaction, he took to the estimation of the demand curve with a redoubled zeal: "Some economists, among whom are to be included not a few members of the institutional school, have, unfortunately, gotten the impression that any attempt to derive a law of demand must needs be based on no better psychology than that of James Mill. A few of them go so far as to deny the existence of the law of demand"(Schultz 1928, 95). But to justify the existence and stability of some such "law" out there susceptible to estimation, Schultz was driven to depend more and more upon the structure of neoclassical theory. In his final book he admitted that doing so entailed a strong divergence from his mentor: "[Moore] could not, as do most of his critics, accept the Cournot-Marshall demand curve at its face value. He questioned the assumptions underlying it, and he did not wish to give it much prominence in his own theoretical structure. To him the problem was much more complex, namely, how to derive the general dynamic demand function from statistical observations" (Schultz 1938, 82).

But this problem of dynamics, with all its central implications for the viability of an economic empiricism, is precisely where Schultz fell down; and he stumbled because of his dependence upon neoclassical theory. Even after he finished his thesis, Schultz was skeptical of Moore's synthetic solution to dynamics; in a letter of 19 December 1924 he wrote to Moore asking "why, in deriving a dynamic law of demand, is it necessary to resort to relative quantities and relative prices? Why may we not correlate the absolute observed quantities with the absolute observed prices?"[19] Unwilling to accept Moore's phenomenological approach, Schultz looked to neoclassical theory to guide his estimation choices; but little guidance was forthcoming. There is, for instance, the embarrassing spectacle of his not knowing what should be regressed upon what (Schultz 1928, 36–38). Schultz reported both price regressed on quantity and vice versa, since his theory gave no justification for the stochastic terms; and he was unfamiliar with early work on the errors in variables approach (Epstein 1987, 22). This was embarrassing because the alternatives generally gave widely varying estimates of the elasticities involved, calling into question the existence of that independent lawlike structure. But if the stochastic terms seemed to dangle perilously about without rationale, the problem of the existence of invariants was even worse.

By the early 1930s Schultz had stumbled upon the fact that neoclassical theory did place some restrictions upon the format of the demand functions and that this had something to do with the integrability conditions. There exists an extensive correspondence between Harold Hotelling and Schultz stretching from 1932 to 1935, in which the two try to rediscover those conditions (which dated back to the work of Antonelli in 1881) and work out their economic meaning.[20] The importance of this issue for econometrics was that the absence of integrability restrictions made the evolution of the system ineluctably path-dependent: in other words, there would be no time-independent laws to be found, no deterministic dynamic regularities to be recovered, and everyone looking for laws of demand would just be chasing after a will-o'-the-wisp (Mirowski 1989b, chapter 7). After years of grappling with this problem, Schultz's final resolution left much to be desired. In *The Theory and Measurement of Demand* (1938) he first insists that integrability is not all that important, then admits that he must generally assume measurable utility for his purposes of estimation (and hence the integrability conditions)—only then to write: "But what equations of motion and what laws of conservation of comparable scope do we have in economics? To ask the question is to answer it. There are none that have the definiteness and universal demonstrability of the corresponding physical laws . . . we can think of the total utility function—if it exists—as corresponding to the energy potential whose partial derivatives measure the forces which guide the movements of the individual. But, unfortunately, we know neither the values nor the forms of the required functions" (57).

The contrast with Moore could not be greater. Moore knew that the neoclassical imitation of energy physics was spurious and therefore understood that it could not provide any solid basis for an empirical economic inquiry, much less a full-fledged stochastic and dynamic economics. Schultz took his whole life to discover that the analogy with potential energy was spurious, but by that time he had invested so much effort in his "theory and measurement of demand" that he went right ahead and persisted in his entirely baseless procedure of "estimating" neoclassical "laws of demand" to the bitter end. This alone, I would argue, signifies that Moore's understanding of science was much more profound than that of Schultz: it was not the mathematics that rendered an inquiry "scientific," but rather the sure grasp of the metaphoric vision of explanation in a particular historical context. But then again, as the story of Moore shows, that is still no guarantee of success, much less of respect in one's own lifetime.

16

Refusing the Gift

These English psychologists—what do they really want? One always discovers them voluntarily or involuntarily at the same task, namely at dragging the *partie honteuse* of our inner world into the foreground and seeking the truly effective and directing agent, that which has been decisive in its evolution, in just that place where the intellectual pride of man would least *desire* to find it . . . what is it that really always drives these psychologists in just this direction? Is it a secret, malicious, vulgar, perhaps self-deceiving instinct for belittling man? Or possibly a pessimistic suspicion, the mistrustfulness of the disappointed idealists grown spiteful and gloomy? Or a petty subterranean hostility and rancor toward Christianity (and Plato) that has not even crossed the threshold of consciousness? . . . The way they have bungled their moral genealogy comes to light at the very beginning, where the task is to investigate the origin of the concept and judgment "good" . . . One sees straightaway that this primary derivation already contains all the typical traits of the idiosyncrasy of the English psychologists—we have "utility," "forgetting," "habit," and finally "error," all as a basis of an evaluation of which the higher man has hitherto been proud as though it were a kind of prerogative of man as such. This pride has to be humbled, this evaluation disvalued: has that end been achieved?—Nietzsche 1967, 24–25

These neoclassical economists—what do they really want? There have been times—and it may have also happened to you—when they say something whose audacity and sheer philistinism just takes my breath away. And I don't mean those sources of garden-variety outrage, as when they claim that the sale of their kidneys by the Filipino destitute is good for their future because it allows them to accumulate capital, or it is useless for the government to mandate seatbelts in passenger autos because people just end up driving more recklessly to "compensate." No, if you happen to be in this business, you rapidly grow inured to a certain level of humdrum apologetics for corporate rapacity; apparently economists unconsciously extrude these gems in prescient advance of their clients' needs. Rather, what I refer to here is closer to what Nietzsche meant when describing the utilitarians: the production of moral genealogies whose whole purpose seems to be to debase any little piety or sympathy left in our fragmented infoculture. Economists revel in their capacity to be "more hard-boiled than thou": no one will ever catch them succumbing to smarmy sentimentality (will they?). Examples could easily be multiplied, but here we shall restrict ourselves to surveying how neoclassical economists talk about "gifts."

I choose an article from the recent *American Economic Review* which by its very triviality elevates the problem into heightened contrast. The topic is an article by Joel Waldfogel called "The Deadweight Loss of Christmas." Any well-trained economist will be able to reconstruct the argument from the bare title alone. Briefly, it is a dogma among neoclassicals that any transfer of resources which was not "chosen" by the recipient through the market will generally be inefficient, by some optimality criteria which we can thankfully ignore for our present purposes. That people give gifts rather than cash equivalents at Christmas fits this paradigm; and Waldfogel proceeds to retail a little "empiricism lite" to offer up his result that "holiday gift-giving destroys between 10 per cent and a third of the value of the gifts." His sense of timing meshing closely with his comic genius, he proceeds to hammer his punchline: "a conservative estimate of the deadweight loss of Christmas is a tenth as large as estimates of the deadweight loss of income taxation," another institution of modern life which conventionally does not meet with the approval of the neoclassical economist. We could also go into detail about the ceremonial function of the attendant regression analysis, as well as his witty synecdoche comparing gift giving to risk aversion, but all this would merely distract us from the primary question.

What is it that we want from neoclassical economists? You might say that this was all a *jeu d'esprit*, the kind of economist's joke one has to endure at conventions of the American Economics Association; but I don't think so. The reader should stop and consider that the *American Economic Review* (unlike, say, the *Journal of Political Economy*) has never betrayed a penchant for the tongue-in-cheek article; but then I first heard about Waldfogel's argument on CNN around Christmas time 1993. The media moguls themselves didn't quite know how to treat it on TV—they opted for one part "There go those frisky madcap economists again . . ." and one part "Isn't this wicked but true?" In other words, they were suspended somewhere between easy irony and a wry admiration for the iconoclastic cheek of the man. The *Chicago Tribune* actually wrote an editorial on the article—but, you might aver, the *Trib* is not a serious newspaper. And then again, as if to telegraph the point that this is not "simply" or "merely" a joke, just as I sat down to write this I discovered in the Christmas edition of the *New York Times* business page a reprise of the story (Herring 1994). That puckish Joel Wald-fogel is at it again! Estimating the differential "yield" from different classes of gift givers! The fellow clearly has got what it takes to succeed at Yale; take it from me, I spent some time there.

———

If Jacques Derrida can start from a postcard as a pretext to discuss everyone from Plato to Austin, maybe I can start with Joel Waldfogel to discuss everyone from Mauss to Derrida. You see I am not offended by this tr[o]ipe; on the contrary, this offal enfolds a pearl of great price, though we may have to reach for the gas masks while we peruse the entrails to read the portents. Much has to be digested to appreciate the fact that our culture is amused by the *likes* of Joel Waldfogel—that he and people like him are one of the primary reasons why neoclassical economics has vanquished all rivals and has become the icon of ra-tional self-knowledge for academics and businessmen alike. By be-queathing to people a stark yet seemingly paradoxical image of what they want, neoclassical economics can get what it wants, which is to subsume or displace all other academic social theory in the name of unified science. To accomplish this task, it is not enough to brandish point set topology and subgame perfect Nash equilibria, though that helps. Neoclassicism must also undermine every possible rival account of exchange by ruthlessly exposing its vulnerability to self-contradic-tion. It is characteristic of these rival accounts that they are usually "non-economic": that is, they arise outside of formal academic eco-nomics and set themselves apart from it; they would like to oppose technocrats with technocrits. People favorably inclined to postmodern-ism and critical theory are especially prone to make these sorts of argu-ments: economic anthropologists, literary critics, French poststructur-alists, science studies scholars, feminist social theorists, and the like.

My argument, in a nutshell, is this. The concept of "the gift" has been constitutive to any number of anti-neoclassical social theories in the last century, but *all* the traditions that have relied upon it to explicate various forms of exchange have been ultimately vanquished *qua* social theory. (Do I really mean *all?* Yes, I do, though this is ultimately a historical question.) The reason is that the modern concept of "the gift" is itself incoherent, the weak link in the quest to define the "non-economic." From this we may extrapolate that all further attempts to capitalize on the gift will go the way of their predecessors, and worse, attempts to base social theory upon it actually serve to strengthen the neoclassical orthodoxy.

My own little *bricolage* points toward an attempt to circumvent the impasse, if not actually transcend it, and not just gesture toward it ineffectually, as I shall accuse Jacques Derrida of doing in his *Given Time I: Counterfeit Money* (1992). The resolution will be sought in a reconfiguration of the theory of value.

––––––––

No More Free Lunch

Now the gift, *if there is any*, would no doubt be related to economy. One cannot treat the gift, this goes without saying, without treating the relation to the economy, even the money economy. But is not the gift, if there is any, also that which interrupts the money economy? That which, in suspending economic calculation, no longer gives rise to exchange? That which opens the circle so as to defy reciprocity or symmetry the common measure, and so as to turn aside the return in view of the no-return? . . . Not that it remains foreign to the circle, but it must *keep* a relation of foreignness to the circle, a relation without relation of familiar foreignness. It is perhaps in this sense that the gift is impossible.—Derrida 1992, 7

––––––––

The Setting: A blow-dried citizen from Generation X strides up to an ATM in some warm climate, probably California, to judge by the withered sleazy stucco of the surrounding building and the cloudless sky. He is stopped by an obvious bum, propping up a plastic shopping bag and searching endlessly for something secreted on his person. As the technonerd fearlessly raises his plastic card to the black slot, the bum says, in a slightly aggressive tone: "Spare change?"

Mr. X: "Look, my man, if I give you a dollar, your income will go up, so average spending will rise without any offsetting rise in production. That will push inflation up, devaluing our currency after worsening our trade deficit, not to mention shifting the tax burden onto the more productive sectors of society. The dollar becomes worthless, and more people are thrown out of work. So I'd like to help ya, guy, but don't you think things are bad enough already?"

Bum: "Wha??"

ATM Door: Bzzzzzz . . . Click

––––––––

There is a trope which is emblematic of neoclassical economics, which we might call the "futility thesis." In all its various manifestations, the common denominator is some assertion that the world is so structured and interlinked that anything one might wish to accomplish will be offset—usually in some unexpected or unanticipated manner—resulting in a return to the original situation. For those remaining *au fait* with such matters, the Ricardian equivalence, the Coase theorem, the Modigliani-Miller theorem, the regulatory capture thesis, and a host of other doctrines will come to mind. There is a long tradition of such arguments in economics, dating back at least to Malthus's assertion that poor relief will only confirm the poor in their status. While many of these arguments are actually disguised restatements of some principle of arbitrage, there is a more restrictive class of futility theses that should warrant more sustained analysis. In this class of *topoi*, one essentially asserts that gifts are impossible.

Let me cite just a few incidents from the postwar economic orthodoxy, although there are many more to choose from. One exemplary instance is a paper by Robert Sugden (1982), in which he argues that the neoclassical case for governmental supplement to philanthropic provision of public goods is based upon a logical inconsistency between the postulates of publicness, utility maximization, and Nash conjectures. His argument is basically a restatement of the futility thesis, but tempered in its harshness by his assertion that people in fact do not seem to conform to the empirical predictions of the model. The tension is purposely left unresolved in this paper: theory says gifts are impossible, but people seem to act contrary to this knowledge; hence (it is hinted) some revision of theory is needed, which will perhaps restore the actors to the vaunted status of rational choosers. If the hoped-for revision of the theory also manages to reinstate the assertion that governmental activity is ineffectual in some larger frame, well, that would be okay with Sugden, too.

Another instance is Gary Becker's *Treatise on the Family* (1981), a compendium of his papers from the previous decade. As is characteristic of Becker, he is much more interested in showing that simple Marshallian stories can be used to "analyze" seemingly non-economic phenomena, thus flexing the imperialistic muscle of neoclassicism, rather than looking more closely at his own theory; in this case, he contradicts himself in the space of twenty pages. First he posits his so-called Rotten Kid Theorem (there is no "theorem" that any mathematician would recognize, but let that pass): "Each beneficiary, no matter how selfish, maximizes the family income of his benefactor and thereby internalizes all effects of his actions on other beneficiaries" (1981, 183). What does this have to do with gift giving? It takes a little economics training to see that this is the *inversion* of the impossibility of the gift: however selfish the individual member of the *oikos*, Becker says that the assembled kinship unit will end up where it would have done in any event, with the maximization of its household utility function. This is just a rehash of the conventional welfare theorem in neoclassicism that is supposed to reveal the superior efficacy of the market, with Becker's added insistence upon the intrusion of virtual markets into every nook and cranny of experience. But if the paterfamilias cannot taketh away, by symmetry neither can he giveth; altruism is thus equally neutralized in this scheme of things. Becker, unfortunately, has some difficulty seeing through his own little model, since on pages 194–95 he proceeds to argue that "altruism is less common in market transactions and more common in families because altruism is less 'efficient' in the marketplace and more 'efficient' in families" [N.B.: his own scare quotes]. Becker's subsequent forays into sociobiology in order to rationalize what he calls "altruism" thus were born under a doubly bad sign: not only did he betray a tenuous grasp of the biology, but he was, in addition, attempting to explain something which he himself had shown not to exist.

This game of acknowledging the existence of something called "altruism," only to then explain it away as simultaneously Natural and nonexistent, has become one of the major academic pastimes of our upbeat *infotainment* scene. Through the instrumentality of sociobiology, which is just neoclassical economics foisted upon some innocent unsuspecting animals and insects, it reveals its ambitions to become a Theory of Everything (Ridley 1996). The theory is as easy to learn as any proleptic two-step: posit an ontology of "individuals" (selfish genes, isolated consciousnesses, strategic organisms, anomic atoms), and then run the numbers in a "disguised self-interest" narrative. This game of "gotcha" resonates nicely with a certain free-floating paranoia which itself thrives in the interstices of the Information Age.

Lest I be accused of picking upon economists of a certain political persuasion, let me choose for my third example Kenneth Arrow's response to Richard Titmuss's book *The Gift Relationship* (1971). Titmuss's book was an attack upon the then-contemporary American blood collection system, which was at that time roughly 25 percent commercial. Titmuss argued that paying for blood led to high rates of blood-borne illness (then hepatitis), but also that it degraded the population of donors in both psychological and structural ways. Arrow, who in the 1960s was concerned to foster the nascent field of "health economics" as an offshoot of neo-Walrasian welfare theory, was uncharacteristically roused to ire by Titmuss's book. His retorts were a curious hodgepodge: for instance, he attacked the quality of Titmuss's empirical work in general terms, even resorting to the code words "precise and empirical language of empirical sociology," though he himself had never done any comparable empirical work. He smugly pointed out that "only" 6 percent of the eligible British population ever gave blood, as though that were prima facie proof of the aberrant nature of a voluntary provision system. He brought in that theorist's favorite bludgeon, conjectural history: "It may be that the spread of commercial services in the United States was itself due to the failure of voluntary services to supply enough blood . . . it would not show that commercial bloodgiving was a cause rather than an effect" (1971, 19). He opined that the problem "really" was one of uncertainty and asymmetric information between buyer and seller, which he would assert economists were learning to handle. He then tried to twin Titmuss with Friedrich von Hayek, which in the early 1970s (before Hayek's Nobel) was by no means a compliment (27). But the real objection behind all the persiflage surfaced in the exact center of the article: "The aspect of Titmuss's work that will probably have the most striking effect both immediately and in the long run is his argument that a world of giving may actually increase efficiency in the operation of the economic system. This is on the face of it a direct challenge to the tenets of the mainstream of economic thought since the time of Adam Smith" (1971, 20).

Ignoring for the moment the attempt to saddle poor Adam with something he never intended, herein lies the heart of the matter. For Arrow, as for any other neoclassical in good standing, it is simply impossible that gift giving, *if it exists*, could outperform the market in any way, shape, or form. Could Arrow really just be Joel Waldfogel with a human face? In Arrow's shooting gallery it seems that the ducks woodenly resist regimentation in a disciplined row: sometimes Arrow accepts Titmuss's assertion that gifts do exist, but insists that his empirical data are wrong; sometimes he wants to deny the existence or at least the widespread prevalence of gift giving; and sometimes he opts to treat gifts as epiphenomena of hidden market forces or as deceptively disguised individual optimization. The best he could manage is a separate-but-unequal brand of segregationist liberalism: "I think it is best on the whole that the requirement of ethical behavior be confined to those circumstances where the price system breaks down as suggested above" (1971, 22).

While Arrow's fusillade contra Titmuss did provoke a small academic literature, mainly in philosophy, it did not have any effect on the health provider community. Instead, in response to Titmuss's book, the U.S. Department of Health, Education and Welfare in 1973 announced a national blood collection policy discouraging the sale of blood, and the system moved decisively toward a donor model (so much for Arrow's empirical instincts!), although the situation has since been complicated by the appearance of AIDS and the rise of a commercial plasma and blood products sector in more recent times (Piliavin and Callero 1991). There was not much in the way of a field of health economics in the early 1970s, but as we perhaps have learned to our dismay from the national health care debate of 1994, neoclassical economists now have managed to gain much more of a purchase upon public policy toward the medical sector, and consequently the treatment of the "gift" becomes more urgent.

The futility thesis on the impossibility of the gift is endemic in modem economics, even though Arrow and Becker seem only to have a semi-conscious appreciation of its force. Is this merely some sort of ideological bad faith, a crude apologetics for the status quo, or is something more complicated going on here? I shall adopt the latter position, for essentially three reasons: (1) There is nothing written in the smooth convex surfaces of the equations of neoclassicism which dictates that the gift must be treated in any specific manner. How it enters into the neoclassical equations is thoroughly underdetermined. (2) While neoclassicals seem to instinctively agree on the impossibility of the gift, the exact way that the impossibility is demonstrated is not at all a subject of agreement. Indeed, as we have seen, one can get two or more different stories within the same article. (3) The futility thesis is not the sole province of neoclassical economists. Many diverse thinkers proposing their own rival theories of exchange also seem to run up against the thesis, though perhaps not with the verve and variety of the neoclassicals. It is their conundrum to which we now turn.

_____

Who Is the Leader of the Club That Is Made for You and Me?

In economic anthropology, all roads to the gift lead back to Marcel Mauss. All the major anthropological theorists of exchange from Sahlins to Gregory, from Douglas to Parry, from Strathern to Gudeman, feel impelled to make their peace with Mauss. More strikingly, many major exponents of French structuralism, and poststructuralism take their departure from Mauss: Lévi-Strauss, Bataille, Baudrillard, Lyotard, and Derrida in his *Given Time*. The urge to shake this shaman's rattle, this 1925 essay, one more time before venturing forth to do battle with the spreading ectoplasm of bourgeois capitalism is a phenomenon which cannot be explained in any simple manner. The enduring legacy of Durkheimian sociological theory in the guise of the "total social fact" certainly is a part of the story. The role of Mauss in providing a contemporary critique of Bolshevik socialism is another (Gane 1992). Nevertheless, the primary attraction of *The Gift* is, self-reflexively, its radical undecidability. People just don't know what they have hold of when they pick up *The Gift*. In the anthropological literature, one can encounter the most bizarre readings of the essay, such as the claim that Mauss demonstrated that "there is no such thing as a free gift" (Parry 1985, 455; Douglas 1990, viii). If a postwar social theorists cannot tell the difference between Marcel Mauss and Gary Becker, then it really must be the end of history.

But of course, it is not. What is needed instead of eschatology is some real history, a narrative account of the sequence of anthropological texts on exchange, something I have tried to initiate in "Tit for Tat" (1994d). The story, all too briefly, goes like this: the question of the gift effectively begins in anthropology with Bronislaw Malinowski, in his classic *Argonauts of the Western Pacific* (1922). Therein Malinowski described the now-famous Kula ring in an attempt to make the case that western approaches to economics were too limited to comprehend such apparently non-utilitarian practices. As a part of his project to propose an alternative analytical framework, he posited that the polar antithesis to market exchange was the "gift." Mauss's essay, not an ethnography but rather a historical survey of work on interpreting the gift, was critical of Malinowski's treatment; indeed, Malinowski's book had clearly elicited the essay. Uncharacteristically, Malinowski took Mauss's strictures to heart, and in his next work, *Crime and Custom in Savage Society* ([1926]1985, 40), he explicitly repudiated the theoretical importance of the gift. In many respects, it was Malinowski's abrupt summary of Mauss which was primarily responsible for the "no free lunch" interpretation of Mauss's essay.

Mauss, however, had produced a much more complex set of propositions. The *Essai sur le don* was written roughly at the same time as a series of articles on Bolshevism in *Le Monde Slave* (see Gane 1992, 165–211) and interventions in debates about socialism (see Mauss 1969, 675). Furthermore, it bore more than a passing resemblance to texts in the German Historicist tradition, laced with a Durkheimian concern over the role of the sacred. Although there was no evidence that Mauss was intimately acquainted with neoclassical doctrines, he did regard himself as undermining Malinowski's tendency to taxonomize exchanges by degrees of interest or disinterest. Mauss sought to explain the logic of obligation in such ethnographic oddities as the potlatch and Maori hau as a corollary of the principle that the things themselves have souls: "Hence it follows that to make a gift of something to someone is to make a present of some part of oneself" (1990, 12). In other words, Malinowski stood accused of an insufficient appreciation that the distinction between things and persons was eminently a western one. Having recourse to philology, the history of ancient laws, and ethnographies, Mauss insisted that gifts were usually a species of aggression: "through such gifts a hierarchy is established. To give is to show one's superiority, to be more, to be higher in rank, *magister*. To accept without giving in return, or without giving more back, is to become client and servant, to become small" (1990, 74). Hence, what enforces the reciprocation is not some utilitarian calculation, but rather the personality of the giver invested in the partible object; indeed it was the giver incarnate, hovering menacingly over the life of the receiver. The religious overtones were intended by Mauss, for they expressed the Durkheimian penchant for uncovering the religious origins of economic value (Parry 1985, 470).

One aspect of the radical undecidability in reading Mauss is that he attacks Malinowski by rendering the gift less of a polar opposite to commodity exchange than in *Argonauts*, but only subsequently to insist that there existed such a thing as a "gift economy" which could be counterposed to a modern exchange economy. An example of the former assimilative moment is his claim that the (then conventional) distinction in anthropology between barter and money economies was misleading, because the origins of credit could be found in gifts rather than in goldsmith's receipts (Gregory 1982, 19). An example of the latter disjunctive moment would be his schema of the three stages of "total prestation gift," and modern economies (20). This duel thesis—that the gift is not what it at first seems, obscuring the calculus of power and aggression which lay just beneath the surface; but, per contra, the gift is an earlier and kinder, gentler form of economic organization (Mauss 1990, 77–78) to be contrasted to the rapacity of developed market culture—this is what allows anyone to walk away from *The Gift* taking whatever he or she wants from it. Nonetheless, in retrospect *The Gift* and the gift reinforce and mirror one another. For, as Mauss was one of the first to point out, the etymology of the English word gift is itself ambiguous. In Old High German, the word is derived from one meaning "poison"—surely an antonym for the meaning conventionally assigned in modern dictionaries. Or is it? In the OED, the etymology is traced to an Old English word meaning "payment for a wife"; and definition 3 reads, "Something, the possession of which is transferred to another without the expectation or receipt of an equivalent" while definition 3c reads, "a fee for services rendered."

Well, what is it? Can we even begin to conceptualize "something for nothing" without backsliding into "trade of equivalents" or worse, "self-interested manipulation"?

————

How the Gift Poisoned Economic Anthropology

Most people who went into anthropology in the postwar period did so partly out of a skepticism about the universality of their own culture's categories and preoccupations; and most shared a worry that the spread of the capitalist market would sooner or later wipe out the diversity of cultures which they cherished. The smaller tribe who decided to become directly engaged in the project of an "economic anthropology" were therefore predisposed to regard the neoclassical orthodoxy as suspect, along with its third-world offshoot known as "development economics" (Lodewijks 1994). But where would an alternative framework for understanding such phenomena come from? By and large, that postwar generation saw its clan organization split between two opposed totems: Malinowski and Mauss. The former, as we have suggested, had essentially repudiated the gift as an anthropological category; and this taboo in turn led to forays into Marxism and the structuralism of Lévi-Strauss. (The fortunes of this clan, however fascinating, lie beyond our present purview.) The Maussketeers, who regarded the adherents of Malinowski as insufficiently distanced from Western preoccupations, descried their "tendency to see exchanges as essentially dyadic transactions between self-interested individuals, as premised on some kind of balance, the tendency to play down supernatural sanctions, and the total contempt for questions of origin—all these constituted an important legacy of Malinowski's teachings" (Parry 1985, 454). The rallying cry became therefore "back to Mauss!" for many postwar economic anthropologists. However, the huzzah might as well have been "quaff the hemlock!," since each aspiring theorist of the gift in economic anthropology ended up dispirited and dejected (and I do mean every Maussketeer from Carrier (1995) to Sahlins; there are signs that the disillusion has set in among the feminists), essentially repudiating the possibility of a theory-driven economic anthropology. The detailed narrative of how this happened still awaits its historian, although I have made a first stab at exploring the terrain (Mirowski 1994d). Here we shall restrict ourselves to the views of two preeminent theorists, Marshall Sahlins and Chris Gregory; a synoptic view would find the field crowded with notables such as Marilyn Strathern, Tim Ingold, Annette Weiner, Nicholas Thomas, Jonathan Parry, Alain Caillé, and yes, even Mary Douglas. It also would encompass attempts to portray the scientific community as a "gift economy" (Hagstrom 1965).

Marshall Sahlins's *Stone Age Economics* (1972) still stands as a landmark for postwar economic anthropologists, so it is all the more distressing to observe that Sahlins has since apparently given up on the conceptual possibility of a thriving economic anthropology. His more recent pronouncements (Sahlins 1992) have been reduced to generic mantras that cultural homogenization cannot triumph in the economic sphere. The earlier Sahlins was much more feisty:

> If the problem in the beginning was the "naive anthropology" of Economics, today it is the naive economics of Anthropology . . . It is a choice between the perspective of Business, for the formalist method must consider the primitive economies as underdeveloped versions of our own, and a culturalist study that as a matter of principle does honor to different societies for what they are . . . the attempt in the end is to bring the anthropological perspective to bear on the traditional work of microeconomics, the explanation of exchange value. (1972, xi, xii)

Sahlins proceeded to divide primitive exchange into the categories of centralized redistribution and reciprocity, à la Karl Polanyi, and insist with regard to the second that "it is precisely through scrutiny of departures from balanced exchange that one glimpses the interplay between reciprocity, social relations and material circumstances" (190). Sahlins's objective was to specify how a continuum from gift to balanced reciprocity to negative reciprocity would be conditional upon a set of inherently cultural factors, primarily kinship and clan or political distinctions. If successful, Sahlins could then have shown that exchange ratios could not be indicators of any single state of primal scarcity or disembodied forces of "supply and demand"; indeed, the ratios themselves would need to be embedded within an expanded vector of considerations, losing their abstract calculative functions. Equivalence would be no longer dyadic, but rather systemic or multiply attainable. What moderns think of as allocation decisions would be replaced by local orderings inherent in cultural structures.

Intrinsic to the argument is the existence of a benchmark of "equivalence" in exchange and a polar extreme of "gift" where calculations of equivalence have no place. The ability to array objects along this continuum (and beyond, to market-like exchange where a surplus is realized) is provided by a sort of proto-calculational device (a Turing machine?) inherent in the patterns of inclusion and exclusion to be found in kinship ties, clan membership, and so on. But the valiant attempt begins to deconstruct itself right at the end of Sahlins's text: "Everything depends upon the meaning and practice of that capital principle, 'generosity.' But the meaning is ethnographically uncertain, and therein lies the weakness of our theory" (1972, 307). What is the nature of the weakness? To put it in slightly formal terms, the ability to posit an equivalence class somewhere in the system is heavily dependent upon the location of the invariant in the system. For Sahlins, initially the posited invariant resides in kinship relations and the like. But then he proceeds to argue that in the event of a pronounced scarcity or other dislocation (shades of the economist's "external shock"), "a supply-demand

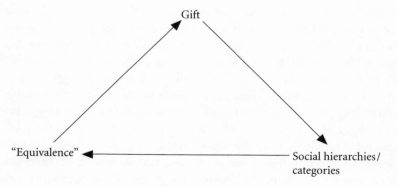

Figure 2. Sahlins causal structure. *Source:* Sahlins 1972

imbalance is resolved by pressure on the trade partners rather than exchange rates" (311). And here is where the corrosive essence of the gift eats away at the system. The role of the gift is to *alter* many of the cultural equivalence classes, such as kinship, political affiliation, and the like, and not simply to ratify prior relationships. Think of the "gift" of women, or the "gift" of territory. In these situations, the cultural patterns are *not invariant* with respect to the system of exchange, and therefore the presumption of an equivalence class is undermined. Value deliquesces at the initiative of the Other; or perhaps worse, it is dissolved in the downpour of external Noise. Nevertheless, from a Western perspective, there remains some notion of intentionality, and perhaps even self-interest, motivating gifts and exchanges; and the temptation is to lodge that intentionality and that calculative index somewhere deep in the human psyche. But, *mirabile dictu*, we are back at the neoclassical theory we tried to escape, or as Sahlins puts it, "In many respects the opposite of market competition, the etiquette of primitive trade may conduct by a different route to a similar result."

Sahlins prefaced his effort with the disclaimer, "I do not attempt here a general theory of value" (1972, 277). Perhaps that was one reason for the collapse of his edifice. However, another more direct cause was his attempt to incorporate the gift into his anthropological economics. One detects a kind of rueful acknowledgment of this in his Radcliffe-Brown Lecture: "And why the necessity for the reconciliation that Mauss discovered in *The Gift*? A pervasive sense of underlying chaos, a kind of Radcliffe-Brownian movement of self-interested atoms, weights like a nightmare on the brains of the living" (1988, 26). Or at least one of the living.

The case of Chris Gregory is equally instructive, because he was coached by his mentors at Cambridge in Sraffian economic theory as a rival tradition to neoclassicism, and subsequently sought to forge an alliance between neo-Ricardianism and Marcel Mauss to produce a theoretically informed economic anthropology. Gregory's *Gifts and Commodities* (1982) returns once more to Melanesia (the primal stomping grounds for economic anthropology ever since Malinowski) to analyze the difference between a "gift economy" and an "exchange economy." He begins by insisting that "the concepts 'gift' and 'commodity' have no meaning within the [neoclassical] approach" (9), an assertion which some earlier sections of this chapter suggest is perhaps a bit too draconian. Then, getting down to business, we are told that "commodity exchange establishes objective quantitative relationships between the objects transacted, while gift exchange establishes personal qualitative relationships between the subjects transacting" (41). Here one detects the influence of Piero Sraffa, although some familiarity with the literature might raise doubts about the hard and fast nature of the dichotomy. The project of the neo-Ricardians to ground prices in the "external" or "physi-

cal" world of technological production specifications was always rather ambivalent, in that it was not always clear to which historical or institutional
referent it applied; in their quest for an "objective" economics it is not so
clear how much the neo-Ricardians differed in this regard from the neoclassicals whom they otherwise so despised.

Nevertheless, for Gregory the Sraffian theory served as a polar opposition
to a specification of the gift economy. In the central section of his text he
proceeded to list a number of criteria for the gift economy, as a prerequisite
for an anthropological theory of exchange. These benchmarks were:

1. People in a gift economy exist in a state of reciprocal dependence, in
   contrast to the relative independence of market participants (42).
2. "Commodities are *alienable* objects transacted by aliens; gifts are *inalienable* objects transacted by non-aliens" (43).
3. "Things are anthropomorphized in a gift economy" (45).
4. "Gift exchange is the exchange of like-for-like . . . commodity exchange is
   different because it involves the exchange of unlike-for-unlike" (46–47).
5. Gift exchange is intrinsically extended through time, unlike commodity
   exchange (47).

The culmination of these considerations is two somewhat variant statements
of the "economic" difference between gift and exchange economies, although both appear on the same page (47):

> Simple commodity exchange establishes a relation of equality between
> heterogeneous things at a given point in time while gift exchange estab-
> lishes a relation of equality between homogeneous things at different
> points in time . . . Commodity exchange—the exchange of unlike-
> for-unlike—establishes relations of equality between the objects ex-
> changed . . . Gift exchange—the exchange of like-for-like—establishes
> an unequal relationship of domination between the transactors.

We are very close to the work of Sahlins here, a proximity which Gregory
acknowledges. It is indeed possible to argue that the resemblance extends
much further, in that within the confines of the single text, the project to
theoretically specify the gift economy deconstructs itself in roughly the same
manner. Like Sahlins, Gregory admits that the five dichotomies above are
better thought of as continua: for instance market transactors are not always
alien uncorrelated atoms, alienability may be restricted by convention in a
market economy, the exchange of commodities extends across time, and so
on. Some of the dichotomies are even a little tendentious: Marx argued that
anthropomorphism was rife even under the capitalist mode. But the crucial
issue in detecting the parallel is that Gregory is striving to establish equivalence classes much in the style of Sahlins, as can be observed from the above

quote. What purportedly demarcates like from unlike, equivalent from non-equivalent, is prior cultural structures: relations of reciprocal dependence, alienability classes, local specifications of identity of objects, agreement on time orderings. However, just as with Sahlins, it is precisely at this point that the corrosive character of the gift seeps into the structure, dissolving difference.

Recall Gregory's final claim that the exchange of like-for-like in the guise of gifts allows the assertion of dominance between transactors. This claim is of course intended to capture Mauss's notion of gift as aggression. As for any good Sraffian, the objective equivalence of things will then serve to underwrite some less specific equivalence class between persons. But is there not here lurking a suspicious circularity, the cultural equivalents determining the equivalence classes of objects underwriting the destabilization of cultural equivalents? The following passage suggests that Gregory caught a whiff of the deliquescence of his system: "So who is superior to whom? This is the problem of rank and the answer depends, in the first instance, on the rank of the objects, i.e., their exchange order. Objects as gifts have this exchange order rather than exchange-value, because the relation between them is ordinal rather than cardinal" (48). This ploy of summoning the dreaded distinction between cardinal and ordinal to conjure away the thorny problems of value theory is really unavailing, if not also excruciatingly embarrassing for Gregory since it is precisely the same move made by the neoclassicals. Combined with the clear possibility that the gift can alter its own equivalence class, Gregory's theory foray tumbles into unceremonious rout: "Thus the principle of like-for-like must be interpreted as rank-for-rank . . . This adds a further complication because it means that some gift exchanges appear as commodity exchanges . . . The redefinition of like-for-like as rank-for-rank also calls for a redefinition of inalienability. While it is conventional to interpret this in a literal sense at the level of pure theory, in practice this must be modified and interpreted in more of a metaphorical sense . . . Strictly speaking, like-for-like exchanges are impossible" (50). Once the gift is given its due, everything that distinguishes it from the commodity melts into air.

How did Gregory go on to write another 150 pages after this Brest-Litovsk? Careful examination of his subsequent work on the "velocity theory of gifts," the trade of women, and so forth reveals that he falls back upon a rather inflexible Sraffian theory of value, in effect treating all value as an embodied "standard commodity." The spectacle of such a timeless physicalist theory supposedly underwriting a culturally sensitive and diverse economic anthropology is enough to make even an economist squirm. Skepticism about a natural invariant inscribed in the commodity (neoclassicals would rather locate it in the "mind') is one of the primary reasons for the failure of neo-Ricardianism in economics.

Dissemination of the Gift, or What Jacques Saw

Jacques Derrida is justly renowned for his notion of the "dissemination" of meaning. For us non-technocrit types, it is enough for this to be defined as a situation where supposedly opposing concepts merge to form a persistently undecidable exchange of attributes, often within the ambit of a single text. This concept was exemplified in his essay "Plato's Pharmacy" (Derrida 1991), in which the contradictory meanings of *Pharmakon* as both "poison" and "remedy" reverberate throughout Plato's dialogue *Phaedrus*. Given the dual meanings of gift as "beneficial donation" and "poison," it is not surprising that the same sort of analysis should be deployed here, or indeed, given the numerous critical readings of Lévi-Strauss, that Derrida himself should carry it out in his *Given Time*. But rather than quote Derrida, it would probably be more helpful for economists to rephrase his insights in more (deceptively?) prosaic terms. The task is to see how the endless displacement of the meaning of the gift obscures, frustrates, and baffles most of those seeking an alternative to neoclassical understandings of exchange.

What do people seem to think a gift is? Most commonly, the gift carries connotations of being the polar opposite of market exchange, that is, a species of non-exchange. Dig a bit deeper, and you will find that what qualifies it for the status of nonexchange is some value principle, because a gift is often defined as a transfer without reciprocal or commensurate value received in exchange. So this must be why the various theorists of the gift economy surveyed above find themselves impelled to discuss equivalence classes, rank orderings, continua of reciprocities, and the like. However, the difficulties of rendering the value principle or principles explicit are not merely the result of some oversight, but rather are inherent in the concept of the gift. Consciousness and intentionality are the source of the problem.

Suppose I drop a $20 bill on the sidewalk. (Derrida does an even more convoluted version of this with Baudelaire's tale of the donation of a counterfeit coin to a beggar.) Is that a gift? Certainly not if I am blissfully unaware that I dropped it—it would simply be a loss. Alternatively, there might be a baroque account where I knew what I was doing when the currency slipped from my grasp. In any event, the gift must have an intentional aspect to be a gift. But one dissemination leads to another with alarming alacrity in this instance. If we tend to conflate intentionality with calculation (and this is the very hallmark of western thought), then this intentionality immediately undoes the gift and instead situates it squarely in the category of market exchange. The gift is poison if it is self-interested; but it is no gift at all if no attention is devoted to future consequences. As Douglas (1990) insists, to give with no discernable interest as to consequences is to deny the very existence of social ties.

Perhaps there is nonetheless some way to circumvent this paradox of intentionality with regard to the gift. Suppose a donor attempts to short-circuit the paradox with profuse expressions of disinterest and grand gestures devoid of self-seeking character (as is quite frequent in ethnographic accounts). In mild versions of this behavior, the contradiction remains quite clear, with the recipient thrust into the unhappy situation of realizing that protestations of disinterest are direct evidence of interest, or at least calculation. This is why the gift is frequently associated with aggression in anthropology and in art from Lascaux to *Lear.* (As a Midwesterner, I recommend Jane Smiley's *A Thousand Acres.*) The ludicrousness of the situation sometimes whips the donor into an even greater frenzy of self-abasement, whereupon one observes orgies of destruction like the potlatch, or complete and utter abnegation of the donor beyond all cultural parameters, as with the hermits of Christian hagiography. But this frenzy of disinterest is all for naught, for it appears that the only successful way to transcend rational calculation is to exit from it, and that is why Western ethnographers often regard orgies of destruction and self-immolation as anti-economic or *irrational,* whereas true asceticism tends to be viewed as the lethargy, indolence, and shiftlessness of traditional societies. We thus come full circle to Durkheim's religious basis of exchange: for westerners the only true gift is the transcendental gift, the one which cannot be given by earthly mortals.

And now Jacques: "If the gift is annulled in the economic odyssey of the circle as soon as it appears as gift or as soon as it signifies itself as gift, there is no longer any "logic of the gift" . . . One can go so far as to say a work as monumental as Marcel Mauss's *The Gift* speaks of everything but the gift" (1992, 24).

Is Jacques a stock character from Molière, speaking liturgical Latin unawares? Russell's set theory paradox has got nothing on this.

———

The Holocaust of the Inanities

The following is taken from Bresnick's *The Six Million Dollar Man*:

> *Schindler's List* uses the Holocaust as its setting, but its affective power may be understood to derive largely from what I take to be the core fantasy of philanthropy—the notion that a gift can be, in the words of Schindler's accountant Itzhak Stern, "an absolute good." The belief in a morally unambiguous philanthropy is writ large in the film's climactic moment . . . the film's apotheosis of Schindler depends on the notion of heroic philanthropy as the only visible way of solving society's ills, whether that society is Nazi Germany or post-Cold War United States. The film is thus truly the product of its historical moment, for in the wake of the eradication of socialism as a viable political and economic counter-system, capitalism is the only game in town, and for those who enjoy the market's spoils, philanthropy is the most potent means of dispelling the moral disquiet occasioned by the enormous disparities of wealth that capitalism produces. Philanthropy, in this account, turns out to be the salve of liberalism's bad conscience, and it is no surprise that Spielberg, who made something on the order of $100 million in 1993, should have directed a film in which the philanthropist is the hero, regardless of the fact that the money that Schindler shells out to save his *Schindlerjuden* accrued to him by virtue of being a war profiteer. (1997, 18)

Bresnick begins his article with the observation: "At the deepest level of its fantasy, Hollywood would like to believe that it is essentially a philanthropy; that what it offers its mesmerized public is the gift of pleasure and, at certain exalted moments, the gift of consciousness itself."

Donner un rien

A frequent complaint against postmodern writers is that they toy with politics, but that their postmodern play serves mainly to avoid political commitment or difficult social analysis. No Tinseltown enthusiasm for those practiced in the arts of reflexivity! While this may be the case, reasoned political action harbors its own paradoxes.

Derrida, more than other writers, is acutely aware of these paradoxes, for he revels in them. In *Given Time* he presents the paradox of intentionality and the resulting impossibility of the gift. He does this primarily through close reading of texts by Mauss and Baudelaire, giving a wide berth to the precincts of social theory in which this paradox becomes painfully apparent. In response, it might then be permitted to put this question to him: To whom does he bequeath his insight, and what is the intended content of his own "gift"?

An obvious retort would be that he does not control the uses of his text, and that he has no idea of who might be on the receiving end of his missive, dissemination being endemic to the project. In other words, he might plead disinterest and ignorance of the consequences of his gift—but he is too smart for that. Tracing the boomerang of reflexivity, that option is closed to him, for it is precisely that reaction which he has relegated to the status of impossibility.

Rather, and characteristically, Derrida chooses consistency in the face of dissemination. In *Given Time* and in much of his other work, he gestures toward the impossibility of the gift, he dances around it, he peers at it from many angles, takes relevant texts from others, appropriates ideas from across centuries as if they were all intended for his edification; but in the final accounting, he leaves us with nothing. Or, as he says, "The general equivalent would be a transcendental signified or signifier" (1992, 52). Yes, we should all be wary of Pie in the Sky, but how about the Gift on the Ground?

And fragging Fukayama after the colonial wars are over hardly constitutes an endorsement of any novel ambitions for social theory (Derrida 1994).

Could it be that Jacques Derrida is the Joel Waldfogel of philosophy?

————

The Road to Perdition

Contrary to Derrida, there is at least one immediate corollary of the impossibility of the gift, and it is a political one. It is that the supposed tradeoff between equity and efficiency in economics is literally meaningless; and furthermore, the attempt to define liberal or left politics as creating a space within economics for ethics or communal goals or generosity or compassion is a tender trap. It is treacherous because it is premised upon the notion that the right is smugly selfish and coldly calculative, whereas the left alone is both capable of and predisposed toward giving a gift. This, of course, is just a replay of the paradox of intentionality, modulo the question of the ontological character of the fundamental actor. As soon as these ideas are mooted in the public arena, they are neutralized by the rhetoric and reality of political endeavor. For to "give" communally one must "give" reasons to get support, and then the actor becomes desperately embroiled in the calculations of cost and benefit, the apparent antithesis of the gift. This constitutes one of the great logical contradictions of democratic political life in the early twenty-first century.

The prognosis that one might draw from the paradox of intentionality is that any combination of gift theory and neoclassical economics is not a viable language for discussing politics. Arrow's attempts to reconcile his vestigial socialist instincts with his Walrasian general equilibrium theory are simply incoherent, for reasons having nothing to do with his own technical "impossibility theorem." The attempt of the "liberal" George Akerlof to present a repackaged neoclassicism with a human face must likewise be judged a minor and insignificant diversion. Indeed, his use of Marcel Mauss to motivate the idea of "labor contracts as partial gift exchange" (1984, 152) only goes to show that an interdisciplinary neoclassical is an oxymoron. The movement by the economics orthodoxy to "take ethics seriously" (Hausman and McPherson 1993) proposes the Sisyphean task of rolling the gift up the utility gradient. Finally, the whole massive literature which endlessly disputes the possibility and nature of altruism (Paul et al., eds., 1993) in an economic or rational-choice framework is merely a make-work project designed to keep a few underemployed academics busy, and should be one of the first targets of any budget cuts. These amendments to rational choice theory serve mainly to make the individual theorists pride themselves in their nobility and broadmindedness; they make no substantial alteration to the "two-step" explanations so prevalent in the culture. (The implications for applied policy areas like "health economics" will be left to the imagination of the reader.)

But does this mean that the death of the gift is the triumph of the theorist of rational self-interest? Is it Joel Waldfogel or nothing? Not at all.

Gift Theory and Value Theory

Derrida asserts that the existence of a general equivalent would be tantamount to the existence of a transcendental signifier. I think this is where he goes wrong, no matter whether one regards it as a rehash of Durkheim or else a translation of Saussure's appropriation of Walrasian general equilibrium. My excursions into economic anthropology, literary criticism, and unorthodox economics were meant to suggest that: (a) their resort to gift theory in order to provide themselves with an alternative theory of exchange has left them hobbled and vulnerable to incursions by neoclassical economists; and (b) the crux of the problem, perhaps unrecognized by all these parties, resides in the specification of the quality and character of the *invariants* which are presumed to govern the actions and interepretations of the participants. To recap: the very definiton of the gift is predicated upon some such invariant, but the gift corrodes and undermines all the posited invariants. Thus far I agree with Derrida. Where we part company is in the implication, never fully explicit in Derrida, that the project of a value theory is futile.

The neoclassicals have a retort to this skepticism, which is why they generally do defeat their rivals. Value invariance, they insist, exists in the mental recesses of individuals; their orderings, while idiosyncratic and personal, are inviolate; thus self-interest is the only possible language suited to the discussion of exchange. The cogency of this response has been attacked and defended *ad nauseam* in the twentieth century; we shall simply pass it by here. Let's save it for another day, a day when the neoclassicals may have read a little bit more than the *AER*.

I should like to propose another possible response to this skepticism, one which resonates much more harmoniously with the prior theoretical inclinations of the anthropologists, critical theorists, and feminists. It posits that value invariance is a socially constructed phenomenon, centered upon the institutions of monetary creation and control, one which is simultaneously acquiesced in and undermined by the self-seeking activities of transactors (Mirowski 1991, 1994c). It displays both elements of intentionality and unintended consequences; indeed, the tensions between the bottom-up and top-down forces are what allow it to be cast in the language of self-organized criticality. Value invariance is enforced from the top down by various monetary and accounting controls; it is homeostatically maintained from the bottom up by means of arbitrage operations. Value invariance is compromised from the top down by the expansion of debt and the need for macroeconomic expansion; it is challenged from the bottom up by all manner of devices aimed at circumventing budget constraints, from transactions innovations to theft. Putative psychological regularities of the transactors play no essential role in the structure. "Value" here simply refers to the outcomes of a system of exchange organized in this manner.

While I have framed some formal aspects of a social theory of value elsewhere, here we will restrict ourselves to the consequences of this framework for the concept of the "gift." They fall under four categories: (1) The gift is yet one more instance of a bottom-up activity which impugns the strict integrity of the value invariant. (2) The relationship of the gift to monetary phenomena is central to its evolution and significance. (3) Gifts are an attempt to simultaneously operate outside the network of exchange and yet remain within it; and as such, stand as yet another class of pragmatic balancing acts which encompass the larger paradox of treating the value unit as invariant while all along acknowledging that it is not. (4) Norms of beneficence and reciprocity are self-referential devices, such as those found in any recursive computational system. Thesis (1) will be sketchily described in this section, while theses (2–4) will be covered in the following 3 sections.

One can use some of the mathematics of networks of the social theory of value to demonstrate that a true gift, *should it exist,* would present obstacles to the numerical constitution of the value invariant.

Briefly, imagine that the nodes of a directed graph are associated with commodities, while the arcs between them designate permitted exchanges. Attached to each arc is a rational number which represents the bilateral barter exchange ratio between the commodities. If the exchange were to be characterized as a gift, then that rational number would either be zero or infinity. While such attributions are technically permissible, they would effectively prevent any circuit of completed arbitrage in the section of the graph encompassing that commodity path. No completed arbitrage means no value invariant; therefore, gifts impugn the integrity of the value principle.

It is important to be clear about what this technical result does and does not mean. It is not a "proof" that gifts don't exist in a capitalist exchange system. Rather, it highlights how gifts will necessarily appear as incompatible with a well-developed market value system. In a sense, it explains why the culture from time to time produces a Joel Waldfogel or Jacques Derrida: people clearly think about and act upon a category of gift activities, but simultaneously are forced to subsume them under the system of commodity exchanges when engaging in valuation. It is the frisson of paradox accompanying this realization which can then be capitalized upon by the irony of a Derrida or a Waldfogel.

_____

No Gifts without Payment Systems

Another implication of the social theory of value is that the very category of "gift" can only have meaning when contrasted to a prior payments system and an instituted value invariant. Thus the great error of anthropologists from Mauss to Gregory, or feminists from Cixous to Strathern, or sociologists of science like Hagstrom, is to posit the existence of a "gift economy" which is somehow prior to and counterposed against an exchange economy. Undoubtedly much of this tendency derives from a problem endemic to the definition of gifts: namely, should they be restricted to closed spheres of exchange which *exclude* money? The uneasy coexistence of gifts and monetization has been shown very nicely for the history of the United States by Viviana Zelizer (1994). Nevertheless, one should not confuse the synchronic quarantine of money from gifts with some diachronic precedence of gifts over money. Gifts are an attempt to transcend the system of value; but that system transcendence already presupposes some form of monetary structure. Without money (or some similar imposition of equivalence classes), there is no "outside" to which to escape.

The major theoretical implication of the gift as a function of a money-based value schema is that the circularity of definition which bedevils other attempts at gift theory (Sahlins, Gregory) is neutralized. One of the signal characteristics of monetary exchange is that gifts do not alter the fundamental algebraic structures, as they often do with exchanges divided into equivalence classes along kinship, clan, or other lines. While gift giving is antithetical to the stability and integrity of the value invariant, that stability and that integrity are maintained outside the sphere of the gift, in markets, banking institutions, and accounting entities.

Unwrapping the Gift

As Derrida reminds us, gifts are an attempt to be both intentional and disinterested, simultaneously a-rational and rational, friendly and hostile. Perhaps a better way to capture the paradox is by noting that the category of gift transactions tries to use the system of social valuation to get outside the system of social valuation. At the most prosaic level, have you ever wondered why modern transactors wrap their gifts before presentation? From this vantage point, the explanation would involve stylized obfuscation. To put it differently, the market origins and the calculation of intentions cannot of course be effectively banished from the act of gift giving in a market culture, but they can be disguised in such a way that the donor signals his willingness to suppress those phenomena. The wrapping of a gift pretends that it is temporarily extracted from the mundane level of commerce, and that its identity and its value (don't leave those price tags on!) are irrelevant to the occasion. That the wrapping of gifts is a custom indicates that an interim solution to the paradox of intentionality, just as with the paradox of value invariance, must equally take place at the societal level. Gift wrap, like accounting, is elevated to the status of a transpersonal semiotic system. No individual protestations of disinterest, no rational argument however impassioned, can have any effective purchase on the paradox; but *institutions* can.

Importance of Something for Nothing

The final task of value theory is to explain why gifts exist at all if they are merely excrescences of a market-based value principle. Here we take a brief look at possible extensions into computational theory. The paradigm of the social theory of value is a vast transpersonal algebra, a kind of finite system of automata with the configuration of exchanges themselves as the analogue of the hardware, allowing the calculation of consequences of economic activities. Anyone familiar with this literature will realize that there is a whole range of results, from Gödel to Turing to algorithmic intractability to complexity theory, which suggests that some results capable of being stated within the system cannot be proven or even calculated within the system. This is especially true in the class of recursive functions, or statements made within the system about statements in the system. In other words, there are some truths which can be discerned from "outside" the system which cannot be adequately encompassed from within it.

I should like to suggest that the category "gift" tends to occupy this relationship to the price system, conceived either as the logic of a system of supply and demand or as a projection of a system of utility maximization, and that the sociologist Alvin Gouldner essentially realized this in a series of essays written in the 1960s on "The Norm of Reciprocity" and "The Importance of Something for Nothing." In the first, he made the telling observation that functionalist social theory must presuppose a purely balanced reciprocity; and if the balance is in any way felt to be lacking, the analyst reimposes it by inventing additional classes of calculative considerations. (This is the best summary of the structure of Gary Becker's style of sociology I have ever encountered, all the more impressive because it was proposed well before the fact.) The equivalent in Gödel's Theorem would be the *post hoc* inclusion of the undecidable statement into the previous structure as a new axiom of the revised system. Nevertheless, this is a mug's game, as Gouldner points out: it is an irreducibly arbitrary procedure, and creates a false sense of comprehensive explanation. Moreover, the achievement of pervasive balance in exchange is also a dead end, in the sense that it creates a rational impasse as to any further motivation to exchange (1973, 252). The vexing "no-trade theorems" of rational expectations theory merely illustrate this point.

In his second essay, Gouldner suggests that the category of gift, or "something for nothing," is the mechanism which breaks the deadlock. A system of pure value invariance, which implies pervasive equivalence in exchange, zero arbitrage, and complete balance, is a paradoxically unstable social system. (If this short-circuits some neoclassical neurons, just think of the "no-trade theorems" of Grandmont and Milgrom-Stokey in the rational expectations literature.) The condition which both initiates new exchange and keeps the system of exchange functioning is the possibility of something outside the value sphere, namely the gift. It is the gift which injects the promise of irrationality, the mirage of transcendence, into the heart of Weberian *Zweck-rationalität*. "The self that wants something for nothing seeks an existence without alienation . . . it wants to be loved for itself" (1973, 271). It is the fabled return to childhood, or perhaps the nostalgia for the lost history of a barely imagined precapitalist era. It is the proposition which can be stated within the system (something for nothing needs a value invariant) but which cannot be computed within the system (the paradox of the gift).

But just as Gödelian paradoxes have led to further fruitful and interesting mathematics in the realm of recursive functions, the paradox of the gift leads to further social structures, perched atop the original institutions of value and exchange. "The paradox of elites is this . . . they exploit and take something for nothing. But what transforms them from merely powerful strata into a legitimate elite, in short, what transforms their domination into hegemony, is that they can and sometimes do give something for nothing" (1973, 274).

No, No, Not Nietzsche!

He who . . . actually practices requital—is, that is to say, grateful and revengeful—is called good; he who is powerful and cannot requite is called bad. The good are a caste, the bad a mass like grains of sand. Good and bad is for a long time the same thing as noble and base, master and slave. On the other hand, one does not regard the enemy as evil: he can requite. (Nietzsche 1986, 37)

Notes

Introduction: Cracks, Hidden Passageways, and False Bottoms

1　Or, in the words of that other famous philosopher, Tom Lehrer, "Once the rockets go up / Who cares where they come down / That's not my department / Says Wernher von Braun."

2　See, for instance, Ziman 1994; Gibbons et al. 1994; Lessig 2001; McSherry 2001; Drahos 2002; Krimsky 2003; and of course Mirowski and Sent 2002.

3　Hands 2001, 373, gives this an especially wicked caricature: "Take a game theoretic model from industrial organization theory; change the firms or players to 'scientists'; add the adjective 'epistemic' in a few places . . . and suddenly you have a philosophical model of scientific knowledge."

4　Ron Giere has glossed this postwar beneficence as: "Don't think about the fact I am a German immigrant or speak with an accent, just consider the validity of my ideas" (quoted in Howard 2003). I discuss the strange history of the meanings of the "social" in twentieth-century philosophy of science in Mirowski 2004.

5　See also Motterlini 1999, 107, where Lakatos cites Latsis as showing that neoclassical economics is a "degenerating program" in his terminology.

6　"I was assigned to the Ninth Bomb Division in Rheims as an advisor on radar counter-measures. That was a . . . what did you call it . . . industrial engineering group?—that's not quite what it was called. These people who applied mathematics and science to strategic and other problems in a rather unsystematic way" (Kuhn 2000, 271). Kuhn's absent-mindedness on his participation in "operations research" should not be taken as evidence of its impact upon such matters as his career choice after returning from the war, as this interview makes clear. Also, one should not be misled into thinking that Kuhn was somehow *more* of a historian than Lakatos; as he admits in the same interview: "It didn't really get me interested in history of science; and there are those who feel, and feel with some justice, that I never really did get to be an historian" (276).

7　The new world of Big Science and its managers is discussed in Galison and Hevly 1992; Galison 1997; Kay 1993; Kohler 1991; and McGrath 2002. Polanyi's own anti-Bush version of the social benefits of science is discussed in chapter 3 below.

8　This is not the place to go into the possible geographical bifurcations between the American academy on the one hand and that of Europe and Asia on the other, something which shows up pronouncedly in the Weintraub volume. Science studies as an academic formation itself appears to be more institutionally robust in the European academic context.

9   It is already provoking comment within the science studies community; see Scott, Richards, and Martin 1990. The anguish is especially evident in the "bioethics for hire" profession, one of the few growth areas for the philosophy of science and ethics in the era of privatized science. See Elliott 2002.

10 For some representative texts see Gross and Leavitt 1994; Koertge 1998; Philip Kitcher 2000; Labinger and Collins 2001.

11 Some useful introductions include Biagioli 2000b; MacKenzie 1996; Mirowski and Sent 2001.

12 I expressly decline to discuss the "actor-network" French school of the sociology of science here, even though its adherents have some explicit things to say about economics and science. Some indications of why I neglect their work might be found in Latour 1999.

13 The inventor of the term "social epistemology," Steve Fuller, does not fit easily into either of these camps. He has been known in the past to make extensive use of the work of the social studies camp, although lately he has taken to criticizing such icons of the group as Bruno Latour and Michel Callon. His original training was as a philosopher, but he sets himself in opposition to the Kitcher style of philosophy of science. His latest attempt to spell out a third way is Fuller 2002a. He is discussed further in chapter 5 below. Another exceptional figure is Brad Wray (2000).

14 More recently, in Philip Kitcher 2002, he denies this characterization; but just like his interlocutor in that instance, Helen Longino, I find his protestations of innocence unconvincing.

15 Dewey and the pragmatists had a lot to say about this, before they were sidelined by Kitcher's forebears, the analytical philosophers of science. On this see Mirowski 2004.

16 "We do better to deploy the notion of aims in its most natural home, referring to the aims of individual agents rather than to some abstraction" (2001, 87). It seems astounding that a philosopher can so blithely dictate that the "individual" is not an abstraction, or that homes are innately "natural." Perhaps this philosopher forgot one of his own earlier incarnations (1996, 282): "Grand rhetoric about human freedom seduces us into thinking that we must, quite literally, make ourselves . . . This conception was always incoherent. If the self that allegedly makes itself is already fully formed, then it does not, after all, *make* itself; if it is not fully formed, then *it* does not make itself. To find our freedom, we have to start acknowledging that we are the people we are because of events that are beyond our control, even beyond our understanding." This doesn't sound like utilitarianism, Toto.

17 One of Kitcher's most irritating ploys is to present himself as a mediator between historicists and analytical philosophers, all the while betraying vast ignorance about the history of arguments over the relationship of science to democracy (Hollinger 1996; Purcell 1973) or indeed the relationship between the history of utilitarian models of science and the philosophy of science.

18 "Behind the often evangelical rhetoric about the value of knowledge stands a serious theology, an unexamined faith that pursuit of inquiry will be good for us" (2001, 166). One is perplexed that Kitcher nonetheless refrains from testifying his own belief in Methodism.

19 "The fundamentals of human reasoning are pretty much everywhere the same . . . So the ways in which arguments are justified (and discovered) in the human sciences should be no different than those employed in the natural sciences" (2001, 175).

20 The precept that there is no such thing as a generic scientific publication, but that one must combine economic, technological, disciplinary, and social factors into account to

understand how both print and electronic journals function in their specific disciplinary settings, is the subject of Scheiding (forthcoming).

21 This paper has already provoked reactions from those who insist that Thornton could not have been such a pivotal figure because he was essentially "atheoretical." See, for instance, Ekelund and Thornton 2001.

1 Confessions of an Aging Enfant Terrible

1 I cannot resist including one example of such offended sensibilities: "The lurid language and the conflation of the cultural atmospheres at the end of our most recent centuries conjure up images of consumptive Parisian cabaret singers sipping absinthe with Nobel Memorial Prize winners . . . It's not that it's repetitive, it's just that there is too much cleverness, obscure references to popular culture, and recherché puns . . . I found it distracting, and my concern is that others will as well. By introducing noise into the communication channel, the author has rendered substance less accessible than it might be . . . Better and clearer expressions can be found by doing a Google search on the web" (Field 2003, 614–15).

2 From this perspective, Walrasian "general equilibrium" is based upon a fallacy, viz. that a general theory of trade must reduce the determinants of prices to a single mechanism, because all agents are uniform and subject to the same cognitive "law." This reveals how the spurious "individualism" of neoclassicism has serious consequences for conceptualizing how markets work.

3 To make his work more accessible, I have edited his major writings (Thornton 1999). His career is described in chapter 13 of this book.

4 This problem is discussed by Stadler, Wagner, and Fontana (2001) and Fontana (2003). The way in which aspects of commodity space preclude adequate characterization of certain economic phenomena is a theme found in the work of Robert Clower, Oskar Morgenstern, and Alfred Sohn-Rethel, among others.

5 The choice of measure of computational complexity will be one of the more contentious areas in this school of economics. To preclude discussion here, but to render our sketch more concrete, imagine that the index used is the Chomsky hierarchy for language recognition. This mode of characterizing market complexity is discussed in Mirowski and Somefun 1998.

6 Indeed one might argue, following Fontana, that a formal model of the various objectives of the market participants would not possess the topological structure of a metric space, but only an accessibility pretopology. See Stadler et al. 2001.

2 On Playing the Economics Card

1 The incident is described in Hodges 1983, 415. Another advocate of an algorithmic approach to science (who also happened to be an economist), namely Herbert Simon, has felt impelled to attack the idea of tacit knowledge in Simon 1974. On the problems of Simon's algorithmic science, see Sent 2001.

2 This opposition is clearly stated in an early lecture, "Popular Education in Economics," dated February 1937. The lecture can be found in the Michael Polanyi papers, Regenstein Library, University of Chicago [hereafter cited as MPP], box 25, folder 9: "The general weakness of utilitarianism . . . is this: that its philosophy makes self-seeking the supreme principle in economic life and assumes that people are happy if their blind acquisitiveness

is transformed into a maximum efficiency. In fact, blind acquisitiveness is repugnant to the social instincts of man. If he co-operates with a community he wants to be conscious of a common purpose. Accordingly, he revolts against the idea that the community should refuse responsibility for giving its citizens opportunity to work and live an educated healthy life." All quotations from the Papers of Michael Polanyi are used with permission of the University of Chicago Library. Utilitarianism is clearly linked to scientism in M. Polanyi 1958, 141–42.

3   The similarities and differences between Polanyi's conception of decentralized market coordination of dispersed knowledge and that of his compatriot Hayek are discussed in chapter 3.

4   In the spirit of Polanyi, one might suggest that modern utilitarianism is perfectly suited to the predicament of the professionalized social sciences and the philosophical profession in modern academia. As a doctrine, its political valence can shift from the most statist bureaucratic planning dogma to the most naturalistic defense of *laissez-faire* at the drop of a hat; its mathematical intricacies act as a barrier to entry to all but the most intrepid; and its empirical emptiness is only surpassed by the delicate subtlety of considerations that can be brought to bear in absorbing the concerns of philosophical traditions that do not even begin to acknowledge the legitimacy of any utilitarian tenets. Utilitarianism manages to arrogate the sobriquet of "rationality" simply because it crudely represses the paradoxes of rationality acknowledged in every other philosophical tradition. It looks like science to those disgusted with interminable indecisive discussions of the character of social reality found in other traditions; and it underwrites a cynical instrumentalism in everyone else. It is the hallmark of the intellectual whose expertise is offered for sale to any and all comers.

5   See, for instance, M. Polanyi 1941, 437: "[The scientist] looks out for a problem to which to apply his special gifts to best advantage and later, when discovery is achieved, puts his claims before his colleagues and tries to gain their acceptance for them, he acts rather like a businessman."

6   See, for instance, the letter to his brother Karl Polanyi dated 3 December 1953 (MPP, box 17, folder 9): "In my opinion, therefore, the classical definition of economics as a logic of choices is wrong. Modern economics is characterised by the interaction of systems of choices operated 'independently' at a large number of centres. This is what I call poly-centricity and I think I have shown that scientific life shows characteristics of poly-centricity in close analogy to the market, the differences being mainly due to the fact that the process of public valuation occurs in a different manner."

7   Polanyi to Gerald Holton, dated 12 November 1963, in MPP, box 6, folder 4.

8   "Each link in these chains and networks will establish agreement between the valuations made by scientists overlooking the same overlapping fields, and so, from one overlapping neighborhood to another, agreement will be established on the valuation of scientific merit throughout all the domains of science" (1969a, 55–56). Since the issue will arise in the next section, it is worthwhile to note here that Philip Kitcher attempts to appropriate Polanyi's conception of overlapping authority to his own conception of "rational author-ity functions" (Philip Kitcher 1993a, 320n). In light of this revival of utilitarianism, one notes the passage immediately subsequent to that quoted above: "Scientific opinion is an opinion not held by any single human mind, but one which, split into thousands of fragments, is held by a multitude of individuals, each of whom endorses the opinion of the other at second hand" (56).

9   This is also a problem for modern normative naturalists like Laudan. See Hands 1994a.

10 See in particular the letter of Polanyi to Karl Mannheim dated 19 April 1944, in MPP, box 4, folder 11: "In regards to the social analysis of the development of ideas, suffice to say that I

reject all social analyses of history which makes social conditions anything more than *opportunities* for a development of thought. You seem inclined to consider moral judgments on history as ludicrous, believing apparently that thought is not merely conditioned, but determined by a social or technical situation. I cannot tell you how strongly I reject such a view."

11 "Nature is given to man ready-made; we may try to elucidate it, but we cannot improve it. But language, literature, history, politics, law and religion, as well as economic and social life, are constantly on the move, and they are advanced by poets, playwrights, novelists, politicians, preachers, journalists and all kinds of other, non-scholarly, writers. These are the primary initiators of cultural change, rather than the Faculties of Arts . . .

We may conclude that the profound distinction between science and technology is but an instance of the difference between the study of nature on the one hand and the study of human activities and the products of human activities, on the other. The universities cannot be the main source of progress either in humanistic or in material culture, as they are in the natural sciences" (1961, 406).

12 Here I must acknowledge the perceptive book by Steve Fuller (2000b), which makes clear the shared problem situation of Polanyi and Kuhn, and in particular its advanced grasp of the thesis that Kuhn's book is ultimately about the defense of science in a situation where it has become inextricably beholden to the state. Where I diverge from Fuller is in the description of the type of economics that one finds in *Structure*. He sees it as Schumpeterian, whereas I find it still essentially orthodox and utilitarian, linked to operations research.

13 "There are limits to proper tolerance. In some cases, epistemic performance is so inflexible that . . . some form of deception or self-deception is occurring. The category of pseudo-scientists is a psychological category . . . Pseudoscientists are those whose psychological lives are configured in a particular way" (Philip Kitcher 1993a, 196).

14 For those interested in what the mathematical model looks like, see chapter 10.

15 "Think of people as part of the natural order. Among their tasks are attempts to represent the natural order. . . . Philosophy has the task of trying to expose, given what we now believe, what are the best ways, individually and collectively, of going on" (Philip Kitcher in Callebaut 1993, 317).

16 "Our species, it seems, can come to terms with wounds to its *amour propre*" (Philip Kitcher 1996, 371).

17 "Molecular genetics currently offers the chance of preventing lives whose quality would inevitably be low and of repairing damage in a small range of cases: The rest is promise. Nevertheless, many reflective people, recalling the extraordinary successes of molecular biology, and comparing them with the recent history of attempts at social policy, believe that the promise will be actualized, that we shall be able to combat the disruptions of defective proteins, but that, lacking comparable expertise with the complexities of social causation, we are doomed to continue blundering (at least for the foreseeable future) from one misguided policy to another" (Philip Kitcher 1996, 312). It is instructive how this position comes very close to that of Polanyi (1961) that all one can really justify in terms of funding at the universities is the natural sciences.

3   Economics, Science, and Knowledge

1 One recent acknowledgement of the political significance of trends in the philosophy of science is Agassi 1995. The political economy of recent philosophers of science is described in Hands 2001. Examples of what is being done with the history of earlier incidents in the philosophy of science include Howard 2003 and Mirowski 2004.

2 Rob Leonard, "Ethics and the Excluded Middle," *Isis* 89 (1998): 1–26; Peter Galison, "Aufbau/Bauhaus," *Critical Inquiry* 16 (1990): 709–52. The locus classicus of this work is, of course, Stephen Toulmin and Alan Janik, *Wittgenstein's Vienna* (New York: Simon and Schuster, 1973).

3 But see Paul Feyerabend, *Killing Time* (Chicago: University of Chicago Press, 1995).

4 This is how he is described in Prosch 1986. This book contains a comprehensive bibliography, revealing two books (1936, 1945) and numerous articles devoted solely to economics, including articles published in the *Manchester School* and the *Review of Economic Studies*.

5 Unpublished transcript of an interview by James Buchanan with Friedrich von Hayek, "F. A. Hayek: Nobel Prize-winning Economist," conducted in 1978 under the auspices of the Oral History Program, University Library, UCLA. Copyright 1983, Regents of the University of California. Text courtesy of Bruce Caldwell.

6 Caldwell 1988. See also Nicolai Juul Foss, "More on Hayek's Transformation," *History of Political Economy* 27 (1995): 345–564, which in my opinion strains too mightly to situate the transformation in 1933 by doggedly keeping the focus upon the narrowly defined business cycle theory. I would especially like to thank Bruce Caldwell for his extensive help with matters germane to the original October 1995 talk (to a group of economists) in Cracow, Poland, that was the basis for this essay; all remaining errors and disagreements are my responsibility alone.

7 The aforementioned articles are reprinted in Hayek, *Individualism and Economic Order* (Chicago: Gateway, 1972); see also Hayek, *The Counter-Revolution of Science* (Indianapolis: Liberty, 1979 [1952]).

8 See, for instance, William Lanouette, *Genius in the Shadows* (New York: Scribners, 1992), 76, noting some evidence of Polanyi's interest in economics before he moved to Manchester.

9 Hayek's memory with regard to the 1950s, as reflected in the passages quoted in the previous section, was a little faulty. Michael Polanyi was offered a position on the Committee on Social Thought at the University of Chicago in 1951 but was blocked from accepting it by the U.S. State Department on the grounds that he had belonged to a "subversive organization" in his youth. On this incident, see material in MPP, box 46, folder 5.

10 *The Recollections of Eugene Wigner*, as told to Andrew Szanton (New York: Plenum, 1992), 157. On his early hesitation in leaving Berlin, see Lanouette, *Genius in the Shadows*, 111, 119. In this he appears to have differed from Hayek, who upon emigration to Britain seems to have become more British than the British. On this, see the numerous comments in *Hayek on Hayek*, ed. Stephen Kresge and Leif Wenar (Chicago: University of Chicago Press, 1994).

11 There are two book-length treatments, the first and best-known being Gary Werskey's *The Visible College* (London: Allen Lane, 1978), which is hampered by its hagiographic approach to the figures of J. D. Bernal and Joseph Needham, its strident Marxist tone, and the lack of provision of deeper context surrounding the whole problem of the relationship of the state to science in Britain. A brief treatment from the other end of the political spectrum is Neal Ward, *Communism and the British Intellectuals* (New York: Columbia University Press, 1959), esp. 131–41, but this provides very little in the way of background at all. The other book-length treatment is McGucken 1984. Chapter 9 is concerned with the Society for Freedom in Science, which Michael Polanyi helped form in 1940. This book is overly concerned with the mechanics of the various British organizations and their response to the Social Relations of Science movement in the 1930s and 1940s, and it lacks the fire and motivation of the other texts. For some primary sources, see MPP, box 15, folders

1–2. Some of the broader issues of Britain's perceived backwardness in science relative to the German context can be found in Tom Wilkie, *British Science and Politics since 1945* (Oxford: Basil Blackwell, 1991).

12   This statement requires much more historical specification than we can devote to it here. What I intend to refer to, crudely, is the "transformation" of the Hayek critique from the more recognizably "economic" version in *Collectivist Economic Planning* to that found beginning with the essay "Economics and Knowledge" and elaborated upon throughout the rest of his life. In this I can only concur with a statement in a letter from Bruce Caldwell, dated 27 June 1995: "What increasingly worried Hayek in the late 1930s was the excitement for all sorts of planning among the non-economist members of the intelligentsia of Britain, the pre-war Laski being a notorious example, but more particularly, the natural scientists whose enthusiasm got popular attention and who were accorded such respect in this heyday of the positivist age. Rather than explaining his critique of socialism, I think that responding to the 'Social Relations of Science' movement helps explain Hayek's move away from economics and towards (1) his 1938 "Freedom and the Economic System" . . . and (2) his critique of scientism."

    The sources of what later became known as Hayek's critique of socialism have yet to be adequately explored. While the standard account, certainly encouraged by Hayek himself, is to trace its genealogy from the Austrian school of economics through Mises, there lingers the problem that many of the early progenitors, such as Menger and Wieser, were not all that hostile to statism, and did not share Hayek's later positions with respect to knowledge. Other more likely sources of the epistemological critique of planning might be found in such collateral figures in Vienna as Oskar Morgenstern and Hans Mayer, or indeed in Polanyi himself. What would seem to emerge from such a reevaluation is a distinctive Austrian approach to epistemology (and especially the question of knowledge and uncertainty) rather than a distinctive Austrian economics.

13   See, for instance, the correspondence between Hayek and Polanyi concerning the attempt to start a "Liberal Journal," "mainly, but by no means exclusively concerned with the problem of economic and social policy and the general questions of individual and particularly intellectual freedom." Hayek to Polanyi, 4 February 1940, MPP, box 4, folder 31. The journal was apparently never published because of a dearth of financial supporters.

14   On this see Werskey, *The Visible College*, chapter 8; McGucken 1984. A phenomenon which requires further research is the role of the "Tots and Quots" club, which brought together many of the main figures of the science planning movement and provided a connection to the Keynesians through the membership of Roy Harrod. Harrod was one of the very few to review Polanyi's book *Full Employment and Free Trade* (1945).

15   The other, entitled "Employment and Money," was even more explicitly Keynesian. The second film was funded by the Rockefeller Foundation, and was screened throughout Britain and the United States. Jacob Marschak even requested to use it in his course on "Monetary Policy" at the New School! MPP, box 4, folder 51. Nevertheless, neither film was very popular with its target audience, the lay public. In the opinion of one educator, it could not be viewed with benefit in the absence of extensive lectures and preparation. H. Shearman to Polanyi, 5 April 1945, MPP, box 4, folder 12.

16   F. A. von Hayek, Review of M. Polanyi, *The Contempt of Freedom*, and Colin Clark, "A Critique of Russian Statistics," *Economica*, n.s. 8 (May 1941): 212. The original articles which eventually became the bulk of *The Counter-Revolution of Science* were published in the same journal in February 1941, n.s. 8:9–36; May 1941, n.s. 8:119–50; August 1941, n.s. 8:281–320; August 1942, n.s. 9:267–91; February 1943, n.s. 10:34–63; February 1944, n.s. 11:27–39.

17 Of course, there were some good reasons for Hayek to maintain a lower profile: "he was forced, for example, to always refer to Germany as the paradigm case of totalitarianism and to mute or veil his opinions about the Soviet ally; also, he was from the German-speaking world, so was going to be viewed by at least some as himself a bit suspect." Bruce Caldwell, letter to Philip Mirowski, 27 June 1995.

18 One letter will have to suffice here to buttress these claims. This is from a letter from J. R. Hicks to Polanyi dated 18 November 1945: "You have certainly done a good work in helping to provide the framework for a new Liberalism. I don't know that I shall end up as 100% Liberal as you are, though I am more on that side than the other. But I agree with Harrod in having sympathy for your vision [rather] than with the ancien regime of Hayek and Fisher." MPP, box 4, folder 13.

19 Michael Polanyi, "The Value of the Inexact," *Philosophy of Science* 3 (1936):233–34.

20 This is the interpretation of Prosch 1986, chapter 20, and Wigner, *The Recollections of Eugene Wigner*, 315. The extent to which this feeling stemmed from Polanyi's perception of the political scene in the late 1960s is not at all clear from the sources, nor from his last work, written with the philosopher Harry Prosch, Polanyi and Prosch 1975.

21 Michael Polanyi, Review of F. A. Hayek, *Individualism and Economic Order*, *Economica*, August 1949, 267.

22 M. Polanyi, Review of F. A. Hayek, *The Counter-Revolution of Science*, *Manchester Guardian*, 2 January 1953, D3.

23 M. Polanyi, Review of F. A. Hayek, *Individualism and Economic Order*, *Economica*, August 1949, 267.

24 Michael Polanyi, *Full Employment and Free Trade*, 2d ed. (Cambridge: Cambridge University Press, 1948), xv–xvi.

25 The quote is not Polanyi's but rather the "central question of all the social sciences" from Hayek's "Economics and Knowledge," *Economica*, n.s. 4 (1937): 54. I switch personas in midstream to make the point that it was not a question that had occurred to people in the social sciences before it had occurred to philosophers of science; and this has some bearing on the "transformation" of the Austrian program.

26 M. Polanyi 1946, 27, 29. It has been common to interpret such passages as references to theological guarantees, but the Jewish Polanyi never strongly committed to any particular religious faith.

27 See "The Republic of Science: Its Political and Economic Theory," reprinted in M. Polanyi 1969a. On this, see chapter 2 of this book.

28 Polanyi bemoaned the ways in which the tabletop science of his youth was largely giving way to "big science," and the extent to which his exit from physical chemistry had something to do with his own disillusionment with this trend. And it is noteworthy that while he would often excoriate the Soviets for the Lysenko affair, he never, to my knowledge, commented upon the various medical "experiments" during the Nazi era, or the development of atomic weapons in the United States, even though some of his Hungarian friends such as Szilard and von Neumann played major roles at Los Alamos. These latter phenomena were relatively free choices by the scientists involved that caused them anguish upon scales previously undreamt of in the West.

29 F. A. Hayek, *The Sensory Order* (Chicago: University of Chicago Press, 1952), 6–7. It is easy to see in this passage another iteration of the aversion to objectivist and behavioralist aspects of scientism which was a major theme of Hayek's in the 1940s.

30 F. A. Hayek, "The Sensory Order after 25 Years," in W. Weimer and D. Palermo, eds., *Cognition and the Symbolic Process*, vol 2 (Hillsdale: Erlbaum, 1982): 291. Those familiar with modern cognitive science, from Dan Dennett's parables about brains in vats to John

Holland's classifier systems, should experience a frisson of recognition here. On a separate note, Walter Weimer recognizes the parallels between Polanyi and Hayek; see 245–47 in the same volume.

31 F. A. Hayek, "The Errors of Constructivism," in *New Studies in Philosophy, Politics, Economics and the History of Ideas* (London: Routledge, 1978), 10. That Polanyi would define this sort of argument as "scientism" can be observed from, e.g., *Personal Knowledge* (Chicago: University of Chicago Press, 1958), 141 et seq.

32 See, for instance, Victor Vanberg, "Spontaneous Market Order and Social Rules," *Economics and Philosophy* 2 (1986): 75–100; Hodgson 1993, chapters 11–12.

33 Jeremy Shearmur, "Hayek and the Case for Markets," in Jack Birner and Rudy van Zijp, eds., *Hayek, Coordination and Evolution* (London: Routledge, 1994), 196.

34 Polanyi and Prosch 1975, 104.

35 Polanyi and Prosch 1975, 110.

4   What's Kuhn Got to Do with It?

1   Popperians were wary of Kuhn from the beginning; see, for instance, Motterlini 1999; Jarvie 1988. But there are fewer and fewer of those around these days; so the modern disaffection should be traced to other sources.

2   All subsequent undated page references are to Fuller 2000b.

3   In a text that Fuller unaccountably neglects to cite in his book, Kuhn wrote: "Forty years ago . . . I came upon a few pieces of the Continental literature on the methodology of social science. In particular, if memory serves, I read a couple of Max Weber's methodological essays . . . as well as some relevant chapters from Ernst Cassirer's *Essay on Man*" (1991, 17).

4   Indeed one can go even further, as Hacking (2000) has done, and attribute the centrality of the doctrine of "incommensurability" in Kuhn to his characterization of the dull algorithmic character of normal science: "Kuhn came to expect incommensurability because he turned flexible ordinary languages into abstract structures between which mutual adaptation or translation had been engineered out." This certainly was the case in Kuhn's career after *The Structure of Scientific Revolutions*.

5   Fuller (2000b, 258) compares Kuhn's "revolutions" to Walt Rostow's own stage theory in economic history; I believe this provides novel insight into the types of arguments that repudiated simplistic rational-choice theories and yet still resonated with cold war mandates. On the hallowed lineage of stage theories, see Meek 1976.

6   The biography by Hershberg (1993) renders this problematic and its consequences with greater clarity than does Fuller himself. Hershberg quotes Conant as writing: "I do not like the atomic age or any of its consequences. To learn to adjust to these consequences with charity and sanity is the chief spiritual problem of our time" (572).

7   See, for instance, Armen Alchian, Kenneth Arrow, and William Capron, "An Economic Analysis of the Market for Scientists and Engineers," RAND Research Memo RM-2190-RC, 1958.

8   On Polanyi's position, see chapter 2 of this book.

9   To find descriptions of this history, as well as outlines of the content of operations research, see Fortun and Schweber 1993; Mirowski 1999; Mirowski 2002 ; Rau 1999.

10 Fuller briefly discusses the connection (327–28) but does not make the links to OR.

11 Fuller even goes so far as to assert that the social sciences provide a more virtuous pedagogical model for science studies, since they "do not launder out ideological disagreements in professional training, but rather enable those disagreements to align with, and often alter conflicts in the society at large" (401). While this is not the place to make the argument in detail, I would suggest that the modern social sciences can be split into two

groups: those that do their laundry in private, and those that scrub in public but have no impact on conflicts in the society at large.

12 One indication of this possibility is the passage on p. 349 that endorsed the neoconservative economist Thomas Sowell's attack on the labor theory of value from a neoclassical standpoint. He writes: "should not STS practitioners ultimately prefer a theory of scientific value based on utility rather than labor?"

13 I am not the first to worry about this. See Steve Downes's review of Fuller's *Science* in *Philosophy of the Social Sciences*, March 2000.

5 The Economic Consequences of Philip Kitcher

1 Philip Kitcher 1993a, 10. All subsequent undated page references are to this book.

2 It is worth noting that the first and last footnotes in *Advancement* refer to Latour, although the latter's position with regard to most of the issues central to Kitcher's work is never explicated in any depth in between.

3 Actually, Hayek's vision of spontaneous order changes quite a bit over the course of his career. A good place to start is the paper by Geoff Hodgson in Mirowski 1994a, and the paper by Caldwell (1988).

4 One might speculate that explicit recourse to Smith or to Hayek would signal a political conservatism that Kitcher, or at least his intended audience, would find repugnant. In any case, there is no attempt to acknowledge any theorist of the invisible hand or spontaneous order in the entire book, a curious omission in so literate an author, one so willing to make numerous generic references to "economics."

5 This grounding of the status of "legitimate epistemic actor" in naturalistic predispositions is much more substantial in the text than one might at first realize, and goes a long way toward explaining various locutions which might otherwise zip by as mere rhetorical figures. For instance: "Few are born antirealists, and those who achieve antirealism typically do so because it is thrust upon them" (Kitchen 1993a, 131). This innuendo that science studies scholars are evolutionarily unfit to be scientists skirts very close to the style of argumentation in Gross and Leavitt 1994.

6 Philip Kitcher's disdain for Freudian psychology may have some relationship to the recent denunciation of it as a pseudoscience by Patricia Kitcher (1993). In any event, to acknowledge psychology as a discipline would be tantamount to the radical naturalism that Kitcher warned against in 1992.

7 The similarity of this description to the projects of noncardinal utilities and "revealed preference" in neoclassical micro theory should set off alarm bells to those who know of its subsequent vicissitudes. Indeed, much of Kitcher reads like a replay of twentieth-century controversies in welfare economics, a fact already noted by Hands (1994a; 2001).

8 Operating from within our own system of capacities, social backgrounds, and experiences, we can explain why our subjects think what they think, do what they do, and succeed to the extent that they succeed. The realist move is to suppose that exactly the same type of account could be given for each or all of us . . . I think the best strategy for responding to powerful objections to realist reliance on reference is to view our understanding of reference as generated by analogy from our assignment of referents to the tokens of others (Philip Kitcher 1993c, 168–69).

9 That Lewontin, in particular, has made the connection between the treatment of evolution as "solving problems" and the projection of a neoclassical economics upon the organism is of the utmost importance in seeing how Kitcher makes many of the same moves in his own work.

10   We discuss the analytical problem to the neglect of possible empirical counterexamples to Kitcher's claim. For instance, James Clerk Maxwell personally relied quite directly upon the existence of an aether to motivate his "displacement current," which led in turn to some of the most dramatic predictions of his theory of electromagnetism. Just because we can now rewrite Maxwell's equations without the aether does not imply that they were *historically* dispensable.

11   I owe these points to a student essay by David Walton and some written comments by Phil Sloan.

12   The issue of the treatment of history in the culture wars would require greater attention than can be devoted to it here. It should be noted, however, that authors like Gross and Leavitt (1994), when refuting "constructivist" history, cannot be bothered to do much more than make vague gestures toward contrary evidence, and by so doing, demonstrate their contempt for the historian's craft.

13   Of course, there are deep problems with this maneuver. See, for instance, Grantham 1994.

14   This raises the frightening prospect that Kitcher and Latour are closer consanguineously than either would care to admit. Both want to reduce science to abstract valuation principles; only Latour wants to go much further than Kitcher in emptying these values of all content and reducing them to simple network configurations. In this, he would more closely follow the historical trend of neoclassical economics itself. This thesis is argued in McClellan (1996).

15   I owe these delightful counterfactuals, as well as the thesis of this paragraph, to Ed Manier.

16   I infer this from comments such as those on p. 312. The canonical source of evolutionary stable strategies is Maynard Smith 1982.

17   "Going on about markets and the failures of neoclassical economics IN GENERAL is thus irrelevant. What is to the point is whether there's a better way of presenting the question of [what kinds of social arrangements favor the acquisition of the cognitive good] by using a 'thicker' notion of society." E-mail of Philip Kitcher to Philip Mirowski, dated 4 September 1994.

18   "There's no real argument in Latour, just rhetorical flourish and, I'm afraid, serious misunderstanding of lots of views. However, I do enjoy talking to him, and I hope that, in time, we can clear some of our disagreements up" (Callebaut 1993, 219).

19   Kitcher's work (1995) on the Human Genome Project perfectly exemplifies this practice. Therein Kitcher first admits that the only sensible prognosis for the HGP is that it will lead to a new eugenics movement, which he attempts to sugarcoat as a "Utopian eugenics." However, rather than see this as a solid reason to oppose such a use of public moneys, he instead asserts that "sources of skepticism about the project are really grounded in sensitivity to broad questions in social philosophy," and since social uses of the natural technology are readily separable, the HGP is really a "good thing."

6   Re-engineering Scientific Credit

1   Hands 2001, chapter 8.

2   As James Boyle (1996, 225) has put it, "Professional economists often talk as though there was a natural suite of property rights which automatically accompanied a free market." The explicit law and economics movement has not made this situation much better. Further, endless debates over the "public good" nature of science are themselves symptomatic of the tendency to ignore the shifting character of authorship in favor of lucubrations over the character of the "output" of science and its difficulty of appropriation.

3 "Once science is properly understood, it turns out that what is good for individual scientists is by and large good for science" (Hull 1988, 304).

4 Choosing an example not entirely at random, consider F. Abe et al., 1992. This is the Collider Detector at Fermilab (CDF) collaboration, one of the two largest experimental particle physics groups in the world. Looking at the entire distribution of multi-authorship, Rob Kling informs me that the median number of authors in the current *Physical Reviews Letters* is 4 to 6. The number of papers with authors numbering in the three digits, once the preserve of high-energy particle physics, is now spreading to the life sciences (Regaldo 1995). You know things are getting out of hand when there are twelve authors on a paper on the problem of scientific authorship, as in, say, Bachrach et al. 1998.

5 The eighteenth-century emergence of the Romantic Author was first pointed out by Martha Woodmansee. For further explication see Woodmansee 1994 and Jaszi 1991.

6 See Keller 1983 on McClintock; Gleick 1992 on Feynman; Mullis 1998 on Mullis; anybody on Hawking . . .

7 Boyle 1996, chapter 6.

8 But not adopted by the United States until 1989: see Halbert 1999, 14.

9 Boyle 1996, 134; Kahin 2001; Lessig 1999.

10 One way to understand the fascination of the philosophy of science in the cold war era with a search for a mechanical set of rules for the "scientific method" was to reify the distinction between the unsystematic search process of the tinkerer and the superior systematic practices of the scientist. The failure of the "received view" in philosophy prepared the way for an erosion of the distinction between the pure and the applied.

11 It is interesting to observe that in another creative yet unavoidably collaborative endeavor, the making of movies, the problem is acknowledged in film credits that distinguish different forms of contributions; Hollywood has even invented an honorific "credit" called "associate producer," which everyone understands can be bestowed as a gift, in much the same way as scientific authorship.

12 In Jon Cohen 1995, 1710.

13 Biagioli 2000a, 87.

14 Biagioli 1999, 510.

15 It is noteworthy that while there is a well-developed subset of economic history devoted to the narrowly construed history of technological change, the major locus of the economic history of science is to be found in the science studies literature. See Shapin 1994; Biagioli 1993; Alder 1997; Kay 1993; Kohler 1991; Smith and Wise 1989. We take this as a symptom of the underdevelopment of a vibrant economics of science.

16 This might be one way to understand the infamous Mertonian "norms" of science, which served to describe the predicament of the cold war scientist without actually confronting any of the actual social structures of accounting and validation.

17 "[Scientific] credit . . . operate[s] (and need[s] to operate) in an economy that is distinct from the capitalist economy" (Biagioli 2000a, 85). "Scientific credit is not about property rights, at least for the time being" (87).

18 See, for instance, Slaughter and Rhodes 1996; Gibbons et al. 1994; Branscomb, Kodama, and Florida 1999; Kneller 1999; Krimsky 2003; Mirowski and Sent 2002.

19 In the interest of hewing to our topic, we must ignore a tremendous amount of detail about distinctions between assemblers, compilers, and applications, not to mention the extreme importance of the rise of the personal computer and a consumer software market.

20 This refers to *Gottschalk v. Benson*, 409 U.S. 63 (1973). The subsequent amendment to the Copyright Act to permit copyright of software was 17 U.S.C. § 101 (1980). Interestingly for

subsequent developments, the case of *Diamond v. Chakrabarty*, 447 U.S. 303 (1980), held that living organisms were patentable. See Kevles 1998.

21 In Branscomb 1994, 150.

22 The Official Draft of UCITA, which is intended to be ratified by state legislatures, can be found at www.law.upenn.edu/ulc/beta/beita/beita200.html, and discussions at www.ucitaonline.com.

23 Drahos 2002. For recent deliberations of WIPO, see www.wipo.int/eng/meetings.

24 149 F.3d 1368 (Fed. Cir. 1998). See www.law.emory.edu/fedcircuit/july98/96–1327.wpd .html.

25 This trend is described in a number of articles included in Mirowski and Sent 2002. While this change has been conceptualized by some in the science studies community as a shift between what has been called "Mode 1/Mode 2" (Gibbons et al. 1994), the author feels, as the reader will observe from the previous citation, that this rubric misses out on many of the major features of the transition.

26 Economists who have discussed science as a market process include Kenneth Arrow in Mirowski and Sent 2002; Ordover and Willig 1978; Zamora Bonilla 2003; and Wible 1998. Philosophers who have used market analogies include Philip Kitcher (1993a), David Hull, Alvin Goldman, and John Ziman. Many of their works are excerpted and discussed in Mirowski and Sent 2002; see also Hands 2001 (chapter 8), where simple conflations of science and market are criticized.

27 Litman 2001, 28.

28 This is also admitted in the business press to be the case in modern times. See, for instance, "Patent Wars," *Economist*, 8 April 2000: "Increasingly, companies realize that among the few remaining barriers to entry are the ones the government hands out in the form of 20-year monopolies."

29 This tends to be the attitude adopted in many of the reports appearing under the rubric of "intellectual property" in the journal *Science*. For a contrary view, see Mirowski and Van Horn 2004.

30 Litman 2001, 131.

31 See Waelde 2001 for this important distinction. It also appears that the EC Directive on Legal Protection of Conditional Access Services is following the lead of the DMCA in this respect.

32 The case of Edward Felten, a Princeton professor who had to withdraw presentation of a paper from a conference after receiving a threatening letter from the Record Industry Association of America, has been documented in the "New Developments" section of Jessica Litman's Web site at www.law.wayne.edu/litman/classes/cyber/newdevo1.html. See also Foster 2001b.

33 For a game theory model of this conundrum in the context of a natural scientist trying to decide whether to encourage or discourage replication of experimental findings, which is just a special case of the problem of identifying reliable research acolytes, see chapter 10.

34 The text of the Database Directive can be found as appendix D to National Research Council 1999.

35 A tabular summary of these differences is provided in National Research Council 1999, 9, table S.2.

36 See, for instance, the accounts in National Research Council 1999; David 2000; and Pamela Samuelson 2001.

37 But a new attempt materialized in March 2001. See Maurer, Hugenholtz, and Onsrud 2001.

38 Pamela Samuelson 2001, 2030.

39 Blumenthal et al. 1996b, 370.

40 Davidoff et al. 2001; Mirowski and Van Horn 2004.

41 Boyle 2000, 2037.

7 Looking for Those Natural Numbers

1   One indication is that the entire September 1988 issue of *Isis* and that of spring 1988 of *Science in Context* were devoted to the problem of historical experiment; other landmarks in interpretation have been Hacking 1983; Shapin and Schaffer 1985; Galison 1987 and 2003; and Wise 1995.

2   The *seterée* was the area of land that could be sown by one *setier* in the vicinity of Bourges. This illustrates how area and volume did not have an abstract existence separate from context.

3   A good introduction to the concept of the group in abstract algebra is Durbin 1985.

4   Joseph Fourier is sometimes given the credit for being the progenitor of "dimensional analysis" because in chapter 2, section 9, of his *Analytical Theory of Heat* (Fourier 1878, 126–30) he notes that physical equations should display dimensional conformity. However, precisely because his comments were not concerned with ideas of "natural measurement" or natural constants, they did not give rise to any further research program in the French context.

5   Under the influence of Rankine and Maxwell, W. S. Jevons tried to import dimensional analysis into his novel mathematical political economy (Jevons [1871] 1970, 118–21); but because he did not understand that his own theory of utility violated dimensional conformity, it was a failure.

6   "We are both in the same boat . . . Instead of reducing economics to physics, I endeavor to impress upon beginners in physics the principles of book keeping." Letter of James Clerk Maxwell to Henry Macleod, quoted in Macleod 1884, 12.

7   Lundgreen states that "it is clearly electricity which represents the main push factor leading to national standardizing bureaus embracing scientific research" (1986, 27). On the importance of Werner von Siemens in prompting the creation of the PTR, see Cahan 1989. The situation in the United States is covered in Cochrane 1966.

8   It should be stressed that these are historical distinctions and not airtight analytical ones. Various theorists (Campbell [1920] 1957; Causey 1969; Krantz et al. 1971) have attempted to settle the issue analytically, but in my opinion none has really been successful.

9   This interest of Einstein's in metrology is curtly denied by Pais (1982, 34), who writes: "The occurrence of dimensionless constants . . . [was] a subject about which he knew nothing, we know nothing."

10 Einstein clarified this further in a letter of 13 October 1945: "In a reasonable theory there are no [dimensionless—P.M.] numbers whose values are only empirically determinable. Of course I cannot prove this. But I cannot imagine a unified and reasonable theory which explicitly contains a number which the whim of the Creator might just as well have chosen differently, whereby a qualitatively different lawfulness of the world would have resulted" (Rosenthal-Schneider 1980, 37).

11 This change in the status of natural measurement has some close parallels with the transition between the earlier and later stances of Wittgenstein toward language.

12 The close formal relationship between the problem of inducing consistency in a set of dimensional constants, the problem of arbitrage in market exchange, and the "subjectivist" justification of probability has not received any attention in the large literature on the "No Dutch Book" condition, to my knowledge. For the probability background, see de Finetti 1974; Heilig 1978. The connection to the concept of arbitrage is outlined in chapter 8.

8   A Visible Hand in the Marketplace of Ideas

1   One author who has begun to sort out the issues is Hands (1994c; 2001).

2   The mathematical model of arbitrage is discussed at greater length in Mirowski 1991a and 1994c. A more elaborate version of the history of physical constants is presented in Mirowski 1993b. That paper can also be read as a companion to chapter 7, which discusses the cultural legitimations of the physical constants. The critique of economics dates from Mirowski 1989b.

3   The modern champion of the Neyman-Pearson school is Mayo (1985). The latest enthusiasts for a Bayesian theory of science are Howson and Urbach (1989) and Franklin (1986; 1990). A very important historical work, one which demonstrates that the two rivals have not been kept as pristinely separate as conventional wisdom supposes, is Gigerenzer and Murray 1987. A more recent work revealing some of the dark sides of the Bayesian ascendancy is Earman 1992.

4   The basic mathematical model is surveyed in Ellerman 1984. Further elaboration and description in the economic context can be found in Mirowski 1991a, 2002, and 1994c.

5   This is true even of more "postmodern" historians, such as many of those gathered at a recent Princeton symposium on the history of precision in quantitative science (see Wise 1995). It is entertaining to observe how much more "radical" are modern physicists than the postmodern historians in this regard: "Modern physics is based on some intrinsic acts of faith, many of which are embodied in the fundamental constants" (Petley 1985, 2).

6   For a discussion of more general central limit theorems and stable distributions, see Zolatarev 1986; and chapters 11 and 12.

7   Take, for instance, Petley's citation of Reich, which turns out to be a verbal report by the president of the Royal Astronomical Society of London on Reich's German experiments (*Philosophical Magazine* 1838, 283–84). On the determination of the gravitational constant, supposedly a repetition of and improvement on Cavendish's experiment, the commentator remarks: "The arm itself appears to have been nearly of the same length as that used by Cavendish, but we are not informed of its weight, nor of the weight of the small balls." Even the gathered company recognized that this might be a source of variance, if not error. While on this topic, the widespread impression that early paradigm determinations of the physical constants might be "restaged" for modern audiences is more a theatrical than an epistemic prospect, given the spotty character of early experimental reports, combined with vast differences in the very character of the materials used between then and now. This point is nicely made for nineteenth-century practices in physics by Stansfield (1990).

8   See, for instance, the discussion in Birge 1957 (43–47). In light of the crusade by Allan Franklin (1986, chapter 5; 1990, 132) to rehabilitate the reputation of Millikan after the problems identified by Holton (1978), this singling out of the Nobel Prize winner is especially interesting.

9   I must here enter a demurrer concerning the way in which error budgets are regarded by Nancy Cartwright. Whereas she views them as evidence of the "totally controlled experiment" (Cartwright 1989, section 2.4.2) in pursuit of novel findings, I see them instead as ultimate evidence of an absence of tight prior knowledge and control, which is stanched by means of a relatively arbitrary assessment of what magnitudes of error will be countenanced. It is an approach of the engineer or the grants administrator, rather than being Cartwright's exemplar of the Millian inquirer after tendencies and capacities.

10   It is necessary to stress that the Birge ratio cannot indicate where the problem lies; nor is a low Birge ratio prima facie evidence of experimental success, since collusion could equally

well produce a $B = 1$. There are also many proposed refinements of the Birge ratio in the metrology literature, discussed in Petley 1985 (305–6). It is prudent to point out that we have only just begun to sketch the social theory of the various options open to the individual scientist when confronted with a large-scale arbitrage opportunity as described above. Mathematically, "error" can indifferently be reduced by throwing out some experiments, reallocating error among existing experiments, or changing the theory and reconfiguring the graph. In real life, the options are not so indifferently available to every scientist. Birge himself is not remembered in standard histories of physics because he did not engage in the high-status occupation of theorists to banish error, nor did he generate more estimates of the relevant constants. To put it bluntly, metrology is not a royal road to a Nobel Prize. This will clearly bias the distribution of reactions to error. (I owe this point to Michael Power.)

11 For claims along these lines, see Morgan 1990 and Cartwright 1989. The problems with these assertions are discussed in Mirowski 1990a and 1995b.

9 Brewing, Betting, and Rationality

1 All subsequent references of the format (B/THB/. . .) are to the Truman archive at the Greater London Record Office.

2 A good description of the beer-making process can be found in Michael Dunn, *The Penguin Guide* (1979). We should also remind the reader that in Britain it was extremely unusual for any firm to have a fixed periodic and consistent closing of its books until the advent of the Company Acts in the mid-nineteenth century.

3 Robert Fogel, in Fogel and Elton, eds., 1983, 26.

4 Brown and Maital 1981; Asch and Quandt 1987; Dokko and Edelstein 1989; Pearce 1984; Weiller and Mirowski 1990.

5 The classic anthology of papers on cointegration is Engle and Granger 1991. A survey is provided by Dickey, Jansen, and Thornton 1991.

6 In some instances, ties were settled by awarding two winners. Also, at the very end of our period, a few new punters were allowed to bet, whom we have excluded from our tables. They were included, however, in the calculations underlying our tables.

7 Now that the top graduate schools in economics have moved on to game theory as their microeconomics of choice, some might read the above comments as simply endorsing that trend. That would be a mistake; but that particular argument is irrelevant to the present intent of this chapter.

8 See Howson and Urbach 1989; Gigerenzer and Murray 1987; Mirowski 1995b.

9 The Bayesian statisticians believe that they have the intellectually superior approach to this problem: but there are good arguments against them as well. See Mirowski 1995b and Gigerenzer and Murray 1987.

10 See the *Dictionary of National Biography* 3:559–61; Buxton 1849. As yet there exists no scholarly biography.

11 In Thomas Fowell Buxton's Observation book (B/THB/G/63) one finds the following comments, dated 29 August 1812: "But above all the foregoing modes of improving the profits of our trade, there is one which I have not a doubt is more especially in our interest. This great invaluable secret is—making our beer the best in the Town. Compared with this the mode of gaining trade by large allowances to the publicans—To put it in the most favourable point of view for allowances, we will admit that in the latter case you have the publican in your favour, and the public against you—in the former the public in your favour, and the publican against you, but it is clear to my mind that it is the consumer who ultimately decides, & that his approbation is worth twenty times as much as the retailer is."

12 The following comments are excerpted from (B/THB/A/129), which was Robert Hanbury's personal memo book. In an entry dated 25 August 1831, he wrote: "It is desirable
that we should relieve Mr. Pryor in the management of the storehouse & that we should
look out for a suitable head clerk. He would be more the worse if he understood Ale
Brewing." On 13 July 1837, upon the naming of Arthur Pryor as a partner on a trial basis,
Hanbury wrote, "We consent to take him only in the hope that his brother being here will
be a cheque upon him & lend to his reform & induce him to render himself useful but if
we are disappointed in the hope of his reform he will not be allowed to remain here."

10 Why Econometricians Don't Replicate

1 This criticism also applies to some recent philosophers of science who have had recourse
to Bayesian learning models, such as Franklin and Howson 1984 and Franklin 1986. To see
an elaboration of our criticism in that context, see Galison 1988.
2 One well-publicized case where the issue of replication seemed to be central to the controversy was the flap over the existence of "cold fusion." If actual replication were simply
defined, then why did *Science* magazine compare an "index of fusion confidence" to the
ups and downs of the stock market (Pool 1989)? It is our impression that the model
presented below could be profitably applied to the *actual* history of this incident, where
many actors were engaged in protracted negotiations over what it was they were claiming
to replicate, resulting in many bizarre twists and turns (Simon 2002). On the more general
lack of replication activity in the history of science, see Collins 1985 and Pinch 1985.
3 Urbach 1981 argues that repeated replication raises the probability that the theory is in fact
true but that the incremental increase in this probability decreases with successive replications. This still runs afoul of Popper's opposition to an inductive logic.
4 We assume that each extender has the same cost function. An appendix available from
the authors shows that the same qualitative results can be obtained while relaxing this
assumption.
5 We do not allow *O* to reveal his information selectively in this model, i.e., whatever he
reveals, he reveals to everyone. If selective disclosure were possible, replication would be
even less likely than our model suggests.
6 We assume that the extender extends if he is indifferent between extending and not
extending.
7 We assume that the replicator replicates if he is indifferent between replicating and not
replicating.
8 This raises the interesting methodological question of whether dependence of the rational
expectations literature upon relatively uncomplicated vector autoregressions encouraged
the rapid profusion of econometric counterevidence.

11 From Mandelbrot to Chaos

1 One may occasionally find an economist working with Hamiltonians; but it is clear that
(a) they are not the favored mode of conceptualization of dynamics in neoclassical theory
(Weintraub 1989) and (b) there is absolutely no agreement upon the proper interpretations of Hamiltonians because of the problems mentioned in Mirowski 1989b, chapter 7;
1989d. As a parenthetical remark, the favored tactic of resort to Liapunov techniques to
discuss dynamics has *never* been plausibly linked to the core neoclassical tenet of optimizing behavior (Bausor 1987).
2 An even more involved (and epicyclic?) procedure takes the format of ARCH models,

which allow variances of Gaussian disturbances to themselves vary in an autoregressive scheme. See Engle (1982). This earned that author the Nobel Prize in 2003. A third way of building in epicycles is to treat the variance of the distribution of prices as if it were the result of a draw from a finite-variance distribution. See Mandelbrot's reaction in Mandelbrot 1973.

3   In conversations Mandelbrot has expressed his reticence with regards to protracted controversy. In that instance, "[a co-worker] had grown impatient with my refusal to reopen old fights that had been won to an acceptable degree, and for my deliberate preference for seeking soft acceptance, with controversy only when it is unavoidable, as opposed to hard acceptance, with unforgiving victims" (conversation with author).

4   We have sacrificed a certain modicum of precision here in the interest of making the cross-disciplinary connections more transparent. In fact, exact self-similarity is a pure geometric concept characterizing such abstract objects as the Koch curve. Statistical self-similarity is more characteristic of phenomena such as coastlines, mountains, etc. Finally, in a strict sense, fractional Brownian motion is self-affine rather than self-similar: if the time axis were to be magnified by a factor $\theta > 1$, the value of the self-affine variable would be magnified by a factor of θH where $H > 1/2$.

5   To be more precise, Mandelbrot wrote, "A fractal is by definition a set for which the Hausdorff Besicovich dimension strictly exceeds the topological dimension" (Mandelbrot 1983, 15). But perusal of the appendices, and particularly pages 357–66, makes one realize in retrospect that the attempt to restrict fractals to a metric conception was leading to a proliferation of dimension definitions. This led in turn to a subsequent realization that a single number is not sufficient to characterize the fractal objects pioneered by Mandelbrot (Mandelbrot 1986; Halsey et al. 1986). But here we are concerned with the recapitulation of the historical road from economics to fractals (and back again), which includes what would now be regarded as errors, detours, etc.

6   The technical terms are all explained at an incredibly non-technical level in Gleick (1987). The rejection of the whole Hamiltonian approach to dynamics is clear from a quote from the physicist Libchaber: "A physicist would ask me, how does this atom come here and stick there? . . . And can you write the Hamiltonian of the system? And I tell him, I don't care, what interests me is the *shape*, the mathematics of the shape and the evolution" (Gleick 1987, 210).

7   One must acknowledge a number of apparently dynamic models in growth theory, capital theory, and the like, but sophisticated neoclassical theorists will admit that these achieve their seeming dynamics by either resorting to single-good models with only one consumer, no production, etc. etc., or else writing everything in terms of "utility units," hence obviating any general equilibrium structure. For a survey of such attempts see Burmeister 1980, Wulwick 1990; Weintraub 1989. The general problem of a full neoclassical dynamics is discussed in detail in Mirowski 1989b; Mirowski 1989d. That is not to say that neoclassical theorists appreciate having this century-long failure pointed out to them: "Everyone knows that economic dynamics isn't in a satisfactory state. Everyone knows that error terms shouldn't just be tacked on to deterministic equations. One more paper that says these things doesn't add anything to the practice of economics." Letter of Hal Varian to Philip Mirowski, June 17, 1988.

8   The Sarkovskii theorem is based upon the following ordering of the natural numbers:

$$3 \succ 5 \succ 7 \succ \ldots \succ 2 \cdot 3 \succ 2 \cdot 5 \succ \ldots \succ 2^2 \cdot 3 \succ 2^2 \cdot 5 \succ \ldots$$
$$\succ 2^3 \cdot 3 \succ 2^3 \cdot 5 \succ \ldots \succ 2^3 \succ 2^2 \succ 2 \succ 1$$

The theorem states that if $f: \mathbb{R} \to \mathbb{R}$ is continuous, and f has a periodic point of prime period k, then if $k \succ \ell$ in above ordering, then f also has a periodic point of period ℓ. See Devaney 1986, 62 et seq.

9   This raises the possible objection that I have just now ignored the contention of Mandelbrot mentioned earlier in this chapter: that the assumption of continuous motion is part of the problem in orthodox economics. To prevent any confusion, I would like to suggest that the issues surrounding table 9 are problems of neoclassical economics, a theory which began by copying the physical metaphor of motion in a commodity space. In a truly alternative economics, one which rejected imitation of physics, such as the one described in chapter 1, these confusions over the meaning of "chaos" would not pose any obstacle.

10   Mitchell Feigenbaum: "The whole tradition of physics is that you isolate the mechanism and all the rest flows. That's completely falling apart. Here you know the right equations but they're just not helpful." Quoted in Gleick 1987, 174. See Barenblatt 1996 for examples.

11   Kelsey (1988, 25) mentions this in passing, but does not seem to realize how it undermines the rest of his article. Undoubtedly this derives from his ignorance of the origins of neoclassical economics in copying energy physics. This is just one of a sequence of examples of the *contretemps* which economic theorists could avoid if they did not hold the history of their discipline in such contempt.

12   Mandelbrot's Economics

1   Mandelbrot himself relates this story in an interview in Albers and Alexanderson 1987, 231–34. I discuss this sequence of papers in chapter 11.

2   It is not even clear that Pareto used least squares or any other statistical procedure to derive his "law." Rather, it seems, he was primarily interested in suggesting that income distribution was generally invariant to human intervention, as a prelude to an argument against the efficacy of socialism. For further historical discussion of the law, see Persky 1992 and Mirowski 1994a, 55–57.

3   Mandelbrot (1983, 335). This problem of economics being dominated by perceptions of what is effective or lawlike in physics has bedeviled neoclassical economics since its origins, as explained in Mirowski 1989b. We shall discover that physicists often play a critical role in shifting the allegiances of mathematical economics, even in the episodes described herein.

4   The relevant citations are in Blattberg and Sargent 1971, Fama 1963, Fama 1965a, and Paul Samuelson 1972. The episode with Sargent is nicely covered in Sent 1998.

5   There is as yet no history of the incorporation of probability theory into economics, although a start has been made by Menard 1987 and Mirowski 1989c and 1997. A nice history of neoclassical approaches to theories of speculative prices written for the general public is in Bernstein 1992. On some evidence that Mandelbrot has been effectively written out of orthodox histories of theories of asset pricing, see Bernstein 1992; for another, see LeRoy 1989. For contrary evidence that the efficient markets hypothesis is no longer in vogue, see Ridley 1993.

6   This seemingly intemperate characterization is supported by many who lived through the era. See, for instance, the retrospective account by Paul Samuelson entitled "Is Real-World Price a Tale Told by the Idiot of Chance?" in Paul Samuelson 1977, 471–75.

7   Mandelbrot's retrospective commentary on this piece makes the point even clearer: "The notion I was propounding around 1964 . . . referred to the conventional wisdom that the

study of weather and of economics is just a bit harder than the study of perfect gases, but that it will eventually achieve the same degree of perfection, by using the same means. To the contrary, my work suggested a profound qualitative distinction between the underlying fluctuations, and suggested that the theories of the corresponding phenomena were bound to differ sharply" (1987, 118).

8   This is all very nicely covered in Sent 1994. In a final interview with Sargent, she confronts him with this curious silence. He responded: "First, it's a pain to do those estimators the way you want to, so you cut yourself off from a lot. But that's not the reason I stopped. I guess the answer is I was interested in other stuff, and also Peter Clark's thing really, really influenced me."

9   Mandelbrot's impatience with economists more readily comes out in conversation: "When a fractal theory really starts moving by itself I tend to become technically underequipped to continue to participate, and it becomes wise to move on. But in economics it is clear that I did not stay long enough" (in Albers and Alexanderson 1987, 224).

10   For precisely this reason, there is no decent survey of this literature bridging the various communities, to my knowledge. For a sampling of studies which support the Mandelbrot hypothesis see Simkowitz and Beedles 1980 and Cornew, Town, and Crowson 1984. For a sampling of studies critical of the hypothesis, see Akgiray and Booth 1988, Gribbin, Harris, and Lau 1992, Hall, Brorsen, and Irwin 1989, and Lau, Lau, and Wingender 1990. For studies which focus upon the presence or absence of long dependence, see Aydogan and Booth 1988, Fang, Lai, and Lai 1994, Greene and Fielitz 1977, and Mandelbrot 1960.

11   This paragraph summarizes the following studies: Akgiray and Booth 1988, Akgiray and Lamoureux 1989, Gribbin, Harris, and Lau 1992, Hall, Brorsen, and Irwin 1989, Jansen and de Vries 1991, Lau, Lau, and Wingender 1990, McCulloch 1994, and Pesaran and Robinson 1993.

12   See, for instance, Bollerslev, Chou, and Kramer 1992, 22–23. See the discussion of the BDS test in the next section of this chapter. Moreover, GARCH does a poor job of miming the "fat-tails" phenomenon: "the conditional normality assumption in ARCH generates some degree of unconditional excess kurtosis, but typically less than adequate to fully account for the fat-tailed properties of the data. One solution to the kurtosis problem is the adoption of conditional distributions with fatter-tails" (Bollerslev, Chou, and Kramer 23). Another solution would be Occam's razor.

13   The major sources are Mirowski 1989b, 1994b, 2002. Another important factor is the rise of the rational expectations movement in orthodox macroeconomics, a topic which cannot be covered here, but which is nicely discussed in Sent 1998. The key to understanding much of the history is to appreciate how much the players at differing junctures were conscious of the degree to which they were willing to imitate physical models. See, for instance, Brock 1991, 233.

14   This was the major thesis of chapter 11, although consciousness of this point is still lacking in many of the major proponents. There is an extensive literature on chaos in overlapping-generations models, covered in Benhabib, ed., 1992, which we shall ignore for the remainder of this chapter. Few seem to assert that chaos has been shown to be theoretically unlikely in economics; most seem to simply presume its presence or absence to be predominantly an empirical question.

15   Strictly speaking, it cannot even be called a test for IID random variables, since there exist some "pathological cases" where BDS will accept the null even when the time series is not IID. See Brock, Hsieh, and LeBaron 1991, 47.

16   The history of the Santa Fe connection is covered in Mirowski 1995a.

13   The Works of William Thomas Thornton

1   For those who require a skeleton key to decode the parallels, here we are referring to the frequent confusion of William Thomas Thornton with Henry Thornton (1760–1815), a leading authority on early British monetary economics. On these confusions, see Peake 1994. And of course, the Danish prince without whom our drama would have no protagonist is none other than John Stuart Mill, and Fortinbras is William Stanley Jevons.

2   These statements refer to the set of arguments referred to as the Sonnenschein-Mantel-Debreu theorems. For the technical discussions, see Sonnenschein 1972; Mantel 1976; Hildenbrand 1994. A good non-technical introduction is provided by Rizvi (1994; 1998).

3   Lest this seem a bootless caricature, we bid the reader to consult the first chapter of Niehans 1990.

4   His intellectual biography is the subject of a forthcoming Notre Dame PhD dissertation by Aida Ramos.

5   We should note that precision in language matters here, a precision lacking in Cournot's English translator. *Débit* has the connotation of retail sales, as from a shop. This is significant, since it was precisely in this era that retail stores with fixed posted prices were becoming prevalent in urban contexts (Alexander 1970; Fairchilds 1993). It is true that in this chapter Cournot states that he regards *débit* and *demande* as synonyms, but the reason is important: "we do not see for what reason theory need take account of any demand which does not result in a sale" (46). Already we are far from the world of neoclassical economics.

6   The need to make these distinctions is provoked by the ubiquitous unreliable accounts to be found in the modern secondary literature on the history of economic thought. Most textbooks simply take any mention of "supply and demand" as making reference to the Marshallian apparatus *avant la lettre*, no matter who the author. Some, such as Samuel Hollander, venture much further beyond the pale in insisting upon a profound continuity between classical and neoclassical writers by spinning interpretations which construct each individual as a more or less conscious Marshallian. (This practice was criticized by Neil de Marchi in Thweatt, ed., 1988, 146.) Elsewhere, one is often confronted by such factually false statements as: "The chief adversary of the labor theory of value in the nineteenth century was always the supply-and-demand theory" (Ekelund and Hebert 1990, 160).

7   "Mill's theory of value shifted the emphasis to the equilibrium of demand and supply" (Niehans 1990, 128). "Mill clearly analysed supply and demand in terms of schedules, thus clearing up much of the confusion present in earlier controversies" (Backhouse 1985, 40).

8   Mill's *Collected Works*, 15:574–75.

9   See, for instance, the footnote on page 123: "In these masterly papers, Mr. Mill will be found to have anticipated many of the remarks in the text, and he has, moreover, discussed, at considerable length, some matters to which my plan required only a slight reference."

10   Comment at the Political Economy Club, December 6, quoted in White 1994, 149.

11   While the exact nature of discussions of the Political Economy Club is not reported in the minutes, they are clear about who held the various positions in the club. Both were officers and Newmarch eventually succeeded Thornton as treasurer of the club.

12   Political Economy Club 1921.

13   Both the timing of Thornton's publications and his having identified in 1866 supply and demand as the theoretical crux of the problem of wages give the lie to ridiculous attempts by Jacob Hollander, following the lead of Wilson (1871) and others, to smear Thornton by

suggesting that he derived his ideas from Francis Longe's *Refutation of the Wages Fund Theory* (1866). Likewise, the attempt by Forget (1991) to sympathetically link Mill and Longe while treating Thornton as somehow external to the Millian tradition will also be shown inconsistent with the evidence.

There are some further tantalizing bits of evidence that Thornton had been pressing Mill on weaknesses in his account of demand and supply even before the papers on wages and unions. On this, see Mill's *Collected Works*, 3:608.

14 Macmillan Archives, British Library, Manuscripts Room. Emphasis in original.

15 Examples of this interpretation can be found in Ekelund 1985; Hollander 1985, 409–17; Schwartz 1972; Vint 1994; Backhouse 1985; Niehans 1990, 129. Hollander's statement can serve as the epitome of this error: "Thornton's book merely provided an opportunity to express publicly the reservations against formulations of the wages fund doctrine such as Fawcett's which Mill already had in mind for several years" (1985, 418n).

16 The footnote is found in the first edition of *On Labour* (1869, 84–85n). This also explains why Longe's *Refutation* (1866) was essentially irrelevant for both Mill and Thornton, contrary to Forget (1991).

17 For a discussion of the central importance of symmetry principles in economic theory, see Mirowski 1989b; Sent 1998.

18 This assessment is shared by the modern proponents of a Whig history of the neoclassical ascendancy. See, for instance, the assessment of the Nobelist John Hicks: "The evidence surely is that after 1848 [Mill] again turned away from economics. There is very little about economics in his correspondence, until we come to his last years (he died in 1873). Then there are letters directed to his friend W. T. Thornton, who had written a book entitled *On Labour*. But it seems to me that these letters show only that by that date he had got so far away from economics that he had lost the grip he had once possessed" (1983, 61).

19 See Mill's comments on William Stanley Jevons in his letter to Cairnes dated 5 December 1871, in O'Brien 1943, 274. The contempt was mutual. On the latter, see Jevons 1878 and his famous complaint in the *Theory of Political Economy* that "that able but wrong-headed man, David Ricardo, shunted the car of economic science on to a wrong line—a line, however, on which it was further urged towards confusion by his equally able and wrong-headed admirer, John Stuart Mill" ([1871] 1970, 72).

20 A very readable summary of Huxley's career is to be found in Desmond 1994. The bearing of the doctrine of Darwinism upon many of the key figures in our narrative, including Cairnes, Fleeming Jenkin, and Jevons, is briefly assayed in section 6 of this chapter.

21 See, for instance, Pelling 1963; Finn 1993; Howell 1890; Webb and Webb 1904; Clements 1961; Biagini 1987.

22 There remains the interesting issue of what Marx thought of Thornton, although one might construct a preliminary conspectus from his scattered remarks on Mill. I have been unable to find any commentary, unusual for one so comprehensive in his critique of political economy.

23 Cairnes: "If this style of reasoning be legitimate, the whole structure of economic doctrine must inevitably go down" (1874, 184). Jevons: "Though Mr. Thornton's objections are mostly beside the question, his remarks have served to show that the actions of the law of supply and demand were inadequately explained by previous economists" ([1871] 1970, 149).

24 All subsequent starred (*) references are to the edition of *On Labour* found in the *Economic Writings of William Thornton*, vol. 4, Pickering and Chatto, 1999.

25 The widespread faith in "Cooperation" as economic panacea was subjected to scathing critique by Frederic Harrison in his "Industrial Cooperation" (1865; reprinted 1908),

323–65. Although Thornton repeatedly refers to this article, it seems to us that he never adequately addressed Harrison's fundamental point, that cooperatives have never been successful outside of retail activities, and the reason for this is that they do not change any aspect of the employment relationship in any substantial manner.

26 The nearest modern thinker to this position is David Ellerman (1995). He is one of few to try to develop some positive economic theory out of the ashes of the pyrrhic Cambridge capital controversy of the 1960s.

27 These are discussed in his essay "Recent Phases of Scientific Atheism" in his *Old Fashioned Ethics*, especially 1873b, 217–23. Thornton's primary difference from those he calls the "Darwinians" is his attempt to preserve some compatible version of creationism.

28 See the articles by Bowler and Hull in Kohn 1985 and Bowler 1988. Jenkin's review appeared in 1867, almost contemporaneously with his work on unions.

29 See note 2 above. The significance of the SMD proofs for the historical attempts to marry Walrasian theory to supply and demand explanations is explored in Mirowski and Hands 1998.

30 "The Marshallian model remains the most useful characterization ever developed of what happens when demand and supply changes . . . What is the alternative proposed and how is it superior in describing or predicting economic motivations?" (Ekelund and Thornton 2001, 517). The answer requires at least another book. Let me recommend Mirowski 2002.

14 Smooth Operator

1 Langford L. Price, Memoirs and Notes on British Economists, 1881–1947, MS 107, 15, Brotherton Library, University of Leeds. Price also relates the following anecdote, which gives some insight into Marshall's character (12):

> I heard that at that time when Marshall was Principal of University College, Bristol, William Ramsay, then a Professor there, solemnly summoned one morning and received with a very grave face, thought that he was going to have intimation of some intended dismissal from his post or something similarly serious. But he was only asked his opinion about the proper place of a new umbrella stand.

That Marshall was humorless when it came to economics would be a characterization which he himself would probably accept. For example, in a letter to Edgeworth dated 6 June 1896, delivering a reprimand on the "best way to conduct a Journal," he wrote: "By the end of your letter I am able to see more fully the dry and caustic humour of your notice: but I don't think the ordinary readers will: & I dislike jokes in an Economic Journal." Letter in Edgeworth-Marshall correspondence, deposited in the London School of Economics Library, manuscript department.

2 This gross caricature must be fine-tuned depending upon the author in question. For instance, in Adam Smith only "unproductive" pursuits destroyed value. For more on this and other distinctions, see Mirowski 1989b, chapter 4.

3 One particularly glaring exemplar of this problem appears in the work of Samuel Hollander, where any appearance of something that might be construed as Marshallian supply and demand is immediately identified as an anticipation of the neoclassical organon, to the extreme extent of claiming that there has been only one coherent unified research program in the entire history of economic thought (Hollander 1987). It will become obvious that the major thesis of this chapter directly questions such practices. But at the opposite end of the spectrum, such otherwise discerning historians as Bharadwaj (1978a)

assert that supply and demand explanations were the thin wedge used to insinuate neo-classical theory into classical discourse. This, too, is denied herein. If in this respect I can make some small contribution to transcending the conflict between the polar positions of Hollander and the neo-Ricardians over value theory, which raged throughout the 1980s, I shall undoubtedly be promoted in my next life to something more exalted, like a lawyer.

4 "At our Rest Dinner in July 1822 whilst we are conversing on the probable prices of Barley and Hops for the following year, it was suggested and agreed to that at our future annual Rest Dinners each of us should put down in writing what we considered would be the prices of Barley & Hops on the first Monday in January in the ensuing year." Greater London Record Office, Ace 73.36 B/THB. These are the subjects of chapter 9.

5 That the requirements of formalization motivated Whewell to a greater degree than any others is suggested not just by the quotation but also by a notebook on political economy, MS no. R. 18.8 in the Whewell papers in the Trinity College Library, Cambridge. There, in a section which seems to be a sketchbook for the 1829 article, he makes a list of various possible equilibrium concepts which might be applied to mathematical formalizations of political economy.

6 In Whewell's *Six Lectures on Political Economy* (1862), 51, he explicitly repudiates mathematical models of supply and demand, which should quash all claims such as that in Henderson (1973) that Whewell should be regarded in any way as a precursor of neoclassicism.

7 This essay was originally published in *Recess Studies*, edited by Sir Alexander Grant and published in Edinburgh in 1870. The version here cited is drawn from Jenkin's collected papers.

8 One example should suffice. In 6 April 1896, Marshall wrote to Edwin Seligman: "On p. 156 you seem to think I was helped out by Fleeming Jenkin's paper. It is a matter of no moment but as a fact my obligations are solely to Cournot; not to Fleeming Jenkin or Dupuit. I had given the main substance of my doctrines in lectures a year or two before he read his paper at Edinburgh" (Dorfman 1941, 407). Seligman, in reply, tried to placate him on this point, only to discover that the matter was of greater moment than a man with an average sense of humor might allow. Marshall wrote in another letter of 10 July 1896 (and not 21 October as stated in Dorfman): "You say you think it was 'natural' to assume that I had borrowed my theory of taxation in relation to consumer's rent—or some part of it—from Fleeming Jenkin. Will you kindly forgive my saying plainly that it seems most unnatural" (407–8).

Although Whitaker (1975, 2:241) writes, "It is unfortunate that evidence on dating is insufficient to justify Marshall's claim that he anticipated Jenkin, but there is nothing in the annotations making such a claim inherently implausible," this should be counter-balanced by evidence such as Foxwell's letter to J. M. Keynes, 24 April 1925 (J. M. Keynes papers, Cambridge): "I happened to come across [Jenkin's 1870 paper] in the Easter vacation of 1870, when I was attending Marshall's lectures on diagrammatic economics, & I shall never forget his chagrin as he glanced through the article as I showed it to him. There was nothing in Cournot which so closely agreed with Marshall's general approach to the Theory of Value & particularly to his statement of the equation of supply & demand." While the decontextualized "diagrammatic" approach could be attributed to Cournot, much of the actual structure of argument came from Jenkin. How anyone could get away with claiming that he had invented something which had been published twenty years before his own book, and which many knew he had seen at that time, is simply a testament to the power of Cambridge in constructing its own genealogy as part and parcel of its orthodoxy.

9   Marshall to Edgeworth, 8 February 1880, London School of Economics Miscellaneous Collection, folder 470: "As to the interpretation of the Utilitarian dogma, I think you have made a great advance: but I still have a hankering after a mode of exposition in which the dynamical character of the problem is made more obvious; which may in fact represent the cultural notion of happiness as a process rather than a statical condition." That the energetics was more important than the utilitarianism has not been previously noted; one would begin to illustrate this thesis by examining Herbert Spencer's *First Principles* and Benjamin Kidd's *Social Evolution*, two works that Marshall admitted were important to his intellectual development. Both deal in the mid-nineteenth-century fascination for the conservation of energy, and both reveal the ties to evolution and biological metaphor so prominent in Marshall's thought.

10   See, for instance, Kreps 1990, 37: "Because Marshallian demand plays a very limited role in the remainder of this book . . . we will give the subject relatively short shrift here."

11   Letter of Marshall to Edgeworth, 28 March 1880, London School of Economics Miscellaneous Collection, folder 470.

15   Problems in the Paternity of Econometrics

1   I hope that no one is offended by the gender of my extended metaphor of paternity. After having read through much of the correspondence concerning the founding of the Econometrics Society in the 1930s, with its persistent and unselfconscious references to "good men," the "best men," and so forth, I think most would agree that the metaphor was apt. See, for instance, Irving Fisher's letter to Edwin Bidwell Wilson dated 4 December 1931: "As you know, all men, and particularly academic men, are partly paid for their efforts in honor, and even if the motive is often unworthy, perverted, or miscarries, it is a real psychological force which ought to be harnessed up." This letter can be found in the Edwin Bidwell Wilson Collection, Harvard University Archives, HUG 4874.203, Correspondence, box 1930/31. Note Fisher's flirtation with sexual metaphor.

2   A description of Moore's course offerings at Columbia in 1904–5 can be found in a letter to Walras published in Walras 1965, 3, letter 1573.

3   In Mills 1924 one finds the same appeal to pragmatism, to Clerk Maxwell, and to Moore himself: "Of contemporary writers, Henry L. Moore has not only clearly described the essential characteristics of statistical laws, but has demonstrated the fruitfulness of the concept when applied to economic problems" (45).

4   Letter of Moore to E. R. A. Seligman, 10 May 1910, Seligman Collection, Columbia University Manuscripts Library.

5   Letters in the Henry Moore Collection at Columbia University Library Manuscripts Department, box 3.

6   Moore Collection, letter of Moore to Henry Schultz, 18 June 1934, box 3. This remark is also revealing concerning Walras's uncertain grasp of physics (discussed in Mirowski and Cook 1990). First, anyone familiar with the history of science would hardly claim that Laplace, who was at the center of the system of *grandes écoles*, was in any sense neglected in his own lifetime. Secondly, it shows that Walras saw himself as imitating rational mechanics before the development of the energy concept, even though the formalism of neoclassicism was predicated on the energy metaphor.

7   In a letter dated 20 September 1924 to Edwin Seligman he compares his entire salary history with that of Harry Seager at Columbia in an apparently unsuccessful plea for a raise. The beleaguered tone is plain: "A few years ago . . . you made a memorable speech in which you went directly to the heart of the matter in saying: 'The only way to promote

research is to find a man who can do it and let him alone.' You were absolutely right. But how does it work in the particular case of our own department? For twenty odd years Professor Seager and myself, who entered Columbia together with the same rank and same salary, have pursued different ends. He has preferred administration and teaching and has justly prospered in honors and income. I have accepted the necessary isolation and incurred the risks of the investigator who attacks new problems and devises new methods, but after nearly a quarter of a century of unremitting labor I have received from the University some thirty thousand dollars less than my honored colleague." Letter in Seligman Collection, Columbia Archives, box 37, folder 100.

8   Moore collection, box "Old Lectures I," no date. From the surrounding material it would seem that it dates from the middle of his career.

9   See Moore 1914, 45, 49. The definition of K appeared to be $\Sigma\,(x_i - \phi_i)\,/\int(\phi - \bar{x})$, where x_i are the observations, $\bar{x}$ the mean, and ϕ the fitted Fourier function. This has no obvious relation to later time series test statistics.

10   Letter of Edwin Bidwell Wilson to Wesley Clair Mitchell, 20 November 1936, Wilson Collection, Harvard Archives. It is relevant to our later argument that Mitchell responded to this praise with skepticism. As a sidelight, Wilson's statistical correspondents were still discussing the merits of Moore's work well into the 1930s. Wilson's own analysis paper in QJE on periodogram in 1934 was prompted by Moore's work. See Wilson's letter to Mitchell, 11 May 1934, Wilson Archives. According to Deutscher (1990, 189), both Mitchell and Moore were among the ten most-cited macroeconomists of the decade 1920–30; but both drop off that list in the 1930s.

11   Memo by Tjalling Koopmans, dated 12 February 1954, Tjalling Koopmans Papers, MS Series no. 1439, box 10, folder 176, Sterling Manuscript Archives, Yale University.

12   Letter dated 26 January 1928, J. M. Clark to Moore, Moore Papers, box 30.

13   Letter of Moore to E. R. A. Seligman, 26 July 1917, Seligman Collection, Correspondence folder "Moore," Columbia University Libraries Manuscript Collection.

14   Letter of Moore to Seligman, 2 August 1918, Seligman Collection, correspondence folders; Stigler 1962, 2. Moore did return to Columbia from Barnard the next year, but only upon taking a salary cut of $500.

15   Letter, Moore to Henry Schultz, 23 April 1928, Moore Collection, box 3. On the friction with Mitchell see note 10 above.

16   The manuscript can be found in box 47 of the Moore Collection.

17   Box 47, Moore Collection; *Good Life*, chapter 7, pp. 1, 3.

18   For instance, it is surely misplaced hyperbole to claim that his work "could well serve as a model for a proper approach to economic analysis today" or that "his statistical analysis is solidly based on mathematical economic theory" (Mosak 1987, 261), as we shall indicate in the text.

19   Letter from Schultz to Moore, Moore Papers, box 2. Moore responded in a letter of 22 December 1924: "The theory of the statical law is so limited by unreal hypotheses . . . that the statical law may only be approached but never reached by inductive investigation. Furthermore even if the static law were known it would be unrealizable practically in a changing society. The laws that interest you and me may be reached inductively and are immediately utilizable in a changing society."

20   Correspondence between Schultz and Hotelling, 16 July 1932 to 17 May 1935, Harold Hotelling Collection, Columbia University Archives. For a description of this incident, see Mirowski and Hands 1998.

References

Abe, F., et al. 1992. Search for Squarks and Ghuinos from pp Collisions . . . 1.8 TeV. *Physical Review Letters* 69, no. 24 (14 December): 3439–43.

Agassi, Joseph. 1995. Contemporary Philosophy of Science as Thinly Masked Antidemocratic Apologetics. In K. Gavroglu et al., eds. *Physics, Philosophy and the Scientific Community*, 153–69. Dordrecht: Kluwer.

Akerlof, George. 1984. *An Economic Theorist's Book of Tales*. New York: Cambridge University Press.

Akgiray, V., and G. Booth. 1988. The Stable Law Model of Stock Returns. *Journal of Business and Economic Statistics* 6:51–57.

Akgiray, V., and C. Lamoureux. 1989. Estimation of Stable Law Parameters. *Journal of Business and Economic Statistics* 7:85–93.

Albers, Donald, and G. Alexanderson, eds. 1987. *Mathematical People*. Boston: Birkhauser.

Alder, Ken. 1997. *Engineering the Revolution: Arms and Enlightenment in France, 1763–1815*. Princeton: Princeton University Press.

Alexander, David. 1970. *Retailing in England in the Industrial Revolution*. London: Athalone.

Amadae, S. M. 2003. *Rationalizing Capitalist Democracy*. Chicago: University of Chicago Press.

Anderson, Elizabeth. 1993. *Value in Ethics and Economics*. Cambridge: Harvard University Press.

Anderston, P., K. Arrow, and D. Pines, eds. 1988. *The Economy as an Evolving Complex System*. Reading, Mass.: Addison-Wesley.

Andreoni, James. 1990. Impure Altruism and Donations to Public Goods. *Economic Journal* 100:464–77.

Anonymous. 1847. Overpopulation and Its Remedy by William Thomas Thornton. *Westminster Review*, January, 161–77.

——. 1869a. On Labour by W. T. Thornton. *British Quarterly Review* 50 (October): 448–74.

——. 1869b. Thornton on Labour. *Athenaeum* 2156 (February 20): 275.

——. 1869c. Labour & Capital. *Westminster Review* 92 (July): 36-56.

——. 1959. *Truman the Brewer*. London.

Arrow, Kenneth. 1951. *Social Choice and Individual Values*. New York: John Wiley and Sons.

Arrow, Kenneth. 1975. Gifts and Exchanges. In E. Phelps, ed. *Altruism, Morality and Economic Theory*. New York: Sage.

Asch, P., and R. Quandt. 1987. Efficiency and Profitability in Exotic Bets. *Economica* 54:289–98.

Ashenfelter, O. 1986. Editorial statement. *American Economic Review* 76:586.

Asner, Glen. 2002. "Corporate Fad or Government Policy?" Paper presented to the Nobel Symposium, Stockholm.

Aumann, Robert. 1985. What Is Game Theory Trying to Accomplish? In K. Arrow and S. Honkapohja, eds. *Frontiers of Economics*. Oxford: Basil Blackwell.

Aydogan, K., and G. Booth. 1988. Are There Long Cycles in Common Stock Returns? *Southern Economic Journal* 55:141–49.

Bachrach, Steven R., et al. 1998. Who Should Own Scientific Papers? *Science* 281, no. 5382:1459–60.

Backhouse, Roger. 1985. *A History of Modern Economic Analysis*. 1988. 2nd ed. Oxford: Basil Blackwell.

Bagehot, Walter. 1880. *Economic Studies*. London: Longmans, Green.

Bain, Alexander. 1882. *James Mill: A Biography*. London: Longmans, Green.

Barenblatt, G. I. 1996. *Scaling Self-similarity and Intermediate Asymptotics*. Cambridge: Cambridge University Press.

Barnes, Donald. 1930. *A History of the English Corn Laws*. London: G. Routledge and Sons.

Barnett, William, Ernst Berndt, and Halbert White, eds. 1988. *Dynamic Econometric Modelling*. New York: Cambridge University Press.

Barnett, William, and Ping Chen. 1988. Deterministic Chaos and Fractal Attractors as Tools for Nonparametric Dynamical Economic Inference. *Mathematical Computation and Modelling*, June, 275–96.

Barnsley, Michael, and Stephen Demko. 1985. Iterated Function Systems and the Global Construction of Fractals. *Proceedings of the Royal Society of London* 399:243–75.

Barrow, J., and F. Tippler. 1986. *The Anthropic Cosmological Principle*. Oxford: Oxford University Press.

Bataille, Georges. 1988. *The Accursed Share*. New York: Zone.

Baumol, William, and Jess Benhabib. 1989. Chaos: Significance, Mechanism, and Economic Applications. *Journal of Economic Perspectives*, winter, 77–106.

Bausor, Randall. 1994. Qualitative Dynamics in Economics and Fluid Mechanics. In P. Mirowski, ed. *Natural Images in Economics*. New York: Cambridge University Press.

———. 1987. Liapunov Techniques in Economic Dynamics and Classical Thermodynamics. Unpublished manuscript, University of Massachusetts.

Becher, Harvey. 1971. *William Whewell and Cambridge Mathematics*. PhD diss., University of Missouri.

———. 1992. The Whewell Story. *Annals of Science* 49:377–84.

Becker, Gary. 1981. *A Treatise on the Family*. Cambridge: Harvard University Press.

Beller, Mara. 1988. Experimental Accuracy, Operationalism, and the Limits of Knowledge. *Science in Context* 2:147–62.

Benhabib, J., ed. 1992. *Cycles and Chaos in Economic Equilibrium*. Princeton: Princeton University Press.

Bernstein, Peter. 1992. *Capital Ideas*. New York: Free Press.

Berreby, D. 1993. Chaos Hits Wall Street. *Discover*, March, 77–84.

Bharadwaj, K. 1978a. *Classical Political Economy and the Rise to Dominance of Supply and Demand Theories*. New Delhi: Orient Longmans.

———. 1978b. The Subversion of Classical Analysis. *Cambridge Journal of Economics* 2:253–72.

Biagini, Eugenio. 1987. British Trade Unions and Popular Political Economy, 1860–80. *Historical Journal* 30:811–40.

Biagioli, Mario. 1993. *Galileo, Courtier: The Practice of Science in the Culture of Absolutism*. Chicago: University of Chicago Press.

———. 1999. Aporias of Scientific Authorship. In Mario Biagioli, ed. *The Science Studies Reader*, 12–30. New York: Routledge.

———. 2000a. Rights or Rewards? Changing Contexts and Definitions of Scientific Authorship. *Journal of College and University Law* 21:83–108.

———, ed. 2000b. *The Science Studies Reader*. London: Routledge.

Binmore, K. 1994. *Game Theory and the Social Contract*. Cambridge: MIT Press.

Birge, Raymond. 1929. Probable Values of the General Physical Constants. *Physical Review Supplement* 1:1–73.

———. 1932. Probable Values of *e*, *h*, *e* / *m* and *a*. *Physical Review* 40:228–61.

———. 1939. The Propagation of Error. *American Physics Teacher* 7:351–57.

———. 1945. The 1944 Values of Certain Atomic Constants. *American Journal of Physics* 13:63–73.

———. 1957. A Survey of the Systematic Evaluation of the Universal Physical Constants. *Nuovo Cimento*, supp. 6:39–67.

Black, R. D. C., ed. 1977. *Papers and Correspondence of W. S. Jevons*. Vol. 7. London: Macmillan for the Royal Economic Society.

———. 1987. Jenkin, Fleeming. In J. Eatwell, M. Milgate, and P. Newman, eds. *The New Palgrave: A Dictionary of Economics*. London: Macmillan.

Blank, S. 1991. Chaos in Futures Markets? *Journal of Futures Markets* 11:711–28.

Blattberg, Robert, and Nicholas Gonedes. 1974. A Comparison of the Stable and Student Distributions as Statistical Models for Stock Prices. *Journal of Business* 47, no. 2 (fall): 244–80.

Blattberg, R., and T. Sargent. 1971. Regression Non-Gaussian Stable Disturbances. *Econometrica* 39:501–10.

Blaug, Mark. 1992. *The Methodology of Economics*. 2nd ed. Cambridge: Cambridge University Press.

———. 2001. No History of Ideas, Please, We're Economists. *Journal of Economic Perspectives* 13:145–64.

Bloor, David. 1982. Durkheim and Mauss Revisited: Classification and the Sociology of Knowledge. *Studies in the History and Philosophy of Science* 13:267–97.

Blumenthal, David, et al. 1996a. Relationships between Academic Institutions and Industry in the Life Sciences. *New England Journal of Medicine* 334, no. 6 (8 February): 368–73.

———. 1996b. Participation of Life-Science Faculty in Research Relationships with Industry. *New England Journal of Medicine* 335, no. 23 (5 December): 1734–39.

Bollerslev, T., R. Chou, and K. Kramer. 1992. ARCH Modelling in Finance. *Journal of Econometrics* 52:5–59.

Bondi, Hermann. Why Mourn the Passing of Determinacy? In A. van der Merwe, ed. *Old and New Questions in Physics*. New York: Plenum.

Booth, William. 1993. *Households*. Ithaca: Cornell University Press.

Bourdieu, Pierre. 1975. The Specificity of the Scientific Field and the Social Conditions of the Progress of Reason. *Social Science Information* 14:19–47.

Bowler, Peter. 1988. *The Non-Darwinian Revolution*. Baltimore: Johns Hopkins University Press.

Bowley, A., and G. Wood. 1905. The Statistics of Wages in the UK during the Last Hundred Years: Engineering and Shipbuilding, a Trade Union Standard Rate. *Journal of the Royal Statistical Society* 68:104–37, 373–91.

———. 1906. The Statistics of Wages in the UK during the Last Hundred Years: Engineering and Shipbuilding, General Results. *Journal of the Royal Statistical Society* 69:148–92.

Boyle, James. 1996. *Shamans, Software, and Spleens: Law and the Construction of the Information Society*. Cambridge: Harvard University Press.

——. 2000. Cruel, Mean or Lavish? Economic Analysis, Price Discrimination and Digital Intellectual Property. *Vanderbilt Law Review* 53, no. 6:2007–39.

——. Forthcoming. *Net Total: Law, Politics and Property in Cyberspace.*

Branscomb, Anne W. 1994. *Who Owns Information? From Privacy to Public Access.* New York: Basic Books.

Branscomb, Lewis M., Fumio Kodama, and Richard Florida, eds. 1999. *Industrializing Knowledge: University-Industry Linkages in Japan and the United States.* Cambridge: MIT Press.

Breit, William. 1967. The Wages Fund Controversy Revisited. *Canadian Journal of Economics and Political Science* 23:509–28.

Brentano, Lujo. 1870. On the History and Development of Gilds. In Joshua Toulmin Smith, ed. *English Gilds.* London: N. Trübner.

Bresnick, Adam. 1997. The Six Billion Dollar Man. *Times Literary Supplement,* July 18:18–19.

Brick, W. 1991. Understanding Macroeconomic Time Series Using Complex Systems Theory. *Structural Change and Economic Dynamics* 2:119–41.

Bridgman, Percy. 1931. *Dimensional Analysis.* 2nd ed. New Haven: Yale University Press.

Brock, William. 1986. Distinguishing Random and Deterministic Systems. *Journal of Economic Theory,* October, 168–95.

——. 1991. Causality, Chaos, Explanation and Prediction in Economics and Finance. In J. Casti and A. Karlqvist, eds. *Beyond Belief.* Boca Raton: CRC.

Brock, W., D. Hsieh, and B. LeBaron. *Nonlinear Dynamics, Chaos and Instability.* Cambridge: MIT Press.

Brock, William, and A. Malliaris. 1989. *Differential Equations, Stability and Chaos in Dynamic Economics.* New York: North-Holland.

Brock, William, and Chera Sayers. 1988. Is the Business Cycle Characterized by Deterministic Chaos? *Journal of Monetary Economics,* July, 71–90.

Brown, Byron, and Schlomo Maital. 1981. What Do Economists Know? *Econometrica* 49:491–504.

Brownlie, A., and M. Lloyd Prichard. 1963. Professor Fleeming Jenkin, 1833–1885: Pioneer in Engineering and Political Economy. *Oxford Economic Papers* 15:204–16.

Buckingham, E. 1914. On Physically Similar Systems. *Physical Reviews* 4:347–76.

Burda, Z., J. Jurkiewicz, and M. Nowak. 2003. Is Econophysics a Solid Science? *Acta Physica Polonia B* 34:87–131.

Burmeister, Edwin. *Capital Theory and Dynamics.* 1980. New York: Cambridge University Press.

Buxton, Charles. 1849. *Memoirs of Sir Thomas Fowell Buxton.* Philadelphia: H. Longstreth.

Cahan, David. 1989. *An Institute for an Empire.* New York: Cambridge University Press.

Caillé, Alain. 1994. *Don, intérêt, et désintéressement.* Paris: La Découverte.

Cairnes, J. E. 1866. The Law of Demand and Supply. *Economist,* October 20, November 3. Repr. with letters by T. E. Cairnes (December 1) and W. T. Thornton (December 15) in *The Economic Writings of William Thornton,* ed. Philip Mirowski and Steven Tradewell. Vol. 1. Brookfield, Vt.: Pickering and Chatto, 1999.

——. 1871. Political Economy and Laissez Faire. *Fortnightly Review* 10:80–97.

——. 1874. *Some Leading Principles of Political Economy Newly Expounded.* New York: Harper.

——. 1875. *The Character and Logical Method of Political Economy.* London: Macmillan.

Caldwell, Bruce. 1988. Hayek's Transformation. *History of Political Economy* 20:513–41.

——. 1991. Clarifying Popper. *Journal of Economic Literature* 29:1–33.

Callebaut, Werner, ed. 1993. *Taking the Naturalistic Turn.* Chicago: University of Chicago Press.

Campbell, Norman. [1920] 1957. *Foundations of Science.* New York: Dover.

——. 1924. Ultimate Rational Units. *Philosophical Magazine* 47:159–72.

Campbell-Kelley, Martin. 1995. The Development of the International Software Industry, 1950–90. *Business and Economic History* 24:73–110.

Canard, Nicolas-François. [1801] 1969. *Principes d'économie politique*. Rome: Bizzarri.

Caneva, Kenneth. 2000. Possible Kuhns in the History of Science: Anomalies of Incommensurable Paradigms. *Studies in the History and Philosophy of Science* 31:87–124.

Cannadine, David. 1984. Past and Present in the English Industrial Revolution. *Past and Present* 103:131–72.

Cardwell, D. 1971. *From Watt to Clausius*. Ithaca: Cornell University Press.

Carr, B., and M. Rees. 1979. The Anthropic Principle and the Structure of the Physical World. *Nature* 278:605–12.

Carrier, James. 1995. *Gifts and Commodities*. London: Routledge.

Cartwright, Nancy. 1989. *Nature's Capacities and Their Measurement*. Oxford: Clarendon.

———. 1990: Replicability and Reproducibility. In M. Blang and N. de Marchi, eds. *Transitions in Research Programs*. Cheltenham: Edward Elgar, forthcoming.

Casdagli, M. 1991. Chaotic and Deterministic versus Stochastic Non-linear Modelling. *Journal of the Royal Statistical Society* B54:303–28.

Causey, Robert. 1969. Derived Measurement, Dimensions, and Dimensional Analysis. *Philosophy of Science* 36:252–70.

Chadwick, David. 1860. The Rate of Wages in Manchester and Salford. *Journal of the Royal Statistical Society* 23.

Chandrasekhar, S. 1937. The Cosmological Constants. *Nature* 139:757–78.

Chen, Ping. 1988. Empirical and Theoretical Evidence of Economic Chaos. *System Dynamics Review* 4:81–108.

Chipman, John. 1965. A Survey of the Theory of International Trade: Part I. *Econometrica* 13:477–519.

Christ, Carl. 1985. Early Progress in Estimating Quantitative Economic Relationships in America. *American Economic Review* 95:39–52.

Chubin, Darryl E., and Edward J. Hackett. 1990. *Peerless Science: Peer Review and U.S. Science Policy*. Albany: State University of New York Press.

Cicchetti, Domenic. 1991. The Reliability of Peer Review for Manuscript and Grant Submissions: A Cross-disciplinary Investigation. *Behavioral and Brain Sciences* 14:119–86.

Cixous, Helène. 1976. The Laugh of the Medusa. *Signs* 1:875–99.

———. 1991. *Coming to Writing, and Other Essays*. Cambridge: Harvard University Press.

Clapp, B. W. 1962. A Manchester Merchant and His Schedules of Supply and Demand. *Economica* 29:185–87.

Clark, P. A. 1973. Subordinated Stochastic Process Model with Finite Variance for Speculative Prices. *Econometrica* 41:135–56.

Clements, R.V. 1961. British Trade Unions and Popular Political Economy, 1850–75. *Economic History Review* 14:93–104.

Cliffe Leslie, T. E. 1868. Political Economy and the Rate of Wages. *Fraser's Magazine* 78:81–95.

———. [1888]. 1969. *Essays in Political Economy*. New York: Kelley.

Cochrane, Rexmond. 1966. *Measures for Progress*. Washington: National Bureau of Standards.

Cohen, Avi. 1984. The Methodological Resolution of the Cambridge Capital Controversies. *Journal of Post Keynesian Economics* 6:614–29.

Cohen, E. R., and B. Taylor. 1987. The 1986 Adjustment of the Fundamental Physical Constants. *Reviews of Modern Physics* 59:1121–48.

Cohen, E. R., K. Crowe, and J. Dumond. 1957. *The Fundamental Constants of Physics*. New York: Interscience.

Cohen, Jon. 1995. The Culture of Credit. *Science* 268 (23 June): 1706–18.

Cohen, Julie. 1998. Lochner in Cyberspace: The New Economic Orthodoxy of Rights Management. *Michigan Law Review* 97, no. 2 (November): 462–67.

———. 2000. Call It the Digital Millennium *Censorship* Act. *New Republic*, 23 May.

Coleman, B. 1987. Science Writing: Too Good to Be True? *New York Times Book Review*, 27 September.

Collins, Harry. 1985. *Changing Order*. Los Angeles: Sage.

Cook-Deegan, Robert, and Stephen McCormack. 2001. Patents, Secrecy and DNA. *Science* 293, no. 5528 (13 July): 217.

Cootner, Paul, ed. 1964. *The Random Character of Stock Market Prices*. Cambridge: MIT Press.

Cornes, R., and T. Sandler. 1986. *The Theory of Externalities, Public Goods and Club Goods*. New York: Cambridge University Press.

Cornew, R., D. Town, and L. Crowson. 1984. Stable Distributions, Futures Prices and the Measurement of Trading Performance. *Journal of Futures Markets* 4:531–57.

Cournot, Antoine-Augustin. [1838] 1971. *Researches into the Mathematical Principles of the Theory of Wealth*. Trans. N. T. Bacon. New York: Macmillan.

Cowen, Tyler. 1993. The Scope and Limits of Preference Sovereignty. *Economics and Philosophy* 9:253–69.

Creedy, John. 1992. *Demand and Exchange in Economic Analysis*. Aldershot: Edward Elgar.

Cunningham, A. 1988. Getting the Game Right. *Studies in the History and Philosophy of Science* 19:365–89.

Daston, Lorraine. 1986. The Physicalist Tradition in Early 19th Century French Geometry. *Studies in the History and Philosophy of Science* 17:269–95.

———.1988. *Classical Probability in the Enlightenment*. Princeton: Princeton University Press.

———. 1992. Objectivity and the Escape from Perspective. *Social Studies of Science* 22:597–618.

Daumas, Maurice. 1963. Precision of Measurement and Physical and Chemical Research in the Eighteenth Century. In A. C. Crombie, ed. *Scientific Change*. London: Heinemann.

David, Paul. 1998. Common Agency Contracting and the Rise of Open Science Institutions. *American Economic Review Papers and Proceedings* 88:15–21.

———. 2000. A Tragedy of the Public Knowledge "Commons"? Global Science, Intellectual Property and the Digital Technology Boomerang. WP 04/00, OIPRC Electronic Journal of Intellectual Property Rights, //www.oiprc.ox.ac.uk/EJWP0400.pdf.

David, Paul, and Partha Dasgupta. 1994. Towards a New Economics of Science. *Research Policy* 23:487–521.

Davidoff, Frank, et al. 2001. Sponsorship, Authorship and Accountability. *Canadian Medical Association Journal* 165, no. 6 (18 September): 786–88.

Davis, H. T. 1941. *The Analysis of Economic Time Series*. Bloomington: Principia.

de Finetti, Bruno. 1974. *Theory of Probability*. New York: John Wiley and Sons.

Defoe, Daniel. [1719] 1941. *Robinson Crusoe*. New York: Walter Black.

DeGrauwe, P., H. Dewachter, and M. Embrecht. 1993. *Exchange Rate Theory: Chaotic Models of Foreign Exchange Markets*. Oxford: Basil Blackwell.

de Marchi, Neil. 1974. The Success of Mill's Principles. *History of Political Economy* 6:119–57.

de Marchi, Neil, and Mary S. Morgan, eds. 1994. *Higgling: Transactors and Their Markets in the History of Economics*. Durham: Duke University Press.

Dennis, Kenneth. 1977. *Competition in the History of Economic Thought*. New York: Arno.

de Quincey, Thomas. 1877. *The Works of Thomas de Quincey*. Riverside ed. Boston: Houghton Mifflin.

Derrida, Jacques. 1991. *A Derrida Reader: Between the Blinds*. Ed. Peggy Kamuf. New York: Columbia University Press.

——. 1992. *Given Time I: Counterfeit Money*. Chicago: University of Chicago Press.

——. 1994. *Spectres of Marx*. New York: Routledge.

Desmond, Adrian. 1994. *Huxley: the Devil's Disciple*. London: Michael Joseph.

Desmond, Adrian, and James Moore. 1991. *Darwin*. London: Michael Joseph.

Deutsch, David. 1986. On Wheeler's Notion of Law without Law in Physics. *Foundations of Physics* 16:565–72.

Deutscher, Patrick. 1990. *R. G. Hawtrey and the Development of Macroeconomics*. Ann Arbor: University of Michigan Press.

Devaney, Robert. 1986. *An Introduction to Chaotic Dynamical Systems*. Menlo Park, Calif.: Benjamin/Cummings.

de Ville, P., and C. Menard. 1989. An Insolent Founding Father? *European Economic Review* 33:494–502.

de Vries, C. 1991. On the Relation between GARCH and Stable Processes. *Journal of Econometrics* 48:313–24.

Dewald, W., J. Thursby, and R. Anderson. 1986. Replication in Empirical Economics. *American Economic Review* 76:587–603.

Dewey, Clive. 1974. The Rehabilitation of the Peasant Proprietor in 19th Century Economic Thought. *History of Political Economy* 6:17–47.

Dickens, Charles. [1854] 1971. *Hard Times*. New York: Signet.

Dickey, David, Dennis Jansen, and Daniel Thornton. 1991. A Primer on Cointegration with an Application to Money and Income. *Review of the Federal Reserve Bank of St. Louis*, March–April, 58–78.

Dimand, Robert. 1993. Alfred Marshall and the Whewell Group. *Manchester School* 61:439–41.

Dirac, Paul. 1937. The Cosmological Constants. *Nature* 139:323.

Divisia, F. 1953. La Société d'économétrie a atteint sa majorité. *Econometrica* 21:1–30.

Dmitriev, V. K. [1902] 1974. *Economic Essays on Value, Competition and Utility*. Cambridge: Cambridge University Press.

Dokko, Y., and R. Edelstein. 1989. How Well Do Economists Forecast Stock Market Prices? *American Economic Review* 79:865–71.

Donoghue, Mark. 1995. The Wages-and-Profits Fund: Classical Remnants in Marshall's Early Theory of Distribution. *European Journal of the History of Economic Thought* 2:355–74.

——. 1997. Mill's Affirmation of the Classical Wage Fund Doctrine. *Scottish Journal of Political Economy* 44:82–99.

——. 2000. Some Unpublished Correspondence of William Thomas Thornton. *European Journal of the History of Economic Thought* 7:321–49.

Dorfman, J. 1941. The Seligman Correspondence. *Political Science Quarterly* 56:407–9.

Douglas, Mary. 1986. *How Institutions Think*. Syracuse, N.Y.: Syracuse University Press.

——.1990. Foreword to Marcel Maus, *The Gift*. New York: W. W. Norton.

Drahos, Peter. 2002. *Information Feudalism*. New York: New Press.

Duhem, Pierre. 1977. *The Aim and Structure of Physical Theory*. New York: Atheneum.

Dunn, Michael. 1979. *The Penguin Guide to Real Draught Beer*. Harmondsworth: Penguin.

Dunning, T. J. 1860. *Trades' Unions and Strikes*. London.

Dupre, J., ed. 1987. *The Latest on the Best*. Cambridge: MIT Press.

Dupuit, Jules. [1844] 1952. On the Measurement of Utility of Public Works. *International Economic Papers* 2:83–110.

Durbin, John. 1985. *Modern Algebra*. 2nd ed. New York: John Wiley and Sons.

Earman, John. 1986. *A Primer on Determinism*. Dordrecht: Reidel.

Earman, John. 1992. *Bayes or Bust*. Cambridge: MIT Press.

Eddington, Arthur. 1930. *The Nature of the Physical World*. London: Macmillan.

———. 1935. *New Pathways in Science*. Cambridge: Cambridge University Press.

———. 1936. *Relativity Theory of Protons and Electrons*. Cambridge: Cambridge University Press.

———. 1939. *Philosophy of Physical Science*. Cambridge: Cambridge University Press.

———. 1941. Group Structure in Physical Science. *Mind* 50:268–79.

Edgeworth, Francis Y. 1912. Review of H. L. Moore's Laws of Wages. *Economic Journal* 22 (March): 66–71.

Einstein, Albert. 1911. Elementare Betrachtungen über die thermische Molekularbewegungen in festen Körpern. *Annalen der Physik* 35:679–94.

Eisenberg, Rebecca. 2001. Bargaining over the Transfer of Research Tools. In R. Dreyfuss, D. Zimmerman, and H. First, eds. *Extending the Boundaries of Intellectual Property*. New York: Oxford University Press.

Ekelund, Robert. 1985. Mill's Recantation Once Again: A Reply to Professor Negishi. *Oxford Economic Papers* 37:152–53.

———. 1997. W. T. Thornton: Savant, Idiot, or Idiot-Savant? *Journal of the History of Economic Thought* 19:1–23.

Ekelund, R., and R. Hebert. 1990. *A History of Economic Theory and Method*. 3rd ed. New York: McGraw Hill.

Ekelund, R., and W. Kordsheimer. 1981. J. S. Mill, Unions and the Wages Fund Doctrine. *Quarterly Journal of Economics* 96:531–41.

Ekelund, R., and Y. Shieh. 1989. Jevons on Utility, Exchange, and Demand Theory. *Manchester School* 57:17–33.

Ekelund, R., and S. Thommesen. 1989. Disequilibrium Theory and Thornton's Assault on the Laws of Supply and Demand. *History of Political Economy* 21:567–92.

Ekelund, R., and Mark Thornton. 1991. Geometric Analogies and Market Demand Estimation: Dupuit and the French Contribution. *History of Political Economy* 23 (fall): 397–418.

———. 2001. William T. Thornton and 19th Century Economic Policy. *Journal of the History of Economic Thought* 23:513–31.

Ellerman, David. 1984. Arbitrage Theory: A Mathematical Introduction. SIAM Review 26:241–61.

———. 1995. *Intellectual Trespassing as a Way of Life*. Lanham: Rowman and Littlefield.

Elliot, Hugh, ed. 1910. *Letters of John Stuart Mill*. 2 vols. London: Longmans.

Elliott, Carl. 2002. Diary. *London Review of Books*, 28 November, 36–37.

Ellis, Robinson. 1878. *Academy*, 29 June.

Engle, Robert. 1982. Autoregressive Conditional Heteroskedasticity with Estimates of the Variance of U.K. Inflation. *Econometrica*, July, 987–1004.

Engle, R., and C. Granger, eds. 1991. *Long-Run Economic Relationships*. Oxford: Oxford University Press.

Epstein, Roy. 1987. *A History of Econometrics*. Amsterdam: North Holland.

Etner, François. 1987. *Histoire du calcul économique en France*. Paris: Economica.

Evans, G., S. Honkapohja, and T. Sargent. 1993. On the Preservation of Deterministic Cycles When Some Agents Perceive Them to Be Random Fluctuations. *Journal of Economic Dynamics and Control* 17:705–21.

Ezrahi, Y. 1990. *The Descent of Icarus*. Cambridge: Harvard University Press.

Fairchilds, Cissie. 1993. The Production and Marketing of Populuxe Goods in 18th Century Paris. In John Brewer and Roy Porter, eds. *Consumption and the World of Goods*. London: Routledge.

Fama, E. 1963. Mandelbrot and the Stable Paretian Hypothesis. *Journal of Business* 36 (October): 420–29.

———. 1965a. The Behavior of Stock Market Prices. *Journal of Business* 38 (January): 34–105.

——. 1965b. Portfolio Analysis in a Stable Paretian Market. *Management Science*, December, 404–19.

——. 1970. Efficient Capital Markets. *Journal of Business* 25:383–417.

——. 1991. Efficient Capital Markets, II. *Journal of Finance* 46:1575–1617.

Fang, H., K. Lai, and M. Lai. 1994. Fractal Structure in Currency Futures. *Journal of Futures Markets* 14:169–81.

Farmer, J. D. 1991. A Rosetta Stone for Connectionism. In S. Forrest, ed. *Emergent Computation*. Cambridge: MIT Press.

Farmer, James, E. Ott, and J. Yorke. 1983. The Dimension of Chaotic Attractors. *Physica* 7D:153–80.

Fawcett, Henry. 1860. Strikes: Their Tendencies and Remedies. *Westminster Review* 18:1–23.

——. 1865. *Economic Position of the British Labourer*. London: Macmillan.

Feige, E. 1975. The Consequences of Journal Editorial Policies and a Suggestion for Revision. *Journal of Political Economy* 83:1291–96.

Feiwel, G., ed. 1989. *Joan Robinson and Modern Economic Theory*. New York: New York University Press.

Feller, William. 1971. *An Introduction to Probability Theory and Its Applications*. New York: John Wiley and Sons.

Fetter, Frank. 1980. *The Economist in Parliament: 1780–1868*. Durham: Duke University Press.

Feyerabend, Paul. 1978. *Science in a Free Society*. London: New Left Books.

——. 1987. *Farewell to Reason*. London: Verso.

Field, Alex. 2003. Mirowski's Machine Dreams. *European Journal for the History of Economic Thought* 10:611–22.

Fine, Terrence. 1973. *Theories of Probability*. New York: Academic Press.

Finn, Margot. 1993. *After Chartism*. Cambridge: Cambridge University Press.

Fisher, Franklin. 1983. *Disequilibrium: Foundations of Equilibrium Economics*. New York: Cambridge University Press.

Floss, S. 1941. An Outline of the Philosophy of A. A. Cournot. PhD diss., University of Pennsylvania.

Fogel, Robert, and G. R. Elton, eds. 1983. *Which Road to the Past?* New Haven: Yale University Press.

Fontana, Biancamaria. 1985. *Rethinking the Politics of Commercial Society: The Edinburgh Review, 1802–1870*. Cambridge: Cambridge University Press.

Fontana, Walter. 2003. The Topology of the Possible. In A. Wimmer and R. Koessler, eds. *Paradigms of Change*. Reading: Addison-Wesley.

Ford, Joseph. 1983. How Random Is a Coin Toss? *Physics Today*, April, 40–47.

Forget, Evelyn. 1991. John Stuart Mill, Francis Longe, and William Thornton on Demand and Supply. *Journal of the History of Economic Thought* 13:205–21.

——. 1992. J. S. Mill and the Tory School. *History of Political Economy* 24:31–59.

——. 1993. J. B. Say and Adam Smith. *Canadian Journal of Economics* 26:121–33.

——. 1994. Disequilibrium Trade as a Metaphor for Social Disorder in J.-B. Say. In N. de Marchi and M. Morgan, eds. *Higgling: Transactors and Their Markets in the History of Economics*. Durham: Duke University Press.

Forsyth, A. R. 1935. Old Tripos Days at Cambridge. *Mathematical Gazette* 19:167.

Fortun, Michael, and Schweber, Silvan. 1993. Scientists and the Legacy of WWII. *Social Studies of Science* 23:595–642.

Foster, Andrea L. 2001a. 2 Scholars Face Off in Copyright Clash. *Chronicle of Higher Education*, 10 August, 45.

——. 2001b. Princeton Cryptographer's Challenge to Music Industry Draws Computer Scientists' Support. *Chronicle of Higher Education*, 16 August.

——. 2001c. Logging In with . . . Jessica Litman. *Chronicle of Higher Education*, 12 October.

Fourier, Joseph. 1878. *The Analytical Theory of Heat*. Cambridge: Cambridge University Press.

Frängsmyr, T., J. L. Heilbron, and Robin Rider, eds. 1990. *The Quantifying Spirit in the Eighteenth Century*. Berkeley: University of California Press.

Frank, M., and T. Stengos. 1989. Measuring the Strangeness of Gold and Silver Rates of Return. *Review of Economic Studies* 56:553–67.

Frank, R., T. Gilovich, and D. Regan. 1993. Does Studying Economics Inhibit Cooperation? *Journal of Economic Perspectives* 7:159–71.

Franklin, Allen. 1986. *The Neglect of Experiment*. New York: Cambridge University Press.

——. 1990. *Experiment Right or Wrong*. New York: Cambridge University Press.

Franklin, A., and C. Howson. 1984. Why Do Scientists Prefer to Vary Their Experiments? *Studies in the History and Philosophy of Science* 15:51–62.

Frieden, B. R. 1986. A Probability Law for Fundamental Constants. *Foundations of Physics* 16:883–903.

Frisch, R. 1950. Alfred Marshall's Theory of Value. *Quarterly Journal of Economics* 64:495–524. Repr. in Wood 1982, 3:61.

Fuller, Steve. 1992. Being There with Thomas Kuhn: A Parable for Postmodern Times. *History and Theory* 31, no. 3:241–75.

——. Mortgaging the Farm to Save the Sacred Cow. *Studies in the History and Philosophy of Science* 25:251–61.

——. 1998. *Science*. Minneapolis: University of Minnesota Press.

——. 2000a. *The Governance of Science*. Buckingham: Open University Press.

——. 2000b. *Thomas Kuhn: A Philosophical History for Our Times*. Chicago: University of Chicago Press.

——. 2000c. Why Science Studies Has Never Been Critical of Science. *Philosophy of the Social Sciences* 30:5–32.

——. 2002a. *Knowledge Management Foundations*. Oxford: Butterworth-Heinemann.

——. 2002b. Prolegomena to a Sociology of Philosophy in the 20th Century English-Speaking World. *Philosophy of the Social Sciences* 32:151–77.

Furbank, P. N. 1993. Confessional Claims. *Times Literary Supplement*, 13 August, 6.

Galison, P. 1987. *How Experiments End*. Chicago: University of Chicago Press.

——. 1988. Review of Franklin 1986. *Isis* 79:467–70.

——. 1997. *Image and Logic: A Material Culture of Microphysics*. Chicago: University of Chicago Press.

——. 2003. *Einstein's Clocks, Poincaré's Maps*. New York: W. W. Norton.

Galison, Peter, and Bruce Hevly, eds. 1992. *Big Science*. Stanford: Stanford University Press.

Gane, Mike, ed. 1992. *The Radical Sociology of Durkheim and Mauss*. London: Routledge.

Garnier, Germain. 1796. *Abrégé des principes de l'économie politique*. Paris: Agasse.

Gherity, James. 1988. Mill's Friendly Critic: Thornton or Whewell? *Manchester School* 56:282–85.

Gibbons, Michael, et al. 1994. *The New Production of Knowledge: The Dynamics of Science and Research in Contemporary Societies*. London: Sage.

Gigerenzer, Gerd. 2000. *Adaptive Thinking*. Oxford: Oxford University Press.

Gigerenzer, Gerd, and David Murray. 1987. *Cognition as Intuitive Statistics*. Hillsdale, N.J.: Erlbaum.

Gilbert, C., and N. de Marchi, eds. 1988. The History and Methodology of Econometrics. *Oxford Economic Papers*. Special issue.

Gildon, Charles. 1719. *The Life and Strange Surprizing Adventures of Mr. D . . . DeF—of London, Hosier*. London.

Glanz, James, and Dennis Overbye. 2001. Cosmic Laws Like the Speed of Light Might Be Changing. *New York Times*, 14 August.

Gleick, James. 1987. *Chaos: Making a New Science*. New York: Viking.

———. 1992. *Genius: The Life and Science of Richard Feynman*. New York: Pantheon.

Gnedenko, B., and A. Kolmogorov. 1954. *Limit Distributions for Sums of Independent Random Variables*. Reading, Mass.: Addison-Wesley.

Gode, D., and S. Sunder. 1993. Allocative Efficiency of Markets with Zero-Intelligence Traders: Market as a Partial Substitute for Individual Rationality. *Journal of Political Economy* 101:119–37.

———. 1997. What Makes Markets Allocatively Efficient? *Quarterly Journal of Economics* 101:603–30.

Goldman, Alvin. 1992. *Liaisons*. Cambridge: MIT Press.

———. 1999. *Knowledge in a Social World*. New York: Oxford University Press.

Goldstein, S., B. Misra, and M. Courbage. 1981. On the Intrinsic Randomness of Dynamical Systems. *Journal of Statistical Physics* 25:111–35.

Gooday, Graeme. 1990. Precision Measurement and the Genesis of Physics Teaching Laboratories. *British Journal for the History of Science* 23:25–51.

———. 1992. The Morals of Measurement: Precision and Constancy in Late Victorian Physics. Paper presented at the December 1992 meeting of the History of Economics Society, Washington.

Gooding, David. 1990. *Experiment and the Making of Meaning*. Boston: Kluwer.

Gooding, D., T. Pinch, and S. Schaffer, eds. 1989. *The Uses of Experiment*. Cambridge: Cambridge University Press.

Gouldner, Alvin. 1973. *For Sociology*. New York: Basic Books.

Gourvish, T. J., and R. G. Wilson. 1994. *The British Brewing Industry, 1830–1980*. Cambridge: Cambridge University Press.

Grandmont, Jean-Michel, and Pierre Malgrange. 1986. Nonlinear Economic Dynamics. *Journal of Economic Theory*, October, 3–12.

Granger, C., and D. Orr. 1972. Infinite Variance and the Research Strategy in Time Series Analysis. *Journal of the American Statistical Association* 67:275–85.

Granger, C., and T. Terasvirta. 1993. *Modelling Nonlinear Economic Relationships*. Oxford: Oxford University Press.

Grantham, T. 1994. Does Science Have a Global Goal? *Biology and Philosophy* 9:85–97.

Grassberger, Peter, and Itamar Procaccia. 1983. Measuring the Strangeness of Strange Attractors. *Physica* 9D:189–208.

Grattan-Guinness, Ivor. 1990. *Convolutions in French Mathematics*. Boston: Birkhauser.

Greene, M., and B. Fielitz. 1977. Long-Term Dependence in Common Stock Prices. *Journal of Financial Economics* 4:339–49.

Gregory, Chris. 1982. *Gifts and Commodities*. New York: Academic Press.

———. 1994. Economic Anthropology. In Tim Ingold, ed. *Routledge Companion Encyclopedia of Anthropology*. London: Routledge.

Gribbin, D., R. Harris, and H. Lau. 1992. Futures Prices Are Not Stable Paretian Distributed. *Journal of Futures Markets* 12:475–87.

Groenewegen, Peter. 1973. A Note on the Origin of the Phrase Demand and Supply. *Economic Journal* 83:505–9.

———. 1995. *A Soaring Eagle*. Aldershot: Edward Elgar.

Gross, Paul R., and Norman Leavitt. 1994. *Higher Superstition: The Academic Left and Its Quarrels with Science*. Baltimore: Johns Hopkins University Press.

Guggenheim, E. 1942. Units and Dimensions. *Philosophical Magazine* 33:479–96.

Guston, D., and K. Keniston, eds. 1994. *The Fragile Contract*. Cambridge: MIT Press.

Guterman, Lila. 2001. 12 Medical Journals Issue Joint Policy on Research Supported by Business. *Chronicle of Higher Education*, 10 September.

Hacking, Ian. 1983. *Representing and Intervening*. New York: Cambridge University Press.

———. 1990. *The Taming of Chance*. New York: Cambridge University Press.

———. 1994. Review of Kitcher. *Journal of Philosophy* 91, no. 4:212–15.

———. 2000. Review of Paul Feyerabend's *Conquest of Abundance*. *London Review of Books*, 22 June, 28–29.

Hacohen, Malachi. 2000. *Karl Popper: The Formative Years, 1902–1945*. Cambridge: Cambridge University Press.

Hadden, Richard. 1994. *On the Shoulders of Merchants*. Albany: State University of New York Press.

Hagstrom, W. O. 1965. *The Scientific Community*. New York: Basic Books.

Halbert, Debora J. 1999. *Intellectual Property in the Information Age: The Politics of Expanding Ownership Rights*. Westport, Conn.: Quorum.

Halevy, Elie. 1972. *The Growth of Philosophical Radicalism*. London: Faber.

Hall, J., B. Brorsen, and S. Irwin. 1989. The Distribution of Futures Prices. *Journal of Financial and Quantitative Analysis* 24:105–16.

Hall, Peter. 1981. A Comedy of Errors: The Canonical Form of the Stable Characteristic Function. *Bulletin of the London Mathematics Society* 13:23–27.

Halsey, Frederick. 1920. *The Metric Fallacy*. 2nd ed. New York: American Institute of Weights and Measures.

Halsey, Thomas, et al. 1986. Fractal Measures and Their Singularities: The Characterization of Strange Sets. *Physical Review* 33:1141–51.

Hamermesh, Daniel. 1992. The Young Economist's Guide to Professional Etiquette. *Journal of Economic Perspectives* 6:169–79.

Hands, W. 1994a. Blurred Boundaries. *Studies in the History and Philosophy of Science* 25:751–71.

———.1994b. Economics and Laudan's Normative Naturalism. Paper presented to New Orleans meetings of the Society for the Social Studies of Science.

———. 1994c. The Sociology of Scientific Knowledge and Economics. In Roger Backhouse, ed. *New Perspectives in the Methodology of Economics*. London: Routledge.

———. 2001. *Reflection without Rules: Economic Methodology and Contemporary Science Theory*. Cambridge: Cambridge University Press.

Hansen, Anders. 1992. Journalistic Practices and Science Reporting in the British Press. *Public Understanding of Science* 3:111–34.

Harrison, Frederic. 1865. The Limits of Political Economy. *Fortnightly Review* 1:356–76.

———. 1889. Socialist Unionism. *Nineteenth Century* 26:433–39.

———. 1908. *National and Social Problems*. New York: Macmillan.

Hausman, Dan, and Michael McPherson. 1993. Taking Ethics Seriously. *Journal of Economic Literature* 21:671–731.

Hayek, F. 1951. *John Stuart Mill and Harriet Taylor*. London: Routledge and Kegan Paul.

Hearn, William. 1863. *Plutology*. Melbourne: G. Robertson.

Hedges, Larry. 1987. How Hard Is Hard Science, How Soft Is Soft Science? *American Psychologist* 42:443–55.

Heilbron, J. L. 1986. *Dilemmas of an Upright Man*. Berkeley: University of California Press.

———. 1990. The Measure of Enlightenment. In Tore Frängsmyr et al., eds. *The Quantifying Spirit in the Eighteenth Century*. Berkeley: University of California Press.

Heilig, Klaus. 1978. The Dutch Book Argument Reconsidered. *British Journal for the Philosophy of Science* 29:325–46.

Held, Virginia. 1990. Mothering versus Contract. In Jane Mansbridge, ed. *Beyond Self-Interest.* Chicago: University of Chicago Press.

Helmholz, Carl. 1990. Raymond Thayer Birge. *Biographical Memoirs of the National Academy of Sciences* 59:73–84.

Henderson, J. 1973. William Whewell's Mathematical Statements of Price Flexibility, Demand Elasticity and the Giffen Paradox. *Manchester School* 41:329–42.

———. 1996. *Early British Mathematical Economics.* Totowa: Rowman and Littlefield.

Hendry, David. 1980. Econometrics: Alchemy or Science? *Economica* 47:387–406.

Henrion, Max, and Baruch Fischoff. 1986. Assessing Uncertainty in Physical Constants. *American Journal of Physics* 54:791–97.

Herhold, Scott. 1999. Patent War Pending. *San Jose Mercury News*, 17 July.

Herring, Hubert. 1994. Dislike Those Suspenders? *New York Times*, December 25.

Hershberg, James. 1993. *James B. Conant: Harvard to Hiroshima.* New York: Alfred A. Knopf.

Hickman, B., ed. 1972. *Econometric Models of Cyclical Behavior.* New York: National Bureau of Economic Research.

Hicks, John R. 1983. *Classics and Moderns.* Oxford: Basil Blackwell.

Hildenbrand, Werner. 1994. *Market Demand.* Princeton: Princeton University Press.

Hilts, Philip. 1999. Law on Access to Research Data Pleases Business, Alarms Science. *New York Times*, 31 July, A1.

Hobson, J. A. 1938. *Confessions of an Economic Heretic.* London: George Allen and Unwin.

Hodge, M. S. 1989. Darwin's Theory and Darwin's Argument. In M. Ruse, ed. *What the Philosophy of Biology Is.* Boston: Kluwer.

Hodges, Alan. 1983. *The Enigma.* New York: Simon and Schuster.

Hodgson, G. 1993. *Economics and Evolution.* Ann Arbor: University of Michigan Press.

Hollander, Samuel. 1985. *The Economics of John Stuart Mill.* Oxford: Basil Blackwell.

———.1987. *Classical Economics.* Oxford: Basil Blackwell.

Hollinger, David. 1996. *Science, Jews and Culture.* Princeton: Princeton University Press.

———. 2000. Paradigms Lost. *New York Times Book Review*, 28 May, 23.

Holton, Gerald. 1978. *The Scientific Imagination.* New York: Cambridge University Press.

———. 1994. On Doing One's Damnedest. In David H. Guston and Kenneth Keniston, eds. *The Fragile Contract: University Science and the Federal Government.* Cambridge: MIT Press.

———. 1995. Michael Polanyi and the History of Science. In K. Gavroglu, ed. *Physics, Philosophy and the Scientific Community.* Boston: Kluwer.

Hon, Giora. 1989. Towards a Typology of Experimental Errors. *Studies in the History and Philosophy of Science* 20:469–504.

Horgan, John. 1996. *The End of Science.* Reading, Mass.: Addison-Wesley.

———. 1997. The Big Bang Theory of Science Books. *New York Times Book Review*, December 14, 39.

Horwich, Paul, ed. 1993. *World Changes.* Cambridge: MIT Press.

Howard, Don. 2003. Two Left Turns Make a Right: On the Curious Political Career of North American Philosophy of Science at Mid-Century. In Gary Hardcastle and Alan Richardson, eds. *Logical Empiricism in North America.* Minneapolis: University of Minnesota Press.

Howell, G. 1890. *The Conflicts of Labour and Capital Historically and Economically Considered.* London: Macmillan.

Howson, C., and P. Urbach. 1989. *Scientific Reasoning: The Bayesian Approach.* La Salle, Ill.: Open Court.

Hsieh, D. 1991. Chaos and Nonlinear Dynamics. *Journal of Finance* 46:1839–77.

Hsu, D., R. Miller, and D. Wichern. 1974. On the Stable Paretian Behavior of Stock Market Prices. *Journal of the American Statistical Association* 69:108–13.

Hughes, Thomas, and Agatha Hughes, eds. 2000. *Systems, Experts and Computers*. Cambridge: MIT Press.

Hull, David L. 1988. *Science as a Process: An Evolutionary Account of the Social and Conceptual Development of Science*. Chicago: University of Chicago Press.

———. 1994. Review of Kitcher's *The Advancement of Science*. *Isis* 85:554–55.

Hyde, Lewis. 1983. *The Gift*. New York: Vintage.

Ingraham, Mark. 1923. On Professor Moore's Mathematical Analysis of the Business Cycle. *Journal of the American Statistical Association* 18:759–65.

Ingrao, B., and G. Israel. 1990. *The Invisible Hand*. Cambridge: MIT Press.

Jaditz, T., and C. Sayers. 1993. Is Chaos Generic in Economic Data? *International Journal of Bifurcation and Chaos* 3:745–55.

Jansen, D., and C. de Vries. 1991. On the Frequency of Large Stock Returns. *Review of Economics and Statistics* 73:18–24.

Jarvie, Ian. 1988. Explanation, Reduction and the Sociological Turn in the Philosophy of Science, or Kuhn as Ideologue for Merton's Theory of Science. In Gerard Radnitzsky, ed. *Centripetal Forces in the Sciences* 2:299–320. New York: Paragon House.

———. 2001. Science in a Democratic Republic. *Philosophy of Science* 68:545–64.

Jasanoff, Sheila, 1995. *Science at the Bar: Law, Science, and Technology in America*. Cambridge: Harvard University Press.

Jaszi, Peter. 1991. Toward a Theory of Copyright: The Metamorphosis of Authorship. *Duke Law Journal*, April, 455–502.

Jeffreys, J. 1945. *The Story of the Engineers, 1800–1945*. London: Lawrence and Wishart.

Jenkin, Fleeming. 1867. The Origin of Species. *North British Review* 46:149–71.

———. [1887] 1931. *The Graphic Representation of the Laws of Supply and Demand, and Other Essays*. London: London School of Economics, Series of Reprints of Scarce Tracts in Economic and Political Science, no. 9.

———. 1887. *Papers Literary, Scientific, etc.* S. Colvin and J. Ewing, eds. London: Longmans, Green.

Jensen, Richard, and Marie Thursby. 2001. Proofs and Prototypes for Sale: The Licensing of University Inventions. *American Economic Review* 91:240–59.

Jeong, J., and G. Maddala. 1991. Measurement Errors and Tests for Rationality. *Journal of Business and Economic Statistics* 9:431–39.

Jevons, William Stanley. 1868. *A Lecture on the Trades' Societies: Their Objects and Policy*. Manchester.

———. 1878. John Stuart Mill's Philosophy Tested. *Contemporary Review* 32:88–99.

———. [1882] 1894. *The State in Relation to Labour*. London: Macmillan.

———. 1890. *Pure Logic and Other Minor Works*. Ed. Robert Adamson. London: Macmillan.

———. 1905. *The Principles of Economics*. Ed. H. Higgs. London: Macmillan.

———. [1874] 1905. *The Principles of Science*. 3rd ed. London: Macmillan.

———. [1871] 1970. *The Theory of Political Economy*. Baltimore: Penguin.

Johnson, George. 2001. New Contenders for a Theory of Everything. *New York Times*, December 4, D1, D5.

Jordan, Pascual. 1939. "Cosmological Theory." *Annalen der Physik* 36:64.

———. 1949. The Formation of the Stars and the Development of the Universe. *Nature* 164:637–40.

Kadvany, John. 2001. *Imre Lakatos and the Guises of Reason*. Durham: Duke University Press.

Kaergaard, Niels. 1984. The Earliest History of Econometrics: Some Neglected Danish Contributions. *HOPE* 16:437–44.

Kagel, John, and Alvin Roth. 1995. *Handbook of Experimental Economics*. Princeton: Princeton University Press.

Kahin, Brian. 2001. The Expansion of the Patent System: Politics and Political Economy. *First Monday* 6, no. 1 (January).

Kahneman, D., P. Slovic, and A. Tversky, eds. 1982. *Judgments under Uncertainty*. New York: Cambridge University Press.

Kaplan, Stephen. 1976. *Bread, Politics and Political Economy in the Reign of Louis XVI*. The Hague: Nijhoff.

———. 1984. *Provisioning Paris*. Ithaca: Cornell University Press.

Kay, Lily. 1993. *The Molecular Vision of Life: Caltech, Rockefeller and the Rise of the New Biology*. New York: Oxford University Press.

———. 1997. Rethinking Institutions: Philanthropy as a Problem of Knowledge and Power. *Minerva* 35:283–93.

Kaye, Norman. 1956. The Pioneer Econometrics of Henry L. Moore. PhD diss., University of Wisconsin.

Keller, Evelyn Fox. 1983. *A Feeling for the Organism: The Life and Work of Barbara McClintock*. San Francisco: W. H. Freeman.

Kelsey, David. 1988. The Economics of Chaos or the Chaos of Economics. *Oxford Economic Papers*, March, 1–31.

Kevles, Daniel. 1998. *Diamond v. Chakrabarty* and Beyond: The Political Economy of Patenting Life. In Arnold Thackray, ed. *Private Science: Biotechnology and the Rise of the Molecular Sciences*, 65–79. Philadelphia: University of Pennsylvania Press.

Keynes, John Neville. 1917. *The Scope and Method of Political Economy*. 4th ed. London: Macmillan.

Kilminster, C. W. 1994. *Eddington's Search for a Fundamental Theory*. New York: Cambridge University Press.

Kirby, Maurice. 2000. Operations Research Trajectories: Anglo-American Experience, 1940–1990. *Operations Research* 48:661–70.

Kirman, A. 1992. Whom or What Does the Representative Individual Represent? *Journal of Economic Perspectives* 6:117–36.

Kitcher, Patricia. 1993. *Freud's Dream*. Cambridge: MIT Press.

Kitcher, Philip. 1982. *Abusing Science: The Case against Creationism*. Cambridge: MIT Press.

———. 1983. *The Nature of Mathematical Knowledge*. Oxford: Oxford University Press.

———. 1985. *Vaulting Ambition*. Cambridge: MIT Press.

———. 1992. The Naturalists Return. *Philosophical Review* 101:53–114.

———. 1993a. *The Advancement of Science: Science without Legend, Objectivity without Illusions*. New York: Oxford University Press.

———. 1993b. Function and Design. In P. French et al., eds. *Midwest Studies in Philosophy*. Vol. 18. Notre Dame: University of Notre Dame Press.

———. 1993c. Knowledge, Society and History. *Canadian Journal of Philosophy* 23:155–78.

———. 1994. Contrasting Conceptions of Social Epistemology. In F. Schmitt, ed. *Socializing Epistemology*. Lanham, Md.: Rowman and Littlefield.

———. 1995. Utopian Eugenics and Social Inequality. Paper presented at Conference on the Human Genome Project, University of Notre Dame, 6 October.

———. 1996. *The Lives to Come*. New York: Simon and Schuster.

———. 2000. Reviving the Sociology of Science. *PSA Proceedings, Philosophy of Science* 67:S33–S44.

———. 2001. *Science, Truth and Democracy*. New York: Oxford University Press.

———. 2002. The Third Way: Reflections on Helen Longino. *PSA Proceedings, Philosophy of Science* 69:549–59, 569–72.

———. 2003. Disciplined Maverick: An Interview with Philip Kitcher. *Columbia Undergraduate Philosophy Review* 53–61.

Klein, Martin. 1977. The Beginnings of Quantum Theory. In C. Weiner, ed. *History of Twentieth Century Physics*. New York: Academic Press.

Kling, Rob, and Geoffrey McKim. 2000. Not Just a Matter of Time: Field Differences and the Shaping of Electronic Media. *Journal of the American Society for Information Science* 51, no. 14 (December): 1306–20.

Kneller, Robert. 1999. Intellectual Property Rights and University-Industry Technology Transfer in Japan. In Lewis M. Branscomb, Fumio Kodama, and Richard Florida, eds. *Industrializing Knowledge: University-Industry Linkages in Japan and the United States*. Cambridge: MIT Press.

Knight, K. 1993. Estimation in Dynamic Linear Regression Models with Infinite Variance Errors. *Econometric Theory* 9:570–88.

Knorr-Cetina, K. 1982. Scientific Communities or Transepistemic Arenas of Research? A Critique of Quasi-economic Models of Science. *Social Studies of Science* 12:101–30.

Koertge, Noretta. 1990. The Function of Credit in Hull's Evolutionary Model of Science. *Proceedings of the Philosophy of Science Association* 2:237–44.

———, ed. 1998. *House Built on Sand*. New York: Oxford University Press.

Kohler, Robert E. 1991. *Partners in Science: Foundations and Natural Scientists, 1900–1945*. Chicago: University of Chicago Press.

Kohn, David, ed. 1985. *The Darwinian Heritage*. Princeton: Princeton University Press.

Kolm, Serge-Christophe. 1984. *La bonne économie: La reciprocité générale*. Paris: Presses Universitaires de France.

Kothari, D. 1938. Cosmological and Atomic Constants. *Nature* 142:354–55.

Koutrouvelis, I. 1980. Regression-Type Estimation of the Parameters of Stable Laws. *Journal of the American Statistical Association* 75:918–28.

Krantz, D., et al. 1971. *Foundations of Measurement*. Vol. 1. New York: Academic Press.

Kreps, D. 1990. *A Course in Microeconomic Theory*. Princeton: Princeton University Press.

Krimsky, Sheldon. 2003. *Science in the Private Interest*. Lanham: Rowman and Littlefield.

Kuhn, Thomas. 1963. The Function of Dogma in Scientific Research. In A. C. Crombie, ed. *Scientific Change*. New York: Basic Books.

———. [1962] 1970. *The Structure of Scientific Revolutions*. Chicago: University of Chicago Press. Rev. ed.

———. 1977. *The Essential Tension*. Chicago: University of Chicago Press.

———. 1991. The Natural and the Human Sciences. In D. Hiley, J. Bohman, and R. Shusterman, eds. *The Interpretive Turn*. Ithaca: Cornell University Press.

———. 2000. *The Road since Structure*. Chicago: University of Chicago Press.

Kula, Witold. 1986. *Measures and Men*. Princeton: Princeton University Press.

Kverneland, K. 1978. *World Metric Standards for Engineering*. New York: Industrial Press.

Kyburg, Henry. 1992. Measuring Errors of Measurement. In C. Savage and P. Ehrlich, eds. *Philosophical and Foundational Issues in Measurement Theory*. Hillsdale, N.J.: Erlbaum.

Labinger, Jay, and Harry Collins, eds. 2001. *The One Culture?* Chicago: University of Chicago Press.

Lakatos, Imre. 1970. Falsification and the Methodology of Scientific Research Programs. In Lakatos and Musgrave, eds. *Criticism and the Growth of Knowledge*. Cambridge: Cambridge University Press.

Lakatos, Imre, and Alan Musgrave, eds. 1970. *Criticism and the Growth of Knowledge*. Cambridge: Cambridge University Press.

Lamperti, John. 1966. *Probability*. New York: Benjamin.

Landa, Janet Tai. 1994. *Trust, Ethnicity and Identity*. Ann Arbor: University of Michigan Press.

Langenberg, D., and B. Taylor. 1971. *Precision Measurement and the Fundamental Constants*. Washington: U.S. Government Printing Office.

Latour, B. 1987. *Science in Action*. Cambridge: Harvard University Press.

———. 1993. *We Have Never Been Modern*. Cambridge: Harvard University Press.

———. 1999. On Recalling ANT. In John Law and J. Hassard, eds. *Actor Network Theory and After*. Oxford: Basil Blackwell.

Latour, Bruno, and Steve Woolgar. 1986. *Laboratory Life: The Construction of Scientific Facts*. Princeton: Princeton University Press.

Lau, A., H. Lan, and J. Wingender. 1990. The Distribution of Stock Returns: New Evidence against the Stable Model. *Journal of Business and Economic Statistics* 8:217–23.

Leamer, E. 1983. Let's Take the "Con" out of Econometrics. *American Economic Review* 73:31–43.

LeBaron, B. 1994. Chaos and Nonlinear Forecastability in Economics and Finance. *Philosophical Transactions of the Royal Society of London (A)* 348:397–404.

Lee, C. 1979. *British Regional Employment Statistics, 1841–1971*. New York: Cambridge University Press.

Leonard, Thomas. 2002. Reflection on Rules in Science: An Invisible Hand Perspective. *Journal of Economic Methodology* 9:141–68.

LeRoy, S. 1989. Efficient Capital Markets and Martingales. *Journal of Economic Literature* 27:1583–1621.

Lessig, Lawrence. 1999. *Code and Other Laws of Cyberspace*. New York: Basic Books.

———. 2001. *The Future of Ideas*. New York: Random House.

Levy, David. 1998. The Premature Death of Path Dependence. Paper presented to the History of Economics Society meeting, Montreal.

Lévy, Paul. 1925. *Calcul des probabilités*. Paris: Gauthier Villars.

Lewis, Gilberg. 1925. Ultimate Rational Units and Dimensional Theory. *Philosophical Magazine* 49:739–50.

Lichtenberg, A., and M. Liebman. 1983. *Regular and Stochastic Motion*. New York: Springer.

Litman, Jessica. 2001. *Digital Copyright: Protecting Intellectual Property on the Internet*. Amherst: Prometheus.

Liu, T., and C. Granger. 1992. Using the Correlation Exponent to Decide Whether an Economic Series Is Chaotic. *Journal of Applied Econometrics* 7:S25–S39.

Lo, A. 1991. Long-Term Memory in Stock Market Prices. *Econometrica* 59:1279–1313.

Lodewijks, John. 1994. Anthropologists and Economists: Conflict or Cooperation? *Journal of Economic Methodology* 1:81–104.

Longe, Francis. [1866]. 1903. *A Refutation of the Wage-Fund Theory*. Baltimore: Johns Hopkins University Press.

Longfield, Mountifort. 1834. *Lectures on Political Economy*. Dublin: Milliken.

Longino, Helen. 2002a. *The Fate of Knowledge*. Princeton: Princeton University Press.

———. 2002b. Science and the Common Good: Thoughts on Kitcher's *Science, Truth and Democracy*. *PSA Proceedings, Philosophy of Science* 69:560–68.

Lundgreen, Peter. 1986. *Standardization, Testing, Regulation*. Bielefeld: Kleine.

Lyons, Gene. 1969. *The Uneasy Partnership*. New York: Russell Sage.

MacIntyre, Alasdair. 1984. *After Virtue*. 2nd ed. Notre Dame: University of Notre Dame Press.

Mackenzie, Donald. 1990. *Inventing Accuracy: A Historical Sociology of Nuclear Missile Guidance*. Cambridge: MIT Press.

——. 1996. *Knowing Machines*. Cambridge: MIT Press.

——. 2001. Physics and Finance. *Science, Technology and Human Values* 26:115–44.

——. 2002. *Mechanizing Proof*. Cambridge: MIT Press.

Macleod, H. 1884. *An Address to the Board of Electors to the Professorship of Political Economy in the University of Cambridge*. London: Blundell.

Magee, James. 1915. Review of Moore's *Economic Cycles*. *Journal of Political Economy* 23:515–17.

Mahoney, Michael. 1988. The History of Computing in the History of Technology. *Annals of the History of Computing* 10:113–25.

Maki, Uskali. 1999. Science as a Free Market: A Reflexivity Test in an Economics of Economics. *Perspectives on Science* 7:486–509.

Malinowski, Bronislaw. 1922. *Argonauts of the Western Pacific*. London: Routledge.

——. [1925] 1985. *Crime and Custom in Savage Society*. Totowa: Rowman and Allanheld.

Maloney, J. 1985. *Marshall, Orthodoxy, and the Professionalism of Economics*. Cambridge: Cambridge University Press.

Malthus, Thomas. [1820] 1966. *Principles of Political Economy*. In vol. II of David Ricardo's *Collected Works*. Ed. Piero Sraffa. Cambridge: Cambridge University Press.

——. 1827. *Definitions in Political Economy*. London: John Murray.

——. 1986. *Essays on Political Economy*. Vol. 6 in *The Works of T. M. Malthus*, ed. E. A. Wrigley and David Souden. London: Pickering and Chatto.

Mandelbrot, B. 1960. The Pareto-Levy Law and the Distribution of Income. *International Economic Review* 1:79–106.

——. 1961. Stable Paretian Random Functions and the Multiplicative Variation of Income. *Econometrica*, October, 517–43.

——. 1962. Paretian Distributions and Income Maximization. *Quarterly Journal of Economics*, February, 57–85.

——. 1963a. New Methods in Statistical Economics. *Journal of Political Economy* 71 (October): 421–40.

——. 1963b. The Variation of Certain Speculative Prices. *Journal of Business* 36 (October): 394–419.

——. 1964. On the Derivation of Statistical Thermodynamics from Purely Phenomenological Principles. *Journal of Mathematical Physics*, February, 164–71.

——. 1966. Forecasts of Future Prices, Unbiased Markets, and Martingale Models. *Journal of Business* 39:242–55.

——. 1967. The Variation of Some Other Speculative Prices. *Journal of Business* 40 (October): 393–413.

——. 1969. Long-Run Linearity, Locally Gaussian Processes, H-Spectra, and Infinite Variances. *International Economic Review* 10:82–111.

——. 1971. When Can Price Be Arbitraged Efficiently? A Limit to the Validity of the Random Walk and Martingale Models. *Review of Economics and Statistics* 53 (August): 225–36.

——. 1972. Statistical Methodology for Non-periodic Cycles. *Annals of Economic and Social Measurement* 1 (July): 259–90.

——. 1973. A Comment on "A Subordinated Stochastic Process Model." *Econometrica*, January, 157–59.

——. 1977. *Fractals: Form, Chance and Dimension*. San Francisco: W. H. Freeman.

——. 1982. The Many Faces of Scaling: Fractals, the Geometry of Nature, and Economics. In William Schieve and Peter Allen, eds. *Self-Organization and Dissipative Structures*. Austin: University of Texas Press.

——. 1983. *The Fractal Geometry of Nature*. New York: W. H. Freeman.

——. 1986. Fractal Measures and Multiplicative Chaos. In G. Mayer-Kress, ed. *Dimensions and Entropies in Chaotic Systems*. Berlin: Springer.

——. 1987. Towards a Second Stage of Indeterminism in Science. *Interdisciplinary Science Reviews* 12:117–27.

——. 1989a. Chaos, Bourbaki and Poincaré. *Mathematical Intelligencer* 11:2, 10–12.

——. 1989b. Fractal Geometry: What Is It and What Does It Do? *Proceedings of the Royal Society of London* A423:3–16.

——. 1997. *Fractals and Scaling in Finance*. Berlin: Springer.

Mandelbrot, Benoit, and Murad Taqqu. 1979. Robust R/S Analysis of Long Run Serial Correlation. Paper presented at the 42nd Session of the International Statistical Institute, Manila.

Mandelbrot, B., and H. Taylor. 1967. On the Distribution of Stock Price Differences. *Operations Research* 15:1057–62.

Manin, Yu. 1981. *Mathematics and Physics*. Boston: Birkhauser.

Mann, Charles. 1998. Who Will Own Your Next Good Idea? *Atlantic* 282, no. 3 (September).

Mantel, Rolf. 1976. Homothetic Preferences and Community Excess Demand Functions. *Journal of Economic Theory* 12:197–201.

Marcet, J. [1816] 1827. *Conversations on Political Economy*. 6th ed. London: Longman, Rees, Orme, Brown and Green.

Markus, G. 1987. Why Is There Hermeneutics of Natural Science? *Science in Context* 1:5–51.

Marshall, Alfred. [1920] 1947. *Principles of Economics*. 8th ed. London: Macmillan.

——. 1975. *Early Economic Writings*. Ed. J. Whittaker. New York: Free Press.

——. 1994. Ye Machine. *Research in the History of Economic Thought and Method*, archival suppl. 4:116–32.

Marx, Karl. 1935. *Value, Price and Profit*. New York: International.

——. 1974. *The First International and After*. Ed. David Fernbach. New York: Vintage.

Mason, John. 1980. Political Economy and the Response to Socialism in Britain, 1870–1914. *Historical Journal* 23:565–87.

Mason, Roger. 1989. *Robert Giffen and the Giffen Paradox*. Totowa: Barnes and Noble.

Mathias, Peter. 1959. *The Brewing Industry in England*. Cambridge: Cambridge University Press.

Maurer, Stephen, Berrt Hugenholtz, and Harlan Onsrud. 2001. Europe's Database Experiment. *Science* 294 (26 October): 789–90.

Mauss, Marcel. 1969. *Oeuvres*. Vol. 3. Paris: Éditions de Minuit.

——. 1990. *The Gift*. Trans. W. Halls. New York: W. W. Norton.

Mayr, Ernest. 1982. *The Growth of Biological Thought*. Cambridge: Harvard University Press.

Maxwell, James Clerk. 1870. Presidential Address to Section A of the British Association. *Nature* 2:419–22.

——. 1871. *The Theory of Heat*. London: Longmans.

——. 1965. *The Scientific Papers*. Ed. W. Niven. New York: Dover.

Mayfield, E., and B. Mizrach. 1992. On Determining the Dimension of Real-Time Stock-Price Data. *Journal of Business and Economic Statistics* 10:367–74.

Maynard Smith, J. 1982. *Evolution and the Theory of Games*. Cambridge: Cambridge University Press.

Mayo, Deborah. 1985. Behavioralistic, Evidentialist, and Learning Models of Statistical Testing. *Philosophy of Science* 52:493–516.

——. 1992. Did Pearson Reject the Neyman-Pearson Philosophy of Statistics? *Synthese* 90:233–62.

McCauley, Joseph. 1993. *Chaos, Dynamics and Fractals*. New York: Cambridge University Press.

McClellan, C. 1996. The Economic Consequences of Bruno Latour. *Social Epistemology* 10:193–208.

McCulloch, J. R. 1825. *Principles of Political Economy*. Edinburgh: Black.

——. [1825] 1864. *Principles of Political Economy*. 5th ed. Edinburgh: Adam and Charles Black.

McCulloch, J. 1994. Financial Applications of Stable Distributions. In G. S. Maddala and C. R. Rao, eds. *Statistical Methods in Finance*. New York: Elsevier, 1996.

McCumber, John. 2001. *Time in the Ditch: American Philosophy in the McCarthy Era*. Evanston: Northwestern University Press.

McFarland, J., R. Petit, and S. Sung. 1982. The Distribution of Foreign Exchange Price Changes. *Journal of Finance* 37:693–715.

McGrath, Peter. 2002. *Scientists, Business and the State, 1890–1960*. Chapel Hill: University of North Carolina Press.

McGucken, William. 1984. *Scientists, Society and the State*. Columbus: Ohio State University Press.

McMullin, E., ed. 1988. *Construction and Constraint*. Notre Dame: Notre Dame University Press.

McSherry, Corynne. 2001. *Who Owns Academic Work?* Cambridge: Harvard University Press.

Meek, Ronald. 1976. *Social Science and the Ignoble Savage*. Cambridge: Cambridge University Press.

Menard, Claude. 1976. *La formation d'une rationalité économique*. Paris: Flammarion.

——. 1980. Three Forms of Resistance to Statistics: Say, Cournot, Walras. *HOPE* 12:524–41.

——. 1987. Why Was There No Probabilistic Revolution in Economic Thought? In L. Krüger et al., eds. *The Probabilistic Revolution*. Vol. 2. Cambridge: MIT Press.

Mendoza, Eric. 1990. Delaroche and Berard and Experimental Error. *British Journal for the History of Science* 23:285–91.

Meyer, John, and R. Glauber. 1964. *Investment Decisions, Economic Forecasting and Public Policy*. Boston: Harvard Business School.

Meyerson, Emile. [1908] 1962. *Identity and Reality*. New York: Dover.

Mill, Anna. 1960. *John Mill's Boyhood Visit to France*. Toronto: University of Toronto Press.

Mill, James. 1966. *Selected Economic Writings*. Ed. D. Winch. Chicago: University of Chicago Press.

Mill, John Stuart. 1897. *Early Essays*. London: Bell.

——. [1848] 1899. *Principles of Political Economy*. New York: Colonial.

——. 1965. *Principles of Political Economy*. Vols. 2 and 3 of *Collected Works*. Toronto: University of Toronto Press.

——. [1869] 1967. Thornton on Labour and Its Claims. Vol. 5 of *Collected Works of John Stuart Mill*, ed. J. M. Robson. Toronto: University of Toronto Press.

——. 1972. *Collected Works*, vol. 14. Toronto: University of Toronto Press.

Miller, Arthur. 1986. *Imagery in Scientific Thought*. Cambridge: MIT Press.

Miller, Daniel, ed. 1993. *Unwrapping Christmas*. Oxford: Clarendon.

Mills, Frederick. 1924. On Measurement in Economics. In Rexford Tugwell, ed. *The Trend of Economics*. New York: Alfred A. Knopf.

Mirowski, Philip. 1983. Review of Russell MacCormmach, *Night Thoughts of a Classical Physicist*. *HOPE* 15:145–46.

——. 1986. Mathematical Formalism and Economic Explanation. In P. Mirowski, ed. *The Reconstruction of Economic Theory*. Norwell, Mass.: Kluwer.

——. 1988. *Against Mechanism: Why Economics Needs Protection from Science*. Totowa: Rowman and Littlefield.

———. 1989a. The Measurement without Theory Controversy. *Économies et sociétés*, série Oeconomia, no. 11:65–87.

———. 1989b. *More Heat Than Light: Economics as Social Physics, Physics as Nature's Economy.* New York: Cambridge University Press.

———. 1989c. The Probabilistic Counter-Revolution: How Stochastic Concepts Came to Neoclassical Economics. *Oxford Economic Papers* 41 (March): 217–35.

———. 1989d. The Rise and Fall of the Equilibrium Concept in Economic Theory. *Recherches économiques de Louvain* 55, no. 4:447–68.

———. 1989e. 'Tis a Pity Econometrics Isn't an Empirical Endeavor: Mandelbrot, Chaos, and the Noah and Joseph Effects. *Ricerche Economisti* 63:76–99.

———. 1990a. From Mandelbrot to Chaos in Economic Theory. *Southern Economic Journal* 57:289–307.

———. 1990b. The Rhetoric of Modern Economics. *History of the Human Sciences* 3:243–57.

———. 1991a. Postmodernism and the Social Theory of Value. *Journal of Post Keynesian Economics* 13:565–82.

———. 1991b. The How, the When and the Why of Mathematical Expression in the History of Economics. *Journal of Economic Perspectives* 5:145–58.

———. 1992. Looking for Those Natural Numbers. *Science in Context* 5:165–88.

———. 1993a. The Goalkeeper's Anxiety at the Penalty Kick. In Neil de Marchi, ed. *Non-Natural Economics.* Durham: Duke University Press.

———. 1993b. Unholy History of Error. Notre Dame Working Paper.

———, ed. 1994a. *Edgeworth on Chance, Economic Hazard and Statistics.* Lanham, Md.: Rowman and Littlefield.

———, ed. 1994b. *Natural Images in Economic Thought: Markets Read in Tooth and Claw.* New York: Cambridge University Press.

———. 1994c. Some Suggestions for Linking Arbitrage, Symmetries and the Social Theory of Value. In Amitava Dutt, ed. *New Directions in Analytical Political Economy.* Aldershot: Edward Elgar, 185–210.

———. 1994d. Tit for Tat: Concepts of Exchange, Higgling, and Barter in Two Episodes in the History of Economic Anthropology. In Neil de Marchi and Mary S. Morgan, eds. *Higgling: Transactors and Their Markets in the History of Economics.* Durham: Duke University Press.

———. 1994e. A Visible Hand in the Marketplace of Ideas. *Science in Context* 7:563–89.

———. 1995a. Do You Know the Way to Santa Fe? In S. Pressman and J. Smithin, eds. *Explorations in Political Economy.* London: Routledge.

———. 1995b. Three Ways of Thinking about Testing in Econometrics. *Journal of Econometrics* 76:25–46.

———. 1997. The History of Classical and Frequentist Theories of Probability. In Jim Henderson, ed. *The State of the History of Economics.* London: Routledge.

———. 1998–89. Economics, Science and Knowledge: Polanyi vs. Hayek. *Tradition and Discovery* 25, no. 1:29–42.

———. 1999. Cyborg Agonistes: Economics Meets Operations Research. *Social Studies of Science* 29:685–718.

———. 2002. *Machine Dreams.* New York: Cambridge University Press.

———. 2004. The Scientific Dimensions of Society and Their Distant Echoes in 20th Century Philosophy of Science. *Studies in the History and Philosophy of Science.*

Mirowski, Philip, and Pamela Cook. 1990. Walras' Economics and Mechanics. In Warren Samuels, ed. *Economics as Discourse.* Norwell: Kluwer-Nijhoff.

Mirowski, Philip, and Wade Hands. 1998. A Paradox of Budgets. In M. Rutherford and M. Morgan, eds. *From Interwar Pluralism to Postwar Neoclassicism*. Durham: Duke University Press.

Mirowski, Philip, and Esther-Mirjam Sent, eds. 2001. *Science Bought and Sold: Essays in the Economics of Science*. Chicago: University of Chicago Press.

Mirowski, P., and Koye Somefun. 1998. Markets as Evolving Computational Entities. *Journal of Evolutionary Economics* 8:329–56.

Mirowski, P., and Robert Van Horn. 2004. The Contract Research Organization and the Commercialization of Science. *Social Studies of Science*.

Mitchell, W. C. 1927. *Business Cycles: The Problem and Its Setting*. New York: National Bureau of Economic Research.

Mokyr, Joel. 2002. *The Gift of Athena*. Princeton: Princeton University Press.

Moore, Henry L. 1894. Von Thünen's Theory of Natural Wages. *Quarterly Journal of Economics* 9:388–408.

——. 1905a. The Personality of A. A. Cournot. *Quarterly Journal of Economics* 19:370–99.

——. 1905b. Review of *A Geometrical Political Economy*, by H. Cunynghame. *Political Science Quarterly* 20:346–47.

——. 1906. Paradoxes of Competition. *Quarterly Journal of Economics* 20:211–30.

——. 1908. The Statistical Complement of Pure Economics. *Quarterly Journal of Economics* 23:1–33.

——. 1911. *Laws of Wages*. New York: Macmillan.

——. 1914. *Economic Cycles: Their Law and Cause*. New York: Macmillan.

——. 1917. *Forecasting the Yield and Price of Cotton*. New York: Macmillan.

——. 1922. Elasticity of Demand and Flexibility of Prices. *Journal of the American Statistical Association* 18:8–19.

——. 1923. *Generating Economic Cycles*. New York: Macmillan.

——. 1926a. The Partial Elasticity of Demand. *Quarterly Journal of Economics* 40:393–401.

——. 1926b. A Theory of Economic Oscillations. *Quarterly Journal of Economics* 41:1–29.

——. 1929. *Synthetic Economics*. New York: Macmillan.

Moore, Walter. 1989. *Schrödinger: Life and Thought*. New York: Cambridge University Press.

Morgan, Mary. 1990. *A History of Econometrics*. Cambridge: Cambridge University Press.

Mosak, Jacob. 1987. Henry Schultz. *The New Palgrave* 4:261–62.

Motterlini, Matteo, ed. 1999. *For and against Method*. Chicago: University of Chicago Press.

Mueller, Iris. 1955. *J. S. Mill and French Thought*. Urbana: University of Illinois Press.

Mullis, Kary B. 1998. *Dancing Naked in the Mind Field*. New York: Pantheon.

Mummery, A. F., and J. A. Hobson. [1889] 1956. *The Physiology of Industry: Being an Exposure of Certain Fallacies in Existing Theories of Economics*. New York: Kelley and Millman.

Musson, A. 1974. *Trades Unions and Social History*. London: Frank Cass.

Myerson, Roger. 1999. Nash Equilibrium and the History of Economic Theory. *Journal of Economic Literature* 107:1067–82.

National Research Council, Committee for a Study on Promoting Access to Scientific and Technical Data for the Public Interest. 1999. *A Question of Balance: Private Rights and the Public Interest in Scientific and Technical Databases*. Washington: National Academy.

Negishi, T. 1985. Comments on Ekelund. *Oxford Economic Papers* 37:148–51.

——. 1986. Thornton's Criticism of Equilibrium Theory and Mill. *History of Political Economy* 18:567–77.

——. 1989. On Equilibrium and Disequilibrium: Reply to Ekelund and Thommesen. *History of Political Economy* 21:593–600.

Nelson, Richard, ed. 1962. *The Rate and Direction of Inventive Activity*. Princeton: Princeton University Press.

Newman, P. K. 1960. The Erosion of Marshall's Theory of Value. *Quarterly Journal of Economics* 74:587–601.

Nickles, T. 1995. Philosophy of Science and History of Science. *Osiris* 10:139–63.

Niehans, Jurg. 1990. *A History of Economic Theory (Thought?)*. Baltimore: Johns Hopkins University Press.

Nietzsche, Friedrich. 1966. *Beyond Good and Evil*. New York: Vintage.

———. 1967. *On the Genealogy of Morals*. Trans. W. Kauffmann. New York: Vintage.

———. 1986. *Human, All Too Human*. Cambridge: Cambridge University Press.

Norman, Eric. 1986. Are the Fundamental Constants Really Constant? *American Journal of Physics* 54:317–21.

Northrop, F. 1941. The Impossibility of a Theoretical Science of Economic Dynamics. *Quarterly Journal of Economics*, November, 1–17.

Novos, Ian, and Michael Waldman. 1984. The Effects of Increased Copyright Protection. *Journal of Political Economy* 92:236–48.

Nunberg, Geoffrey. 1993. The Places of Books in an Age of Electronic Reproduction. *Representations* 42 (spring): 13–37.

O'Brien, G. 1943. J. S. Mill and J. E. Cairnes. *Economica* 10:273–85.

O'Connell, Joseph. 1993. Metrology: The Creation of Universality by the Circulation of Particulars. *Social Studies of Science* 23:129–74.

Ohanian, Hans. 1977. Cosmological Changes in Atomic and Nuclear Constants. *Foundations of Physics* 7:391–403.

Olesko, Katheryn. 1988. Michelson and the Reform of Physics Instruction. In S. Goldberg and R. Stuewer, eds. *The Michelson Era in American Physics*. New York: American Institute of Physics.

———. 1991. *Physics as a Calling*. Ithaca: Cornell University Press.

Ordover, Janusz, and Robert Willig. 1978. On the Optimal Provision of Journals as Sometimes Shared Goods. *American Economic Review* 68:324–38.

Osborne, D. 1978. On Dimensional Invariance. *Quantity and Quality* 12:75–89.

Ott, E. 1993. *Chaos in Dynamical Systems*. New York: Cambridge University Press.

Packe, Michael. 1954. *Life of J. S. Mill*. London: Secker and Warburg.

Pais, Abraham. 1982. *Subtle Is the Lord . . .* Oxford: Oxford University Press.

Parker, William, ed. 1986. *Economic History and the Modern Economist*. Oxford: Basil Blackwell.

Parry, Jonathan. 1985. The Gift, the Indian Gift and the "Indian Gift." *Man* 21:453–73.

Paul, Ellen, et al., eds. 1993. *Altruism*. New York: Cambridge University Press.

Peake, Charles. 1994. A Note on John Stuart Mill, William Thornton, and William Whewell. *Manchester School* 62:319–23.

Pearce, Douglas. 1984. An Empirical Analysis of Expected Stock Price Movements. *Journal of Money, Credit and Banking* 16: 317–27.

Peirce, C. S. 1879. Note on the Theory of the Economy of Research. *United States Coast Survey for the Fiscal Year Ending June 1876*. Washington: U.S. Government Printing Office.

Pelling, Henry. 1963. *A History of British Trades Unionism*. London: Macmillan.

Persky, J. 1992. Pareto's Law. *Journal of Economic Perspectives* 6:181–92.

Pesaran, B., and G. Robinson. 1993. The European Exchange Rate Mechanism and the Volatility of the Sterling-Deutschemark Exchange Rate. *Economic Journal* 103:1418–31.

Petley, Brian. 1985. *The Fundamental Physical Constants and the Frontiers of Measurement*. Bristol: Adam Hilger.

Pickering, Edward. 1873. *Elements of Physical Manipulation*. Boston: Houghton Mifflin.

Pigou, A. C., ed. 1925. *Memorials of Alfred Marshall*. London: Macmillan.

Piliavin, Jane, and Peter Callero. 1991. *Giving Blood*. Baltimore: Johns Hopkins University Press.

Pimbley, Joseph. 1997. Physicists in Finance. *Physics Today*, January, 42–47.

Pinch, T. 1985. Towards an Analysis of Scientific Observation. *Social Studies of Science* 15:3–36.

Planck, Max. 1931. *The Universe in Light of Modern Physics*. New York: W. W. Norton.

———. 1949. *Scientific Autobiography*. New York: Philosophical Library.

———. 1959. *The Theory of Heat Radiation*. New York: Dover.

Poirier, D. 1988a. Casual Relationships and Replicability. *Journal of Econometrics* 39:213–34.

———. 1988b. Frequentist and Subjectivist Perspectives on the Problems of Model Building in Economics. *Journal of Economic Perspectives* 2:121–44.

Polanyi, Karl. [1944] 1957. *The Great Transformation*. Boston: Beacon.

Polanyi, Michael. 1941. The Growth of Thought in Society. *Economica* 8:428–55.

———. 1946. *Science, Faith and Society*. London: Oxford University Press.

———. 1958. *Personal Knowledge*. Chicago: University of Chicago Press.

———. 1959. *The Study of Man*. Chicago: University of Chicago Press.

———. 1961. Science: Academic and Industrial. *Journal of the Institute of Metals* 89:401–6.

———. 1969. *Knowing and Being*. Chicago: University of Chicago Press.

———. 1974. *Scientific Thought and Social Reality*. Psychological Issues Monograph no. 32. Ed. Fred Schwartz.

———. [1940] 1975. *The Contempt of Freedom*. New York: Arno.

Polanyi, Michael, and Harry Prosch. 1975. *Meaning*. Chicago: University of Chicago Press.

Political Economy Club. 1921. *Political Economy Club Centenary Volume*. London.

Pool, R. 1989. How Cold Fusion Happened—Twice! *Science* 244:420–23.

Popper, K. 1965. *Conjectures and Refutations*. New York: Harper and Row.

———. 1976. *Unending Quest*. London: Fontana.

Porter, Theodore. 1985. The Mathematics of Society. *British Journal of the History of Science*, March, 51–69.

———. 1986. *The Rise of Statistical Thinking*. Princeton: Princeton University Press.

———. 1992. Objectivity as Standardization. *Annals of Scholarship* 9:19–59.

———. 1995. *Trust in Numbers*. Princeton: Princeton University Press.

Posner, Richard. 1980. A Theory of Primitive Society. *Journal of Law and Economics* 23:1–53.

Preston, John, Gonzalo Munevar, and David Lamb, eds. 2000. *The Worst Enemy of Science?* New York: Oxford University Press.

Pribram, Karl. 1983. *A History of Economic Reasoning*. Baltimore: Johns Hopkins University Press.

Prigogine, Ilya. 1980. *From Being to Becoming*. New York: W. H. Freeman.

Prigogine, Ilya, and Isabelle Stengers. 1984. *Order out of Chaos*. New York: Bantam.

Proctor, Robert. 1991. *Value Free Science?* Cambridge: Harvard University Press.

Prosch, Harry. 1986. *Michael Polanyi: A Critical Exposition*. Albany: State University of New York Press.

Purcell, Edward. 1973. *The Crisis of Democratic Theory: Scientific Naturalism and the Problem of Value*. Lexington: University Press of Kentucky.

Radnitzky, G. 1989. Falsificationism Looked at from an Economic Point of View. In K. Gavroglu, Y. Goudaroulis, and P. Nicolacopoulos, eds. *Imre Lakatos and Theories of Scientific Change*. Boston: Kluwer Academic.

Radnitzsky, G., and P. Bernholz, eds. 1987. *Economic Imperialism*. New York: Paragon.

Raffaelli, Tiziano. 1994. Marshall's Analysis of the Human Mind. *Research in the History of Economic Thought and Method*, archival suppl. 4:57–93.

Rai, Arti K. 1999. Regulating Scientific Research: Intellectual Property Rights and the Norms of Science. *Northwestern University Law Review* 94:77–152.

Rai, Arti K., and Rebecca S. Eisenberg. 2001. The Public and the Private in Biopharmaceutical Research. www.law.duke.edu/pd/papers/raieisen.pdf.

Rankine, W. 1881. *Miscellaneous Scientific Papers*. London: Charles Griffin.

Rau, Erik. 1999. Combat Scientists: The Emergence of OR in the US in World War II. PhD diss., University of Pennsylvania.

Regaldo, Antonio. 1995. Multiauthor Papers on the Rise. *Science* 268 (7 April): 25.

Reichenbach, Hans. 1938. *Experience and Prediction*. Chicago: University of Chicago Press.

Reichman, J. H., and Paul F. Uhlir. 1999. Database Protection at the Crossroads: Recent Developments and Their Impact on Science and Technology. *Berkeley Technology Law Journal* 14, no. 2:799–821.

Rescher, N. 1978. *Scientific Progress*. Pittsburgh: University of Pittsburgh Press.

———. 1989. *Cognitive Economy*. Pittsburgh: University of Pittsburgh Press.

Richards, J. 1988. *Mathematical Visions: The Pursuit of Geometry in Victorian England*. New York: Academic Press.

Richardson, Alan. 2002. Engineering Philosophy of Science. *PSA Proceedings, Philosophy of Science* 69:S36–S47.

Richmond, Lesley, and Alison Turton. 1990. *The Brewing Industry*. Manchester: Manchester University Press.

[Rickards, G. K.] 1869. Thornton on Labour. *Edinburgh Review* 130 (October): 198–212.

Ridley, M. 1993. Survey: Frontiers of Finance. *Economist*, October 9, S1–S25, 329.

———. 1996. *The Origins of Virtue*. New York: Viking.

Ringer, Fritz. 1969. *The Decline of the German Mandarins*. Cambridge: Harvard University Press.

Rizvi, Abu. 1994. The Microfoundations Project in General Equilibrium Theory. *Cambridge Journal of Economics* 18:357–77.

———. 1998. Responses to Arbitrariness in Contemporary Economics. In John Davis, ed. *New Economics and Its History*. Durham: Duke University Press.

Robinson, J. V. 1973. *Collected Economic Papers*. Vol. 4. Cambridge: MIT Press.

———. 1979. *Collected Economic Papers*. Vol. 5. Cambridge: MIT Press.

[Rogers, Edward.] 1822. *An Essay on Some General Principles of Political Economy*. London.

Rorty, Richard. 1992. Trotsky and the Wild Orchids. *Common Knowledge* 1:140–53.

Rose, Andrew. 1986. Four Paradoxes in GNP. *Economics Letters*, nos. 2–3:137–41.

Rosenberg, Alex. 1996. A Field Guide to Recent Species of Naturalism. *British Journal for the Philosophy of Science* 47:1–29.

Rosenfeld, Arthur. 1975. The Particle Data Group. *Annual Review of Nuclear Science* 25:555–98.

Rosenthal-Schneider, Ilse. 1980. *Reality and Scientific Truth*. Detroit: Wayne State University Press.

Rucker, A. 1889. On the Suppressed Dimensions of Physical Quantities. *Philosophical Magazine* 27:104–14.

Ruelle, David. 1989. *Chaotic Evolution and Strange Attractors*. Cambridge: Cambridge University Press.

———. *Chance and Chaos*. 1991. Princeton: Princeton University Press.

———. 1994. Where Can One Hope to Profitably Apply Ideas of Chaos? *Physics Today*, July, 24–30.

Ruger, Alexander. 1988. Atomism from Cosmology. *Historical Studies in the Physical Sciences* 18:376–401.

Rutherford, M. 1993. *Institutions and Economics*. New York: Cambridge University Press.

Sahlins, Marshall. 1972. *Stone Age Economics*. Chicago: Aldine.

———. 1988. Cosmologies of Capitalism. *Proceedings of the British Academy* 74:1–51.

———. 1992. Economics of Develop-Man in the Pacific. *Anthropology and Aesthetics* 22:12–25.

Samuelson, L. 1993. Does Evolution Eliminate Dominated Strategies? In K. Binmore et al., eds. *Frontiers of Game Theory*. Cambridge: MIT Press.

Samuelson, Pamela. 2001. Anticircumvention Rules: Threat to Science. *Science*, 14 September, 2028–31.

Samuelson, Paul. 1970. Classical and Neoclassical Monetary Theory. In Robert Clower, ed. *Monetary Theory*. Baltimore: Penguin.

———. 1972. *The Collected Scientific Papers of Paul Samuelson*. Vol. 3. Cambridge: MIT Press.

———. 1977. *The Collected Scientific Papers of Paul Samuelson*. Vol. 4. Cambridge: MIT Press.

Say, Jean-Baptiste. 1830. *Treatise on Political Economy*. Trans. C. Princep. 4th ed. Philadelphia: Grigg.

———. 1852. *Cours complet d'économie politique pratique*. Vol. 2. Paris: Guillaumin.

Schabas, M. 1989. Alfred Marshall, Stanley Jevons, and the Mathematization of Economics. *Isis* 80:60–73.

Scheiding, Tom. Forthcoming. Publish *and* Perish: Electronic Publication and the Serials Crisis. PhD diss., University of Notre Dame.

Scheinkman, J. 1990. Nonlinearities in Economic Dynamics. *Economic Journal* 100:33–48.

Scheinkman, J., and B. LeBaron. 1989. Nonlinear Dynamics and Stock Returns. *Journal of Business* 62:311–38.

Schmidt, Frederick, ed. 1994. *Socializing Epistemology*. Lanham, Md.: Rowman and Littlefield.

Scholtz, Carter. 2002. *Radiance*. New York: Picador.

Schultz, Henry. 1928. *Statistical Laws of Demand and Supply*. Chicago: University of Chicago Press.

———. 1931. Review of G. Evans, *Mathematical Introduction to Economics*. *Journal of the American Statistical Association* 26:484–91.

———. 1933. A Comparison of Different Elasticities of Demand Obtained by Different Methods. *Econometrica* 1:274–301.

———. 1938. *The Theory and Measurement of Demand*. Chicago: University of Chicago Press.

Schumpeter, Joseph. 1933. The Common Sense of Econometrics. *Econometrica* 1:5–12.

———. 1954. *A History of Economic Analysis*. New York: Oxford University Press.

Schuster, Heinz. 1989. *Deterministic Chaos*. 2nd ed. Weinheim: VCH.

Schwartz, Pedro. 1972. *The New Political Economy of J. S. Mill*. London: Weidenfeld and Nicholson.

Scott, Pam, Evelyn Richards, and Brian Martin. 1990. Captives of Controversy: The Myth of the Neutral Social Researcher in Contemporary Scientific Controversies. *Science, Technology and Human Values* 26:229–44.

Scrope, G. Poulette. [1833] 1969. *Principles of Political Economy*. New York: Kelley.

Senior, Nassau. [1836] 1965. *An Outline of the Science of Political Economy*. New York: Kelley.

Sent, Esther-Mirjam. 1994. Resisting Sargent. PhD diss., Stanford University.

———. 1998. *The Evolving Rationality of Rational Expectations Theory*. New York: Cambridge University Press.

———. 2001. Sent Simulating Simon Simulating Scientists. *Studies in the History and Philosophy of Science* 32, no. 3:479–500.

Serres, Michel. 1982. *The Parasite*. Baltimore: Johns Hopkins University Press.

Shapin, Steven. 1991. The Mind in Its Own Place. *Science in Context* 4:191–218.

———. 1994. *Social History of Truth*. Chicago: University of Chicago Press.

Shapin, S., and S. Schaffer. 1985. *Leviathan and the Air Pump*. Princeton: Princeton University Press.

Shi, Yanfei. 2001. *The Economics of Scientific Knowledge*. Cheltenham: Edward Elgar.

Sholtz, Paul. 2000. Economics of Personal Information Exchange. *First Monday* 5, no. 9 (September).

Shopes, Lina. 2001. Historians and Human Subjects Research. *Recent Science Newsletter* 2, no. 3 (spring): 6–7.

Sidgwick, Henry. 1879. The Wages Fund Theory. *Fortnightly Review*, n.s., 153.

Silva, James G. 2000. Copyright Protection of Biotechnology Works: Into the Dustbin of History? *Boston College Intellectual Property and Technical Forum*. http://www.be.edu/be.org/abp/law/st.org/ipu/articles.content/2000012880html.

Simkowitz, M., and W. Beedles. 1980. Asymmetric Stable Distributed Security Returns. *Journal of the American Statistical Association* 75:306–12.

Simon, Bart. 2002. *Undead Science: Science Studies and the Afterlife of Cold Fusion*. New Brunswick: Rutgers University Press.

Simon, Herbert. 1974. Brodie on Polanyi on the Meno Paradox. *Philosophy of Science* 43:147–50.

Sims, C. 1971. Linear Regression with Non-normal Error Terms. *Review of Economics and Statistics* 53:204–5.

Slaughter, Sheila, and Gary Rhoades. 1996. The Emergence of a Competitiveness R&D Policy Coalition. *Science, Technology and Human Values* 21:303–39.

Smith, Adam. [1776] 1976. *An Inquiry into . . . the Wealth of Nations*. Chicago: University of Chicago Press.

Smith, Crosbie, and M. Norton Wise. 1989. *Energy and Empire: A Biographical Study of Lord Kelvin*. Cambridge: Cambridge University Press.

Smith, Helen Lawton, ed. 2002. *The Regulation of Science and Technology*. Basingstoke: Palgrave.

Smith, Vernon E. 1951. The Classicists' Use of Demand. *Journal of Political Economy* 59:242–57.

———. 1956. Malthus' Theory of Demand. *Scottish Journal of Political Economy* 3:205–20.

Smith, Vernon L. 1991. *Papers in Experimental Economics*. New York: Cambridge University Press.

Smyth, R., ed. 1962. *Essays in Economic Method*. London: Duckworth.

So, J. 1987. The Sub-Gaussian Distribution of Currency Futures. *Review of Economics and Statistics* 69:100–107.

Sonnenschein, Hugo. 1972. Market Excess Demand Functions. *Econometrica* 40:549–63.

Sox, Harold C., Martin B. Van Der Weyden, and Michael S. Wilkes. 2001. Sponsorship, Authorship and Accountability. *Canadian Medical Association Journal* 165, no. 6 (18 September): 786–88.

Spencer, Herbert. 1872. *Essays: Moral, Political and Aesthetic*. New York: Appleton.

Stadler, B., G. Wagner, and Walter Fontana. 2001. The Topology of the Possible. *Journal of Theoretical Biology* 213:241–74.

Stansfield, Ronald. 1990. Could We Repeat It? In John Rocke, ed. *Physicists Look Back*. Bristol: Adam Hilger.

Stephan, Paula. 1996. The Economics of Science. *Journal of Economic Literature* 34:1199–1235.

Sterelny, K. 1994. Science and Selection. *Biology and Philosophy* 9:45–62.

Stewart, Thomas. 1997. *Intellectual Capital: The New World of Organizations*. New York: Doubleday.

Stigler, George. 1941. *Production and Distribution Theories*. New York: Macmillan.

———. 1962. Henry L. Moore and Statistical Economics. *Econometrica* 30:1–21.

———. 1965. *Essays in the History of Economics*. Chicago: University of Chicago Press.

Stigler, Stephen. 1986. *A History of Statistics*. Cambridge: Harvard University Press.

Stoney, G. Johnstone. 1881. On the Physical Units of Nature. *Philosophical Magazine* 11:381–90.

Stoppard, Tom. 1967. *Rosencrantz and Guildenstern Are Dead*. New York: Grove.

Strathern, Marilyn. 1988. *The Gender of the Gift*. Berkeley: University of California Press.

Sturrock, John. 1993. *The Language of Autobiography*. Cambridge: Cambridge University Press.

Sugden, Robert. 1982. On the Economics of Philanthropy. *Economic Journal* 92:341–50.

Swijtink, Zeno. 1987. The Objectification of Observation. In L. Krüger et al., eds. *The Probabilistic Revolution*. Vol. 1. Cambridge: MIT Press.

Taubes, Gary. 1996. Science Journals Go Wired. *Science* 271 (9 February): 764–68.

Taussig, Frank. 1897. *Wages and Capital*. New York: Appleton.

Taylor, B., and W. Phillips, eds. 1984. *Precision Measurement and Fundamental Constants II*. Washington: National Bureau of Standards, Special Publication no. 617.

Taylor, Lester. 1974. Estimation by Minimizing the Sum of Absolute Errors. In Paul Zarembka, ed. *Frontiers in Econometrics*. New York: Academic Press.

Thagard, P. 1993. Societies of Minds: Science as Distributed Computing. *Studies in the History and Philosophy of Science* 24:49–67.

Theocharis, Reghinos. 1983. *Early Developments in Mathematical Economics*. 2nd ed. London: Macmillan.

Thompson, E. P. 1993. *Customs in Common*. New York: New Press.

Thornton, Thomas. 1807. *The Present State of Turkey; Or, A Description of the Political, Civil and Religious Constitution, Government and Laws of the Ottoman Empire*. London: Joseph Mawman.

Thornton, William. 1846. *Over-population and Its Remedy*. London: Longman, Brown, Green and Longmans.

———. 1848. *A Plea for Peasant Proprietors*. London: John Murray.

———. 1850. Equity Reform. *Westminster Review*, April.

———. 1854. *Zohrab; Or, A Midsummer's Day's Dream; And Other Poems*. London: Longman, Brown, Green and Longmans.

———. 1857. *Modern Manicheism, Labour's Utopia, and Other Poems*. London: John Parker and Sons.

———. 1862. On the Income Tax. *British Association for the Advancement of Science Report*.

———. 1863. Maritime Rights of Belligerents and Neutrals. *Macmillan's Magazine*, January.

———. 1864. Strikes and Industrial Cooperation. *Westminster Review* 25:349–83.

———. 1866. A New Theory of Supply and Demand. *Fortnightly Review* 6:420–34.

———. 1867. What Determines the Price of Labour or the Rate of Wages? *Fortnightly Review* 7:551–66.

———. 1869a. Indian Railway Reform. *Westminster Review*, July.

———. 1869b. Labour and Capital. *Fortnightly Review*, July.

———. 1869c. *On Labour*. London: Macmillan.

———. 1870a. Anti-Utilitarianism. *Fortnightly Review*, September.

———. 1870b. *On Labour*. 2nd ed. London: Macmillan.

———. 1871a. National Education in India. *Cornhill Magazine*, September.

———. 1871b. Natural Rights, Abstract Justice. *Fortnightly Review*, September.

———. 1871c. Neutrality for Neutrals. *Contemporary Review*, November.

———. 1871d. Technical Education in England. *Cornhill Magazine*, September.

———. 1872. Huxleyism. *Contemporary Review*, October.

———. 1873a. His Career in the India House. In *John Stuart Mill: His Life and Works*. Boston: James Osgood.

——. 1873b. *Old-fashioned Ethics and Commonsense Metaphysics.* London: Macmillan.

——. 1875a. Economic Definition of Wealth. *Fortnightly Review,* April.

——. 1875b. *India Public Works; And Cognate Indian Topics.* London: Macmillan.

——. 1876. Professor Cairnes on Value. *Contemporary Review* 28 (October): 813–35.

——. 1878. *Word for Word from Horace: The Odes Literally Versified.* London: Macmillan.

——. 1879a. The Bright Clauses of the Irish Land Act. *Fortnightly Review,* April.

——. 1879b. The Wages Fund. *Nineteenth Century,* August.

——. 1880a. Indian Exchange Difficulty. *Westminster Review,* July.

——. 1880b. Parliament without Parties. *Macmillans Magazine,* January.

Thweatt, William. 1983. Origins of the Terminology of Supply and Demand. *Scottish Journal of Political Economy* 30:287–94.

——, ed. 1988. *Classical Political Economy.* Boston: Kluwer.

Tiles, Mary. 1984. *Bachelard: Science and Objectivity.* New York: Cambridge University Press.

Tilling, Laura. 1973. The Interpretation of Observational Errors in the Eighteenth and Early Nineteenth Centuries. PhD diss., University of London.

——. 1975. Early Experimental Graphs. *British Journal for the History of Science* 8:193–213.

Tintner, Gerhard. 1953. The Definitions of Econometrics. *Econometrica* 21:31–39.

Tintner, G., and I. Sengupta. 1972. *Stochastic Economics.* New York: Academic Press.

Titmuss, Richard. 1971. *The Gift Relationship: From Human Blood to Social Policy.* New York: Vintage.

Turner, Stephen. 1994. *The Social Theory of Practices.* Chicago: University of Chicago Press.

——. 1999. Does Funding Produce Its Effects? In T. Richardson and D. Fisher, eds. *The Development of the Social Sciences in the U.S. and Canada: The Role of Philanthropy.* Stamford: Ablex.

——. 2001. What Is the Problem with Experts? *Social Studies of Science* 31:123–50.

Uebel, Thomas. 2000. Some Scientism, Some Historicism, Some Critics: Hayek's and Popper's Critiques Revisited. In M. Stone and J. Wolff, eds. *The Proper Ambition of Science,* 151–73. London: Routledge.

——. 2004. The Political Philosophy of Science of the Other Logical Empiricism. *Studies in the History and Philosophy of Science.*

Uemiya, S. 1981. Jevons and Fleeming Jenkin. *Kobe University Economic Review* 27:45–57.

Urbach, P. 1981. On the Utility of Repeating the "Same" Experiment. *Australasian Journal of Philosophy* 59:151–62.

van Helden, Albert. 1983. Roemer's Speed of Light. *Journal of the History of Astronomy* 14:137–41.

Vassilicos, J., A. Demos, and F. Tata. 1993. No Evidence of Chaos but Some Evidence of Multifractals in Foreign Exchange and Stock Markets. In A. Crilly, R. Earnshaw, and H. Jones, eds. *Applications of Fractals and Chaos.* Berlin: Springer.

Vint, John. 1994. *Capital and Wages: A Lakatosian History of the Wages Fund Doctrine.* Aldershot: Edward Elgar.

Waelde, Charlotte. 2001. The Quest for Access in the Digital Era: Copyright and the Internet. *Journal of Information Law and Technology.* http://ch.warwick.ae.uk/ph/014/waelde.html.

Waldfogel, Joel. 1993. The Deadweight Loss of Christmas. *American Economic Review* 83:1328–37.

Waldrop, Mitchell. 1992. *Complexity.* New York: Simon and Schuster.

Wallis, Roy, ed. 1979. *On the Margins of Science: The Social Construction of Rejected Knowledge.* Sociological Review Monograph 27. University of Keele.

Walras, L. 1965. *Correspondence of Leon Walras and Related Papers.* Ed. W. Jaffé. Amsterdam: North Holland.

Wang, Jessica. 1999. Merton's Shadow: Perspectives on Science and Democracy since 1940. *Historical Studies in the Physical Sciences* 30, no. 1:279–306.

Warwick, Andrew. 2003. *Masters of Theory: Cambridge and the Rise of Mathematical Physics.* Chicago: University of Chicago Press.

Waterman, Anthony. 1998. Reappraisal of Malthus the Economist. *History of Political Economy* 30:293–334.

Webb, Sydney, and Beatrice Webb. 1904. The Assize of Bread. *Economic Journal* 14:196–218.

Weiller, K., and P. Mirowski. 1990. Rates of Interest in Eighteenth Century England. *Explorations in Economic History* 27:1–28.

Weinberg, Stephen. 1998. The Revolution That Didn't Happen. *New York Review of Books*, 8 October, 48–52.

Weintraub, E. Roy. 1989. *Stabilizing Economic Knowledge.* Unpublished manuscript, Duke University.

——, ed. 1992. *Towards a History of Game Theory.* Durham: Duke University Press.

——, ed. 2002. *The Future of the History of Economics.* Durham: Duke University Press.

West, E. G., and R. W. Hafer. 1978. J. S. Mill, Unions and the Wages Fund Recantation. *Quarterly Journal of Economics* 92:603–19.

Whewell, W. 1829. Mathematical Exposition of Some Doctrines of Political Economy. *Transactions of the Cambridge Philosophical Society.* Repr. in Whewell 1971.

——. 1831. Mathematical Exposition of Some of the Leading Doctrines in Mr. Ricardo's *Principles of Political Economy and Taxation. Transactions of the Cambridge Philosophical Society.* Repr. in Whewell 1971.

——. [1862] 1967. *Six Lectures on Political Economy.* New York: Kelley.

——. 1971. *Mathematical Exposition of Some Doctrines of Political Economy from the Transactions of the Cambridge Philosophical Society.* New York: Augustus Kelley.

Whitaker, J. K., ed. 1975. *Early Economics Writings of Alfred Marshall, 1867–1890.* New York: Free Press for the Royal Economic Society.

——. 1987. The Continuing Relevance of Alfred Marshall. In R. D. C. Black, ed. *Ideas in Economics.* London: Macmillan.

White, Michael. 1982. Reading and Rewriting: The Production of an Economic Robinson Crusoe. *Southern Journal* 15:115–42.

——. 1989a. Cuckoo or Bowerbird? Jevons, Physics and the Marginalist Revolution. Unpublished paper, Monash University.

——. 1989b. Invention in the Face of Necessity: Marshallian Rhetoric and the Giffen Goods. Unpublished paper, Monash University.

——. 1989c. Why Are There No Demand and Supply Curves in Jevons? *History of Political Economy* 21:425–56.

——. 1994. That God-Forgotten Thornton: Exorcising Higgling after *On Labour.* In N. de Marchi and M. Morgan, eds. *Higgling: Transactors and Their Markets in the History of Economics.* Durham: Duke University Press.

——. 1998. Obscure Objects of Desire? Paper presented at the Duke Conference on Economics of Art.

——. 2003. *A Mechanization of Victorian Values.* PhD diss., Monash University.

Whittaker, Edmund. 1945. Eddington's Theory of the Constants of Nature. *Mathematical Gazette* 29:137–44.

——. 1951. *Eddington's Principle in the Philosophy of Science.* Cambridge: Cambridge University Press.

Wible, James R. 1998. *The Economics of Science: Methodology and Epistemology as if Economics Really Mattered*. London: Routledge.

[Wilson, John.] 1871. Economic Fallacies and Labour's Utopias. *London Quarterly Review* 131 (July): 121–39.

Wise, M. N. 1988. Mediating Machines. *Science in Context* 2, no. 1:77–114.

——. 1993. Mediations: Enlightenment Balancing Acts. In Paul Horwich, ed. *World Changes*. Cambridge: MIT Press.

——, ed. 1995. *The Values of Precision*. Princeton: Princeton University Press.

Wise, M. N., and C. Smith. 1989. Work and Waste: Political Economy and Natural Philosophy in 19th Century Britain. *History of Science* 27:263–301.

Wood, J. C., ed. 1982. *Alfred Marshall: Critical Assessments*. London: Croom Helm.

Woodmansee, Martha. 1994. *The Author, Art and the Market: Rereading the History of Aesthetics*. New York: Columbia University Press.

Wolpert, Lewis. 1993. *The Unnatural Nature of Science*. Cambridge: Harvard University Press.

Wray, K. Brad. 2000. Invisible Hands and the Success of Science. *Philosophy of Science* 67:163–75.

Wright, Philip. 1924. Review of Moore's *Generating Economic Cycles*. *Journal of the American Statistical Association* 19:103–8.

Wulff, Sonja. 2001. Shy about the Public Domain? Scientific Publishing Isn't What It Used to Be. *Daily Twist*. http://www.doubletwist.com/news/columns/article.jhtml?secton=weekly01&name=weekly015.

Wulwick, Nancy. 1990. The Stylized Facts of Growth. Unpublished working paper, Jerome Levy Institute.

Youden, W. 1972. Enduring Values. *Technometrics* 14:1–11.

Young, R. 1985. *Darwin's Metaphor*. Cambridge: Cambridge University Press.

Zamora Bonilla, J. P. 2002. Scientific Inference and the Pursuit of Fame. *Philosophy of Science* 69:300–323.

——. 2003. Peddling Science. *Philosophy of Science* 70:833–39.

Zastoupil, Lynn. 1994. *John Stuart Mill and India*. Stanford: Stanford University Press.

Zelizer, Viviana. 1994. *The Social Meaning of Money*. New York: Basic Books.

Ziman, John. 1993. Review of Philip Kitcher's *The Advancement of Science*. *Nature* 364 (22 July): 295–96.

——. 1994. *Prometheus Bound*. Cambridge: Cambridge University Press.

Zolatarev, V. 1986. *One-Dimensional Stable Distributions*. AMS Translations no. 65. Providence: American Mathematical Society.

Index

The Advancement of Science, 102–4; economic objections to, 111–15
Kjeldsen, Tinne, 42
Klamer, Arjo, 42
Klein, Martin, 157
Koopmans, Tjalling C., 369
Kuhn, Thomas, 15–16, 22, 60, 78, 94–96, 220; operations research and, 16–17, 92–94; organization of science and, 17, 18; Kitcher compared to, 24, 25; freedom in science and, 54, 62, 65, 66–68; Fuller on, 85–88, 89; allure of, 85–91
Kula, Witold, 147, 149

Laplace, Pierre Simon, 290
Latour, Bruno, 98, 100, 114, 115, 175
Law, John, 285
Leonard, Rob, 42
Lessig, Lawrence, 130
Levy, Paul, 235, 252
Lewontin, Richard, 105
Lexis, Wihelm, 358
Lipsitz, Imre, 14–16, 22, 87
Litman, Jessica, 130
Longfield, Mountifort, 298

MacIntyre, Alasdair, 47, 55
MacKenzie, Donald, 20, 127
Malthus, Thomas, 292, 294, 304, 327; supply and demand theory and, 296, 297–98
Mandelbrot, Benoit, 32, 230, 241–42, 249–50, 251–52; modern economics and, 232–41; chaos and fractal dimensions in economics and, 262
Manheim, Karl, 77
Marcet, Jane, 296
Marginalist Revolution, 41
market metaphor, 32, 53–54, 56, 59–64, 66, 67, 68, 74, 82–83, 101, 102, 109–10, 116, 141, 169, 215
Marshall, Alfred, 33, 274, 277, 279, 288, 315, 324, 336, 346, 349, 360, 365, 366; supply and demand theory and, 238–39, 337, 352–56; Thornton and, 315, 327; Moore and, 363, 365
Marx, Karl, 320, 321, 323
material transfer agreement (MTA), 139
Mathias, Peter, 195–96

Mauss, Marcel, 382, 386
Maxwell, James Clerk, 151–53, 158, 231, 361
McCulloch, J. R., 296, 340
McSherry, Corynne, 21
measurement, in Britain and Germany, 155–68
Menard, Claude, 288, 291, 292, 364
Menger, Karl, Jr., 73
metaphor, 41–42; biological, 353–54
Mill, James, 292, 293–94, 373
Mill, John Stuart, 275, 294, 327, 332, 336; wages fund and, 274, 279, 320, 324, 346; supply and demand theory and, 296, 299–302, 311–12, 329–30, 340, 353; Thornton and, 304–6, 307, 309, 310–16, 328, 333, 346; union organization and, 318, 323, 326
Millikan, Robert, 184–85
Mitchell, Wesley Clair, 358, 361, 372
Moore, Henry Ludwell, 33, 355, 357, 358, 360, 365; life of, 359, 361; efficiency theory of wages of, 362–64; supply and demand theory and, 366–74
Morgenstern, Oskar, 44, 73, 112
Myerson, Roger, 43

Nash, John, 49
National Institutes of Health, 131, 141
Negishi, Takashi, 332, 333
Neurath, Otto, 5, 13
Newton, Isaac, 181, 285, 286
Neyman-Pearson doctrine, 171–72, 269
Nietzsche, Friedrich, 376, 390

operations research (OR), 16–17, 91–94, 95, 171

Pareto, Vilfredo, 107, 252, 356, 359, 360, 361, 372; law of stable distributions of, 252–62, 361
Pauli, Wolfgang, 161
Petley, Brian, 179, 182
Peirce, Charles Saunders, 102
Physiocrats, 283–84, 286
Pickering, Andrew, 21
Pigou, Arthur Cecil, 324, 335
Pinch, Trevor, 21, 29, 127
Planck, Max, 156–57, 159–60, 167
Poirier, Dale, 213, 214
Polanyi, Karl, 73, 77, 383

Waddington, Conrad, 92

wages fund doctrine, 279, 301, 302, 303, 312–15, 320, 323, 346

Walras, L., 336, 359, 360, 361, 364, 371

Weaver, Warren, 5, 91, 92

Webb, John K., 28

Weber, Max, 156

Weinberg, Stephen, 85

Weintraub, Roy, 42

Whewell, William, 321, 341, 342–43, 344, 345, 348, 353

Whitaker, P. H., 336

White, Michael, 42, 48

Wicksteed, P. H. , 353

Wise, Norton 148, 284, 322, 338

World Copyright Treaty, 135

World Intellectual Property Organization, 129

Wright, Gavin, 40

Philip Mirowski is the Koch Professor of Economics and
the History of Science at the University of Notre Dame.

Library of Congress Cataloging-in-Publication Data
Mirowski, Philip, 1951–
The effortless economy of science? / Philip Mirowski.
p. cm. — (Science and cultural theory)
Includes bibliographical references and index.
ISBN 0-8223-3310-4 (cloth : alk. paper)
ISBN 0-8223-3322-8 (pbk. : alk. paper)
1. Research—Economic aspects. 2. Science and state.
I. Title. II. Series.
Q180.55.E25M57 2004   338.9′26—dc22   2004003274